Introduction to Microsoft Dynamics™ GP 10.0: Focus on Internal Controls

Terri E. Brunsdon, CPA, JD

Marshall B. Romney, PhD

Paul John Steinbart, PhD

Prentice Hall

Upper Saddle River, New Jersey 07458

Cataloging data for this publication can be obtained from the Library of Congress.

Editor: Julie Broich
Editorial Director: Sally Yagan
Editor in Chief: Eric Svendsen
Product Development Manager: Ashley Santora
Editorial Project Manager: Kierra Kashickey
Marketing Manager: Andy Watts
Marketing Assistant: Ian Gold
Permissions Project Manager: Charles Morris
Senior Managing Editor: Judy Leale
Production Project Manager: Kerri Tomasso
Senior Operations Specialist: Arnold Vila
Operations Specialist: Benjamin Smith
Art Director: Jayne Conte
Cover Designer: Nancy Thompson
Cover Illustration/Photo: Photodisc
Printer/Binder: Bind-Rite Graphics/Robbinsville

Credits and acknowledgments borrowed from other sources and reproduced, with permission, in this textbook appear on appropriate page within text.

Pearson Education Ltd., London
Pearson Education Singapore, Pte. Ltd
Pearson Education, Canada, Inc.
Pearson Education–Japan
Pearson Education Australia PTY, Limited
Pearson Education North Asia, Ltd., Hong Kong
Pearson Educación de Mexico, S.A. de C.V.
Pearson Education Malaysia, Pte. Ltd
Pearson Education Upper Saddle River, New Jersey

Prentice Hall
is an imprint of

PEARSON

www.pearsonhighered.com

10 9 8 7 6 5 4 3 2 1
ISBN-13: 978-0-13-609804-1
ISBN-10: 0-13-609804-5

PREFACE

INTRODUCTION TO MICROSOFT DYNAMICS 10.0: FOCUS ON INTERNAL CONTROLS is designed to illustrate practical application of the theory taught in an accounting information systems course. The text includes Microsoft Dynamics GP version 10.0 software and sample databases used with the text. Students gain "hands on" experience with the software by capturing financial transactions, analyzing company performance, and instituting internal controls in a general ledger software environment.

This text integrates GP training in accordance with guidelines recommended by the Committee of Sponsoring Organizations' (COSO) Enterprise Risk Management model.[1] In conjunction with this text, students should also refer to materials in an accounting information systems text such as *Accounting Information Systems,* co-authored by Marshall B. Romney and Paul John Steinbart (11th ed., Pearson Prentice Hall 2009).

INTRODUCTION TO MICROSOFT DYNAMICS GP 10.0: FOCUS ON INTERNAL CONTROLS expands student skills beyond basic transaction posting and typical reporting. Students explore issues affecting compliance with internal control objectives such as setting software control options and using control reports to monitor activities. Each chapter exposes students to topics at two different levels. Level One focuses on task oriented processes such as transaction entry, controlling transaction entry, and reporting on activities performed in the cycle. Level 2 delves deeper into Series setup by illustrating internal control options in the software that enforce compliance with company internal control policies. Each chapter concludes with exercises and questions that reinforce skills learned at both levels.

The text is accompanied by two identical sample databases, namely S&S, Incorporated and S&S, Inc Project DB. The text uses the S&S, Incorporated database to illustrate tasks performed in the chapter. Students can then use the second database for end-of-chapter materials. With this approach, students can feel confident that practicing transactions while reading the chapter will not affect the outcome of graded materials. The text also contains instructions so that students can detach and copy databases to a removable drive for porting work between the classroom and home.

How Chapters Are Organized

The text is designed to teach accounting software from a cycle-based approached. The first three chapters illustrate installing the software and sample database and navigating the software. In Chapter 4, students are introduced to the first cycle, namely revenue. Remaining

[1] See Romney and Steinbart, *Accounting Information Systems* (11th ed., Pearson Prentice Hall 2009), Chapter 6, for more information on COSO's ERM model.

chapters cover the expenditure and payroll cycles and conclude by illustrating the general ledger and reporting system. GP Series covered in the text are the System Manager, Inventory Control, Sales Order Processing and Receivables Management, Purchase Order Processing and Purchasing, Payroll, and Financial.

- **Chapter 1:** Level One illustrates installing the software, logging in and out of the software, and attaching, detaching, backing up and restoring sample databases. This level also introduces students to working in the software interface by practicing home page navigation, transaction inquiry, and basic reporting. The GP Series installed with the education edition of the software is also discussed. Level Two looks at decisions impacting the purchase of computerized accounting software and GP and the importance of adhering to software licensing and "rights of use."

- **Chapter 2:** Level One focuses on understanding the S&S sample company chart of accounts. Students review the general ledger account framework used to create the chart of accounts and identify departments. Illustrations also cover creating general ledger accounts, printing the chart of accounts and trial balance reports, and opening and closing monthly accounting periods. This level concludes with an illustration using GP's SmartList to export data to Microsoft Excel. Level Two looks at the database management system's role in coordinating transaction processing, GP Series integration, and relational database concepts and terminology.

- **Chapter 3:** This chapter focuses on GP security and internal control options affecting the system. Level One looks at security installed during software installation, internal control options for posting setup, the audit trial, and activity tracking. Level Two illustrates configuring user software access and activity permissions as well as security reporting.

- **Chapter 4:** This chapter focuses on inventory items used by the sample company and is intended for readers of both levels. The chapter discusses setting up and pricing items. It also illustrates assigning vendor to items, conducting a physical count, adjusting inventory, and reporting.

- **Chapters 5 through 8:** These chapters illustrate transaction processing and reporting by cycle. Chapter 4 looks at the revenue cycle; Chapter 5 the expenditure cycle; and Chapter 6 the payroll cycle. Chapter 8 concludes cycle based activities by performing tasks that close the accounting period and report results. Level One of each chapter focuses on task oriented processes such as capturing transactions, posting transactions, controlling transaction posting, reporting, and closing the period. Students begin with reviewing an activity diagram of the cycle, which becomes the roadmap for discussions on cycle activities, threats, and controls. Level Two of each chapter looks at configuring Series setup options that implement internal controls.

- **Appendix A** repeats instructions in Chapter 1 covering backing up and restoring databases. **Appendix B** provides tables illustrating company chart of accounts, customers, vendors, inventory items, and employees. **Appendix C** contains instructions on correcting posting errors. **Appendix D** contains solutions for in-chapter exercises that appear throughout the text.

To Instructors and Students

Microsoft Dynamics GP Education Edition version 10.0 software and sample databases illustrated in the chapters accompany the text. Instructors may install the software on lab machines and students may install the software on a home computer. Moreover, sample databases are portable so that students can conveniently transport data between school and home.

When exiting the software, users will be prompted to unload sample databases. If you are using the data at home and do not need to copy it to a removable drive then you do not need to unload data. However; if using on a lab machine then databases must be unloaded or the next user will have access to your data. You may also want to copy your data on the lab machine to a removable drive to protect it from loss.

For you convenience, Appendix A restates Chapter 1 instructions on backing up and restoring databases. Appendix B provides detailed lists of the sample company customers, vendors, employees, inventory, and general ledger accounts. Appendix C contains error correction procedures. You will also find solutions for in-chapter exercises in Appendix D. An instructor's manual is also available.

Students are encouraged to experiment while learning to use GP. In the real world, posting and processing errors frequently occur. This text emphasizes implementing internal control procedures that timely detect errors and provides procedures for correcting these errors.

What is New in the Text

Students will find more step-by-step guidance on performing software tasks. Furthermore, version 10.0 of the software improves the user interface by implementing home page layouts of menu commands on the screen.

Icons Signaling Special Attention

The textbook incorporates symbols to signal chapter exercises, special issues, and additional ideas on approaching a task. This table appears on the inside front cover of the text.

About the Authors

Terri Brunsdon is a Certified Public Accountant with undergraduate degrees in accounting and computer programming and a Juris Doctorate in Law and Masters in Tax from the University of Akron. Terri has over twenty years of accounting experience and specializes in recommending and implementing accounting software solutions. Terri also has six years of higher education teaching experience in accounting information systems and computer software applications. She is a member of the American Institute of Certified Public Accountants (AICPA) and an AICPA Certified Information Technology Professional (CITP). Terri authors the Pearson Prentice Hall's Brunsdon Learning Series texts that include *Learning QuickBooks Pro, Learning Peachtree Complete*, and *Learning Microsoft Office Accounting*.

Marshall B. Romney, PhD, CPA, CFE, is the John and Nancy Hardy Professor of Accounting and Information Systems in the Marriott School of Management at Brigham Young University. Marshall has published 23 books, including the leading text on Accounting Information Systems. Marshall is a past president of the Information Systems section of the AAA and was a member of both the Information Technology Executive Committee and the IT Practices Subcommittee of the American Institute of Certified Public Accountants. He was an advisor to the National Commission on Fraudulent Financial Reporting. At BYU, Marshall is the Associate Director of the School of Accountancy and Information Systems and is the director of both the graduate and undergraduate Information Systems programs.

Paul John Steinbart is Professor of Information Systems at Arizona State University where he teaches courses on accounting information systems and computer security. He is co-author of the leading Accounting Information Systems textbook. Professor Steinbart's research has appeared in leading academic journals including *MIS Quarterly*, *The Accounting Review*, *Decision Sciences*, and the *Journal of Information Systems*.

TABLE OF CONTENTS

Chapter 1 INSTALLING AND USING DYNAMICS GP

CHAPTER OVERVIEW

This chapter contains step-by-step instructions for installing Microsoft Dynamics GP: 10.0 Education Edition software as well as loading, backing up, and restoring sample databases included with the text. Databases provided are ***S&S, Incorporated*** and an exact replica of this database, named ***S&S, Inc Project DB***. With two copies of the database, you can use the S&S, Incorporated database as a "sandbox" for practicing skills while reading the chapter and then use the S&S, Inc Project DB for completing tasks graded by professors.

After reading this chapter, you will have:

- Installed GP and understand the Series included with your edition of the software;
- Loaded, backed up, and restored the sample company databases; and
- Logged into GP, opened a company database, navigated software home pages, posted basic transactions, performed database inquiries, and prepared basic reports.

Level One covers:

- Installing GP and loading, backing up and restoring databases
- Navigating the user interface to post transactions, perform inquiries, and print reports
- An explanation of GP Series installed with the education edition

Level Two covers:

- Identifying and evaluating general ledger software features that impact a company's internal control environment and operating needs
- Adherence to software licensing and "rights of use"

LEVEL ONE

HARDWARE AND OPERATING SOFTWARE REQUIREMENTS

The minimum hardware and operating software requirements for installing GP 10.0 are outlined in Table 1:1.

Hardware:	Pentium IV 2.4 GHz or higher
	512 MB Ram (1 GB recommended)
	2 GB of available hard disk space
	SVGA (800 x 600) video with 16-bit driver
	DVD-Rom or CD-Rom drive
Operating Software:	Windows® XP Profession with SP 2
	Windows Vista® Business, Ultimate, or Enterprise
	Windows Server® 2003 with SP 2

Table 1:1 Hardware and Operating Software Requirements

INSTALLING DYNAMICS GP

In this topic you will install the GP software that accompanies your text. This software is licensed for a single user.

Insert the ***Microsoft Dynamics™ GP 10.0*** CD into your computer drive and the software automatically begin installation.

Alternative procedure for installing software.

Note: If installation does not begin automatically, right click Window's Start menu and select Explore. Click to select the CD-Rom drive for your computer (normally labeled D) to open the contents of the C. Locate the file named Setup and double click the file to begin installation.

If the window illustrated in Figure 1:1 appears, click **Install** and then after receiving a green checkmark in front of the Dexterity component click **Close**. You will then have to reboot your computer to continue installation. Installation should automatically continue after the computer restarts.

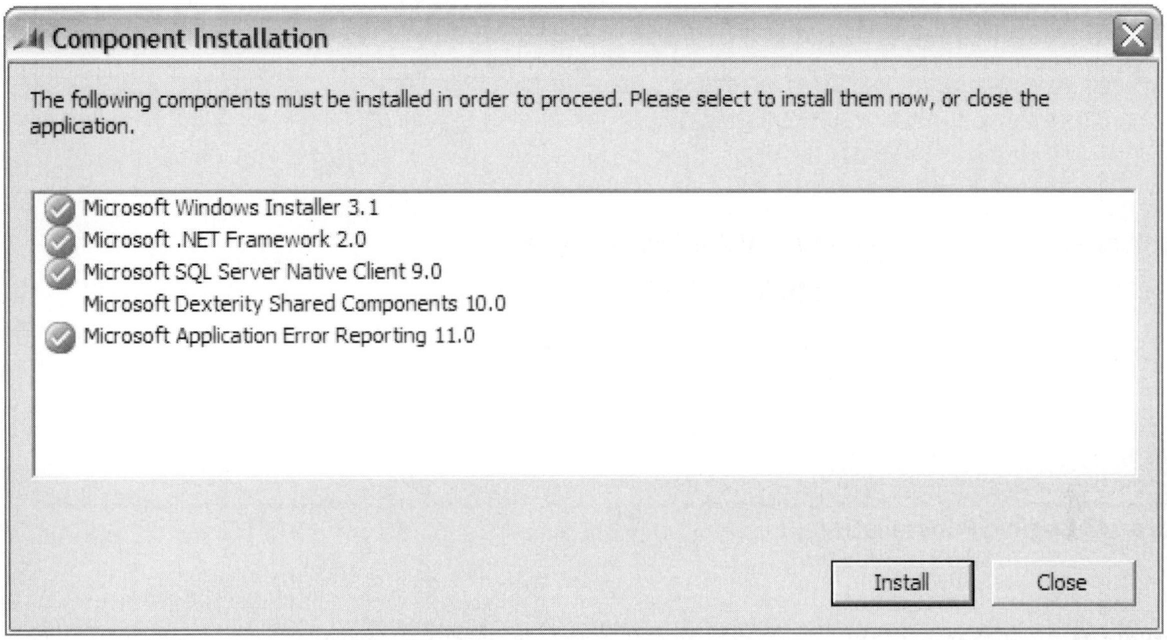

Figure 1:1 Optional Installation Screen

Click **Next** when you receive the screen illustrated in Figure 1:2.

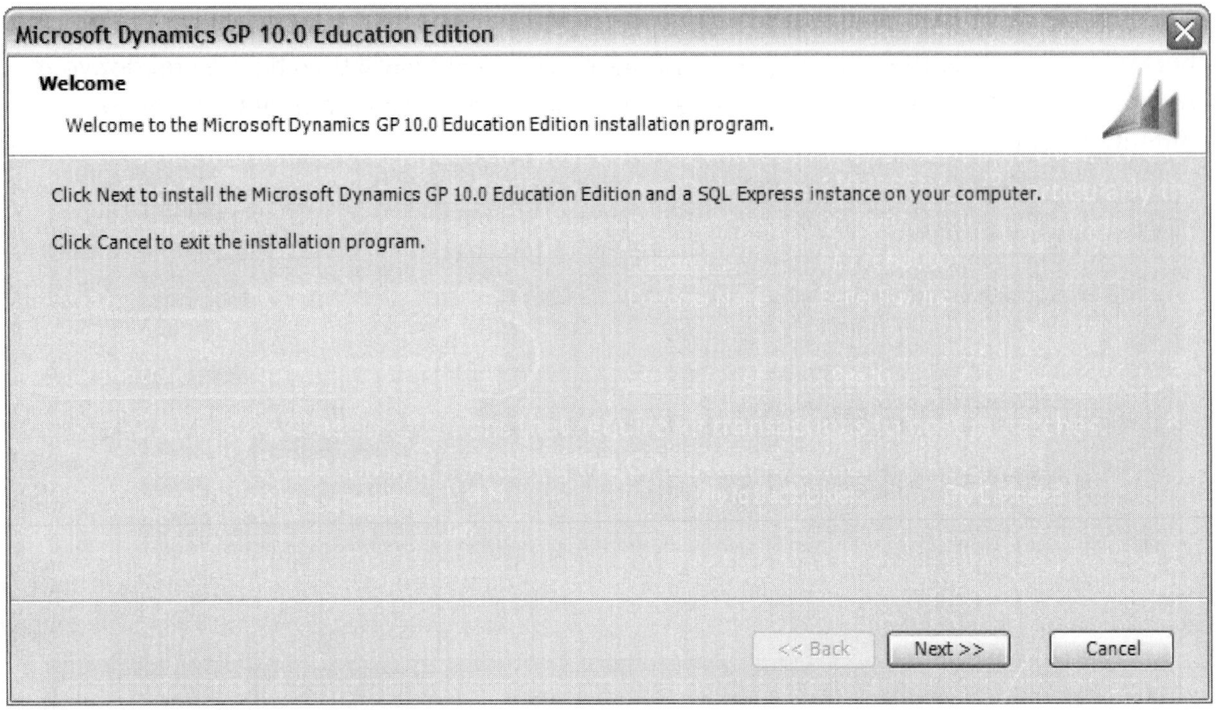
Microsoft Dynamics GP 10.0 Education Edition
Welcome
Welcome to the Microsoft Dynamics GP 10.0 Education Edition installation program.
Click Next to install the Microsoft Dynamics GP 10.0 Education Edition and a SQL Express instance on your computer.
Click Cancel to exit the installation program.
<< Back
Next >>
Cancel

Figure 1:2 Begin GP Installation

Highlight **United States** as the country and click **Next**. (See Figure 1:3.)

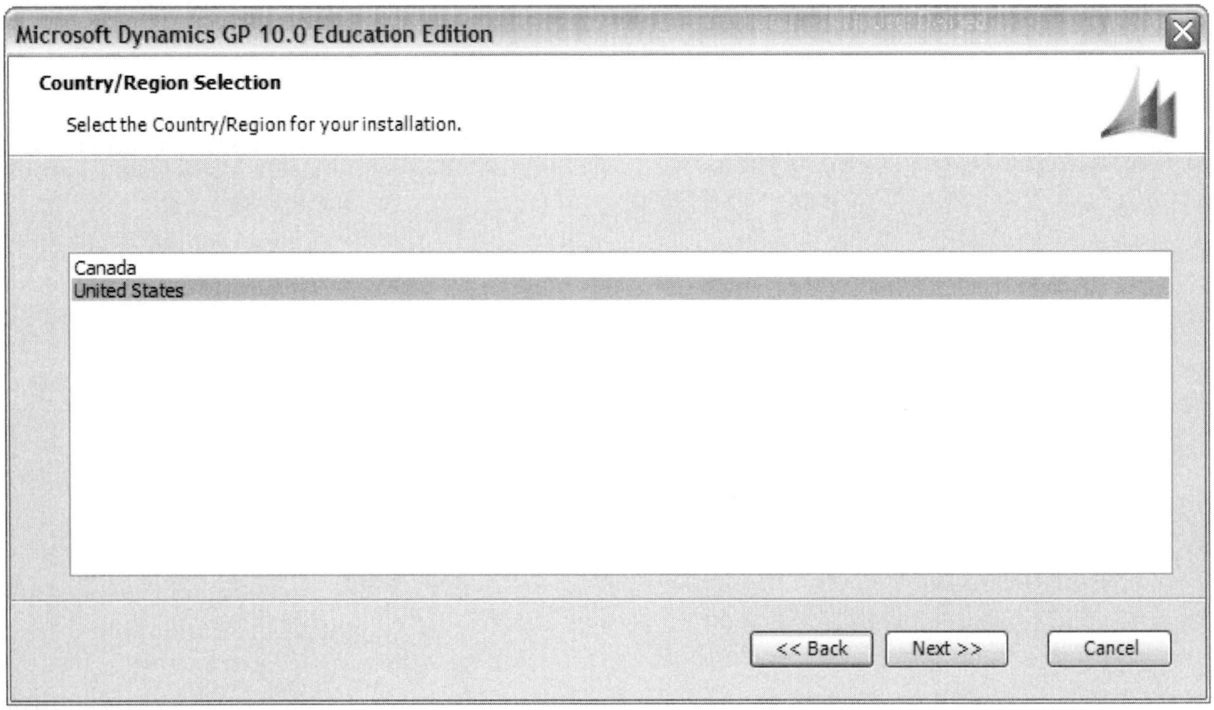
Microsoft Dynamics GP 10.0 Education Edition
Country/Region Selection
Select the Country/Region for your installation.
Canada
United States
<< Back
Next >>
Cancel

Figure 1:3 Select Country

When the Software License Agreement appears (Figure 1:4), scroll through and read the agreement. Acceptance confirms your promise to use the software as provided in the terms of the agreement. (*Note: Software licensing is further discussed in Level Two of this chapter.)* Click the **I Accept** option and then click **Next** to continue installation.

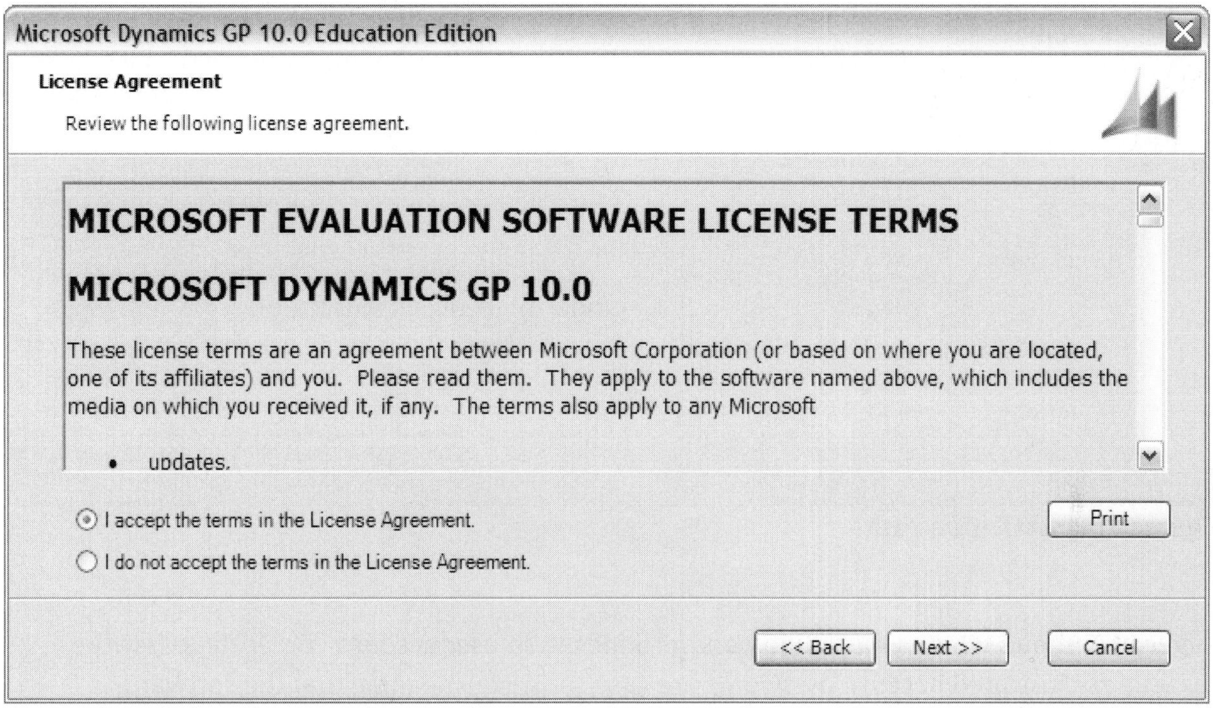

Figure 1:4 Software License Agreement

You will next select a directory path for installing GP. Type in the path illustrated next and click **Next**.

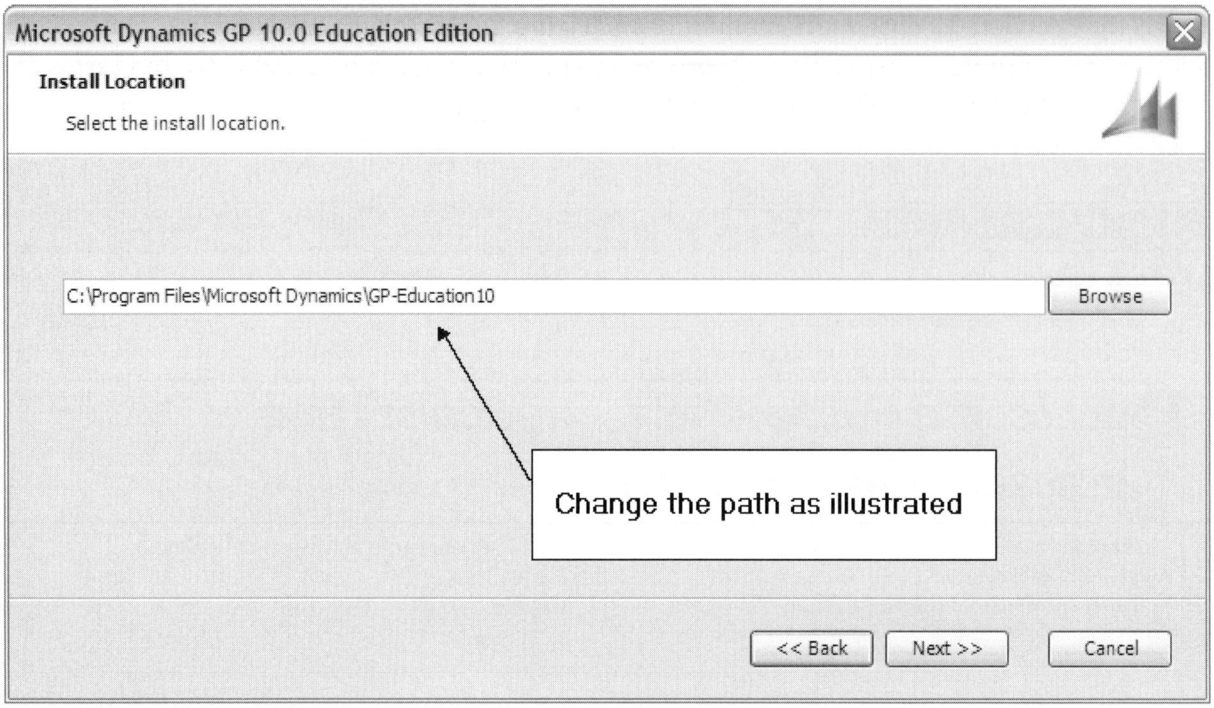

Figure 1:5 Installation Path

Figure 1:6 shows where you enter a password for the ***sa*** user account. Enter the password exactly as illustrated because passwords are case sensitive, meaning that the software differentiates between upper and lower case letter. Click **Next** when finished.

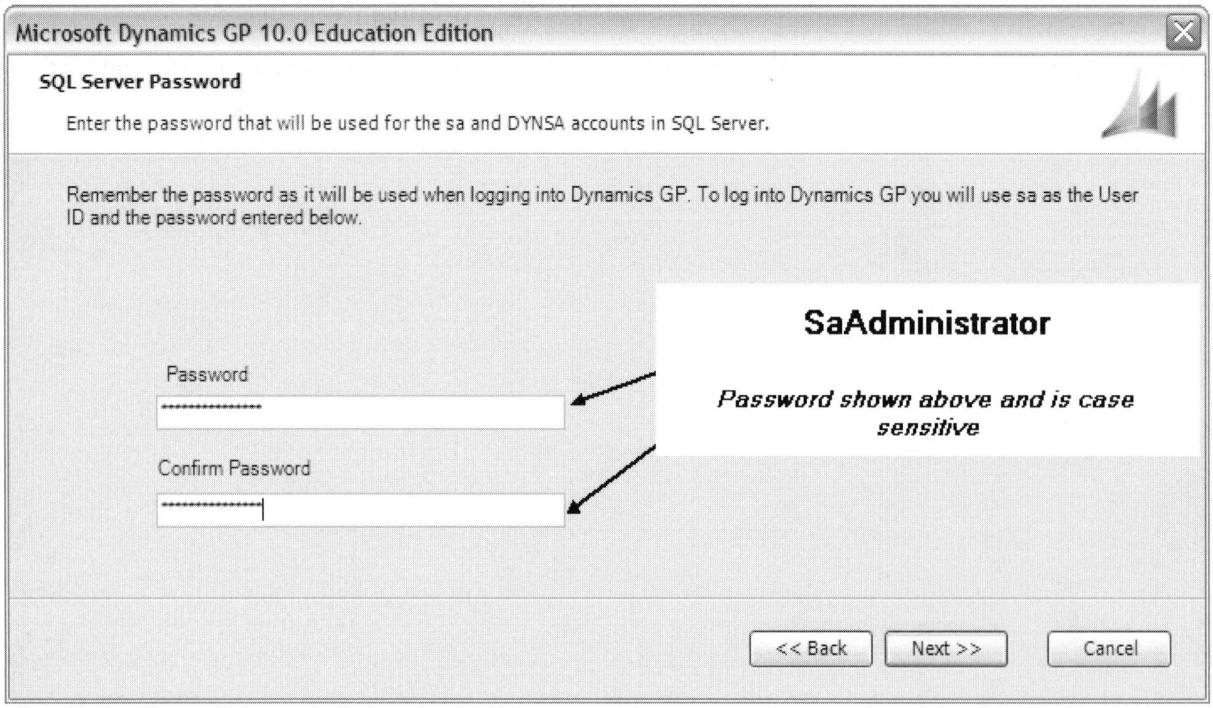

Figure 1:6 Password for sa Account

You are now ready to complete installation. Click **Install** on the window illustrated in Figure 1:7. Do not interrupt installation; otherwise, you must use the Control Panel to remove partially installed files and begin installation again.

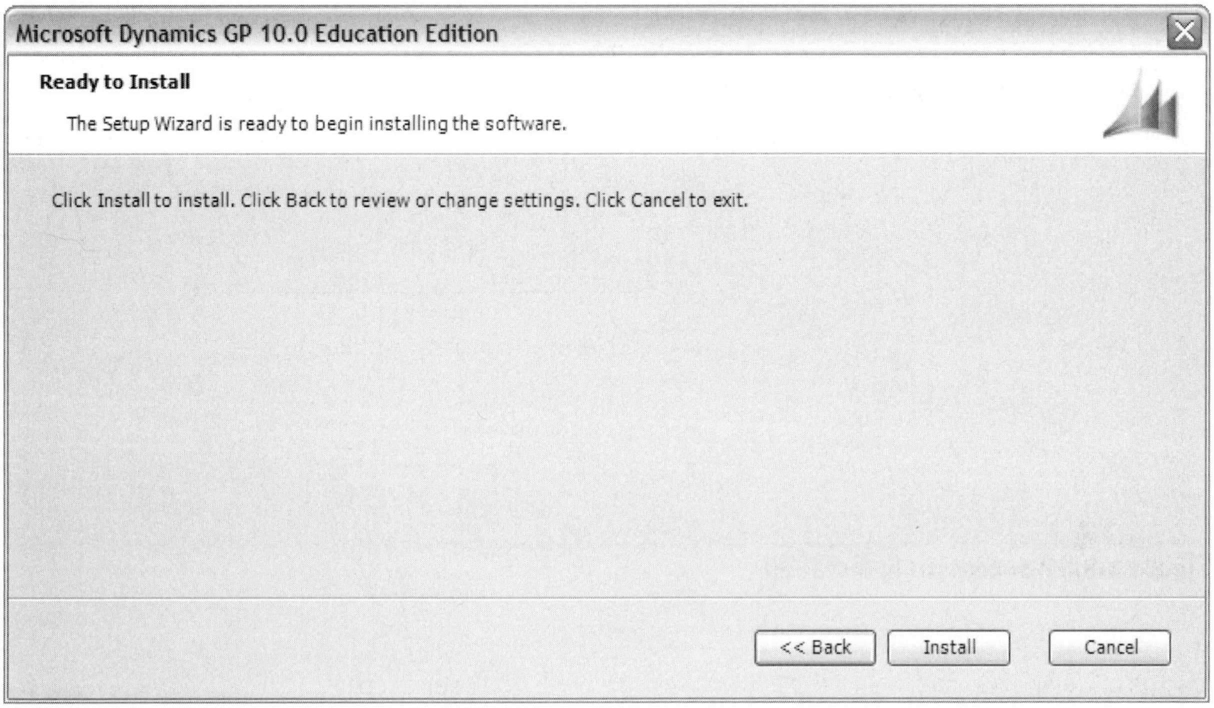
Microsoft Dynamics GP 10.0 Education Edition
Ready to Install
The Setup Wizard is ready to begin installing the software.
Click Install to install. Click Back to review or change settings. Click Cancel to exit.
<< Back
Install
Cancel

Figure 1:7 Install GP

When notified that installation is complete (Figure 1:8), click **Exit**. You can now remove the software CD from your computer and store it in a safe place. In the next topic you will load sample databases onto your computer.

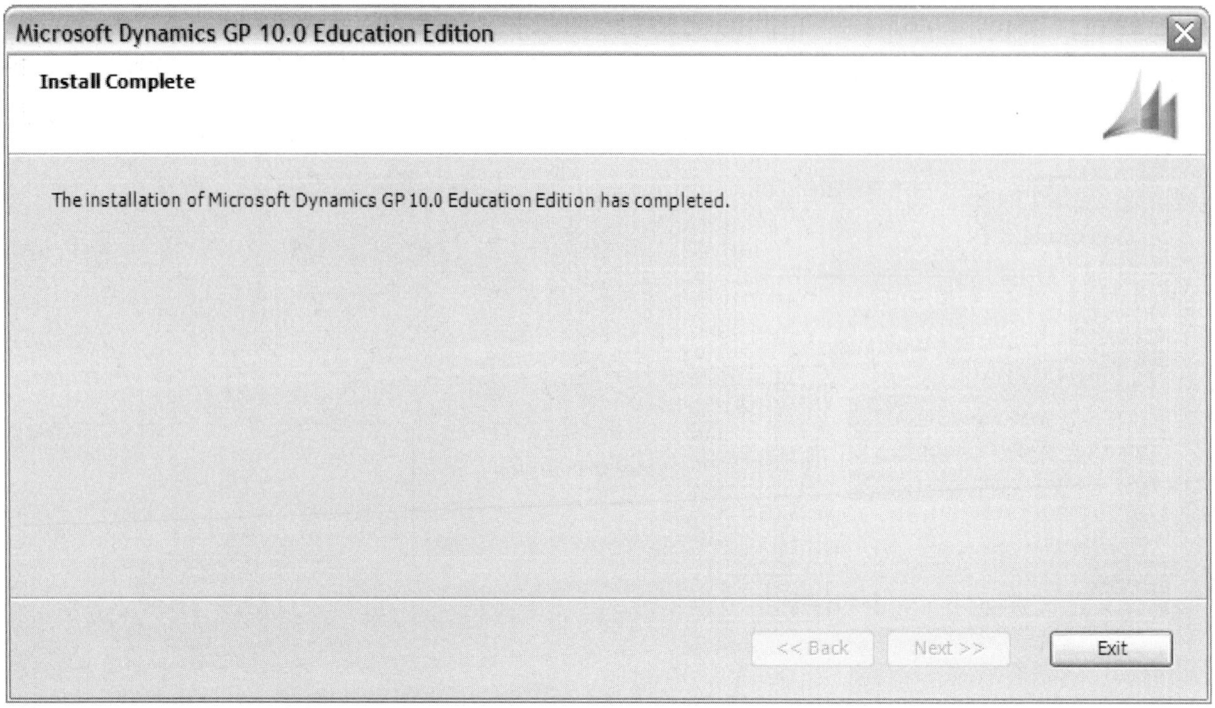

Figure 1:8 GP Successfully Installed

COPY SAMPLE DATABASES TO THE COMPUTER

The sample databases used in the text are located on the **Student CD**. Insert this into your CD-Rom drive and right click the **Start** menu to select **Explore**. (See Figure 1:9.)

Figure 1:9 Window Explorer

Under the **Folders** pane, click **My Computer** and then double click to open your CD drive. (See Figure 1:10.)

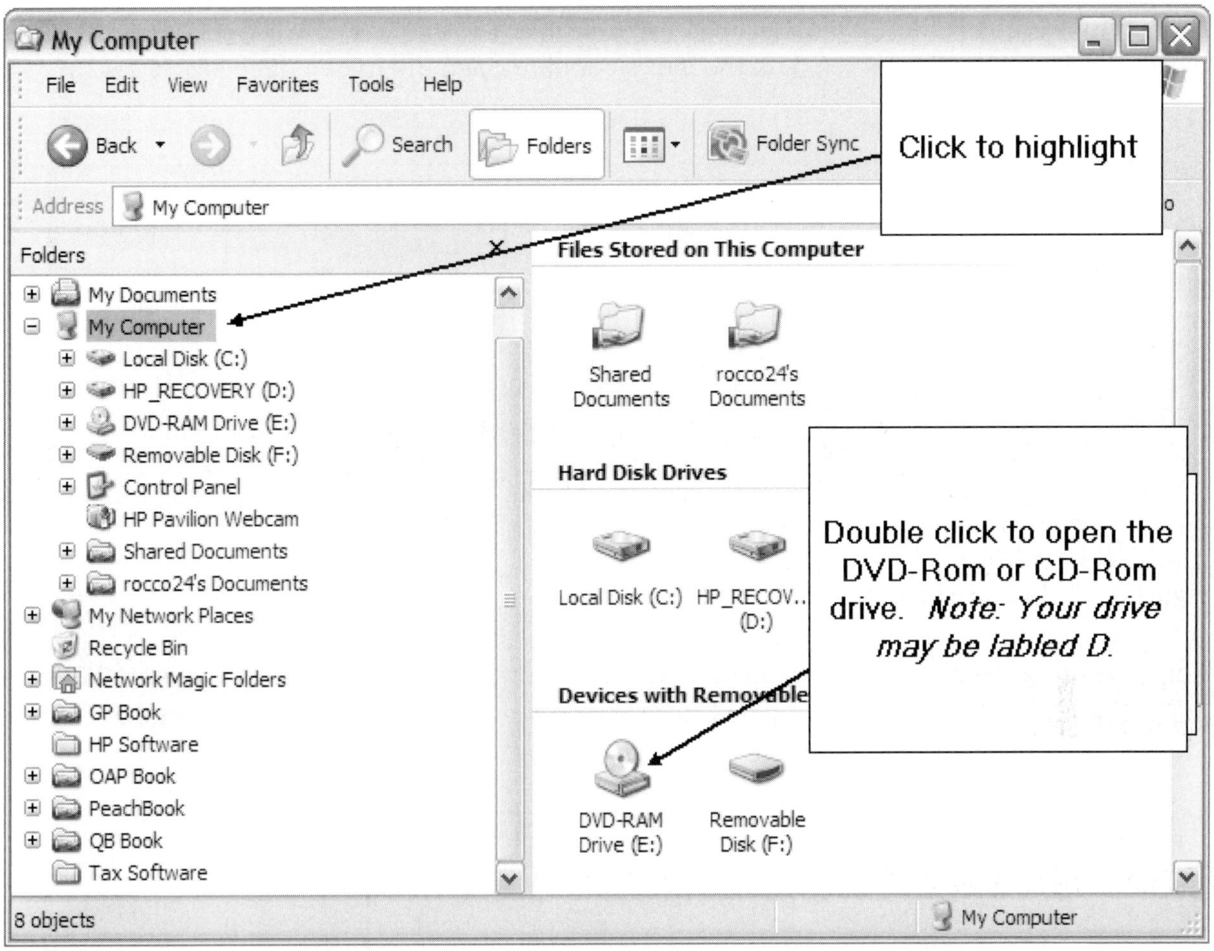

Figure 1:10 Explorer Window

Use the menu to select ***View>>List*** so that your view of data files will display file extensions as illustrated in Figure 1:11. Use your mouse to browse the CD until you locate these files.

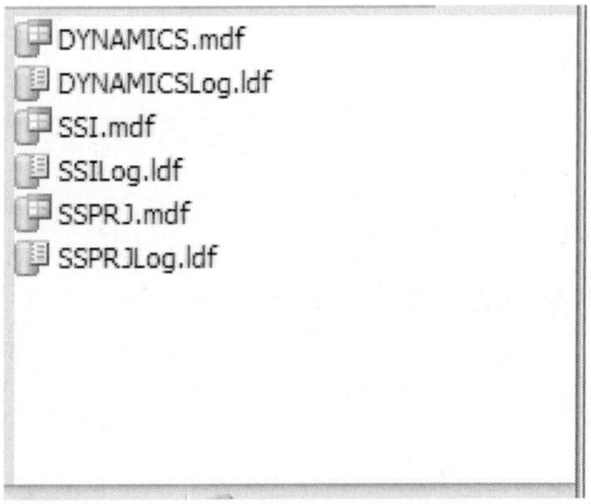

Figure 1:11 Sample Databases

Next, return to the Folders pane and locate your **C** drive. Scroll down the list of folders to locate the **Program Files** folder. Use the plus symbol to open the folder. (See Figure 1:12.)

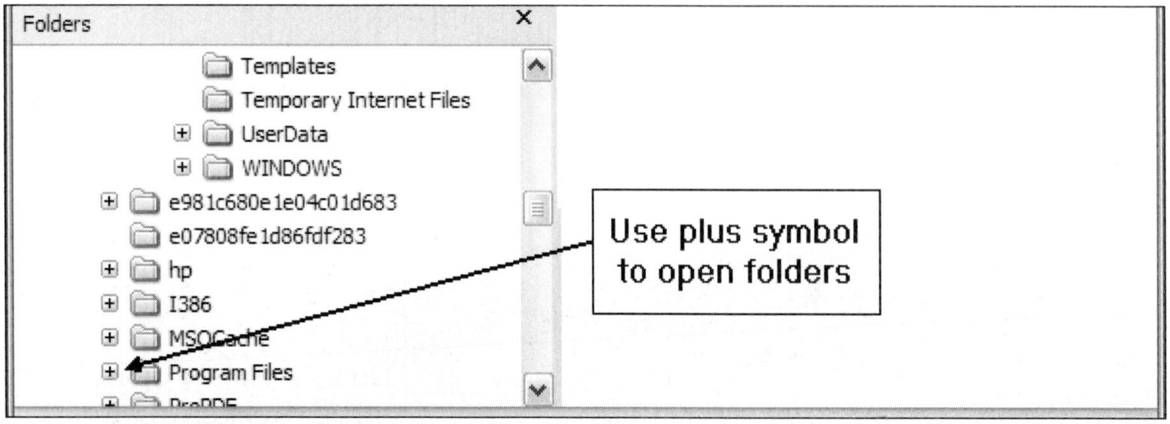

Figure 1:12 Locating Program Files Folder

Continue using the plus symbol to open folders until you locate the **Microsoft Dynamics\GP-Education10\Student Data** folder (See Figure 1:13.) Drag all six files on the Student CD to the Student Data folder on your machine.

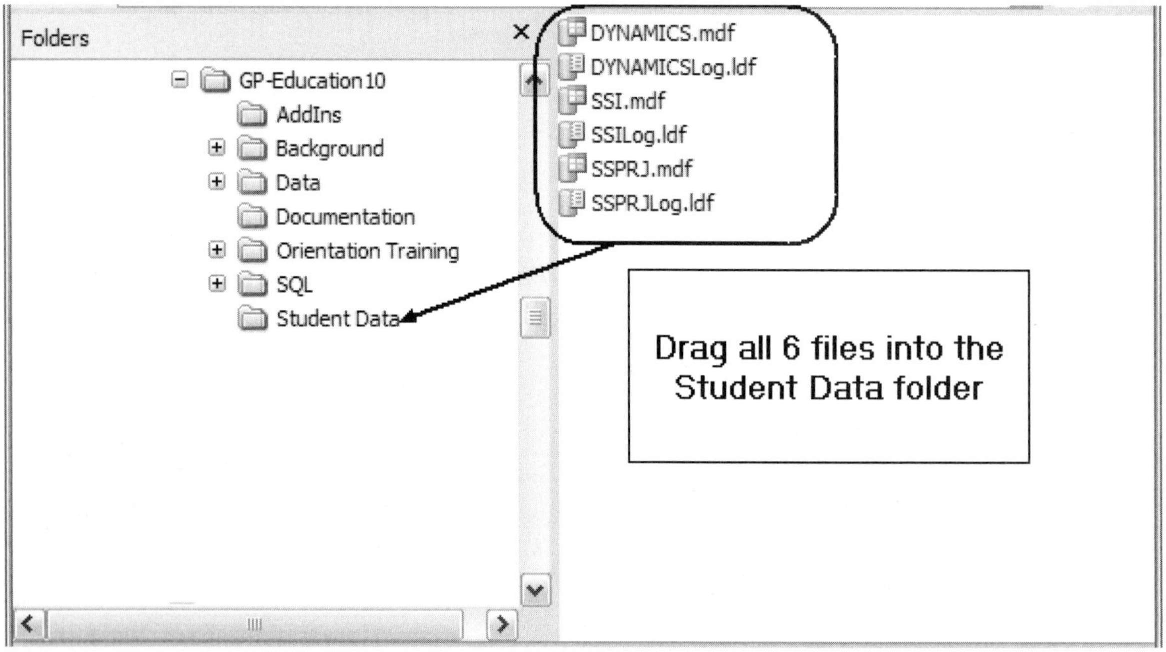

Figure 1:13 Explorer Window

Click **X** to close the Explorer window. You can now remove the Student CD from your computer and store in a safe place.

ATTACHING DATABASES TO GP

You will now attach sample databases to GP. Return to the Start menu and click **Programs>>Microsoft Dynamics>>GP-Education 10.0** to select **GP-Education**. This path is used each time you open GP.

When the Login screen appears as illustrated in Figure 1:14 the Server name will be provided. Enter **sa** as the User ID, **SaAdministrator** as the password, and click **OK**.

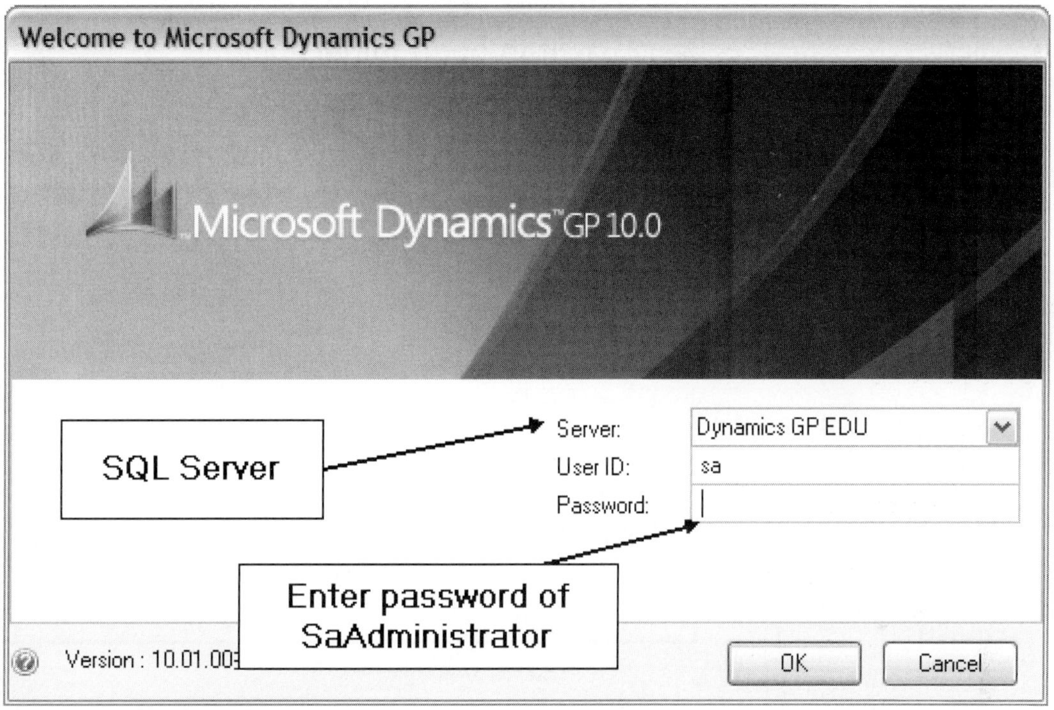

Figure 1:14 Login Screen

GP next opens the window illustrated in Figure 1:15, prompting you to attach company databases. Click **Yes**.

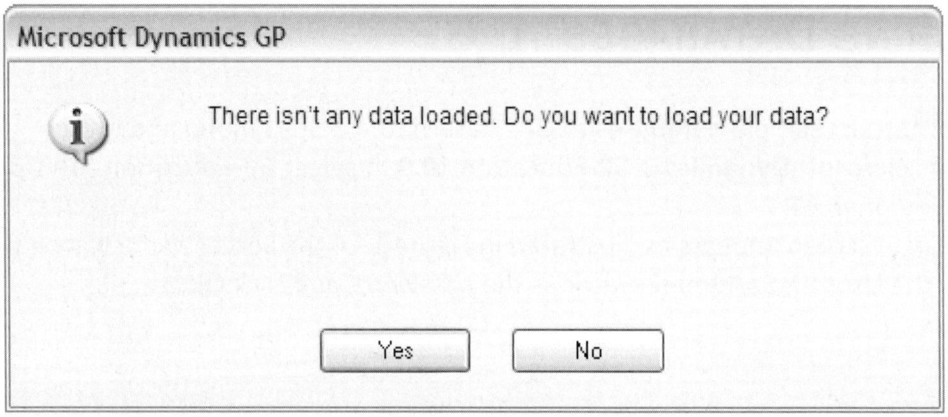

Figure 1:15 Loading Company Databases

You next browse to the folder containing the sample databases copied to your computer and select the **DYNAMICS.mdf** file. (See Figure 1:16.) Click **Open**.

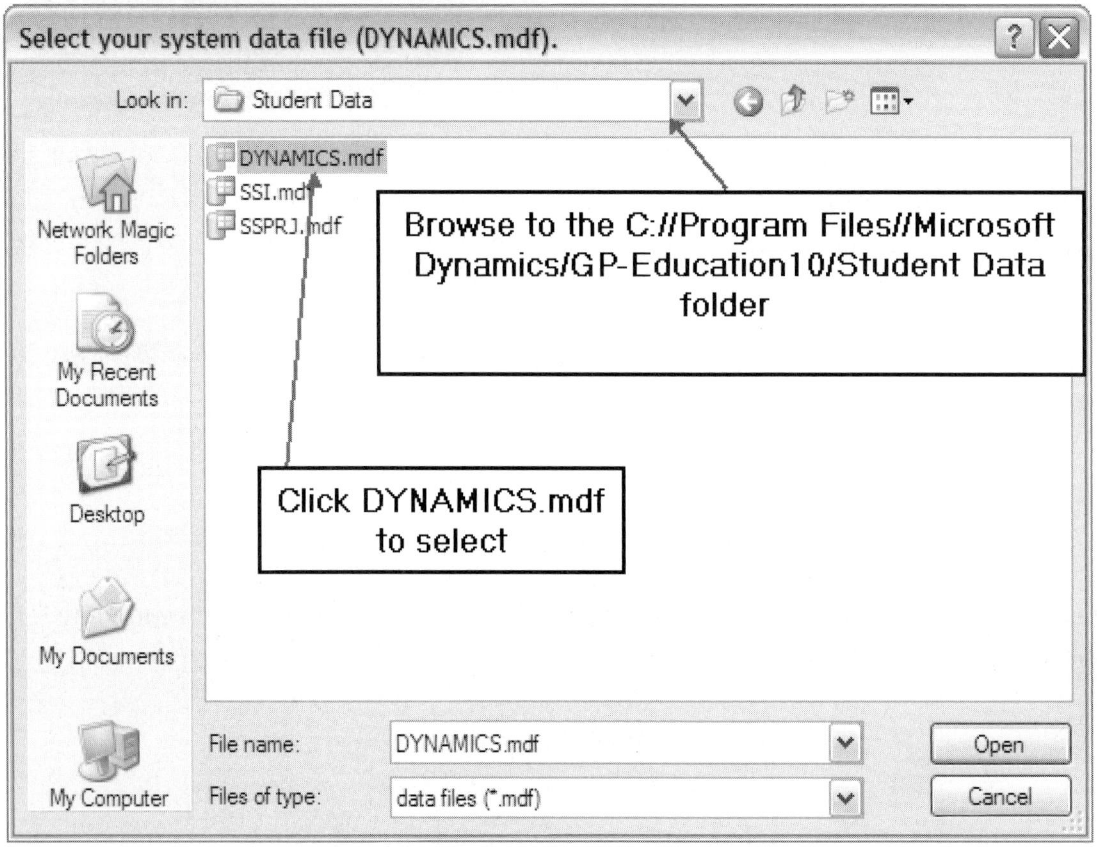

Figure 1:16 Attach Dynamics.mdf Database

It may take a few minutes for GP to load the databases. You will then be prompted to select a company to open. (See Figure 1:17.)

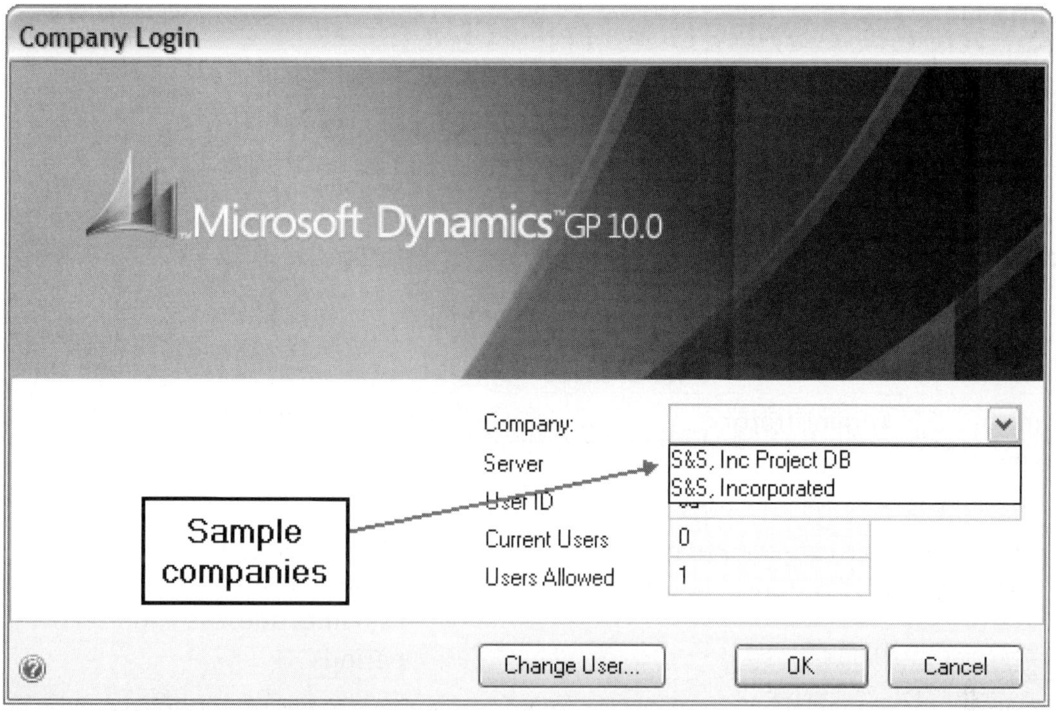

Figure 1:17 Select Company

Click the dropdown icon to view available databases, namely *S&S, Inc Project DB* and *S&S, Incorporated*. Remember that the first database is used for completing projects and assignments graded by your professor. The second database is used while reading the text and practicing your GP skills so choose **S&S, Incorporated** and click **OK**.

As illustrated next, GP sets a software expiration date the first time you open a sample database. Click **OK**.

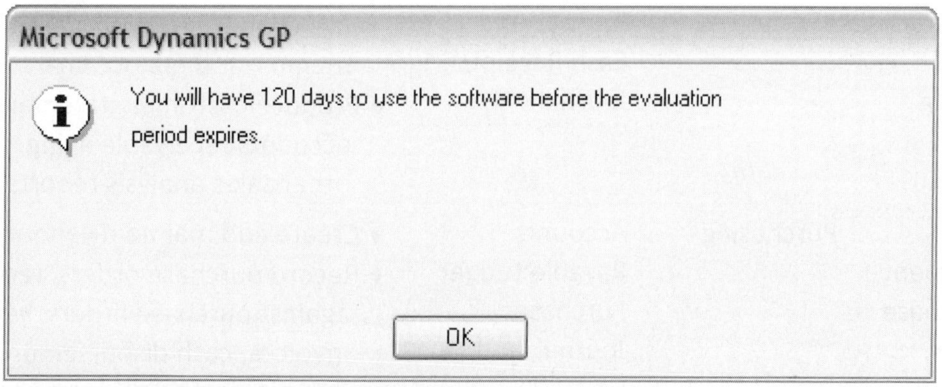

Figure 1:18 Evaluation Period Expiration Notification

Congratulations! You have now completed installation and are ready to begin using the software.

GP Series Covered in the Text

Your copy of GP comes with the Series outlined in the next table. You also have the Human Resources and Fixed Asset Series, which are not covered in this text.

Series	**Home Page Name**	**Traditional Journal and Ledger References**	**Series Tasks**
System Manager	Administrator		♦ Used by all Series to manage overall software behavior such as user IDs, passwords, security and audit trails ♦ Establishes company defaults such as name, address and fiscal periods
Financial	Financial	General Ledger, General Journal, and Chart of Accounts	♦ Create and maintain the chart of accounts ♦ Record adjusting and correcting journal entries ♦ Produce trial balance, financial statements, worksheets, and other financial analysis reports
Receivables Management, Invoicing, and Sales Order Processing	Sales	Accounts Receivable Ledgers, Sales Journal, and Cash Receipts Journal	♦ Create and maintain customers ♦ Record sales orders, order shipments, invoices, cash receipts, merchandise returns, debit memos, and finance charges ♦ Produce customer statements, accounts receivable aging, and other sales analysis reports
Payables Management and Purchase Order Processing	Purchasing	Accounts Payable Ledger, Purchases Journal, and Cash Disbursements Journal	♦ Create and maintain vendors ♦ Record purchase orders, receipts against purchase orders, vendor invoices, cash disbursements, returns, and credit memos ♦ Produce accounts payable aging, cash requirement report, and other purchasing analysis reports

Series	Home Page Name	Traditional Journal and Ledger References	Series Tasks
Inventory Control	Inventory	Inventory Ledgers	♦ Create and maintain inventory items ♦ Establish inventory valuation method ♦ Record inventory adjustments ♦ Produce inventory analysis reports
Payroll	HR & Payroll	Payroll Journals	♦ Create and maintain employees ♦ Record payroll data and produce paychecks ♦ Produce tax liability and other payroll analysis reports

Table 1:2 GP Series Covered In Text

You can think of each Series as serving individual accounting and reporting cycle needs, except for the System Manager Series, which controls Series integration and software security. The previous table also outlines home page names for each Series as well as references to traditional accounting ledgers and journals and tasks performed in a Series.

You will not be downloading security patches to update the education software. However, in the real world you should make security a priority and continually apply security patches and software updates.

BACKING UP AND RESTORING DATABASES

You should backup the Dynamics and company databases every time you finish a GP session.

To backup databases, click the GP button 

and select ***Maintenance>>Backup***. GP prompts for a password to access system security and this password is **sa**. Figure 1:19 illustrates the backup window displaying the list of company and system databases. You should back up each company database used during a session and always back up the system database.

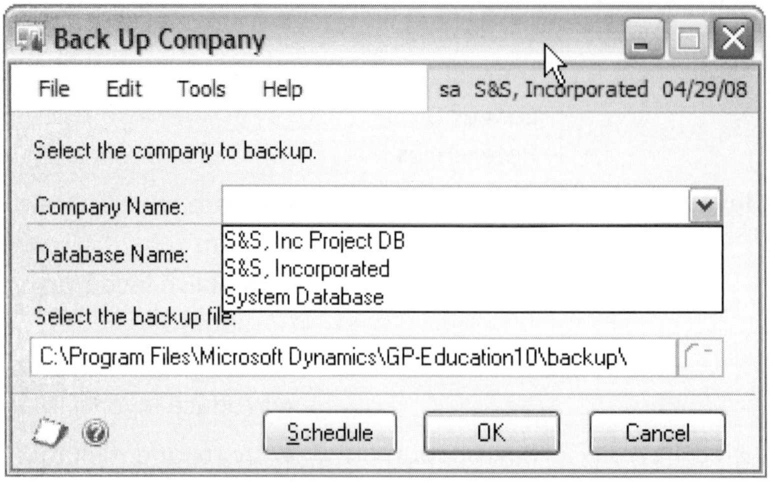

Figure 1:19 Back Up Window

After selecting a company name to back up, GP automatically sets the backup path to the folder illustrated in Figure 1:20 and provides a default backup file name.

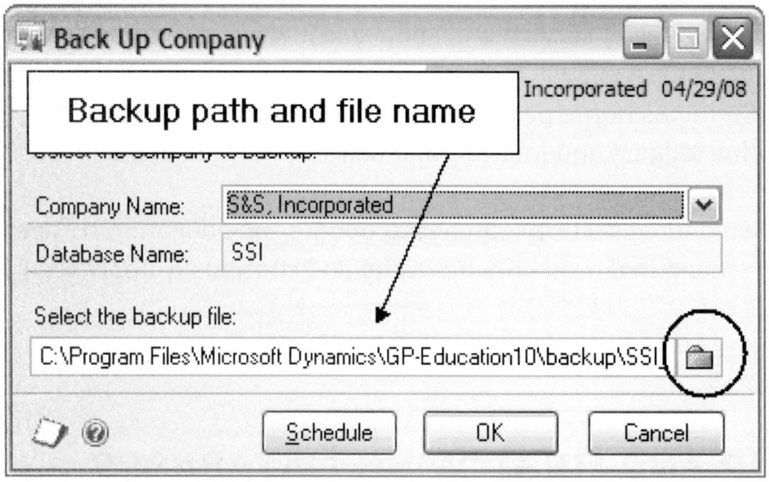

Figure 1:20 Backup Folder

You can change the default folder and file name by clicking the folder icon to open the window illustrated in Figure 1:21. Click **Save** after making your selections to return to the Back Up Window. Thereafter, click **OK** to perform the backup.

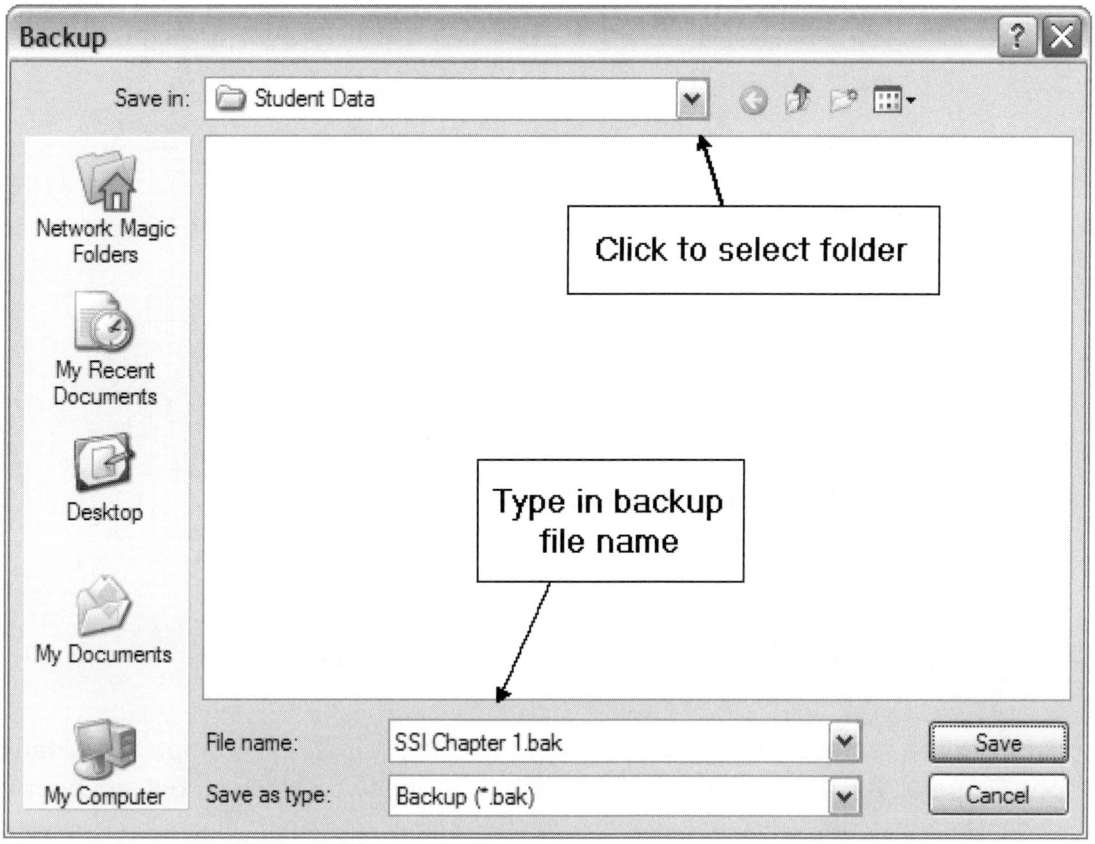

Figure 1:21 Set Back Up Folder and File Name

It is important to practice good backup procedures. If a database is corrupted, you can only restore work saved in the backup file. ***IN OTHERWORDS, YOUR WORK WILL BE LOST IF YOUR DATABASES BECOME CORRUPT AND YOU HAVE NOT BACKED THEM UP.*** However, you can always begin again by recopying original databases from the Student CD onto your computer.

If you need to restore a database, click the GP button to choose ***Maintenance>>Restore***. The password remains the same (i.e., **sa**.) The Restore window resembles the Back Up window. You choose the company name to be restored and also select the backup path and file name to restore to. You will need to restore both the system database and company databases.

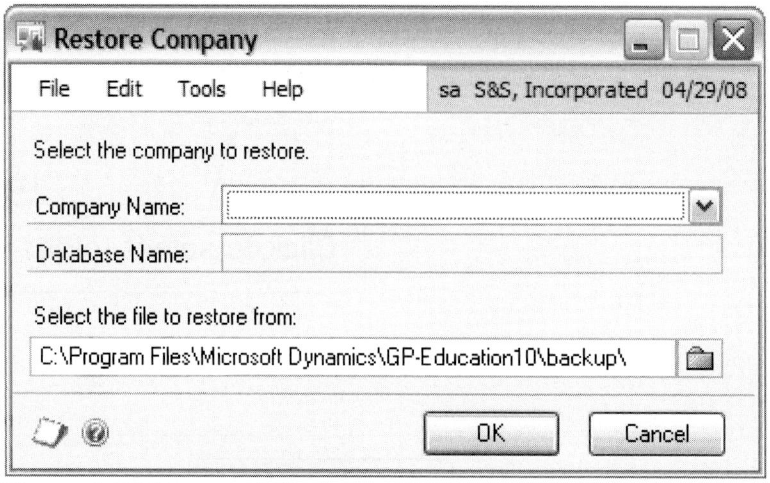

Figure 1:22 Restore Window

EXITING GP AND UNLOADING DATABASES

You will now exit the software. Click the GP button and select ***Exit***. GP prompts to unload your data. (See Figure 1:23.) Databases are unloaded for portability between school and home. If you plan on using the company databases on your home machine then select **No**. However, you MUST unload databases on a school lab or the next user will have access to your data.

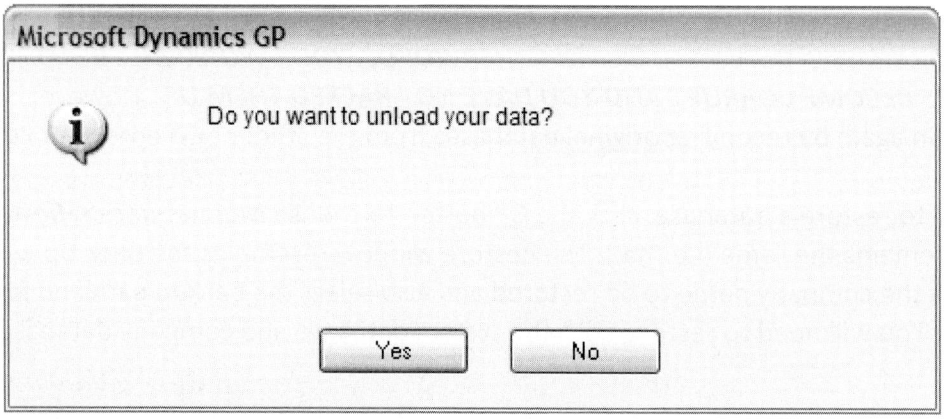

Figure 1:23 Unload Databases

Warning on reattaching databases in the lab.

If you unload your databases and leave them in a lab folder, you may encounter a permissions error when trying to reattach databases. To correct this error, copy the databases to a different folder on the lab machine's hard drive or to a removable drive and recopy back into the original lab machine folder. This procedure seems to clear a data access permissions issue created by SQL server when users are not administrators on the machine (i.e., you are not an administrator on a machine used in a school lab).

After unloading your databases, you can copy data files onto a removable storage device such as a flash drive and then recopy them to a different computer. You must copy all six data files illustrated previously. *(Note: You do not have to remove data files from a lab computer. As long as files are unloaded, the next user will not be able to access to your data).*

GP always prompts to unload (i.e., detach) your data when exiting the software. GP will also prompt to load your data if no data is attached.

RETURNING TO GP

You return to the software by selecting the GP-Education menu from the Start menu as illustrated previously. Each time you open the software, GP prompts to enter the User ID and password. If company database were previously unloaded then GP prompts to reload the databases.

Note: In the event that your last session ended abruptly (i.e., a hardware system crash or software closed improperly), GP prompts to delete your previous login. See Appendix A to resolve this issue.

Company Background

Before beginning tasks in this text, become familiar with the sample company. S&S operates a mid-sized distribution company in Northeast Ohio. It operates on a calendar year and the open accounting period is March of 2007. The company's inventory includes small electronics, televisions, cameras, and audio equipment. S&S's chart of accounts, customers, vendors, inventory items, and employees are listed in Appendix B. Take a few minutes to review this information before continuing.

Introduction to the Interface

When the software first opens you will see the main Home Page, which is activated by clicking Home and is illustrated in Figure 1:24. This figure is labeled so you can identify elements of a home page. The table that follows explains these elements.

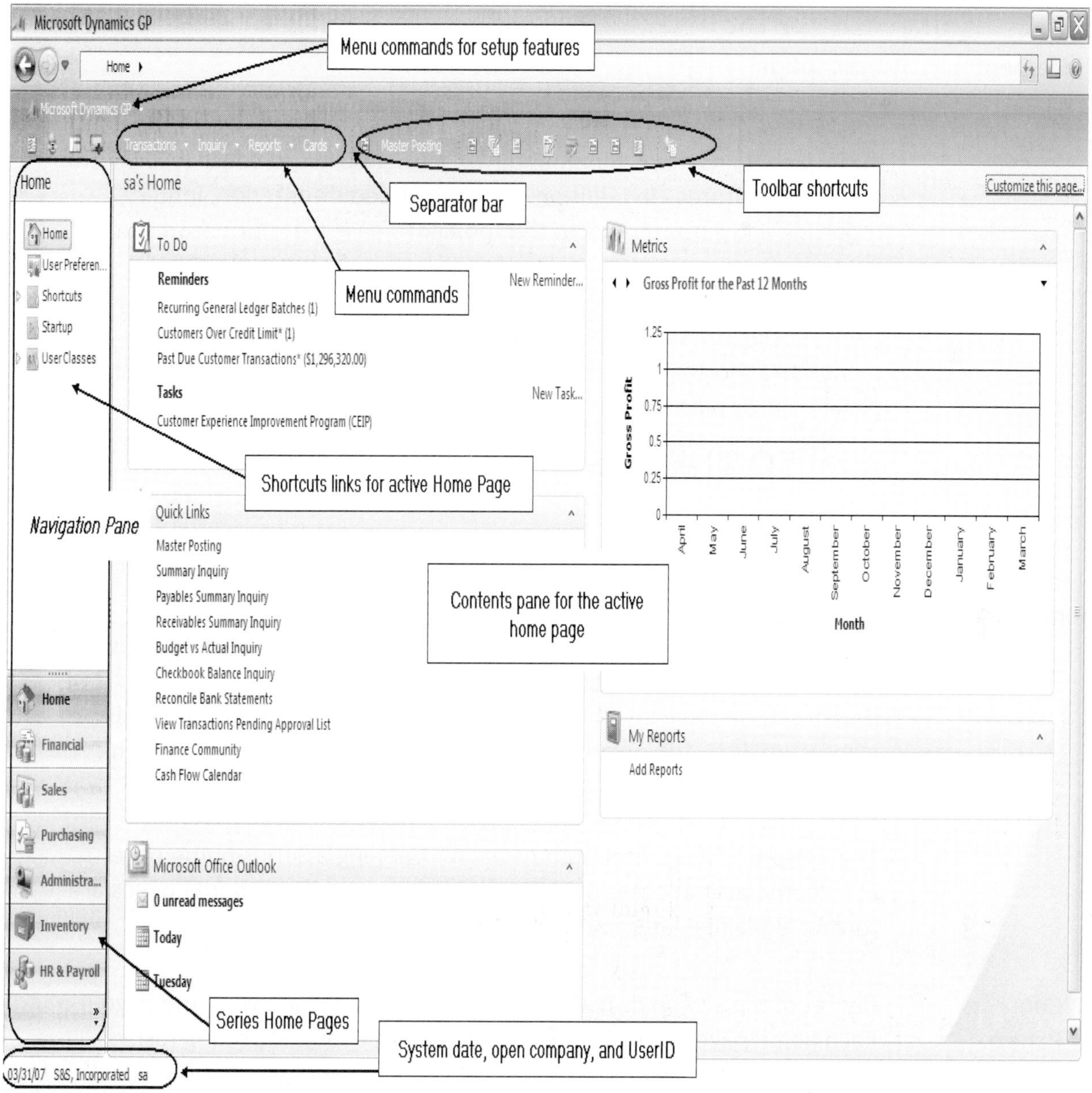

Figure 1:24 Main Home Page

Element	**Description**
Menus	The Microsoft Dynamics GP button  (GP button) contains menu commands for setting up users, security, printers and other features. In addition, we have added transaction, inquiry, reporting and cards menus to the toolbar to ease transition from version 8.0 to 10.0. Right clicking the toolbar allows you to add/remove and customize menus and shortcuts for the toolbar. You can also rearrange toolbar placement by placing your cursor over a separator bar until it changes to this  symbol and dragging a group to reposition.
Navigation Pane	The Navigation Pane appears to the left and remains docked regardless of the active home page. This pane contains two sections. The top section displays shortcut links for the active home page. You can customize links by right clicking the section and selecting Add. Depending on the active home page, this section also displays links to transaction lists; for instance, the Sales home page has links for listing sales transactions. The bottom section displays buttons for opening a Series home page. Each home page focuses on tasks for that Series. Series home pages are further explained later in the chapter.
Contents Pane	Center of the screen displays menu content for the active home page. Each home page provides different commands for performing tasks unique to that Series.
System Date	Accesses the System Date GP uses as the default date on transactions and reports. You can click the date to change it.
Open Company	Displays name of open company. You can double click this name to open a different company.
User ID	Displays the current User ID.

Table 1:3 Elements of the User Interface

The next table describes commands located under the GP button. GP help is accessed by clicking this  symbol in the upper right hand corner of the screen. Toolbar shortcuts are discussed later in the chapter.

GP Button Menu Command	Description
1) User and Company	1) Change user or company
2) User Date	2) Menu access for changing the system date
3) Edit	3) Basic editing commands such as copy and paste
4) Maintenance	4) Routines for repairing databases, setting software security, and backing up or restoring databases
5) Smart List	5) Menu access for opening the Smart List
6) Reminders and Task List	6) Menu access for opening reminders and tasks
7) User Preferences	7) Access to changing user preferences that set display colors and keyboard behavior
	Print Setup and Exit are self-explanatory. The Process Monitor control is for distributed network printing and is not covered in this text.

Figure 1:25 Menus under GP Button

Click the **Financial** home page button in the Navigation Pane to activate the home page for this Series. Figure 1:26 illustrates menu command categories for the Contents Pane on this home page. Categories group menu commands by task (i.e., Transactions, Reports, and Inquiry). You can expand or collapse category details by clicking the icon illustrated. The table that follows has information on tasks performed under each category.

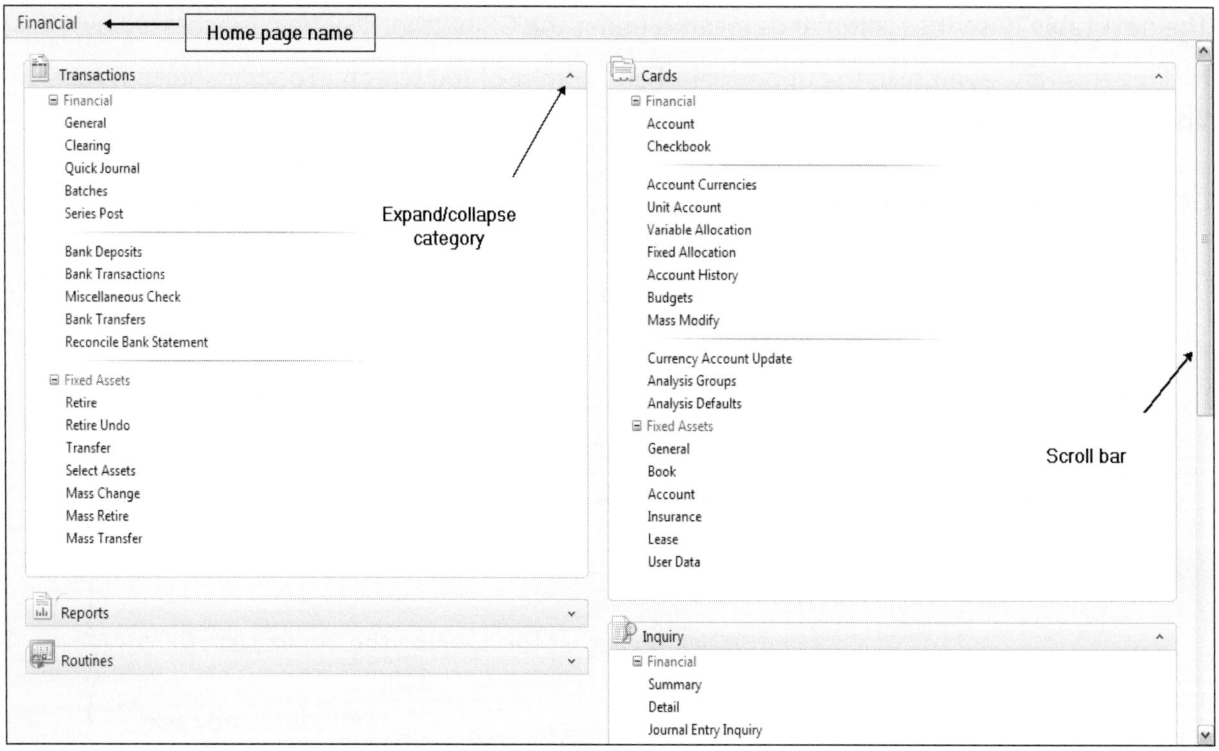

Figure 1:26 Financial Series Home Page

Menu Categories	Tasks
Transactions	Commands for processing transactions. *(Note: This category is not found on the Administration home page.)*
Inquiry	Commands for opening read-only views of transaction data and account balances
Reports	Commands for preparing reports
Cards	Commands for creating and managing master records in the Series
Setup	Commands for setting up Series security and internal controls
Utilities	Commands for deleting/purging records in Series data tables
Routines	Commands for performing routine tasks such as year ending a Series

Table 1:4 Contents Pane Categories

SYSTEM DATE

This topic calls attention to the System Date by emphasizing the importance of changing this date each time you begin a GP session. Click the system date appearing in the bottom left corner of the screen. This date remains docked so it is accessible from any home page.

After opening the date, you can click the calendar icon and scroll through months and years to select a date or you can simply type in a date. Type in "03312007" and click **OK**. This date now appearing at the bottom left. All tasks performed in this text occur in March of 2007. Therefore, make sure to set the system date to a date in March of 2007 before performing a task.

IMPORTANCE OF THE SYSTEM DATE:

Warning: Transactions may be posted to the wrong accounting period if you fail to set the system date.

GP uses the system date as the default date for transactions, inquiries, and reports. The software initially sets this date to your computer's system date. Because tasks in this text occur in March 2007, initially setting the system date to a date in March 2007 helps ensure that you are posting to the correct accounting period. You may also want to change the system date to match the date for a particular task. Always remain conscious of the system date before performing a task. We will try to alert you to changing this date by supplying the date symbol illustrated to the right at the beginning of exercises.

FIELD LOOKUP WINDOWS, HYPERLINKS, AND DROPDOWN LISTS

Users frequently need quick access to transaction information and account balances. Lookup windows assist in selecting information for a field. Hyperlinks are shortcut links for opening other windows related to the field. Dropdown Lists set options for a field. Let us illustrate.

S&S's accountant, Ashton, needs to locate details about a transaction posted to the cash account on January 8, 2007. With the **Financial** home page active, click **Detail** under the **Inquiry** category to open the window illustrated in Figure 1:27.

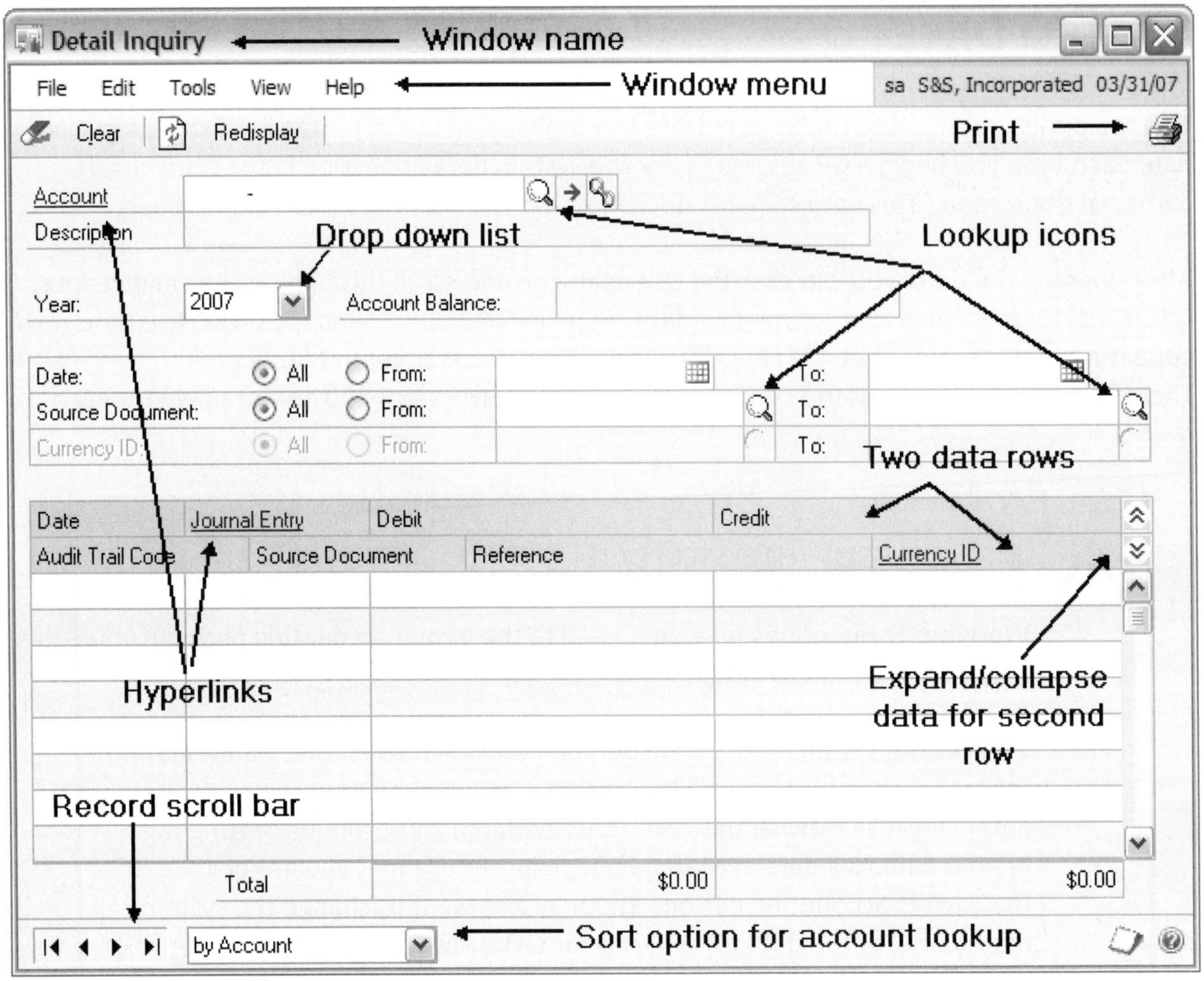

Figure 1:27 Detail Inquiry Window

The window is labeled so you can identify features. The window name displays in the Title bar at the top and window menus appear beneath the Title Bar. This window also contains a printer icon.

There are lookup icons for selecting Account and date range data. The hyperlinked field name for Journal Entry opens a window to view the transaction. Finally, the dropdown list on Year will change the view of data to a different year. *(Note: You must click Redisplay after changing the year.)*

The record scroll bar has record pointers for scrolling through records in a table. In this example, you are viewing the table containing general ledger accounts so clicking the first record pointer displays the first general ledger account and clicking the last record pointer display the last general ledger account. The two record pointers in the middle sequentially scroll backward and forward through general ledger accounts one at a time.

Finally, after selecting an account, this window displays two rows of transaction data in the bottom grid. The headings in each row identify field data in the row. You can expand the view of data on the second row by clicking the row expansion button and collapse the view by clicking the row condense button.

Ashton cannot remember the account number for the cash account so click the **Lookup icon** on the **Account** field to open the window illustrated in Figure 1:28.

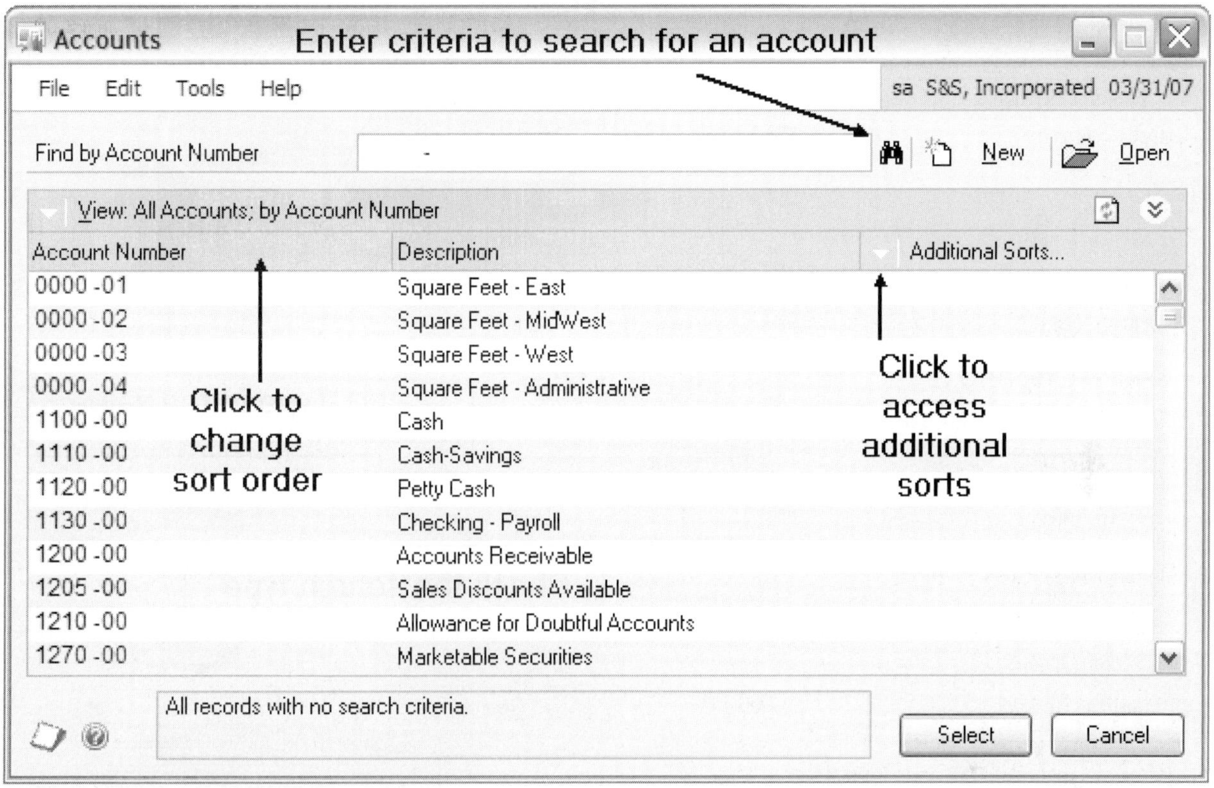

Figure 1:28 Account Lookup Window

The Accounts window lists all general ledger accounts and is currently sorted by account number. You have several options for locating an account.

First, you can change the sort order by clicking column names in the header row. If you click Account Number then account numbers resort from ascending to descending order. If you click Description then accounts sort by alphabetical description. Clicking Additional Sorts allows you to specify other sorting options.

You can also search for an account number or name using the binoculars. Click the **binoculars** so we can practice. (See Figure 1:29.)

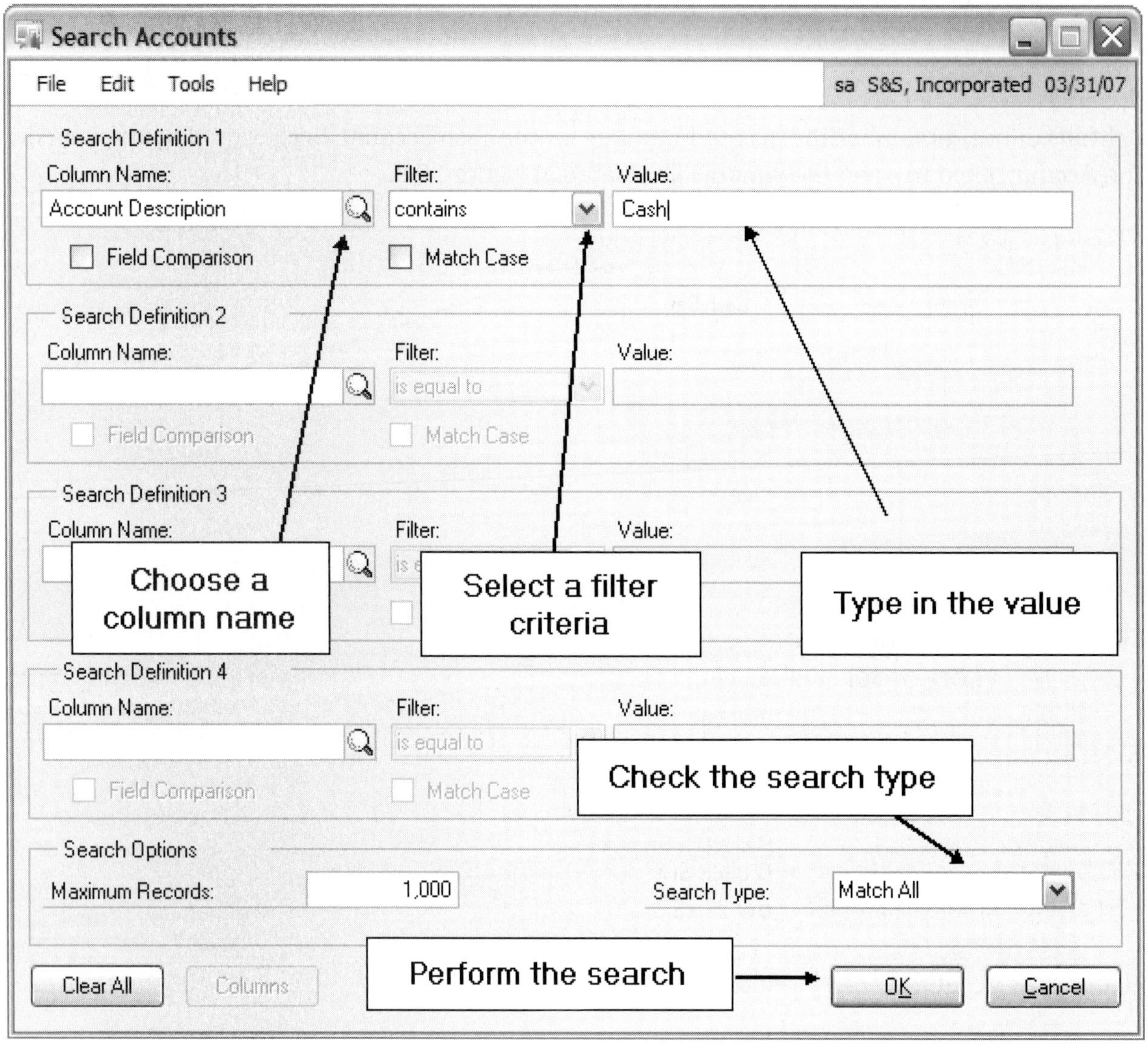

Figure 1:29 Account Search Window

The window illustrated above can conduct a search using four different criteria. Enter the values shown and click **OK**. Upon returning to the Accounts window you find three accounts containing Cash in the description. (See Figure 1:30.)

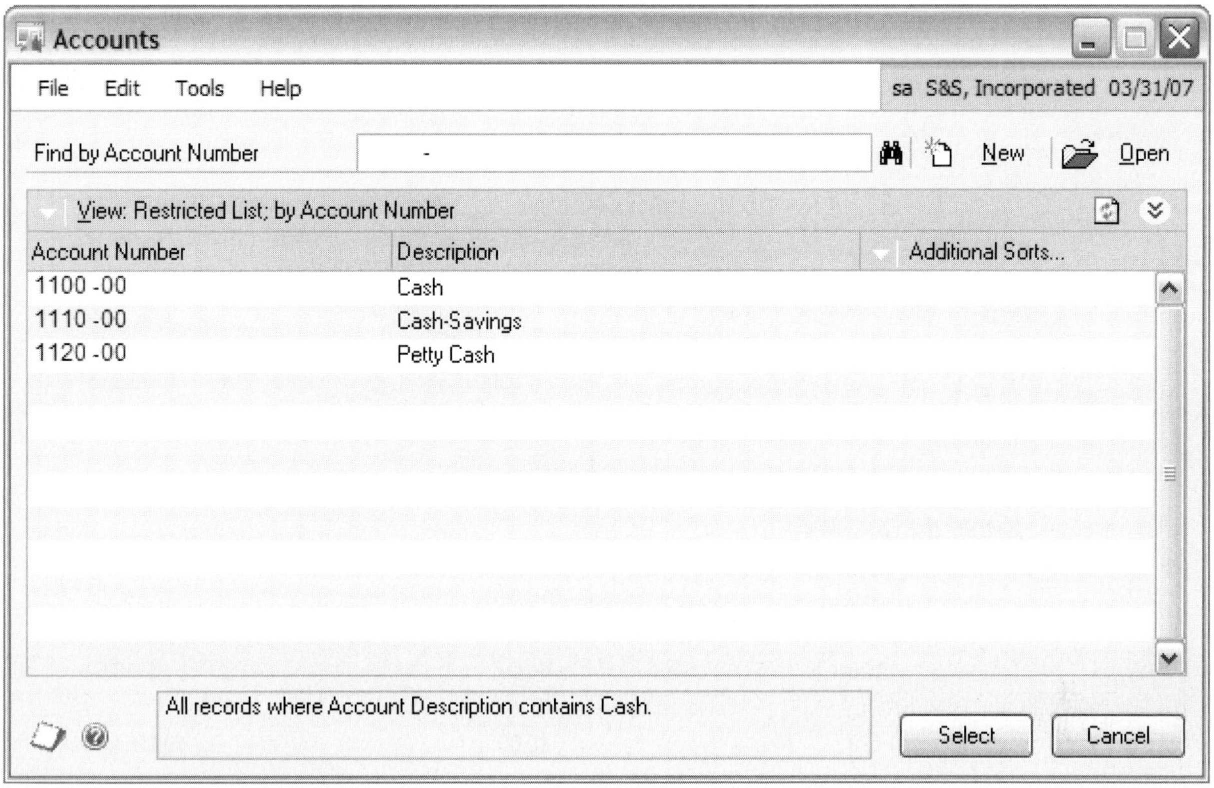

Figure 1:30 Search Results

Highlight account 1100-00 and click **Select** or double click the account. Confirm that Year is 2007 and expand details for row 2. (See Figure 1:31.)

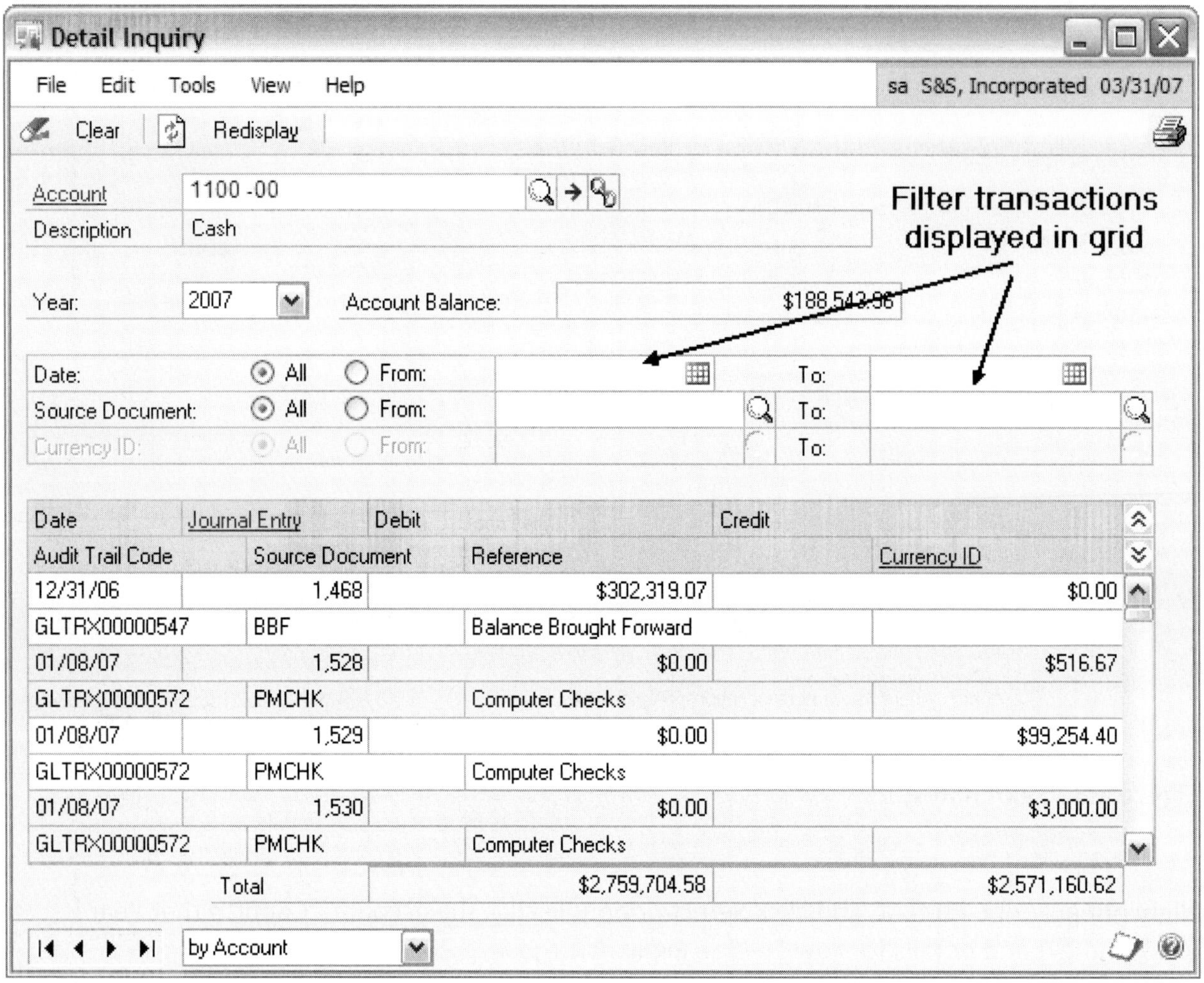

Figure 1:31 Details for Cash Account

The grid lists transactions posted in 2007. You can filter for specific date ranges or by specific source documents using the fields indicated on the illustration.

Highlight the second transaction in the grid (i.e., Journal Entry 1528) and click the Journal Entry hyperlink to see the actual transaction. Open details for the second row so you can view general ledger account names. (See Figure 1:32.)

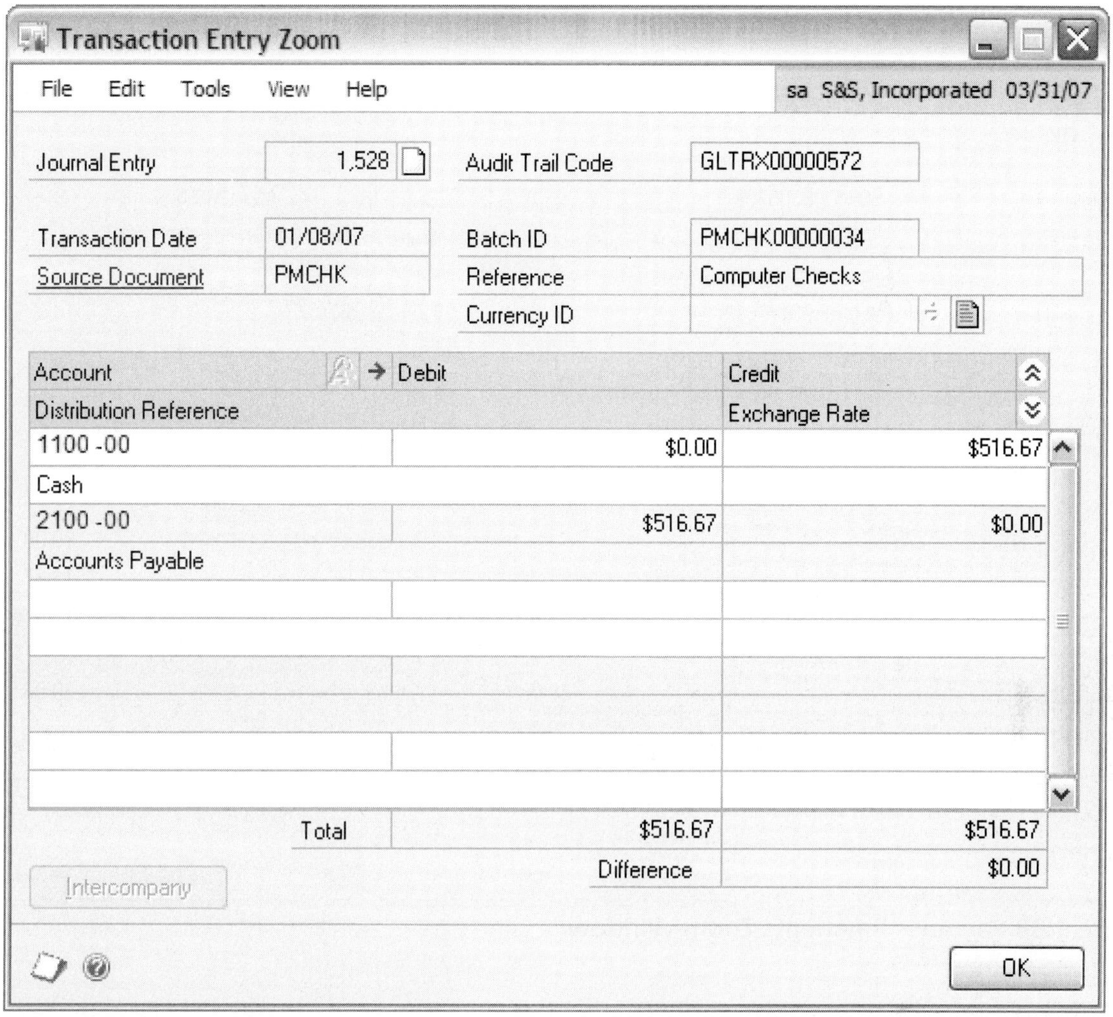

Figure 1:32 Transaction Entry Zoom

The Transaction Entry Zoom window lists all accounts debited and credited by the transaction. It also displays the Batch ID and Reference so we know that this transaction posted as a computer check paying a vendor invoice in accounts payable.

Click the **Source Document** hyperlink to zoom into check details. (See Figure 1:33).

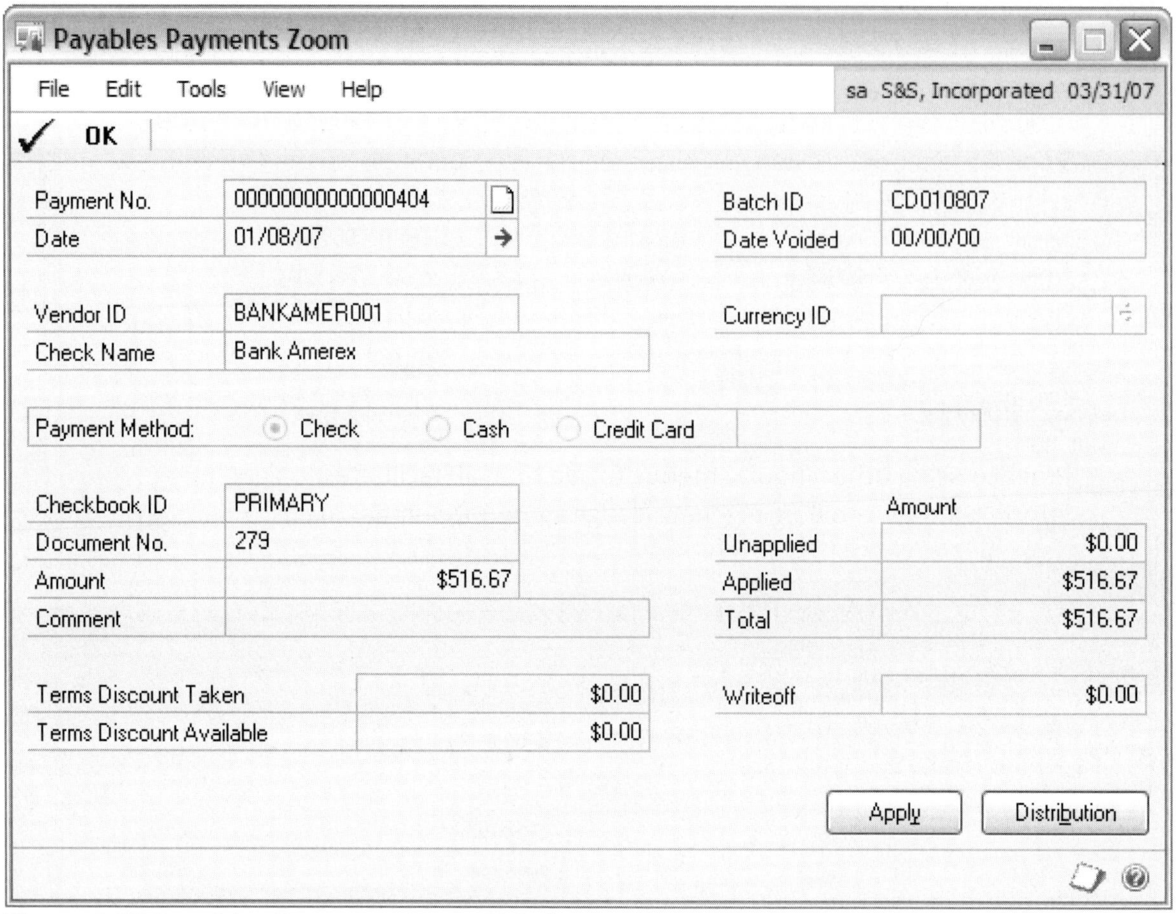

Figure 1:33 Payables Payments Zoom Window

You now know that the payment was on check number 279 sent to Bank Amerex. Click **X** to close the Payables Payment Zoom window and the Transaction Entry Zoom window. Now practice looking up information in the next exercise.

Ashton asks you to inquire into a transaction recorded on January 25, 2007 for $138,412.50 posted in the sales account for the East. He would like to know the customer billed, the invoice number, and the inventory items sold.

After locating this information, experiment looking up the same transaction using the Sales home page. Begin your search by selecting either the Transaction by Customer or Transaction by Document link under the Inquiry category.

Practice using other Inquiry menus to see that GP facilitates looking up information by knowing a general ledger account number, a customer name, or a specific invoice number.

E1:1 Practice Lookups and Hyperlinks

Toolbar Shortcuts

Toolbar shortcuts can be added to the Toolbar to provide quick links to often-used menu commands. Shortcuts are grouped and separated by a separator bar. Holding your mouse over a shortcut displays a description of the shortcut as illustrated next.

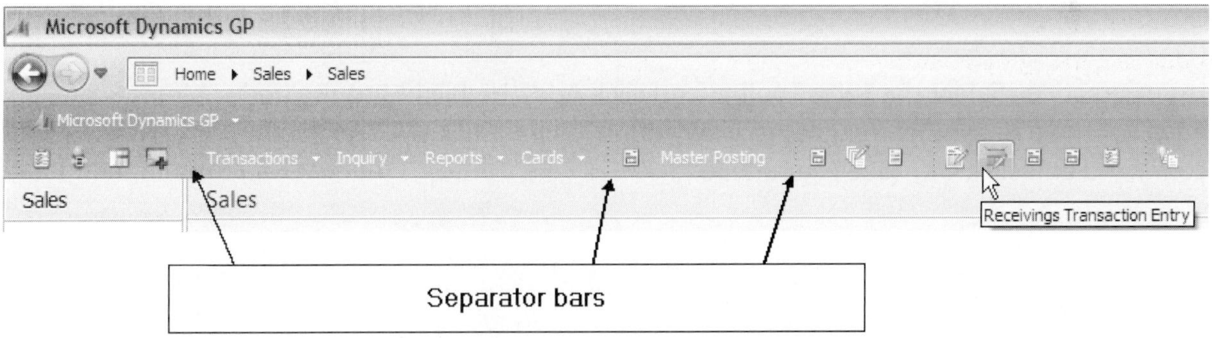

Figure 1:34 Toolbar Shortcuts

You can easily customize shortcuts by right clicking on the Toolbar and selecting **Customize**. You then choose a Toolbar to modify and select an action such as Add or Delete (Figure 1:35).

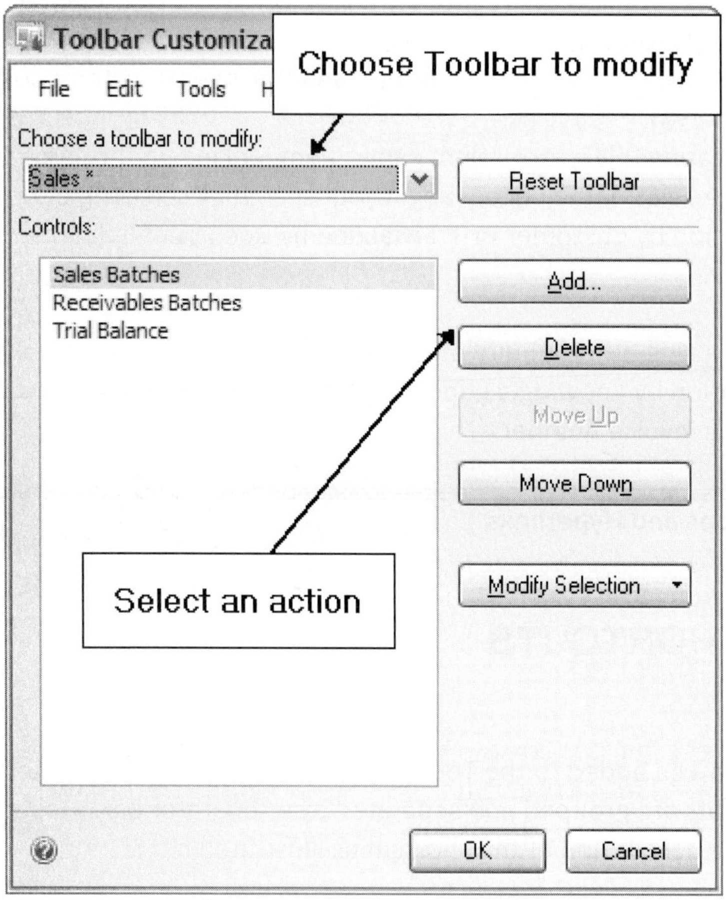

Figure 1:35 Toolbar Customization Window

Let us practice. Select the **Sales** Toolbar and click **Add**. Highlight **Inquiry** under Menu Groups and click the plus symbol for Sales to view your choices. Click the **Transaction by Customer** command and click **OK**. (See Figure 1:36.)

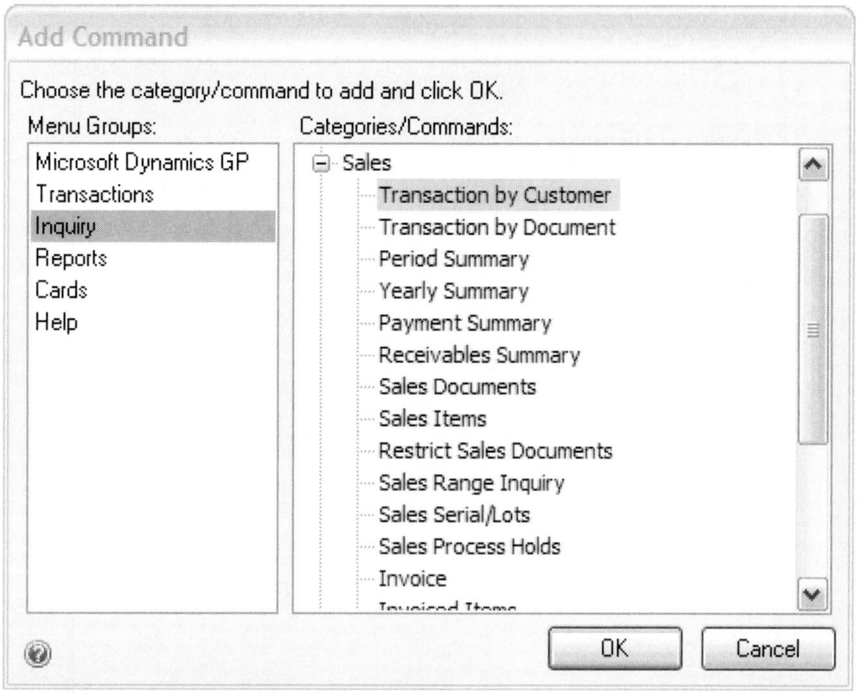

Figure 1:36 Add Toolbar Command

Upon returning to the Toolbar Customization window, keep clicking **Move Down** until the newly added command appears at the bottom. (See Figure 1:37.)

Figure 1:37 New Toolbar Command Added

Click **OK** to save the changes and then hold your mouse over the Toolbar until it displays the new shortcut description illustrated in Figure 1:38.

Figure 1:38 New Shortcut on Toolbar

Click the shortcut to open the inquiry window. *Note: You viewed this window in a previous exercise.* You now see the benefits of creating Toolbar shortcuts so feel free to customize the Toolbar to meet your needs. Close the Inquiry window.

FINANCIAL ACCOUNTS

In relational database terms, general ledger accounts, customers, vendors, inventory, and employees are the master records of an accounting system.[2] In GP, you create these records using **Cards** menus. Master records must be created before recording transactions because transaction records must link to master records. For instance, a sales transaction must link to a customer record, inventory records, and general ledger account records.

Let us now explore creating and modifying general ledger account records. Activate the **Financial** home page and click **Accounts** under the **Cards** category. The Account Maintenance window for general ledger accounts is shown in Figure 1:39 with the first cash account displayed.

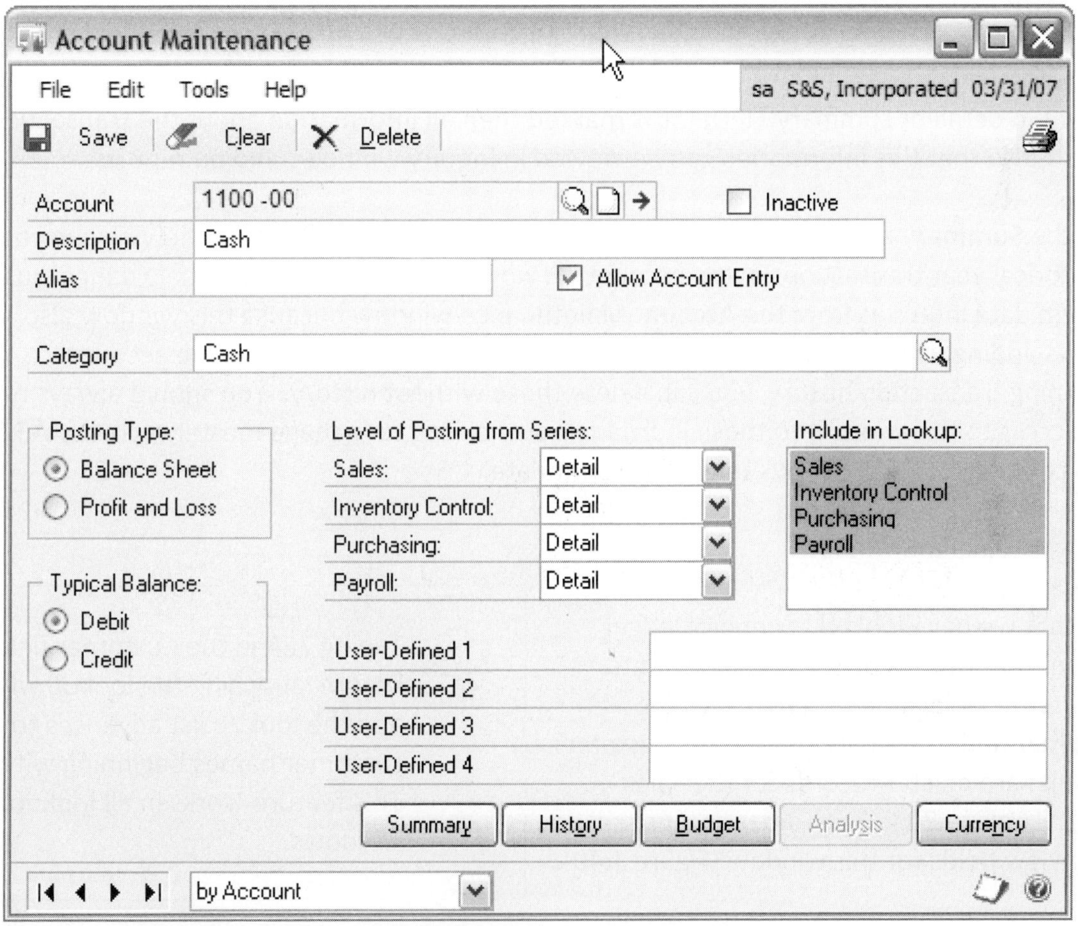

Figure 1:39 Account Maintenance Window

Description defines the account on reports whereas Alias is an optional field that can be to sort lookup windows. *(Note: You previously practiced using sort options in the lookup window.)*

[2] See Chapter 2 for more information on master records.

The account has options for setting Posting Type and Typical Balance. **Posting Type** determines where an account appears on financial statements whereas **Typical Balance** instructs GP on whether the account balance is increased by a debit or credit. You see that creating general ledger accounts requires accounting knowledge.

Category is used to group accounts on financial statements. For instance, this account appears under the Cash category of the Balance Sheet alongside other accounts in this category.

The **Allow Account Entry** option determines if you can post transactions to the account. When the option is marked then transactions can be posted.

The Series highlighted under **Include in Lookup** means the account will display in lookup windows for that Series.

Finally, the **Level of Posting from Series** option determines if transactions will post to the account in detail or summary. If Detail is marked then all information about the transaction will be stored so that this information can be viewed in inquiry windows and on reports.

Note the **Summary** and **History** buttons. These buttons open windows for viewing current year or historical year transactions in the account. A word of caution, it is extremely dangerous to perform data inquiries from the Account Maintenance window because this window also permits adding, changing and deleting accounts. Although GP will not delete accounts containing transaction history, you can delete those without history. You should always restrict user access to this window to those individuals authorized to manage master records. All other users can use Inquiry windows to view account data. [3]

Click **X** to leave the window.

Now that we have looked at general ledger accounts, let us look at customer accounts. Activate the **Sales** home page and click **Customer** under the Cards category. Customer accounts are master records for the Sales Series. Look up Zears' customer account so we can review fields for this window (Figure 1:40).

> Typing ZEA in the Customer field before launching the lookup window and the lookup list advances to customer names beginning with ZEA. This feature works in all lookup windows.

[3] Accounting controls are discussed in Chapter 3.

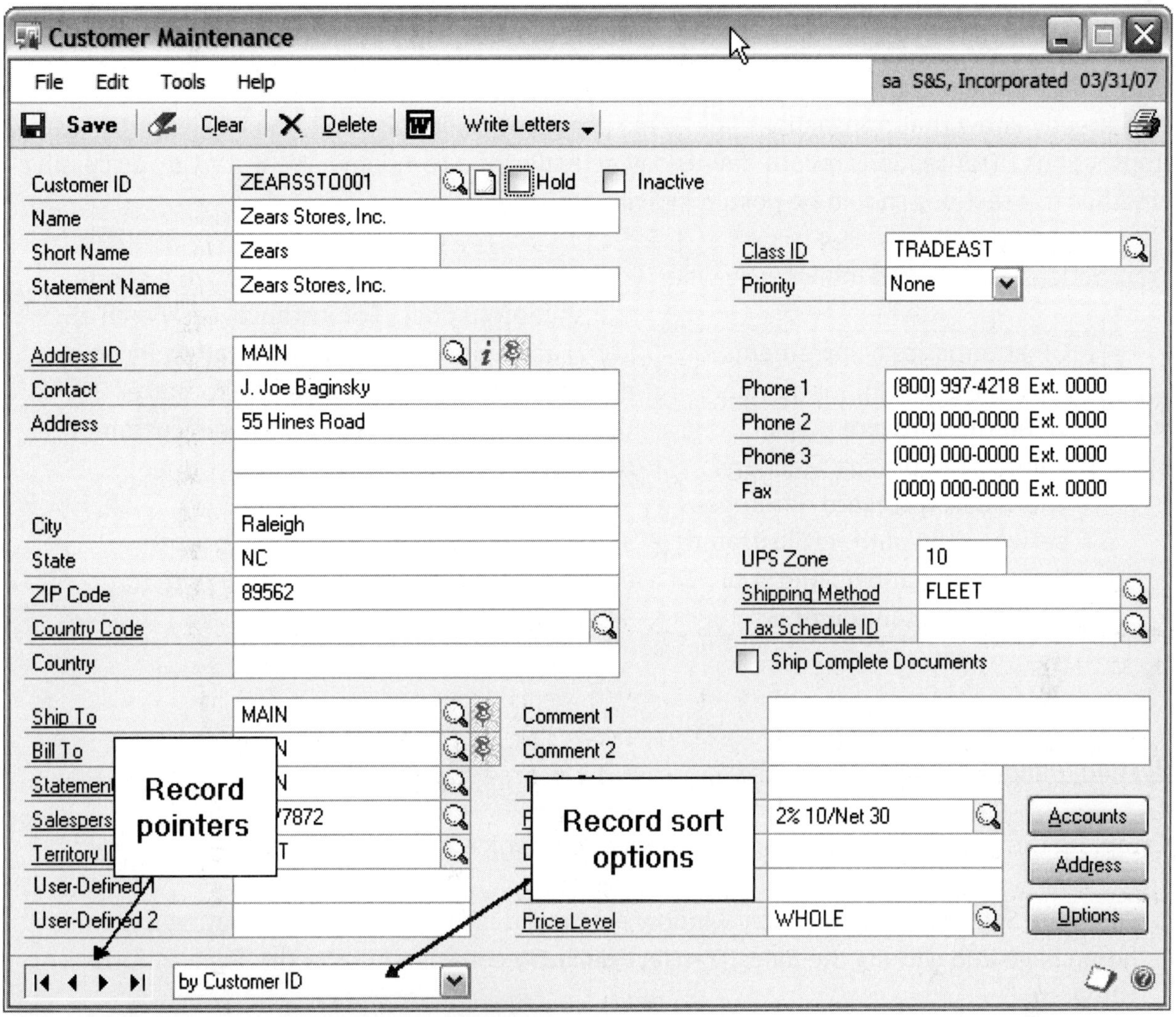

Figure 1:40 Customer Maintenance Window

Customer card fields are more fully explained in Chapter 5 so, for now, note the record pointers located at the bottom of the window that allow sequential movement through customer accounts. Furthermore, you can change the way these pointers move through the records by using the sort dropdown list to choose a different sort option. Click **X** to close the window.

Before moving to the next topic, take time to explore master records for other Series. You will always open main accounts for the Series by clicking the first command under the Cards category.

TRANSACTIONS

You already know that transactions link to master records. In this topic you will learn to post transactions. Transactions record day-to-day activities of a company. We'll start by discussing whether transactions should be posted individually or in batches.

Transactions are entered individually when you need to immediately post or have just one transaction to post. For instance, on March 15, 2007, accounts receivable clerk, James Richmond, needs to immediately post a sale to Better Buy so that shipping can immediately begin customer delivery.

> GP automatically increments auto-filled document numbers when the software posts, deletes, or voids transactions. Therefore, disregard differences between the authors illustrated document numbers and your actual document numbers.

Perform the steps that follow to post this entry. *(Note: Change your system date to 3/31/2007.)*

<u>Posting Individual Sales Transactions</u>

Complete the next steps to post an individual sales invoice.

1. Open the Sales Transaction Entry window illustrated in Figure 1:41 by activating the **Sales** home page and clicking the **Sales Transaction Entry** command under the Transactions category.

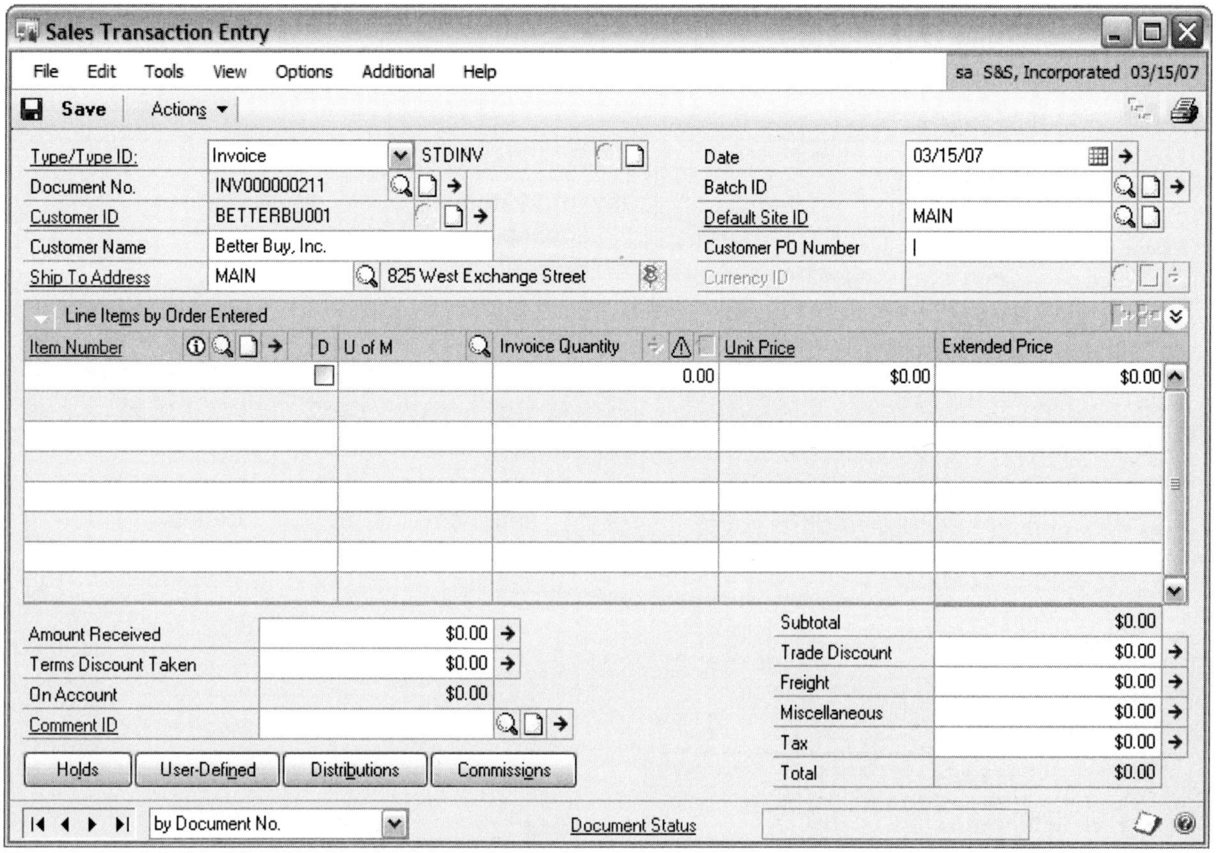

Figure 1:41 Sales Transaction Entry Window

2. Select **Invoice** for **Type/Type ID** and tab to **Customer ID**. Notice that as you tabbed past Document No. the value autofilled. This field is a document control feature to be discussed in Chapter 5.

3. Look up **Better Buy** as the customer and verify that the transaction **Date** is 3/15/2007.

> ⚠ If you select the wrong Customer ID it cannot be changed because GP has already linked this transaction to the customer's record. To select a different customer, click the Actions button and select either Delete or Void.

4. Tab to **Item Number** for the first inventory line item and look up to select **AUDSNCDMP3**. (See Figure 1:42.)

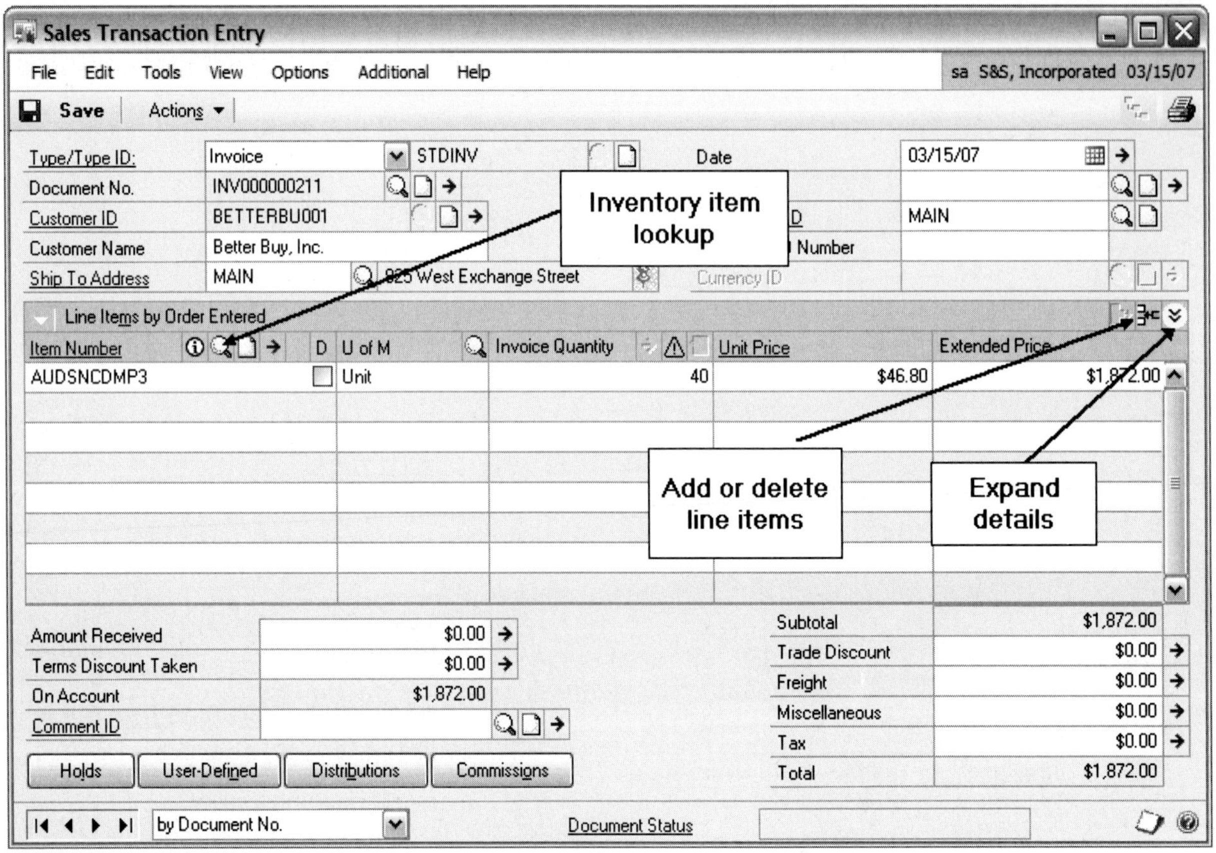

Figure 1:42 Inventory Items on Sales Transaction

> ⚠ If you select the wrong Item Number it cannot be changed. Instead, click the icon illustrated in Figure 1:42 to delete the line item and then reselect an item.

5. Tab to **Invoice Quantity** and enter 40.

6. Expand details for this line item to verify that the quantity is available and that the Qty Fulfilled equals 40. (See Figure 1:43.)

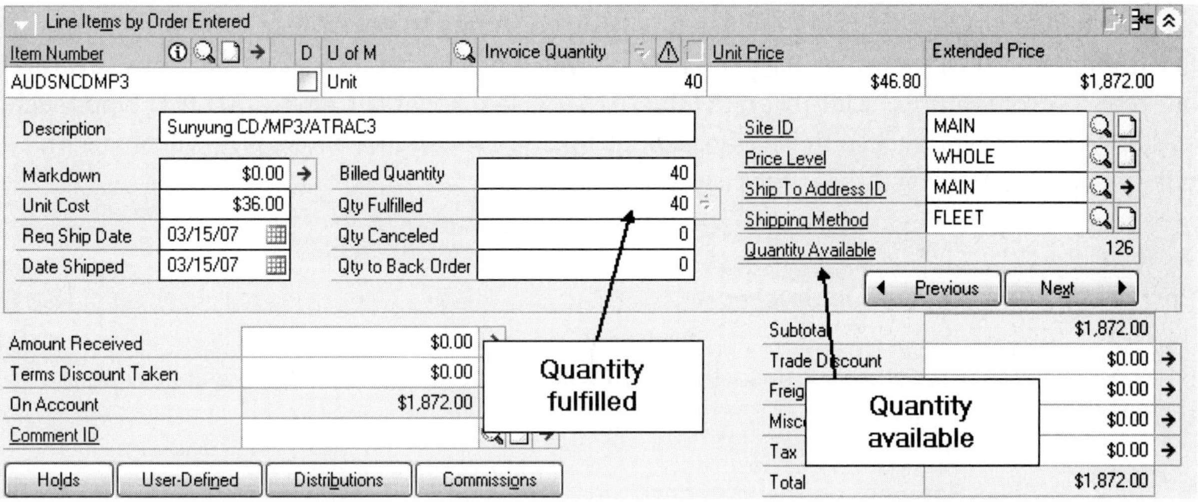

Figure 1:43 Line Item Details

7. Now click **Save** to try and save the transactions. GP prompts as illustrated in Figure 1:44. Click **OK**. Because this transaction in not stored in a batch, you can only post, delete, or void it.

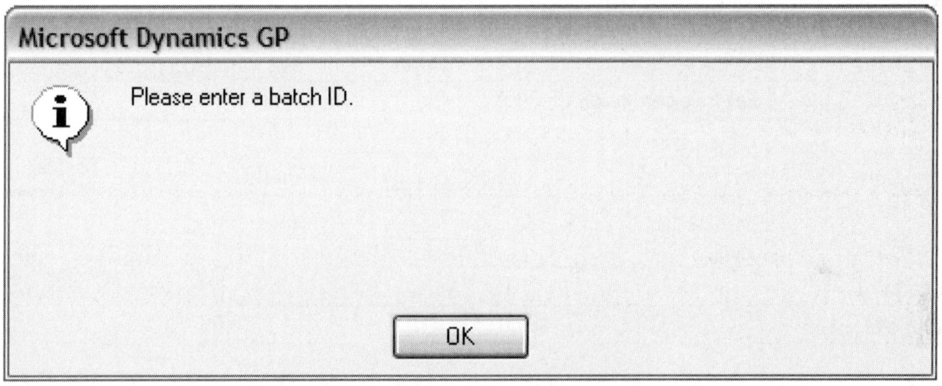

Figure 1:44 Sales Transaction Save Error Message

8. Click the **Actions** button and select **Post**.

9. Click **X** to close the window and posting reports print to the screen. These are control reports listing the transaction's effect on inventory, customer, and general ledger accounts. Subsequent chapters discuss posting reports and the purpose of control reporting in detail. For now, close each report and return to the home page.

> ⚠ After posting an individual transaction, posting reports print only after you close the transaction window. Moreover, these reports will not print to the screen if another report is already open. If it seems like you are waiting a long time for a report to appear then verify that no other reports are open by looking at your Window task bar.

Posting individual transactions is inefficient when processing large numbers of transactions. Furthermore, you will learn in Chapter 3 that posting individual transactions bypasses several internal control features. Moreover, in Chapter 5 you learn that certain transaction types such as sales orders never post so these transactions must be saved to a batch. We will next turn our attention to posting transactions saved in a batch.

Posting Sales Transactions In Batches

Batches are folders for storing transactions you will post at a later time. You will now post a transaction using a batch.

1. Click the **Sales Batches** command under Transactions and enter the information illustrated in Figure 1:45.

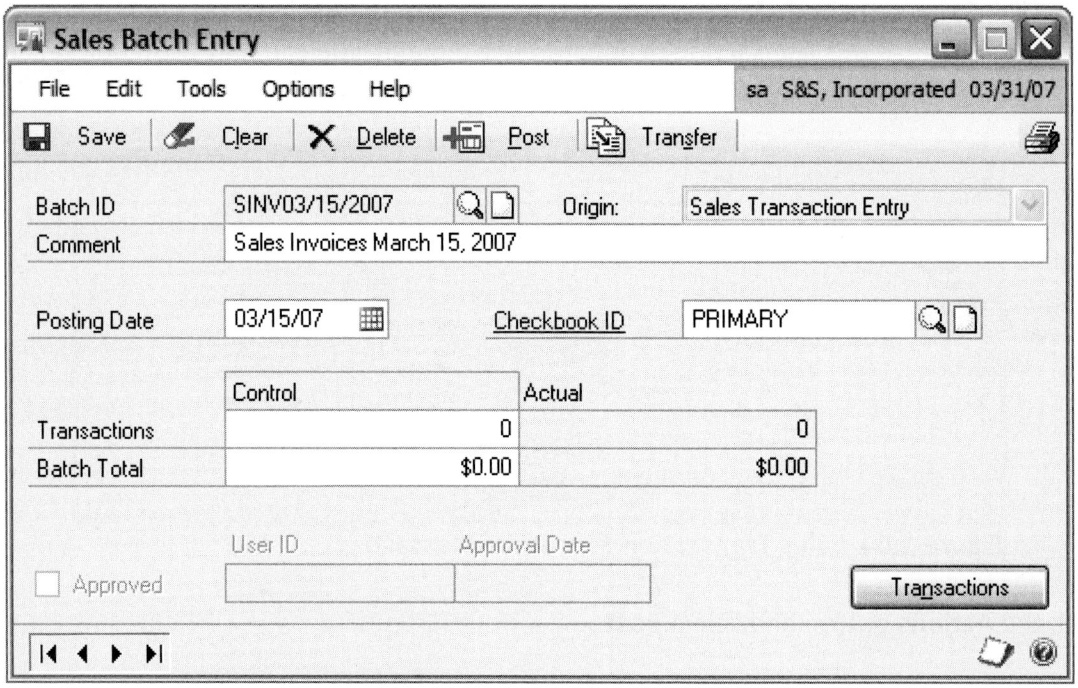

Figure 1:45 Creating a Sales Batch

2. The **Batch ID** value is chosen by the user and should uniquely identify transactions stored in the batch. **Origin** identifies the type of transactions to be stored in the batch. **Comment** is additional text that can be used to describe transactions in the batch. Also, always verify the **Posting Date**. You learn later in the text that this date functions separately from the date on transactions.

3. Click the **Transactions** button.

4. You will now create a sales invoice using the same steps previously illustrated. Refer to Figure 1:46 and create this invoice to Book Buy Earnest for 50 digital camcorders. Note that

the Batch ID from the Sales Batch Entry window appears in the Batch ID for the transaction because you opened the transaction window from the Sales Batch Entry window.

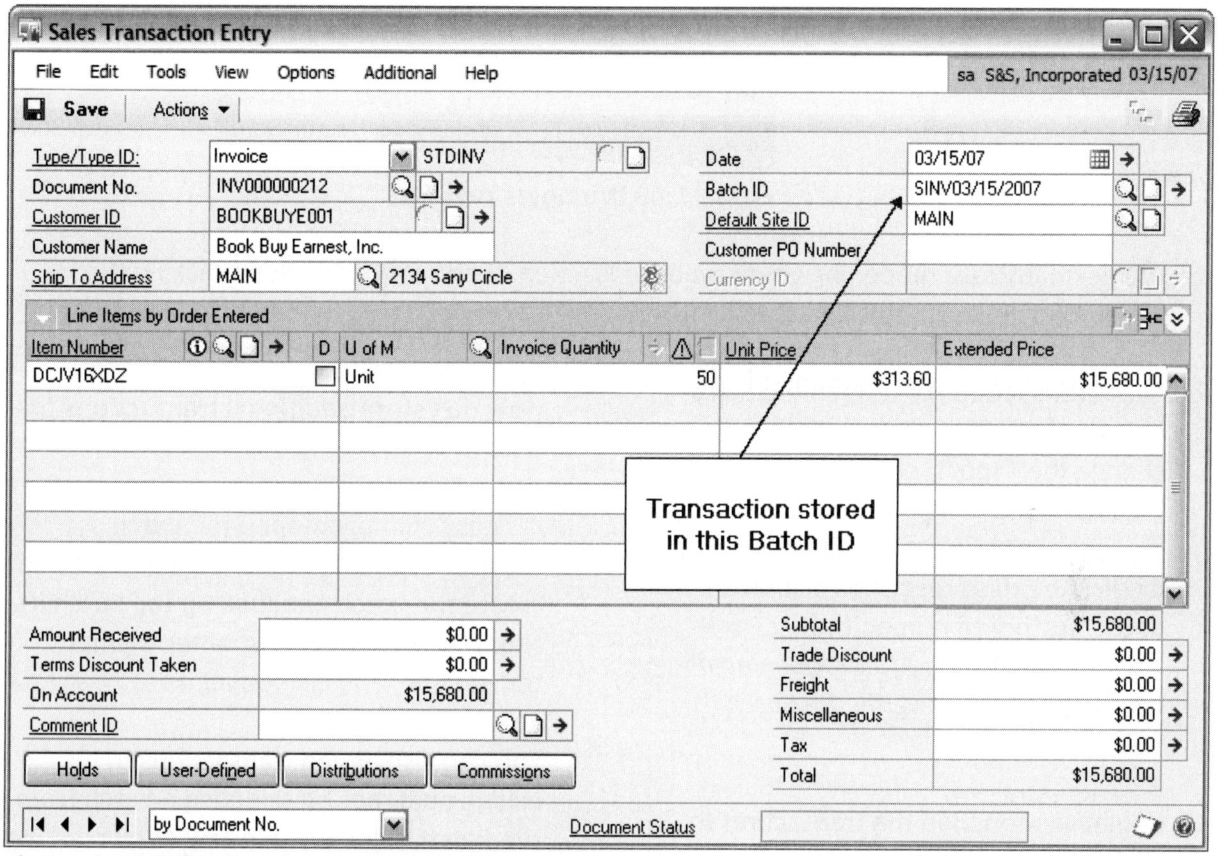

Figure 1:46 Sales Invoice to Book Buy Earnest

5. Click **Actions** and select **Post** to receive the message illustrated in Figure 1:47. Click **OK**. Transactions containing a value in the Batch ID field cannot be posted individually. If you wanted to post this transaction individually then you must delete the Batch ID.

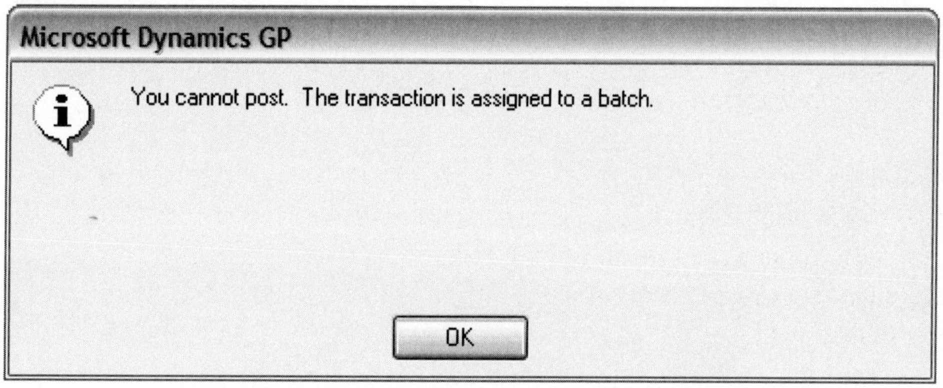

Figure 1:47 Posting Message for Transactions in a Batch

6. Click **Save** to store the transaction and then click **X** to close the transaction window.

7. Return to the Sales Batch Entry window. If you do not see this window, then activate it from the task bar. (See Figure 1:48.)

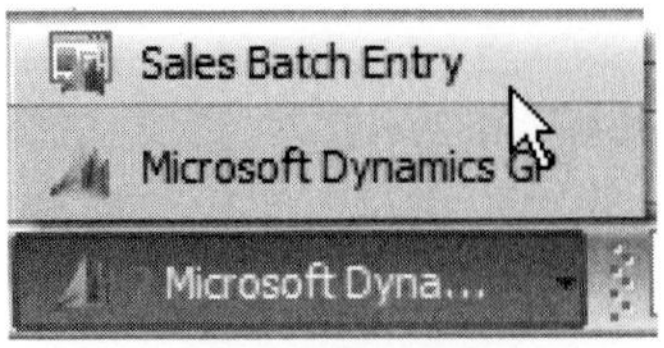

Figure 1:48 Windows Task Bar

8. We next illustrate reopening your saved transaction. Reopen the batch by clicking the Batch ID lookup icon to select batch SINV03/15/2007.

9. Click **Transactions** to reopen the Sales Transaction Entry window. Either change the Type/Type ID field to Invoice and use the Document No. lookup icon to select INV00000000212 or click the third record scroll button at the bottom to reopen the transaction. (*Note: After reopening a transaction always verify the Batch ID value.)*

10. You have reopened the transaction so click **X** to close the transaction.

11. You are now ready to post the batch. Reopen the batch folder as previously illustrated. Click **Post**. Notice that this time posting reports print immediately to the screen and before closing the Sales Batch Entry window. Close each report and close the Sales Batch Entry window.

> How do I store additional transactions to a batch?
>
> It's easy. Simply reopen the batch window using the menu originally used to create the batch and look up the Batch ID. Next, click Transactions, enter the new transaction, and click Save.
>
> You can also assign transactions to existing batches by selecting a batch from the Batch ID lookup window or by creating typing a new batch ID into the Batch ID field and saving the batch when prompted.

DATES...DATES...DATES!! Why do we enter dates so many times?

By now you have entered dates on transactions and on batches. These dates do not have to be the same; however, both impact financial records differently.

How is the batch date used?

When setting up GP, the accountant determines whether to use the batch or the transaction date as the date entries post to the general ledger. *(Note: This posting setup option is discussed in Chapter 3.)* Thus, batch dates determine the posting date on general ledger accounts.

How is the transaction date used?

The transaction date is the date entries post in the Sales, Purchasing, Inventory, and Payroll Series. Thus, a sales invoice posts to the customer account as of the transaction date so that the invoice due date, discount date, and number of days outstanding ages by the actual date of the transaction.

RUNNING REPORTS

Reports are the heart of analyzing financial performance. GP offers different types of report but all reports are generated using commands found under a home page's Reports category. In subsequent chapters we will look at reports in greater depth. In this topic we will illustrate steps for creating and printing reports.

Let us begin by running S&S's financial statements. Complete the next steps.

1. Activate the **Financial** home page and click **Financial Statements** under the **Reports** category. Click the lookup icon on Report to view financial statement types. (See Figure 1:49.)

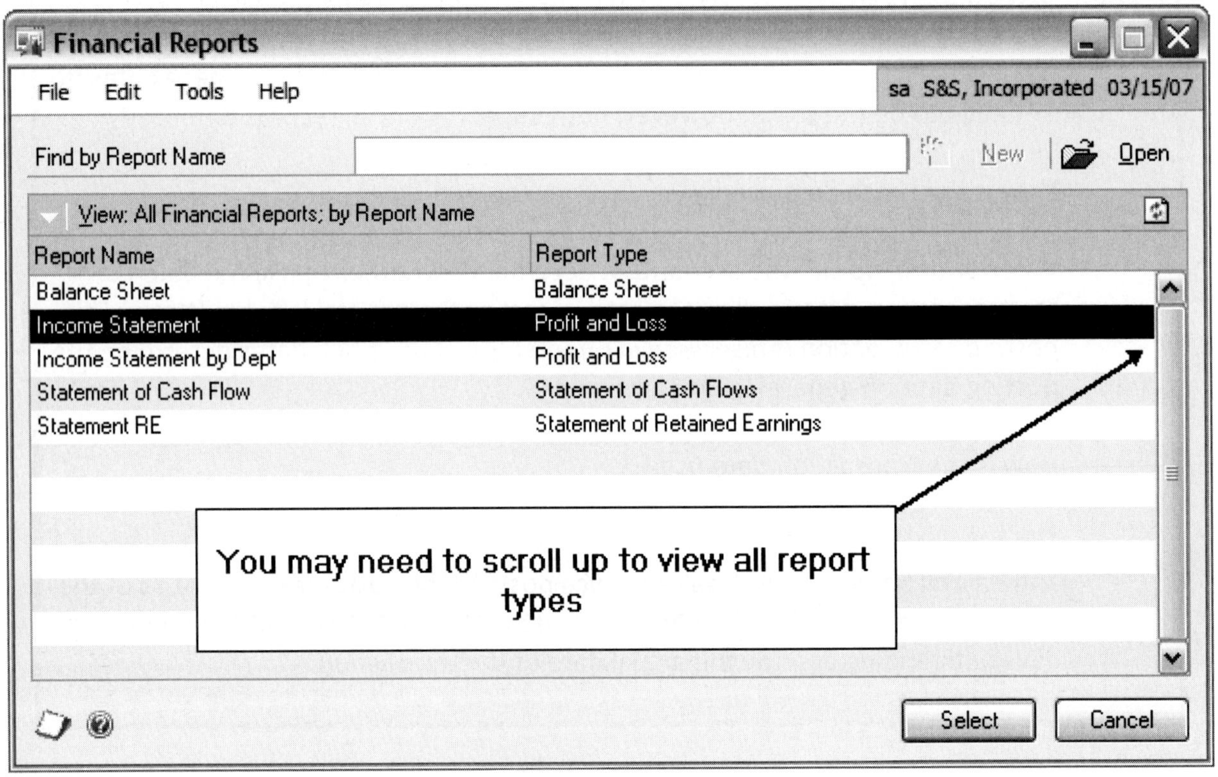

Figure 1:49 Financial Statement Report Types

2. Highlight **Income Statement** and click **Select** to return to the Financial Statement Report window. (See Figure 1:50.) The report category appears in Report and the customized reports for this category appear under Options.

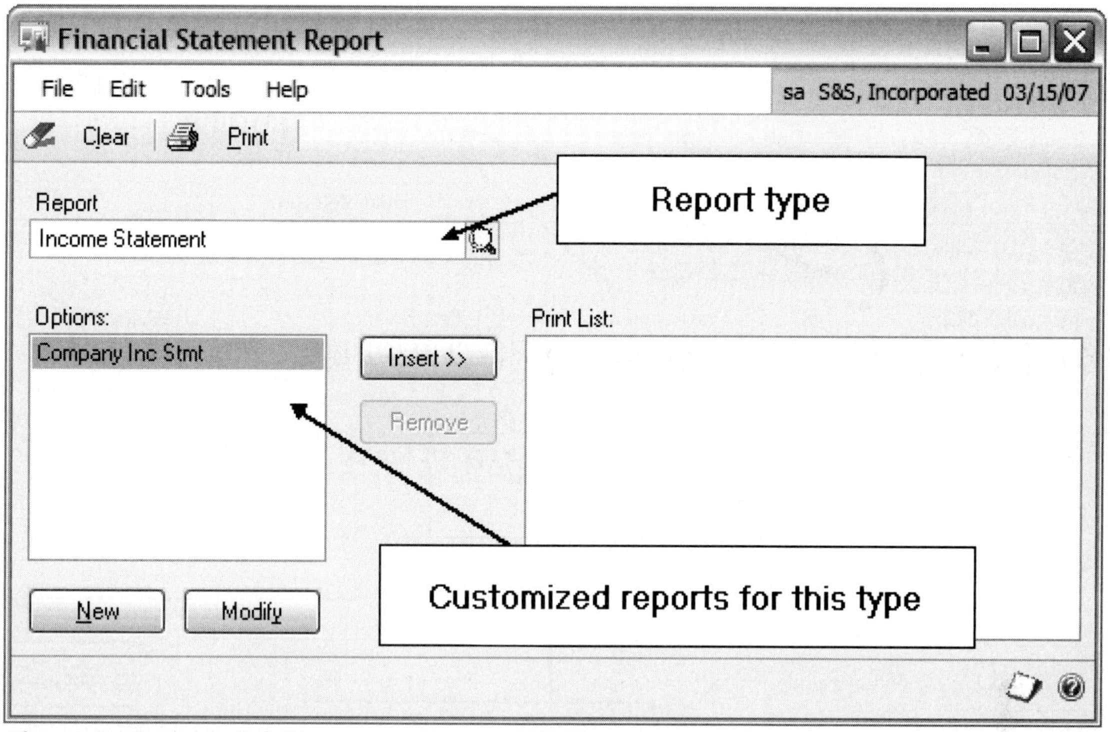

Figure 1:50 Financial Statement Report Window

3. Highlight the report under Options and click **Modify** to open the window illustrated in Figure 1:51. Options windows vary by report because settings and filters for manipulating output are based on the report type.

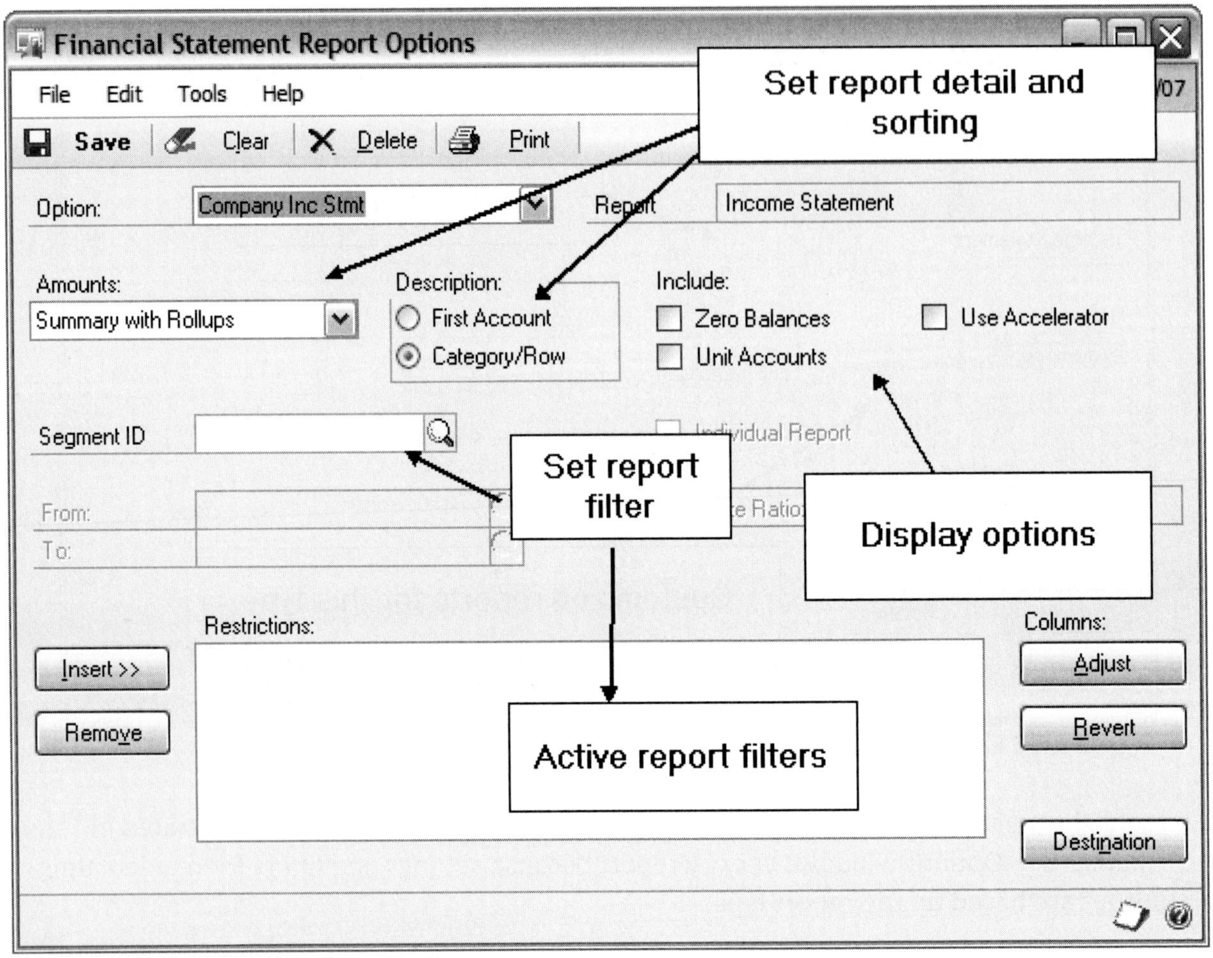

Figure 1:51 Options Window for Reports

4. Notice that there is no option for entering a date range for the income statement. *(Note: You will not be able to set a date for any financial statement report.)* If your system date falls on a date in March 2007 then the income statement prints for the period of January through March 2007. If you want to change the reporting date range then change the system date.

5. We will first print the report using its current options. Click **Destination** to verify where output will be sent. The income statement is set to print to the screen (Figure 1:52) so click **OK**.

⚠ If your system date falls on a date outside of 2007 an error appears on the report stating:

"The user date falls within a fiscal year that hasn't been set up."

To correct, close the report and change the system date before reprinting.

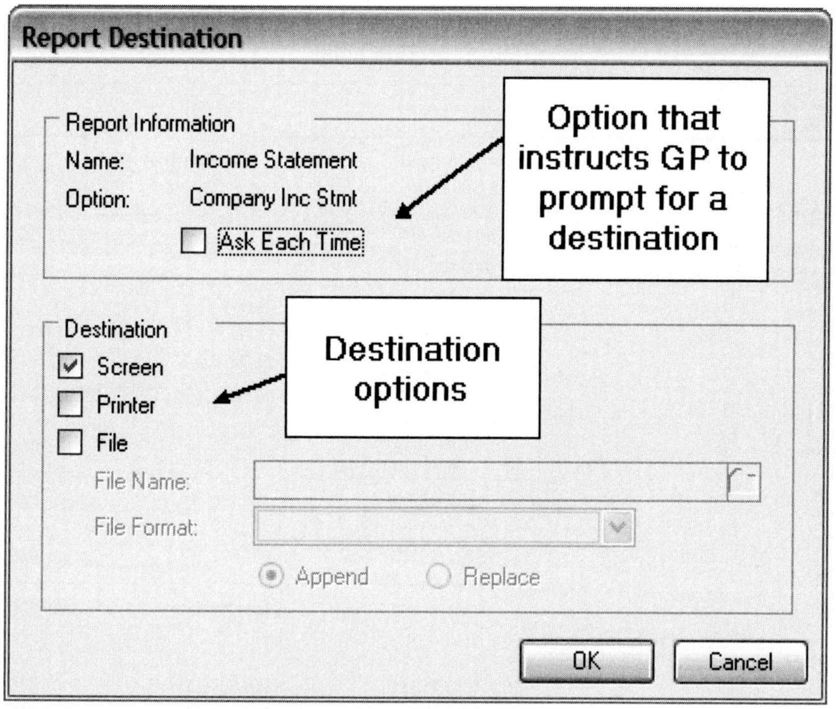

Figure 1:52 Report Destination Window

6. Now click **Print**. (See Figure 1:53.)

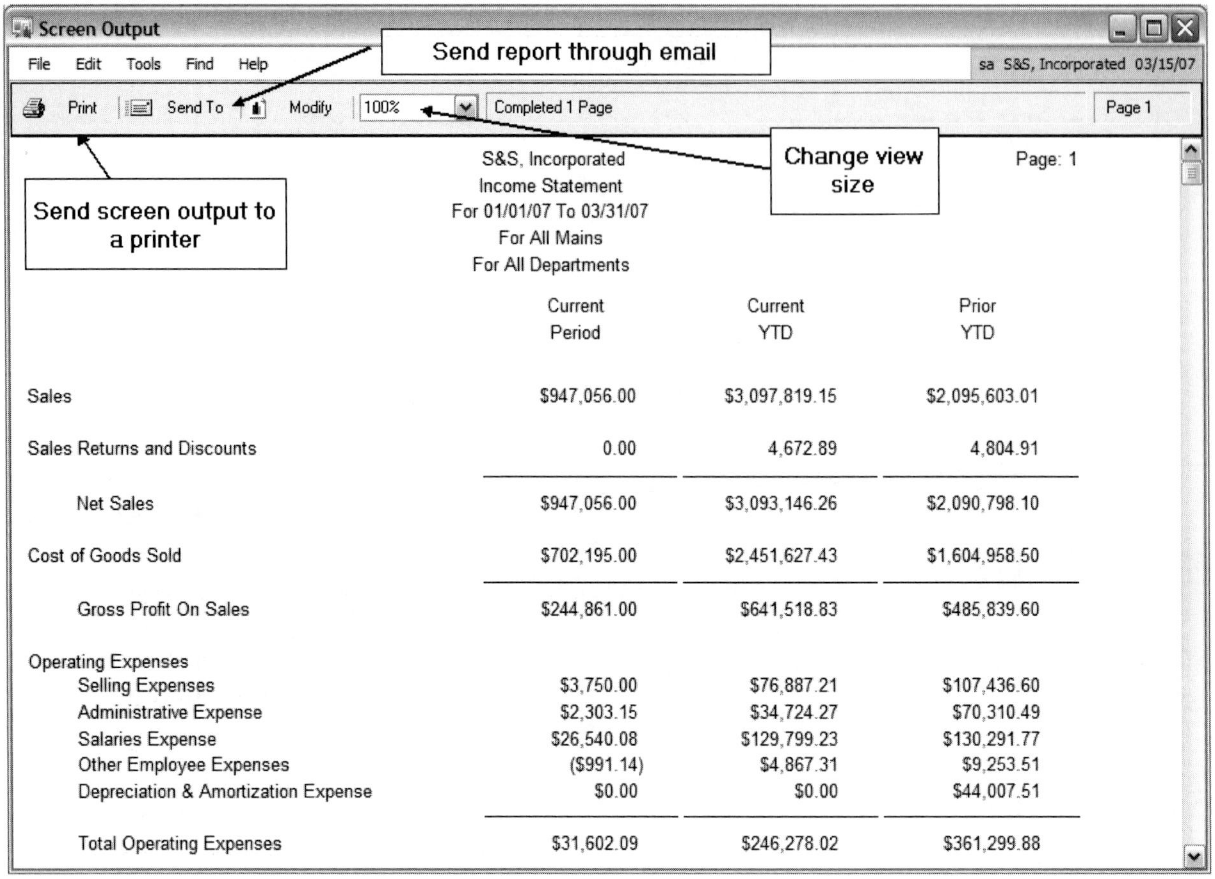

S&S, Incorporated
Income Statement
For 01/01/07 To 03/31/07
For All Mains
For All Departments

	Current Period	Current YTD	Prior YTD
Sales	$947,056.00	$3,097,819.15	$2,095,603.01
Sales Returns and Discounts	0.00	4,672.89	4,804.91
Net Sales	$947,056.00	$3,093,146.26	$2,090,798.10
Cost of Goods Sold	$702,195.00	$2,451,627.43	$1,604,958.50
Gross Profit On Sales	$244,861.00	$641,518.83	$485,839.60
Operating Expenses			
Selling Expenses	$3,750.00	$76,887.21	$107,436.60
Administrative Expense	$2,303.15	$34,724.27	$70,310.49
Salaries Expense	$26,540.08	$129,799.23	$130,291.77
Other Employee Expenses	($991.14)	$4,867.31	$9,253.51
Depreciation & Amortization Expense	$0.00	$0.00	$44,007.51
Total Operating Expenses	$31,602.09	$246,278.02	$361,299.88

Figure 1:53 Screen Output of Income Statement

7. Close the report so we can test a few of the options. Change the option under **Amounts** to Detail with Rollups and print the report. Notice that the report provides more detailed information. (See Figure 1:54.) Close the report.

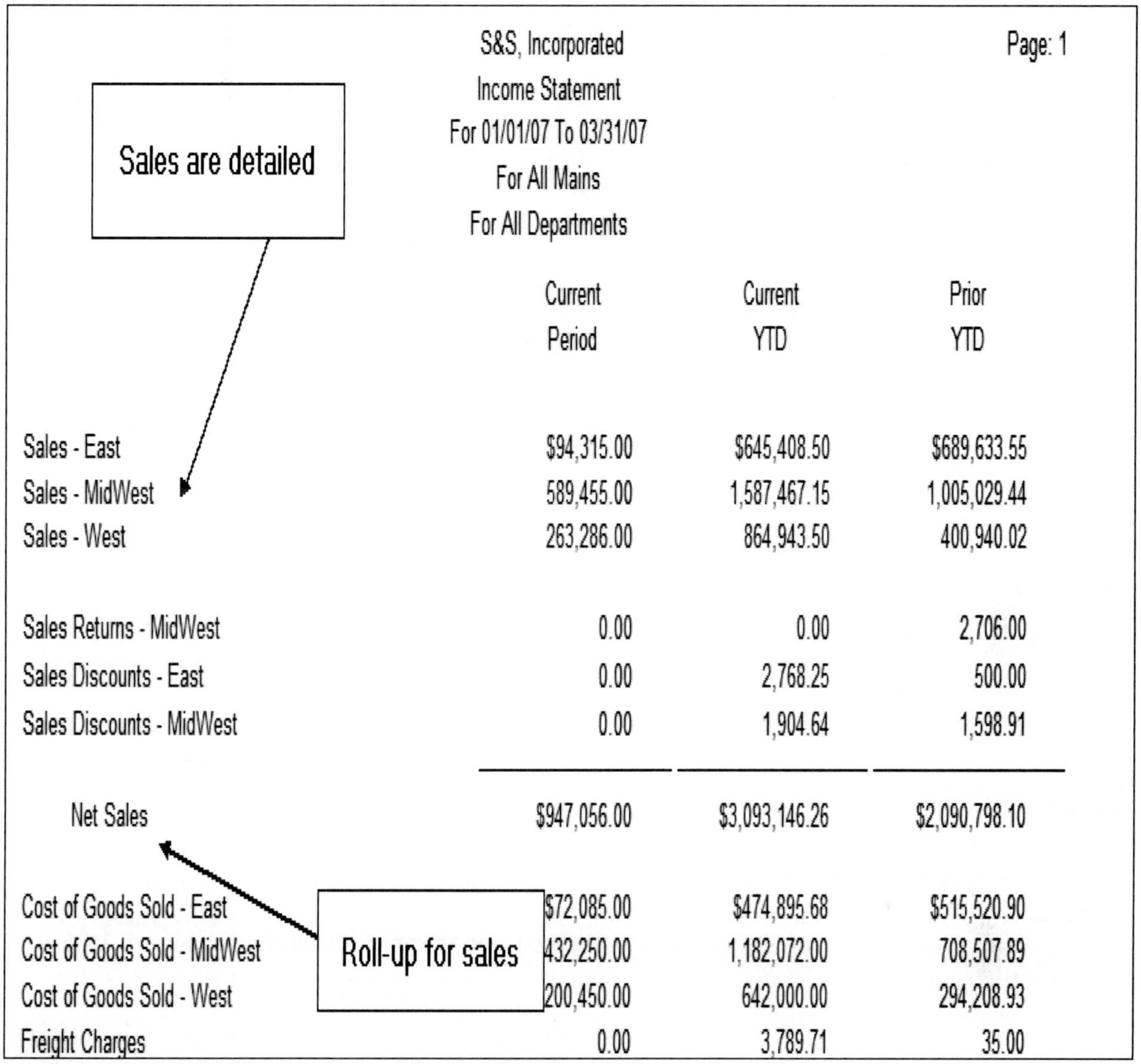

S&S, Incorporated
Income Statement
For 01/01/07 To 03/31/07
For All Mains
For All Departments

Page: 1

	Current Period	Current YTD	Prior YTD
Sales - East	$94,315.00	$645,408.50	$689,633.55
Sales - MidWest	589,455.00	1,587,467.15	1,005,029.44
Sales - West	263,286.00	864,943.50	400,940.02
Sales Returns - MidWest	0.00	0.00	2,706.00
Sales Discounts - East	0.00	2,768.25	500.00
Sales Discounts - MidWest	0.00	1,904.64	1,598.91
Net Sales	$947,056.00	$3,093,146.26	$2,090,798.10
Cost of Goods Sold - East	$72,085.00	$474,895.68	$515,520.90
Cost of Goods Sold - MidWest	432,250.00	1,182,072.00	708,507.89
Cost of Goods Sold - West	200,450.00	642,000.00	294,208.93
Freight Charges	0.00	3,789.71	35.00

Figure 1:54 Income Statement with Detail Rollups

8. We will now set criteria that filters the report so information on one department. Click the lookup icon on **Segment** and select **Department**. In **From**, look up and select **01** (i.e., East). This selection then fills in for **To**. Click **Insert** to place the criteria into **Restrictions**. (See Figure 1:55.) *(Note: You must always insert criteria before it is active for the report.)*

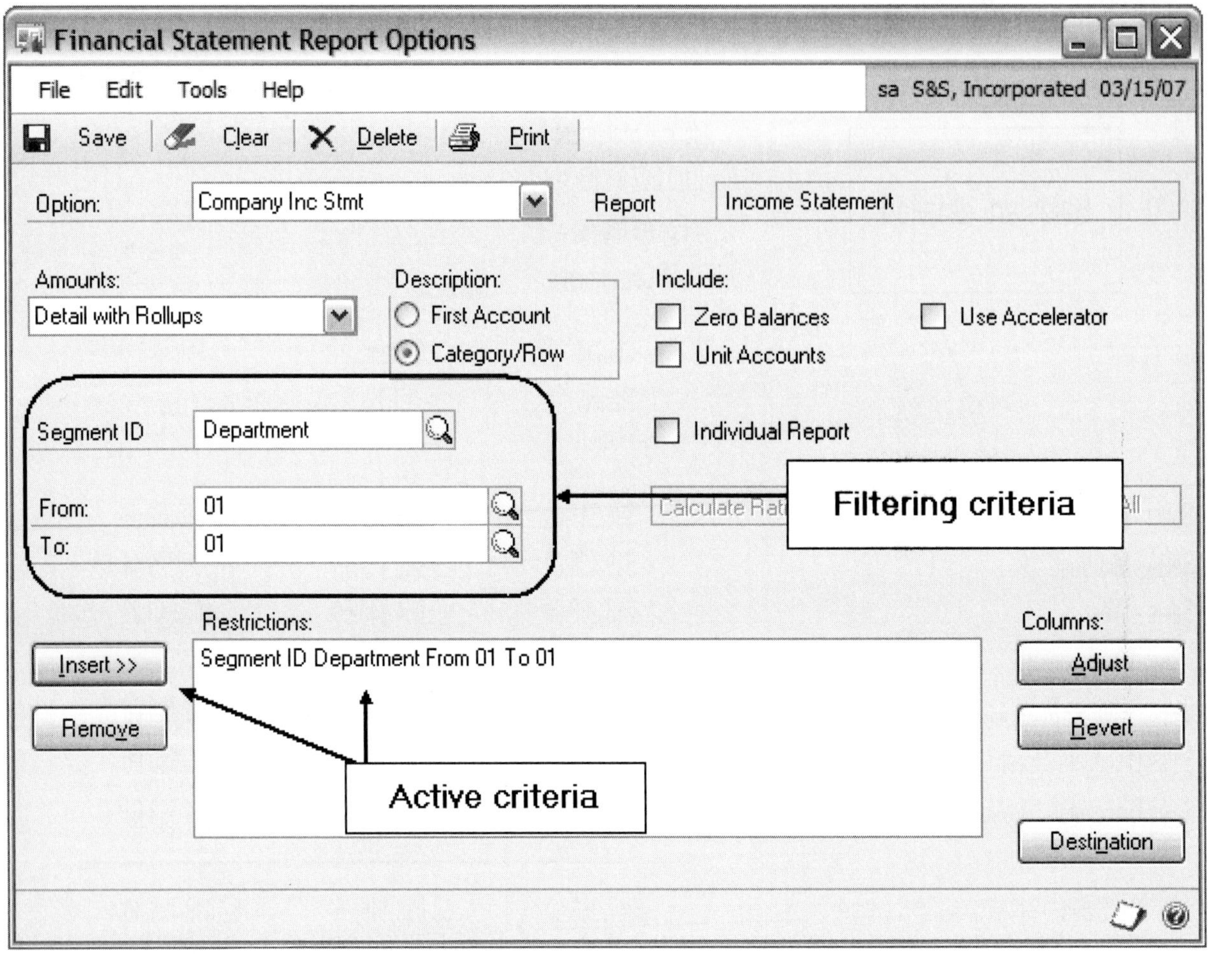

Figure 1:55 Criteria for Income Statement

9. Click **Print** and the income statement for the East department displays. (See Figure 1:56.) Close the report.

S&S, Incorporated
Income Statement
For 01/01/07 To 03/31/07
For All Mains
For Department East To East

Page: 1

	Current Period	Current YTD	Prior YTD
Sales - East	$94,315.00	$645,408.50	$689,633.55
Sales Discounts - East	0.00	2,768.25	500.00
Net Sales	$94,315.00	$642,640.25	$689,133.55
Cost of Goods Sold - East	$72,085.00	$474,895.68	$515,520.90
Gross Profit On Sales	$22,230.00	$167,744.57	$173,612.65

Figure 1:56 Income Statement for East

10. Close the Financial Statement Report Options window and GP prompts to save customized settings for the report. Click **Discard**.

11. You are returned to the original report window where we can practice creating a new income statement report. Click **New** and, in **Option**, type **IS For West**. Enter the criteria illustrated in Figure 1:57 and set the **Destination** to Screen.

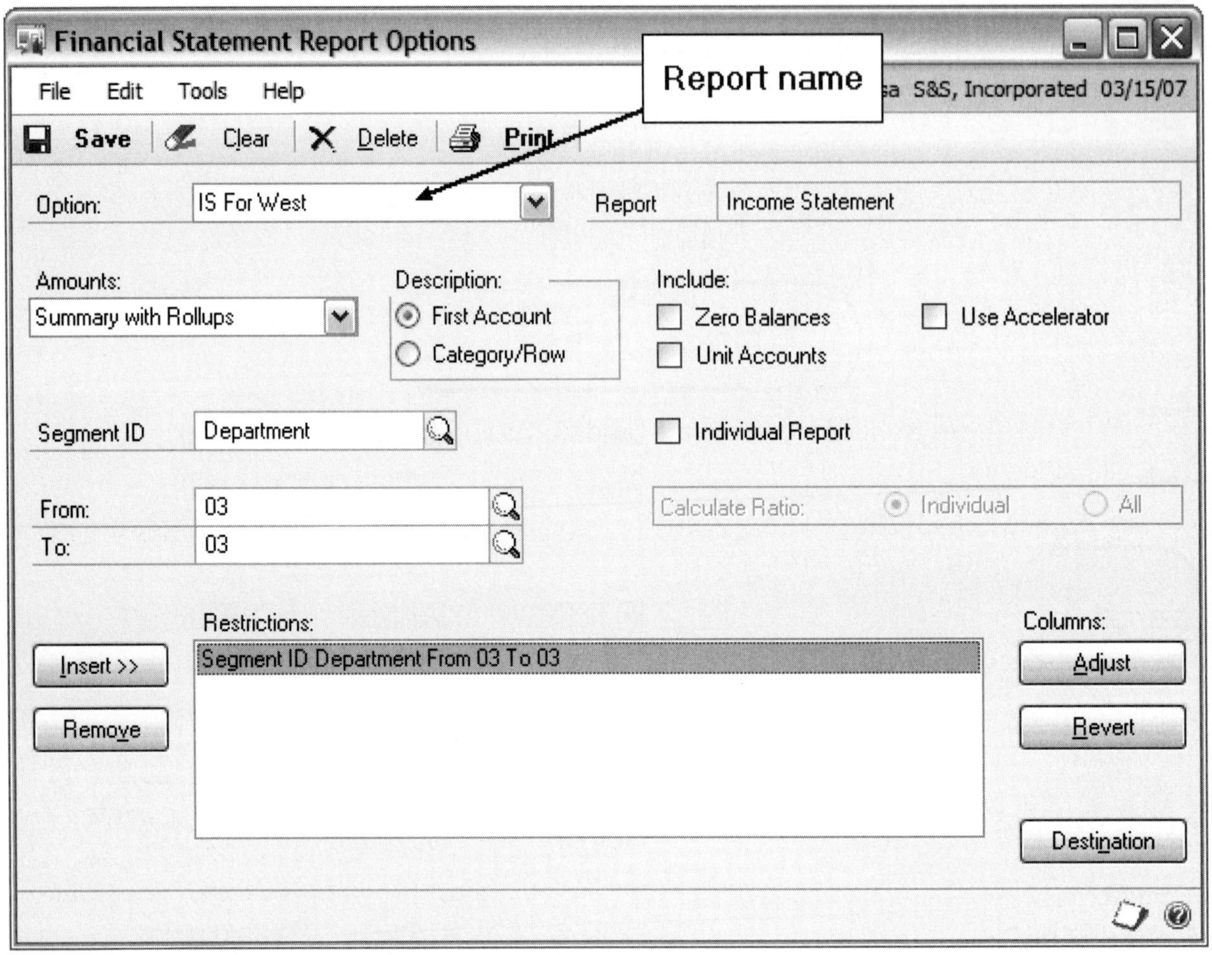

Figure 1:57 New Income Statement Report

12. Print the report to check the output and then click **Save** to store the new report. Close the window to find the new report listed under Options.

Reporting works the same in other Series. Just remember that options vary by report type and you must have a report listed under Options before you can print it. When you want to print a report without modifying it first then highlight the report under Options and click Insert to place into the Print List. You can then click Print to produce the output. You can also insert multiple reports from different reporting categories and print all reports simultaneously.

Close the Financial Statement Report window.

Try printing multiple financial statements.

First, select the Income Statement report category and insert the Company Inc. Stmt into the Print List.

Next, change the report type to Balance Sheet and insert the Company BalSheet into the Print List.

Click the Print button to view the reports. As you close one report the other appears.

E1:2 Practice Printing Multiple Reports

SETTING USER PREFERENCES

Preference options allow users to customize screen display, keyboard behavior, and printer options for local installations of GP. Open the User Preferences window by clicking the **GP Button** and selecting **User Preferences**. Figure 1:58 illustrates the window where you can set preferences for the user.

Your preferences are currently set to use the Screen as the default report destination and to move between fields on a form by pressing Tab. When you open a sales transaction the default document type to display is a sales Order.

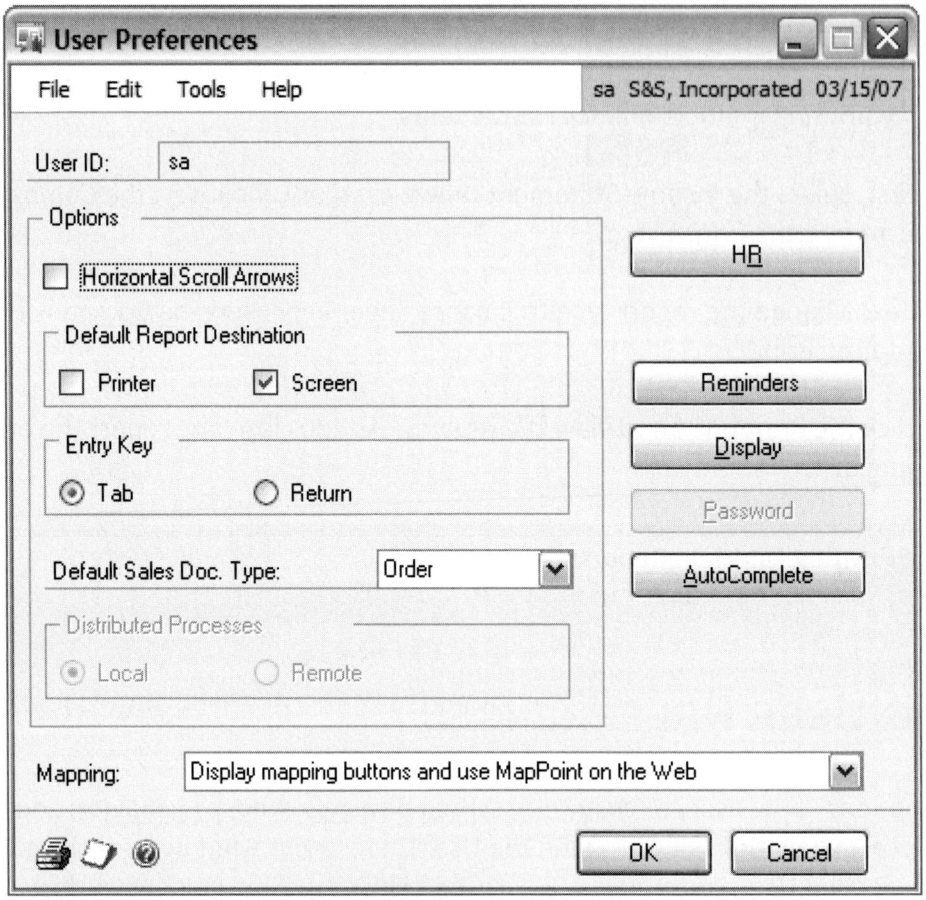

Figure 1:58 User Preferences Window

The Reminders button lets you set "to do" reminders. Click the **Display** button and set the options illustrated in Figure 1:59. These options instruct GP to display required fields for windows in red.

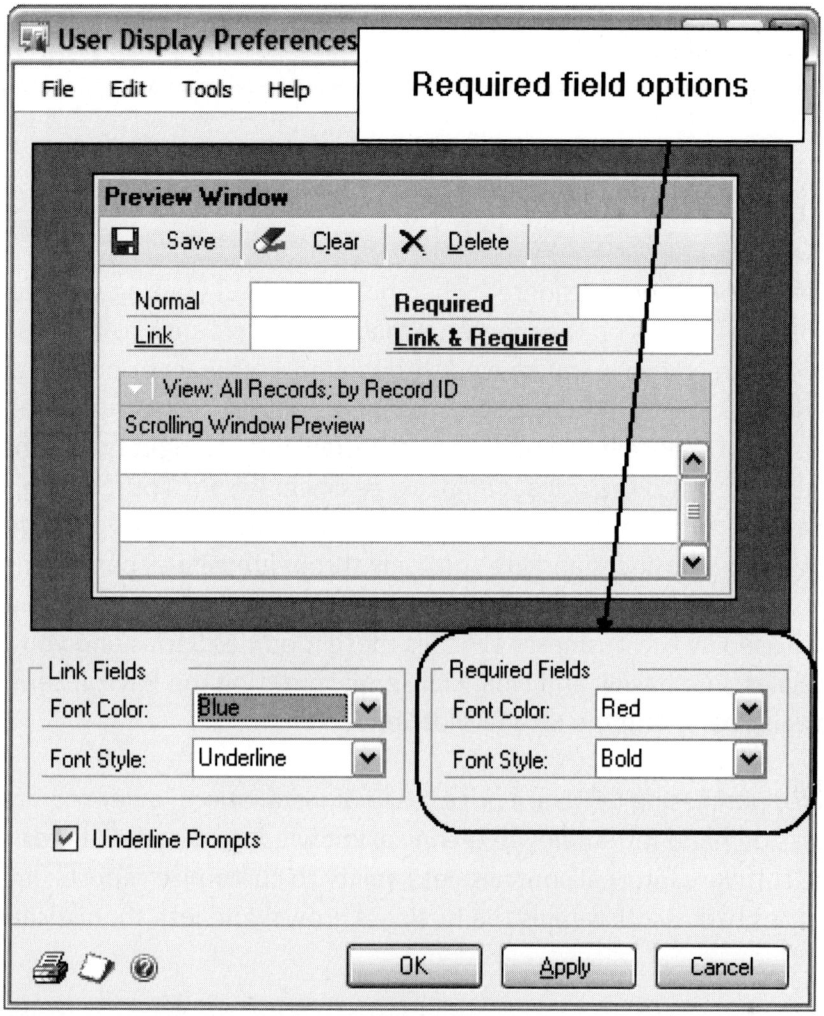

Figure 1:59 Display Required Fields in Red

Click **OK** to save your changes. *(Note: Cancel discards any changes.)*

You have now completed this chapter level. The next level explains selecting accounting software and software licensing.

LEVEL TWO

ACCOUNTING SOFTWARE AND COMPANY OBJECTIVES

This topic looks at factors to be considered when purchasing accounting software. There are a variety of accounting packages on the market. Smaller products such as Microsoft Office Accounting® or Peachtree® can be purchased through local retailers or on-line and are designed to serve the needs of a small business. Such packages are often called "commercial-off-the-shelf" (COTS) software because it is ready for installation and use right out of the box with most features already bundled into the price (i.e., packages include sales, purchasing, payroll, inventory, fixed assets, and financials) . On the other hand, mid-market packages such as GP serve the needs of larger business and are sold only through business partners (sometimes called VARs or resellers). These products are purchased in modules so you can purchase only the features to be used by the business. GP calls these modules Series and you could purchase just the System, Sales, Purchasing and Financial Series, omitting the Payroll Series when payroll is prepared by a third party and the Fixed Asset Series.

The advantages for purchasing COTS are price; ease of installation; lower requirements for hardware; and less demand for employee technical knowledge. Disadvantages are less control over customizing software internal controls; less ability to customize reports; limitations on later adding features to the software as the business grows; and less sophistication on audit trail reporting.

For small businesses, purchasing COTS software is a wise decision because less financial resources are needed to meet financial reporting needs for the business. But as a company grows it has greater reporting needs and internal control requirements. While mid-market software may cost more, it offers significantly more features and greater flexibility in scaling the software by adding features as the business grows or strategies change. Furthermore, sophisticated database management systems that drive these packages accommodate customizing internal controls and expanding data analysis capabilities.

To illustrate, let us assume that you are a regional accounting firm providing auditing, consulting, and tax services to area firms. Your client base is primarily small to mid-size firms with annual sales ranging from $100,000 to $3,000,000. One of your clients is experiencing rapid growth and needs to purchase a computerized accounting solution. The owner is seeking your assistance in selecting a general ledger software package. This client currently provides management consulting services to customers in a tri-state area and would like to eventually expand into selling related products. The company employs 50 people in the tri-state region with only 5 people staffing the accounting department. Payroll is outsourced to a third party. The client is a privately held limited liability company (LLC), thus no SEC reporting requirements;

however, there are loan covenants with an area bank requiring the company to submit monthly financial reports within two weeks after closing the accounting records for the month.

This client has prepared a feasibility study and developed a budget for the project. The project team's report outlines budget figures for general ledger software, hardware, operating software, and user training. The budget can accommodate $20,000 to $30,000 for general ledger software.

Your first meet with the client to demonstrate several COTS packages. The price for such software ranges between $230 to $500 dollars. Your firm is also a mid-market software reseller so you demonstrate features in these packages. Prices here range between $15,000 to $25,000 dollars. Your client comments on the price difference. You caution that price is only one factor to consider when purchasing accounting software. The client should weigh other factors such as scalability (i.e., ability to add features in the future), financial resources to acquire needed hardware, reporting requirements, and internal control needs. You also advise the client that adopting a mid-market package increases user training costs and the client assures you that funding for such training is built into the project budget.

Your client emphasizes that the software it purchases must fit current and future needs of the business. The client plans on opening remote offices in other states and wants these offices to be able to input sales orders and prepare sales reports. All other accounting tasks and reporting will be performed at the corporate office. During this conversation, you discover that the client also wants strong software accounting controls and flexibility in designing reports and user security. You also note that the client plan to sell inventory in the tri-state region, thus will need to collect and report sales taxes for multiple states.

After further discussion, the client decides to purchase GP. All packages reviewed can accommodate multi-state sales tax reporting and remote access to the software. The deciding factors were a need for strong internal controls, flexible financial reporting, and future scalability. The client will initially purchase the System, Financial, Sales, and Purchasing Series because payroll is currently prepared by a third party and fixed assets are tracked in another software package. If the client decides to later bring payroll in-house or to integrate fixed assets it can easily add these modules.

While this is an oversimplification of the process, it provides insight into some of the issues involved in evaluating accounting software. It is important that customers have an opportunity to "test drive" any software before buying and, oftentimes, accountants play a pivotal role in guiding companies through this process.

SOFTWARE LICENSING AND "RIGHTS OF USE"

Accountants are often responsible for assessing threats to a company and instituting policies that minimize such threats. In the software arena, companies are continually exposed to two specific threats. First, employees may install software without the company owning a license to the software. Second, employees may be using software outside the "rights of use" listed in the software license. Both threats expose companies to legal action, often resulting in monetary loss that compensates the software company for the theft of intellectual property. Violators may also face criminal sanctions for their actions.

Before we begin, let's clear up a frequent misnomer about software. Software purchasers often believe that they own the software purchased, thus are free to resell, copy, use, or distribute as needed. But after we explain software industry's business model, you will understand why software companies cannot sell ownership to software and remain viable. To assist in this explanation, we will contrast the software industry business model to the automobile manufacturer business model.

Automobile manufacturers invest in their products by purchasing raw materials (i.e., steel, rubber and paint), paying for employee labor, and paying for overhead (i.e., utilities and insurance). Software companies make similar investments in employee labor and overhead but their raw materials primarily consist of the intellectual contributions made by talented employees. Hence, software is called intellectual property. This term also extends to products produced by the music and movie industries.

Both the automobile and software industries rely on product sales to sustain operations and further investments to research and development that enhance their products. However, unlike the automobile industry, the software industry (as well as the music, and movie industries) face threats to sales because their products are easily reproduced and freely shared with the original purchaser retaining his or her benefits to purchasing. You do not have the resources to duplicate your car now would can you give your car to someone else and continue using it. Yet, these are the realities facing the manufacturers of intellectual property. To mitigate threats to future sales, the intellectual property industry protects profits by licensing its products instead of selling outright ownership. Thus, the buyer of software, music, or movies purchases a license to use the product and agrees to use the product within the purchasers "rights of use" license.

For instance, GP's standard license legally grants the purchaser a right to use and install the software on any machine located at the purchasing company's location(s) and to create as many different company databases needed to run the licensing company's operations. The purchaser's "rights of use" license does not permit the company to lease, rent, or give the software to others. In addition, GP's standard "rights of use policy" does not give the licensing company a right to use an unlicensed Series or to use the product for commercial purposes such as maintaining unrelated company financial records for compensation. Nor does the licensing company own the right to install the product on a Web server for use by other companies. While it is possible to use GP in such fashion, the licensing company must purchase a different "rights of use" policy.

In addition to a "rights of use," license, a company contracts to access the software in accordance with the license agreement. Not all companies license products the same. Some software is licensed on a per-user basis whereas others are licensed on a per-seat basis. Larger packages, like GP, are client/server models, meaning that the "brain" of the software is installed on a computer functioning as a central server and the client piece of the software is installed on individual terminals that access data stored on the central server. Thus, the server holds the main processing software and the GP data while client machines simply process new and retrieve existing data.

Generally, a company using client/server software buys licenses to access the software on a per-user basis. Per-user refers to the number of concurrent users (i.e., simultaneous client machines) permitted to access software and data on the server. With client/server software, the server piece controls the number of concurrent users accessing the server. Your copy of GP licenses one concurrent user so when you log into GP the software displays "1" as the total number of authorized users. Furthermore, your machine is functioning as both client and server.

Suppose that a company needed to installs GP's client piece on ten client computers but needs only five users to have simultaneous access to GP. In this hypothetical, the company would purchase a five-user license to the GP server because the purchaser's "rights of use" license already grants installing the client piece on an unlimited number of client machines located at the purchasing company's site. Although the company may have ten client machines for using GP, a five-user license fulfills its concurrent needs to access the server. The company can purchase additional user licenses when concurrent access requirements increase.

Let's contrast this to software sold on a per-seat basis. Software such as Microsoft Office is sold in this fashion. Per-seat licensing means that you must purchase a separate license for each computer installation. You can think of this a purchasing a license for the seat setting in front of a computer containing the software. So, referring to our previous hypothetical, the company would purchase ten licenses to install Microsoft Office on ten computers. (Note: Companies can purchase bulk licensing without purchasing separate copies of the software.) Unlike the access controls to the server built into client/server software, per-seat software poses a greater threat to controlling the installation of unlicensed software. To compensate, companies should institute preventative controls by configuring a computer's operating system to deny users the right to install software on the machine.

Regardless of whether software is licensed on a per-seat or per-user basis, it is important that companies track software licenses to ensure that products are used within the "rights of use" agreement and that all software on the machine is licensed. Installing pirated software (unlicensed software) is a serious legal offense subjecting companies, **and you**, to the threat of significant financial losses, criminal sanctions, and public scrutiny. Just remember the next time you are offered an unlicensed piece of software, a free movie or a free music download (or witness any so-called “free” products being used by others) that every industry is entitled to the profits earned by manufacturing its products and that no industry exists without profits. As an accountant, you understand the impact lost profits have on a business. Moreover, as an accountant, you understand that using an unlicensed product not only carries legal ramifications but also violates professional ethics.

Level One Questions

True/False

____ 1. Transactions entered individually can be saved or posted.

____ 2. Batch IDs are created by GP.

____ 3. Item Number on the Sales Transaction Entry window refers to an inventory item number.

____ 4. Employee accounts are master records.

____ 5. A paycheck issued to an employee is a transaction record.

____ 6. You can enter four different search criteria to locate a general ledger account by using the binoculars located on the lookup window.

____ 7. Hyperlinks open other task windows.

____ 8. You can use the S&S, Inc. Proj DB to complete tasks that will be graded by your professor.

____ 9. GP will treat transaction dates different from batch dates.

____10. Once you set the system date it remains the same even after exiting the software.

Menu Navigation Exercises

1. Name the home page and command for creating new vendor accounts.

2. You need a summary trial balance report listing general ledger accounts. Name the home page and command to open the Trial Balance Report window. List the name of the summary report and print the report. Describe what information this report contains.

3. You would like to turn on toolbar shortcuts for the Purchasing Series. Explain how to accomplish this.

4. An employee's address has changed. Name the home page and command that allows you to update the address.

5. You need to enter a purchase order. Name the home page and command that lets you complete the task.

Drill Down and Lookup Exercises

1. Ashton requests that you inquire into the total sales for 2007 to customer Fillard's, Inc.

   a. Explain how you would open the window containing this information.

   b. What are total sales for fiscal year 2007 to this customer? *(Hint: After selecting the customer, change the Summary View, type in the year, and click Calculate.)*

2. One of your suppliers, Canyon Cam, wants to know if S&S submitted payment for invoice INV23453 sent in February of 2007. What is your response? *(Hint: After you locate the document, open details on the transaction using the icon illustrated earlier in the chapter and confirm that the unapplied amount is zero.)*

Level Two Questions

1. Your client decided to purchase GP and wants your recommendations on the Series they should initially purchase. List any questions you would ask the client that may impact your recommendation.

2. Your client seeks information on the number of GP user licenses to purchase. The company owns a total of 25 laptops and desktops. The shipping department has three desktops that will access GP during day and evening shifts. Ten full-time salespeople will need access to GP on their laptops. Six full-time accounting clerks need to use GP, but these clerks work in two shifts with three to a shift. Finally, the controller needs access to GP on his workstation. What is the optimal number of user licenses that you recommend your client to purchase? Will your recommendation permit your client to install the client software on all machines it owns? Explain.

Chapter 2 THE S&S COMPANY DATABASE

CHAPTER OVERVIEW

In Chapter 1 you loaded company databases and practiced navigating the software. This chapter provides information about the company database that prepares you for posting transactions.

After reading this chapter you will be familiar with:

- S&S's chart of accounts and departments
- GP general ledger account types such as posting, fixed allocation, variable allocation, and unit
- Printing a chart of accounts, summary trial balance, and detailed trial balance report
- Opening and closing accounting periods
- GP Series integration and a relational database model

Level One covers:

- The general ledger account framework used to create S&S's to create its chart of accounts
- Creating general ledger accounts and understanding account types
- S&S departments and account segments that identifying such departments
- Printing the chart of accounts and trial balance reports
- Creating, opening, and closing monthly accounting periods
- Establishing payment terms, shipping methods, and bank accounts
- Using the Smart List to export data to Excel

Level Two covers:

- The role played by GP's database management system
- Series integration
- Relational database concepts and terminology

Level One

General Ledger Account Framework

Please review the tables located in Appendix B before reading this topic to become familiar with S&S's chart of accounts (COA). The COA lists general ledger account used when posting transactions. We begin by explaining the structuring of account numbers and explain posting types and account categories later in the chapter.

Begin by clicking the GP Button and selecting ***Tools>>Setup>>Company>>Account Format*** to open the Account Format Setup window illustrated in Figure 2:1.

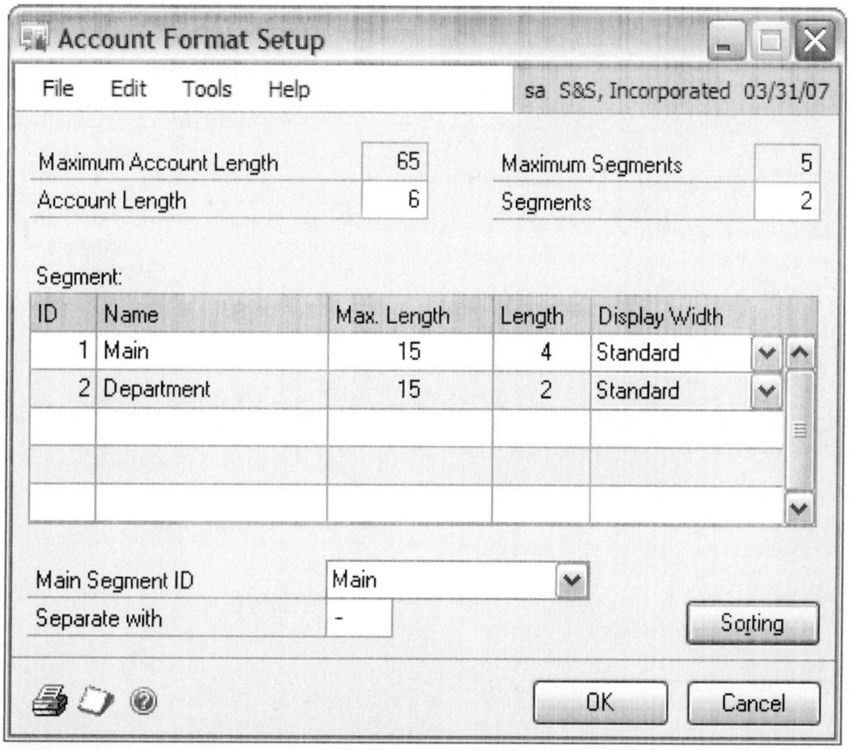

Figure 2:1 Account Format Setup Window

Account numbers are governed by two factors; the maximum framework and the actual framework. The maximum framework is established during installation of GP and governs the overall account length and number of segments for any company created in the software. *(Note: Your version of the software did not require completing this step.)* You cannot change this maximum after installation so you want to make it broad enough to accommodate any possibility. For our purposes the maximum account length is 65 and this length can be subdivided into a maximum of 5 segments.

After establishing a maximum framework, the actual account framework for a company database is set. These parameters are stored in Account Length and Segments. S&S use an actual account length of 6 digits that is subdivided into 2 segments. Additionally, the first segment is called "Main" and the second is called "Department." The Main segment is four digits with a Department segment of two digits.

Click **X** to close the Account Format Setup window.

So what does the account framework tell you? In Appendix B you can view that the Cash account is numbered 1100-00. The main segment is 1100 and the department segment is 00. Locate the Sales – East account to see that its department is 01 so we must further explore S&S's account numbering.

Click the GP button again to select ***Tools>>Setup>>Financial >>Segment***. Look up and select Department as the Segment ID. *(Note: You will need to scroll up the lookup window to make this selection.)* Next, look up information for the Number. (See Figure 2:2.)

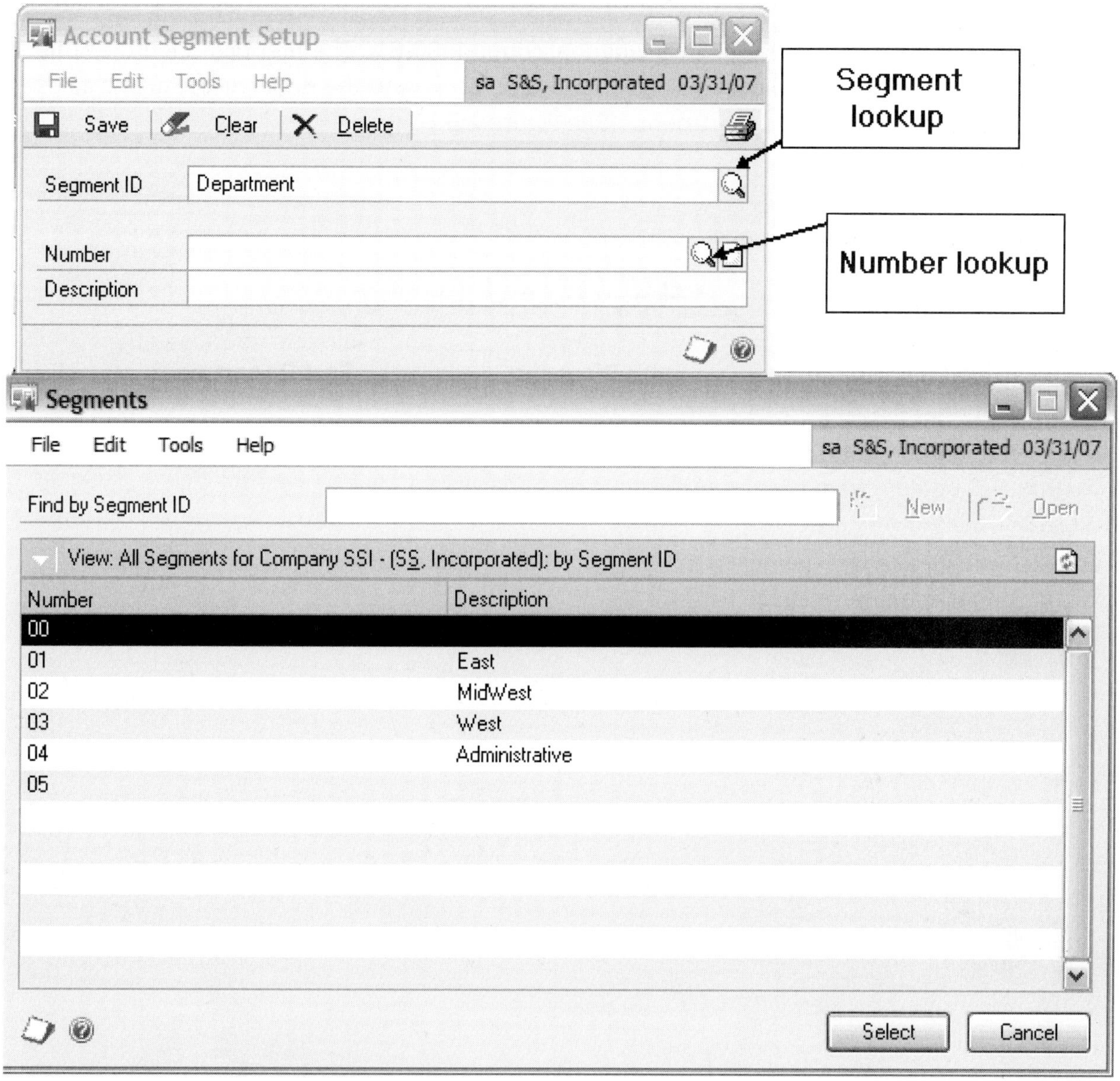

Figure 2:2 S&S Department Segments

You see department segments 01 through 04 have been assigned specific departmental descriptions. Segment 00 is not assigned a description because it is used on general ledger accounts not used for departmental reporting. Segment 05 is also not assigned a description because this segment identifies allocation accounts discussed later in the chapter.

Click **X** to close the lookup window and then **X** to close the Account Segment Setup window.

Aside from department segments, S&S has established account numbering policies that identify main segment account numbers. These policies require the first digit to identify if an account is an asset, liability, equity, revenue, or expense. The second digit further classifies an account into groups such as cash, receivables, inventory, short-term and long-term liabilities. Remaining digits in the main segment sequentially number multiple accounts within a group.

Given these rules, let us identify general ledger account 4400-01. The first digit identifies this as a sales account; the second digit a sales discount account, and the department digit a sales discount account for the East department. (See Figure 2:3.)

Figure 2:3 Account Numbering

Table 2:1 outlines general ledger numbering policies for the main segment and Table 2:2 explains department numbers.

Main Segment	
First Digit	**Second Digit**
0 = Unit Account	Account containing nonfinancial data
1 = Asset	1 = Cash 2 = Accounts Receivable 3 = Inventory 4 = Prepaid Assets 5 = Fixed Assets
2 = Liability	1 = Short-term Trade Payables and Debt 2 / 3 = Other Short-term Liabilities 4 = Long-term Liabilities
3 = Equity	0 = Stock 1 = Additional Paid-in-capital 3 = Retained Earnings
4 = Revenue	1 = Sales 3 = Sales Return 4 = Sales Discount 5 = Cost of Goods Sold 6 = Purchase Discounts
5 = Operating Expense	1 = Wages/Salaries 2 = Commissions 3 = Payroll Expenses 4 = Employee Benefits 5–8 = Other Operating Expenses
6 = Not assigned	
7 = Other Income	0 = All Other Income
8 = Other Expense	0 = All Other Expenses
9 = Taxes	0 = Income Tax Accounts

Table 2:1 Main Account Number

Department Segment	
01	*East*
02	*Mid-West*
03	*West*
04	*Administrative*
05	*Allocation Accounts*

Table 2:2 Account Departments

Did you notice the 9999-00 Suspense account? This account is used when posting transactions and the account affected by one side of the entry is unknown at the time of recording. For instance, you are posting a payable invoice and are unsure of whether to debit a fixed asset account or an office expense account. Instead of postponing posting the invoice, you can post the amount for the account in question to the suspense account.

Using a suspense account serves several purposes. First, you maintain control over the transaction by timely posting it. Second, the liability is recognized as soon as it is known. Finally, suspended transaction can easily be reviewed by monitoring the balance in the suspense account. In theory, the suspense account should be zero unless a transaction is awaiting reclassification.

You now have the knowledge to create and maintain general ledger accounts.
Open the Account Maintenance window (Figure 2:4) and look up the salaries account for the East department. *(Note: In Chapter 1 we illustrated that this window is opened from the Financial home page by clicking Account under Cards.)*

Because you understand S&S's account structure you can rapidly locate the Salaries Expense account by typing a 5 in the Account field before clicking the lookup icon.

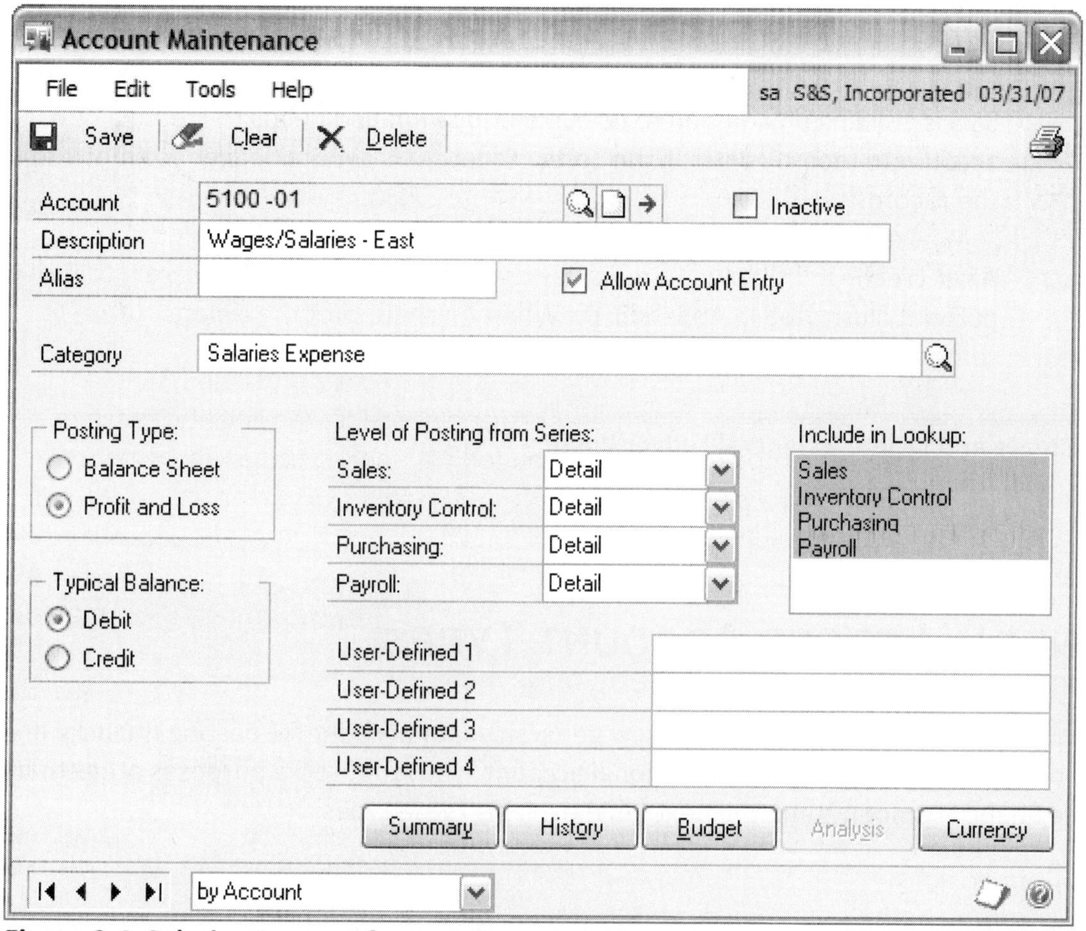

Figure 2:4 Salaries Account for East Department

We explained fields in this window in Chapter 1. Notice that this is a Profit and Loss account, meaning it prints on the profit and loss (i.e., income) statement. Furthermore, it will appear on this statement under the Category of Salaries Expense. Finally, the account balance is increased with a debit (i.e., Typical Balance).

We revisit the Account Maintenance window to emphasize one last point. This window is used to maintain posting accounts, which are account types that store financial amounts. GP offers other account types, which is the subject of our next topic. Complete the exercise that follows before moving onto that topic.

S&S is building an addition to its current location and needs to create a new account to record construction costs. Create this general ledger account and save the record.

After creating, drilldown to redisplay the new account and compare it to the account illustrated in Appendix D. When finished, click the Delete button to remove the new account.

E2:1 Create and Delete a General Ledger Posting Account

GENERAL LEDGER ACCOUNT TYPES

In the previous exercise you created a new general ledger account for posting financial amounts (i.e., posting accounts). GP offers additional account types that serve purposes other than posting financial amounts and the next table explains these types.

Account Type	Description
Posting	Accounts used for posting financial amounts and for storing budget projections. These are the only accounts that appear on financial statements. Accounts are created using the Account command under Cards.
Fixed Allocation	Accounts used for posting financial amounts that will be allocated to posting accounts by using a fixed percentage. Accounts are created using Fixed Allocation command under Cards. For instance, insurance expense can be allocated to four departmental expense posting accounts by using the fixed percentages of 20%, 20%, 20%, and 40%. When an expense is posted to the fixed allocation account GP then redistributes the amount to the departmental posting accounts using the percentages provided. Fixed allocation accounts do not appear on financial statements because balances are fully allocated to posting accounts.

Account Type	Description
Variable Allocation	These accounts function similar to fixed allocation accounts except that financial amounts are allocated based on factors that change over time. These factors are stored in breakdown accounts. The Variable Allocation command under Cards is used to create these accounts. Breakdown accounts can be posting accounts, such as sales and expense accounts, or unit accounts such as the number of employees per department or office square footage. When transactions post to a variable allocation account the financial amount is spread to posting accounts using the percentages calculated by GP. These percentages are calculated by dividing the balance for one breakdown account by the total balances in all breakdown accounts. For instance, S&S tracks revenue and expense by sales department. The wage expense for warehouse workers is distributed to three departmental wage posting accounts based upon monthly revenue for each sales department. GP calculates the percentage used to allocate these wages by dividing each department's revenue by total revenue. Again, like fixed allocation accounts, variable allocation accounts do not appear on financial statements.
Unit Accounts	Unit accounts store quantities rather than financial amounts. These accounts can also store historical and budget information. These accounts do not appear on financial statements and are created using the Unit Account command under Cards. Unit accounts can be used to compare financial and nonfinancial information. For instance, you can create calculations on customized reports that show sales per employee by storing the number of employees in a unit account. Unit accounts also serve as breakdown accounts for calculating variable allocations. For instance, you can instruct GP to allocate rent expense based on a department's square footage by creating a unit account for each department's square footage.

Table 2:3 Account Types

GP

Open the fixed allocation account for utilities. List the posting accounts that receive expense allocations along with the percentage allocated to each.

Open the variable allocation account for the wages/salaries of truckers and warehouse employees. What breakdown accounts are used to allocate transactions? What are the general ledger account numbers for the accounts receiving the allocated expense?

E2:2 Variable and Fixed Allocation Accounts

Let us now print the COA report. Click **Account** under **Reports** to open the window illustrated in Figure 2:5. Select the report dropdown list to view report categories.

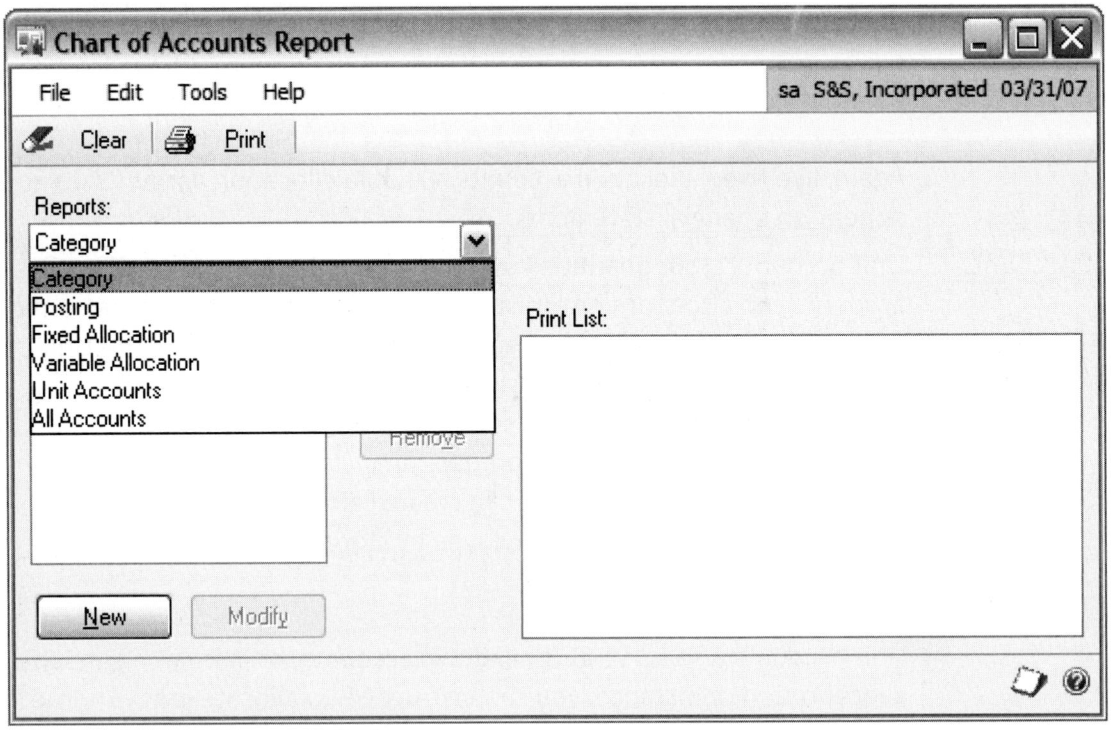

Figure 2:5 COA Report Window

Notice that COA reports are grouped by account type. Select **Posting** and highlight the report named **COA**. **Insert** this report to the **Print List** area and click **Print** to send output to the screen. *(Note: You can click Print on the Preview window to send the report to a printer.)* Compare your first page results to that illustrated in Figure 2:6.

User Date: 03/31/07

POSTING ACCOUNTS LIST
S&S, Incorporated
General Ledger

Page: 1
User ID: sa

Ranges: From: To:
Account: First Last
Account Description: First Last
Category: First Last

Sorted By: Main
Include:

Account User-Defined 1	Description User-Defined 2	Alias	Category User-Defined 3	Active	Account Type	Posting Type User-Defined 4	Typical Balance
1100-00	Cash		Cash	Yes	Posting Account	Balance Sheet	Debit
1110-00	Cash-Savings		Cash	Yes	Posting Account	Balance Sheet	Debit
1120-00	Petty Cash		Cash	Yes	Posting Account	Balance Sheet	Debit
1130-00	Checking - Payroll		Cash	Yes	Posting Account	Balance Sheet	Debit
1200-00	Accounts Receivable		Accounts Receivable	Yes	Posting Account	Balance Sheet	Debit
1205-00	Sales Discounts Available		Accounts Receivable	Yes	Posting Account	Balance Sheet	Debit
1210-00	Allowance for Doubtful Accounts		Accounts Receivable	Yes	Posting Account	Balance Sheet	Credit
1270-00	Marketable Securities		Short-Term Investments	Yes	Posting Account	Balance Sheet	Debit
1310-00	Inventory		Inventory	Yes	Posting Account	Balance Sheet	Debit
1410-00	Prepaid Insurance		Prepaid Expenses	Yes	Posting Account	Balance Sheet	Debit
1430-00	Prepaid - Other		Prepaid Expenses	Yes	Posting Account	Balance Sheet	Debit
1500-00	Land		Property, Plant and Equipment	Yes	Posting Account	Balance Sheet	Debit
1510-00	Buildings		Property, Plant and Equipment	Yes	Posting Account	Balance Sheet	Debit
1515-00	Accum Depr - Buildings		Accumulated Depreciation	Yes	Posting Account	Balance Sheet	Credit
1520-00	Office Furniture/Fixtures		Property, Plant and Equipment	Yes	Posting Account	Balance Sheet	Debit
1525-00	Accum Depr - Office Furn/Fixtures		Accumulated Depreciation	Yes	Posting Account	Balance Sheet	Credit
1530-00	Vehicles		Property, Plant and Equipment	Yes	Posting Account	Balance Sheet	Debit
1535-00	Accum Depr - Vehicles		Accumulated Depreciation	Yes	Posting Account	Balance Sheet	Credit
1540-00	Computer Hardware		Property, Plant and Equipment	Yes	Posting Account	Balance Sheet	Debit

Figure 2:6: Page 1 of COA Report

Notice that the report lists Posting Account as the account type. This report also displays information on posting type and typical balance (i.e., normal balance).

Click **X** to close the report.

> Ashton has not created a report for fixed allocation accounts. He asks that you create this report. You can refer to Chapter 1 if you do not remember the steps for creating new reports.
>
> Print the report to the screen after creating it and compare your results to those in Appendix D. Take the time to create and review reports for other account types.

E2:3 Generate Fixed Allocation Report

GENERAL LEDGER TRIAL BALANCE

The COA report lists company general ledger accounts (posting accounts) whereas the trial balance lists these accounts along with beginning and ending balances, debits and credits for the period, and net changes to accounts. Before the advent of computers the trial balance was an essential tool for testing whether a company's general ledger accounts were in balance. That is to say when

Assets = Liabilities + Equity + Net Income (Loss)

It was easy to make errors when manually posting financial transactions. For instance, you might enter a debit instead of a credit or compute an account balance incorrectly. Computer software has replaced the tedious process of balancing the general ledger. GP requires transactions to balance (i.e., debits to equal credits) before posting a transaction and accurately calculates account balances internally. The trial balance report in GP will not be out of balance unless the software was interrupted during posting. *(Note: Interruptions can occur during hardware failure, electrical outages, or improper system shutdown and may corrupt data files. You can fix corrupted databases by restoring a backup. Data backup and restore procedures were covered in Chapter 1 and are repeated in Appendix A. These procedures are important, so please take the time to read this information.)*

You print the trial balance report by clicking **Trial Balance** under **Reports**. Like COA reports, trial balance reports are grouped into report categories (Figure 2:7) that supply different reporting options.

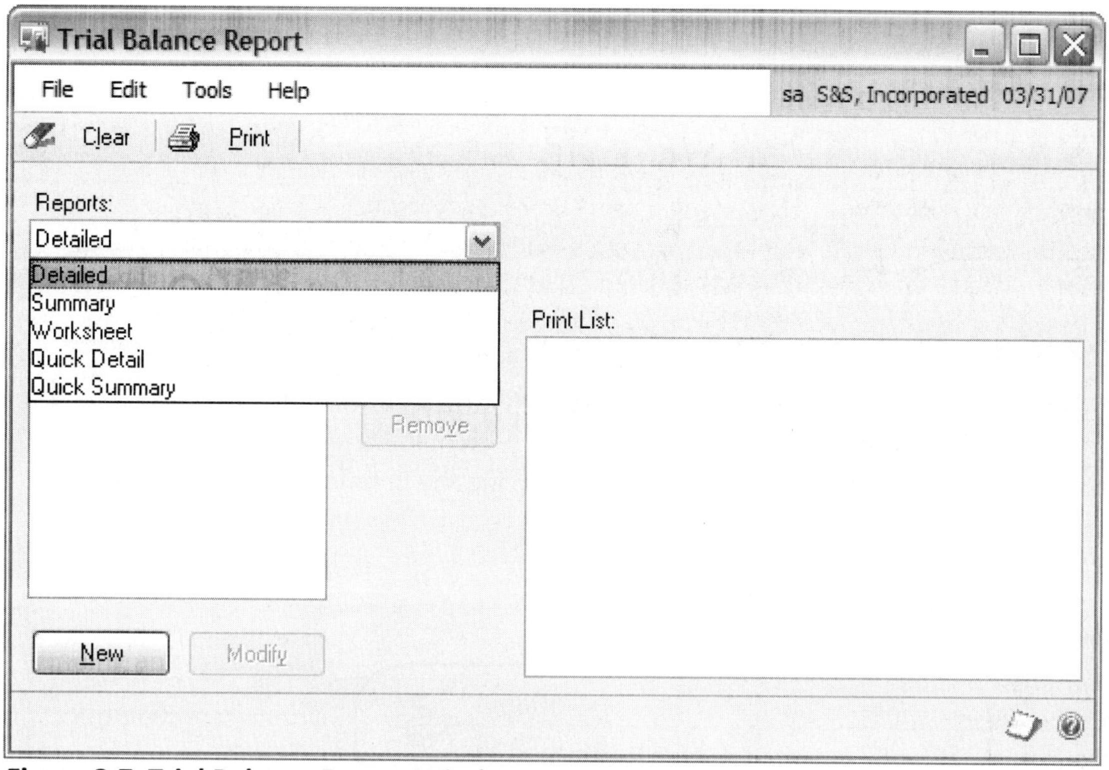

Figure 2:7 Trial Balance Report Window

Choose the **Summary** category and highlight the **Trial Balance** report. Click **Modify** to open the window illustrated in Figure 2:8 and set the report options indicated.

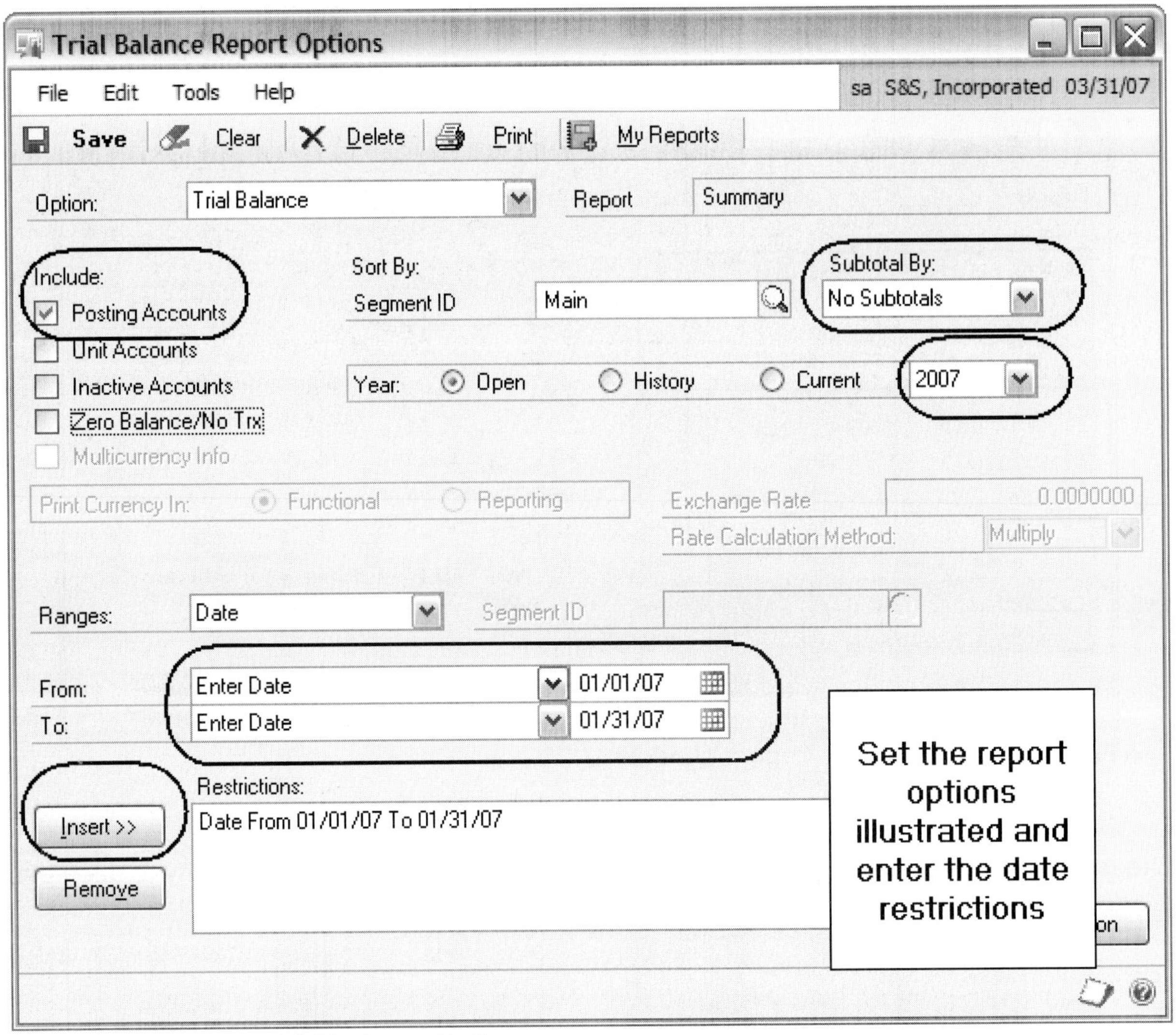

Figure 2:8 Summary Trial Balance Options

If you get an error message stating . . .

"The user date falls within a fiscal year that hasn't been set up."

. . . make sure that your system date falls within a date in fiscal year 2007 and then reprint the report.

Print the report to the screen and compare your results to those in Figure 2:9. Note that the report is "in balance" when the ending balance on the last page of the report equals zero. Close the report, discarding your changes, and the report window when finished.

User Date: 03/31/07

TRIAL BALANCE SUMMARY FOR 2007

S&S, Incorporated

General Ledger

Page: 1
User ID: sa

Date range

Ranges: From: To:
Date: 01/01/07 01/31/07
Account: First Last

Sorted By: Main
Include: Posting

Inactive	Account	Description	Beginning Balance	Debit	Credit	Net Change	Ending Balance
	1100-00	Cash	$302,319.07	$667,325.25	$948,545.12	($281,219.87)	$21,099.20
	1110-00	Cash-Savings	$120,908.11	$520.97	$0.00	$520.97	$121,429.08
	1120-00	Petty Cash	$1,287.01	$1,000.00	$828.00	$172.00	$1,459.01
	1130-00	Checking - Payroll	$1,597.60	$30,000.00	$30,233.90	($233.90)	$1,363.70
	1200-00	Accounts Receivable	$676,239.25	$1,037,799.40	$667,325.25	$370,474.15	$1,046,713.40
	1205-00	Sales Discounts Available	$0.00	$2,768.25	$0.00	$2,768.25	$2,768.25
	1210-00	Allowance for Doubtful Accounts	($19,982.00)	$0.00	$0.00	$0.00	($19,982.00)
	1310-00	Inventory	$983,796.69	$1,096,287.20	$766,272.00	$330,015.20	$1,313,811.89
	1410-00	Prepaid Insurance	$16,275.00	$0.00	$2,325.00	($2,325.00)	$13,950.00
	1500-00	Land	$120,000.00	$0.00	$0.00	$0.00	$120,000.00
	1510-00	Buildings	$765,000.00	$0.00	$0.00	$0.00	$765,000.00
	1515-00	Accum Depr - Buildings	($21,675.00)	$0.00	$0.00	$0.00	($21,675.00)
	1520-00	Office Furniture/Fixtures	$165,000.00	$0.00	$0.00	$0.00	$165,000.00
	1525-00	Accum Depr - Office Furn/Fixtures	($33,392.93)	$0.00	$0.00	$0.00	($33,392.93)
	1530-00	Vehicles	$367,876.00	$0.00	$0.00	$0.00	$367,876.00
	1535-00	Accum Depr - Vehicles	($104,231.59)	$0.00	$0.00	$0.00	($104,231.59)
	1540-00	Computer Hardware	$175,790.22	$0.00	$0.00	$0.00	$175,790.22
	1545-00	Accum Depr - Computer Hardware	($59,156.86)	$0.00	$0.00	$0.00	($59,156.86)
	1550-00	Computer Software	$67,000.00	$0.00	$0.00	$0.00	$67,000.00
	1555-00	Amortization - Computer Software	($31,638.87)	$0.00	$0.00	$0.00	($31,638.87)
	2100-00	Accounts Payable	($329,899.39)	$918,233.96	$1,254,555.15	($336,321.19)	($666,220.58)
	2105-00	Purchase Discounts Available	$0.00	$11,207.12	$13,412.72	($2,205.60)	($2,205.60)
	5610-04	Utilities - Administrative	$0.00	$5,053.84	$0.00	$5,053.84	$5,053.84
	5620-04	Insurance Expense - Administration	$0.00	$2,325.00	$0.00	$2,325.00	$2,325.00
	5700-00	Bank Charges & Fees	$0.00	$311.16	$0.00	$311.16	$311.16
	7020-00	Interest Income	$0.00	$0.00	$520.97	($520.97)	($520.97)
	8010-00	Interest Expense	$0.00	$28,494.45	$14,239.85	$14,254.60	$14,254.60
	9010-00	Income Tax Expense	$0.00	$24,000.00	$0.00	$24,000.00	$24,000.00

	Accounts	Beginning Balance	Debit	Credit	Net Change	Ending Balance
Grand Totals:	108	$0.00	$4,821,191.38	$4,821,191.38	$0.00	$0.00

Last page of report

Figure 2:9 Trial Balance Summary Report

Question?

Why does my report show revenue and expense accounts with a zero beginning balance?

Read on to find the answer.

COMPANY FISCAL PERIODS

You can only post transactions to open accounting periods; therefore, it is important to understand identifying open periods. Click the GP button to select ***Tools>>Setup>>Company>> Fiscal Periods***. The Fiscal Periods Setup window is illustrated in Figure 2:10.

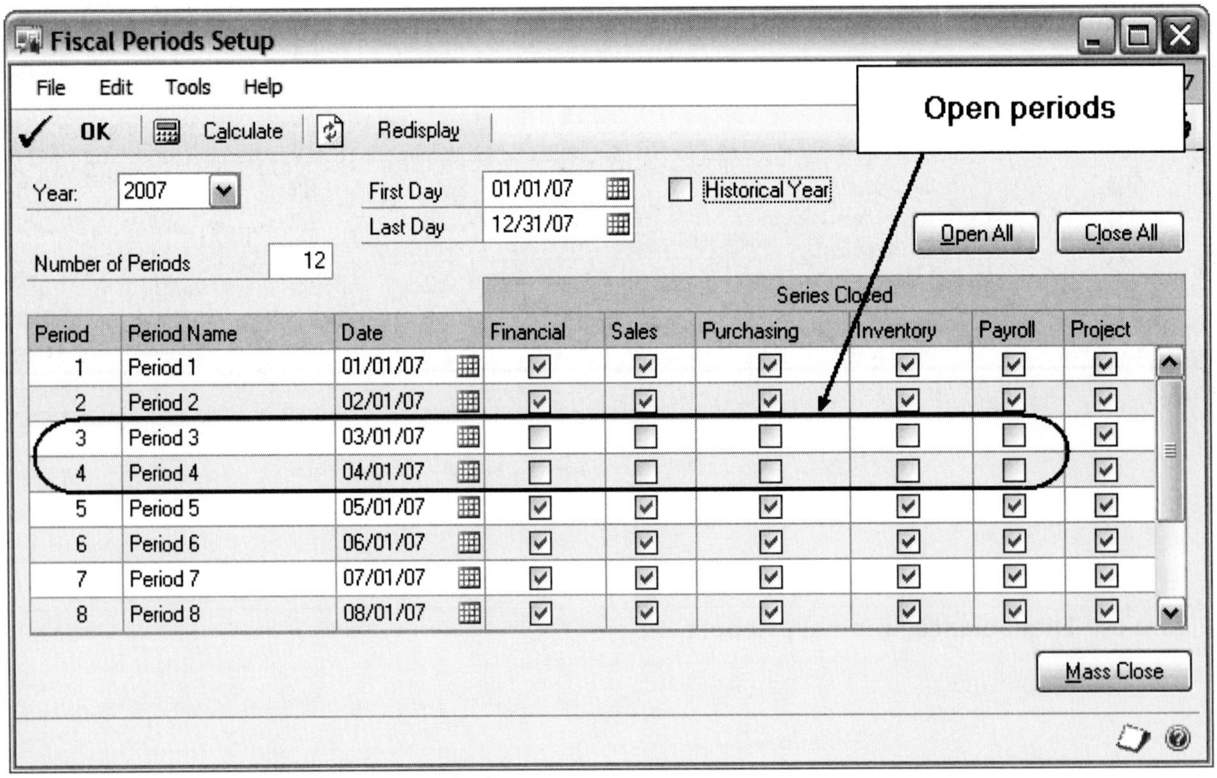

Figure 2:10 Fiscal Periods Setup Window

The dropdown list on Year selects the year to display. Verify that the year is 2007 because this is S&S's current accounting year. The dates in First Day and Last Day reveal that S&S operates on a calendar year.

Look at the Series Closed columns. Option boxes correspond to a Period and each Series operates independent of the other. Periods marked with a checkmark are closed meaning you can no longer post transactions to that period for the corresponding Series. Thus, S&S currently permits transaction posting for March and April of 2007 (i.e., Period 3 and 4) for the unmarked Series.

Now change the year to 2006 to see that this year is an Historical Year with all periods closed to posting.

Answer:

The trial balance report begins at January 1, thus revenues and expenses for the prior year were closed to the Retained Earnings account during the closing process.

The opening and closing of accounting periods is an important internal control procedure that mitigates posting errors. Because GP posts transactions only to open accounting periods, any transaction attempting to post to a closed period will generate an error explained later in the chapter. Closing a period is especially important to protecting the integrity of financial reporting. The last thing a company wants is to issue financial and management reports and then have results changed by posting transactions to the reported period. Besides closing reported periods, you should also close future periods until needed. This mitigates erroneous postings to a future period.

Accountants keep open only those periods required to process transactions, usually one month. However, during the beginning of a month, you will often keep two periods open for a few days.

To control the length of time two periods remain open, accountants set a cutoff date for processing transactions for a prior month. After the cutoff date, the accountant closes the previous month and posts reversing journal entries to accrue remaining transactions for the closed period. We will discuss reversing journal entries in Chapter 8.

As previously mentioned, GP generates warning and error messages if attempting to post to a closed period. First, GP warns the user during transaction entry as illustrated in Figure 2:11. This warning appears after entering a closed period date on a batch or a transaction.

How do I set up a new fiscal year?

You may have noticed that S&S has only two fiscal periods, the closed year of 2006 and the open year of 2007. To create the next year, you would type 2008 year into the Year field and click the Calculate button.

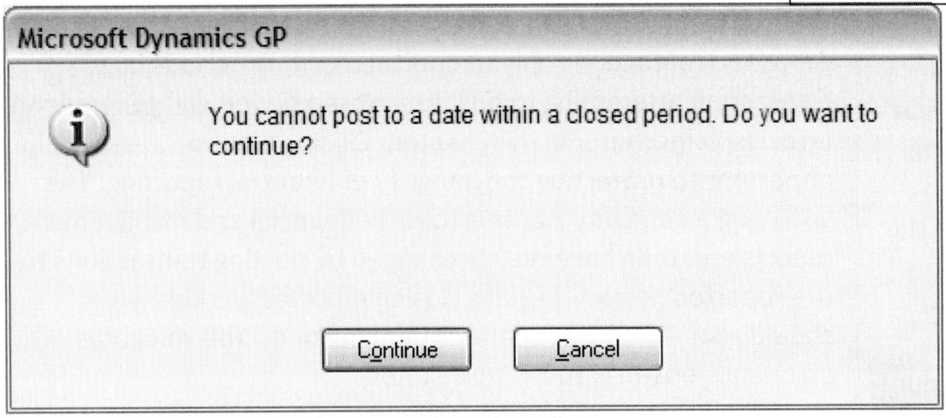
Microsoft Dynamics GP
You cannot post to a date within a closed period. Do you want to continue?
Continue
Cancel

Figure 2:11 Closed Period Warning

If entering an individual transaction and the user ignores the previous message, the next message appears when the user attempts to post. Clicking OK returns you to the transaction to change the date.

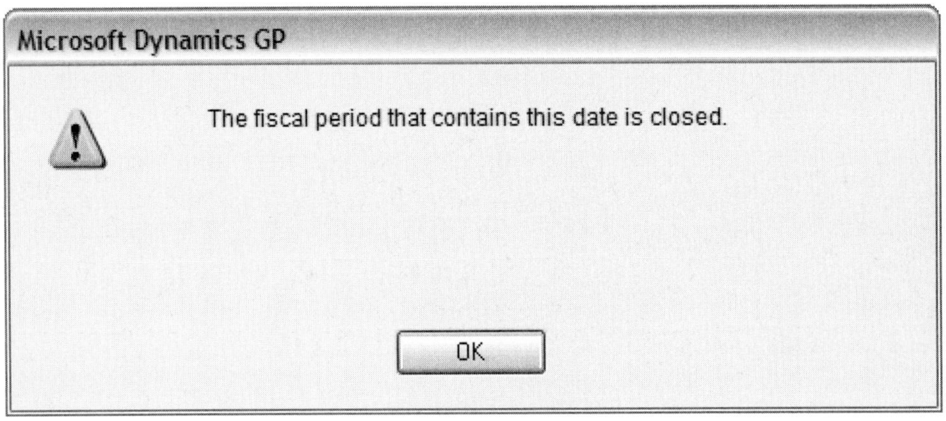
Microsoft Dynamics GP
The fiscal period that contains this date is closed.
OK

Figure 2:12 Posting Error for Single Transaction

If the transaction is saved to a batch and the user ignores the closed period warning and posts the batch the GP generates the following report after posting and suspends posting the batch.

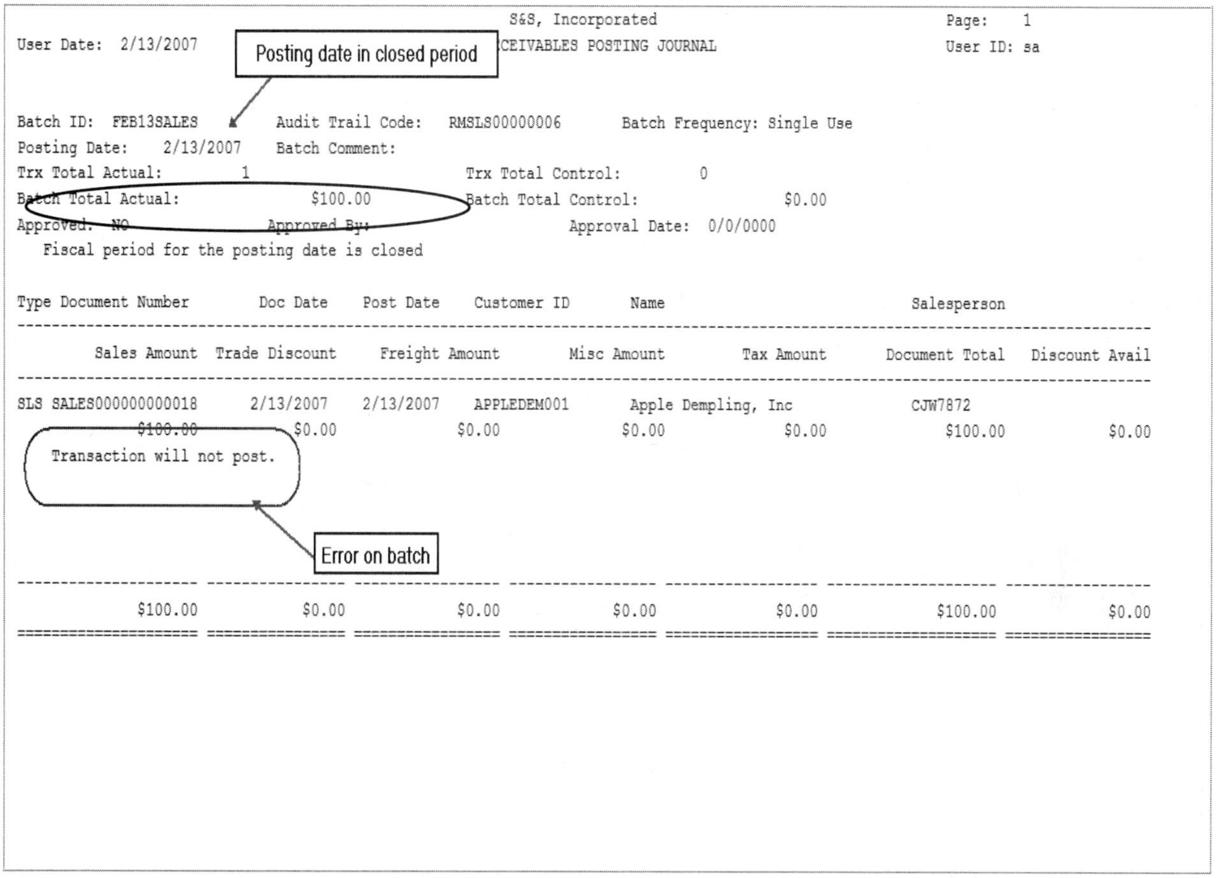

Figure 2:13 Posting Report with Error on Batch

After closing the posting report, GP supplies the following error message to let you know that the batch must be recovered.

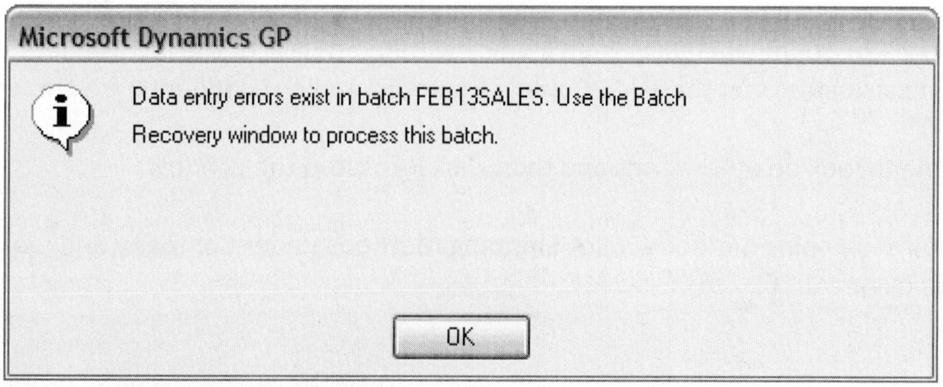

Figure 2:14 Suspended Batch

You recover the batch using instructions in Appendix C under the Common Errors topic. After recovering, reopen the batch and change the posting date. Also reopen the transaction to change the date.

Payment Terms, Shipping Methods, and Bank Accounts

We now discuss three remaining company setup items. First, let us look at payment terms. Activate the **Administration** home page and focus on the **Setup** section. Click **Payment Terms** under **Company**. Look up and select the **2% 10/Net 30** terms (Figure 2:15).

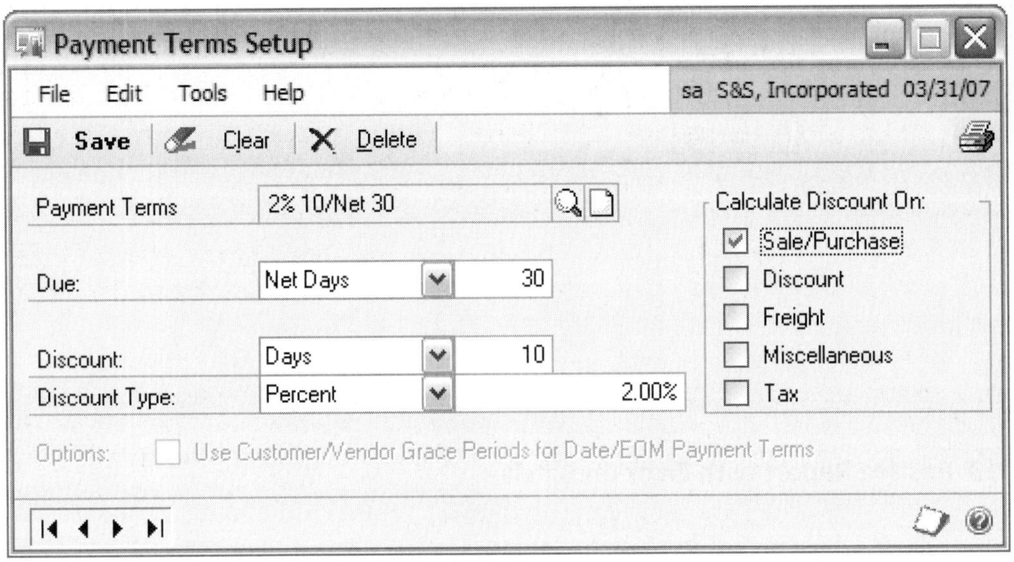

Figure 2:15 Payment Terms Setup Window

Payment terms apply to customer invoices and vendor bills. The 2% 10/Net 30 term offer customers a 2% discount when paying an invoice within ten days of the invoice date. Note that the discount calculates from the Sales/Purchase amount and not discounts, freight, etc.

Take the time to look up other terms and then click **X** to close the window.

We next look at shipping methods. Click **Shipping Methods u**nder **Company** and look up the **FLEET** terms (Figure 2:16).

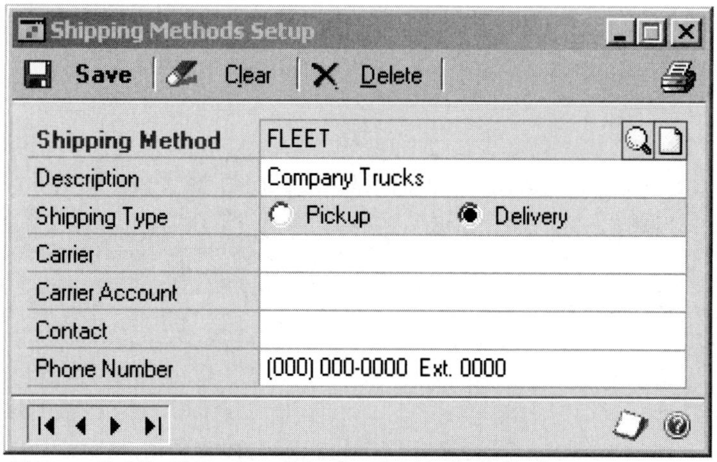

Figure 2:16 Shipping Method Setup Window

Shipping methods apply to both customer and vendor transactions; however, serve merely informational purposes because GP does not automatically compute shipping charges. You must enter any shipping charges during transaction entry. S&S trucks most customer orders with company owned trucks so use the FLEET Shipping Method as the default. Close this window.

Finally, let us review banking information. Click **Bank** under **Company** and open the **FNB** account (Figure 2:17). S&S does all of its banking with First National Bank and this window stores basic information about the bank.

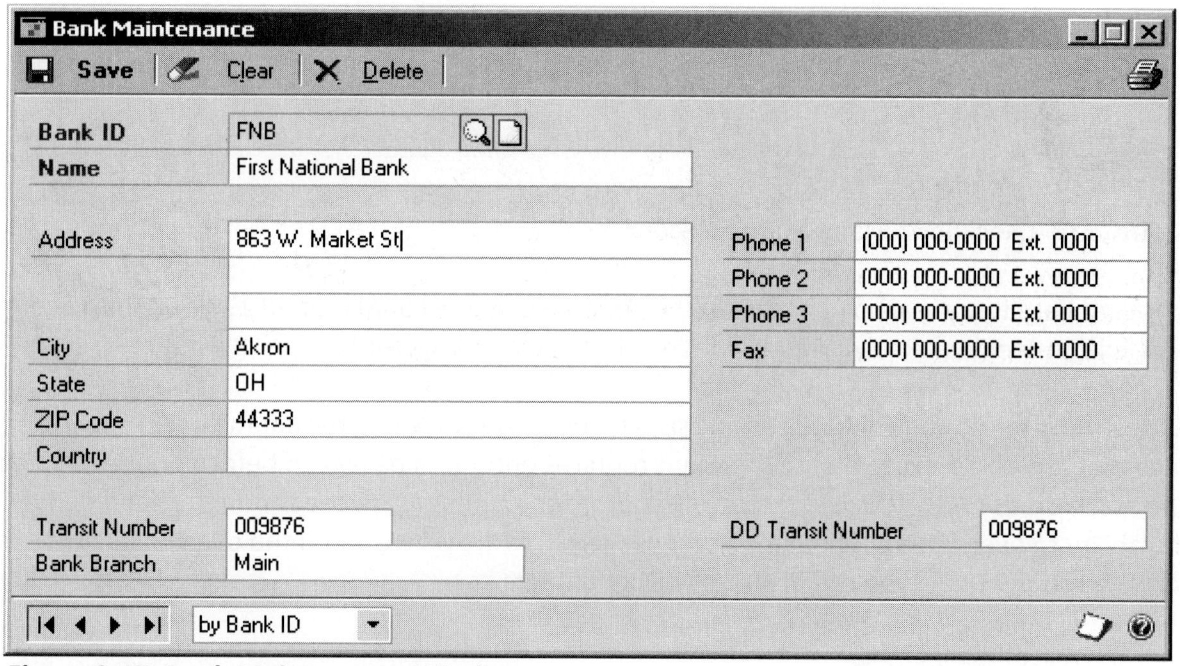

Figure 2:17 Bank Maintenance Window

Close the Bank Maintenance window so we can review information on specific bank accounts. Activate the **Financial** home page and click **Checkbook** under **Cards**.

Click the lookup icon to find that S&S maintains two bank accounts, namely PAY and PRIMARY. The first account is used to issue paychecks and the second account for all other checks. Select the **PRIMARY** account. (See Figure 2:18.)

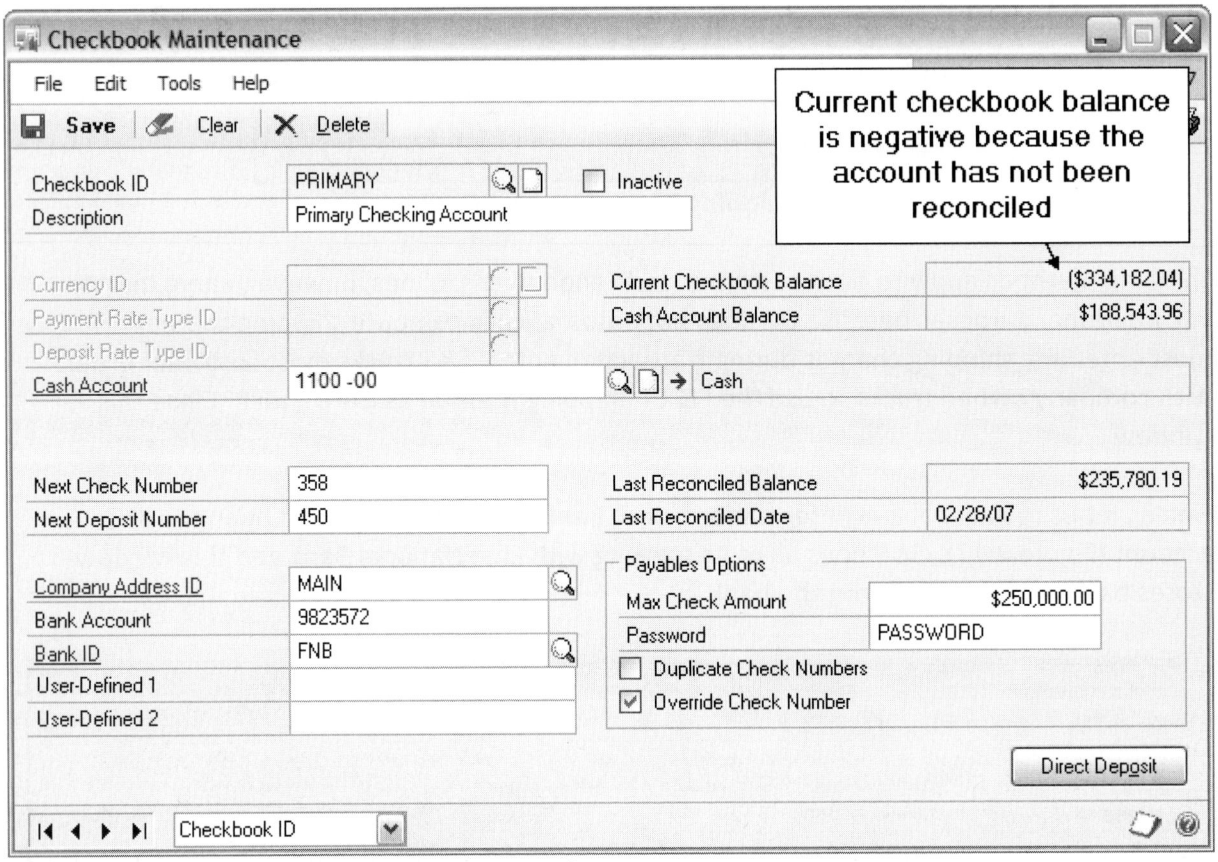

Figure 2:18 Checkbook Maintenance Record

This card links to transactions posted in the general ledger account named 1100-00 Cash and also links to the Bank Reconciliation window illustrated in Chapter 8.

Notice the internal control features on this window. You can set a maximum check amount such that any check exceeding this amount requires enter of a password before printing. *(Note: The password is PASSWORD.)* You can also deny printing duplicate check numbers and deny the ability to override a check number. These features are active when the checkmark is removed so right now you can override check numbers.

Click **X** to close the window.

SMARTLIST

The Smart List is a great tool for querying data and exporting it to Excel. Often the SmartList is the quickest way to generate views of data and is also a great way to get data for additional analysis. Look on the toolbar for the light bulb icon  and click it to open the SmartList window illustrated in Figure 2:19.

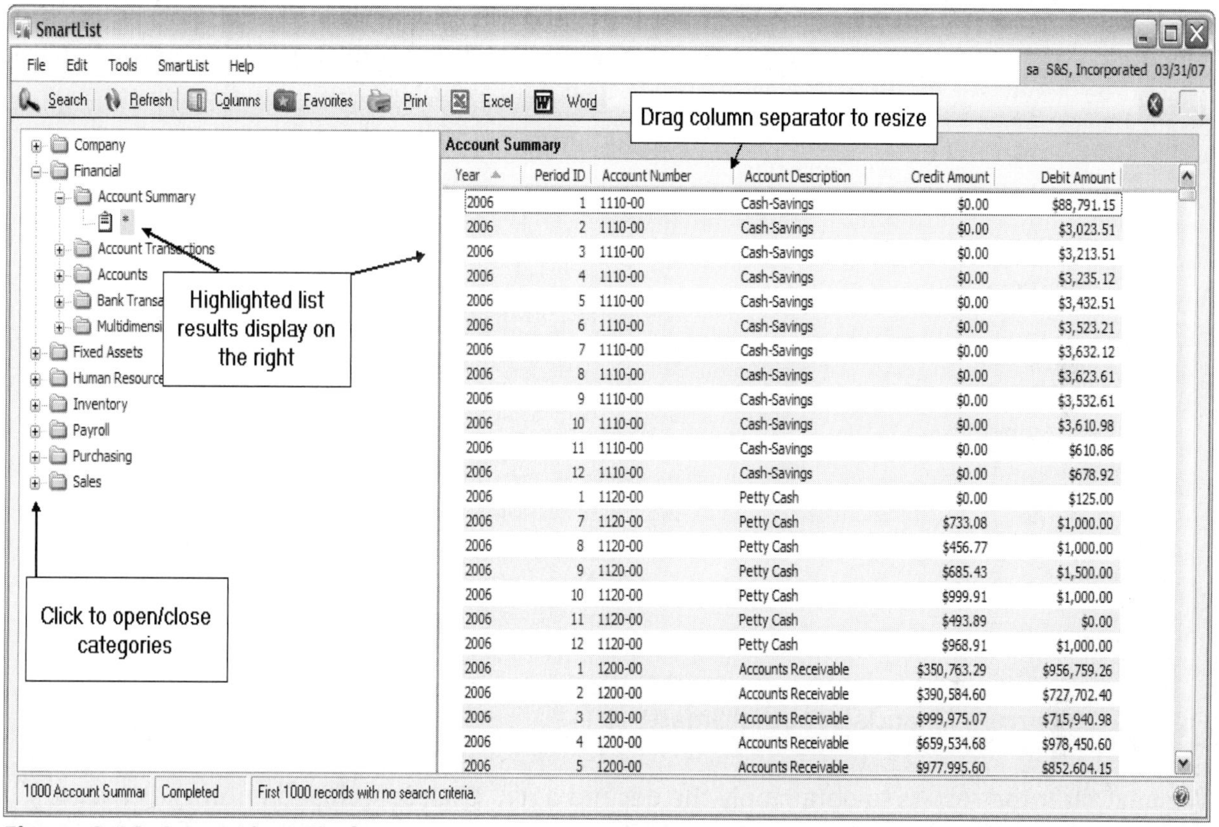

Figure 2:19 SmartList Window

Clicking the plus/minus symbol on a category folder displayed to the left opens/closes folder contents. You can then click on a list in the folder to display the results to the right.

The toolbar 

allows you manipulate the data as well as export it.

Click the plus sign to expand the **Account Summary** category and click the * list as illustrated above. The right side of the window operates like an Excel spreadsheet. Columns can be expanded by dragging a column separator and data can be sorted by clicking a column heading.

You can add or remove column of data by clicking the **Columns** button and can enter criteria to filter the data using the **Search** button. Once you have the desired results you can export the data to **Excel** or **Word** or send the results to the printer.

Let's illustrate the usefulness of this tool. Assume that there is a problem reconciling the Accounts Receivable Aging report to the balance in the accounts receivable general ledger account in January 2007. You decide to create a SmartList that displays all entries in the accounts receivable general ledger account in January and export the results to Excel.

First, we will open an initial view into all general ledger account transactions. Expand the **Account Transactions** folder on the left and click the **Current Financials Journal** SmartList. (See Figure 2:20.)

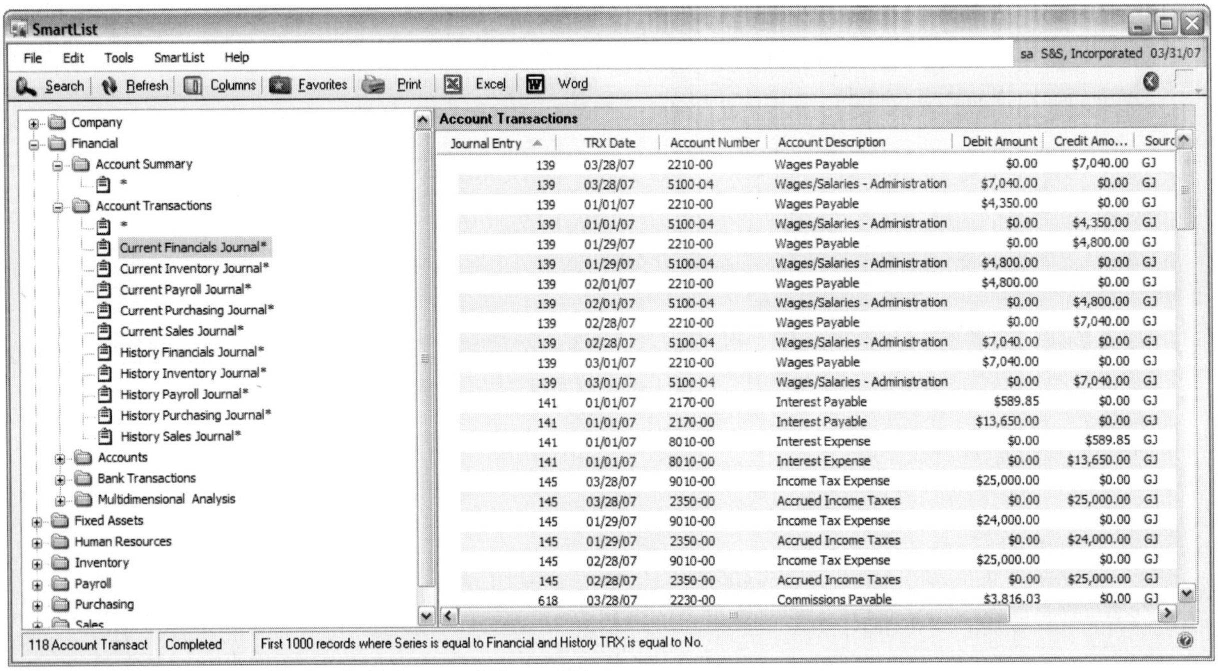

Figure 2:20 Current Financials Journal SmartList

We next filter the results to obtain only the desired data. Click **Search** and enter the criteria illustrated in Figure 2:21.

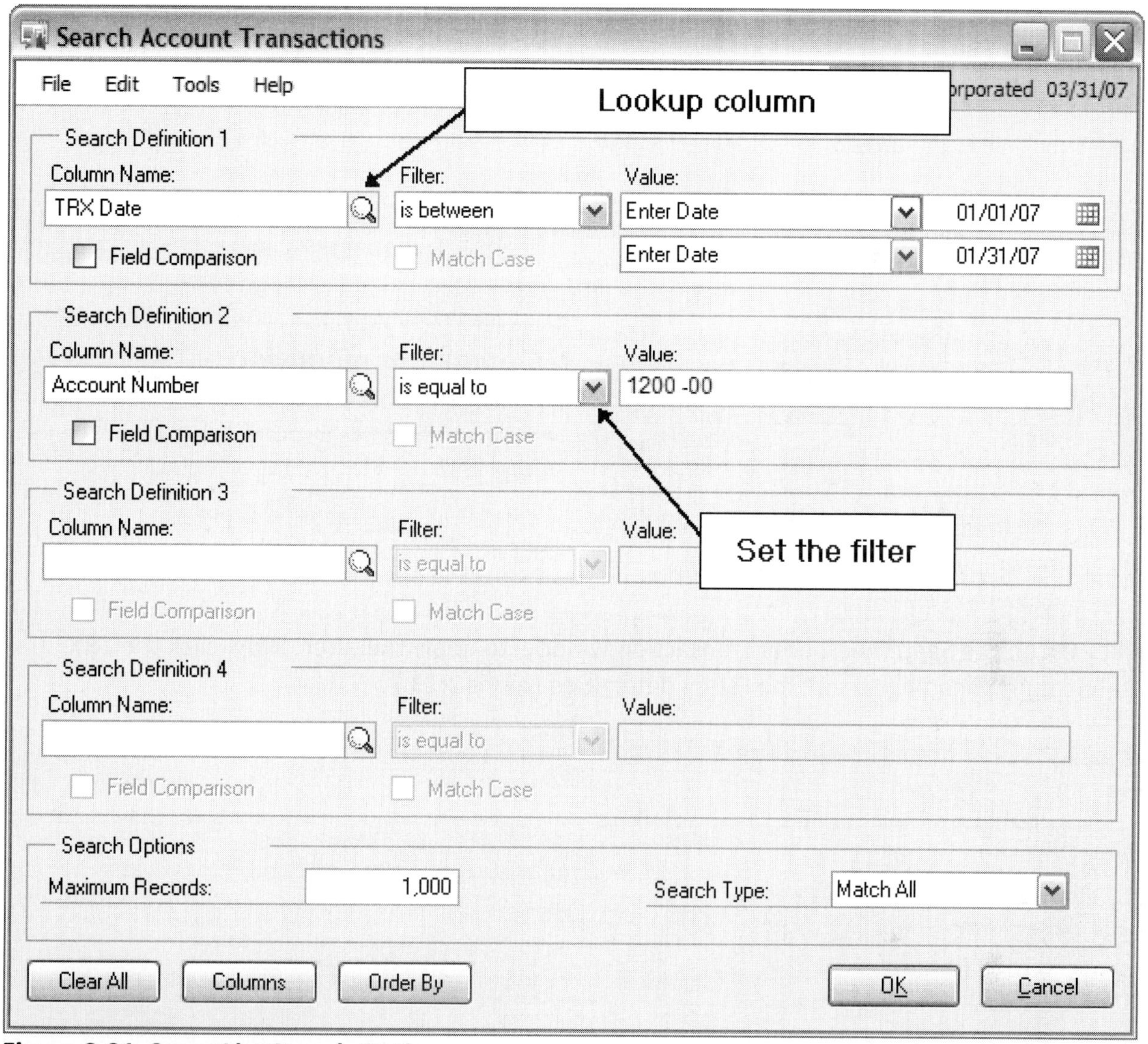

Figure 2:21 SmartList Search Options

Note: The column name you search on must be present in the SmartList view. When you need to add another column to search on, activate the SmartList window and click the Columns button to open the window illustrated in Figure 2:22.

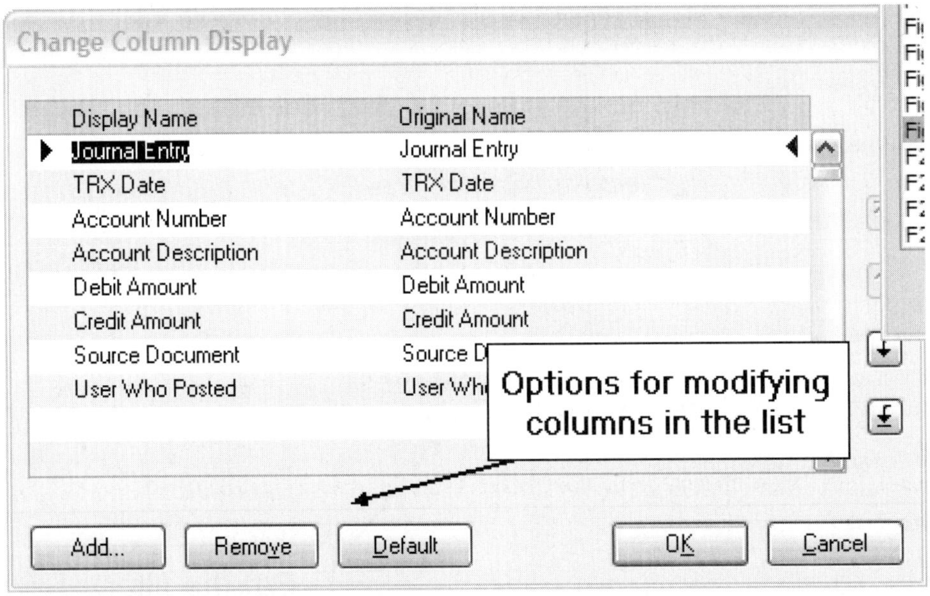

Figure 2:22 SmartList Columns

Click **OK** on the Search Accounts Transaction window to apply the filter. Now click the **TRX Date** column heading to sort the list by date. (See Figure 2:23.)

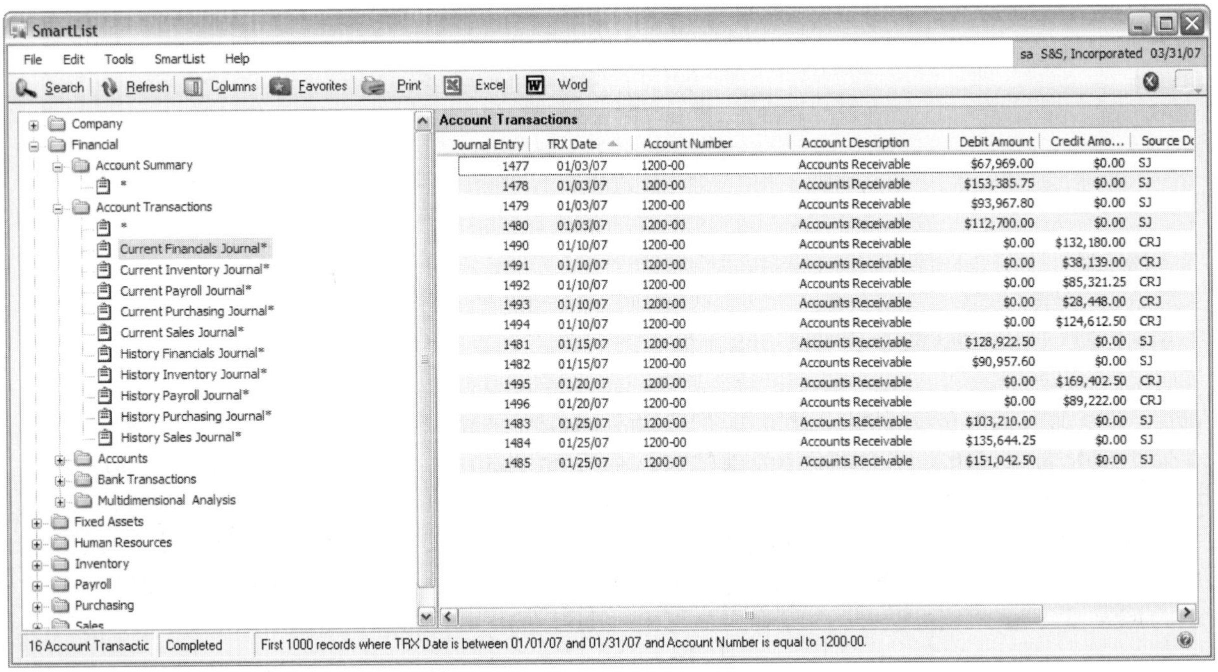

Figure 2:23 Search Results Sorted by Date

Let us now save the list for future use. Click **Favorites,** enter the **Name** illustrated in Figure 2:24, and click **Add** to select **Add favorite**.

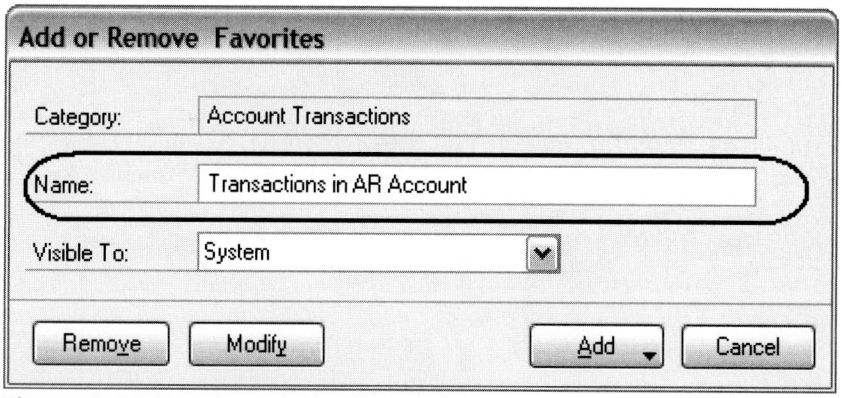

Figure 2:24 Naming a New SmartList

Your new SmartList is now listed under Account Transactions (Figure 2:25) and because we saved the list as visible to the System anyone using GP may access the list.

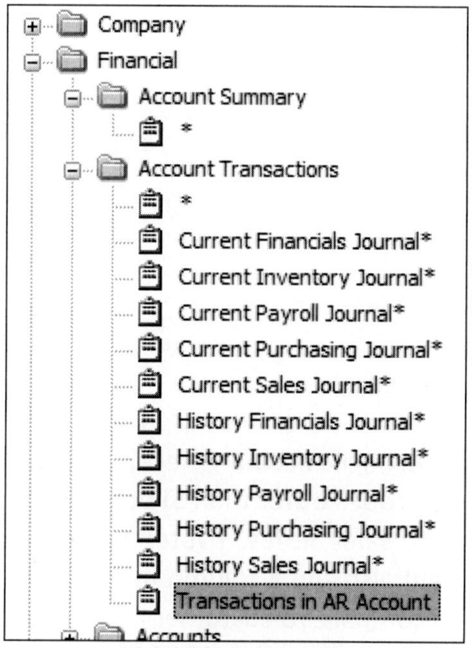

Figure 2:25 New Smart List

Before exporting the data you determine that the problem extends into March. Click **Search** and change the TRX Date to cover 1/1/2007 to 3/31/2007. Click **OK** to display the results. Resave the list by clicking **Favorites** and this time clicking **Modify**.

We are now ready to export the data by clicking Excel. *(Note: You must have Excel on your computer to use this feature.)* When Excel opens the data appears in a new workbook ready for data manipulation and analysis. (See Figure 2:26.)

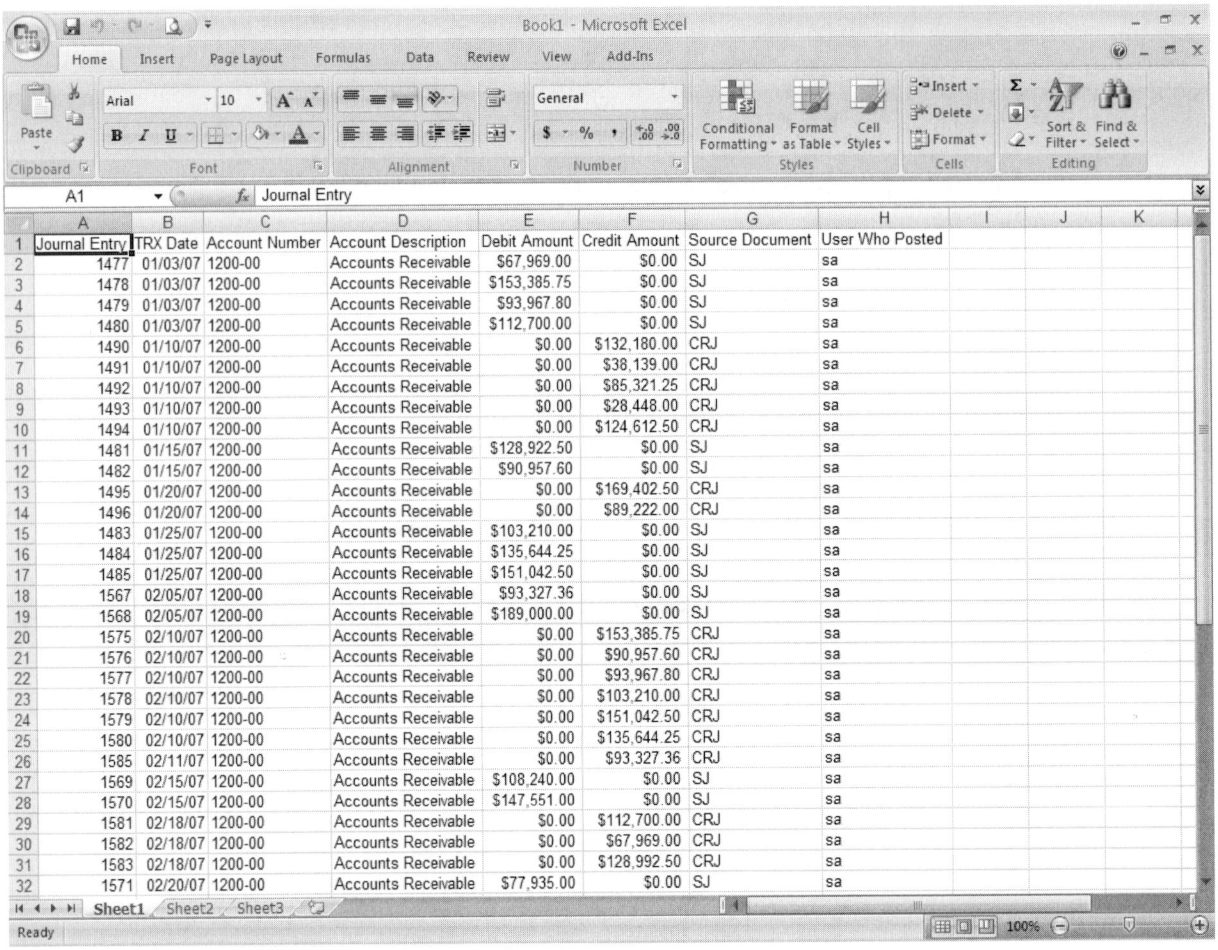

Journal Entry	TRX Date	Account Number	Account Description	Debit Amount	Credit Amount	Source Document	User Who Posted
1477	01/03/07	1200-00	Accounts Receivable	$67,969.00	$0.00	SJ	sa
1478	01/03/07	1200-00	Accounts Receivable	$153,385.75	$0.00	SJ	sa
1479	01/03/07	1200-00	Accounts Receivable	$93,967.80	$0.00	SJ	sa
1480	01/03/07	1200-00	Accounts Receivable	$112,700.00	$0.00	SJ	sa
1490	01/10/07	1200-00	Accounts Receivable	$0.00	$132,180.00	CRJ	sa
1491	01/10/07	1200-00	Accounts Receivable	$0.00	$38,139.00	CRJ	sa
1492	01/10/07	1200-00	Accounts Receivable	$0.00	$85,321.25	CRJ	sa
1493	01/10/07	1200-00	Accounts Receivable	$0.00	$28,448.00	CRJ	sa
1494	01/10/07	1200-00	Accounts Receivable	$0.00	$124,612.50	CRJ	sa
1481	01/15/07	1200-00	Accounts Receivable	$128,922.50	$0.00	SJ	sa
1482	01/15/07	1200-00	Accounts Receivable	$90,957.60	$0.00	SJ	sa
1495	01/20/07	1200-00	Accounts Receivable	$0.00	$169,402.50	CRJ	sa
1496	01/20/07	1200-00	Accounts Receivable	$0.00	$89,222.00	CRJ	sa
1483	01/25/07	1200-00	Accounts Receivable	$103,210.00	$0.00	SJ	sa
1484	01/25/07	1200-00	Accounts Receivable	$135,644.25	$0.00	SJ	sa
1485	01/25/07	1200-00	Accounts Receivable	$151,042.50	$0.00	SJ	sa
1567	02/05/07	1200-00	Accounts Receivable	$93,327.36	$0.00	SJ	sa
1568	02/05/07	1200-00	Accounts Receivable	$189,000.00	$0.00	SJ	sa
1575	02/10/07	1200-00	Accounts Receivable	$0.00	$153,385.75	CRJ	sa
1576	02/10/07	1200-00	Accounts Receivable	$0.00	$90,957.60	CRJ	sa
1577	02/10/07	1200-00	Accounts Receivable	$0.00	$93,967.80	CRJ	sa
1578	02/10/07	1200-00	Accounts Receivable	$0.00	$103,210.00	CRJ	sa
1579	02/10/07	1200-00	Accounts Receivable	$0.00	$151,042.50	CRJ	sa
1580	02/10/07	1200-00	Accounts Receivable	$0.00	$135,644.25	CRJ	sa
1585	02/11/07	1200-00	Accounts Receivable	$0.00	$93,327.36	CRJ	sa
1569	02/15/07	1200-00	Accounts Receivable	$108,240.00	$0.00	SJ	sa
1570	02/15/07	1200-00	Accounts Receivable	$147,551.00	$0.00	SJ	sa
1581	02/18/07	1200-00	Accounts Receivable	$0.00	$112,700.00	CRJ	sa
1582	02/18/07	1200-00	Accounts Receivable	$0.00	$67,969.00	CRJ	sa
1583	02/18/07	1200-00	Accounts Receivable	$0.00	$128,992.50	CRJ	sa
1571	02/20/07	1200-00	Accounts Receivable	$77,935.00	$0.00	SJ	sa

Figure 2:26 SmartList Exported to Excel

If you were really attempting to reconcile accounts receivable the first step might be to sort the Source Documents and search for codes other than SJ or CRJ because this indicates that a transaction did not originate in the Sales Series. *(Note: Source documents for a Series are discussed in Chapter 3.)* You might also add a column to display customer names and then use Excel to subtotal by customer to compare to customer account balances on the aging report. Or better yet, you learn in Chapter 5 that version 10 of GP added a tool to help reconcile the accounts receivable aging report to the general ledger account.

Click **X** on the Excel workbook and select **No** to exit without saving. Click **X** to close the SmartList.

Level Two

DATABASE MANAGEMENT SYSTEM (DBMS)

GP runs atop Microsoft SQL, which is a database management system (DBMS). This DBMS manages table creation and linking as well as data manipulation, queries, forms, and reporting. When users create new company databases, the DMBS calls upon a GP template to establish all the necessary database components. You might think of this as similar to establishing a new database in Microsoft Access by using a database wizard.

Students studying database concepts are familiar with relational database terminology. It also helps to understand this terminology when using accounting software. We begin by identifying the tables involved in a relational database, namely master, transaction, and linking. Master tables store the main records in a relationship whereas transaction tables contain activity records related to the master records. The database may also need a third table (i.e., linking table) to establish a many-to-many relationship between master and transaction tables.

GP stores customer, vendor, employee, and general ledger records in separate master tables. Day-to-day transactions are then stored in transaction tables that are linked directly or via linking tables to the master records. This means that creating a new customer affects the master table whereas creating a new invoice affects a transaction table as well as a linking table.

All records have primary keys used to ensure that each record in a table is unique. For customer records, the primary key is Customer ID. (See Figure 2:27.) Records may also contain foreign keys used to link the record to a record in another table. The Address ID in a customer record is a foreign key linking the customer to address records in the address table. In GP, a field name labeled with "ID" indicates either a primary or foreign key although not all foreign keys use this labeling. You must always supply a value for a primary key field and may also be required to provide a value for a foreign key field before GP permits saving the record.

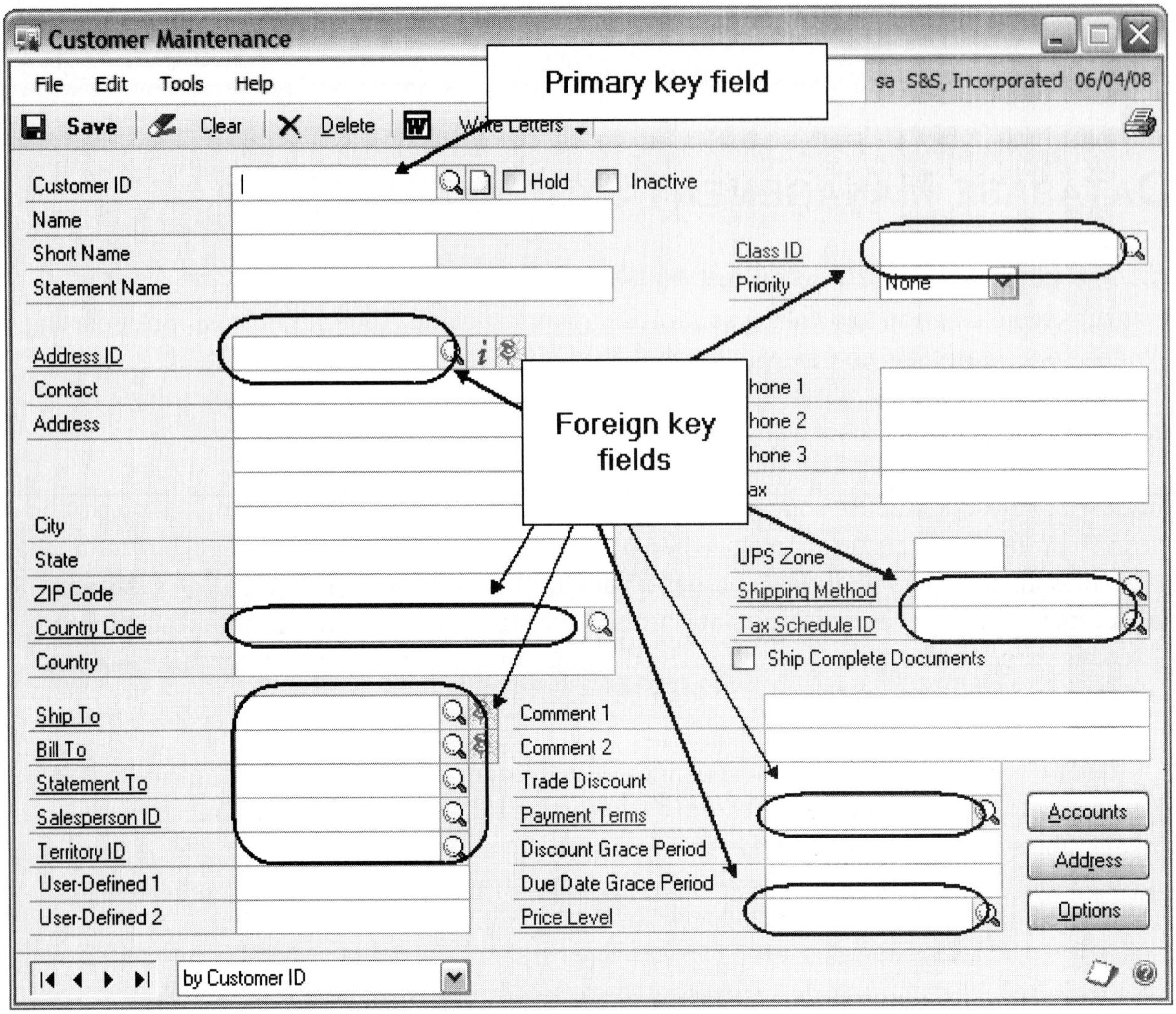

Figure 2:27 Primary and Foreign Keys on Customer Record

You do not need to know specific GP tables and relationships. We are simply explaining terminology you will encounter in the text and conveying a message that data entry can affect multiple tables. As illustrated, master records may interact with several tables. In addition, transaction records supply data to multiple tables and reports pull data from multiple tables. Such information helps when creating user access privileges in Chapter 3 and emphasizes the point of our next topic on series integration and error correction.

Series Integration

In a manual accounting system the accountant would post a sales invoice on the sales journal and then post it again on the customer account ledger. The accountant then totaled the sales journal and posted these totals to general ledger accounts. Audit trails had to be entered so that auditors could trace transactions from the source journal to financial accounts and vice versa. Imagine the errors that could occur. You could post an entry backwards (i.e., debit as a credit), subtotal incorrectly, or forget to post in all the places.

Accounting software solves the problem of multiple postings and mathematical calculations. Transactions are entered once and then processed from the original entry. This also means that subsidiary journals must integrate with financial journals. Such integration for GP is illustrated in Figure 2:28.

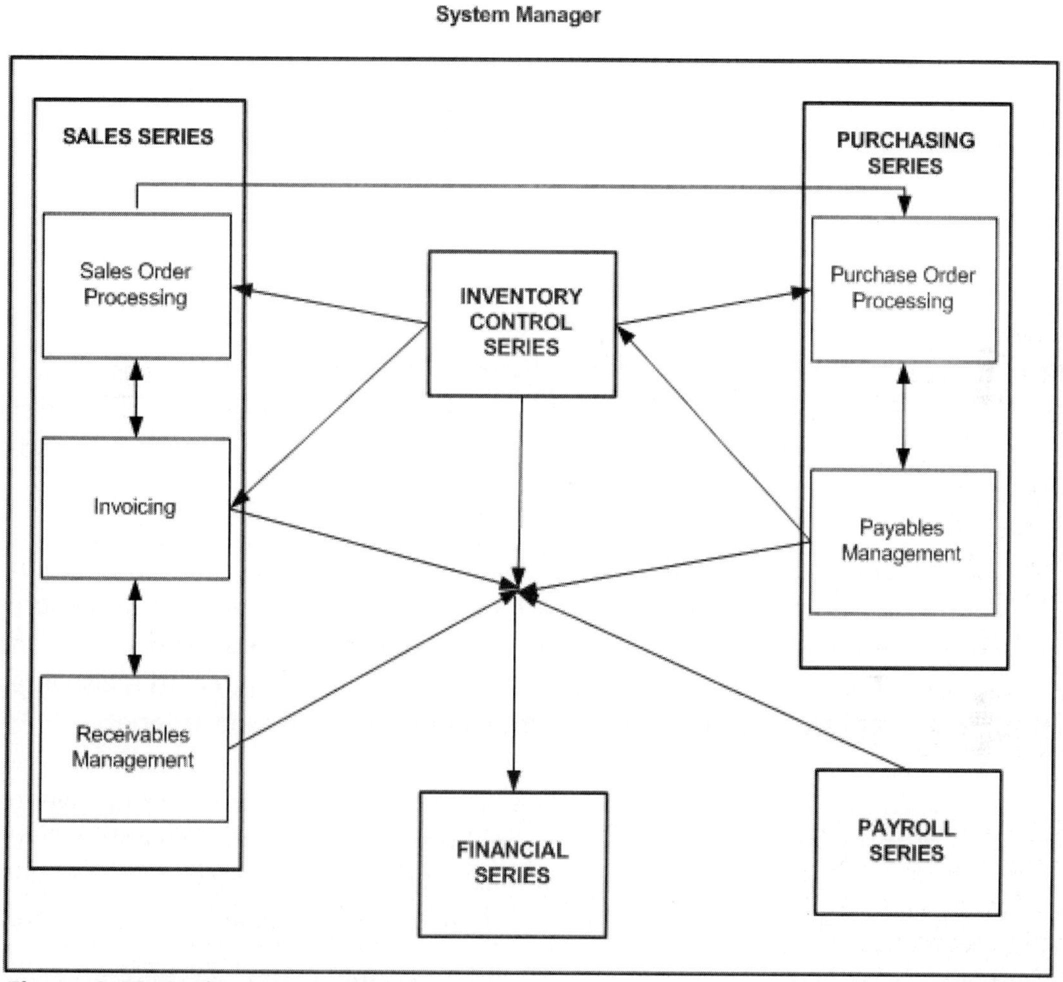

Figure 2:28 Series Integration

This figure shows that the System Manager Series functions as the "brain" for integration by managing system-wide settings for security, audit trails, and activity tracking. It also shows how Series integrate transactions among themselves. Thus, a sales invoice entered in the Sales Series integrates this transaction with records maintained by the Inventory Control and Financial Series. While each Series maintains its own set of master records, transaction records are linked to tables in multiple Series. Series integration makes it possible to post data in one Series to records stored in other Series.

This also means that error correction procedures must ensure that you are correcting data across multiple Series and the following example illustrates this.

Sales Processing Illustration

Step One: A salesperson or order entry clerk enters a sales order for inventory. During order entry, a customer master record, one or more inventory master records, and possibly a salesperson master record are linked to the order transaction record. GP then "flags" quantities on inventory master records as unavailable for other orders[4] but the transaction is not posted because orders are only commitments to ship to customers. Transaction records are only posted after changing the order into an invoice in Step Three (i.e., the order is shipped to the customer).

Assume that the order has the wrong item or incorrect quantity. You can easily correct the error by modifying the order. If you placed the order on the wrong customer then the error can be corrected either deleting or voiding it and entering a new order.

Step Two: The warehouse fills and ships the order to the customer. An employee in the shipping department opens the order to change data that indicates items have shipped so that the transaction is ready for invoicing. Again, the transaction record is not posted so modifying the order corrects the error.

Step Three: An accounts receivable clerk transfers the order to a customer invoice and then posts the invoice. At this point an economic exchange occurs and a financial transaction record is recognized [5] by creating an invoice transaction record that is linked to the customer and salesperson master records stored in the Sales Series. This transaction record is also integrated (i.e., linked) to master records stored in the Inventory Control and Financial Series.

At this point, an error has affected multiple Series. If an error exists for the wrong inventory item, incorrect quantity, or wrong customer it cannot be corrected by making entries in the Inventory Control or Financial Series. Instead, it must be corrected by correcting the sales invoice that originated in the Sales Series. You will find instructions to guide you on correcting errors in Appendix C.

---

[4] The behavior of inventory commitments depends upon setup options set under the Inventory Control Series. GP provides different options for handling inventory commitments and this example uses the setup selections set in the S&S database.

[5] The basis for such recognition is found in the Accounting Conceptual Framework. The revenue recognition principal states that revenue is recognized when earned or deemed to have been earned. For our purposes, revenue is earned when legal title to the inventory transfers (i.e., when inventory ships assuming FOB shipping point.) Thus, posting an invoice triggers recognition in financial accounts because title transferred upon shipping. Auditors test the proper recognition of transactions, thus audit shipping records.

Step Four: The customer remits payment on the invoice. An accounts receivable clerk posts the payment and applies it to the outstanding invoice transaction record using the Receivables Management Series. The posting process creates a cash receipts transaction record that is linked to the customer master record in the Sales Series and to general ledger and banking master records in the Financial Series. Thus, to correct an error, you must correct the cash receipts transaction that originated in the Receivables Management Series.

REA Data Model: Master, Transaction, and Linking Tables

This topic provides further guidance on understanding master, transaction, and linking table relationships. Refer to the REA data model of the revenue cycle[6] illustrated in Figure 2:29 to visualize table interaction in the Sales Series.

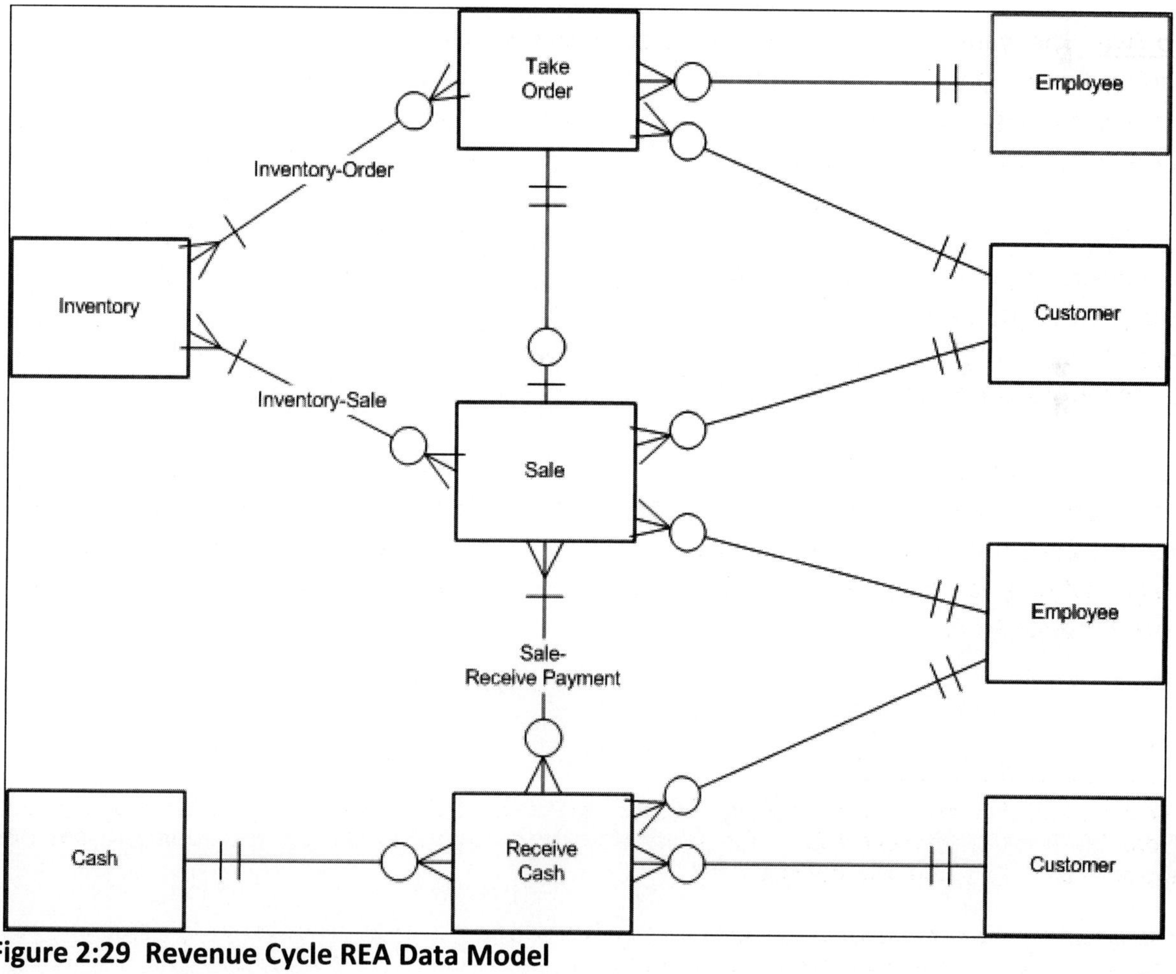

Figure 2:29 Revenue Cycle REA Data Model

[6] Data model is from Romney and Steinbart, *Accounting Information Systems,* (11th ed., Pearson Prentice Hall 2009), p. 569.

Squares on the left represent company resources, those in the middle represent events affecting resources, and squares to the right represent agents taking part in events. In database terms, each square represents a table. Resource and agent squares represent master tables and event squares represent transaction tables. In addition, lines with a label indicate the existence of a linking table that establishes a many-to-many relationship. So why should you care when the DBMS handles table interaction behind the scene? Because such knowledge helps you implement software internal controls.

Master tables are permanent tables requiring minimal data maintenance. In addition, all transaction records link to one or more master records. Thus, maintaining master records authorizes transactions, which means access to these tables is an authorization function in terms of internal controls. On the other hand, transaction tables store records produced by day-to-day posting activities and access to these tables is a recording function.[7] Keep these concepts in mind when reading Chapter 3 on internal controls.

[7] For more understanding on data modeling, refer to Romney and Steinbart, *Accounting Information Systems* (11th ed., Pearson Prentice Hall 2009), Chapters 15 and 16.

Level One Questions

True/False

____ 1. S&S could use 4411-00 to number a general ledger account number entitled Prepaid Rent.

____ 2. A general ledger account number of 5100-03 could be used for posting Salary expense for the West department.

____ 3. Marking the Purchasing Series as closed in the Fiscal Periods window means that you can no longer post vendor invoices for the closed period.

____ 4. Setting an Account Length of 8 and Segments of 3 in the Account Format Setup window means you can number a general ledger account with 100-000-00.

____ 5. Unit is the account type used to designate accounts that store square footage for a department.

Exercises

1. S&S Controller, Ashton, needs to begin allocating company insurance to three sales departments. Currently all insurance expense is recorded in 5620-04 Insurance Expense–Administration. He asks that you create three departmental expense accounts for insurance and establish an allocation account for spreading costs 25% across the board to the new accounts plus the present account.

2. S&S's owners want an income statement for January 2007 by department. They ask that you create these reports using the departmental segment on accounts.

3. Ashton is performing a month-end closing as of February 2007. He needs you to review transaction details in the general ledger for February. Prepare the report that assists you with this task.

4. Create an Excel spreadsheet to analyze customer sales growth by region using the following steps.
    a. Open the existing SmartList named Posted Invoices found under the Sales Transactions folders.
    b. Modify the list to add the Customer Class column so that you can identify regions.
    c. Filter the list so that only the Customer Class equal to BBMID displays.
    d. Export data to Excel and use Excel tools to sort by date.
    e. Add a column named Month and use an Excel function to extract the month from the date into this column. Add another column to store the name of the month to use as the legend for the axis.
    f. Use Excel's subtotal feature to determine sales totals by month and then graph results that compare sales for 2006 to 2007.

Level Two Questions

1. Open a vendor card. Have you accessed a master or transaction table? Please explain.

2. The vendor card contains numerous data fields. List the field name storing the vendor record's primary key and also list any foreign key fields on the record. Explain why the vendor record uses primary and foreign keys.

3. Click the Accounts button on the vendor card. These accounts are integrated into which Series?

4. Open a Sales Transaction Entry window from the Sales home page, select the invoice document type, and then review data entry fields.

    a. Besides the Sales Series, list other Series integrated with the invoice transaction. (Remember to click the Distributions button.)

    b. Will this invoice record be stored in a master or transaction table?

    c. Use database terminology to describe the Customer ID field on the invoice record.

5. Open a purchase order transaction using the Purchase Order Entry command on the Purchasing home page and identify the primary key and foreign keys on the transaction.

Chapter 3 INTERNAL CONTROLS AND GP SECURITY

CHAPTER OVERVIEW

This chapter focuses on internal control settings in the System Manager Series, including user access to the software and Series posting and reporting controls. The controls set in the System Manager Series as pervasive, meaning these controls govern all aspects of GP. Along with System Manager Series controls, GP provides internal control options for the Sales, Purchasing, and Financial Series. We will explore these options in subsequent chapters.

As we discuss internal controls throughout this text, it is important to understand COSO's Enterprise Risk Management (ERM) framework. This framework is a guide for implementing user security because it explains segregation of duties[8] and the role of independent checks on performance. In light of recent developments in accounting oversight, particularly the Sarbanes-Oxley Act of 2002 (SOX) and subsequent revisions, accountants must be able to implement and evaluate whether software internal controls comply with SOX Section 404 requirements. For additional information on the COSO's ERM framework, SOX, and internal control objectives see Chapters 6 through 8 of *Accounting Information Systems*, Romney and Steinbart, (11th ed., Pearson Prentice Hall 2009).

GP topics covered in this chapter deal with user access permissions, activity tracking, posting setup, and the audit trail. Such tasks are usually performed system administrators or accountants charged with responsibility for setting internal controls and security policies.

Level One covers:

- Security implemented during installation of the software
- Internal control features in Posting Setup
- The audit trail and activity tracking

Level Two covers:

- System administration security
- Setting user software access and activity permissions and security reporting

---

[8] Segregation of duties separates employee responsibilities into the functional areas of authorization, recording, and custody. When setting software controls, the tasks a user is permitted to perform should fall under just one of these functional areas.

SECURITY INSTALLED DURING GP INSTALLATION

You might remember setting a password when installing GP for the *sa* User ID to access the software. In fact, this is the password you use to login to the system and is the initial security installed during installation.

The *sa* User ID is an acronym for system administrator. By default, this User ID is the owner of the database and has full control over database administration. Some of the tasks illustrated in this chapter can only be performed by someone logged in as the *sa*. The *sa* user can create or delete company databases, create new users, and perform database maintenance tasks such as data integrity checks and database backups and restores. Therefore, it is important to protect the password for this account and, in the real world, change it frequently.

GP incorporates a separate password for opening additional security features accessed through clicking the GP Button and selecting ***Tools>>Setup>>System***. Select this menu path and focus on the commands illustrated in Figure 3:1.

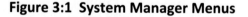

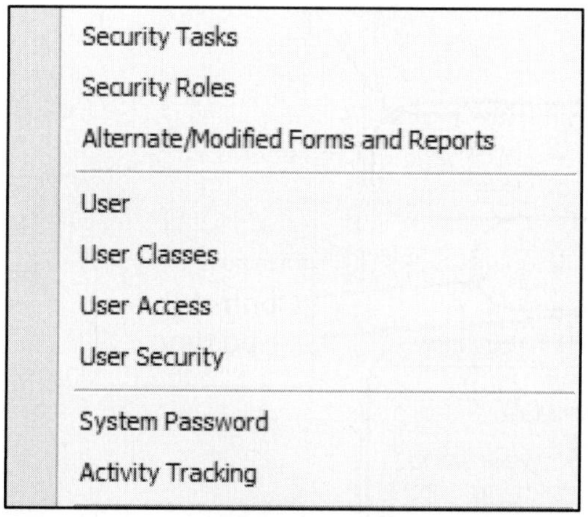

Figure 3:1 System Manager Menus

To open any of these menus you will need to enter a system password that is different from the *sa* login password. GP will prompt you for this password each time you select any of the illustrated menus. The system password functions independent from the login password so that responsibility for setting certain internal control features may be delegated to accountants not having login access through the *sa* account.[9] We have set the System password to ***sa.*** Note that this password can be changed by clicking the System Password menu.

[9] For an in-depth discussion on the COBIT Framework, refer to Romney and Steinbart, *Accounting Information Systems* (11th ed., Pearson Prentice Hall 2009), pgs. 203-204.

POSTING SETUP CONTROLS

Before discussing security, we will look at menus controlling posting behavior and documenting the audit trail. Commands for accessing these features are found under the GP Button by selecting ***Tools>>Setup>>Posting***. (See Figure 3:2.)

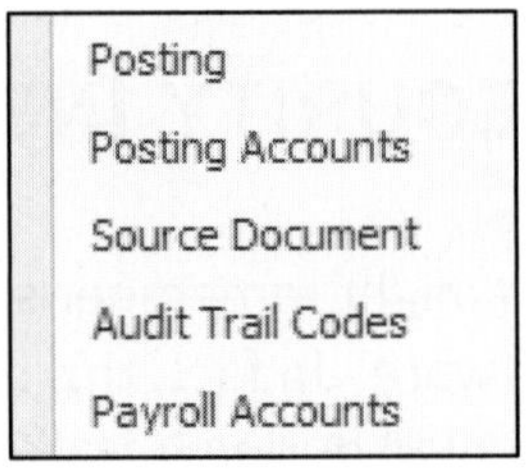

Figure 3:2 Posting Setup Menus

Click the Posting menu and choose **Sales** as the Series and **Invoice Entry** as the Origin. (See Figure 3:3.) The window displays posting options for sales invoice transactions. Posting setup determines posting internal controls and control reports that print after posting. There are posting controls for each Series as wells as for each origin of a transaction in that Series.

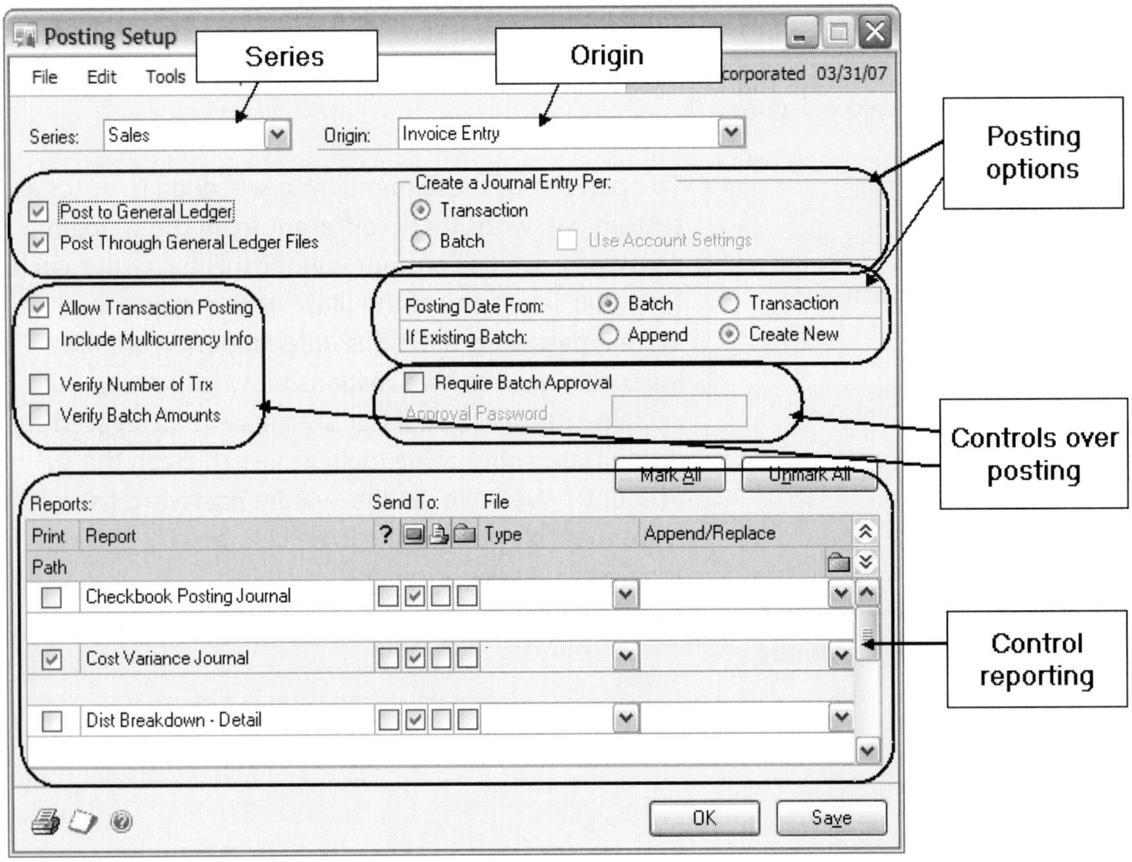

Figure 3:3 Posting Setup for Sales Series Invoices

The dropdown on Origin reveals that controls are set by type of task performed in a Series. From this figure, we know that Sales Series invoices:

1) Posted in batches make entries directly to general ledger accounts and these entries

post as individual transactions in the accounts.

2) Post to the general ledger using the date on the batch.
3) Can be posted individually (i.e., do not have to post in a batch).
4) If posted in a batch, are not required to include control totals or batch approval before posting.

You will have a better understanding of the list after reading this topic

The Reports section at the bottom of the window lists the control reports that print after posting. You can use the scroll bar to view all journals marked for printing.

Click **X** to close the Posting Setup window. The following provides more information on the internal control effect of these options.

I. ***Options of Post to General Ledger and Post Through General Ledger Files***

These options represent two distinct methods of posting transactions to general ledger accounts.

Post to General Ledger is always marked and instructs GP to post transactions in the selected Series but not to post in the Financial Series. Instead; transactions are suspended in a Financial Series batch that must be separately posted before transactions affect general ledger accounts. *(Note: Remember that general ledger accounts are stored in the Financial Series.)* You want to pay close attention to this feature because it also means that you will not view your posted transactions in general ledger accounts until after you perform a second post. To view Financial Series suspended batch, activate the Financial Series home page and click Series Post under Transactions. *(Note: We illustrate posting suspended batches later in the text.)* Selecting this method lets companies review transactions prior to posting them to general ledger accounts; however, making changes to suspended batches is not recommended because such changes alter the audit trail from the originating Series.

Post to General Ledger Files instructs GP to post ***batched transactions*** directly to general ledger accounts. To implement this method, both posting options are marked. Notice our emphasis on batched transactions. GP still suspends transactions posted individually so you must always perform a second post in the Financial Series before viewing these transactions in general ledger accounts.

Another key point, posting options are set by Series and by Origin so posting treatment can be tailored to meet a company's internal control objectives. S&S has opted to use the second posting method for all Series and Origins. We will next illustrate these settings by posting an individual transaction first and then posting a batched transaction.

Posting an Individual Transaction

1. Activate the **Sales** home page and click **Invoice Entry**. Enter the invoice transaction as illustrated in Figure 3:4. *(Note: Your invoice number may vary from that illustrated but remaining fields are identical.)*

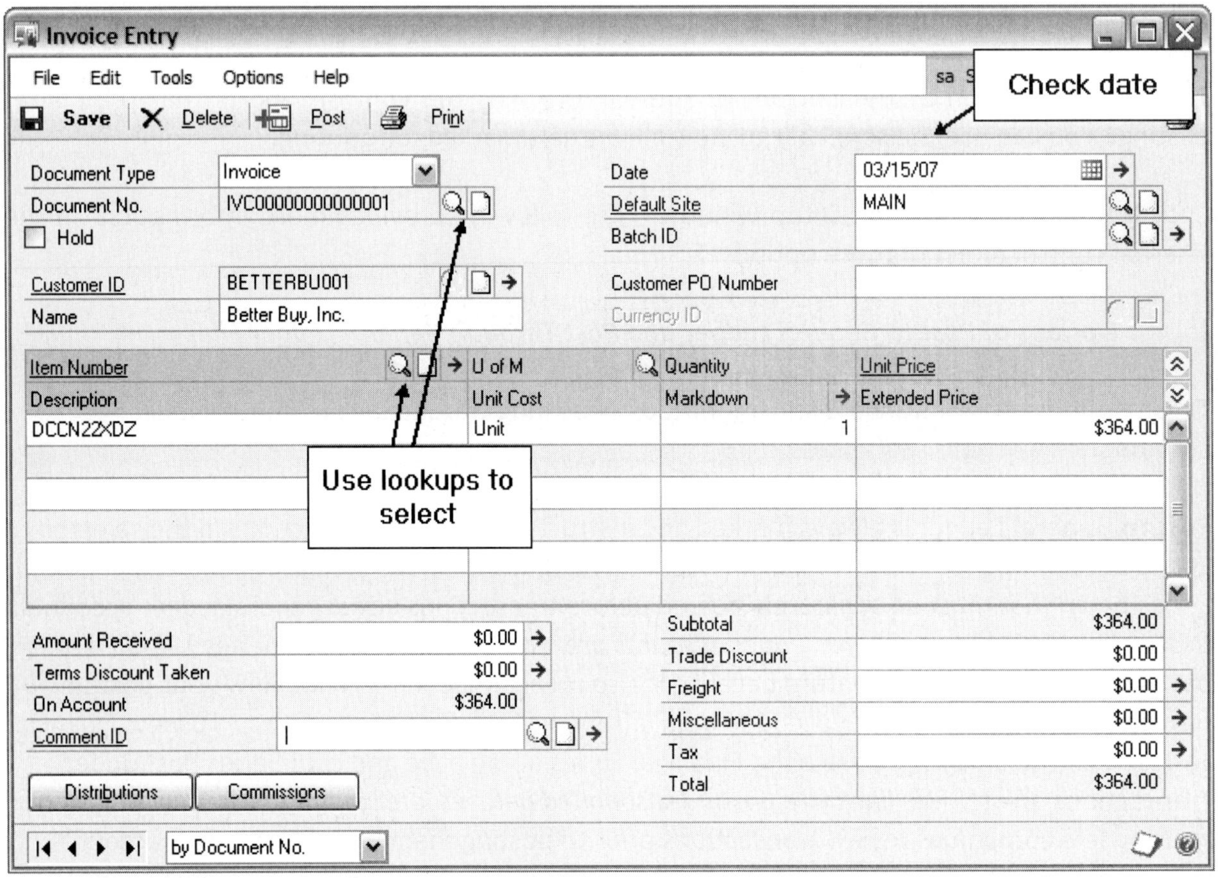

Figure 3:4 Invoice Transaction to Better Buy

2. When finished, click **Post** and then close the window to print the posting reports. *(Note: Posting reports often print only after closing the active window.)*

   The Invoice Posting Journal prints first, listing general ledger accounts affected by posting. (See Figure 3:5.) Do not be fooled by the presence of these accounts. We will later discover that this invoice has not been finalized to general ledger accounts.

```
                                    S&S, Incorporated                           Page:    1
User Date:  03/31/07             INVOICING POSTING JOURNAL                      User ID: sa
                                         Invoicing

Batch ID: sa                 Audit Trail Code: INVCE00000001        Batch Frequency: Single
                             Batch Comment:

Batch Total Actual:          $0.00     Batch Total Control:          $0.00
Trx Total Actual:                0     Trx Total Control:                0
Approved:                       No     Approved By:                              Approval Date:  00/00/00

Type   Document Number    Doc Date    Post Date   Customer ID     Name                          Salesperson
-------------------------------------------------------------------------------------------------------------
           Subtotal    Trade Discount    Freight Amount      Misc Amount       Tax Amount      Document Total   Discount Av
-------------------------------------------------------------------------------------------------------------

IVC    IVC00000000000001  03/15/07    03/15/07    BETTERBU001     Better Buy, Inc.              ASL6677
           $364.00          $0.00           $0.00          $0.00            $0.00          $364.00            $7

Item Number                      Description                                                  Markdown
                                 U of M    Site                          Quantity            Unit Price        Extended P
DCCN22XDZ                        Canyon DigCamcord 22X Optical / 440X Digital Zoom                  0.00
                                 Unit      MAIN                                 1                 364.00              36
                                                                                                            ---------------
                                                                                                                      36

Account Distributions
Account Number                   Account Description               Account Type             Debit Amount          Credit Am
1200-00                          Accounts Receivable               RECV                         356.72
4100-02                          Sales - MidWest                   SALES                          0.00                36
5200-00                          Commission Expense                COMMEXP                        1.09
2230-00                          Commissions Payable               COMMPAY                        0.00
```

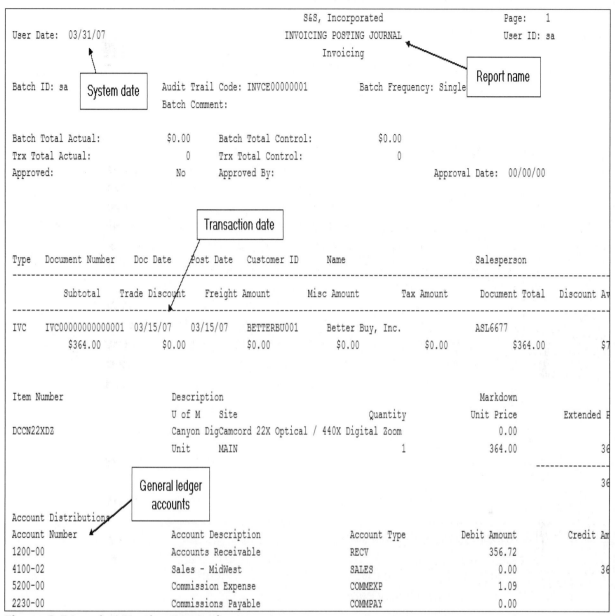

Figure 3:5 Invoice Posting Journal

Close this report and the Inventory Sales Register prints. Review information on the report and then close it. Finally, the Cost Variance Journal prints. Close it.

(Note: When several posting reports are to be printed, one report must be closed before the next appears. The reports that print after posting are determined by Report options illustrated previously in Figure 3:3 and we discuss selecting reports later in the chapter.)

Before checking on the status of this posting, let us next post the same transaction using a batch.

Posting Transaction in a Batch

1. First, create the batch. Click **Invoicing Batches** and enter the information as illustrated in Figure 3:6.

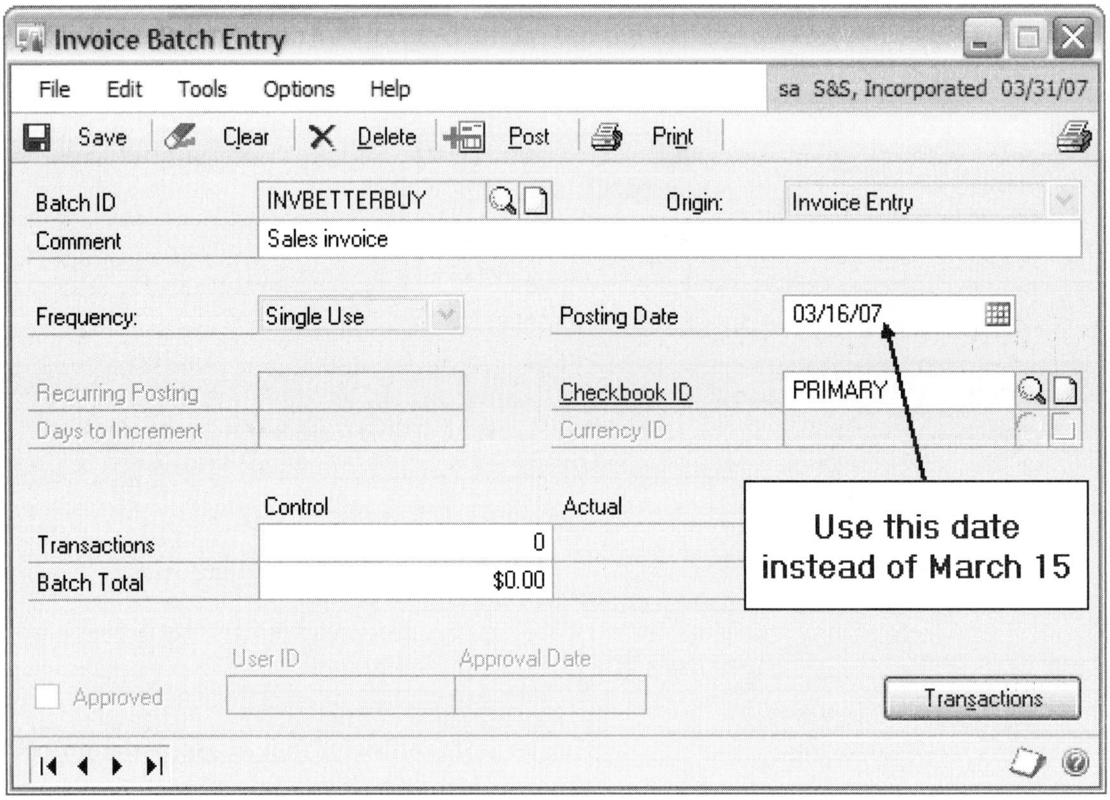

Figure 3:6 Invoice Batch Entry Window

2. Click **Transactions** and enter the invoice as illustrated in Figure 3:7. *(Note: The invoice is identical to the invoice previously entered.)*

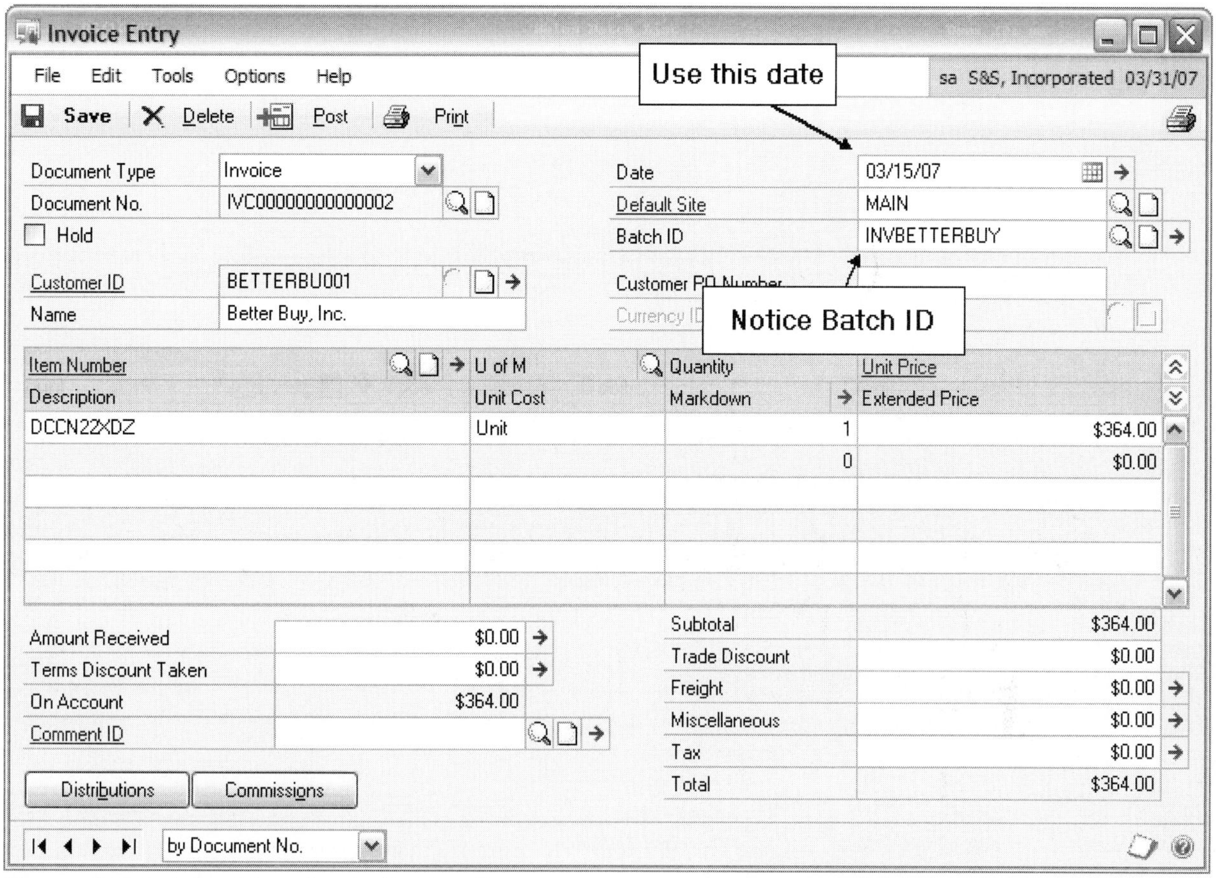

Figure 3:7 Batched Invoice to Better Buy

3. Click **Save** and close the transaction window.

4. Return to the Invoice Batch Entry window and look up the **INVBETTERBUY** batch. Click **Post**. Review the posting reports, this time noting that the last report to print is called the General Posting Journal. (See Figure 3:8.)

S&S, Incorporated
GENERAL POSTING JOURNAL
General Ledger

Page: 1
User ID: sa

User Date: 03/31/07

* Voided Journal Entry

Batch ID: INVCE00000002
Batch Comment: Sales invoice

Transaction date in general ledger accounts

Approved: No	Batch Total Actual: $1,290.18	Batch Total Control:	$0.00
Approved by:	Trx Total Actual: 1	Trx Total Control:	0
Approval Date:			

Journal Entry	Transaction Type	Transaction Date	Reversing Date	Source Document	Transaction Reference	Audit Trail Code	Reversing Audit Trail Code
1,700	Standard	03/16/07		INVCE	Invoice Entry	GLTRX00000642	

Account	Description	Debit	Credit
1200-00	Accounts Receivable	$356.72	
4100-02	Sales - MidWest		$364.00
5200-00	Commission Expense	$1.09	
2230-00	Commissions Payable		$1.09
1205-00	Sales Discounts Available	$7.28	
1310-00	Inventory		$280.00
4500-02	Cost of Goods Sold - MidWest	$280.00	
Total Distributions: 7	Totals:	$645.09	$645.09

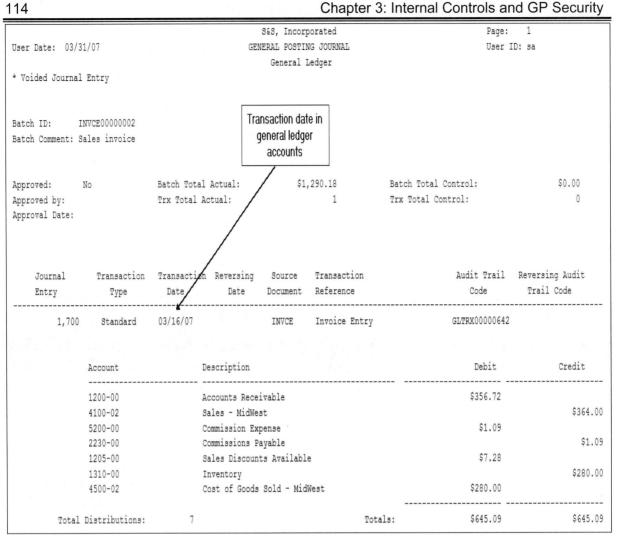

Figure 3:8 General Posting Journal

The presence of this report always signals transactions have finalized to general ledger accounts. Notice that the posting date for general ledger accounts is March 16 (i.e., the date on the batch) instead of the invoice date of March 15.

Why did this occur? Let us return to the beginning of this topic, namely, the portion of the Posting Setup window illustrated in Figure 3:9.

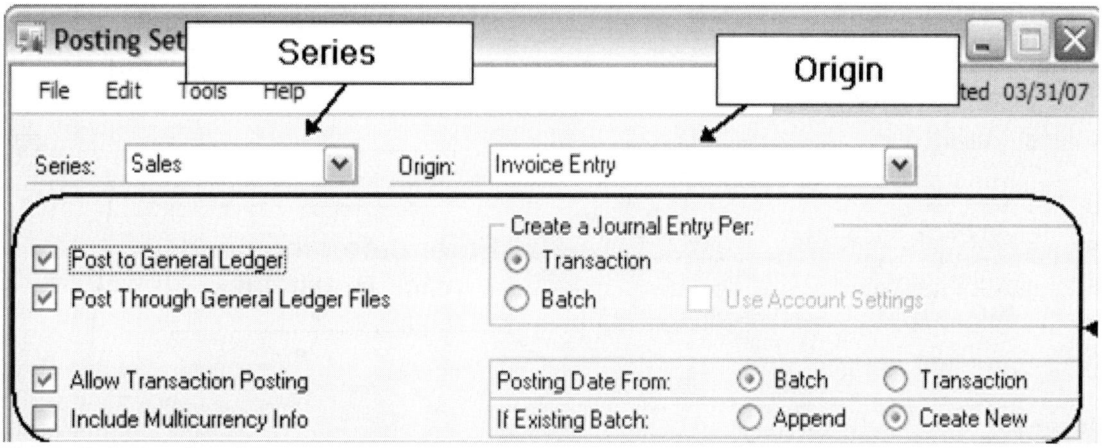

Figure 3:9 Posting Setup Dates

Notice that Posting Date From is marked Batch, meaning that general ledger transactions use the batch date, unless the transaction is posted individually. The posting date in the Sales Series always remains the transaction date because this date properly ages the invoice. You see why it is important to pay attention to dates.

Let us now focus on viewing these postings in the general ledger accounts. Close any open window or report and activate the **Financial** home page.

Click **Detail** under Inquiry. Refer to the next illustration and look up account 1200-00 Accounts Receivable, filtering for transactions posted on March 15 and March 16. You find one invoice transaction dated March 16, 2007. *(Note: The original invoice amount totaled $364.00 but only $356.72 posted to accounts receivable because the invoice carried a 2% early payment discount and the discount posted to a different account. In Chapter 5 we discuss the Sales Series option that tracks potential discounts.)*

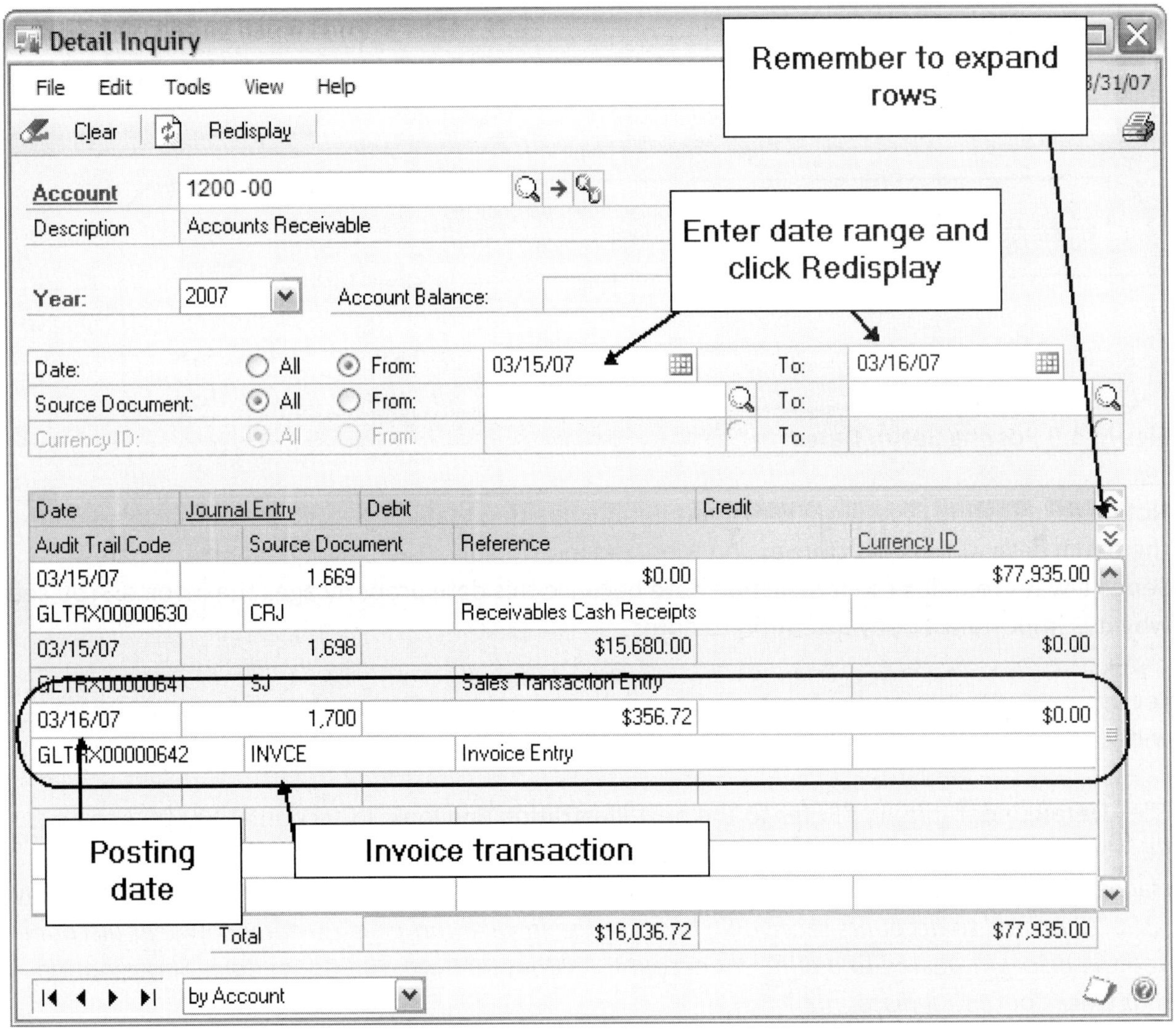

Figure 3:10 Detail Inquiry Window

Highlight the transaction and click the **Journal Entry** hyperlink to open the window illustrated next.

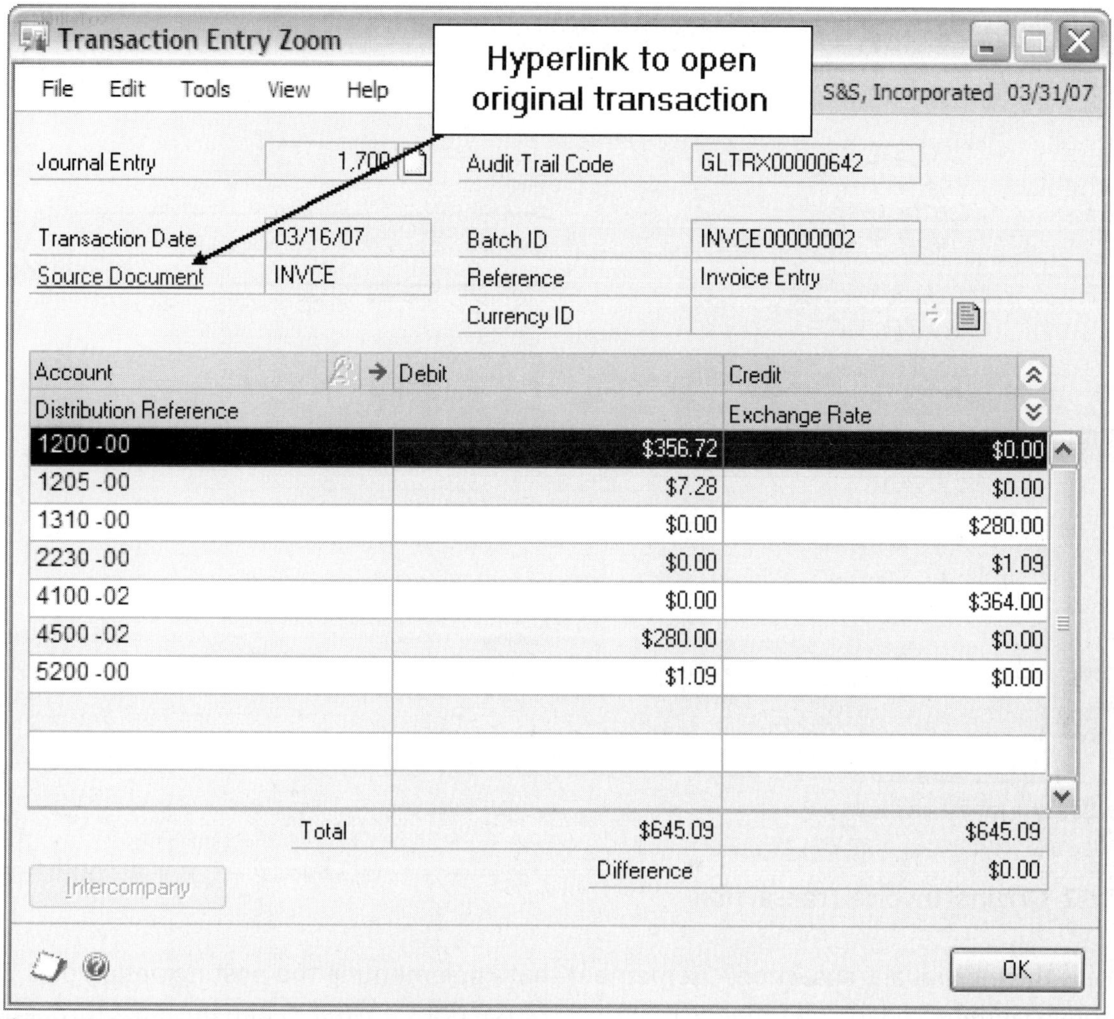

Figure 3:11 Transaction Entry Zoom Window

Click the **Source Document** hyperlink to reopen the original transaction and locate the Batch ID information. (See Figure 3:12**.)** You have now verified that this transaction originated from the INVBETTERBUY batch. Close the Invoice Inquiry and Transaction Entry Zoom windows but keep the Detail Inquiry window open.

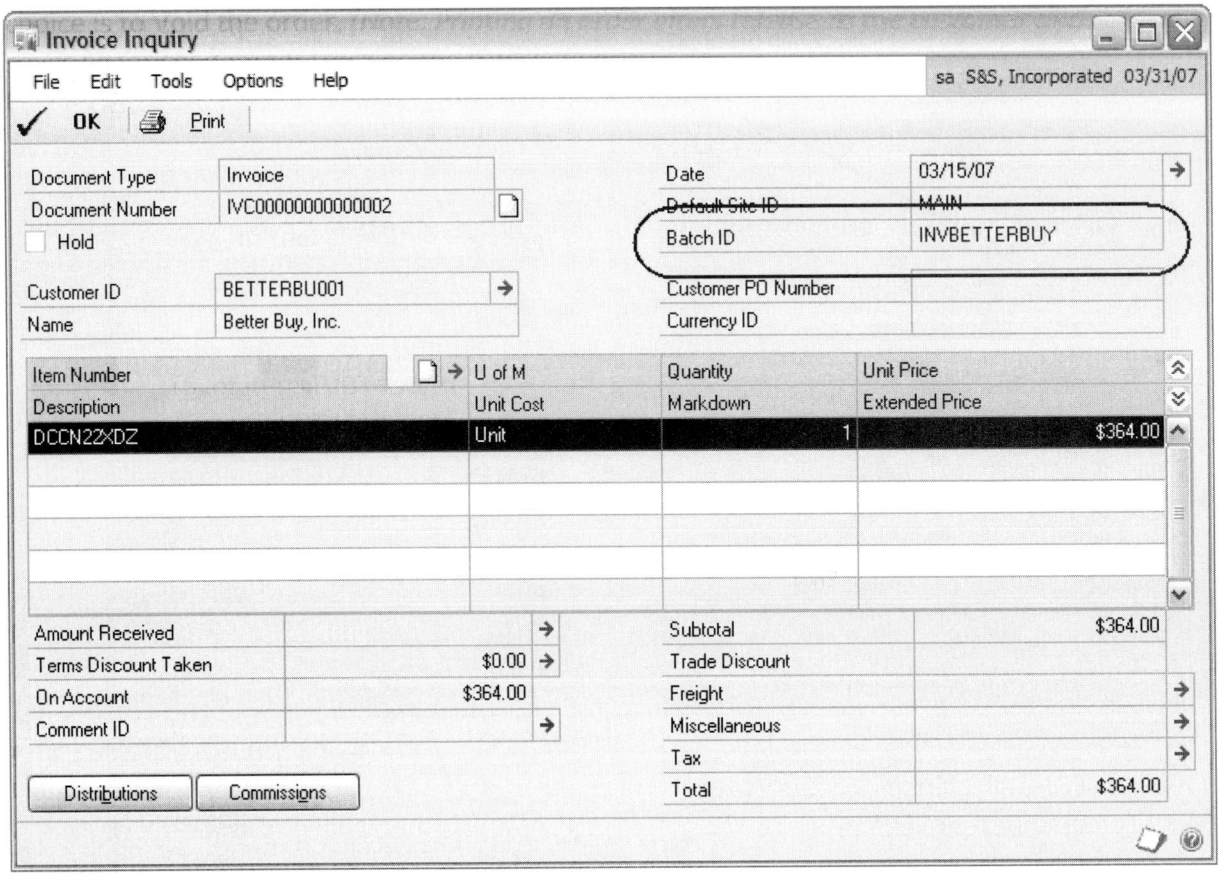

Figure 3:12 Original Invoice Transaction

So where is the individual transaction? Remember that implementing the posting option of Post Through General Ledger Files means that only transactions posted in batches post through to general ledger accounts. You must still perform a second post for transactions posted individually.

On the Financial home page, click **Series Post** under Transactions to open the window illustrated in Figure 3:13.

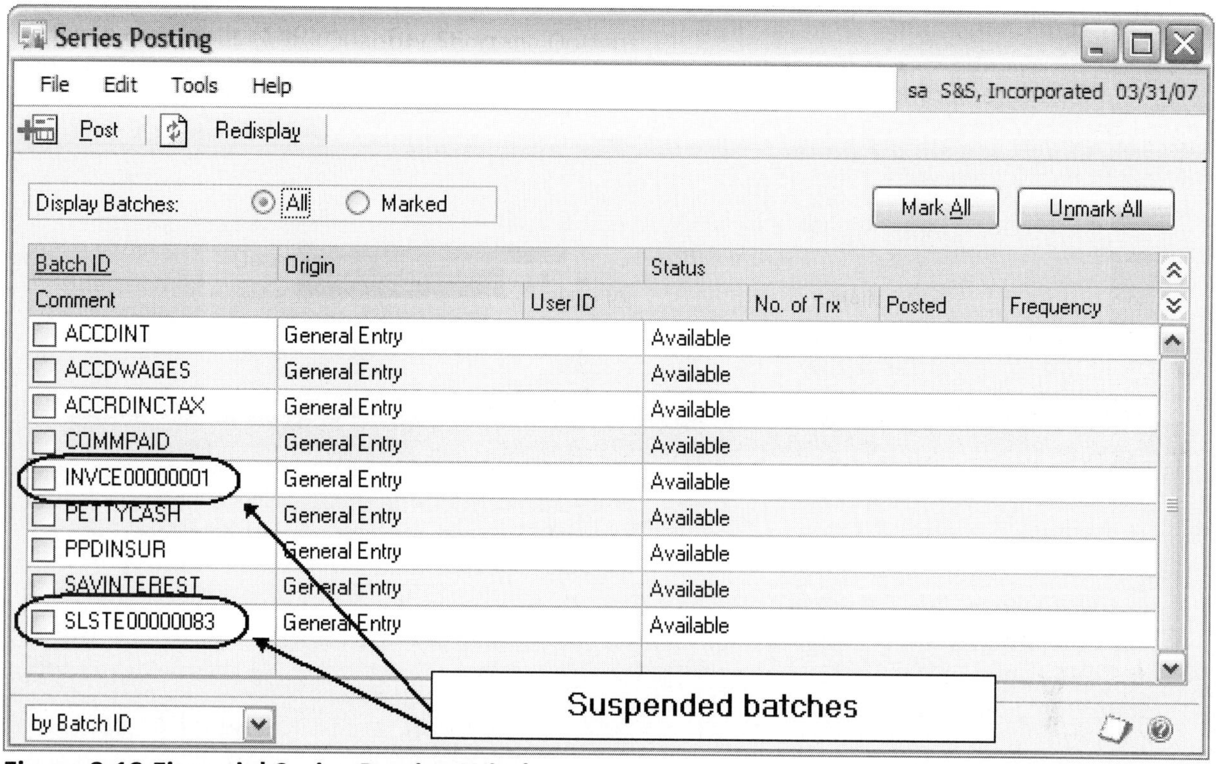

Figure 3:13 Financial Series Posting Window

This window lists batches available for posting in the Financial Series. Batches may be pending or suspended. Pending batches are those created in the Financial Series to store journal entry transactions for later posting. Suspended batches are those created by GP when posting individual transactions in other Series. *(Note: INVCE is the audit trail code for posted sales invoices. Audit trail codes are discussed later in the chapter.)* Therefore, you identify suspended batches by looking at the Batch ID.

Follow the next steps to open the suspended batch.

1. Click the **Batch ID** hyperlink. *(Note: This is a shortcut to opening the Batch Entry window.)*

2. Look up Batch ID "INVCE00000001" and click **Select** to reopen the batch. (See Figure 3:14.)

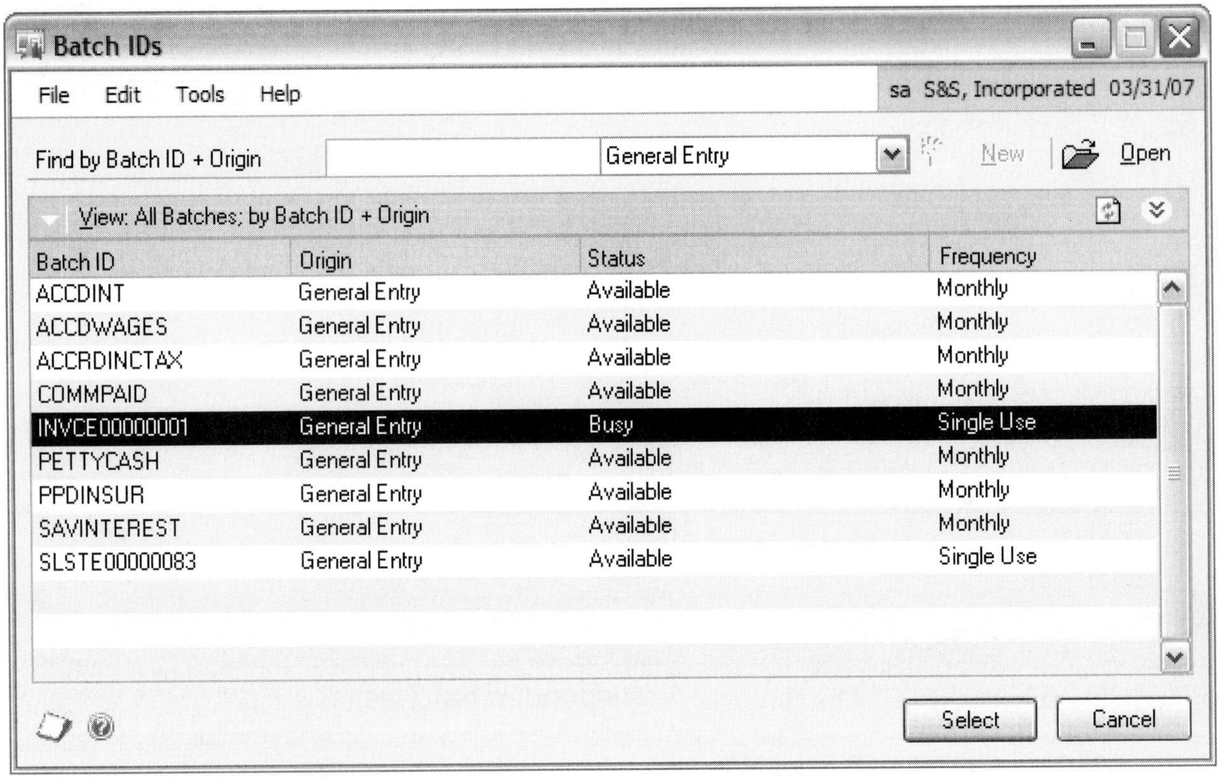

Figure 3:14 Batch ID Lookup

3. Click **Transactions**.

4. Use the Journal Entry lookup icon to locate "INVCE00000001". (See Figure 3:15.) Highlight the transaction and click **Select**.

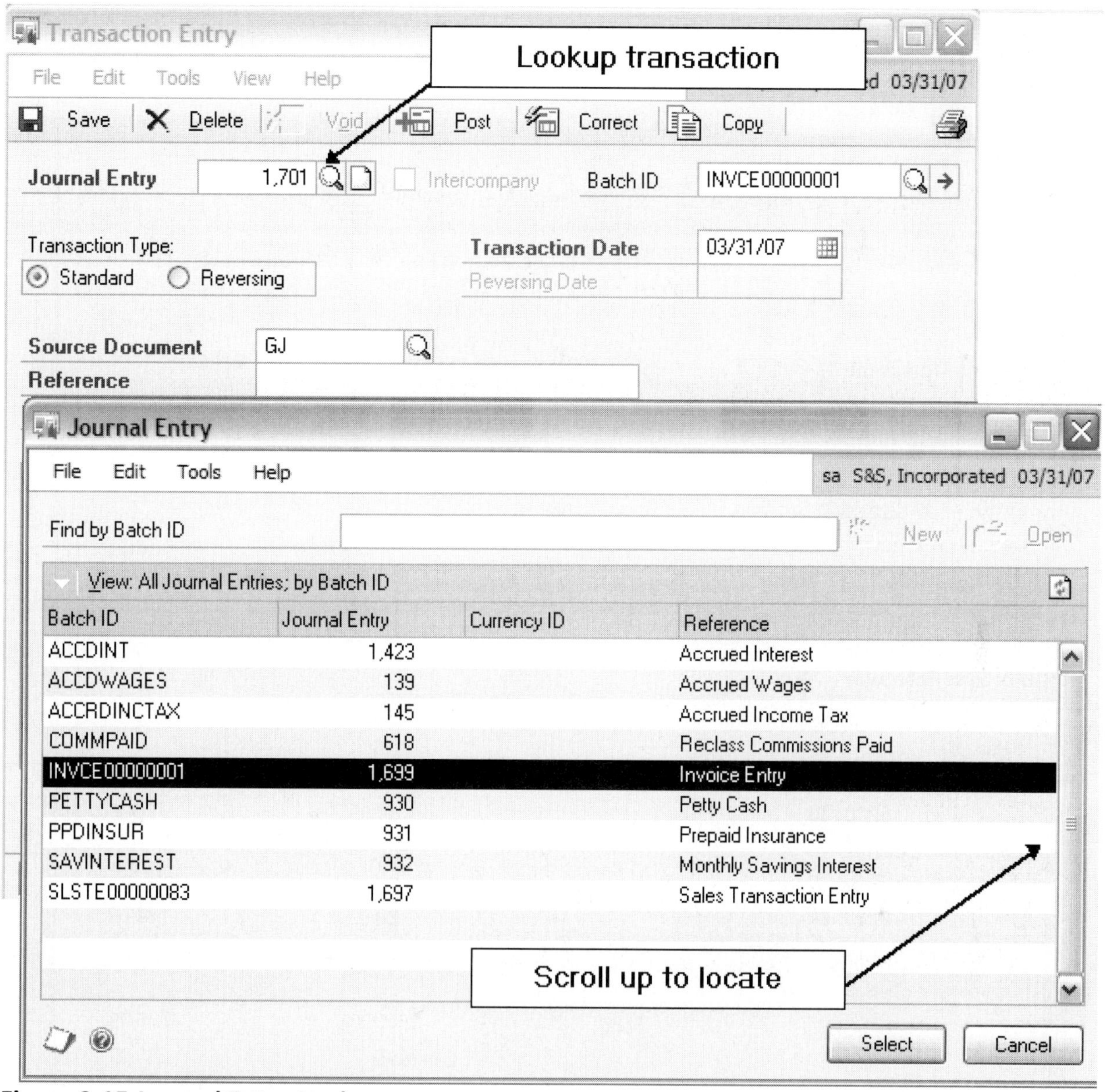

Figure 3:15 Journal Entry Lookup

5. You are now viewing the suspended transaction. (See Figure 3:16.) Expand row details to view addition information.

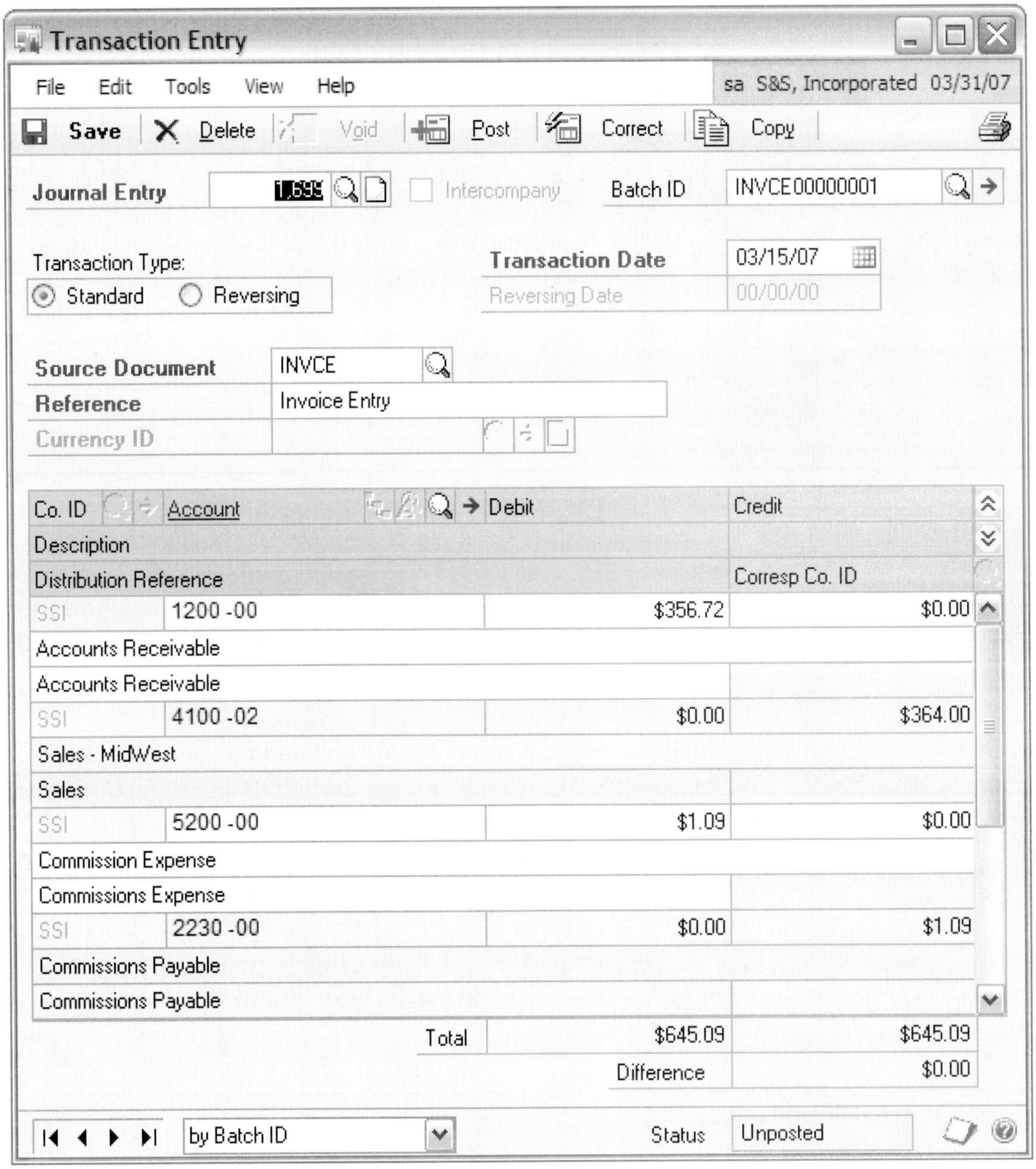

Figure 3:16 Suspended Invoice Transaction

6. You must be very careful in this widow. If you accidently delete the transaction then the Sales Series no longer balances with the Financial Series. See additional warnings that follow. Click **X** to close the Transaction Entry Window and **X** to close the Batch Entry window.

> ⚠ Changing general ledger accounts on suspended transactions is not recommended because data integrity issues may arise.
>
> First, inquires on posting details in the originating Series will not reflect actual accounts affected in the Financial Series. Second, and most important, you can accidentally delete the suspended transaction so that it never posts in the Financial Series (i.e., general ledger accounts) and now the Sales Series no longer balances with the Financial Series. This out-of-balance condition becomes apparent when you reconcile the balance in the accounts receivable account with the outstanding balance on the Accounts Receivable Aging report. We perform this reconciliation procedure in Chapter 5.

Return to the Series Posting window and click the box on INVCE00000001 to mark it for posting. Click **Post.** The General Posting Journal now prints, confirming that the transaction posted to the general ledger.

To verify this, click **X** to close the Series Posting window and return to the Detail inquiry window. Click **Redisplay** to find a second invoice has posted, this time dated March 15, 2007. Close the Detail Inquiry window.

So keep in mind that a second post must be performed to finalize individually posted transactions to general ledger accounts. When transactions remain suspended, account balances are not adjusted and financial statements are incorrect. To avoid this mistake, verify that the General Posting Journal prints after posting and always review the Financial Series Posting window for suspended transactions.

II. *Options that Allow Transaction Posting, Verify Number of Trx, Verify Batch Amounts, and Require Batch Approval*

We will now focus on the following options in the Posting Setup window.

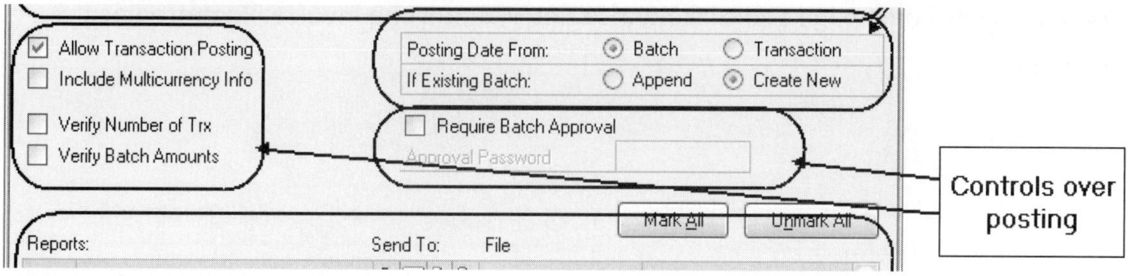

Figure 3:17 Posting Setup Controls

Allow Transaction Posting permits users to post transactions individually instead of requiring all transactions to post in batches. **Verify Number of Trx** and **Verify Batch Amounts** are not marked so employees can post batches without entering control totals. Finally, **Require Batch Approval** is not marked so employees can post batches without independent approval. These options affect S&S's compliance with COSO's recommended control activities,[10] particularly the independent checks on performance that protect data integrity.

Denying Individual Transaction Posting

We now focus on implementing options that require all transactions to post in batches. Reopen the Posting Setup window by clicking the GP Button to select ***Tools>>Setup>>Posting>>Posting***.

Select the Sales Series and Invoice Entry Origin and uncheck **Allow Transaction Posting**. (See Figure 3:18.) Click **Save**. Keep the Posting Setup window open so we can change other options.

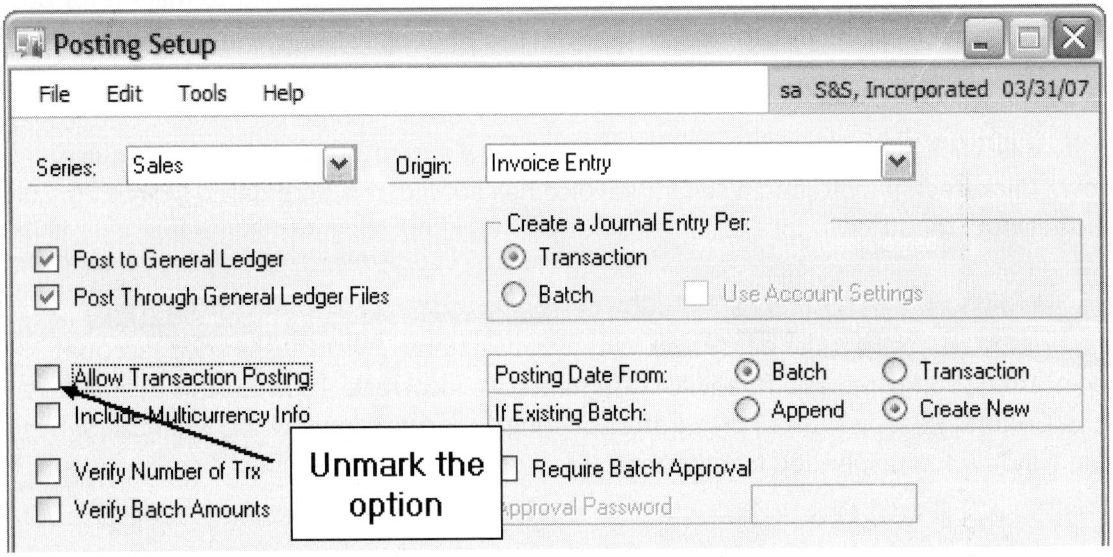

Figure 3:18 Option to Deny Individual Transaction Posting

Now test this setting.

1. Activate the Sales home page and click **Invoice Entry**. Enter the invoice illustrated next.

[10] For an in-depth discussion on COSO's ERM Framework, refer to Romney and Steinbart, *Accounting Information Systems* (11th ed., Pearson Prentice Hall 2009) pgs. 204-207.

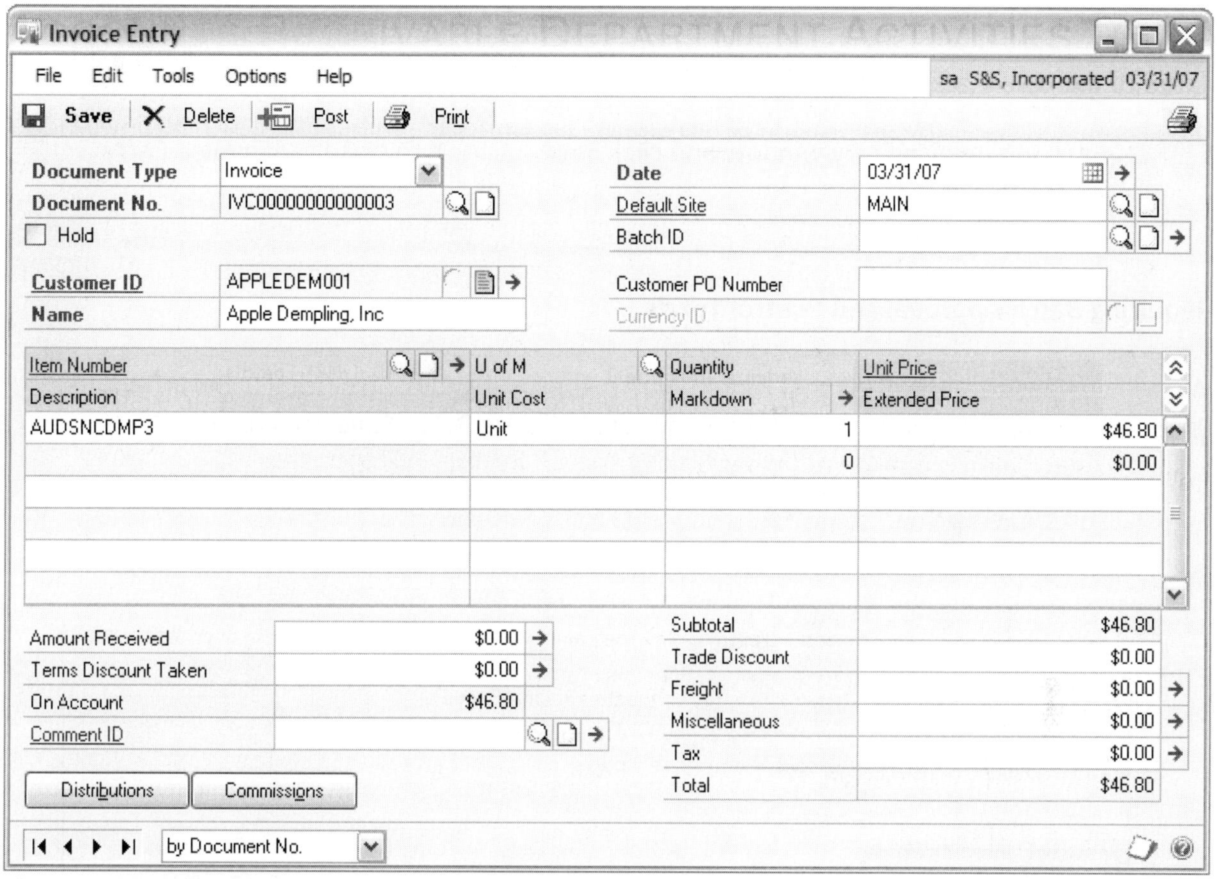

Figure 3:19 Sales Invoice

2. Click **Post** and you receive the message in Figure 3:20 because individual transaction posting is no longer permitted. Click **OK** to return to the transaction. You now can only save or delete the transaction. We will save it in the next step.

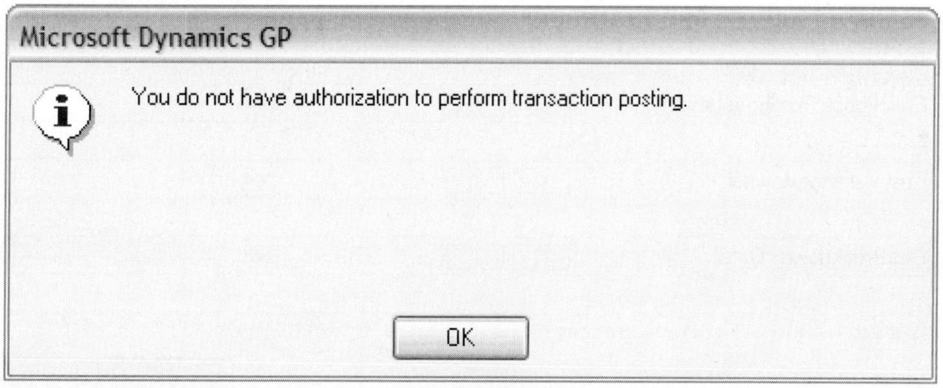

Figure 3:20 Individual Transaction Posting Not Permitted

3. Type **BATCHCONTROL** into the Batch ID field and press tab. Click **Add** to create a new batch. *(Note: This illustrates that you can create a batch after creating a transaction.)*

4. Set the **Posting Date** on the batch to 3/16/2007. *(Note: This is a different date from the date on the transaction.)* Click **Save**.

5. Return to the Invoice Entry window and click **Save**. Click **X** to close the Invoice Entry window.

Requiring Batch Approval and Control Totals

We will now institute controls that require batch approval and control totals. Return to the Posting Setup window and set the options shown in Figure 3:21. **Save** the changes.

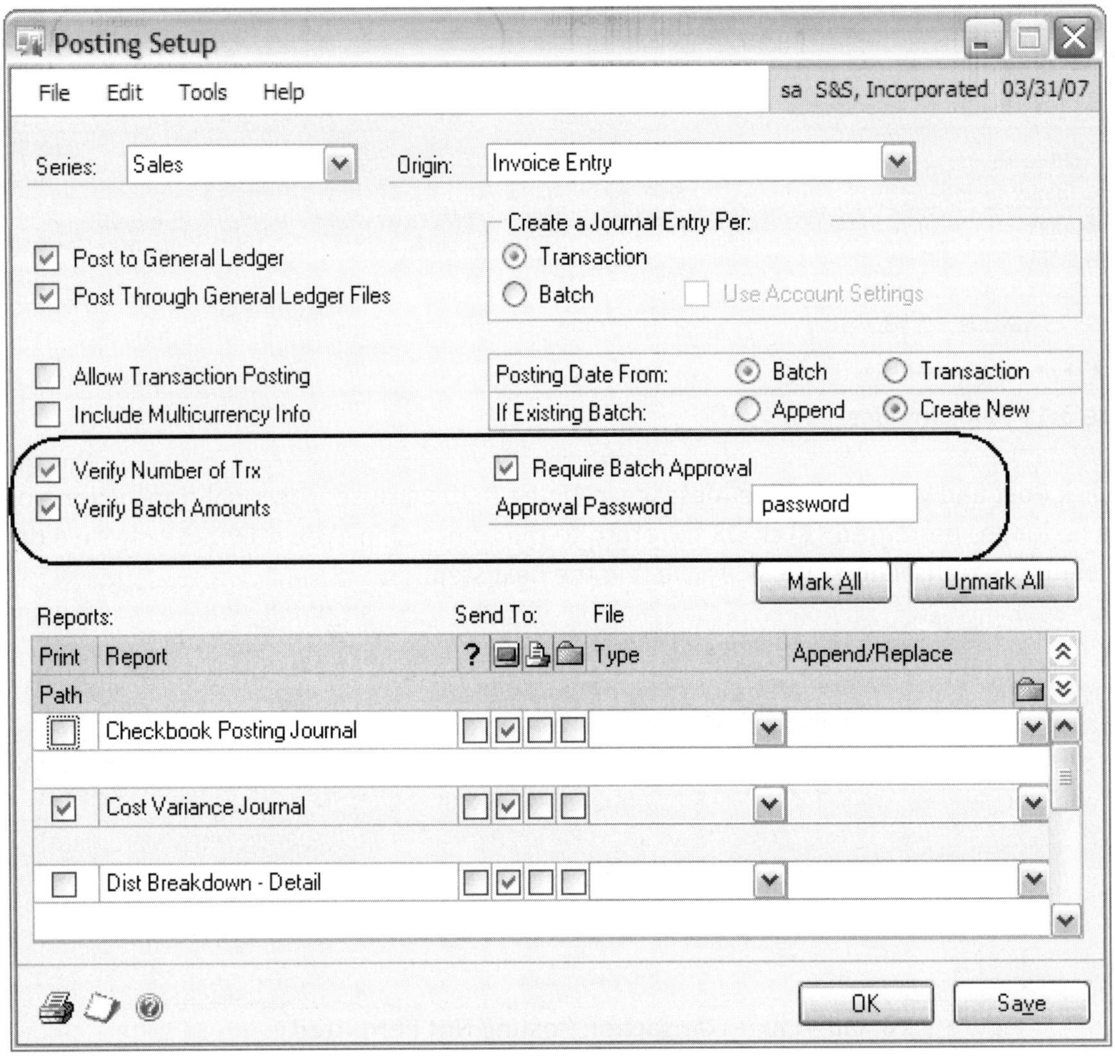

Figure 3:21 Control Totals and Authorization Options

Now test these options by reopening the previous batch. Click **Invoicing Batches** and look up the **BATCHCONTROL** batch. Click **Post** and you receive the message illustrated next.

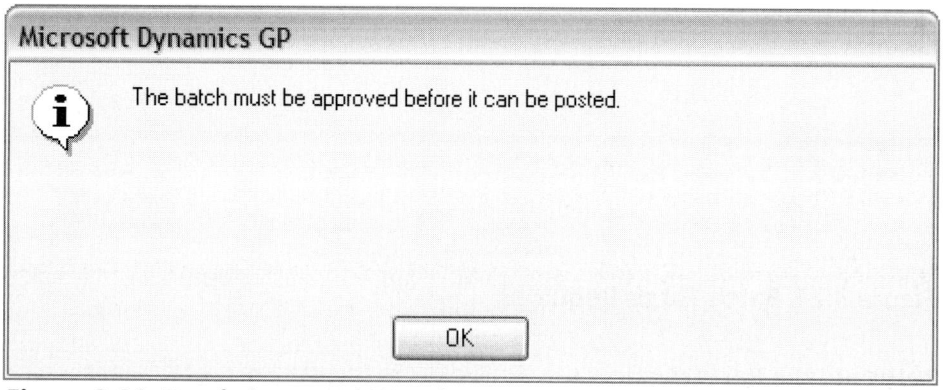

Figure 3:22 Batch Approval Warning

Click **OK** to return to the Batch window. Click the **Approved** option (Figure 3:23) and enter the password when prompted.

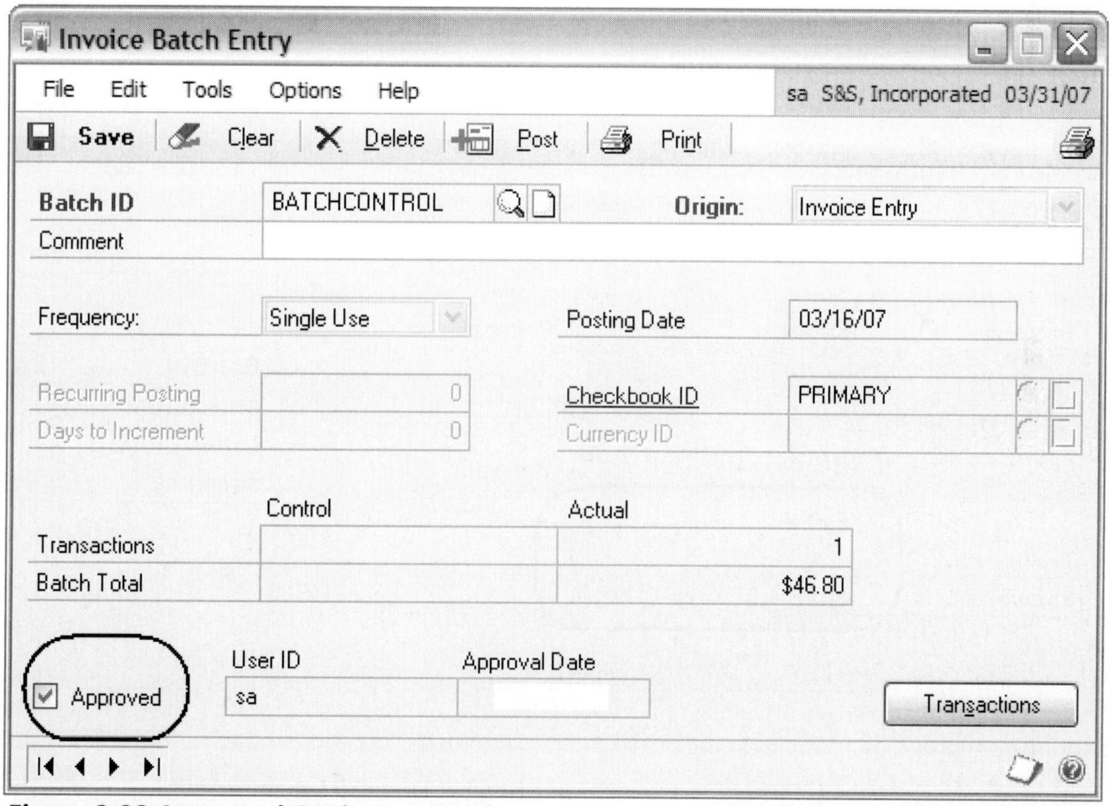

Figure 3:23 Approved Option on Batch

The transaction is now approved for posting so click **Post.** You receive a second message (Figure 3:24) stating that batch totals are required.

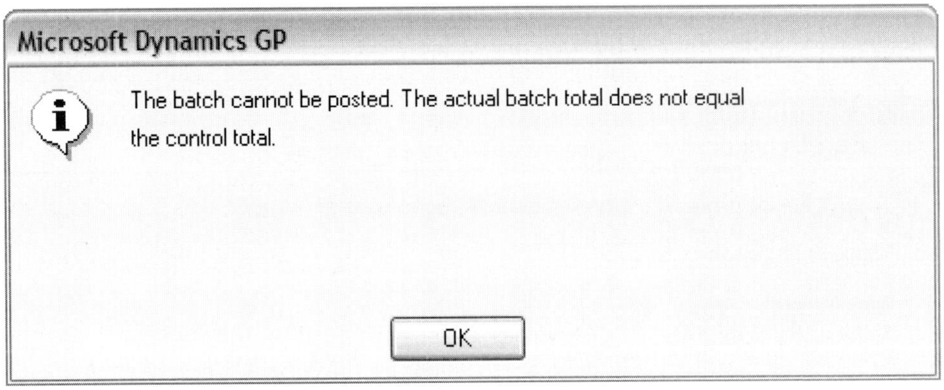

Figure 3:24 Batch Totals Required

Click **OK** to return to the Batch window.

Unmark the Approved option to reset the batch and then enter control totals that correspond to the total number and amount of transactions saved in the batch. (See Figure 3:25.) Again, select **Approved** and enter the password. Click **Post** to process the batch.

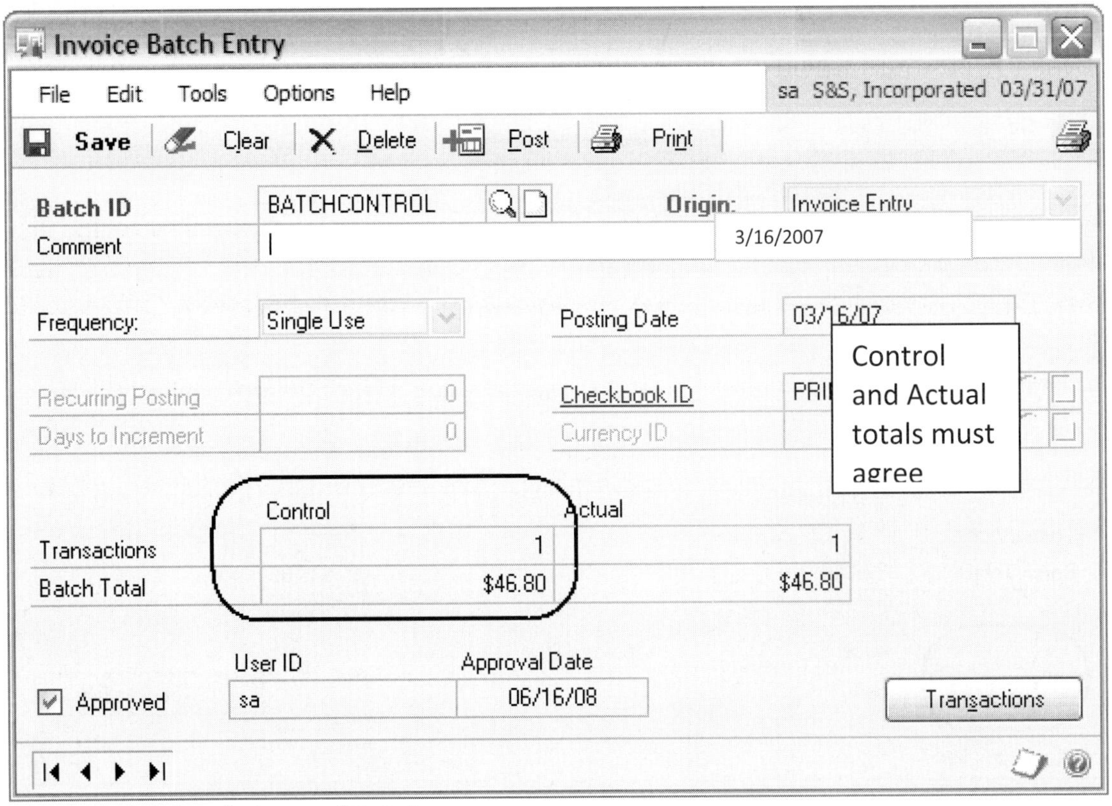

Figure 3:25 Batch Control Totals

You have just experienced GP's batch control features that implement control totals and independent checks on performance. To implement these controls for all transactions you must combine batch controls with the control that forces all transactions to post in batches.

Before leaving this discussion, turn off control options to simplify future exercises. Return to the Posting Setup window and mark Allow Transaction Posting and unmark Require Batch Approval, Verify Number of Trx, and Verify Batch Amounts. Save the changes.

So why not wait until all transactions have been entered in the batch and then fill in batch control fields?

We just illustrated that GP permits this; however, this procedure fails to serve internal control objectives. Control totals should reconcile to totals for external documents to protect the integrity of data entry. Normally, invoice totals and transaction counts are prepared prior to data entry and attached to the documents. This is where approval comes in. Supervisors approving batches for posting should compare external document totals with control totals on the batch.

This also illustrates that internal control procedures rely on both software and external controls.

III. ***<u>Effect of Journal Entry Per, Posting Date From, and If Existing Batch Options</u>***

Return to the Posting Setup window for sales invoices (Figure 3:26). We illustrated the effect of setting the **Posting Date From** option to **Batch** when demonstrating post to and post through options. You know that dates on batches and transactions can differ and have different effects on financial records. We now reemphasize this point.

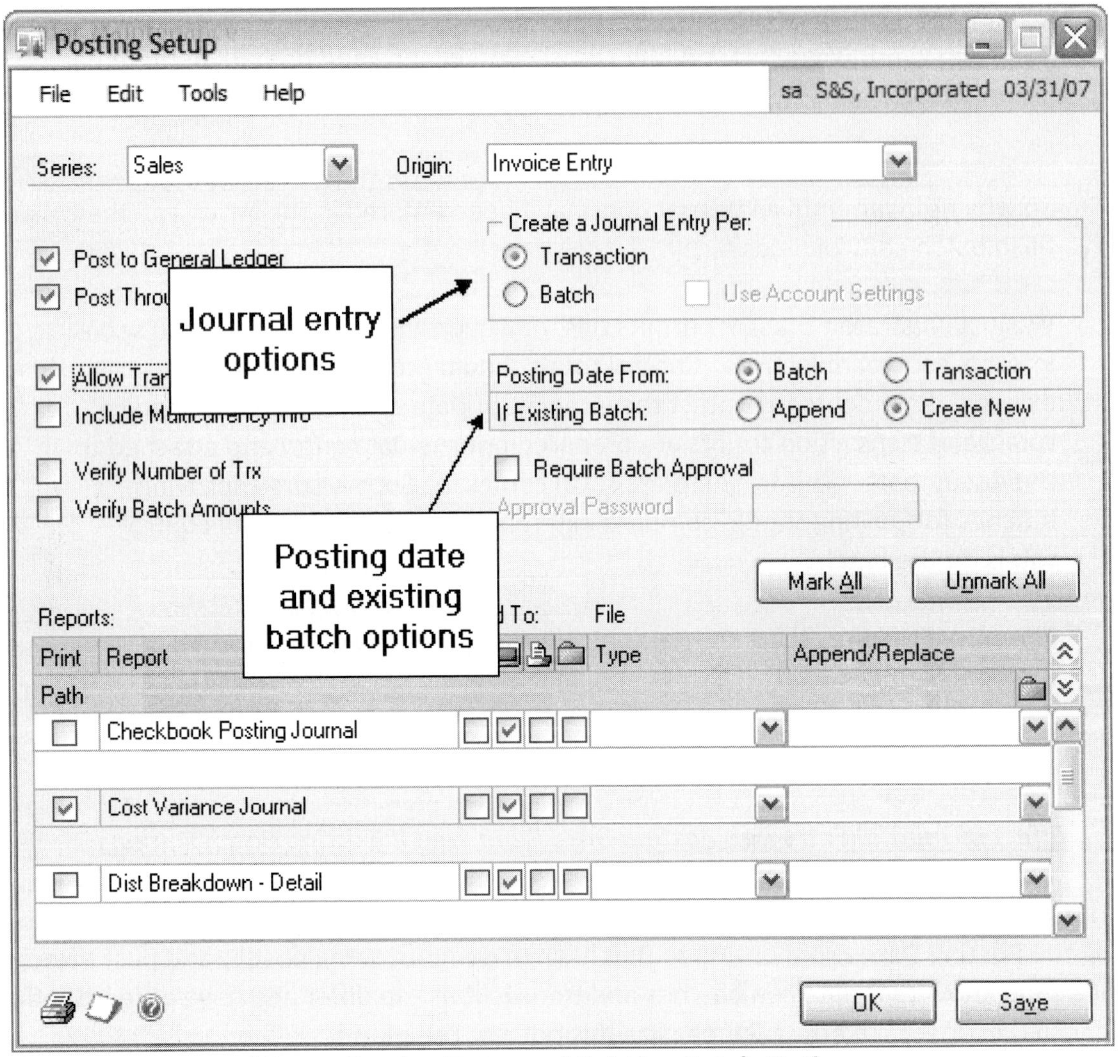

Figure 3:26 Journal Entry, Posting Date, and Existing Batch Options

The date on sales invoice transactions reflects the date of a sale. The Sales Series knows to use transaction dates for calculating the age of an invoice, the invoice due date, and the discount date.

In contracts, the date option under Posting Setup tells the Financial Series which date (i.e., transaction or batch) to use as the posting date on general ledger accounts. The figure above shows that S&S uses the batch date when transactions post through batches; otherwise, individual transaction dates are used.

This posting date setting impacts S&S's posting procedures, especially around month-end and year-end. For instance, if a clerk created a batch dated 10/31/2007 and then entered transactions dated both October and November all transactions will post to the general ledger as of 10/31/2007. The company now has November transactions on October financial statements, thus, impacting financial reporting and decision making. If these erroneous postings were material, the company would have to restate its financial statements. Financial markets react poorly to restated financials because it indicates a lack of internal controls that raises other investor concerns. Furthermore, management reports are erroneous and can impact company decisions.

These issues do not infer that GP should be configured differently; rather, emphasize the importance of documenting and complying with internal control procedures and training employees on these procedures.

Next turn your attention to the **If Existing Batch** option. This option impacts suspended batches. When Create New is marked GP creates a new (i.e., separate) batch for storing suspended transactions. If you were to post several individual invoices then each suspended transaction will be listed with a separate Batch ID in the Financial Series Posting window.

In contrast, marking Append instructs GP to place all suspended invoice transactions into one batch until this batch is posted. This option is fine when you diligently perform a second post on suspended transactions; however, if you fail to timely post then you will end up with transactions for several months placed into the same batch. S&S uses the Create New option for all Series and Origins; therefore, your suspended transactions will be placed into separate batches.

Finally, let's focus on **Create a Journal Entry Per Transaction**. With Transaction marked, GP posts each transaction for a batch as separate entries to general ledger accounts rather than posting one entry for the batch total. This way you retain greater detail and have the ability to drill down to specific transactions.

We now illustrate. Activate the Financial home page and click **Trial Balance** under Reports. Choose the **Detailed** report category and highlight the **Detailed TB** report. Click **Modify** and insert options illustrated in Figure 3:27.

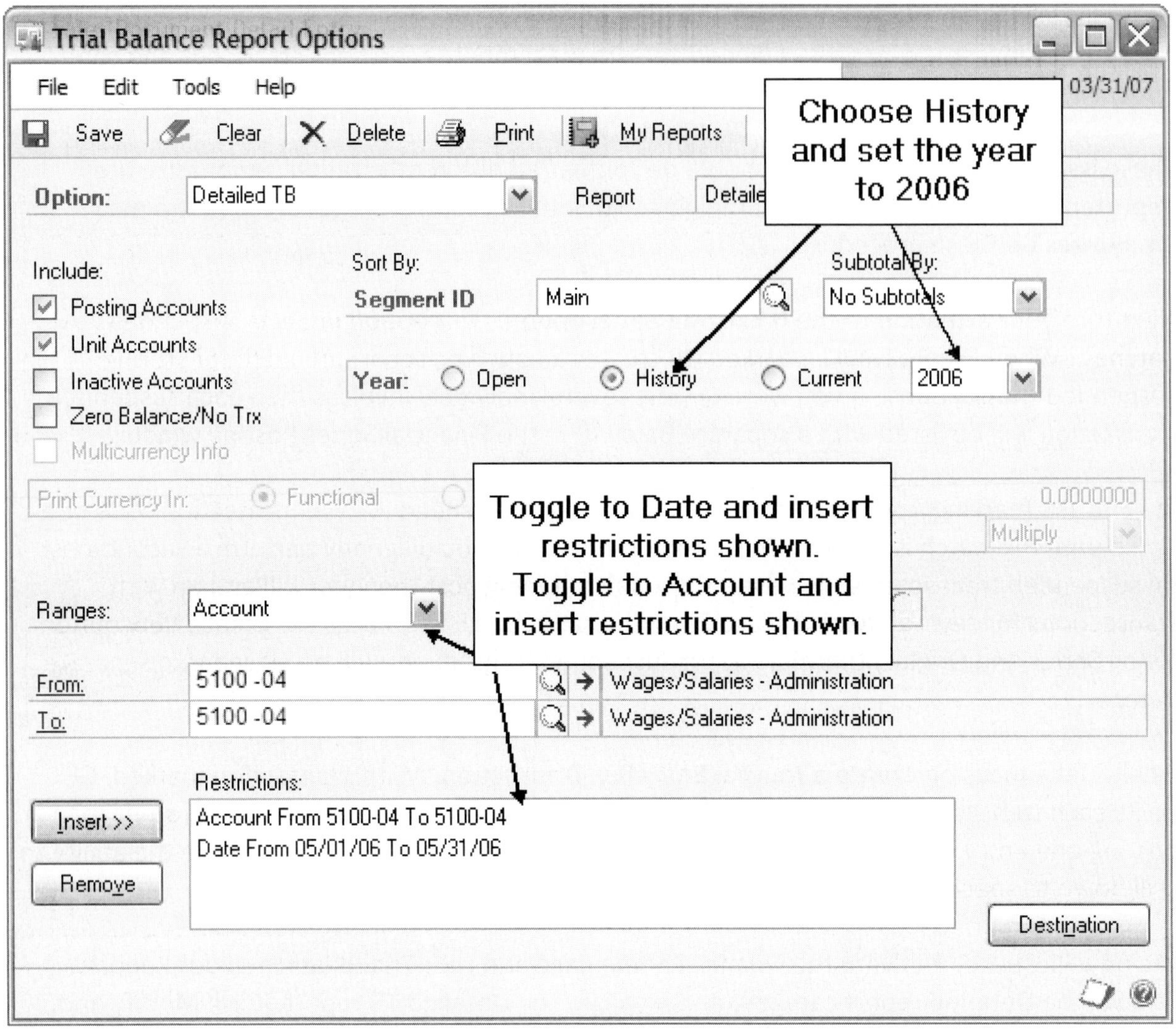

Figure 3:27 Detail Trial Balance Options

You have set options that print details for the payroll expense account. S&S originally set Payroll Series posting options to Create a Journal Entry Per Transaction and then, after recording payroll expense for May 15th, discovered that employee paycheck information posted in detail, compromising the confidentiality of payroll information. To correct this breach, S&S changed the posting option to Create a Journal Entry Per Batch. Print the report and review the output (Figure 3:28), noting the difference before and after May 15th.

User Date: 03/31/07

HISTORICAL DETAILED TRIAL BALANCE FOR 2006

S&S, Incorporated

General Ledger

Page: 1
User ID: sa

Ranges: From: To:
Date: 05/01/06 05/31/06 Subtotal By: No Subtotals Include: Posting, Unit
Account: 5100-04 5100-04 Sorted By: Main

Account: 5100-04 Description: Wages/Salaries - Administration Beginning Balance: $89,031.64

Trx Date	Jrnl No.	Orig. Audit Trail	Distribution Reference	Orig. Master Number	Orig. Master Name	Debit	Credit
05/01/06	139	GLREV00000193					$3,100.00
05/12/06	637	UPRCC00000019	Payroll Computer Checks			$3,240.00	
05/15/06	595	UPRCC00000018		73755	Fleming, Ashton P.	$2,291.67	
05/15/06	599	UPRCC00000018		73759	Parry, Scott J.	$2,708.33	
05/15/06	600	UPRCC00000018		73760	Gonzalez, Susan M.	$2,708.33	
05/26/06	638	UPRCC00000020	Payroll Computer Checks			$3,240.00	
05/29/06	139	GLTRX00000233				$3,253.21	
05/31/06	639	UPRCC00000021	Payroll Computer Checks			$7,708.33	

		Net Change	Ending Balance	Debit	Credit
Account: 5100-04	Totals:	$22,049.87	$111,081.51	$25,149.87	$3,100.00

	Accounts	Beginning Balance	Net Change	Ending Balance	Debit	Credit
Grand Totals:	1	$89,031.64	$22,049.87	$111,081.51	$25,149.87	$3,100.00

Detail per paycheck on May 15

Figure 3:28 General Ledger Pay Details

One final point, the Transaction option requires more disk space than the Batch option; however, the ability to view transactions in detail often outweighs additional disk space requirements.

Close the report and the Trial Balance Report Options window, clicking **Discard** to saving changes. Finally, close the Trial Balance Report window.

IV. ***Reports Options***

Open the Posting Setup window and review the reports selected for Sales Series Invoice Entry. The bottom section of the Posting Setup window determines the control reports that print after posting and selects the printers to receive output. These options provide flexibility in customizing output. For instance, payroll reports and checks can be sent to a printer with controlled access over output while accounts payable checks can be sent to a different printer containing check stock. In addition, companies can customize control report printing to meet internal control objectives.

Take the time review options for other Series and Origins. Be sure to look at report options. Posting reports are invaluable internal control tools used in subsequent chapters.

THE AUDIT TRAIL

The audit trail is an integral part of internal controls because it documents the source of general ledger postings. Accountants and auditors use the audit trail to trace transactions from the point of origin to the general ledger and vice versa. In GP, the audit trail functions automatically and can be customized to a limited extent.

Source document codes are the first component of GP's audit trail. These codes identify the originating source for a transaction; for example, whether a transaction originated in the Sales or Purchasing Series. GP supplies source document codes and permits some customization. These are viewed by clicking the GP button to select ***Tools>>Setup>>Posting>>Source Document***. (See Figure 3:29.) Each Series maintains its own codes to identify transactions originating in that Series.

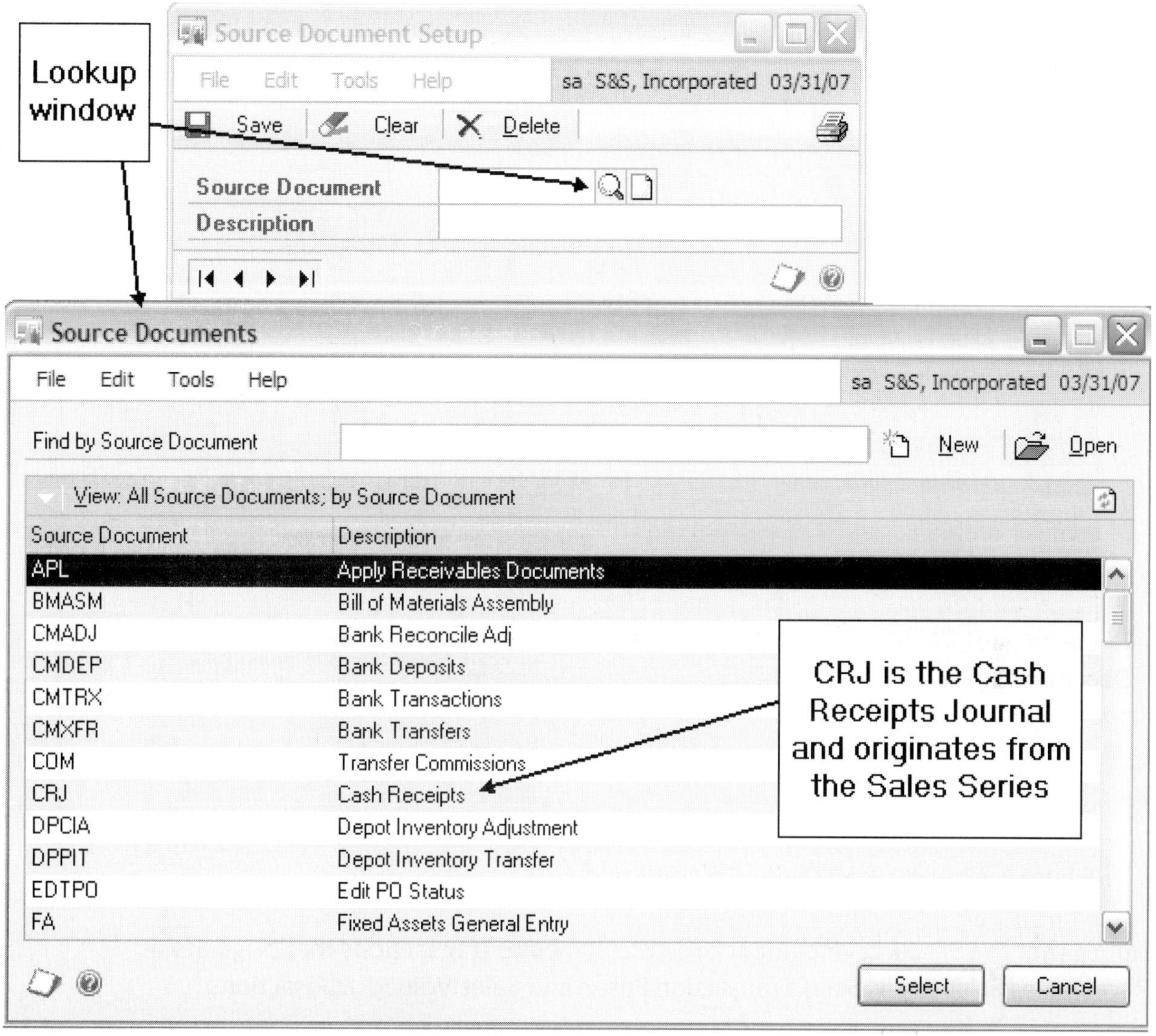

Figure 3:29 Source Document Setup Window

Scroll through source codes in the lookup window to locate code SJ. This is the source code for transactions originating on the Sales Journal maintained by the Sales Series. Close the lookup window and the Source Document window.

We next illustrate how the SJ source document code crossreferences to audit trail codes. Click the GP button and select ***Tools>>Setup>>Posting>>Audit Trail Codes*** The Audit Trail Codes Setup window is illustrated in Figure 3:30 with the Sales Series displayed.

Figure 3:30 Audit Trail Codes Setup Window

Notice that the SJ source document code is assigned to transactions that originate as Receivables Sales Entry, Sales Transaction Entry, and Sales Voided Transactions.

Next, look at the Prefix column to identify audit trail prefixes that distinguish the origination source. Notice that Sales Transaction Entry is assigned a prefix of SLSTE and the Next Number (i.e., document number) added to this prefix will be 85. Hence, the next time a sales transaction posts, the audit trail for this transaction will be SLSTE00000085.

(Note: GP adds leading zeros to document numbers and automatically increments the number each time a transaction posts. Your number may differ from that illustrated.)

Close the Audit Trail Codes Setup window and we next trace the audit trail for a sales transaction. From the Financial home page, click **Detail** under Inquiry and look up account 1200-00 Accounts Receivable. Expand information for the second row and highlight the sales transaction posted on January 3, 2007. (See Figure 3:31.)

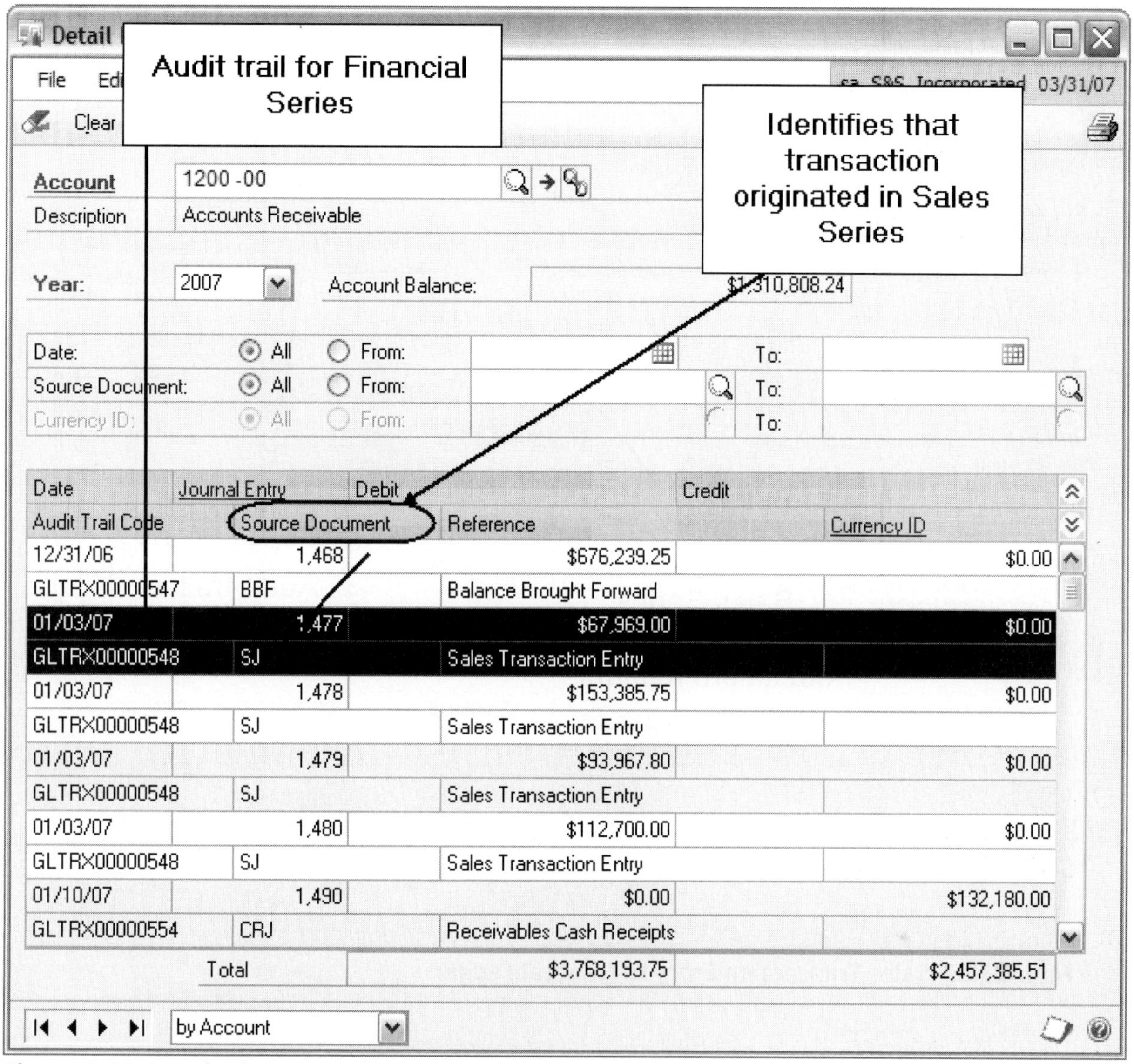

Figure 3:31 Inquiry into Accounts Receivable

You see that SJ is the Source Document for this transaction and Reference shows it as a Sales Transaction Entry. Also note the audit trail code assigned by the Financial Series as well as the journal entry code.

Click **Journal Entry** to zoom to the entry posted to general ledger accounts and review the information on Figure 3:32.

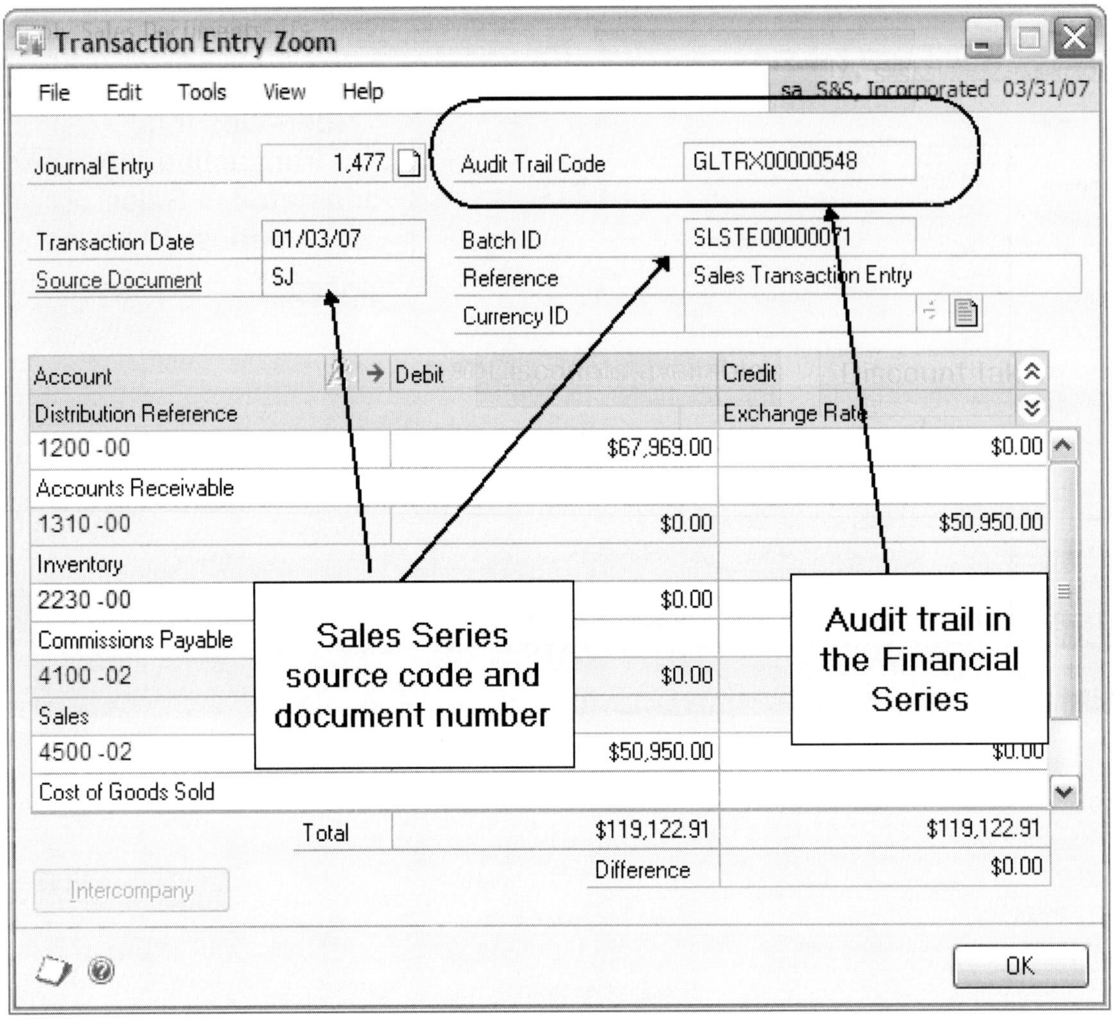

Figure 3:32 Sales Transaction Entry to General Ledger

Close all open windows. Audit trail codes also appear on the detailed trial balance report. (See Figure 3:33.)

DETAILED TRIAL BALANCE FOR 2007

Page: 1
User ID: sa

S&S, Incorporated

General Ledger

Ranges:	From:	To:				
Date:	01/01/07	01/31/07	Subtotal By:	No Subtotals	Include:	Posting, Unit
Account:	1200-00	1200-00	Sorted By:	Main		

Account: 1200-00 Description: Accounts Receivable Beginning Balance: $6

Trx Date	Jrnl No.	Orig. Audit Trail	Distribution Reference	Orig. Master Number	Orig. Master Name	Debit
01/03/07	1,477	SLSTE00000071	Accounts Receivable	INV000000184	Precise Markets, Inc	$67,969.00
01/03/07	1,478	SLSTE00000071	Accounts Receivable	INV000000185	Electronic Town, Inc.	$153,385.75
01/03/07	1,479	SLSTE00000071	Accounts Receivable	INV000000186	GG HREGG Stores, Inc.	$93,967.80
01/03/07	1,480	SLSTE00000071	Accounts Receivable	INV000000187	Kollister's, Inc.	$112,700.00
01/10/07	1,490	RMCSH00000042	Accounts Receivable	PYMNT000000000165	Apple Dempling, Inc	
01/10/07	1,491	RMCSH00000042	Accounts Receivable	PYMNT000000000166	Discount Electronics,Inc.	
01/10/07	1,492	RMCSH00000042	Accounts Receivable	PYMNT000000000167	GG HREGG Stores, Inc.	
01/10/07	1,493	RMCSH00000042	Accounts Receivable	PYMNT000000000168	Lerneers & Lowers, Inc.	
01/10/07	1,494	RMCSH00000042	Accounts Receivable	PYMNT000000000169	Pink House Electronics ,Inc.	
01/15/07	1,481	SLSTE00000072	Accounts Receivable	INV000000188	Small Screen Sales, Inc.	$128,922.50
01/15/07	1,482	SLSTE00000072	Accounts Receivable	INV000000189	Fillards, Inc.	$90,957.60
01/20/07	1,495	RMCSH00000043	Accounts Receivable	PYMNT000000000170	Rick's Specialty Goods, Inc.	
01/20/07	1,496	RMCSH00000043	Accounts Receivable	PYMNT000000000171	Teddi Gower, Inc.	
01/25/07	1,483	SLSTE00000073	Accounts Receivable	INV000000190	Traders Table, Inc.	$103,210.00
01/25/07	1,484	SLSTE00000073	Accounts Receivable	INV000000191	Zears Stores, Inc.	$135,644.25
01/25/07	1,485	SLSTE00000073	Accounts Receivable	INV000000192	Tubes & Turners, Inc.	$151,042.50

		Net Change	Ending Balance	
Account: 1200-00	Totals:	$370,474.15	$1,046,713.40	$1,037,799.40

	Accounts	Beginning Balance	Net Change	Ending Balance	Debit
Grand Totals:	1	$676,239.25	$370,474.15	$1,046,713.40	$1,037,799.40

Figure 3:33 Audit Trail on Detailed Trial Balance

Audit trail codes help you identify posted transactions. From the Financial home page, click **Cross-Reference** under Reports. Select the **Journal Entry** report category and modify the **JOURN ENTRY** report as shown in Figure 3:34.

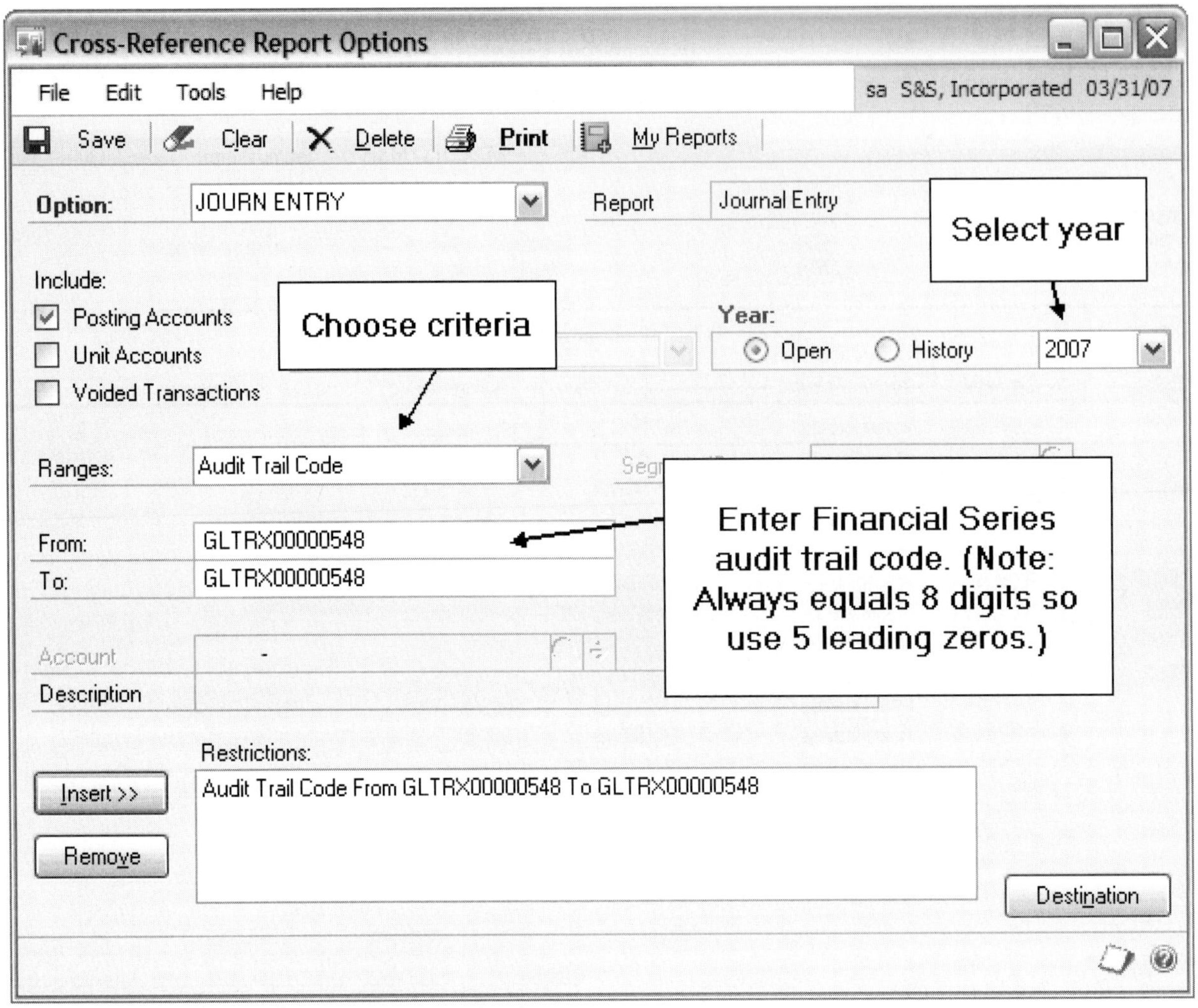

Figure 3:34 Cross-Reference Report Options

Print the report to the screen. (See Figure 3:35.)

S&S, Incorporated   Page: 1

User Date: 03/31/07   CROSS-REFERENCE REPORT BY JOURNAL ENTRY FOR 2007   User ID: sa

General Ledger

* Voided Journal Entry

Ranges:	From:	To:		From:
Journal Entry	First	Last	Date	First
Source Document	First	Last	Account	First
Audit Trail Code	GLTRX00000548	GLTRX00000548		

Include: Posting   Sort by: Journal Entry

Four invoices were in the batch so all assigned the same audit trail code; however, each assigned a differenct journal entry number. (Note: Scroll down report to see all the invoices.)

Journal Entry	Trx Date	Source Document	Audit Trail Code		
Account	Description			Debit	Credit
1,477	01/03/07	SJ	GLTRX00000548		
1200-00	Accounts Receivable			$67,969.00	
1310-00	Inventory				$50,950.00
2230-00	Commissions Payable				$203.91
4100-02	Sales - MidWest				$67,969.00
4500-02	Cost of Goods Sold - MidWest			$50,950.00	
5200-00	Commission Expense			$203.91	
Total Distributions:	6		Totals:	$119,122.91	$119,122.91
1,478	01/03/07	SJ	GLTRX00000548		
1200-00	Accounts Receivable			$153,385.75	
1310-00	Inventory				$113,175.00
2230-00	Commissions Payable				$460.16
4100-02	Sales - MidWest				$153,385.75
4500-02	Cost of Goods Sold - MidWest			$113,175.00	
5200-00	Commission Expense			$460.16	
Total Distributions:	6		Totals:	$267,020.91	$267,020.91

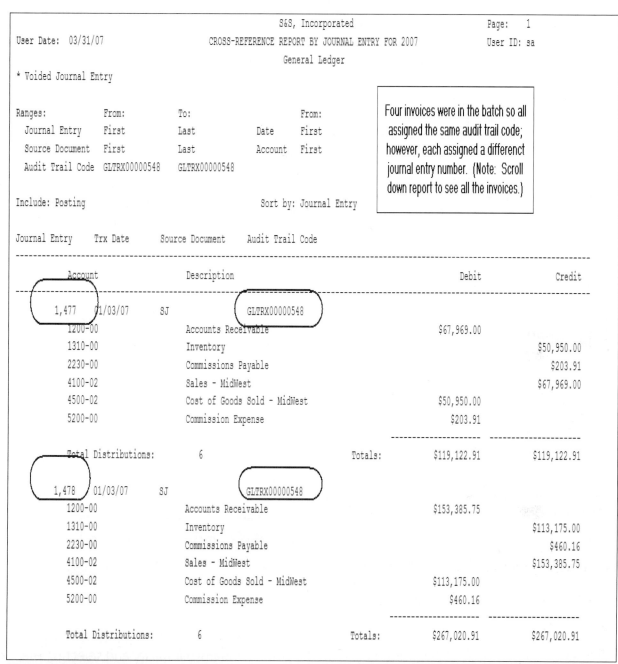

Figure 3:35 Cross-Reference Report

You can also filter the cross-reference report by Source Document and Journal Entry number. Remember that this report is generated from the Financial home page so you must filter by Financial Series audit trail codes.

Close the report and any open window.

You can become familiar with GP audit trail codes by printing them. Simply click ***File>>Print*** on the window menu while in the Audit Trail Codes Setup window.

ACTIVITY TRACKING LOG

Activity tracking logs user activity in the software but must first be activated. Click the GP button, select ***Tools>>Setup>>System>>Activity Tracking***, and enter ***sa*** as the password. (See Figure 3:36.)

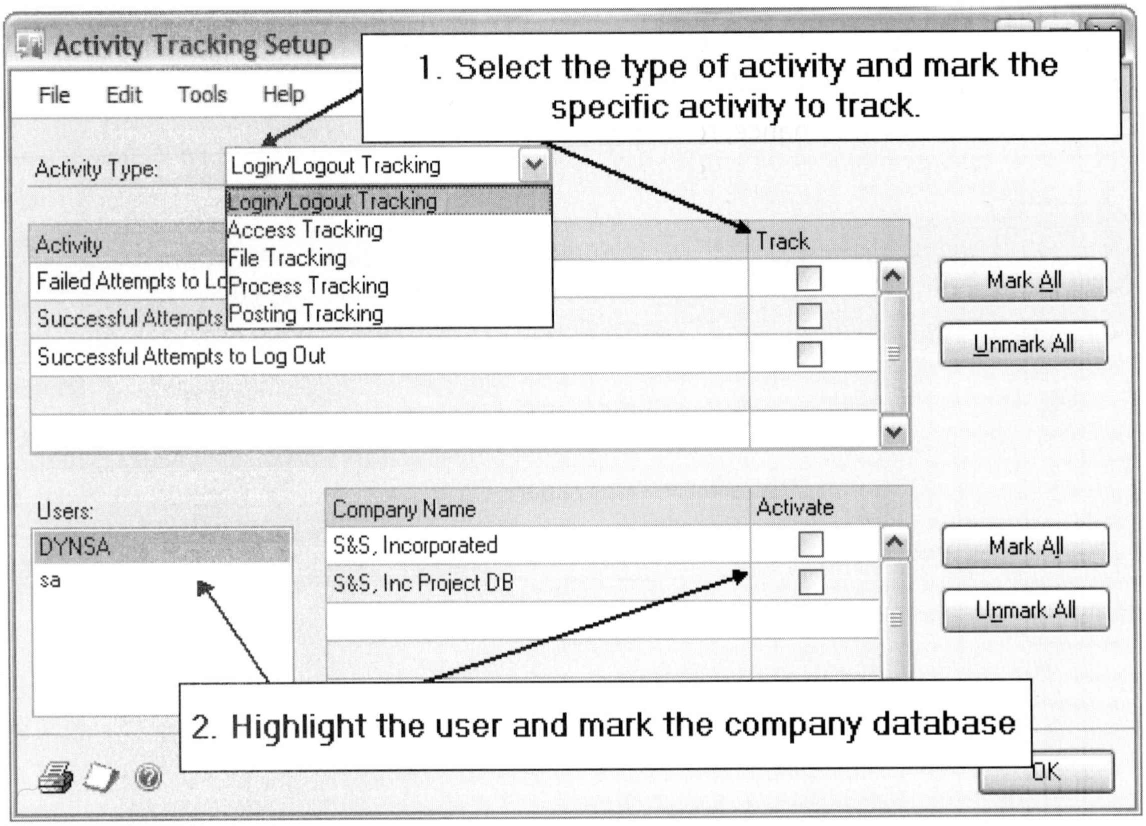

Figure 3:36 Activity Tracking Setup

You activate tracking by highlighting a user, marking the company database, and selecting the tracking. After activating, you can run reports from the Administration home page by selecting General under Reports. Since tracking consumes additional hard drive space, companies seldom activate successful attempts to log in or out of GP.

Table 3:1 that follows describes tracking categories.

Category	Activity Tracked	Description
Login/Logout Tracking	Successful login/logouts and failed logins	Reports login and logout activities.
Access Tracking	Successful and failed attempts to open a table, window, or print a report	Tracks successful and denied attempts to log into the software.
File Tracking	Additions/deletions/ modifications to master, setup and transaction tables.	Reports Save, Delete, and OK button selections by users.
Process Tracking	Table maintenance, routines, and utilities processes	Reports on table maintenance routines such as rebuilding files, checking links, clearing data, and shrinking file sizes.
Posting Tracking	Posting activities	Reports transaction postings by Series.

Table 3:1 Activity Tracking Categories

After reporting, you may want to clear history to save disk space. This is done by clicking Activity Details under Utilities.

Tracking activity is an important internal control tool. At a minimum you should track unsuccessful logins to identify threats to the accounting system.

Close any open windows. You have completed Level One in this chapter.

Level Two

SYSTEM MANAGER SECURITY

The System Manager Series controls GP security. You implement security by creating user IDs and then granting permission to access company databases and to perform tasks in the database. Some companies assign responsibility for implementing security to controllers or chief financial officers (CFOs) whereas other companies employ chief information officers (CIOs) over security and have internal auditors that review compliance with security. Because accountants play such a vital role in developing and monitoring security, it is important for you to understand implementing security in a software environment.

Prior to implementing security, an Access Control Matrix is developed to identify software users and permissions. In GP, you must be logged in as the *sa* user to implement security. When developing your matrix, it helps to think of categorizing user permissions by following the internal control objective of segregation of duties. Table 3:2 is provided as an aide in understanding segregation of duties from a GP perspective.

Category	GP Activity	Examples
Authorization	Create or delete master records	Add customer, delete vendor, create general ledger account, etc.
	Implement security	Create/delete users and assign permissions.
	Approve Transactions	Approve batches, perform write-offs, enter a discount, etc.
	Modify field controls	Establish customer credit limits, payment terms, override pricing, permit sales exceeding credit limit, etc.
Recording	Enter and post transactions	Enter sales orders, change purchase orders, post transaction, etc.
	Change non-critical master file data	Update customer addresses, employee address, etc.
	Reconcile	Prepare bank reconciliations, perform comparisons of aging reports to control accounts, etc.
Custody	Possession of forms	Possession of company checks, preprinted purchase orders forms, etc.

Table 3:2 GP Activities Segregated into Duties

The table is not all-inclusive. Additionally, reporting and inquiries may appear under both authorization and recording. The key to remember is every activity performed in GP fits within a segregation of duties category. Chapter 6 of *Accounting Information Systems*[11] provides more information on segregating duties. You should also review Chapters 10 through 14 for information on internal control concerns by accounting cycle.

The next topic illustrates implementing security by creating users, controlling company access, and setting permissions. The Financial, Sales, Purchasing, Inventory Control, and Payroll Series provide additional internal controls that are discussed in subsequent chapters.

PREDEFINED SECURITY ROLES

Security is implemented on the Administration home page. Activate this home page and remember to use ***sa*** as the password to access windows. We will focus on the Setup category, particularly commands illustrated in Figure 3:37.

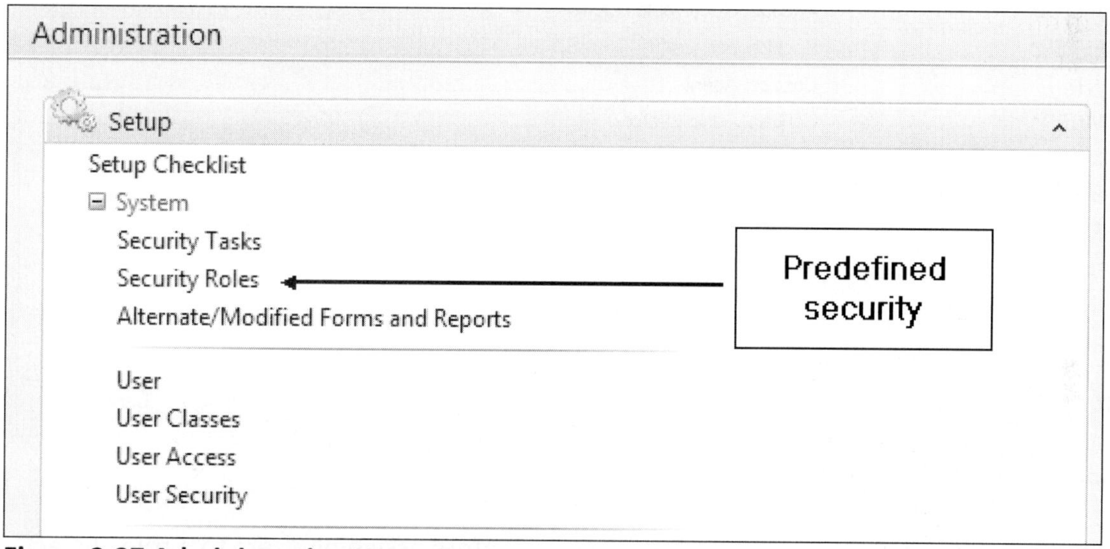

Figure 3:37 Administration Home Page

We need to first understand GP predefined security before completing an exercise to implement security. **Security Roles** are user roles classified by job description. Click this command and use the lookup icon to view predefined roles. (See Figure 3:38.)

[11] See Romney and Steinbart, (11th ed., Pearson Prentice Hall 2009), pgs. 221-224.

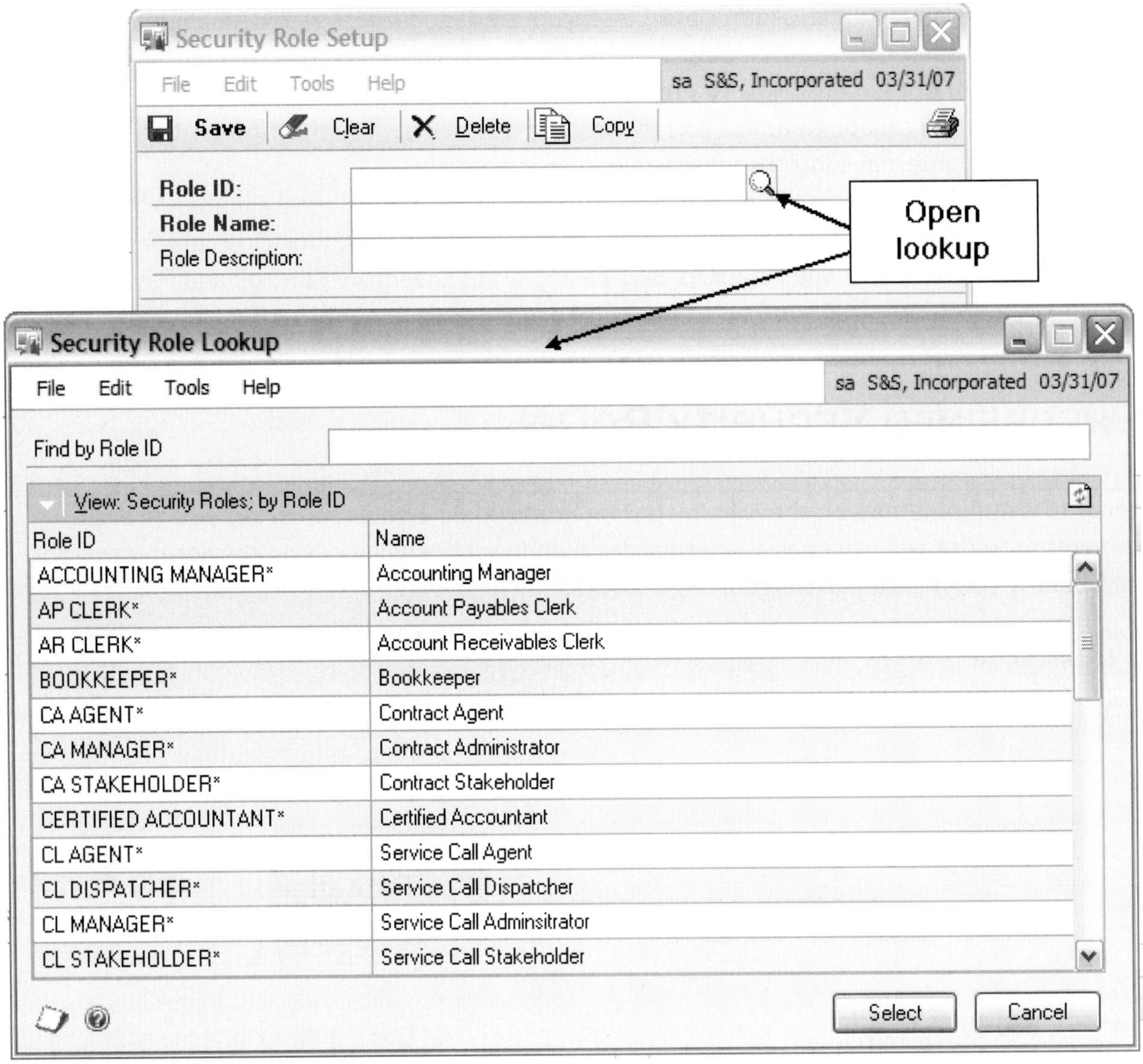

Figure 3:38 Predefined Security Roles

We need to identify permissions granted to these roles before assigning users to a role. Select **AP CLERK**, change the **Display** to **Purchasing**, and scroll down to the tasks illustrated in Figure 3:39.

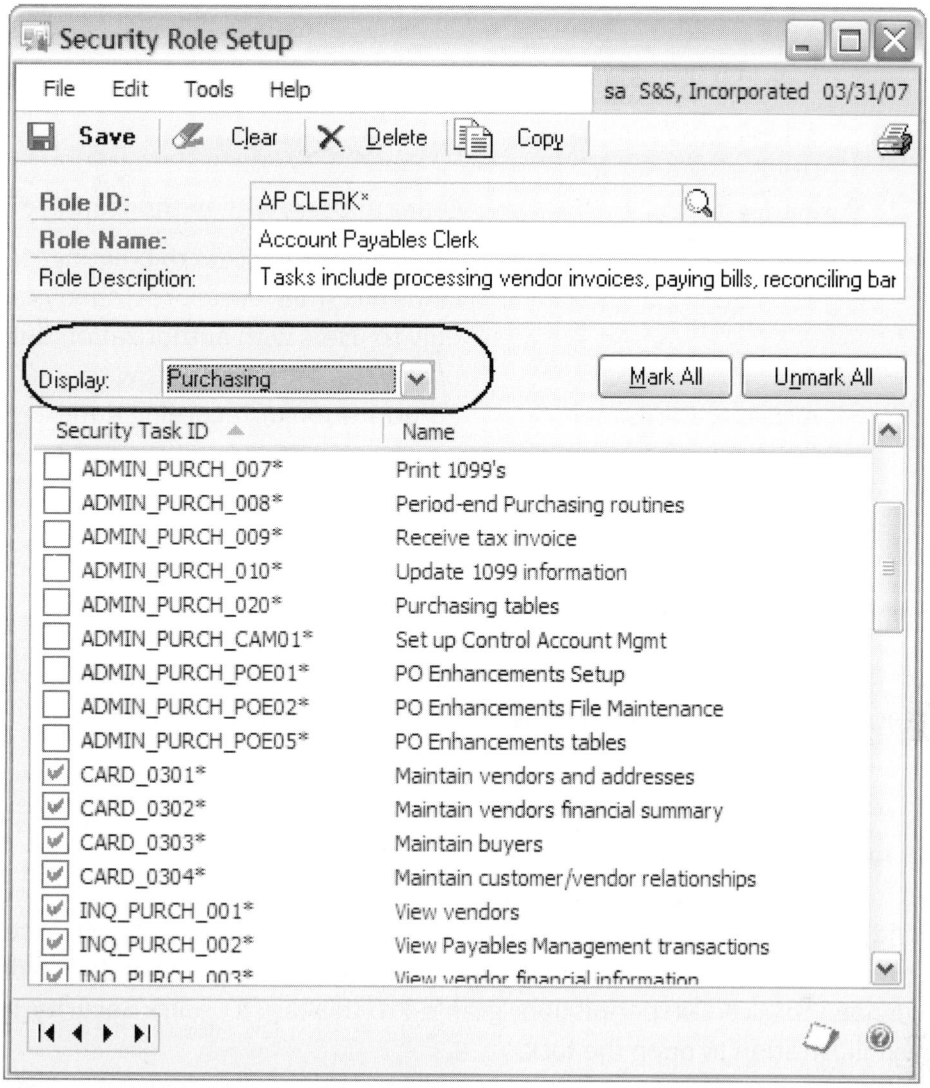

Figure 3:39 AP CLERK Security Role

Under segregation of duties, AP Clerk is a recording function. You need to determine whether permissions granted to this role are correct. Before that, we need to understand GP prefixes on Security Task IDs. The following table provides insight.

Task ID Prefix	Role	Segregation by Duties
ADMIN	Access to Routines, Utilities, and Setup menus	Grant to users with authorization duties.
CARD	Access to Cards menus	When permits access to creating/deleting cards (i.e., master records) then grant only to users with authorization duties; otherwise, grant to users with authorization or recording duties.
INQ	Access to Inquiry menus	Grant to users with authorization, recording, or custody duties.
LIST	Access lists in the Navigation Pane of a home page	Grant to users with authorization, recording, or custody duties.
RPT	Access to reports menus	Grant to users with authorization, recording, or custody duties.
TRX	Access to transaction menus	Grant to users with recording duties.

Table 3:3 GP Activities Segregated by Duties

After reviewing the table, concern exists on whether to grant the AP CLERK role access to the CARD_0301* task ID because this may grant access to creating/deleting vendor cards. Therefore, we need to ascertain permissions granted to this task ID. Click **Security Tasks** and follow the next illustration to open the task.

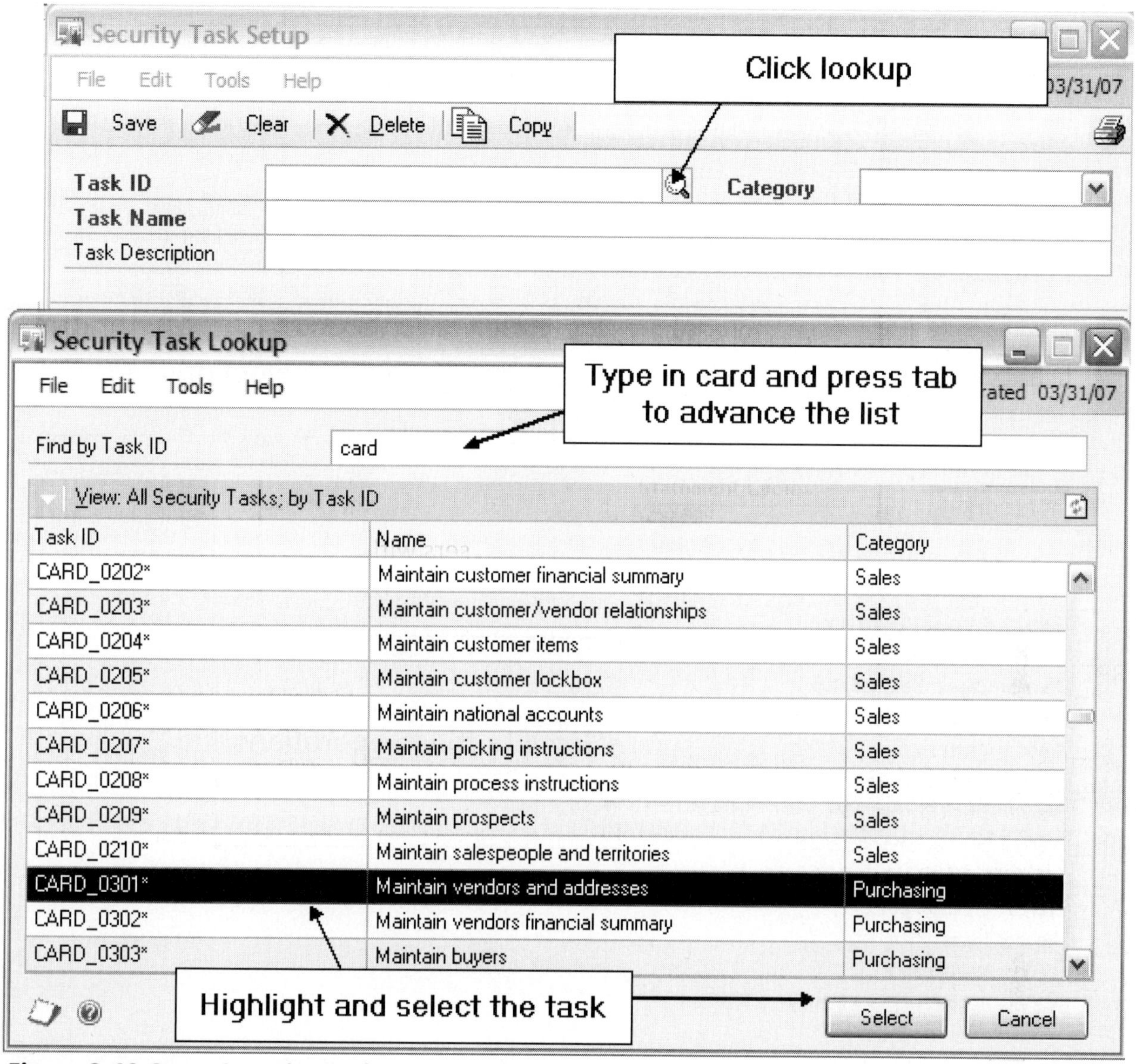

Figure 3:40 Open Security Task

After selecting, follow the next illustration to view permissions for this task.

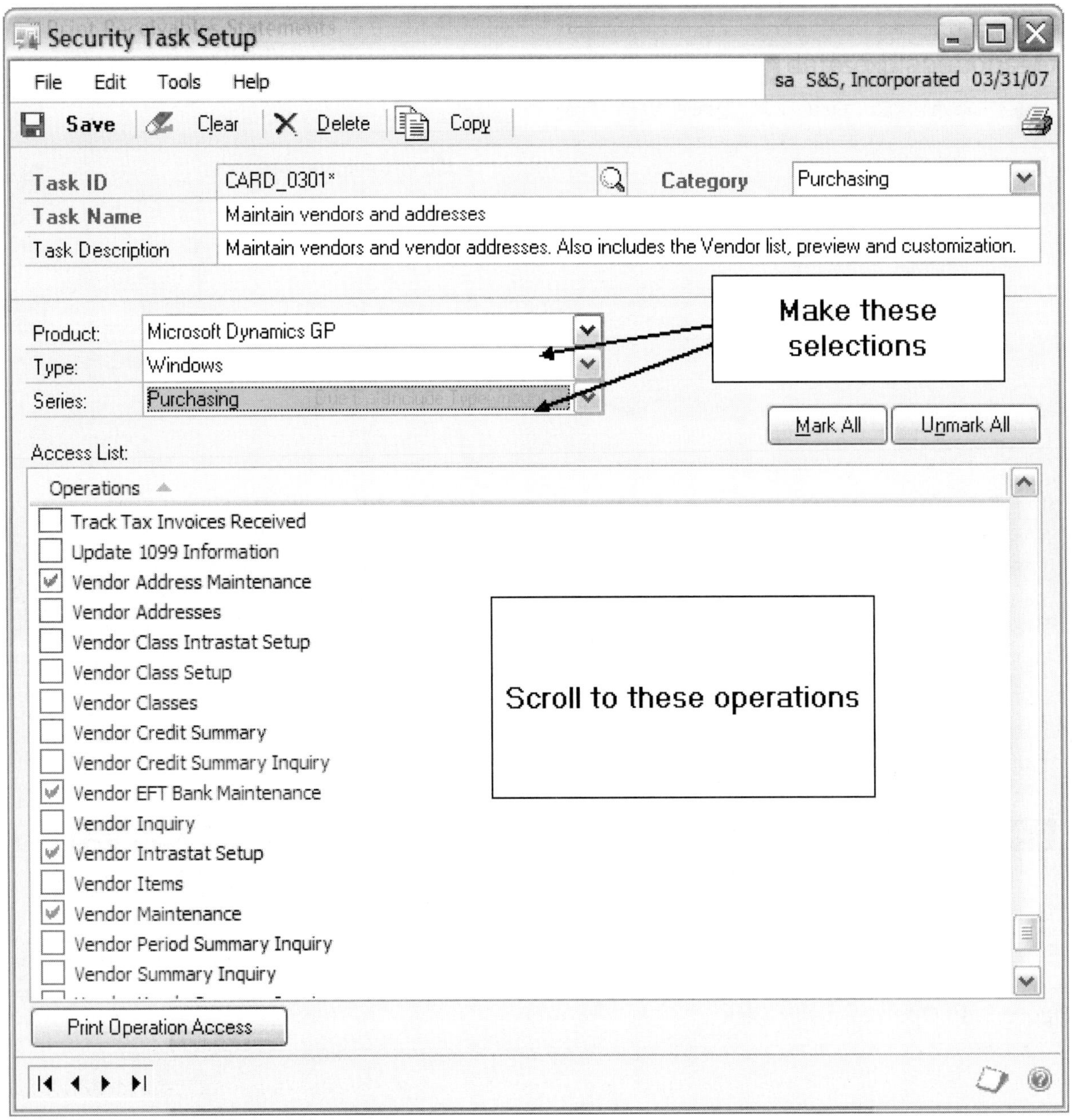

Figure 3:41 Security Task Permissions

We chose Windows in the Purchasing Series so that we can identify the windows this task is permitted to access. Our concern centers on accessing **Vendor Maintenance**. Double click this operation to open the window associated with it. (See Figure 3:42.)

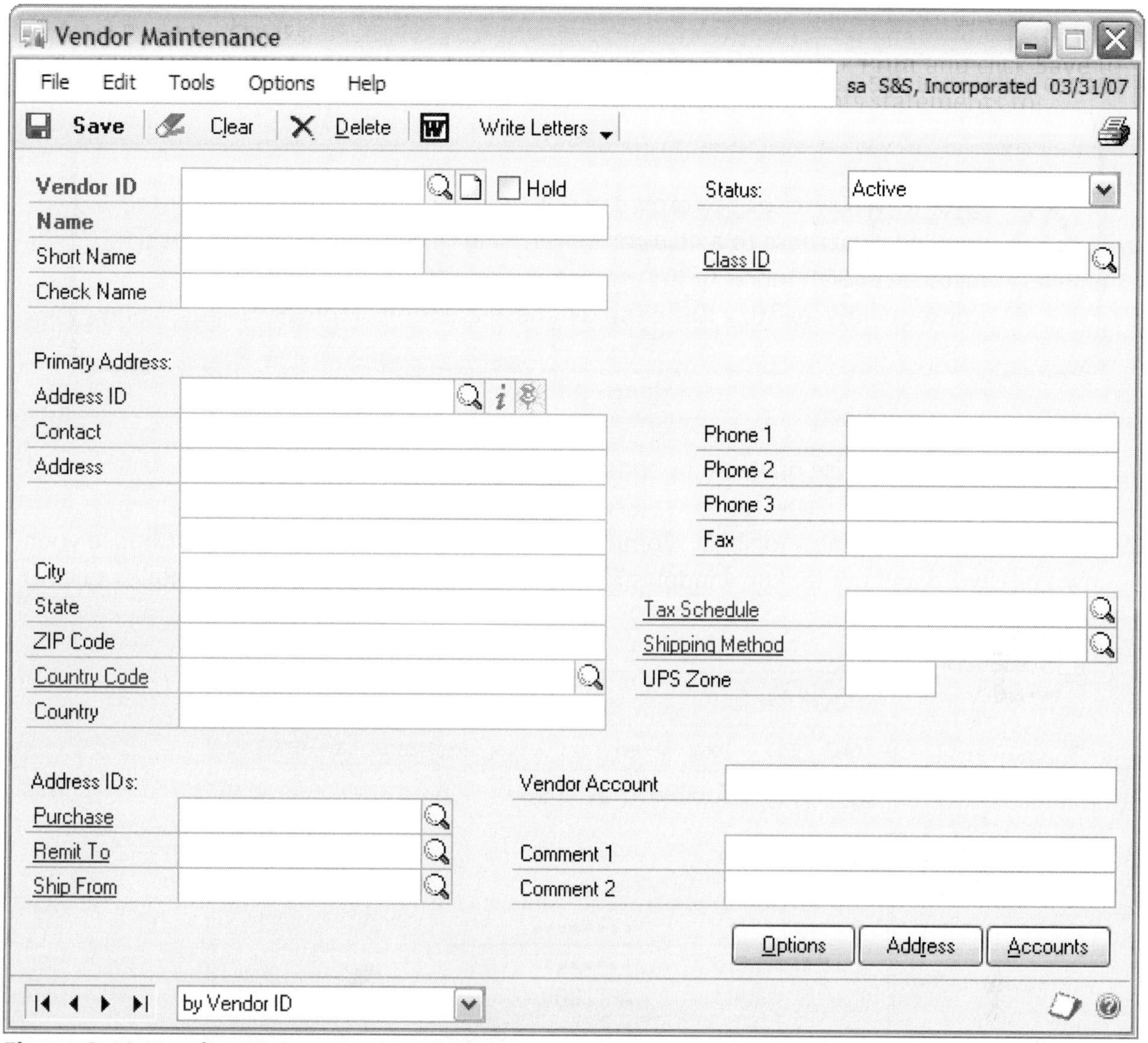

Figure 3:42 Vendor Maintenance Window

Our concerns have been justified because the operation grants access to the Vendor Maintenance Window (i.e., an authorization function). Close the window and return to the Security Task Setup window.

Click **Vendor Maintenance** to unmark it, thus, denying permission to access this window. Click **Save** and then close the window.

Return to the Security Role Setup window and close it.

You now have an understanding of identifying and managing predefined security in GP. We will next implement security.

IMPLEMENTING SECURITY

CAUTION: Exercises performed in this topic must be completed prior to copying a database to a new computer. User IDs are stored by the local instance of SQL Server so IDs are not copied with the database files. Consequently, existing IDs in the database are for illustrative purposes only

We now provide an exercise on implementing security.

1. Click **User** to create a new login ID. Complete the window as illustrated next. Choose your own password and use lookup windows to select the Class ID and Home Page Role. Click **Save**.

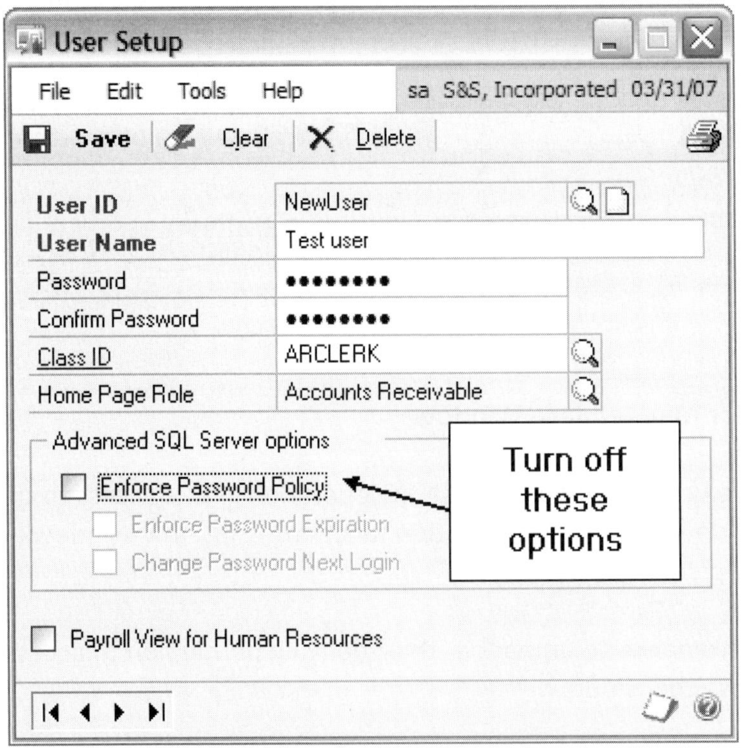

Figure 3:43 New User Account

Note: Class ID places users into groups. You can open the window for creating classes by clicking the hyperlink. Home Page Role customizes a user's home page view to commands the user may access. Advanced SQL Server options enforce password policies but only work with Windows Server 2003 or higher.

2. We must next grant permissions for the new user to access a company database. Click **User Access** and complete the steps illustrated next. Click **OK** when finished.

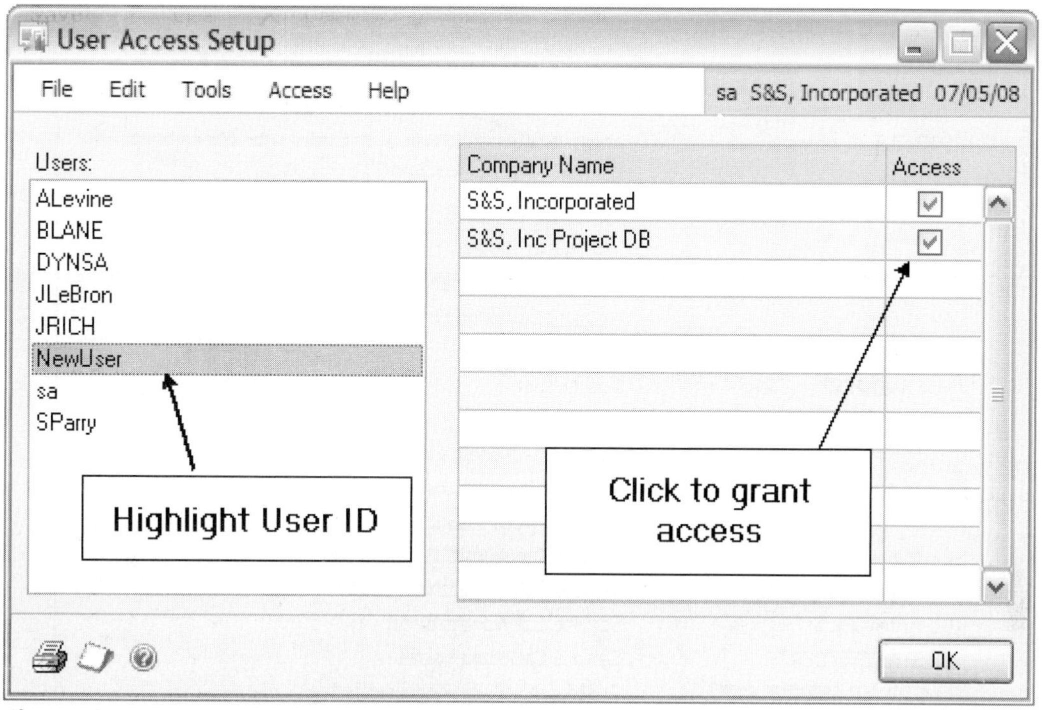

Figure 3:44 User Access to Databases

3. Finally, grant the user permissions to perform tasks. Click **User Security** and perform the steps illustrated next. Click **Save** and remember to repeat these steps for the other database.

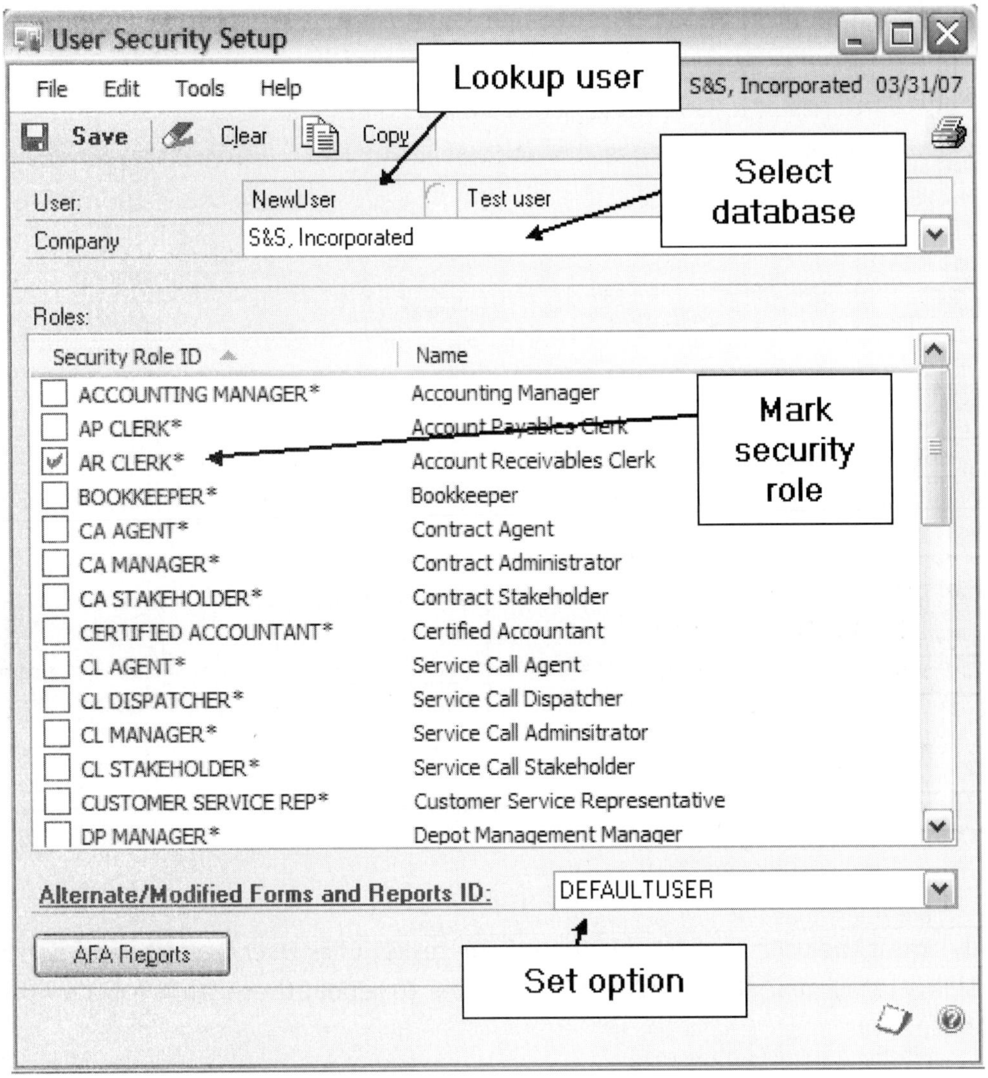

Figure 3:45 Grant User Permissions

Test this user account when you have the time by logging in with the new ID and password. You will then discover the tasks not accessible to the user.

> The final step to activating security is to activate it by marking the Security option found in the Company Setup window. This window is accessed by clicking Company under the Setup category on the Administration home page. This feature is already activated for the sample companies. If left unmarked, GP reminds you to activate security upon exiting the User Security Setup window.

SECURITY REPORTING

Security reporting is accessed from the Administration home page under the Reports category. Reports are classified into user, general, and group categories. These categories are explained in Table 3:4.

Report Categories	Purpose
User	Reports on user permissions, class assignments, and company access permissions.
General	Reports on system-wide settings and current activity.
Groups	Groups the above reports for printing multiple reports simultaneously.

Table 3:4 Security Reporting Categories

Reports are printed to document security and review for compliance with internal controls objectives.

You have now completed Level Two.

Level One Exercises

1. Review the Posting Setup for the Payroll Series and list the control reports that print after period ending the Series.

2. You are training a new accounts payable clerk. Describe batch processing to the clerk and explain the month-end procedures for posting vendor invoices when the company uses the Batch as the option for Posting Date From in the Purchasing Series.

3. The controller, Ashton, asks that you explain the difference between the Post to General Ledger and Post Through General Ledger options under Posting Setup.

4. The only information you have on a transaction comes from the following detail trial balance.

Trx Date	Jrnl No.	Orig. Audit Trail	Distribution Reference	Orig. Master Number	Orig. Master Name	Debit
5/16/2006	666	PMCHK00000012	Accounts Payable	983	Office Rex, Inc.	$2,303.15

   a. What can you tell Ashton about this transaction by simply looking at the report?

   b. Can you provide additional information after using GP to research the transaction? Please explain.

Level Two Exercises

1. S&S hired a new accounts receivable clerk to process invoices and customer payments. Does this person have authorization, recording, or custody duties?

2. Review the ARCLERK security role and list any permissions granted to this role that conflict with your answer to Question 1.

3. You are asked to create a user ID for the new clerk. Create a User ID of BLANE and complete steps that grant access to the S&S, Incorporated database and permissions to tasks. (Note: You can disregard issues raised in Question 2.)

   Print a report to document completing this question. This report is created by clicking Security and selecting User Security as the reporting category. You will need to create a new report in this category and filter for the new user ID.

4. You are asked to recommend internal control procedures for a company. This company has one owner, one accounting clerk, and two salespeople. Recommend who should be assigned duties for the following tasks and explain why you made that recommendation.
   a. Opening the mail
   b. Setting credit limits for new customers
   c. Taking sales orders
   d. Preparing customer invoices
   e. Posting customer checks
   f. Depositing customer checks
   g. Approving vendor bills
   h. Posting vendor bills
   i. Printing checks to vendors
   j. Signing checks to vendors
   k. Approving inventory orders
   l. Ordering inventory
   m. Reconciling bank statements
   n. Preparing financial statements

Chapter 4 INVENTORY CONTROL SERIES

CHAPTER OVERVIEW

Our journey thus far has traveled the traditional path of implementing a computerized accounting system. First, we installed the software and then became familiar with using GP's interface. We next learned to create company master records such as general ledger accounts and customers. We then gathered knowledge about Series integration and transaction posting. Finally, we implemented GP security and worked with posting setup controls and the audit trail. We are now ready to focus on managing the inventory sold to customers.

As discussed in Chapter 1, S&S is a distributor of small electronics, thus company business activities revolve around inventory. Accordingly, our task is to learn the Inventory Control Series. Ashton has already created inventory master records and recorded current stock levels. Just a reminder, a list of inventory items appears in Appendix B. One last reminder, S&S sells to customers located throughout the United States and owns a fleet of delivery trucks for shipping customer orders.

This chapter covers:

- Inventory setup, including valuation, pricing, unit of measure schedules, and inventory classes
- Maintaining inventory items, price lists, and associating preferred vendors with inventory items
- Recording inventory adjustments and physical counts
- Performing inventory inquiries and printing reports

This chapter is directed at both Level One and Level Two readers.

Levels One and Two

INVENTORY SETUP

Before using the Inventory Control Series, we need to become familiar with Series setup. Activate the Inventory home page and click **Inventory Control** under the Setup category to open the window illustrated in Figure 4:1. The following describes relevant options for this window.

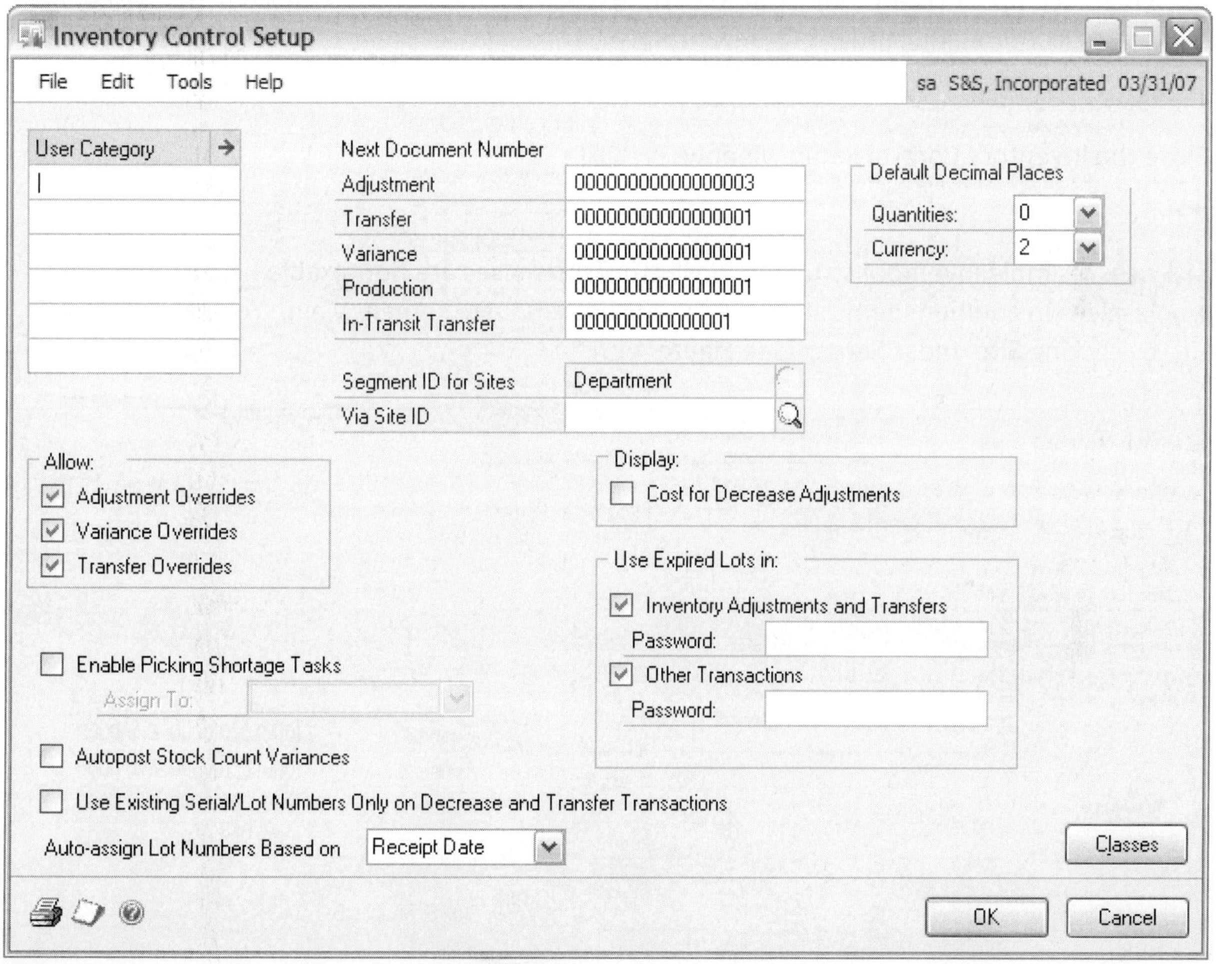

Figure 4:1 Inventory Control Setup Window

User Category is used to create optional fields on inventory items, such as special handling procedures for items containing hazardous materials or requiring refrigeration.

Next Document Number lists the next number to be assigned to the specific transaction types identified (i.e., adjustment, transfer, variance, production, and in-transit transfer). Document control numbers are part of the audit trail for the Inventory Control Series.

Default Decimal Places shows the number of decimal places permitted for quantities of and monetary value for (i.e., price and cost) inventory items.

Allow indicates that S&S permits users to override adjustments, variances, and transfers during transaction entry.

Autopost Stock Count Variance instructs GP to post variances that result when entering physical inventory counts. If left unmarked then GP creates a batch for the variance that you must then post.

Display – Cost for Decrease Adjustments, when marked, instructs GP to display the costs related to decrease adjustments for inventory.

Close the Inventory Control Setup window.

S&S uses a simple inventory structure. Inventory purchases are nontaxable because S&S is a wholesaler. In addition, items are stored in one warehouse, namely Main. You can view this site by clicking **Site** under Cards. (See Figure 4:2.)

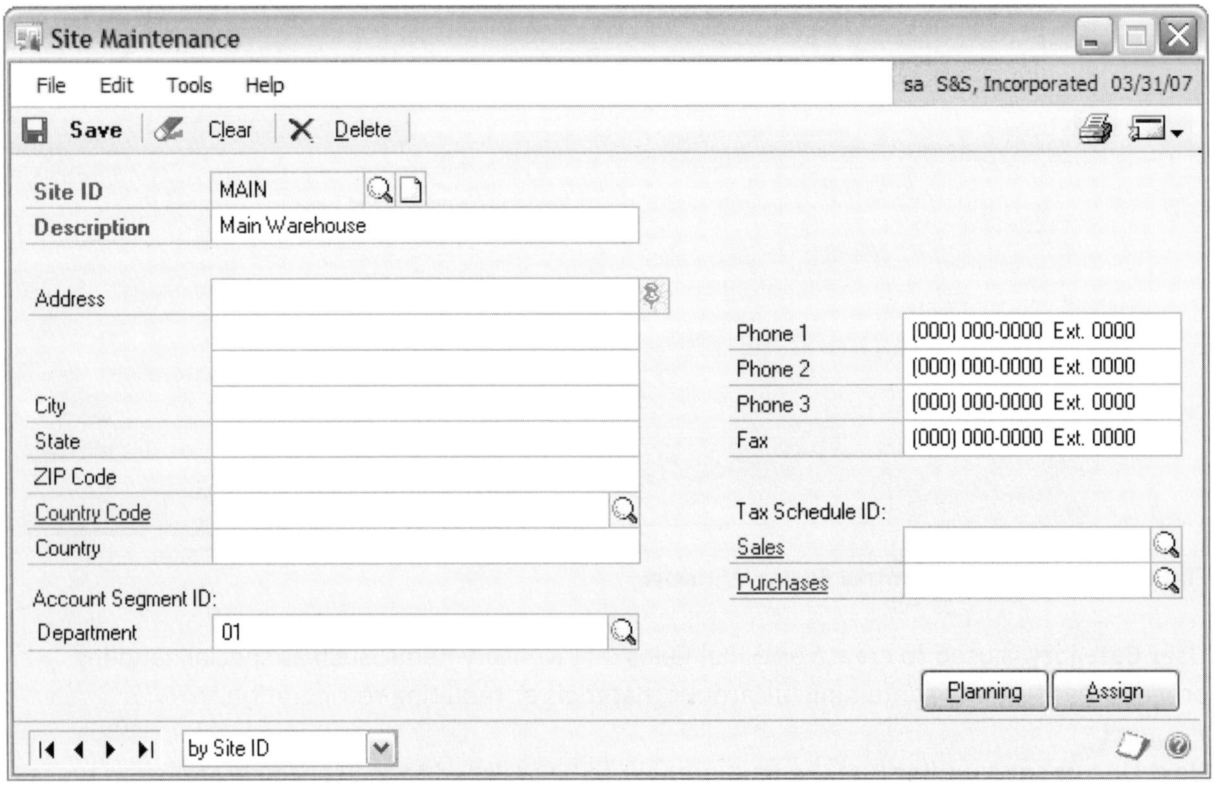

Figure 4:2 Inventory Site Maintenance Window

S&S does not currently use bins or serial numbers to track inventory; however, GP is scalable and these features can be activated at any time in the future.

S&S uses only one price level, namely WHOLE. Price levels are viewed by clicking Price Level under Setup. (See Figure 4:3.)

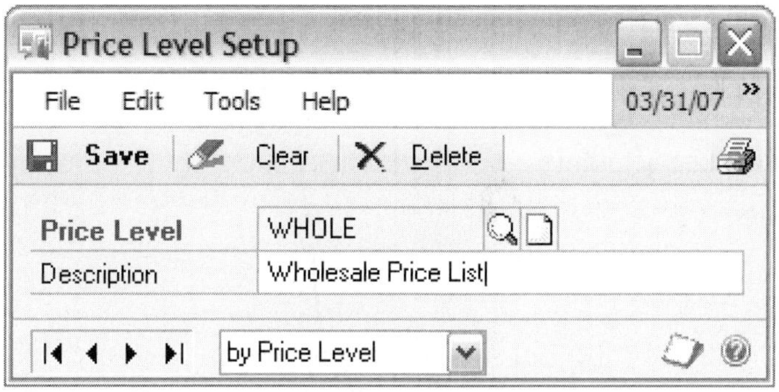

Figure 4:3 Inventory Price Levels

S&S is a bulk distributor so it purchases inventory in large quantities. This inventory comes in different units of measure (UOM). You can view these measurement units by clicking **Unit of Measure Schedule** under Setup. (See Figure 4:4.) You will see the interplay of these schedules when performing tasks in the Purchasing Series chapter.

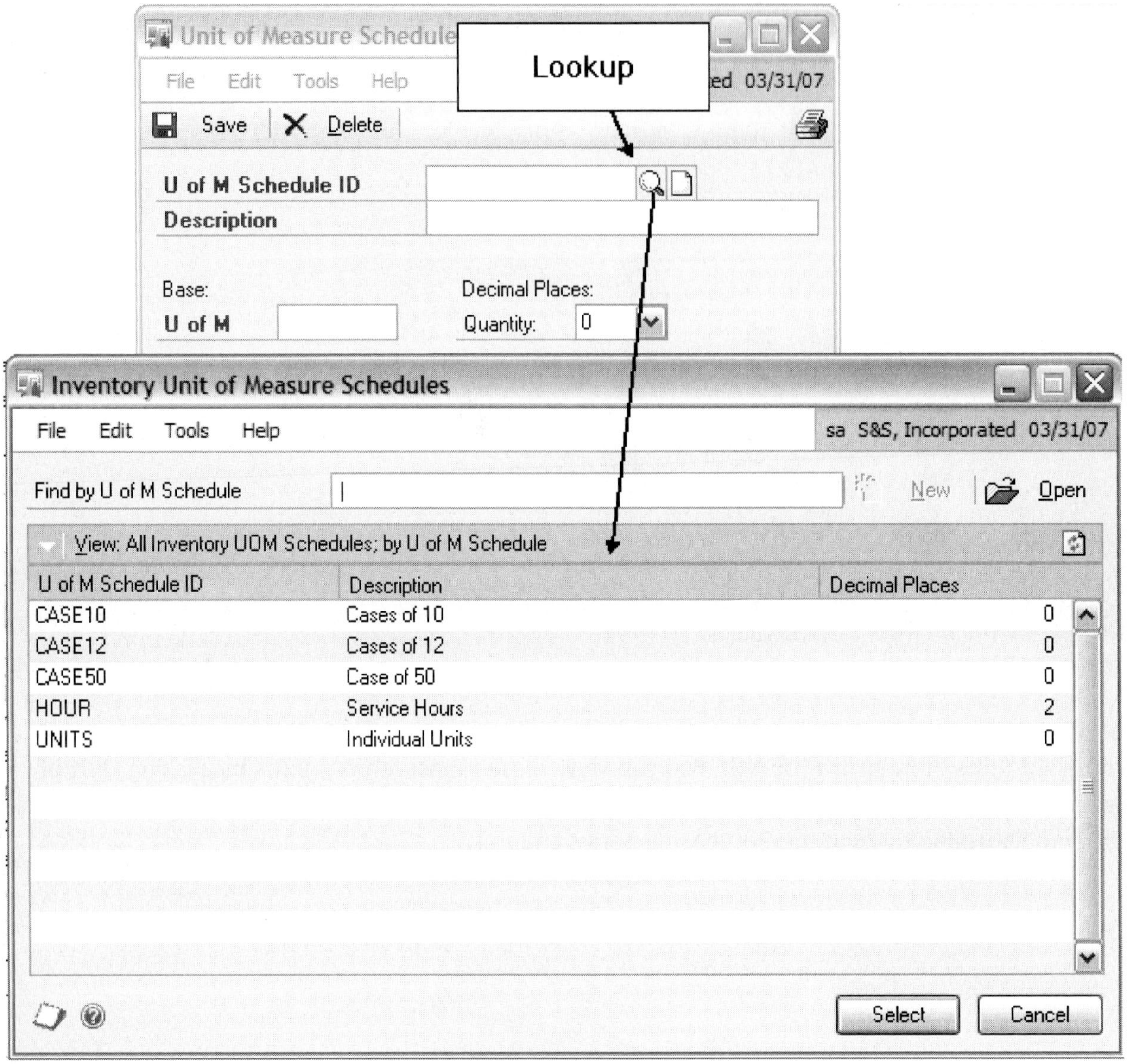

Figure 4:4 Unit of Measure Schedule Setup Window

Finally, Ashton created item classes for grouping inventory items sharing similar attributes. The Item Class Setup window is accessed by clicking **Item Class** under Setup. *(Note: You can also open this window using the Classes button on the Inventory Control Setup window previously illustrated.)*

Open the Item Class Setup window and look up CARAUD. (See Figure 4:5.)

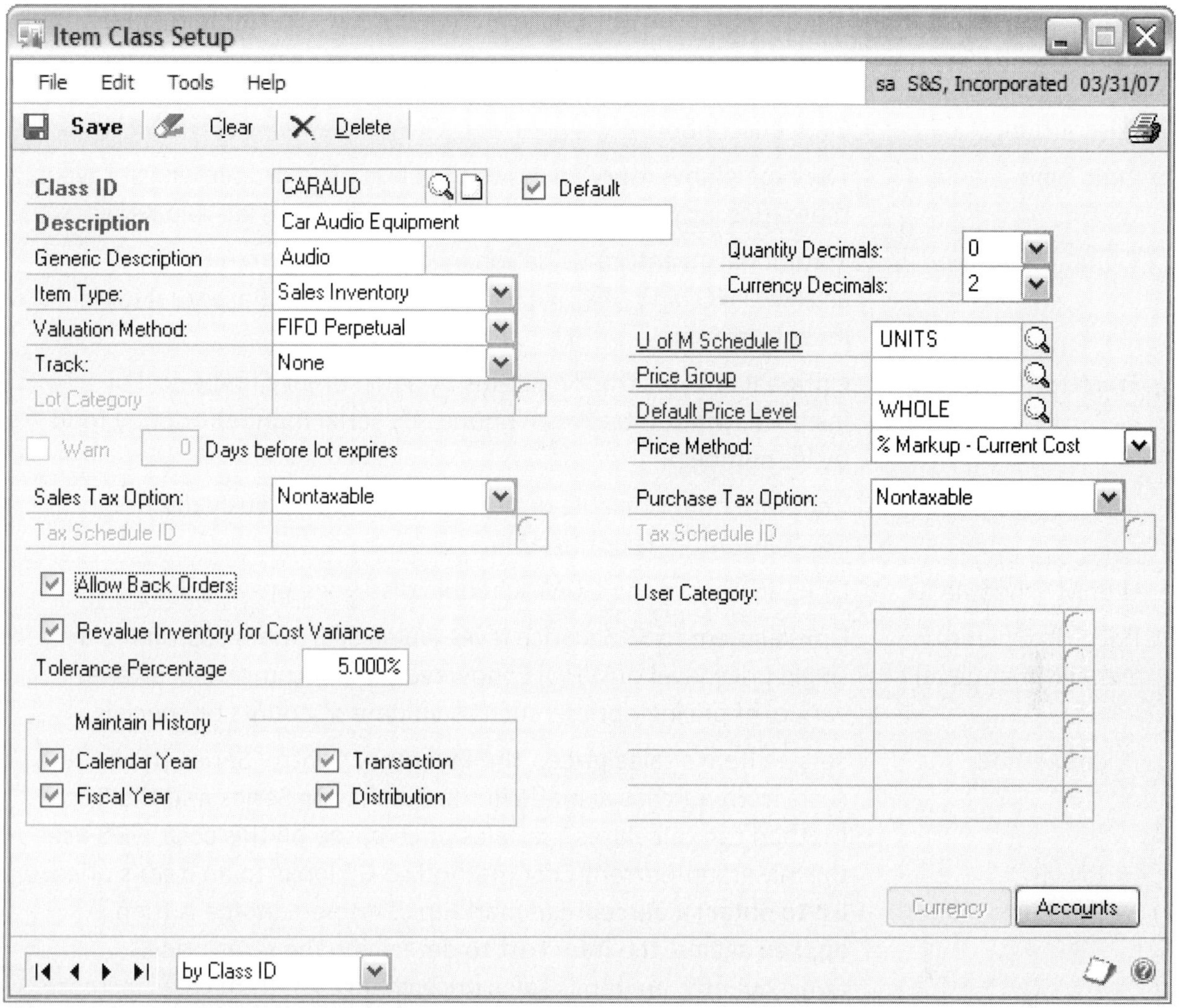

Figure 4:5 CARAUD Inventory Class

Item classes speed data entry for new items by supplying default values for the item. Additionally, classes help ensure data consistency among similar items and assist in analyzing inventory sales and purchasing data. Review the next table for descriptions on class fields.

Item Class Field	Description
Class ID	Primary key that uniquely identify the class.
Description	Class description.
Item Type	The type of inventory linked to the class. The dropdown list reveals that types include sales inventory, discontinued, kit, and services.
Valuation Method	Traditional inventory valuation methods recognized by GAAP such as LIFO, FIFO, and Average Cost. S&S uses FIFO Perpetual for all inventory items.
Track	Optional field for tracking items by serial or lot numbers. For instance, you can track cell phones by serial number or baby food by lot number.
Sales Tax Option	Items are either taxable or nontaxable. As previously discussed, S&S's inventory is nontaxable.
U of M Schedule ID	Links an item to the UOM schedule discussed previously.
Price Group and Default Price Level	Links an item to S&S's price level table. S&S offers customers a single price level of WHOLE; however, many companies offer a variety of pricing options such as volume discounts or specials.
Price Method	Sets an item's sales price. The Inventory Control Series tracks item costs from purchases made in the Purchasing Series and the Price Method can calculates the sales price based on this cost. S&S uses the %Markup-Current Cost method so GP looks to an item's price list to obtain a percentage mark-up. This percentage is then applied against the item cost to determine the sales price. Consequently, an item's sales price changes as item costs increase or decrease.
Allow Back Orders	Option that permits back orders for sales of out-of-stock items.
Revalue Inventory for Cost Variance with Tolerance Percentage	Revalues an item's cost when the purchase variance exceeds a set tolerance percentage. For CARAUD, GP revalues the item's cost when the purchase price for the item exceeds 5 percent of its current cost. This also means that the purchase price variance posts to the inventory asset account instead of the purchase variance expense account. In Chapter 6, we demonstrate the effect of this setting on inventory sales pricing.
Maintain History	Options for retaining details on historical transactions. Marking options lets S&S print historical reporting.

Table 4:1 Item Class Field Descriptions

Before closing the class window, click the **Accounts** button. GP will use these general ledger accounts (Figure 4:6) when posting inventory transactions.

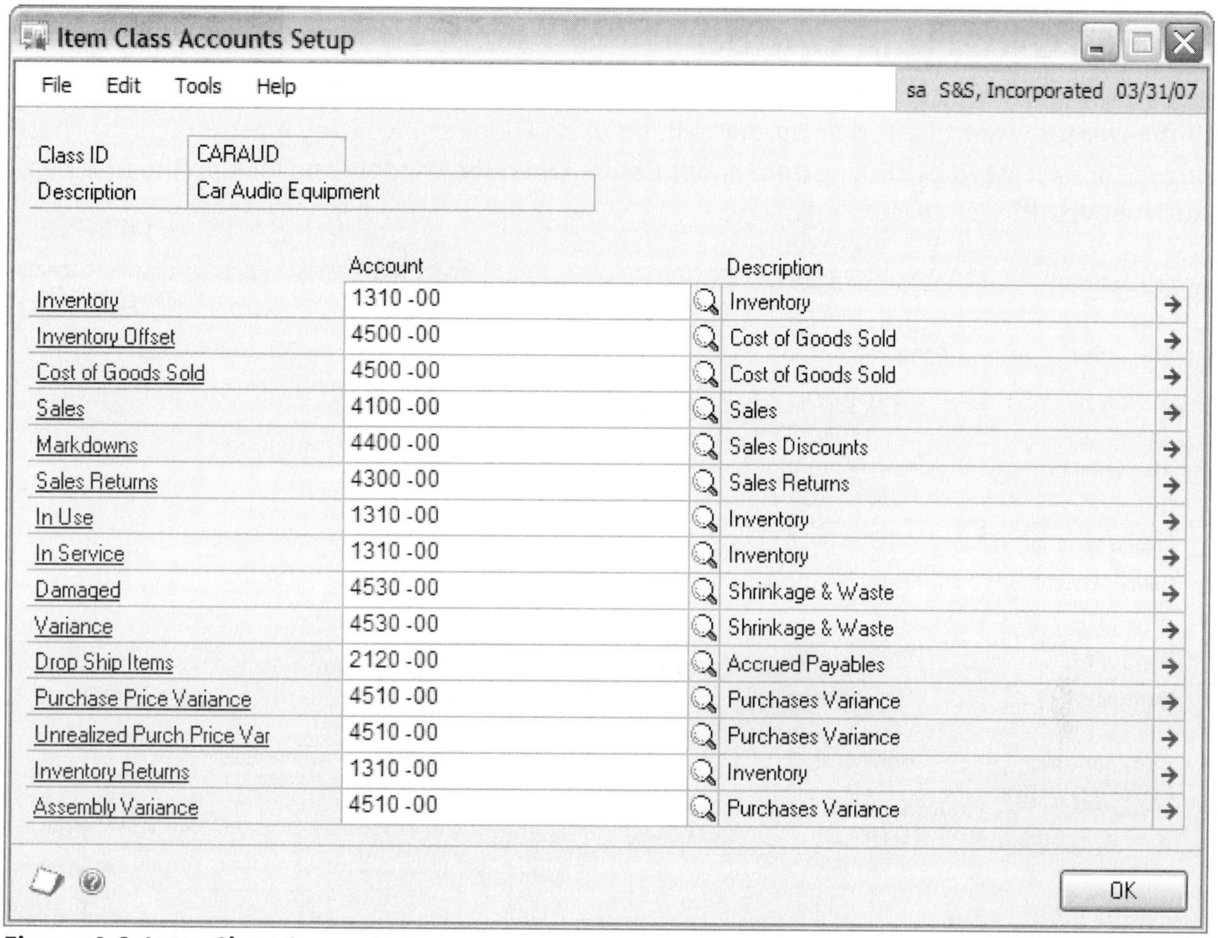

Figure 4:6 Item Class Accounts

In subsequent chapters, you will discover that other Series also contains default accounts. In addition, default accounts are stored under the ***Tools>>Setup>>Posting>>Posting Accounts*** menu.

We will differentiate between the various locations for storing default general ledger accounts in Chapter 6. For now, simply understand that GP cannot post a transaction without being supplied a general ledger account. Furthermore, S&S has instructed GP to post sales transactions by looking at default accounts on customer cards instead of inventory cards. Therefore, the default accounts appearing on inventory items are used only when posting transactions originating in the Inventory Control Series.

Close all open windows and move to the next topic.

INVENTORY ITEM CARDS

With inventory control setup under our belt, let us now look at inventory master records. These records are accessed by clicking **Item** under Cards. Open the window and look up the first item, **AUDJV50WMP3**. (See Figure 4:7.)

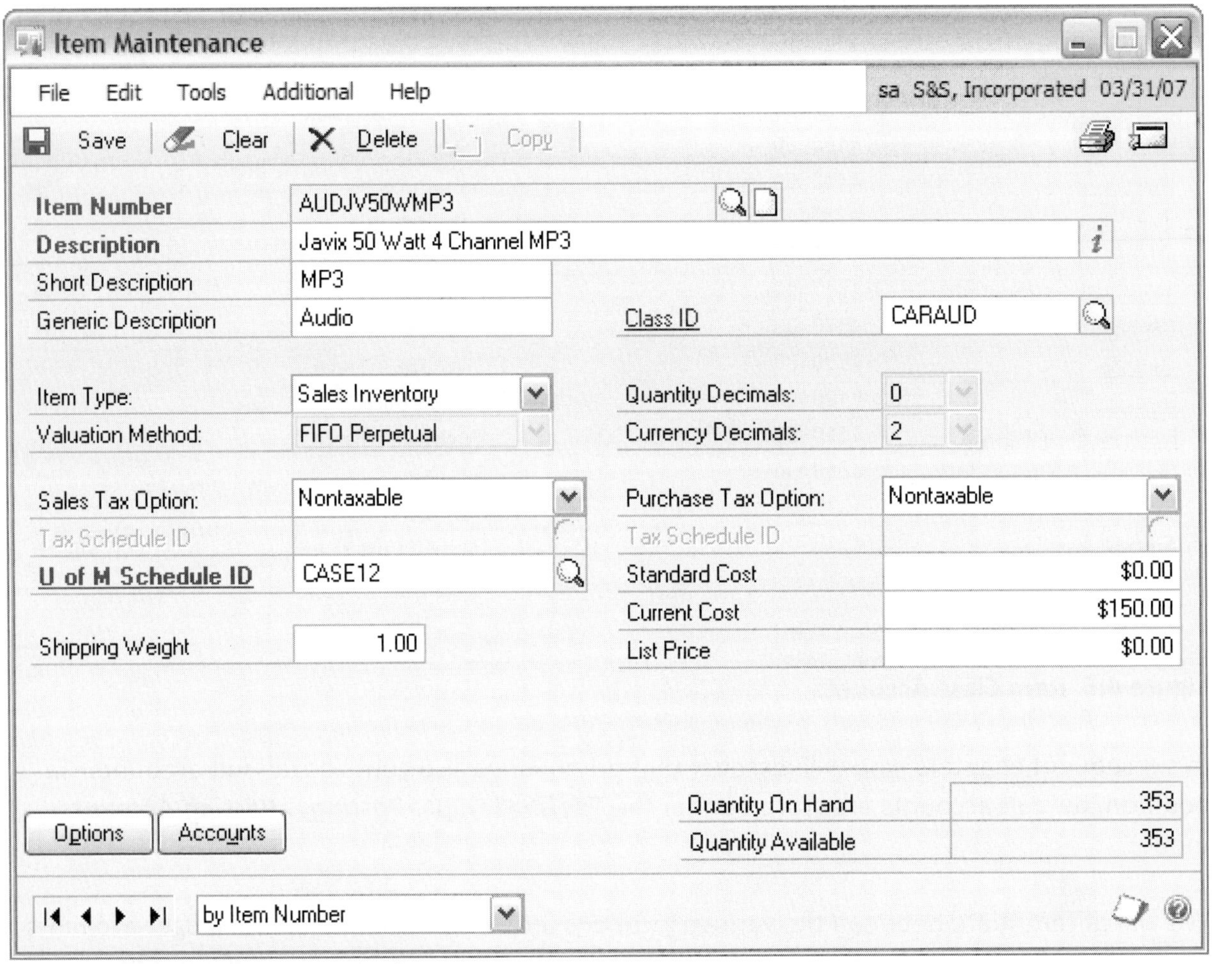

Figure 4:7 Inventory Item Card

Many of the fields were discussed in the previous topic. Notice that this item is assigned to the CARAUD class and many field values defaulted from this class. *(Note: You can always change field values on the item without affecting the class.)*

The item also lists the **Quantity On Hand** and the **Quantity Available**. *(Note: Your quantities will differ if you have practiced posting transactions.)* The quantity available will be less than the quantity on-hand when there are outstanding sales orders for the item. GP does not reduce on hand quantities until the customer is invoiced; however, reduces the quantity available to mitigate the threat of selling items already promised to a customer.

Click the **Accounts** button to view default general ledger accounts. (Not illustrated.) These accounts transferred from the item class and can be changed in this window without affecting the class. Close the Accounts window.

Notice the item's **Standard Cost**. A value is supplied for this field when the item uses a standard cost pricing method. S&S does not use this pricing method so the field is empty. Notice the value under **Current Cost**. This value defaults from the last purchase price paid for the item (i.e., posting a vendor invoice). Remember that, under S&S's pricing structure, this cost affects inventory sales pricing.

Click the **Options** button to open the window shown in Figure 4:8. This window contains additional fields relevant to the item.

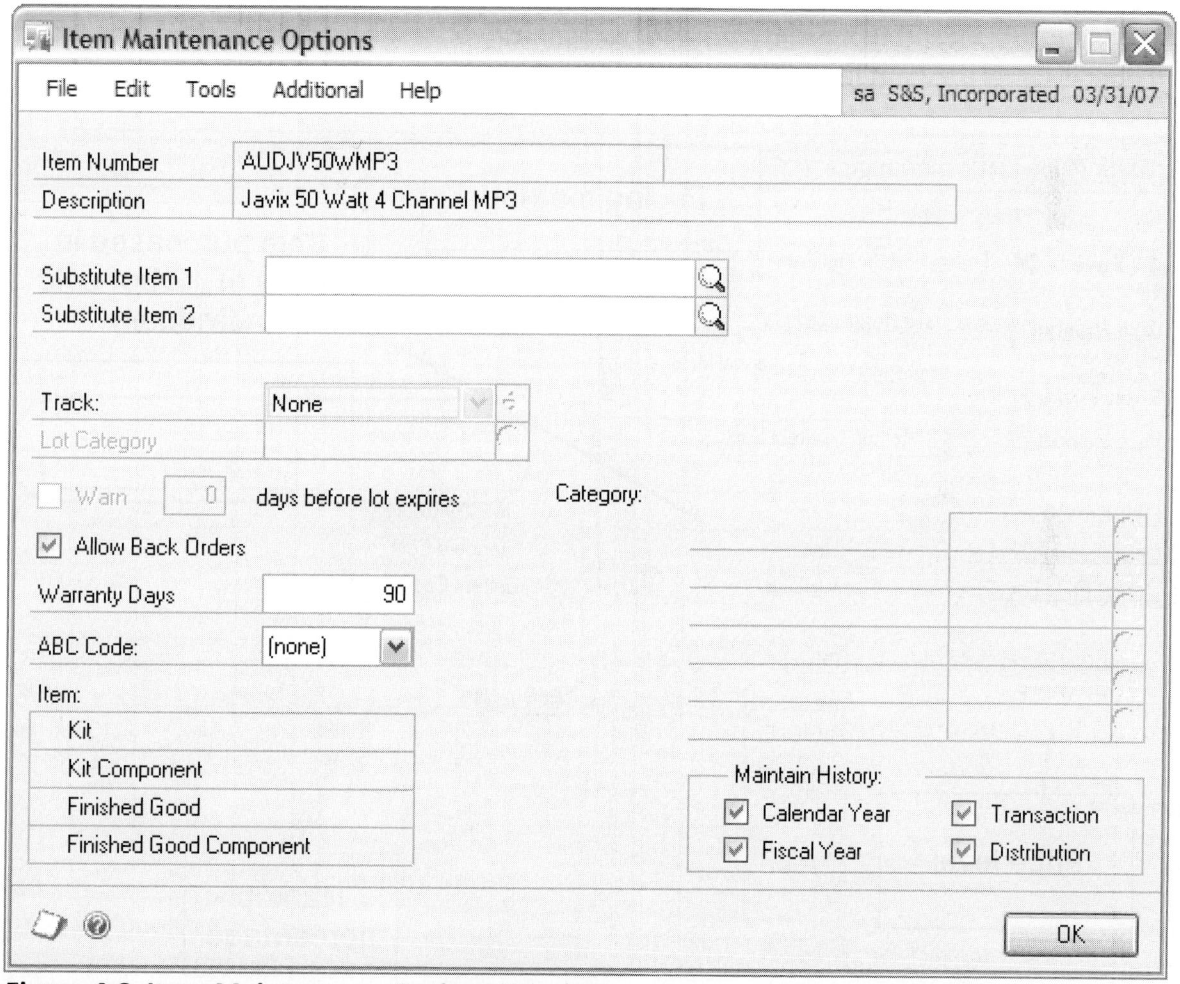

Figure 4:8 Item Maintenance Options Window

Maintain History options defaulted from the class and **Allow Back Orders** defaulted from inventory setup options. Close this window.

Finally, scroll buttons (Figure 4:9) on the lower left of the item window moves you to other records in the inventory table. You can change the default scroll order for moving through records by selecting an order from the dropdown list. Take a few minutes to review other items and then close the window.

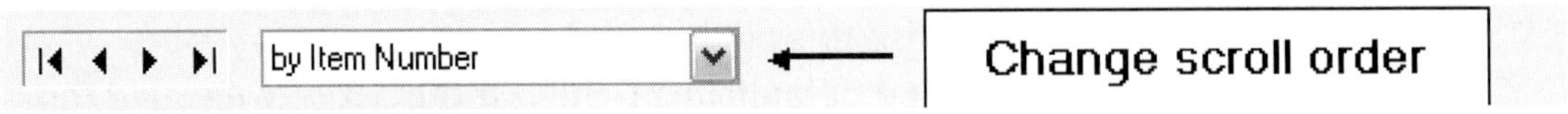

Figure 4:9 Record Scroll Bar

Inventory Pricing

We will now look at setting up and maintaining inventory prices. Click **Price List** under Cards and open item **AUDJV50WMP3**. (See Figure 4:10.)

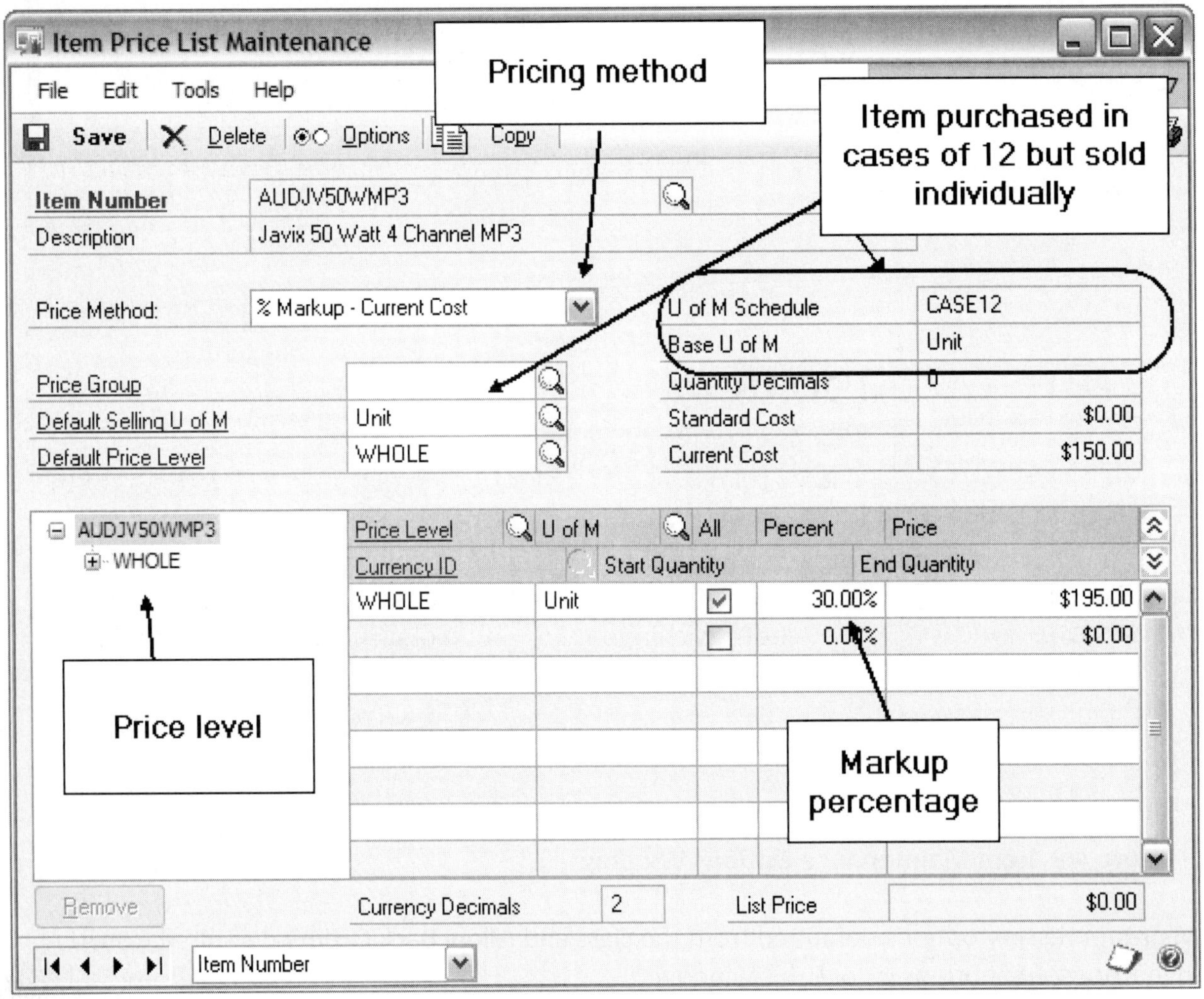

Figure 4:10 Price List Maintenance Window

Remember that S&S uses a percentage markup on current cost to calculate item sales prices. The price list record illustrated supplies the markup percent at each price level. WHOLE is the only price level used by S&S and this item is priced at 30 percent above current cost. Accordingly, the $195 selling price is calculated by multiplying the current cost of $150 by 130 percent (i.e., 1.30).

Scroll through other records and note that items have different markup percentages but always the same pricing method. Close the window when finished.

Try this exercise to test an item's sales price.

Create a sales invoice by clicking Invoice Entry under Transactions on the Sales home page. Select any customer and enter the sale of one unit of AUDJV50WMP3.

Did the $195 sales price appear? Delete the sales invoice when finished.

E4:1 Test an Item's Sales Price

INVENTORY VENDORS

S&S links item records to vendors selling the item. This link will then restrict purchases of the item in the Purchasing Series to only those vendors assigned to the item.

Click **Vendors** under Cards to open the window illustrated in Figure 4:11 and look up item **AUDJV50WMP3**. Change the **Vendor Lookup** option to Assigned and click the **Vendor ID** lookup icon to select the vendor linked to this item.

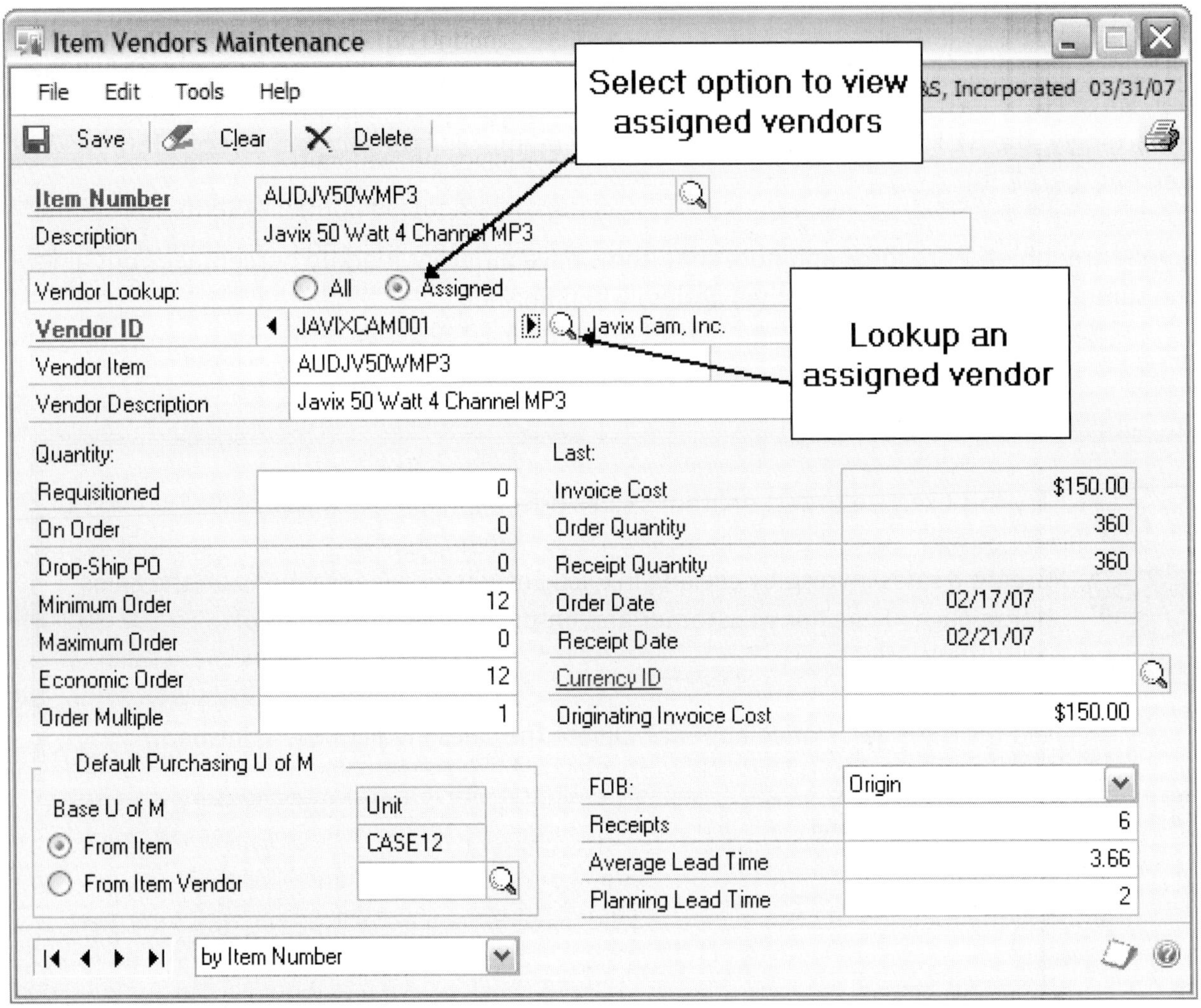

Figure 4:11 Item Link to Vendors

The item-vendor link supplies defaults for orders placed with this vendor as well as information on the last purchase made from the vendor. You can assign multiple vendors to the item by changing the Vendor Lookup option to All, clicking the vendor lookup icon, and selecting another Vendor ID. Close the window

Along with assigning vendors, S&S sets the vendor it prefers (i.e., preferred vendor) to buy the item from. S&S makes this selection after analyzing inventory reports and ranking vendors based on product quality, price, and reliability. We will next view the preferred vendor for AUDJV50WMP3.

Click **Quantities/Sites** under Cards to open the window illustrated in Figure 4:12 and look up the item. Select **Site ID** and look up **MAIN**. *(Note: Preferred vendors are assigned by warehouse site.)*

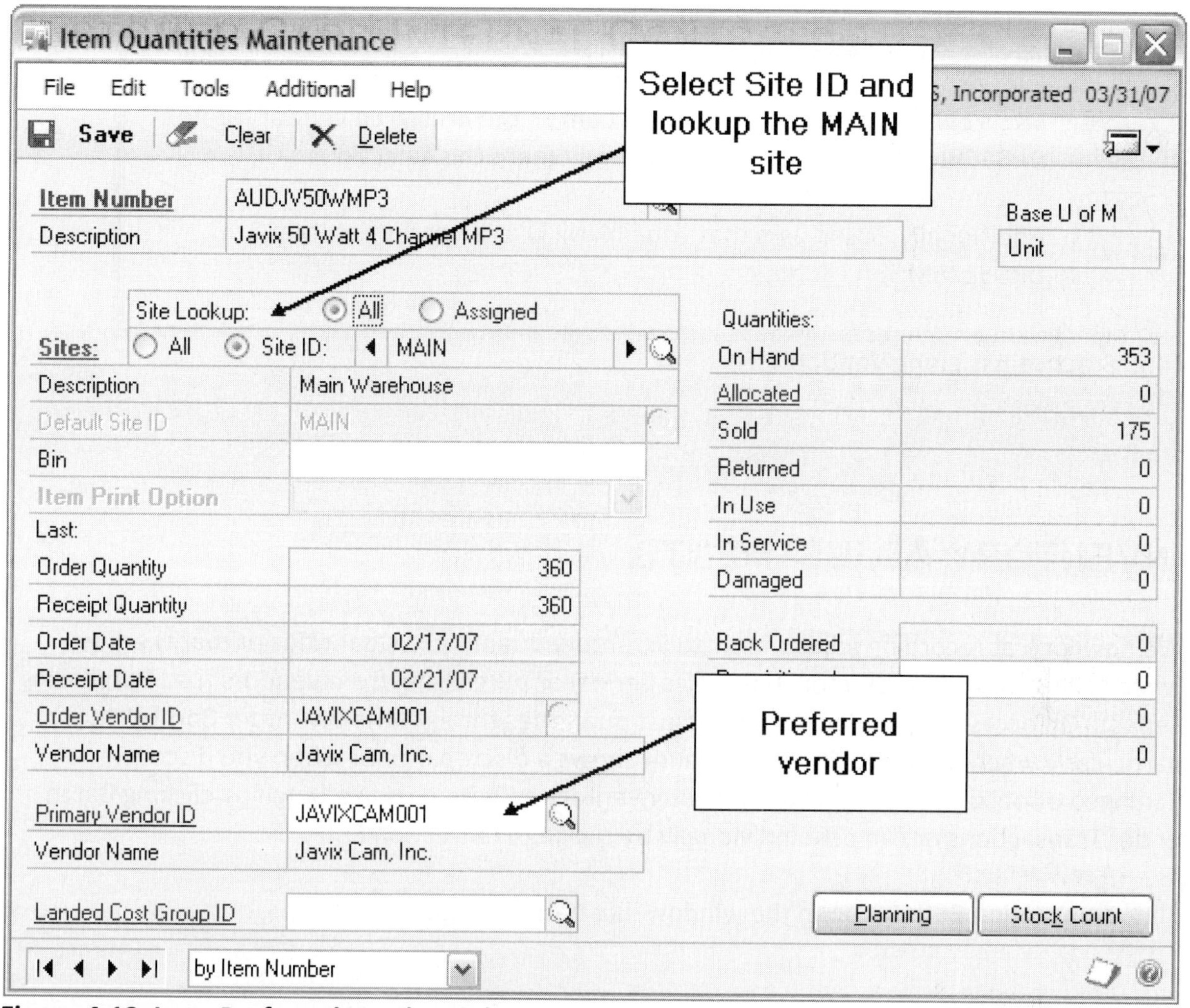

Figure 4:12 Item Preferred Vendor Link

Primary Vendor ID displays the linked vendor whereas **Order Vendor ID** displays the vendor last used to purchase the item from.

We just illustrated the process of linking items to vendors and then setting a preferred vendor for the item. You could just as easily set the preferred vendor first and then GP will create link the item to the vendor.

The item-vendor link and preferred vendor settings play different roles in controlling inventory purchases. When generating a purchase order in the Sales Series, GP places the order with the preferred vendor. We will illustrate this feature in Chapter 5. When generating a purchase order in the Purchasing Series, you can assign the order to any vendor linked to the item. We will illustrate this feature in Chapter 6.

S&S's owner, Susan, selected Nikki Cam as the preferred vendor for item DPD128MCARD and asks that you implement this selection in GP.

Additionally, Susan asks that you link Nikki as a vendor for item DPDS128MGST.

E4:2 Practice Assigning Vendors

INVENTORY ADJUSTMENTS

We now look at recording adjustments to inventory quantities. Quantities primarily adjust when selling items to customers (i.e., Sales Series) or purchasing from vendors (i.e., Purchasing Series). On occasion you may need to adjust quantities through the Inventory Control Series, particularly when a physical inventory count shows a discrepancy or when you discover damaged or obsolete items. You can post inventory adjustments in a batch by clicking Batch under Transactions or can post individually by clicking Transaction Entry.

Click **Transaction Entry** to open the window illustrated in Figure 4:13.

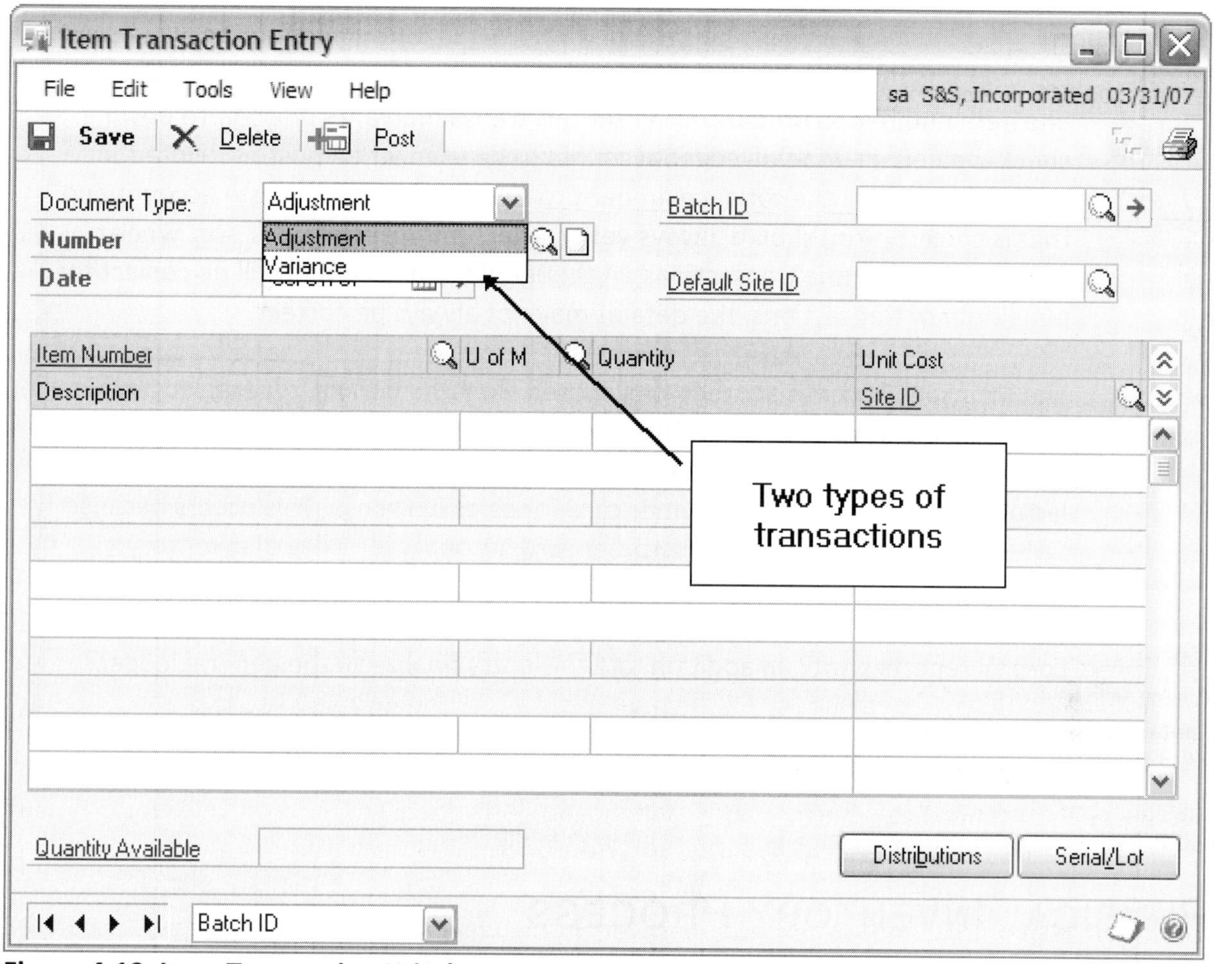

Figure 4:13 Item Transaction Window

Note that there are two types of transactions. Adjustment is used to record a decrease or increase in on-hand quantities for changes due to vendor purchases or customer sales. For instance, if after paying a vendor invoice items are returned then you will need to post a decrease adjustment in quantities. You will also post a vendor credit memo in the Purchasing Series; however, this transaction does not adjust inventory. Adjustments that decrease on-hand quantities are entered as negative amounts. GP will post the dollar value for the adjustment to the general ledger account selected for inventory.

On the other hand, variances are posted when changes to on-hand quantities are due to differences detected through a physical count, damage, or obsolescence. These entries are also entered as negative amounts when reducing on-hand quantities; however, GP will post the dollar value for these changes to the general ledger account selected for shrinkage and waste.

On March 18, 2007, Ashton discovered one damaged Nikki digital camcorder. The item number is DCNK4XDZ. Enter this transaction and, but before posting, check the default general ledger accounts to be used when posting. Note that this entry will post the variance amount to the shrinkage and waste account and that is correct. You should always verify where a transaction will post when recording nonroutine transactions. Although default accounts will be correct for a majority of transactions, the default may not always be correct.

The shrinkage and was account was chosen from the default general ledger account assigned to the item. This is an example of GP choosing general ledger accounts from the item card. In Chapter 5 you will see that GP chooses general ledger accounts from the customer card for sales of items. This occurs because S&S has instructed GP to use customer card accounts for sales of inventory.

Review the posting reports that print after closing the window. Why did these control reports print? In addition, did this entry finalize to the general ledger?

E4:3 Practice Recording Inventory Variance

PHYSICAL INVENTORY PROCESS

GP makes it possible for S&S to use a perpetual inventory system (i.e., quantity counts are constantly updated); however, the company must still conduct a periodic physical count to confirm that physical on-hand quantities agree with quantities in the system. Physical counts also test the effectiveness of internal controls and confirm the accuracy of inventory.

Ashton scheduled a physical count to occur at the end of March. Normally companies conduct such counts close to year-end. Furthermore, many companies perform a smaller scale count at six-month or quarter intervals.

Before conducting this count, you need to prepare a schedule of items to count. First, **set your system date to March 31, 2007**. Click **Stock Count Schedule** under Transactions and follow the instructions illustrated in Figure 4:14.

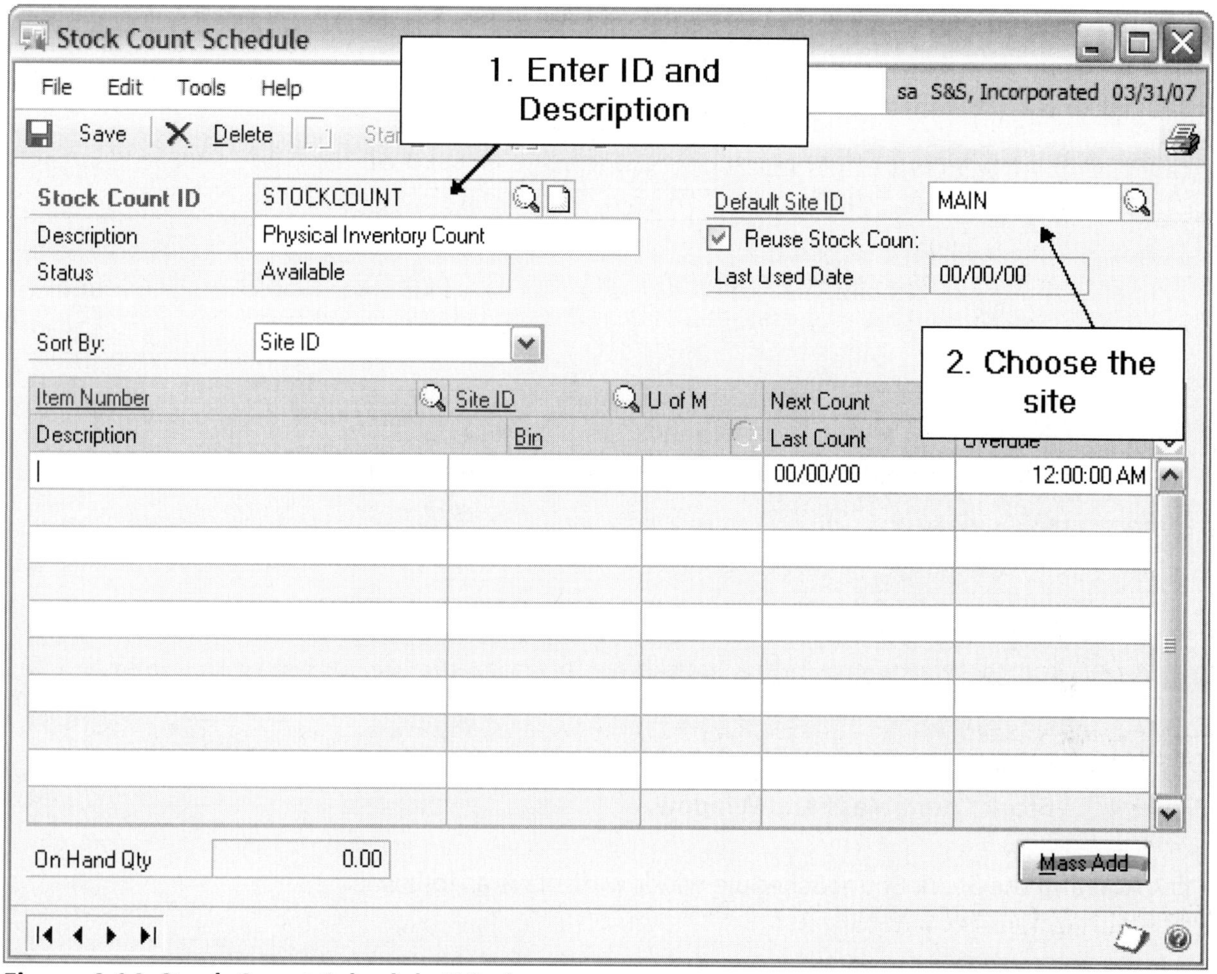

Figure 4:14 Stock Count Schedule Window

You will next add items to the count. Click **Mass Add** and enter the selection criteria illustrated in Figure 4:15.

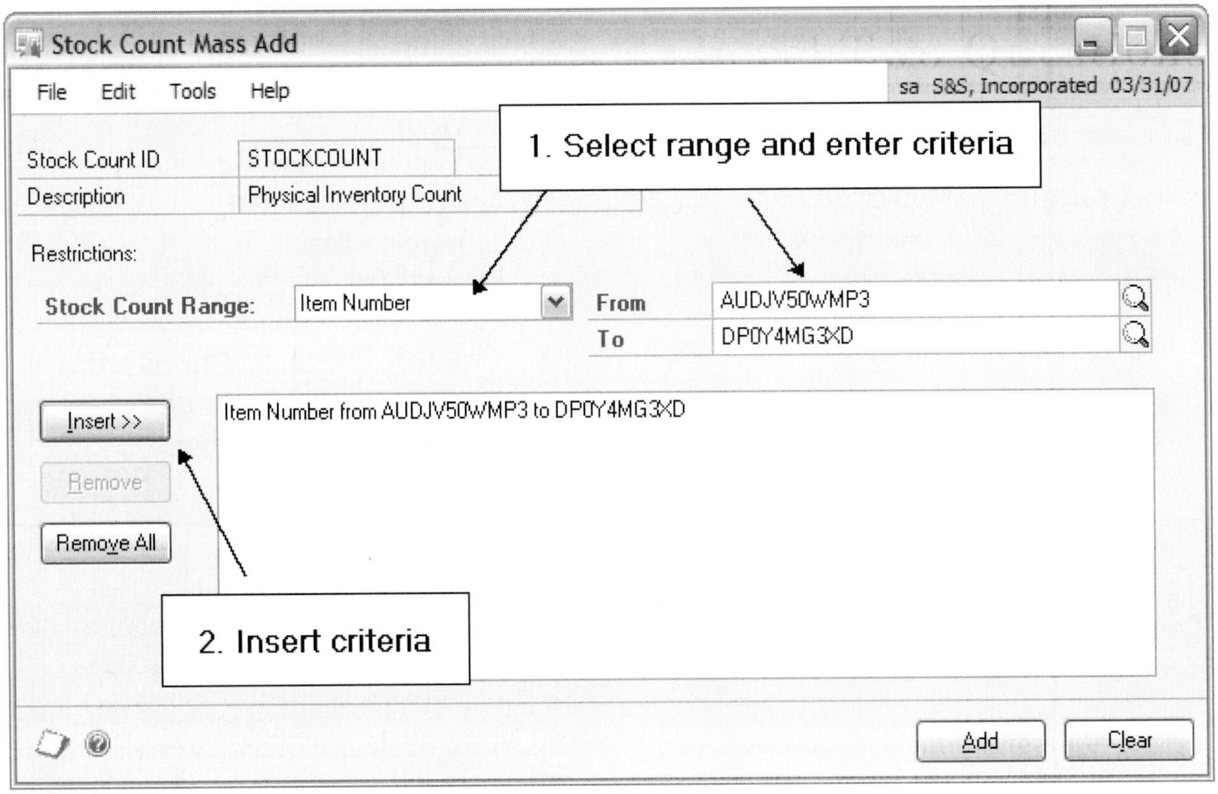

Figure 4:15 Stock Count Mass Add Window

Click **Add** and the Stock Count Schedule window displays as follows.

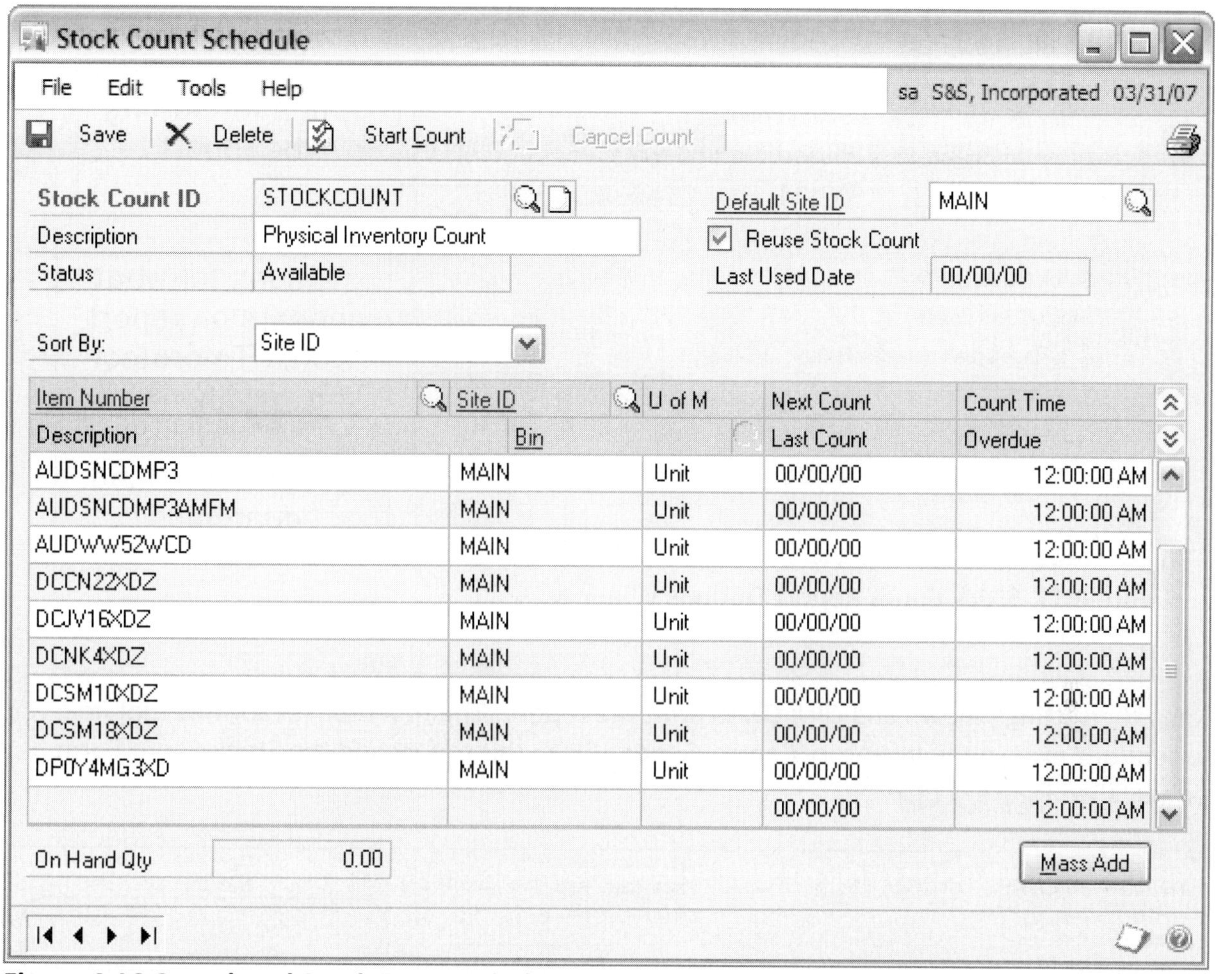

Figure 4:16 Completed Stock Count Window

Click **Save** to store the schedule. Look up the schedule and click **Start Count** to schedule the count.

Click **OK** to print the Stock Count Exception List to the screen. You are next presented with the Stock Count Print Options window. (See Figure 4:17.)

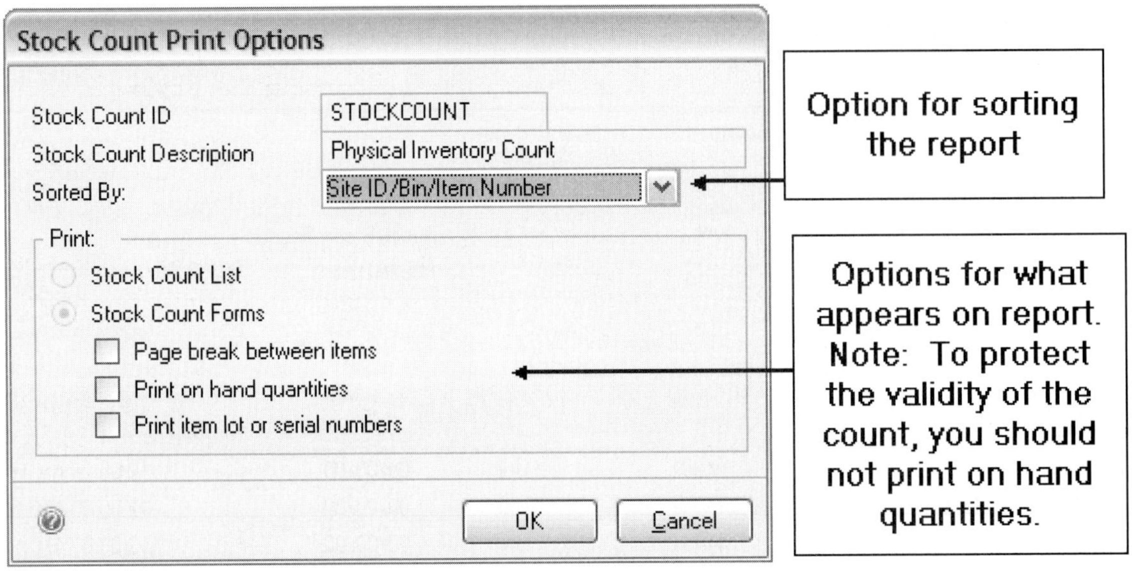

Figure 4:17 Stock Count Report Options Window

Keep the settings shown and click **OK** to print the report. The first report confirms that no exceptions exist in the Inventory Control Series. Close this report and the Stock Count Form prints. (See Figure 4:18.)

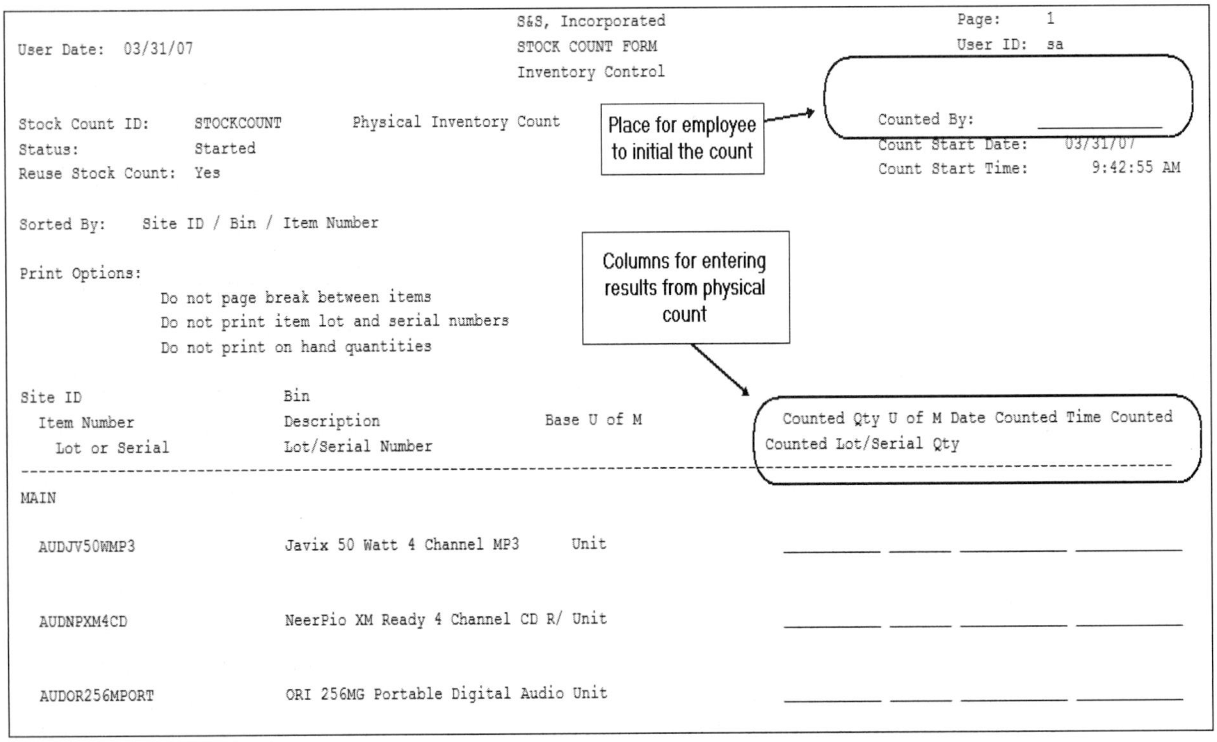

Figure 4:18 Stock Count Form

There are several internal control features to this report. First, items do not reveal GP quantities on hand so employees must actually count items to enter quantities. This controls employee performance. Secondly, there are places for initialing and date/time stamping the count; thus, implementing employee accountability. Ashton will distribute a copy of this report to each employee conducting the count.

Close the report and the Stock Count Schedule window.

After the count, Ashton inputs employee results in GP using the Stock Count Entry window. Verify that your system date is **March 31, 2007**. Click **Stock Count Entry** under Transactions and look up the **STOCKCOUNT** schedule as illustrated next.

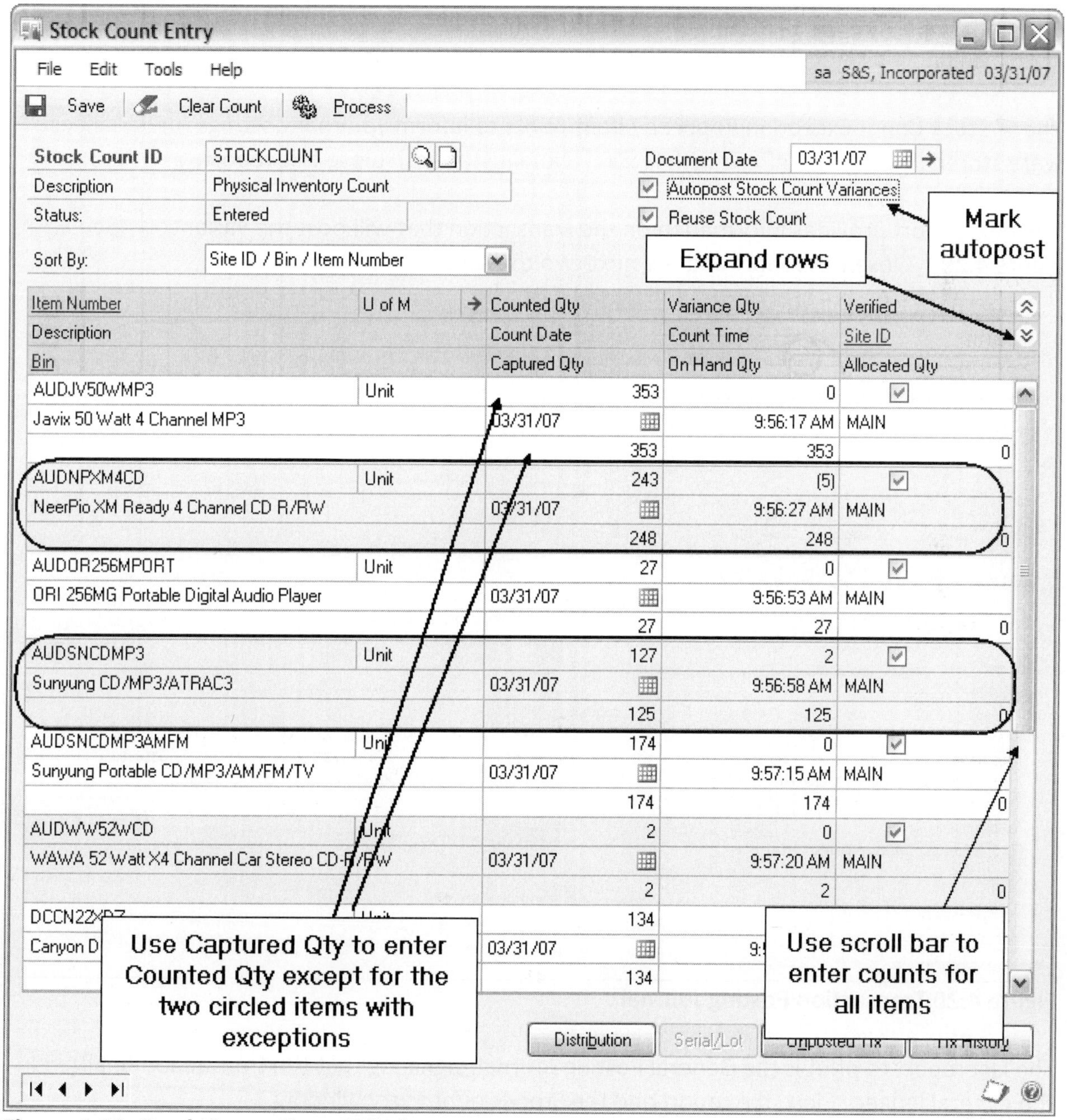

Figure 4:19 Stock Count Entry Window

Reports turned in by employees indicate that two items have quantity discrepancies. These variances occurred in items AUDNPXM4CD (down 5) and AUDSNCDMP3 (up 2).

Follow instructions on the illustration to enter counted quantities into the **Counted Qty** field. Your counted quantities may vary from those illustrated based on your activity in the software. Therefore, enter your Captured Qty as your Counted Qty, except on the two items with discrepancies. For these items, make sure that AUDNPXM4CD displays (5) and AUDSNCDMP3 displays 2 under **Variance Qty**.

Before posting, select the **Autopost Stock Count Variances** option. Also, place your cursor in one of the Counted Qty fields and click **Distribution** to verify that variances will post to the shrinkage and waste account. When finished, click **Process** to post.

The IV Stock Count Exception Report by Item prints to inform you that postings for variances were stored in a batch prefixed with IVSTC. (Not illustrated.) Close this report.

The next report provides information on the transaction that will post the variances. (See Figure 4:20.) Close this report and the next two that open.

```
User Date:  03/31/07                        TRANSACTION POSTING JOURNAL                              User ID: sa
                                                 Inventory Control

Batch ID:  IVSTC0000000001   Comment: STOCKCOUNT                                     Audit Trail Code: IVADJ00000004
Frequency: Single Use        GL Posting Date: 03/31/07
Trx Total- Actual:                       1  Control:                  0
Qty Total- Actual:                 7.00000  Control:            0.00000


Document Number        Document Date  GL Posting Date  Document Type
--------------------------------------------------------------------------------------------------------------
     Item Number                        U of M           Quantity   Site             Unit Cost          Extended Cost
--------------------------------------------------------------------------------------------------------------
          Description                                                          Inventory Account          Offset Account
--------------------------------------------------------------------------------------------------------------
                 Serial/Lot Number                 Quantity
--------------------------------------------------------------------------------------------------------------
00000000000000002      03/31/07        03/31/07          Variance

     AUDNPXM4CD                         Unit                  (5)  MAIN                    $102.00            $510.00
          NeerPio XM Ready 4 Channel CD R/RW                                   1310-00                   4530-00

     AUDSNCDMP3                         Unit                    2  MAIN                     $36.00             $72.00
          Sunyung CD/MP3/ATRAC3                                                1310-00                   4530-00


     Total Items:  2

Total Documents:  1
```

Figure 4:20 Transaction Posting Journal

The last report to print is the General Posting Journal, signaling that the transaction finalized in the general ledger. Close the report and the Stock Count Entry window.

INVENTORY INQUIRIES AND REPORTING

Employees need to review inventory to gather such information as receipts of items, item allocations, and quantities on-hand. This information is available from the Inquiry category on the Inventory home page. *(Remember from Chapter 3 that inquiry menus open windows for viewing information.)*

Let us view some of the information available in these windows. First click **Item** and look up the item illustrated in Figure 4:21.

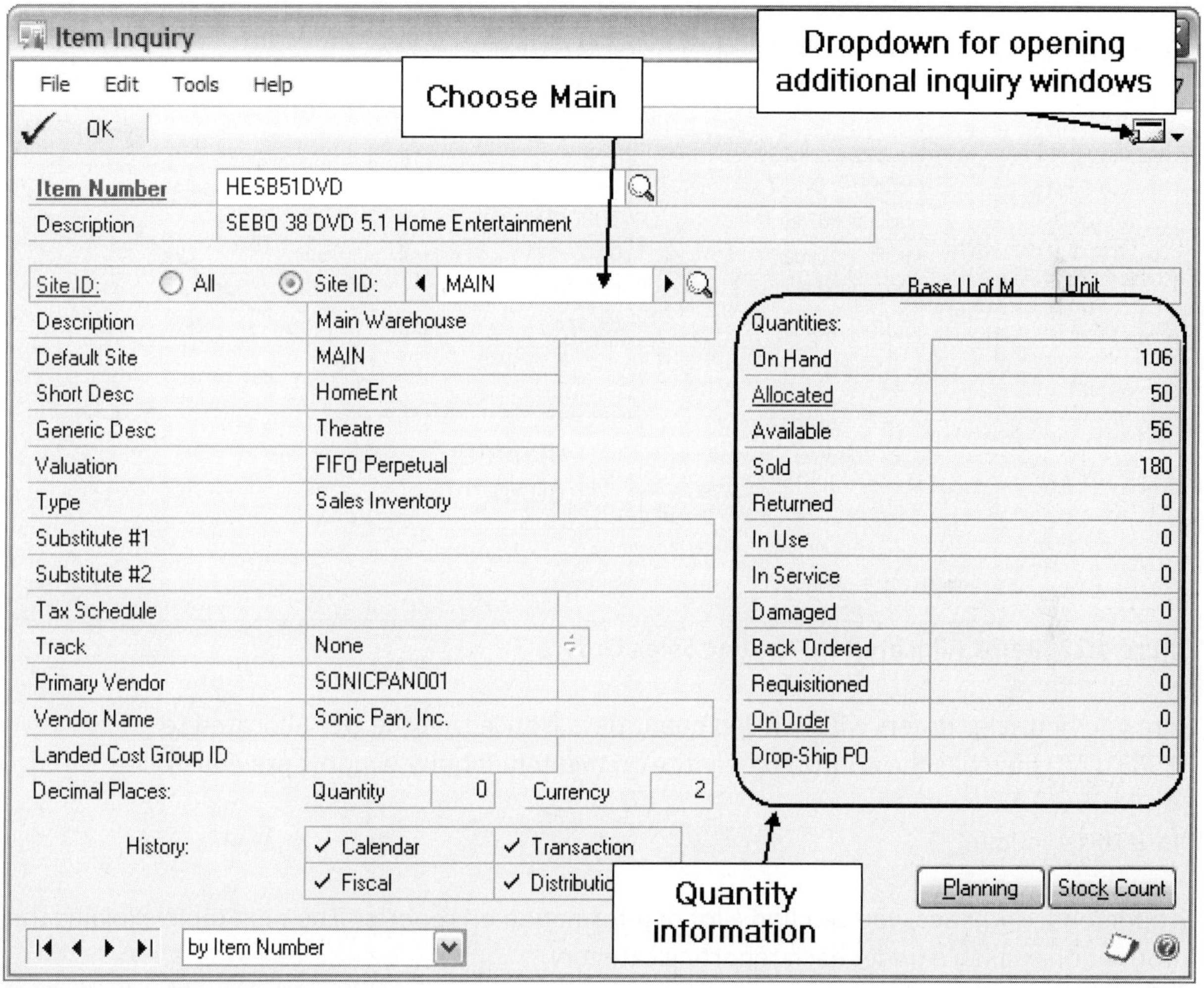

Figure 4:21 Item Information

You can review quantity information in this window. **On Hand** is the total quantity in inventory. **Allocated** is the quantity committed to sales orders (i.e., fulfilled items on the orders). The on hand will reduce after invoicing the order. **Available** is the remaining quantity available for sale (i.e., the difference between On Hand and Allocated). On Order lists the quantity on Purchase Orders.

Close the previous window and click **Item Allocation**. Follow the instructions on Figure 4:22.

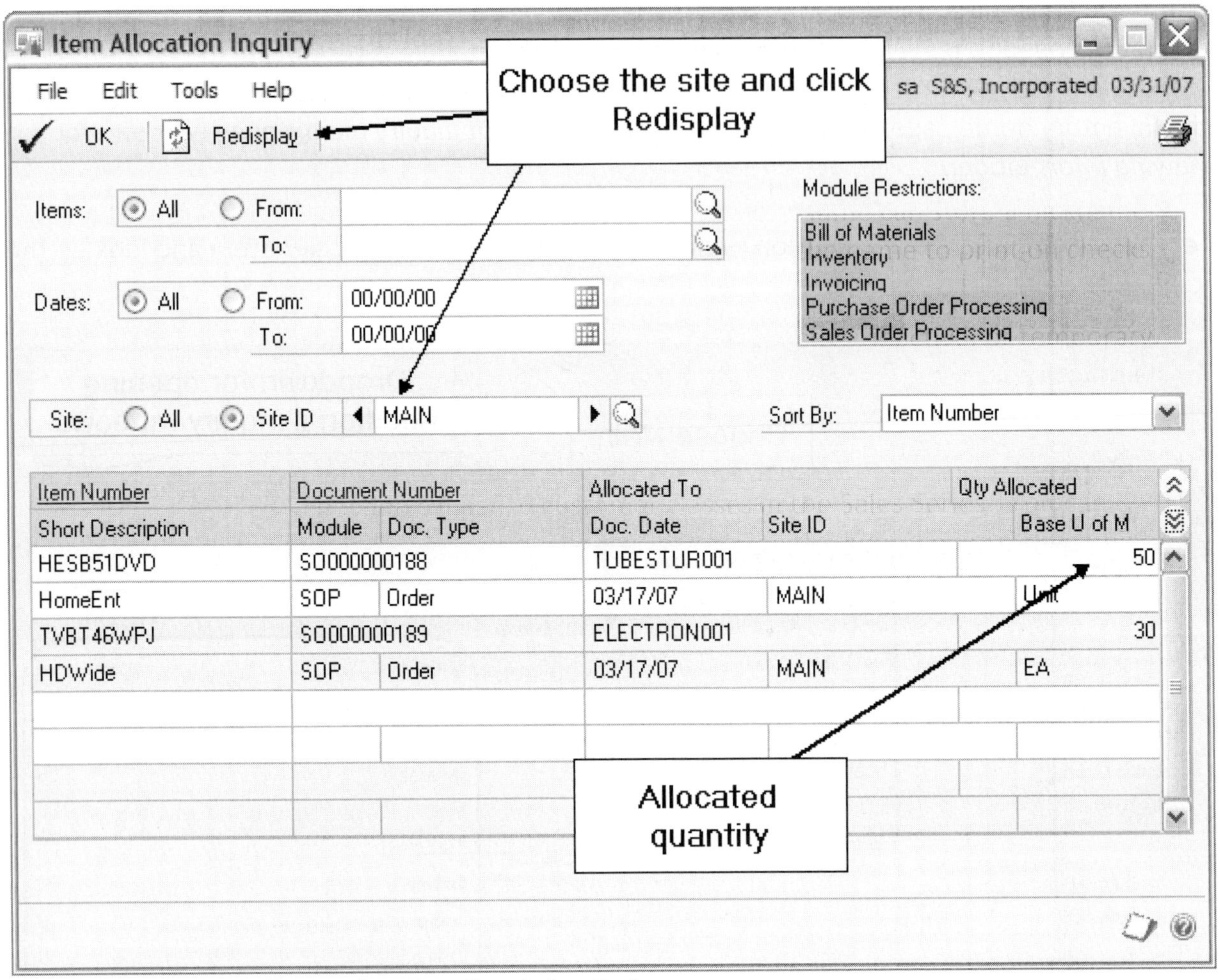

Figure 4:22 Items Allocated to Pending Sales Orders

Here you find sales orders with fulfilled quantities. Notice that the Qty Allocated to HESB51DVD matches the Allocated quantity on the Item Inquiry window previously illustrated.

Close this window.

In addition to inquiries, you can find a lot of information on reports. The next table explains the information available under each reporting category.

Inventory Report Category	Information Available
Item	Item details, price lists, and purchasing options
Activity	Stock status, vendor activity, and physical inventory checklist
Analysis	Inventory turnover and other analysis reports
History	Transaction, distribution, and sales history
Posting Journals	Reprints of reports printed after posting
Setup	Reports on item setup, classes, and pricing levels

Table 4:2 Inventory Report Categories

Click **Activity** and select **Stock Status**. Highlight the report named **CurrStockReport** and print it to the screen. Scroll to the last page of the report and locate **Inventory Value**. (See Figure 4:23.)

User Date: 03/31/07 — Note the system date

STOCK STATUS REPORT
S&S, Incorporated

Page: 3
User ID: sa

Item Number	Item Description	Qty Back Ordered	Qty On Order	Qty Requisitioned	Qty On Hand	Qty Allocated	Current Cost	Inventory Value
TVPS60HDTV	Pasanovic 60 Inch Widescreen HDTV	0	0	0	23	0	$1,905.00	$43,815.00
TVSB52W	Subishi 52 Inch Widescreen DLP	0	0	0	9	0	$1,860.00	$16,740.00
TVSN34W	Sunyung 34 Inch Widescreen	0	0	0	35	0	$2,200.00	$77,000.00
TVSN42W	Sunyung 42 Inch Widescreen Projection	0	0	0	7	0	$1,365.00	$9,555.00
TVSN50W	Sunyung 50 Inch Widescreen Projection	0	0	0	30	0	$1,610.00	$48,300.00
TVSP37P	SonicPan 37 Inch Plasma	0	0	0	10	0	$1,070.00	$10,700.00

Grand Totals: Items 38 — Inventory Value $1,050,713.01

Figure 4:23 Last Page of Stock Status Report

This is a vital report for reconciling the Inventory Control Series to the inventory general ledger account. The value circled on the above illustration must match the balance in the general ledger inventory account on the report date (i.e., March 31, 2007).

We will now confirm that it does. Activate the **Financial** home page. First, click **Series Posting** and post any suspended transactions Next, click **Summary** under **Inquiry** and look up the inventory account. (See Figure 4:24.) *(Note: Your balances will differ from those illustrated if you have practiced transactions; however, your balances should still reconcile to each other.)*

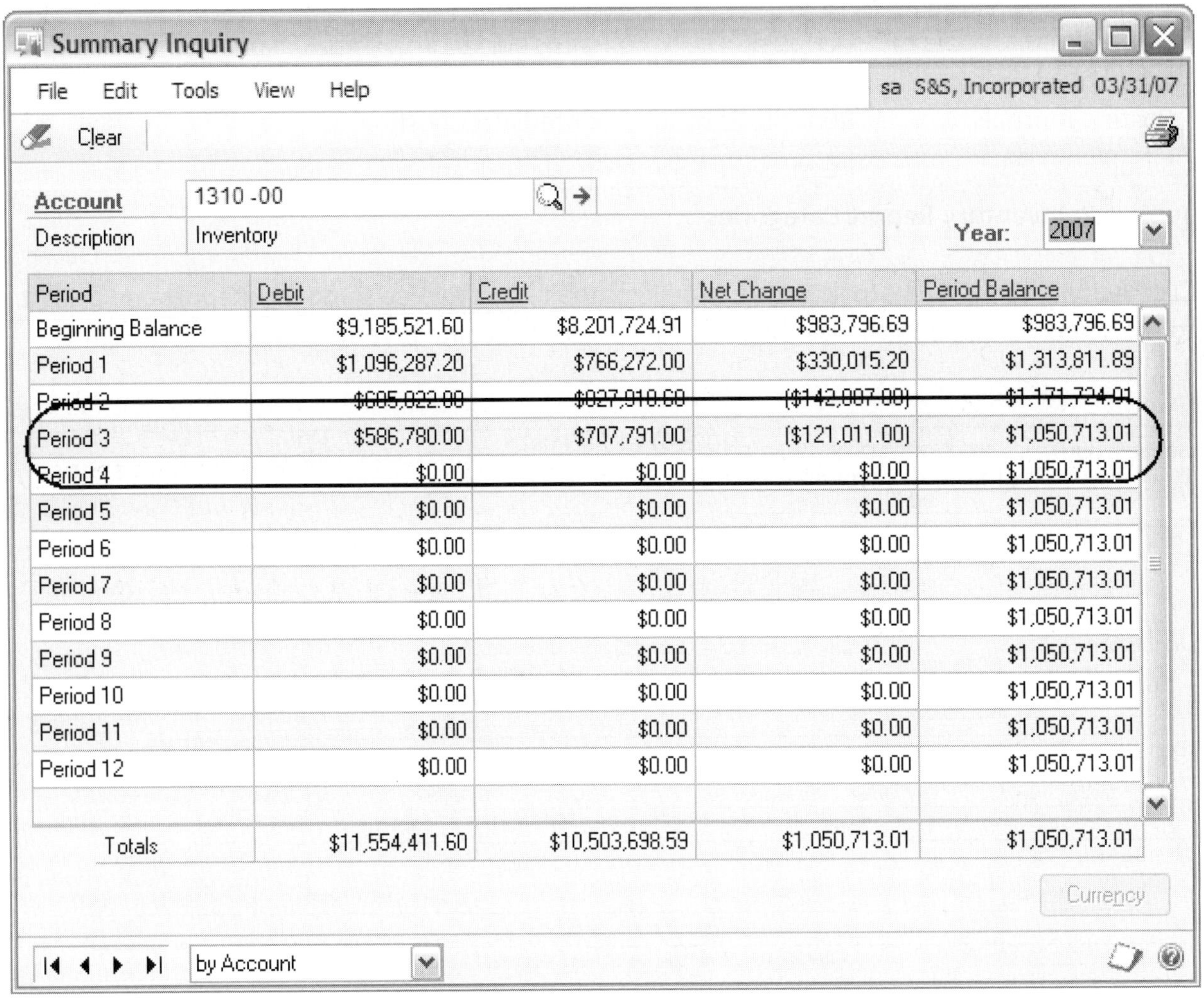

Period	Debit	Credit	Net Change	Period Balance
Beginning Balance	$9,185,521.60	$8,201,724.91	$983,796.69	$983,796.69
Period 1	$1,096,287.20	$766,272.00	$330,015.20	$1,313,811.89
Period 2	$605,022.00	$827,910.60	($142,087.88)	$1,171,724.01
Period 3	$586,780.00	$707,791.00	($121,011.00)	$1,050,713.01
Period 4	$0.00	$0.00	$0.00	$1,050,713.01
Period 5	$0.00	$0.00	$0.00	$1,050,713.01
Period 6	$0.00	$0.00	$0.00	$1,050,713.01
Period 7	$0.00	$0.00	$0.00	$1,050,713.01
Period 8	$0.00	$0.00	$0.00	$1,050,713.01
Period 9	$0.00	$0.00	$0.00	$1,050,713.01
Period 10	$0.00	$0.00	$0.00	$1,050,713.01
Period 11	$0.00	$0.00	$0.00	$1,050,713.01
Period 12	$0.00	$0.00	$0.00	$1,050,713.01
Totals	$11,554,411.60	$10,503,698.59	$1,050,713.01	$1,050,713.01

Figure 4:24 Inventory General Ledger Balance

The value on the report matches the balance in the account. Reconciling the Inventory Control Series to the Financial Series is an important internal control procedure. If you want to run a Stock Status Report as of a specific date then choose the Historical Stock Status reporting category.

You have now finished the chapter. Close all open windows and move to the exercises that follow.

Level One and Two Questions

1. Review information for item DCSM10XDZ. When S&S sells 10 of these items to a customer, what amount posts to the cost of goods sold account? (Assume there are no additional purchases before the sale posts.)

2. What is the sales price for one item of TVSP37P?

3. Explain why companies may want to incorporate a variety of inventory pricing levels.

4. Ashton wants to ensure that Ori Corporation delivers items on time. Use a report in the Inventory Control Series that shows the average lead time for deliveries from the vendor.

5. Ashton is concerned that idle inventory is tying up cash. Use a report in the Inventory Control Series to analyze his concerns.

Chapter 5 REVENUE CYCLE AND GP SALES SERIES

CHAPTER OVERVIEW

We are now ready to begin processing sales transactions and performing other revenue cycle activities using the Sales Series. This chapter presents information as follows:

- Level One: Use GP to perform revenue cycle activities. Begin with an overview of cycle activities and departments and then proceed to capturing transactions, posting, and reporting. Along this path, you will encounter internal control procedures for the revenue cycle. You will also perform month-end and year-end closing procedures for the Series.

- Level Two: Shift focus to internal control options set under Sales Series setup. These options affect compliance with internal control objectives.

Level One covers:

- Overview of Sales Series home page and its connection to revenue cycle activities portrayed in an REA diagram.
- Performing revenue cycle activities, including managing customer, entering sales order entry, fulfilling orders, invoicing customers, posting credit and debit memos, recording returns of inventory, writing-off invoices, and posting customer payments.
- Using reports as control tools for monitoring performance and triggering department activities
- Month-ending and year-ending the Sales Series

Level Two covers:

- Implementing internal controls through Sales Series setup
- Implementing additional controls through customer cards

Level One

Before performing revenue cycle activities, we must first understand activities for this cycle.[12] Figure 5:1 depicts revenue cycle activities as performed by departments and the triggers that initiate department activities. Ovals signify commencement and termination of an activity, rectangles denote activity processes, and parallelograms represent documents triggering or controlling activities. Additionally, threats in the cycle are listed beneath each department along with internal controls that mitigate these threats. The revenue cycle diagram forms a roadmap for discussions to follow and should be referred to frequently while reading this chapter.

Let's begin at the point of initiating cycle activities, namely customers place orders with the sales department. Throughout the day, sales employees enter customer orders in the Sales Series and assess inventory availability, issue back orders for out-of-stock items, check customer credit, answer customer inquiries, and print sales order documentation.

Employees print sales documentation immediately for sales needing to immediately ship or at the end of the day. Documentation includes sales orders and picking tickets. Sales orders serve as customer confirmation of the order and internal control over order processing. Picking tickets trigger activities in the warehouse.

Upon receipt of a picking ticket, warehouse employees begin filling the order by pulling inventory for the ticket. The ticket provides item descriptions, warehouse locations, and quantities ordered. As they pull items, employees enter fulfilled quantities through terminals accessing GP. The owners would like to fully automate the fulfillment process next year by adding barcode scanners, but for now employees pull up the order and manually enter fulfillment data. After entering this data, warehouse employees reprint the packing slip and send it with the items to the shipping department to trigger customer delivery.

Shipping activities begin by performing an inspection for quality and quantity. Employees recount quantities and compare items with the picking slip. Employees also spot-check merchandise for noticeable defects. After inspecting, employees prepare an external bill of lading because GP does not produce this document.[13] Finally, employees retrieve the original sales order from GP, enter any shipping costs from the bill of lading, and print a packing slip. The packing slip is boxed with the inventory and the order is then placed onto company trucks.

---

[12] For additional information on revenue cycle activities, refer to Romney and Steinbart, *Accounting Information Systems* (11th ed., Pearson Prentice Hall 2009), Chapter 10.

[13] GP resellers can create a customized report that prints bill of ladings.

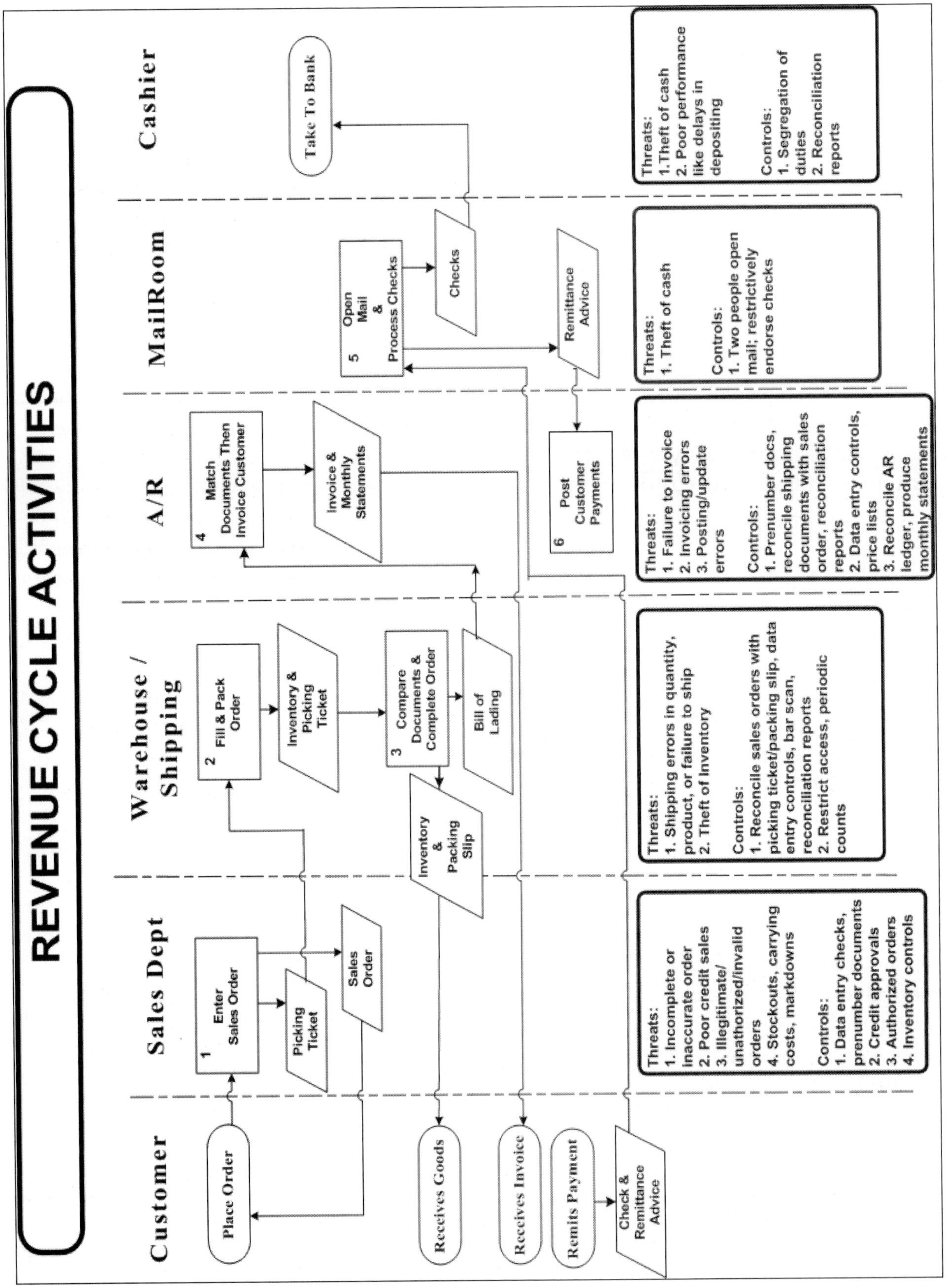

Figure 5:1 Revenue Cycle Activities

The driver carries a copy of the bill of lading for customer signature. Another copy is forwarded to accounts receivable; thus, triggering customer invoicing.[14]

Control over finalizing an order lies within the accounts receivable department. Upon receipt of the bill of lading, department employees independently check shipping department performance by comparing the bill of lading to the original sales order in GP. Employees pull up the fulfilled order, verify shipping charges, and then transfer the order to an invoice. The invoice triggers recognition of sales revenue and cost of goods sold. The invoice is then mailed to the customer and all documents cancelled and filed.

INTERNAL CONTROLS

While S&S implements internal controls early in the cycle, our explanation on the shipping department's order inspection is your first encounter with an independent check on performance. This check serves to control order quality, accuracy, and customer satisfaction. For companies with large sales volume, shipping employees do not usually perform an inspection of every order because this would be and inefficient use of employee time. However, these companies may institute quality control inspection programs that statistically sample orders throughout the day to control warehouse performance.

Accounts receivable employees are also responsible for mailing customers monthly statements that list invoices and payments. S&S offers 30 day payment terms to most of its customers, inferring that invoice payments should arrive approximately 30 days after invoicing.

S&S pays close attention to cash flow as well as revenue because cash is required to pay vendors for inventory purchases and employees for services. Consequently, any inefficiency in entering sales orders, fulfilling, shipping, and/or invoicing negatively impact cash flow. In turn, this can result seeking external financing to meet operating requirements.

After invoicing, revenue cycle activities shift focus towards collecting. Customer payments arrive in the mailroom. For internal control reasons, S&S always has two employees open the mail. One will process remittance advices while the other will process customer payments. For payments sent without a remittance advice, the employee processing remittances prepares a substitute document listing customer name, check number, and payment.[15] This employee then totals remittances and sends advices, along with the control total, to the accounts receivable

[14] While invoicing a customer before actual delivery creates revenue recognition issues, S&S adjusts timing differences by posting adjusting entries prior to issuing financial statements. The cash flow benefits of invoicing at the point of shipping offset any costs of posting adjusting entries.

[15] For customers paying with a two-part check, the top portion of the check normally tears off and serves as the remittance advice. The remittance advice lists the invoices paid by the check. S&S also uses a preprinted monthly statement with a tear-off portion that can serve as a remittance advice.

department. Meanwhile, the second employee restrictively endorses customer checks.[16] Checks are then sent, along with a control total, to the cashier department for depositing.

Segregating mailroom activities mitigates threats to cash. Furthermore, recording customer remittances in the accounts receivable department and depositing checks in the cashier department segregates recording from custody. Recall from Chapter 3 that we explained segregation of duties.[17]

This completes our discussion on the roadmap of revenue cycle activities. We have provided only a glimpse into the flurry of activities performed in the cycle. Moreover, the challenge facing departments using GP is implementing this roadmap while enforcing strong internal controls.

Because cycle activities begin with customers placing orders, our discussion next turns to managing Sales Series customer records.

BILL OF LADING

The bill of lading is a legal contract between S&S and its customer. This document defines ownership of in-transit inventory and liability for shipping costs.[18] Ownership of in-transit inventory impacts accounting information and liability insurance for losses occurring during shipment.[19] Remember from earlier discussions that S&S transports customer orders so it uses FOB destination point. In Level Two we discuss this delivery method's impact on closing procedures. Furthermore, because S&S ships orders, it does not charge customers for delivery unless an order is rush delivered by an outside carrier.

---

[16] Restively endorsing a check means to stamp the back of the check "For Deposit Only." The stamp includes the bank name and account number.

[17] For additional information on segregating duties in the revenue cycle, refer to Romney and Steinbart, *Accounting Information Systems* (11th ed., Pearson Prentice Hall 2009), pgs. 221-223.

[18] Refer to the bill of lading example in Romney and Steinbart, *Accounting Information Systems* (11th ed., Pearson Prentice Hall 2009), p. 381.

[19] Title transfer affects revenue and asset recognition for the customer and the selling company. For the customer, inventory is not capitalized and liability not recognized until title transfers. For the seller, revenue is not recognized and inventory remains capitalized until title transfers.

CUSTOMER CARDS

As learned in Chapter 2, transaction records link to master records.
We will now review master records for the Sales Series, namely customer cards. Activate the Sales home page and click **Customer** under Cards. We will begin by managing existing customers and then create new customers. Remember that Appendix B provides a list of S&S's customers.

Look up customer **Rick's Specialty Goods**. (See Figure 5:2.)

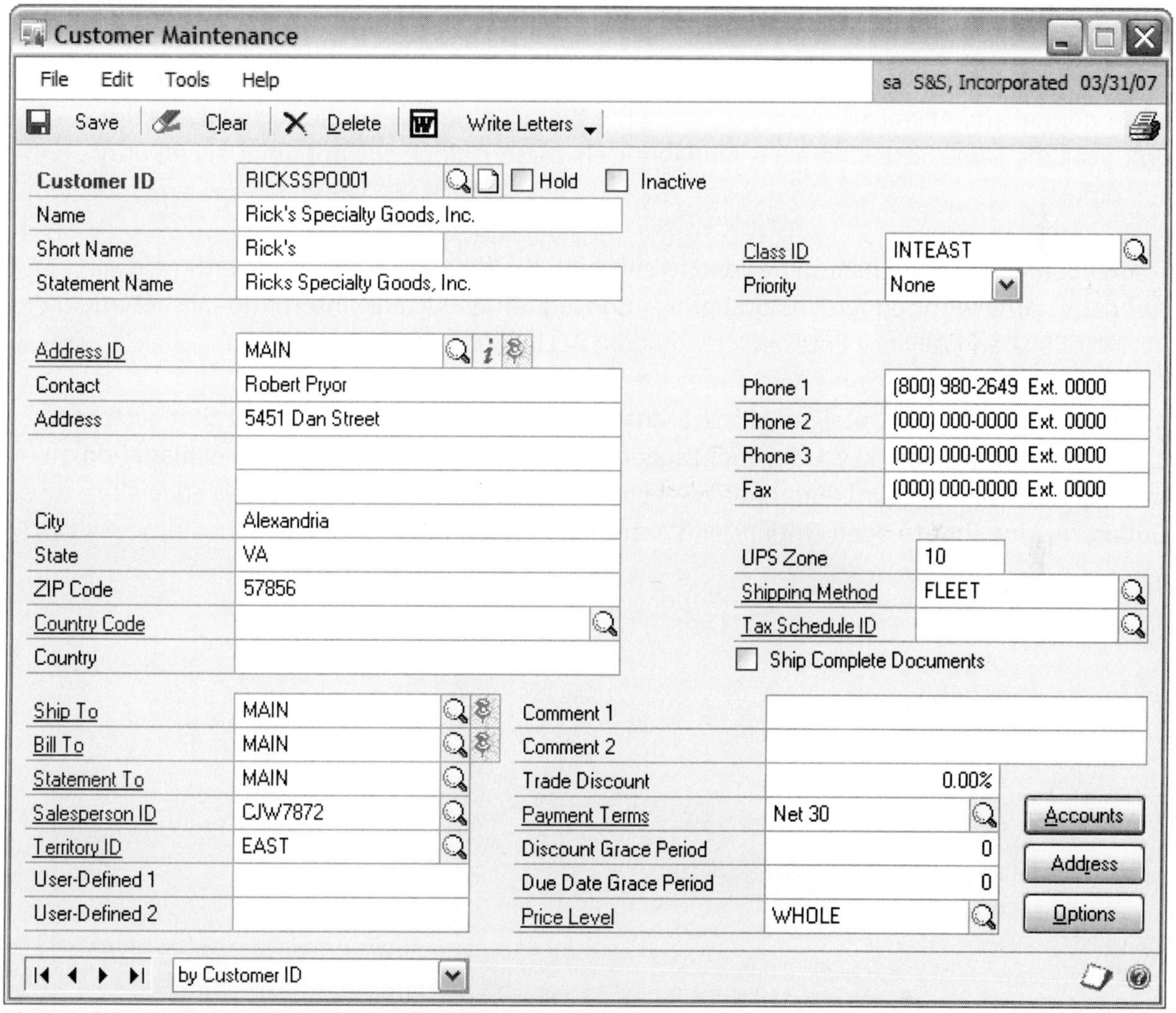

Figure 5:2 Customer Card for Rick's Specialty Goods

The window displays permanent information for the customer such as address and phone. **Customer ID** is the primary key and enforces entity integrity by helping to ensure that customers appear just once in the table. However, the primary key alone cannot ensure uniqueness. Companies must also institute strong controls over assigning Customer IDs.

Creating customer IDs is different from creating employee IDs. With the latter, you can use employee social security numbers as the primary key whereas customers do not come with candidate primary key information. To compensate, companies implement what is called a primary key assignment scheme.

> You can type RIC in the Customer ID field before launching the lookup window to advance to lookup list to customer IDs beginning with RIC.

Ashton has responsibility for developing an assignment scheme. When developing, he remembered that lookups are faster when you type the first few characters into the field before launching the lookup. So he decided to use something that would be easy to remember, namely the first eight letters of a customer's name. However, Ashton soon discovered that alphabetic characters alone will not work. For instance, if you had two customers, Alliance International and Alliance Enterprises, using the first eight letters of the company name produces the same letters. Hence, alphabetic characters alone will not uniquely identify customers.

To overcome this issue, Ashton decided to combine the first eight alphabetic letters in the company name with sequential numbering. Consequently, Alliance International's ID would be ALLIANCE001 and Alliance Enterprises would be ALLIANCE002.

Review the primary keys assigned to S&S' customers in Appendix B and notice that customer IDs employ this primary key assignment scheme. Also review Table 5:1 for an explanation on fields in a customer record. Continue to explore the customer record for Rick's Specialty Goods, making sure to open Options and Accounts windows.

Field	Description
Customer ID	Primary key for uniquely identifying customers.
Name, Short Name, and Statement Name	Company name is the legal name of the business. Short name can be used to shorten or nickname the company name. Statement name appears on printed customer statements.
Class ID	Links customers to a class for grouping those with similar attributes. Classes are also used for reporting and assigning defaults such as credit limit, general ledger accounts, and salesperson. Aside from speeding data entry when creating new customers, customer classes help to ensure data consistency among customers with similar attributes. Customer classes are managed by clicking Customer Class under Setup. Open this window to see that S&S groups customers by business operations such as big box stores, traditional retailers, and internet sellers.
Multiple Address fields	Address ID that identifies customer addresses. You can store multiple addresses for a customer such as a billing address and a business address. This is a required field because customers must be linked to at least one address. S&S uses the ID of Main to identify customer primary addresses. The Ship To, Bill To, and Statement To fields can be linked to other address IDs for the customer.
Shipping Method	Links customers to shipper records. You can open the maintenance window for shipper records by clicking the hyperlinked field name. Examples of shipping methods include UPS, FEDEX, or Fleet. GP does not automatically generate shipping costs so this link is for informational purposes only.
Tax Schedule ID	Links customers to sales tax records. You can open the maintenance window for sales tax records by clicking the hyperlinked field name. S&S is a wholesale distributor so customers are not linked to a Tax Schedule ID.
Salesperson ID	Links customers to the salesperson table. You can open the maintenance window for this table by clicking the hyperlinked field name or by clicking Salesperson under Cards. Salesperson records can be linked to either an Employee ID or a Vendor ID. If linked to a vendor, GP integrates sales commission liabilities with the vendor account. This integration is not available for employees.
Territory ID	Links customers to the territory table. You can open the maintenance window for this table by clicking the hyperlinked field name or by clicking Sales Territory under Cards. Territories enable regional sales reporting and S&S uses territories named East, Mid, and West.

Field	Description
Payment Terms	Links customers to the payment terms table. You can open the maintenance window for this table by clicking the hyperlinked field name. Payment terms are illustrated later in the chapter.
Price Level	Links customers to the inventory pricing table discussed in Chapter 4.
Accounts Button	Opens a window that stores default general ledger accounts used during Sales Series posting. As discussed in Chapter 4, S&S has chosen to use general ledger accounts on customer cards for sales transactions instead of accounts on inventory item cards. This option is viewed by clicking Sales Order Processing under Setup and noting that Customer is the option selected under Posting Accounts From.
Address Button	Opens a window for creating new and managing existing customer addresses.
Options Button	Opens a window for setting internal controls such as credit limit and maximum write-off. Contains other options that assess finance charges and set other defaults.

Table 5:1 Customer Record Fields

Managing existing customer information is easy. After retrieving the record, simply type in the new data and click Save. Customer ID is the only field that cannot be changed because it is the primary key and is linked to transaction records.

When you close the Customer Maintenance window before saving changes to the customer record, GP prompts you to save, discard, or delete the record. Of course, the Delete button removes a customer record, unless the customer has transaction history. When you inadvertently change information, use either the Clear button on the Customer Maintenance window or close the window using the x icon and click the Discard button when prompted.

We must emphasize that opening the Customer Maintenance window is an authorization function. Hence, permission to access should only be granted to employees with authorization duties. Granting access to unauthorized employees exposes the company to threats of poor credit sales, unauthorized sales, lost inventory, and lost cash.

For instance, suppose that a salesperson gets paid by commissions on sales. He/she would like a bigger paycheck and boosting sales would do the trick. This salesperson just received a big order from a customer but the order exceeds the customer's credit limit. Not wanting to lose the sale, he/she increases the credit limit so the sale goes through. The customer subsequently files bankruptcy and S&S never collects payment. You can resolve this issue two ways. First, pay commissions only after the customer pays. Better yet, deny salesperson permission to access the Customer Maintenance window.

Here is another scenario. This salesperson creates a fraudulent customer with his/her address, grants a high credit limit, and permits a high write-off amount. The salesperson then enters an order that ships to him/her and later posts a transaction to write-off the invoice. Here, motivation may be theft of inventory rather than commission boosting.

While continued concealment in either of the preceding scenario relies on lax controls in other areas of the cycle, the best way to mitigate these types of threats is controlling access to the Customer Maintenance window. Departments illustrated in our roadmap of the cycle should not have access to the Customer Maintenance window because these employees are involved with recording sales (sales department), custody of assets (warehouse/shipping /cashier departments), or recording invoices (accounts receivable department).

Try the next exercise on managing customer cards.

GP

1. Giggle Place, Inc. wants to add a new address for receiving shipments. This address is 1865 Illinois Avenue, Nashville, TN 47568. Create the new address and link it to the appropriate field(s) on the customer card. Note: Data involving UPS zone, shipping method, and salesperson remain the same.

2. Susan has approved increasing the credit limit of Fillards, Inc. to $300,000. In addition, she wants Fillards' payment terms extended to a 2% discount on payments made within 10 days. She asks that you make these changes on the customer card.

3. List three companies in the Midwest region. Which salesperson handles sales to these customers?

4. Which department should have authorization for creating new and managing existing customer cards?

5. Name the department that should have permission to modify noncritical customer data such as addresses or phone numbers? How can employees change noncritical data without accessing the Customer Maintenance window?

E5:1 Practice Managing Customer Cards

The only difference between managing customers and creating new customers is assigning a value to the Customer ID field. Now practice adding a new customer.

GP

The Controller of Electronic Connections, Susan Jones, is opening a new account with S&S. The company is located at 35 Park Avenue, Chicago, IL 60609. The phone number is 605-878-9970. Electronic Connections wants shipments sent to its warehouse located at 265 West Main Street, Menlo Park, Chicago 60610. The phone number at this location is 605-865-3304 and Alan Keith is the warehouse supervisor.

Ashton asks that you create the new account using his primary key assignment scheme. Electronic is in the TRADMID class. Accept all the defaults assigned by this class except change the credit limit to $100,000. Save the customer when finished. Why are the default general ledger accounts already present on the customer's card?

E5:2 Practice Adding a New Customer

SALES SERIES TRANSACTIONS

We have finally arrived at capturing sales transactions. Recall from our roadmap discussion that several departments perform revenue cycle activities. Accordingly, the Transaction category on the home page divides into tiers corresponding with cycle activities depicted in our roadmap. (See Figure 5:3.)

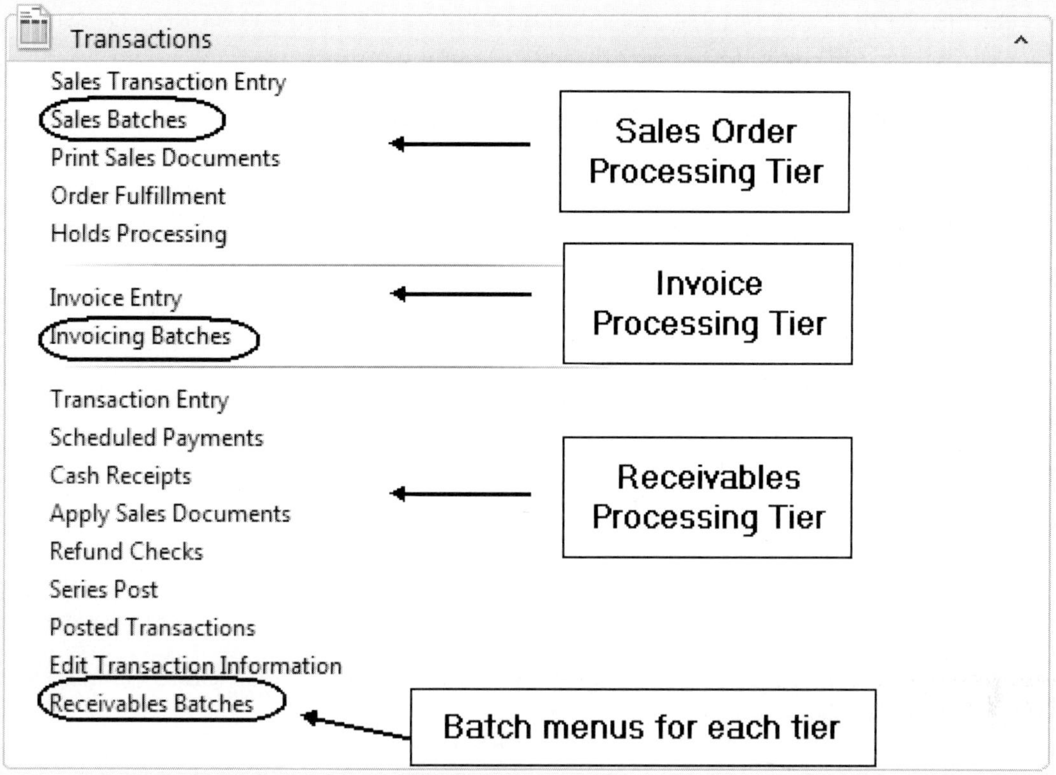

Figure 5:3: Sales Transaction Menu Tiers

Take a moment to become familiar with this tiered structuring. The Sales Order Processing Tier has menus for capturing sales orders, printing order documentation, and fulfilling orders. Employees in the sales, warehouse, and shipping departments work primarily in this tier. In addition, accounts receivable employees use this tier when transferring orders to invoices.

The Invoice Processing Tier has menus for creating invoices without creating a sales order first. The Receivables Processing Tier has menus for posting customer payments, credit memos and invoices for noninventoried sales. Accounts receivable employees work primarily in these two tiers.

Notice that each tier contains a separate menu for creating batches. Individual transactions are created by clicking Sales Transaction Entry, Invoice Entry, or Transaction Entry, depending on the tier. Transaction windows for each tier function differently and are illustrated in Figure 5:4.

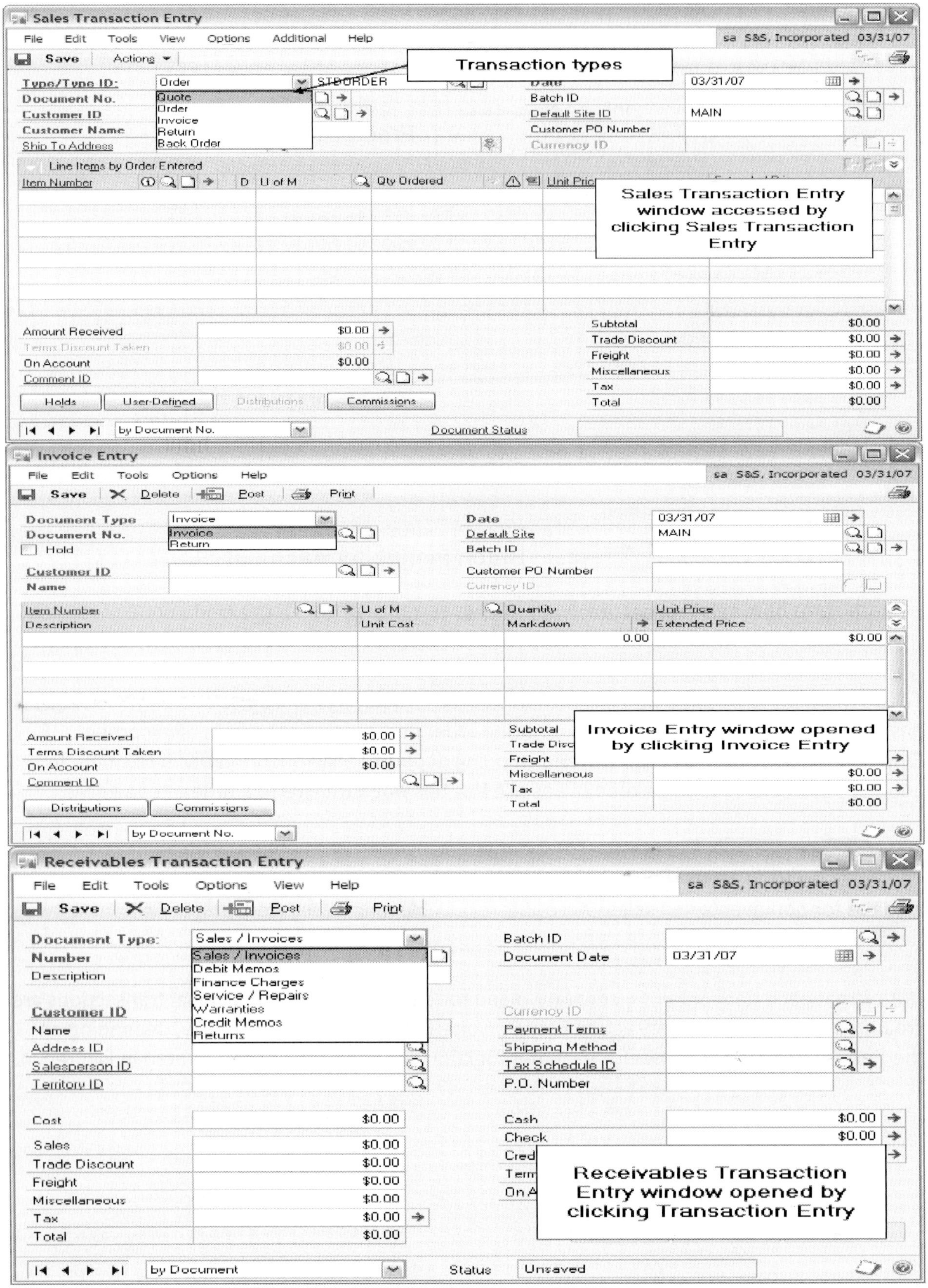

Figure 5:4 Sales Series Transaction Windows

Note that each window originates a different transaction type and may contain different fields. All windows can originate invoice transactions; however, the Receivables Transaction Entry window does interface with inventory items because it lacks an Item Number field. Additionally, sales orders can only be originated from the Sales Transaction Entry window.

To understand how tiers function differently, review an REA diagram for the revenue cycle.[20] (See Figure 5:5.)

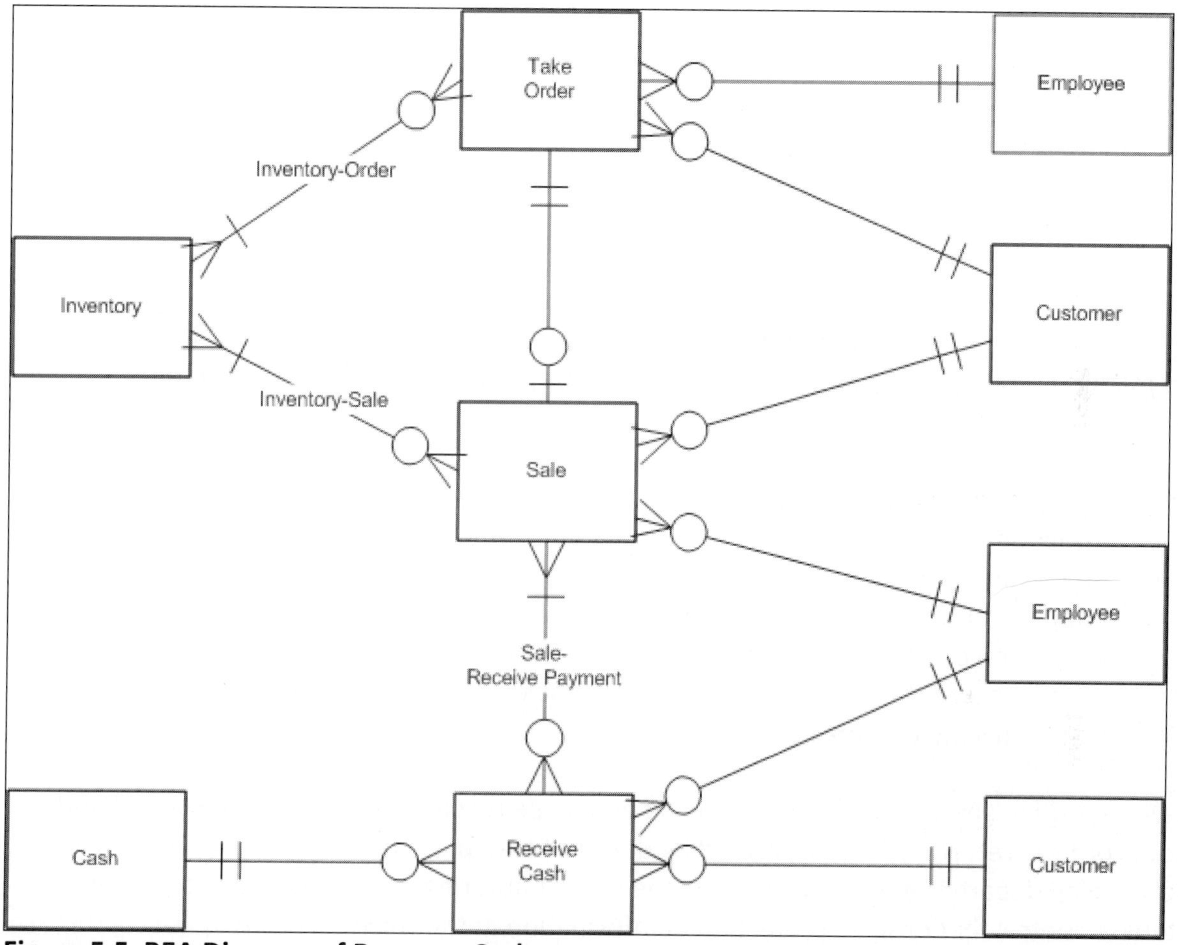

Figure 5:5 REA Diagram of Revenue Cycle

The diagram is read from left to right and as three distinct columns. The first column are company Resources (i.e., inventory and cash). The second shows Events (i.e., order, sale and receive cash transactions) affecting resources. The last are the Agents (i.e., employees and customers) participating in events. Squares and named lines represent separate entities (i.e., table).

In GP terms, resource and agent squares are master tables whereas event squares are transaction tables. Named lines connecting resources to events are also transaction tables (i.e.,

[20] See Romney and Steinbart, *Accounting Information Systems* (11th ed., Pearson Prentice Hall 2009), p. 569.

linking tables). You can think of the Sales Order Processing Tier as corresponding to the Take Order event; the Invoice Processing Tier as corresponding to the Sale event, and the Receivables Processing Tier as corresponding to the Receive Cash event. Accordingly, sales order (i.e., Sales Order Processing Tier) link to the inventory table. Sales invoices (i.e., Invoice Processing Tier) link to the inventory table. However, invoices entered under receive cash (i.e., Receivables Processing Tier) cannot link to the inventory table. Likewise, cash can only be entered through the Receivables Processing Tier because these are the only transactions linked to the Cash table.

So how do you know where to record a customer return of inventory because all the windows originate Returns? You now know that the Receivables Transaction window does not link to inventory so we have ruled out this window. Remaining tiers interact with inventory and either can be used to record the return. The window to use becomes a function of operating procedures and internal control policies.

Let's look at internal control scenarios for handling a customer return of inventory to the shipping department where the salesperson is unaware of the return. *(Note: Either scenario that follows is implemented by setting the user access permissions discussed in Chapter 3.)*

Scenario One: Company policies require shipping employees to enter the return through the Sales Transaction Entry window but permission to post the return is denied. Instead, the accounts receivable department posts the return after contacting the sales department for authorization. In other words, this scenario separates inventory custody, return authorization, and transaction recording. An accounts receivable employee contacts the salesperson for authorization because the salesperson initiated the sale and holds a stake in protecting commissions and satisfying the customer.

However, you might ask, "Didn't the shipping employee receive the inventory (custody) and also record the return?" Actually, recording does not take place until the transaction posts. The shipping department merely captured the data. Capturing data as early as possible is a database control that ensures protection of information at the source. When assessing threats, you should always recognize the possibility of losing control over a transaction. Internal control policies that capture returns in shipping ensure monitoring transactions through GP reporting, thus mitigating the threat of lost data.

Scenario Two: Company policies require shipping employees to notify the salesperson upon receipt of returned inventory. Sales employees use the Sales Transaction Entry window to enter the data while posting remains in the accounts receivable department. However, this policy threatens data loss should the salesperson forget to enter the return. Failing to capture the data means that monitoring resides only in the employee's memory. *(Note: Policies should require the sales department to enter returns when the customer contacts a sales employee before returning inventory.)*

Scenario Three: Company policies require shipping employees to notify the accounts receivable department. Accounts receivable clerks enter the return using the Invoice Entry window. Once again, we have the threat of data loss by delaying capturing the transaction.

You will better understand Sales Series menu tiers after finishing this chapter. For now, know that each tier serves a distinct purpose and that transactions initiated in one tier must be finalized in that tier. For instance, a return entered through the Invoice Processing Tier must be posted using that tier.

SALES DEPARTMENT ACTIVITIES

The sales department serves as the primary point of contact for customers. Sales personnel interact with customers by taking orders and responding to customer inquiries on pricing, inventory availability, anticipated delivery dates, outstanding account balances, payment terms, and pricing discounts. Furthermore, salespeople analyze sales trends, focus on customer satisfaction, and search for additional ways to enhance company revenue. Given that customer orders initiate revenue cycle activities, we begin with capturing orders before moving to other sales department activities.

Sales Orders and Batches

All sales orders must be saved to a batch. To understand this requirement, return to our roadmap discussion and note that a sales order is processed by several departments. First, the order is created by the sales department. Next, it is filled by the warehouse and shipped by the shipping department. Finally, the accounts receivable department transfers it to an invoice. To complete all these steps, you must save the order and, in GP, that means you must assign it to a batch.

There is another reason for this requirement, namely the revenue recognition principal stating that revenue is recognized when earned or deemed to have been earned. For inventory sales, revenue is not earned until legal title transfers per the bill of lading. This means that revenue is earned upon shipment of the inventory. Hence, GP will not post sales orders. Instead, you must transfer the order to an invoice and then post the invoice to recognize revenue.

One last concept before we begin capturing sales orders. S&S uses company trucks to ship inventory to customers and its shipment terms are FOB destination point, meaning title legally transfers when inventory is received by the customer. This also means that S&S bears the risk of loss for in-transit inventory.

These shipping terms contradict with company procedures that posts invoices upon shipment. However, recall that a company must also focus on cash flow as well as revenue. Invoicing customers upon shipment speeds up customer collection and any timing difference that conflicts with the revenue recognition principle can be adjusted through reversing journal entries made prior to issuing financial statements.

Let us now begin capturing orders.

1. Click **Sales Batches** and refer to Figure 5:6 to create a batch. *Note: Naming the batch with a prefix of SO identifies the batch as containing sales orders.*

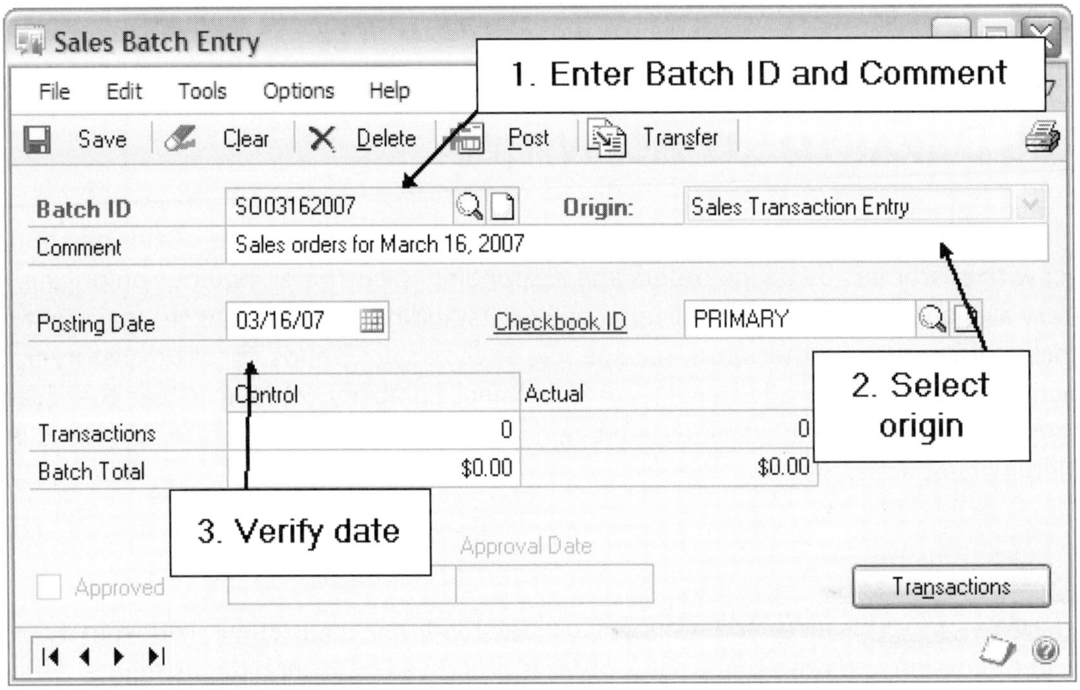

Figure 5:6 Sales Batch Entry

2. Click **Transactions** and refer to Figure 5:7 to create an order to Better Buy.

> Note that the Distributions button in the Sales Transaction Entry window is grayed out, reinforcing the point that sales orders do not post.

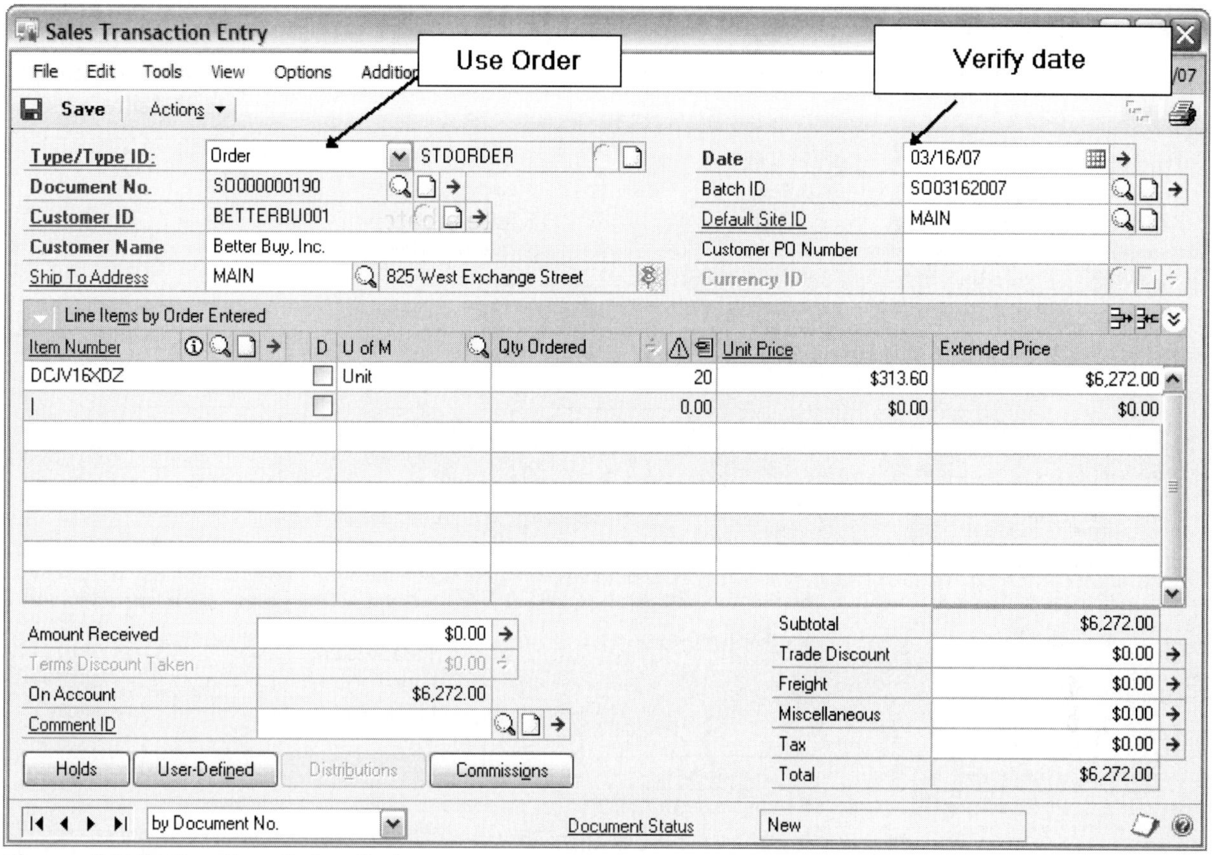

Figure 5:7 Better Buy Sales Order

3. Click to expand line item details as illustrated next and review Table 5:2 describing fields in this window.

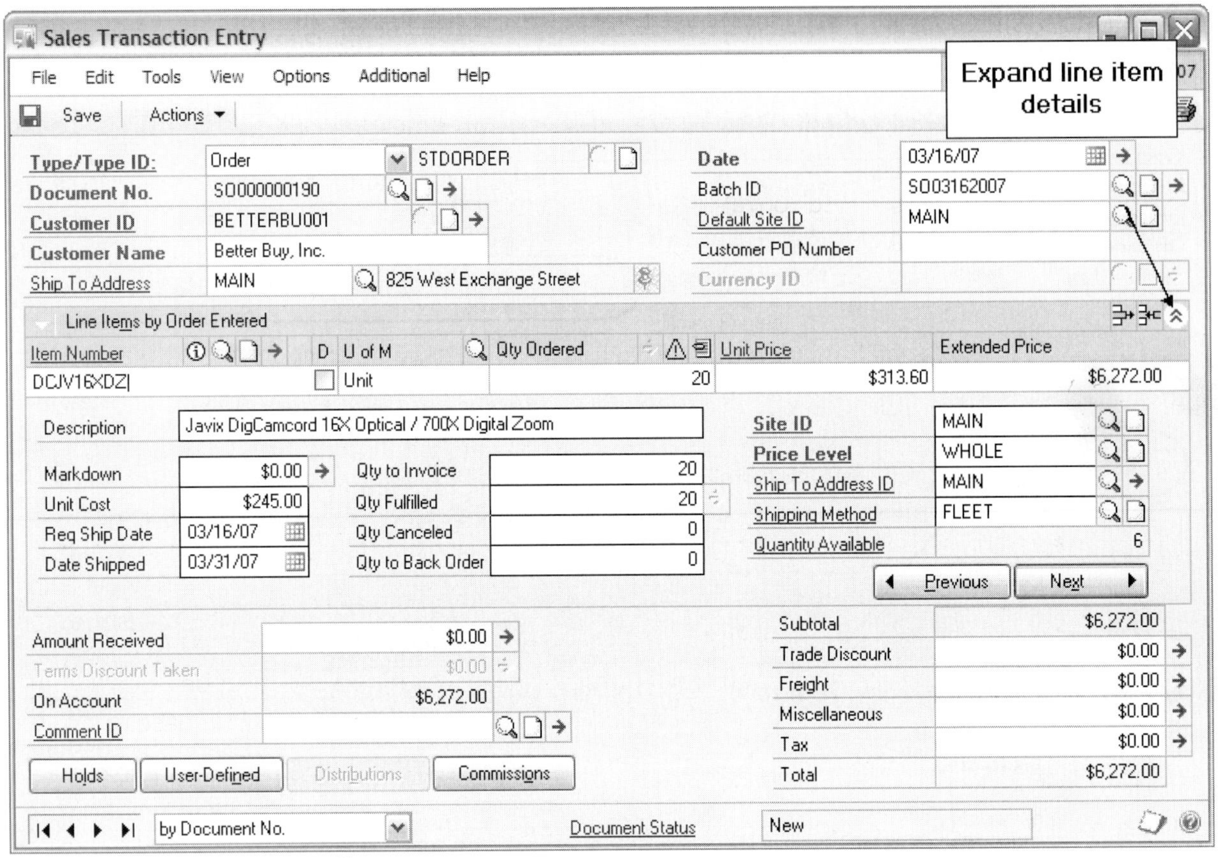

Figure 5:8 Line Item Details

> Did you want what information is located under the Commissions button?
>
> The Commission window stores the sales commission percentage and amount. The salesperson defaults from the customer card and the commission rate defaults from salesperson card. The salesperson and rate can be changed on the transaction without affecting defaults. For orders that split commissions, enter additional salespeople and adjust commission percentages.

4. Click **Save** to store the order and then close the Sales Transaction Entry window. Keep the Sales Batch Entry window for the next exercise.

Field	Description
Actions Button	Contains commands to Transfer, Purchase, Delete, and Void. **Transfer** is used to transfer an order to an invoice. **Purchase** is used to generate a purchase order in the Purchasing Series. **Delete** is used to remove all traces of the transaction. **Void** is used to cancel the transaction and retain history of it.
Type/ Type ID	Document type identifies the transaction source and determines subsequent transaction processing. Choices are Quote, Order, Invoice, Return, and Back Order. **Quote** is used to store information given to customers seeking to buy. You can then report on and track potential sales. This type can later be transferred to an order or invoice if the customer decides to purchase. **Order** is used to capture customer sales requiring inventory shipment. After shipping, the document is transferred to an invoice. **Invoice** can be used instead of Order when sales are immediate (i.e., no shipping required). Invoices are also created by transferring a Quote or Order. **Return** is used for processing customer returns of inventory. **Back Order** is used when on-hand inventory is insufficient to fill the quantity ordered (i.e., for inventory currently out of stock). You can instruct GP to automatically generate back orders when entering the order or invoice.
Document No.	Uniquely identifies the transaction. GP autofills and sequentially increments these numbers. Document numbers form part of the audit trail discussed in Chapter 4.
Customer ID	Customer ID links the transaction to the customer. Transactions can be entered for existing or new customers created "on the fly." *(Note: creating a customer "on the fly" means to enter a new Customer ID so that GP prompts to add the customer record. Remember that proper segregation of duties dictate that customer creation remain separate from transaction recording, so "on the fly" creation should be prohibited.)*
Customer Name	Auto-fills from the customer record. This feature is called closed loop verification, meaning that the selection of data for one field (i.e., Customer ID) automatically fills in data for related fields.

Field	Description
Ship To Address	Address for shipping the inventory and functions as the shipping address for the entire transaction. Autofills from the default shipping address on the customer card. You can change the address when needed without affecting the default on the customer card. To change, click the hyperlinked field name and select a different Address ID from the customer card.
Date	This is called the transaction date. For Quotes and Orders, this date is used to monitor future processing of the transaction. For all other types, this date determines when the transaction was posted to financial records.
Batch ID	Assigns the transaction to a batch. Transactions without a Batch ID must be posted immediately. You can create a new batch from this field by typing a unique Batch ID. You can also assign a transaction to a different batch by looking up to select an existing batch.
Default Site ID	Default location storing the inventory. Remember, S&S maintains one location, namely Main.
Customer PO Number	Stores the customer purchase order number. Companies often request PO numbers to validate authorization to place the order. POs also serve as legal documents to enforce the transaction. This field is not required because not all customers use a PO system.
Item Number	Stores either an Item ID linked from the inventory table or a free-form description for noninventoried items. In Level Two, we illustrate that S&S inventories all items it sells, including service charges, so entering a free-form description is denied.
D check box	Box checked when drop shipping items to a customer. Drop shipments are items shipped directly to the customer by the vendor (i.e., the inventory never comes into the selling company's warehouse). Drop shipments are often used for selling out of stock items.
U of M	Links to Unit of Measure table discussed in Chapter 4 and defaults from the item card.
Qty Ordered	The quantity to enter must be coordinated with the U of M field. For instance, if UOM is Unit (i.e., individual items) and quantity is 30 then the customer ordered 30 individual items. However, if UOM is Case12 and quantity is 30 then the customer ordered 360 individual items (i.e., 30 times 12).
Unit Price	Price per unit, which defaults from the item price list discussed in Chapter 4.
Extended Price	Item quantity times item price.
Site ID	Defaults from the item; however, can be changed if shipping the item from a different warehouse.

Field	Description
Price Level	Defaults from customer card and used to implement tiered sales pricing (i.e., discount or wholesale price). You can use a different price level for each line item. S&S uses one price level, namely WHOLE.
Ship To Address ID	Defaults from Ship To Address entered in the top section of the transaction. Changing the ID on a line item directs that portion of the order to ship to a different location.
Shipping Method	Method used to ship inventory. Defaults from the customer card and can be changed to customize shipping.
Quantity Available	Quantity available displays the remaining quantity available for sale after entering the order quantity on the line item. This quantity excludes items on outstanding customer orders.
Markdown	Clicking the arrow on the field opens a window for entering markdowns on price. Markdowns can be entered as a percent of the unit sales price or as a specific dollar discount.
Unit Cost	Cost per item, which defaults from the item card. The amount displayed will not always equal the amount that posts to cost of goods sold when invoicing because inventory cost layers or average costs may change between the time of placing the order and invoicing the customer.
Req Ship Date	Ship date that needs to be met to deliver the order on time. S&S strives to ship customer orders on the date placed.
Date Shipped and Qty Fulfilled	Date S&S actually ships the order and quantity shipped. For S&S, the Sales Series is set to fulfill orders during order entry; however, many companies use a separate fulfillment process that requires performing a second step to enter the ship date and quantities shipped.
Qty Canceled	Used to cancel quantities on order after printing the order. This field is useful for tracking lost sales due to order cancellations.
Qty to Back Order	Difference between ordered quantities and on-hand quantities. The Purchase command under Actions creates purchase orders for back ordered items.
Transaction totals at bottom right	Subtotal automatically calculates based on line item totals. You must manually enter Trade Discount, Freight, and Miscellaneous charges. Tax defaults from the sales tax rate on the customer card.

Table 5:2 Descriptions for Fields in Sales Transaction Entry Window

Printing Batch and Edit Lists

You will now print control reports that verify data entry by following the next instructions.

1. Return to the Sales Batch Entry window and look up batch SO03162007.

2. Click the **Printer** icon located on the top right of the window. Click the dropdown on Print to view printing options and review the table that follows explaining these options.

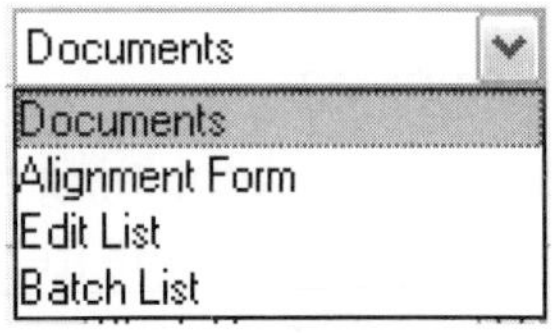

Figure 5:9 Batch Window Print Options

Print Option	Description
Documents	Prints sales order, picking ticket, packing slip, invoice, return, and backorder forms.
Alignment Form	Sends a test pattern to the printer to align preprinted stock before printing forms.
Edit List	Prints transaction details for invoices and returns in the batch (i.e., documents that post).
Batch List	Print details for all transactions in the batch.

Table 5:3 Batch Window Print Options

3. You will print sales order documents in the next exercise so choose **Edit List** and click Print Print . Send output to the screen. The report lists no transactions because the batch contains only sales orders, which do not post. Close the report.

4. Return to the Sales Batch Entry window and click the **Printer** icon again. This time choose **Batch List** and click **Print**. This report displays details for transactions in the batch. (See Figure 5:10.)

```
                                        S&S, Incorporated                               Page:     1
User Date:  03/16/07                    Sales Batch List                                User ID: sa
                                     Sales Order Processing

Batch ID:        SO03162007
Batch Comment: Sales orders for March 16, 2007

Approved:                         Batch Total Actual:          $6,272.00     Batch Total Control:              $0.00
Approved By:                      Trx Total Actual:                    1     Trx Total Control:                    0
Approval Date:        00/00/00

* Allocation Attempted      ^ Repeating Document

Type   Document Number   Doc Date   Post Date  Customer ID      Name                          Salesperson      Workflow Status
-------------------------------------------------------------------------------------------------------------------------------
           Subtotal      Trade Discount     Freight Amount       Misc Amount          Tax Amount        Document Total   Discount Avail
-------------------------------------------------------------------------------------------------------------------------------
ORD    SO000000190       03/16/07   00/00/00   BETTERBU001      Better Buy, Inc.              ASL6677          Workflow Not Activated
          $6,272.00           $0.00              $0.00               $0.00              $0.00         $6,272.00            $0.00

Approved:                         Batch Total Actual:          $6,272.00     Batch Total Control:              $0.00
Approved By:                      Trx Total Actual:                    1     Trx Total Control:                    0
Approval Date:        00/00/00

* Allocation Attempted      ^ Repeating Document

Type   Document Number   Doc Date   Post Date  Customer ID      Name                          Salesperson      Workflow Status
-------------------------------------------------------------------------------------------------------------------------------
           Subtotal      Trade Discount     Freight Amount       Misc Amount          Tax Amount        Document Total   Discount Avail
-------------------------------------------------------------------------------------------------------------------------------
ORD    SO000000190       03/16/07   00/00/00   BETTERBU001      Better Buy, Inc.              ASL6677          Workflow Not Activated
          $6,272.00           $0.00              $0.00               $0.00              $0.00         $6,272.00            $0.00

Item Number                       Description                                                    Markdown
                                  U of M    Site                          Quantity           Unit Price        Extended Price
------------------------------    --------  ----------          --------------------   --------------------  --------------------
DCJV16XDZ                         Javix DigCamcord 16X Optical / 700X Digital Zoom                  $0.00
                                  Unit      MAIN                                20                $313.60             $6,272.00
                                                                                                          --------------------
                                                                                                                    $6,272.00

Salesperson Name                  Sales Territory ID          Comm %      % of Sale          Sales Amount     Commission Amount
------------------------------    ------------------------  -----------  -----------   --------------------  --------------------
Levine, April                     MID                            0.30%      100.00%              6,272.00                 18.82
                                                                                       --------------------  --------------------
                                                                                                $6,272.00                $18.82

           Subtotal      Trade Discount     Freight Amount       Misc Amount          Tax Amount        Document Total   Discount Avail
   ----------------  ----------------  ----------------  ------------------  ------------------  --------------------  ----------------
          $6,272.00           $0.00              $0.00               $0.00              $0.00         $6,272.00            $0.00
   ================  ================  ================  ==================  ==================  ====================  ================
```

Totals for transctions in the batch

Figure 5:10 Batch List Report

5. Close the report and the Sales Batch Entry window.

Edit Lists are control reports that document batch transactions ready to post to general ledger accounts. This report should be printed and verified prior to posting.

On the other hand, Batch Lists are control reports that document all transactions in a batch and should be printed prior to printing sales documents.

Control reports are tools used to ensure the integrity of data entry. These reports permit a visual review of transactions prior to printing sales order documents and posting transactions.

To illustrate the importance of printing a Batch List prior to printing sales documents, we now discuss the types of errors that can occur during sales order entry.

First, you can select the wrong customer. If the order ships, the company will incur added costs or perhaps even a loss in attempting to recover the items. Moreover, the company can lose the customer waiting for their order.

Second, you could select the wrong item or quantity on the order. Again, the company risks losing the customer and bears added costs to correct the shipment. A review of batch lists prior to producing sales order documents mitigates this risk.

You will print sales documents in the next exercise. Although you can print these documents from the Sales Batch Entry window, we want to show you another way to print.

Printing Sales Order Documents

You will now print sales order documents that confirm orders with customers and trigger activities in other departments.

1. Click **Print Sales Documents** under Transactions, choose **Order**, and mark all three **Include** options. Also enter criteria to select the batch. (See Figure 5:11.) *(Note: You have a choice of printing Quote, Order, Invoice, Return, Back Order, and In-Trans Transfer document types.)*

   Note that Include options print all the sales documents we discussed in our roadmap.

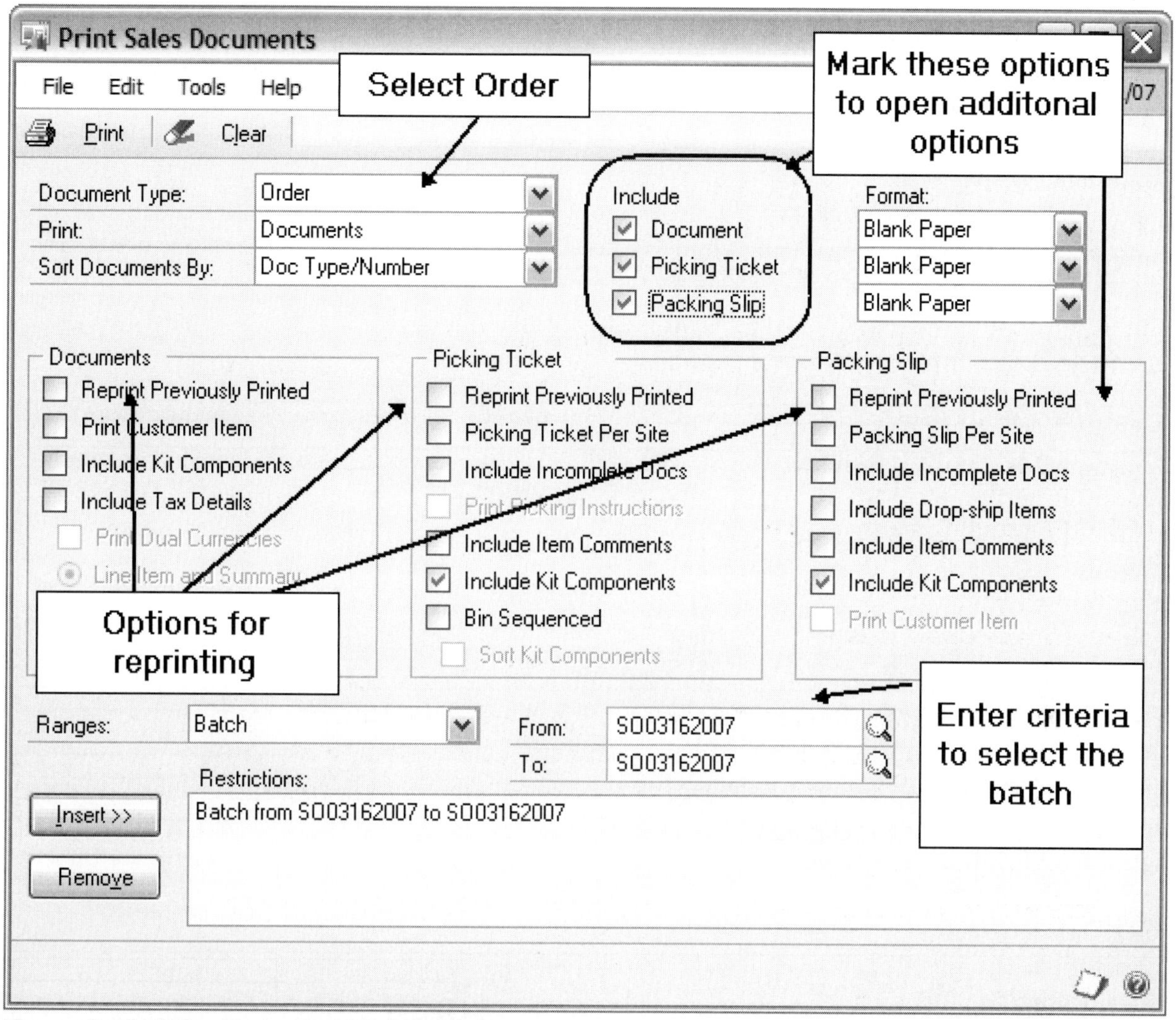

Figure 5:11 Sales Document Print Options

2. Click **Print** and send the documents to the screen. The sales order prints first (Figure 5:12), then the packing slip (Figure 5:13), and finally the picking ticket (Figure 5:14).

S&S, Incorporated

Order	SO000000190
Date	03/16/07
Page	1

Bill To:

Better Buy, Inc.
825 West Exchange Street
Chicago IL 60609

Ship To:

Better Buy, Inc.
825 West Exchange Street
Chicago IL 60609

Purchase Order No.	Customer ID	Salesperson ID	Shipping Method	Payment Terms	Req Ship Date	Master No.
	BETTERBU001	ASL6677	FLEET	2% 10/Net 30	03/16/07	194

Ordered	Shipped	B/O	Item Number	Description	Discount	Unit Price	Ext. Price
20	20	0	DCJV16XDZ	Javix DigCamcord 16X Optical / 700X Digital	$0.00	$313.60	$6,272.00

Subtotal	$6,272.00
Misc	$0.00
Tax	$0.00
Freight	$0.00
Trade Discount	$0.00
Total	$6,272.00

Figure 5:12 Printed Sales Order

S&S, Incorporated

Packing Slip	SO000000190
Document Date	03/16/07
Page	1
Who Printed	sa
Date/Time Printed	[illegible]

Bill To:

Better Buy, Inc.
825 West Exchange Street
Chicago IL 60609

Ship To:

Better Buy, Inc.
825 West Exchange Street
Chicago IL 60609

* Item Shipped Directly from Vendor

Purchase Order No.	Customer ID	Salesperson ID	Shipping Method	Payment Terms	Req Ship Date	Master No.
	BETTERBU001	ASL6677	FLEET	2% 10/Net 30	03/16/07	194

Ordered	Shipped	B/O	Item Number	Description	Site	UOM
20	20	0	DCJV16XDZ	Javix DigCamcord 16X Optical / 700X Digital	MAIN	Unit

Figure 5:13 Printed Packing Slip

Bill To:

Better Buy, Inc.
825 West Exchange Street
Chicago IL 60609

Ship To:

Better Buy, Inc.
825 West Exchange Street
Chicago IL 60609

* Printed Previously on Individual Ticket
** Printed Previously on Bulk Ticket

Purchase Order No.	Customer ID	Salesperson ID	Shipping Method	Payment Terms	Req Ship Date	Master No.
	BETTERBU001	ASL6677	FLEET	2% 10/Net 30	03/16/07	194

Item Number	Description	SiteID/Bin No.	Pick Qty	UOM	Qty Picked
DCJV16XDZ	Javix DigCamcord 16X Optic	MAIN	20	Unit	
		Bin not found	20	Unit	

Figure 5:14 Printed Picking Ticket

The sales order is the only document to list price and is sent to the customer as confirmation of the order. The packing slip is enclosed with the inventory shipped to the customer whereas the picking ticket is sent to the warehouse to use in pulling inventory to fill the order. Notice that the packing slip provides locations for the stock and a column for entering the quantity of items picked to fill the order.

Close the Print Sales Documents window. We next look at modifying saved orders.

Modifying Saved Sales Orders

What happens if a customer wants to change quantities or items on the original order? If you have not printed the order then simply reopen it, enter the changes, and save the order. If you need to change quantities, place your cursor in the field and type in the new amount. If you need to change an item, click ***Edit>>Delete Row*** on the window menu to remove the existing item and reenter a new item.

You can also use this method to change printed orders if the company has not set the internal control option requiring a password to modify printed sales orders. *(Note: Setup topics are discussed in Level Two.)* S&S has not set this option.

What if the customer wants to cancel the entire order? If the order has not been printed then reopen it and select Delete under the Actions button. *(Note: There is also a setup option to deny deleting any order and this option is discussed in Level Two.)* If the order has been printed then GP institutes internal controls by removing Delete as an option under Actions. Your only

choice is to Void the order. *(Note: Printing an order infers release to the customer and voiding it saves historical data for tracking the transactions.)*
Now try the next exercise on processing sales orders.

> On March 19, 2007, the following customer places an order for the items listed.
>
> Laufmans, Inc. ordered the following items:
> 15 of item TVBT46WPJ
> 25 of HESN51DVDVCR
>
> Enter this order. Print the control report for this transaction and the sales documents.

E5:3 Sales Order Processing

Out-of-Stock Inventory

Our orders thus far have always had enough inventory quantities to fill the order. This is not always the case in the real world so we will now illustrate handling sales where the quantity ordered by the customer exceeds the quantity on-hand.

1. Click **Sales Transaction Entry** and select **Candy Bowl Catalog, Inc.** as the customer. Date the transaction for **March 28, 2007**.

2. Expand the rows for line items and look up item **TVSN34W**. Note that there is currently no information for Quantity Available.

3. Tab to **QTY Ordered** and enter 50. Upon entering this quantity, GP opens the Sales Quantity Shortage Options window (Figure 5:15) requesting instructions for allocating the shortage in inventory. On the left are options for allocating this shortage. On the right is information on the current quantity in stock.

   Note: Sales Order setup (covered in Level Two) contains default options for allocating inventory shortages. S&S has set the option to allocate by line item, meaning to allocate during transaction entry.

Figure 5:15 Sales Quantity Shortage Options Window

4. Highlight **Back Order Balance** and click **OK**. Return to the Sales Transaction Entry window and notice that the Quantity Available field has been updated to zero. (See Figure 5:16.) There are also 15 items in the Qty to Back Order field.

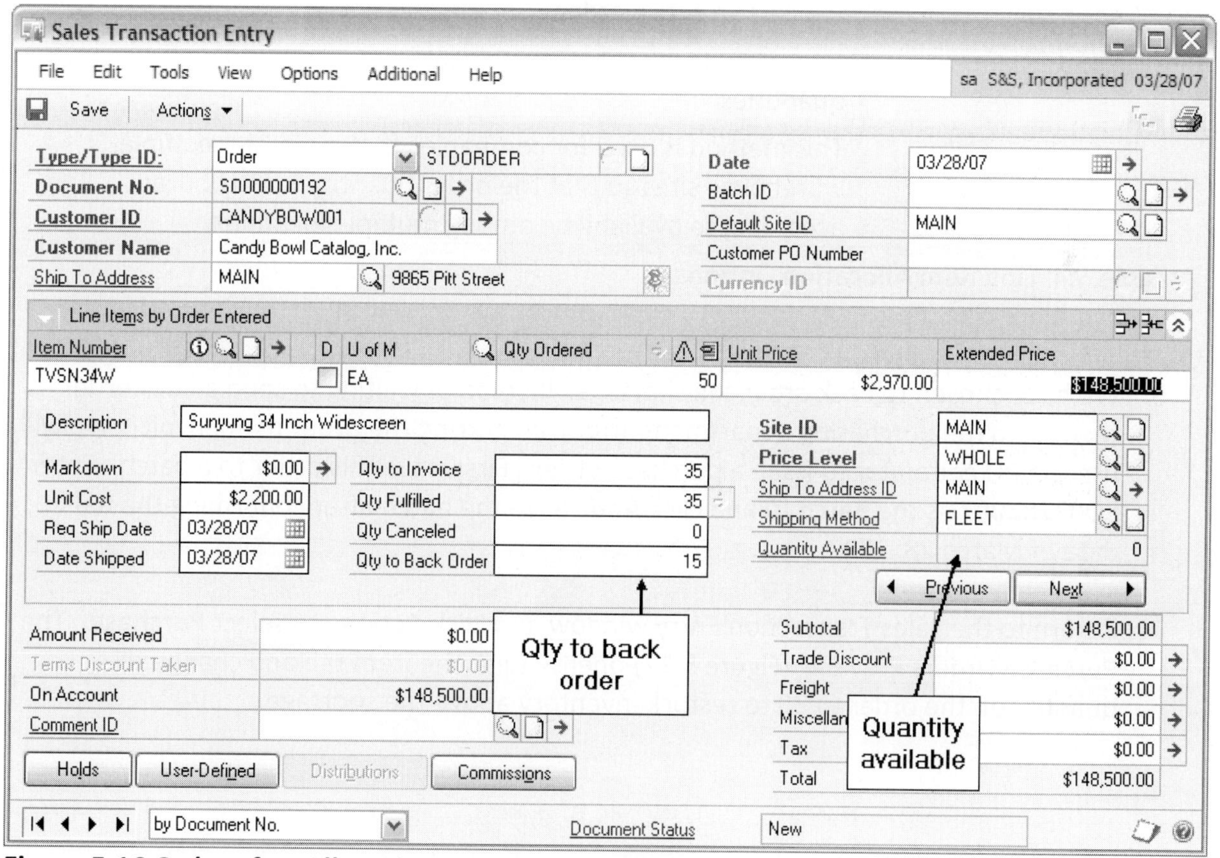

Figure 5:16 Order after Allocating Inventory Shortage

5. Now review options for allocating shortages in Table 5:4. It helps to remember that sales orders only flag inventory as unavailable for other orders. The entry that actually reduces on-hand quantities does not occur until posting an invoice.

Allocation Options	Description
Sell Balance	Allocate remaining quantities in inventory (i.e., available quantities). Quantity available will then reflect zero.
Override Shortage	Disregard the shortage and allocate the entire quantity ordered. The available balance then displays a negative quantity.
Back Order All	Do not allocate any quantity and back order the entire quantity ordered. With this method, GP will create a separate back order document when you transfer the order to an invoice. (Note: Transferring orders is illustrated later in the chapter.)
Back Order Balance	Allocate the quantity available and back order the remaining quantity needed to fill the order. Again, GP will create a back order document when transferring to an invoice. (See previous option.)
Cancel All	Cancel the entire order.
Cancel Balance	Allocate the quantity available and cancel remaining quantities.
Distribute	This method is used for companies that maintain multiple warehouse sites so that the order quantity is distributed, according to availability, among multiple locations.

Table 5:4 Line Item Allocation Options

6. We have chosen to back order the shortage. Instead of waiting to send a back order request to the purchasing department after transferring the order to an invoice, we will use the PO generator to issue a purchase order. First, save this order to a batch. Enter **SO03282007** as the **Batch ID** and click **Add**. Save the batch after confirming the batch date of March 28, 2007.

7. Return to the Sales Transaction Entry window and click **Actions** to select **Purchase**. The Purchase Orders Preview (Figure 5:17) opens. Click the **Item** tab and change the quantity on the order to 30 to restock inventory above the shortage.

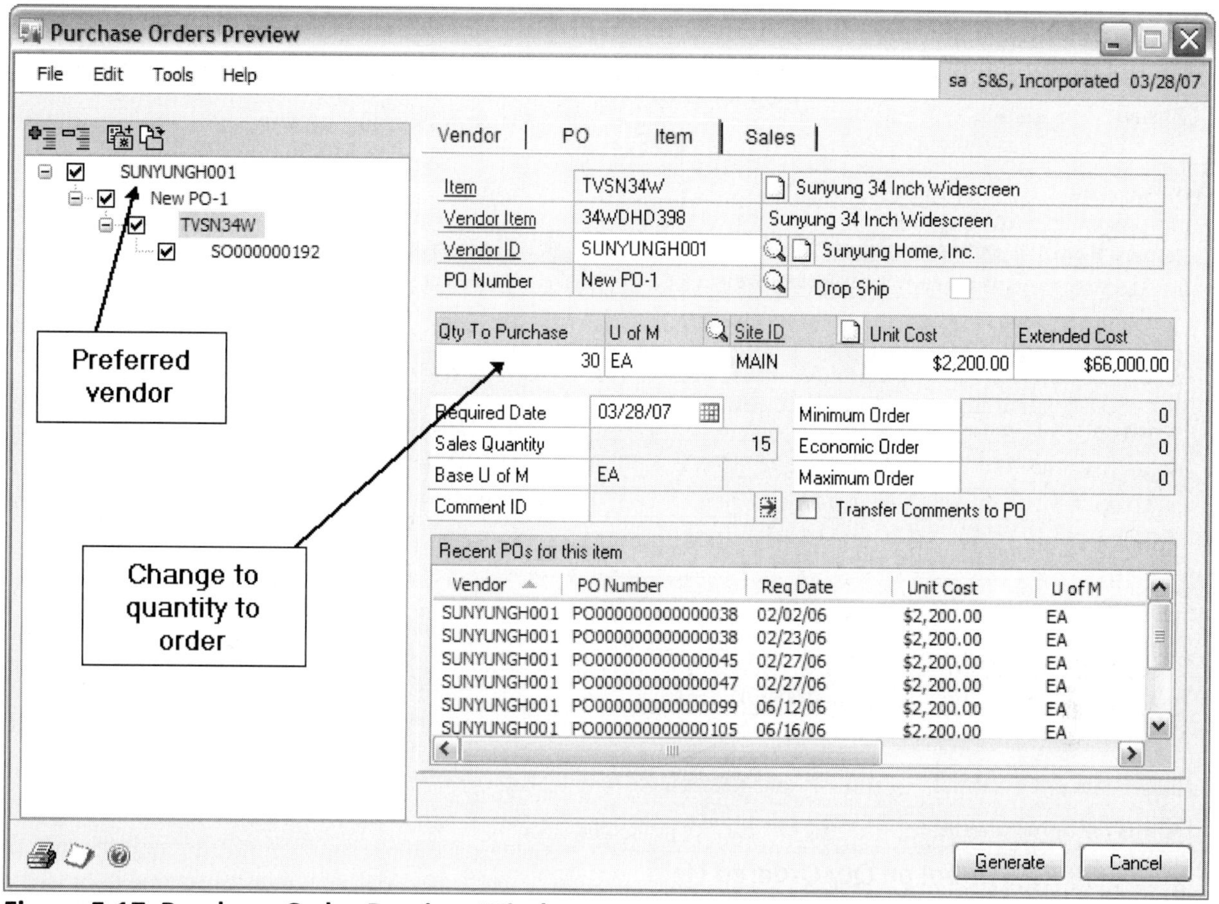

Figure 5:17 Purchase Order Preview Window

8. The purchase order was issued to Sunyung because this is the preferred vendor on the item card. (Note: Preferred vendors were discussed in Chapter 4.) Click **Generate** and print the Purchase Orders Generation Register to the screen. This report can be sent to the Purchasing Department to trigger printing the PO or the department can run its own report.

9. Return to the transaction window and reopen the order. Notice the PO indicator symbol on the Qty Ordered field. (See Figure 5:18.)

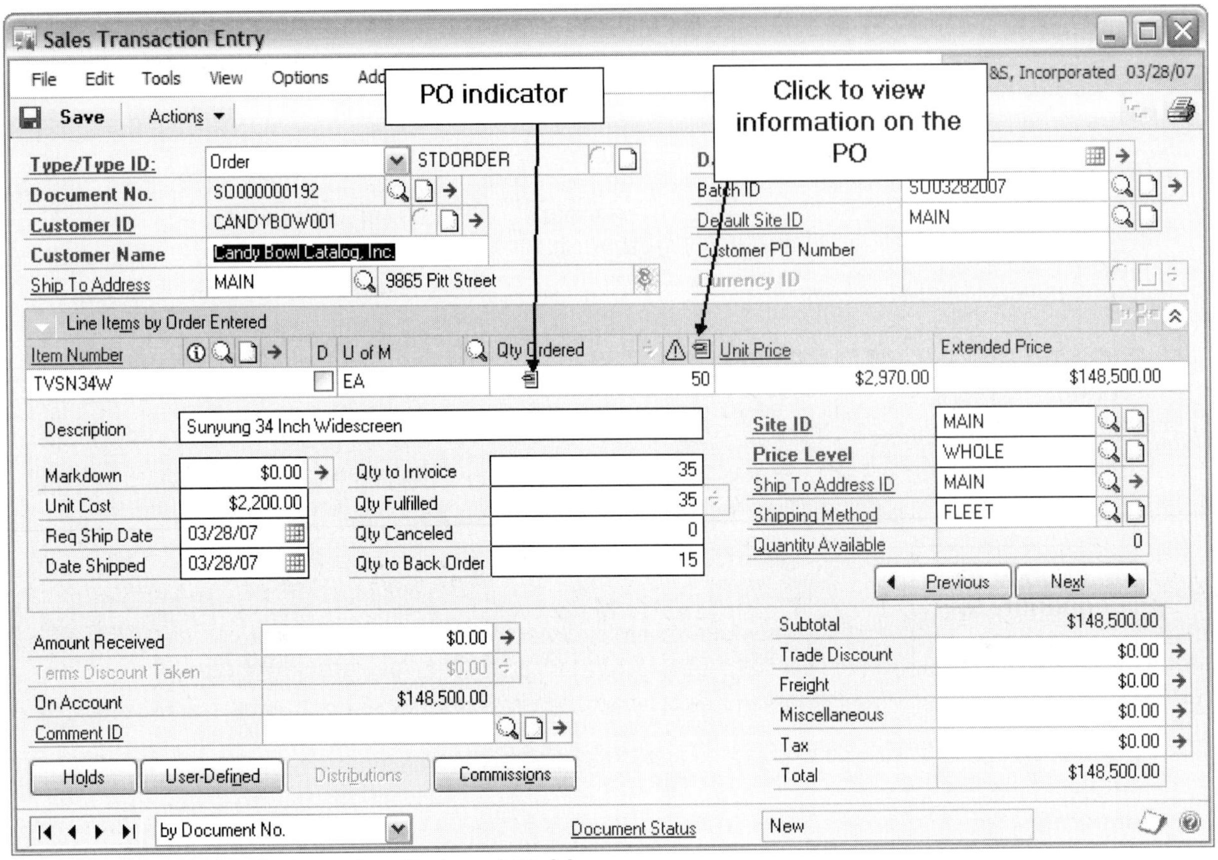

Figure 5:18 PO Symbol on Qty Ordered Field

10. Place your cursor in the Qty Ordered field and click the PO symbol for viewing information. (See Figure 5:19.) When the inventory is received from the vendor, fifteen of the items will automatically be allocated to the Candy Bowl order. The PO generator is an efficient method of managing inventory shortages.

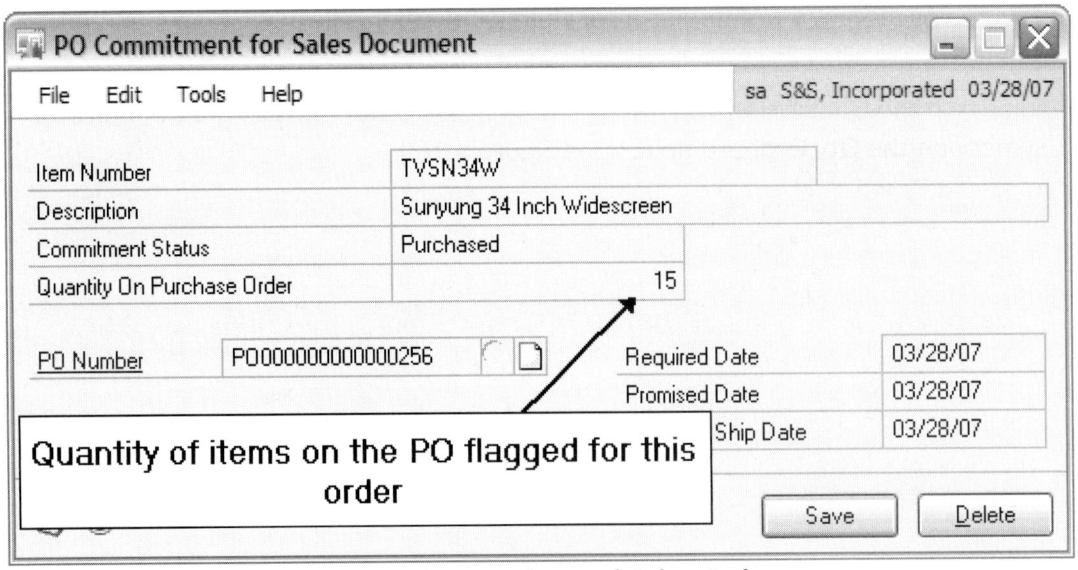

Figure 5:19 PO Items Committed to Candy Bowl Sales Order

11. Click **Save** and return to the transaction window. Save the order and close the window.

We are now ready to discuss activities performed by the warehouse and shipping departments.

WAREHOUSE AND SHIPPING DEPARTMENT ACTIVITIES

When the picking ticket arrives at the warehouse, employees begin filling the order and entering quantities picked onto the ticket. When finished, picked inventory and the picking ticket are sent to the shipping department.

A shipping employee then prepares the bill of lading and checks inventory for any defects. He/she will also verify that items and quantities match the picking ticket. The employee then enters fulfillment and ship data into GP. The next exercise illustrates this process.

Entering Fulfillment Data

1. Click **Order Fulfillment** under Transactions and look up the sales order. (See Figure 5:20.)

2. The employee then enters picked quantities into the Qty Fulfilled field and fulfillment and ship dates. *(Note: To minimize steps you need to take when practicing transactions, we have selected the Sales Series option that automatically enters fulfillment data during sales order entry; thus, the order will already display Qty Fulfilled and Date Fulfilled data.)* There are also fields for entering quantities to back order or cancel.

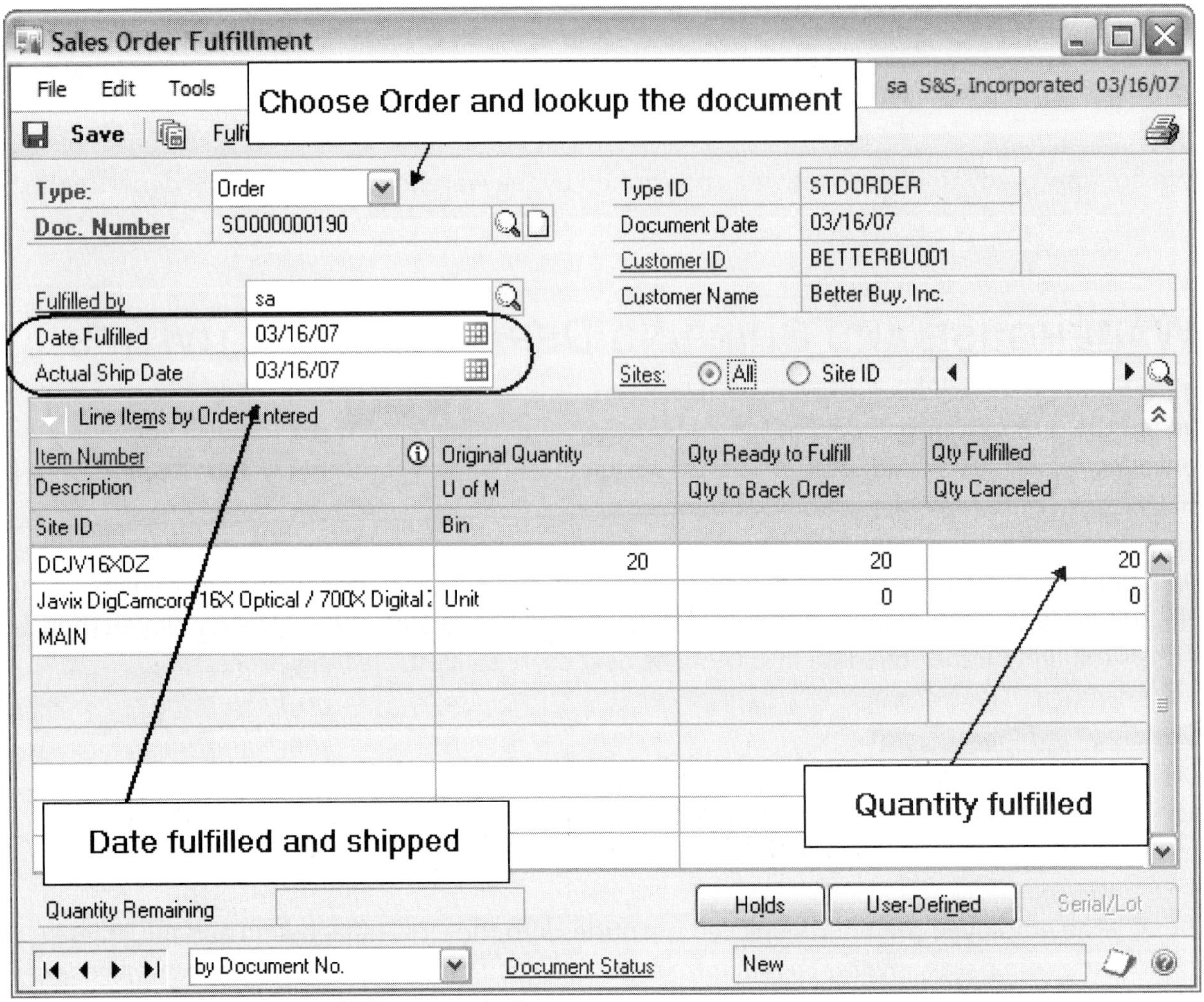

Figure 5:20 Sales Order Fulfillment Window

3. When finished, the employee prints a packing slip. You can print for a single order by selecting ***File>>Print*** on the window menu or print multiple orders by clicking Print Sales Documents as previously illustrated. The packing slip is then boxed with inventory and the order placed on company trucks. A copy of the bill of lading is sent to the accounts receivable department to trigger invoicing.

Close the Sales Order Fulfillment window. We next look at activities performed by the accounts receivable department.

ACCOUNTS RECEIVABLE DEPARTMENT ACTIVITIES

Upon receiving the bill of lading, accounts receivable clerks finalize the order by transferring it to an invoice. This is the process triggering payment by the customer and revenue recognition (i.e., posting revenue, cost of goods sold, and other related charges to general ledger accounts.) The next exercise illustrates this process.

Invoicing Sales Orders

1. There are two ways of transferring orders to invoices.

   First, you can click Sales Batches, look up the batch, and click Transfer to turn all ***fulfilled*** orders in the batch into invoices. *(Note: Only line items that are fulfilled will be invoiced.)*

   Second, you can click Sales Transaction Entry (or go to Transactions from the Sales Batch Entry window) and look up an order to transfer it individually. This method is time consuming if several orders are to be invoiced.

2. We will illustrate the batch method first. Click **Sales Batch Entry** and look up the batch illustrated containing two fulfilled orders.

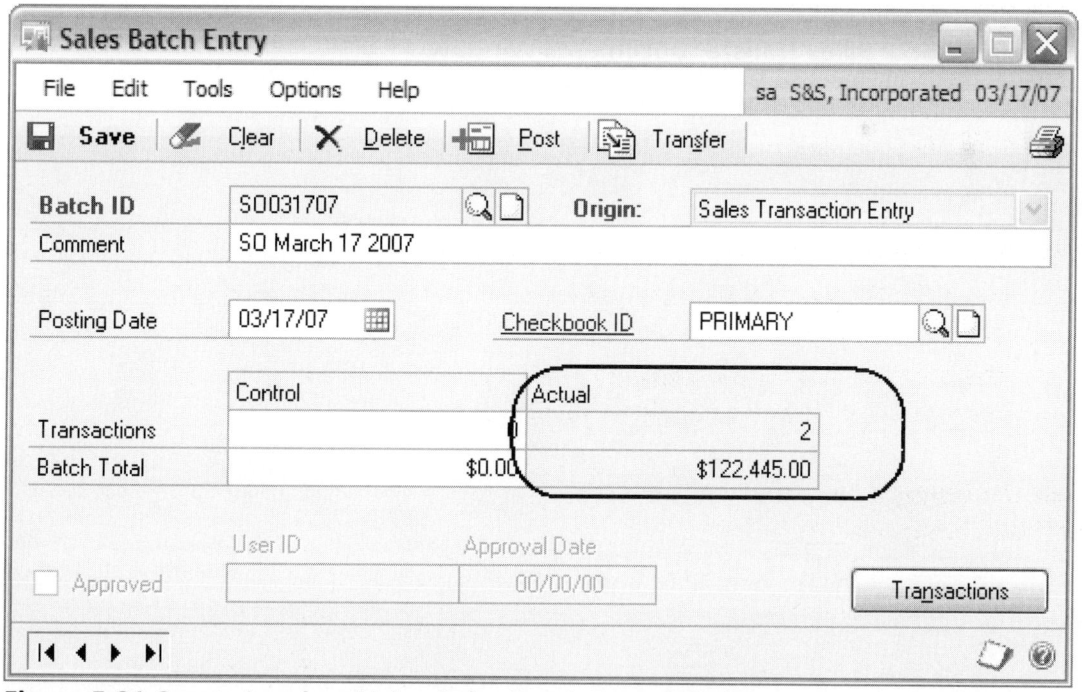

Figure 5:21 Create Invoices Using Sales Batch Entry Window

3. Click **Transfer** and mark the option indicated in Figure 5:22. Review Table 5:5 for an explanation on these options.

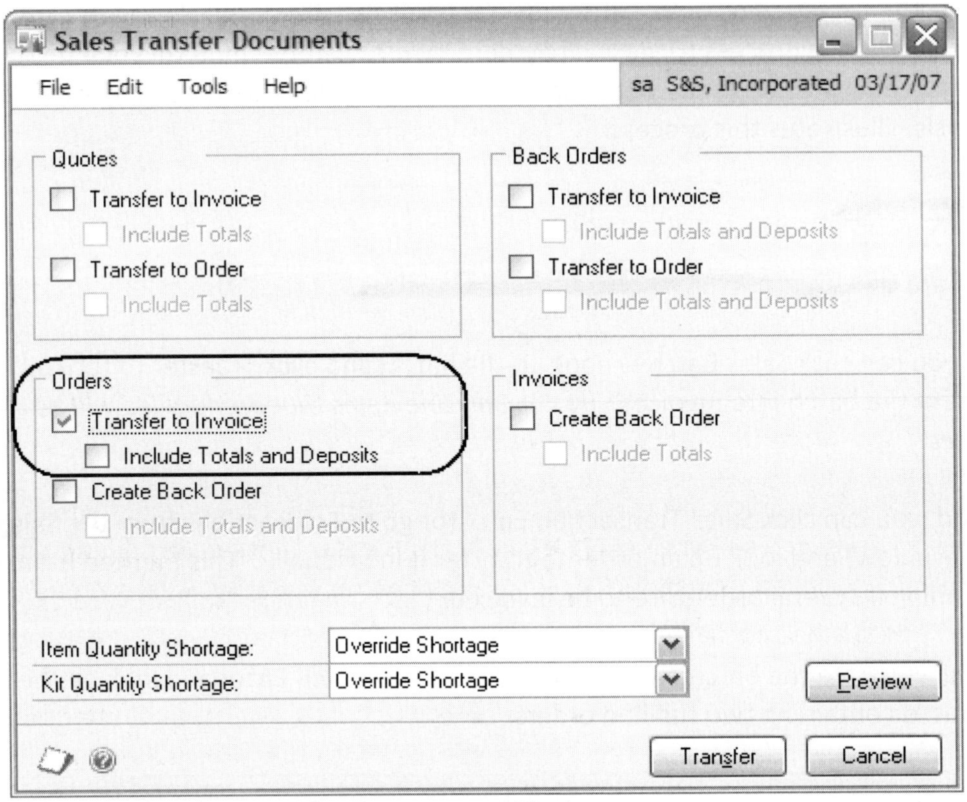

Figure 5:22 Sales Transfer Documents Window

Transfer Option	Purpose
Quotes	Transfer Quotes in the batch to either an Invoice or Order.
Orders	Transfer fulfilled Orders to an Invoice and/or create Back Order document for orders with a quantity entered in the back order field.
Back Orders	Transfer Back Orders to either an Invoice or Order.
Invoices	Create Back Order documents for Invoices having a quantity entered in the back order field.
Include Totals / Include Totals and Deposits	Available for each document type and transfers freight and miscellaneous charges on the original document to the new document. *(Note: Discounts and Taxes always transfer.)* If not marked, you must enter these charges on the new document before posting. Also, you can transfer these charges just once. If the option also transfers deposits then deposit amounts no longer appears on the original document. You can reenter a deposit on the new document.

Table 5:5 Sales Document Transfer Options

4. Let us next focus on options for handling quantity shortages that occur during transfer. Click the dropdown list illustrated (Figure 5:23) and review the table that follows.

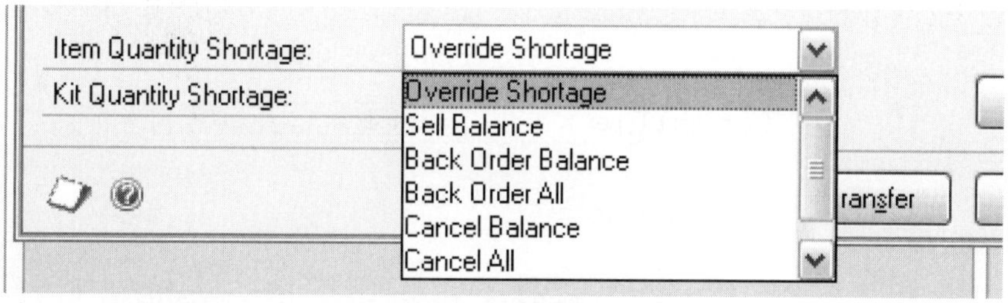

Figure 5:23 Quantity Shortage Options

Note: Recall that when processing orders we illustrated that S&S chose to allocate during line item entry, thus, the option selected during transfer will not change selections made during order entry. S&S chose this method to provide instant feedback for customers. Furthermore, choosing to allocate during line item entry means that inventory is no longer available for sale to other customers.

Allocation Options	Purpose
Override Shortage	Disregard inventory shortages and transfer all quantities on the original document to the new document.
Sell Balance	Transfer only available quantities to the new document and retain the original document to transfer when quantities become available.
Back Order Balance	Transfer only available quantities to the new document and enter shortage quantities to the back order field of the original document. You will also want to mark the Create Back Order option to create a back order document.
Back Order All	Enter all quantities to the back order field of the original document.
Cancel Balance	Transfer only available quantities to the new document and enter remaining quantities to the cancel field of the original document.
Cancel All	Enter all quantities to the cancel field of the original document.

Table 5:6 Sales Document Transfer Options

5. Click **Preview** and select **Order** to view quantities that will be transferred to an Invoice. (See Figure 5:24.) Click **OK**.

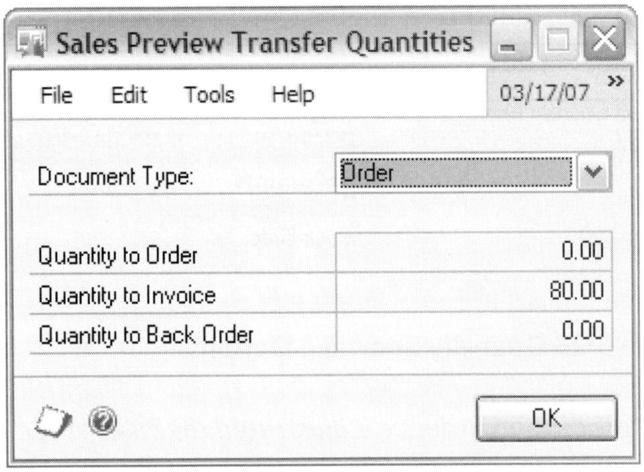

Figure 5:24 Transfer Preview Window

6. Now click **Transfer** and print the SOP Transfer Log to the screen. This report (Figure 5:25) displays the new documents created and reports any errors during transfer.

```
                                     S&S, Incorporated                              Page:     1
User Date:  03/17/07                 Sales Transfer Log                             User ID:  sa
                                    Sales Order Processing

Order SO000000188 successfully transferred to Invoice INV000000213.
Order SO000000189 successfully transferred to Invoice INV000000214.

       0 Error(s) during transfer
       2 Document(s) transferred successfully
```

New documents created

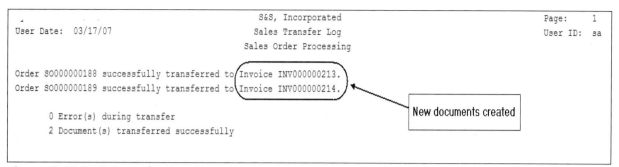

Figure 5:25 SOP Transfer Log

7. Close the report and return to the Sales Batch Entry window. Look up batch **SO031707**. *(Note: The new invoices remain in the original batch and retain the same transaction date as on the order. If you need to change this date then click Transactions to reopen the invoice and change the date. You can also assign the invoice to a different batch by changing the Batch ID. You will also need to open transactions to enter any shipping or miscellaneous charges for the invoice.)*

8. Click ***File>>Print*** on the window menu and choose **Edit List**. Click **Print** and send output to the screen. The Sales Edit List (Figure 5:26) is a control report over posting to the general ledger and should be reviewed for accuracy. Accounts affected when posting are highlighted.

```
                                        S&S, Incorporated                                   Page:     1
User Date:  03/17/07                     SALES EDIT LIST                                    User ID:  sa
                                      Sales Order Processing

Batch ID:        SO031707                                          Audit Trail Code:
Batch Comment:  SO March 17 2007

Approved:                      Batch Total Actual:       $122,445.00    Batch Total Control:        $0.00
Approved By:                   Trx Total Actual:                   2    Trx Total Control:              0
Approval Date:       00/00/00


Type  Document Number    Doc Date   Post Date   Customer ID     Name                        Salesperson
--------------------------------------------------------------------------------------------------------------
         Subtotal    Trade Discount    Freight Amount       Misc Amount       Tax Amount     Document Total   Discount Avail
--------------------------------------------------------------------------------------------------------------
INV   INV000000213       03/17/07   03/17/07    TUBESTUR001     Tubes & Turners, Inc.       MTM3987

Type  Document Number    Doc Date   Post Date   Customer ID     Name                        Salesperson
--------------------------------------------------------------------------------------------------------------
         Subtotal    Trade Discount    Freight Amount       Misc Amount       Tax Amount     Document Total   Discount Avail
--------------------------------------------------------------------------------------------------------------
INV   INV000000213       03/17/07   03/17/07    TUBESTUR001     Tubes & Turners, Inc.       MTM3987
         $94,500.00          $0.00          $0.00              $0.00           $0.00        $94,500.00          $0.00


Item Number                  Description                                          Markdown
                             U of M    Site                       Quantity        Unit Price      Extended Price
---------------------------  --------  ----------  --------------------  ------------------  ------------------
HESB51DVD                    SEBO 38 DVD 5.1 Home Entertainment                       $0.00
                             Unit      MAIN                             50        $1,890.00          $94,500.00
                                                                                             ------------------
                                                                                                     $94,500.00
                             U of M    Site                       Quantity        Unit Price      Extended Price
---------------------------  --------  ----------  --------------------  ------------------  ------------------
HESB51DVD                    SEBO 38 DVD 5.1 Home Entertainment                       $0.00
                             Unit      MAIN                             50        $1,890.00          $94,500.00
                                                                                             ------------------
                                                                                                     $94,500.00

Account Number               Account Description              Account Type      Debit Amount       Credit Amount
---------------------------  -------------------------------  ------------  ------------------  ------------------
                             Unit      MAIN                             50        $1,890.00          $94,500.00
                                                                                             ------------------
                                                                                                     $94,500.00

Account Number               Account Description              Account Type      Debit Amount       Credit Amount
---------------------------  -------------------------------  ------------  ------------------  ------------------
1200-00                      Accounts Receivable              RECV              $94,500.00               $0.00
4100-03                      Sales - West                     SALES                  $0.00          $94,500.00
5200-00                      Commission Expense               COMMEXP              $283.50               $0.00
2230-00                      Commissions Payable              COMMPAY                $0.00             $283.50
                                                                            ------------------  ------------------
                                                                                $94,783.50          $94,783.50
1200-00                      Accounts Receivable              RECV              $94,500.00               $0.00
4100-03                      Sales - West                     SALES                  $0.00          $94,500.00
5200-00                      Commission Expense               COMMEXP              $283.50               $0.00
2230-00                      Commissions Payable              COMMPAY                $0.00             $283.50
                                                                            ------------------  ------------------
                                                                                $94,783.50          $94,783.50
Salesperson Name             Sales Territory ID         Comm %     % of Sale      Sales Amount   Commission Amount
---------------------------  ---------------------  ----------  ----------  ------------------  ------------------
Murphy, Mary                 WEST                        0.30%     100.00%          94,500.00              283.50
                                                                            ------------------  ------------------
                                                                                $94,500.00             $283.50

INV   INV000000214       03/17/07   03/17/07    ELECTRON001     Electronic Town, Inc.       ASL6677
         $27,945.00          $0.00          $0.00              $0.00           $0.00        $27,945.00          $0.00


                                                                                $94,500.00             $283.50

INV   INV000000214       03/17/07   03/17/07    ELECTRON001     Electronic Town, Inc.       ASL6677
         $27,945.00          $0.00          $0.00              $0.00           $0.00        $27,945.00          $0.00


Item Number                  Description                                          Markdown
                             U of M    Site                       Quantity        Unit Price      Extended Price
         $27,945.00          $0.00          $0.00              $0.00           $0.00        $27,945.00          $0.00


Item Number                  Description                                          Markdown
                             U of M    Site                       Quantity        Unit Price      Extended Price
---------------------------  --------  ----------  --------------------  ------------------  ------------------
TVBT46WPJ                    Batoshi 46 Inch Widescreen Projection                    $0.00
                             EA        MAIN                             30          $931.50          $27,945.00

Item Number                  Description                                          Markdown
                             U of M    Site                       Quantity        Unit Price      Extended Price
---------------------------  --------  ----------  --------------------  ------------------  ------------------
TVBT46WPJ                    Batoshi 46 Inch Widescreen Projection                    $0.00
                             EA        MAIN                             30          $931.50          $27,945.00
                                                                                             ------------------
                                                                                                     $27,945.00
Account Number               Account Description              Account Type      Debit Amount       Credit Amount
---------------------------  -------------------------------  ------------  ------------------  ------------------
1200-00                      Accounts Receivable              RECV              $27,945.00               $0.00
4100-02                      Sales - MidWest                  SALES                  $0.00          $27,945.00
5200-00                      Commission Expense               COMMEXP               $83.84               $0.00
2230-00                      Commissions Payable              COMMPAY                $0.00              $83.84
                                                                            ------------------  ------------------
                                                                                $28,028.84          $28,028.84
1200-00                      Accounts Receivable              RECV              $27,945.00               $0.00
4100-02                      Sales - MidWest                  SALES                  $0.00          $27,945.00
5200-00                      Commission Expense               COMMEXP               $83.84               $0.00
2230-00                      Commissions Payable              COMMPAY                $0.00              $83.84
                                                                            ------------------  ------------------
                                                                                $28,028.84          $28,028.84
Salesperson Name             Sales Territory ID         Comm %     % of Sale      Sales Amount   Commission Amount
---------------------------  ---------------------  ----------  ----------  ------------------  ------------------
Levine, April                MID                         0.30%     100.00%          27,945.00               83.84
                                                                            ------------------  ------------------
                                                                                $27,945.00              $83.84

         Subtotal    Trade Discount    Freight Amount       Misc Amount       Tax Amount     Document Total   Discount Avail
  ---------------  ---------------  ---------------  ---------------  ---------------  ---------------  ---------------
      $122,445.00            $0.00            $0.00            $0.00            $0.00      $122,445.00            $0.00
  ===============  ===============  ===============  ===============  ===============  ===============  ===============
```

Figure 5:26 Sales Edit List

9. Close the report and return to the Sales Batch Entry window. Click **Post** and review the posting reports that print to the screen.

10. Return to the Sales Batch Entry window and look up **SO03162007**. We will now illustrate transferring individual orders.

11. Click **Transactions** and look up the order as illustrated in Figure 5:27. Click the document arrow to open the window illustrated next.

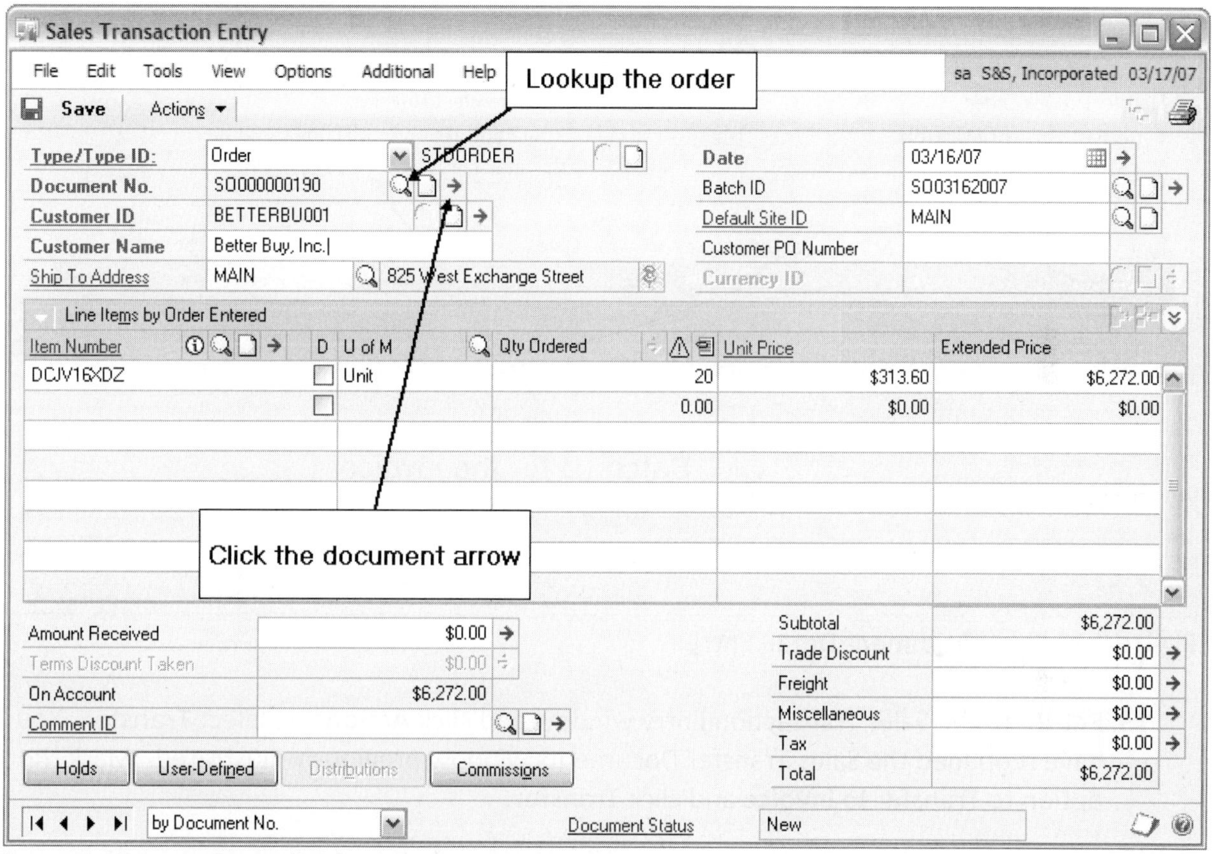

Figure 5:27 Transfer Individual Order to an Invoice

12. In this window (Figure 5:28) you can assign the invoice created upon transfer to a different batch. Type in the **Batch ID** name as indicated and click **Add** to create the batch. Change the batch date to March 16, 2007 and **Save** it. Click **OK** to close the Sales Document Detail Entry window.

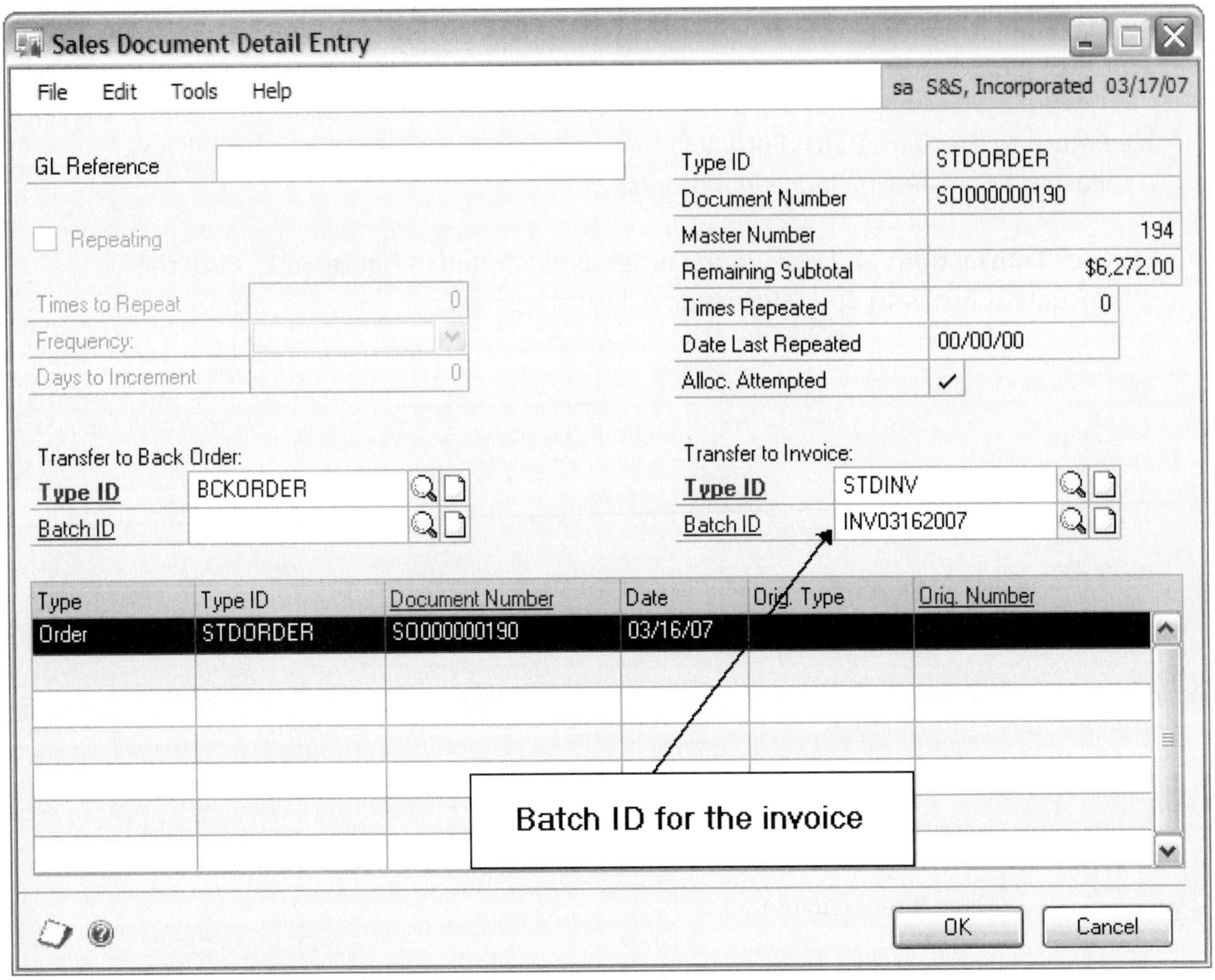

Figure 5:28 Sales Document Detail Entry

13. Return to the Sales Transaction Entry window and click **Actions** to select **Transfer**. You have reopened the Sales Transfer Documents window previously illustrated. Mark the option to **Transfer to Invoice** and click **Transfer**.

14. Review the SOP Transfer log to verify that no errors occurred. Also note the invoice number. Close the report

15. Return to the Sales Transaction Entry and notice that the document is now an Invoice and has been placed in the INV03162007 batch. (See Figure 5:29.)

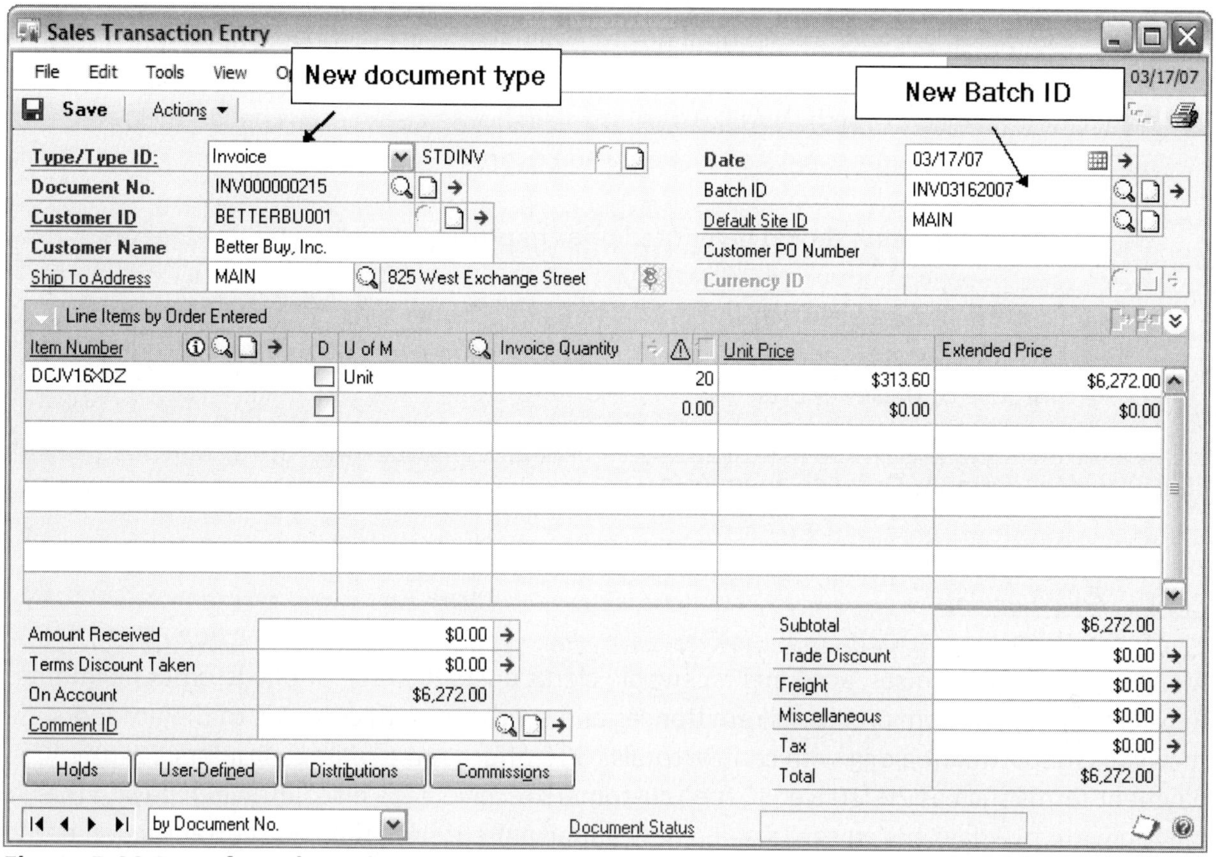

Figure 5:29 Transferred Invoice

16. You could post the transaction by clicking Actions if it were not saved to a batch. Instead **Save** the transaction and close the window.

17. You will now post the invoice. During posting, revenue is recognized and inventory relieved with the costs posted to cost of goods sold. [21] Return to the Sales Batch Entry window, look up the INV03162007 batch, and post it. Close the window.

Now practice transferring orders with the next exercise.

---

[21] The matching principle explains why cost of goods sold is not recognized until invoicing. GAAP provides several methods for recognizing expense. Expenses are recognized when recognizing revenue for those costs bearing a direct relationship to revenue. Costs that cover a period of time are recognized as the benefit derived from those costs expire (i.e., period costs such as prepaid insurance). Capitalized costs are recognized using a systematic and rational allocation method (i.e., depreciating fixed assets). Direct relationship is the correct method for recognizing cost of goods sold because inventory costs bear a direct relationship to the revenue earned from selling inventory.

On March 20, 2007, the Laufmans order in batch SO03192007 from the previous exercise is ready for invoicing. Update the order for invoicing and transfer the new invoice to batch INV03202007. Explain how a clerk could change the default general ledger posting accounts prior to posting.

What documents should be printed prior to posting?

Post the invoice and identify general ledger accounts affected by the transaction. Name the posting control reports that printed and explain the internal control purpose of these reports.

E5:4 Transfer Laufmans Order to an Invoice

Posting Cash Receipts

Along with posting invoices, accounts receivable clerks posts the receipt of customer payments. Recall that the mailroom processes remittances and sends these documents to the accounts receivable department along with control totals. S&S offers some of its customers early payment terms such as 2%/10 Net 30 (i.e., customers receive a 2% discount when paying the invoice within 10 days.) You can imagine how important entering the correct transaction date is when posting cash receipts. Being off just one day can either mistakenly grant or deny the customer this discount.

We will now illustrate posting cash receipts.

1. Change the system date to March 26, 2007 and click **Cash Receipts** under Transactions. Tubes and Turner remitted check number 896912 for $94,500.00 so enter the transaction as illustrated in Figure 5:30.

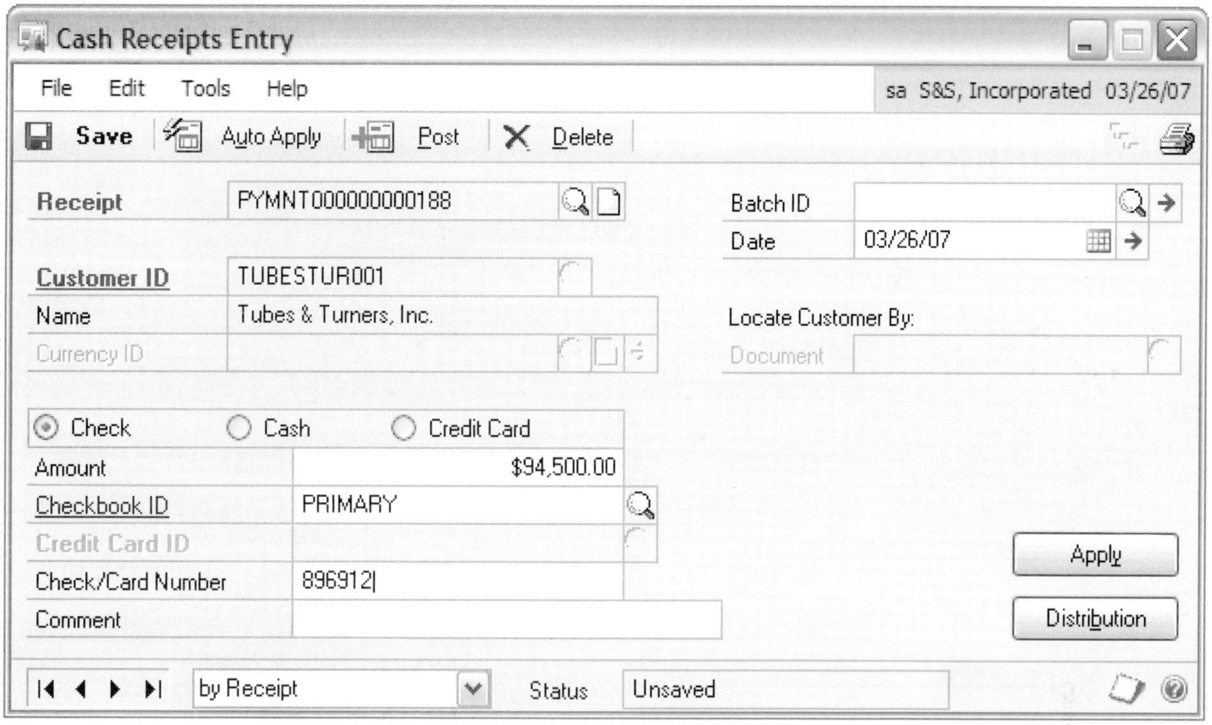

Figure 5:30 Tubes and Turner Cash Receipt

2. Click **Apply** to open so you can choose an invoice to apply the payment to. (See Figure 5:31.)

> **Auto Apply Warning**
>
> Be very careful if using the Auto Apply button. This button will auto apply payments to outstanding invoices so that GP marks for payment either the invoice with the oldest due date or earliest document number. *(Note: The option is set in Sales Series setup.)* This may not always correspond to the invoices intended to be paid by the customer.

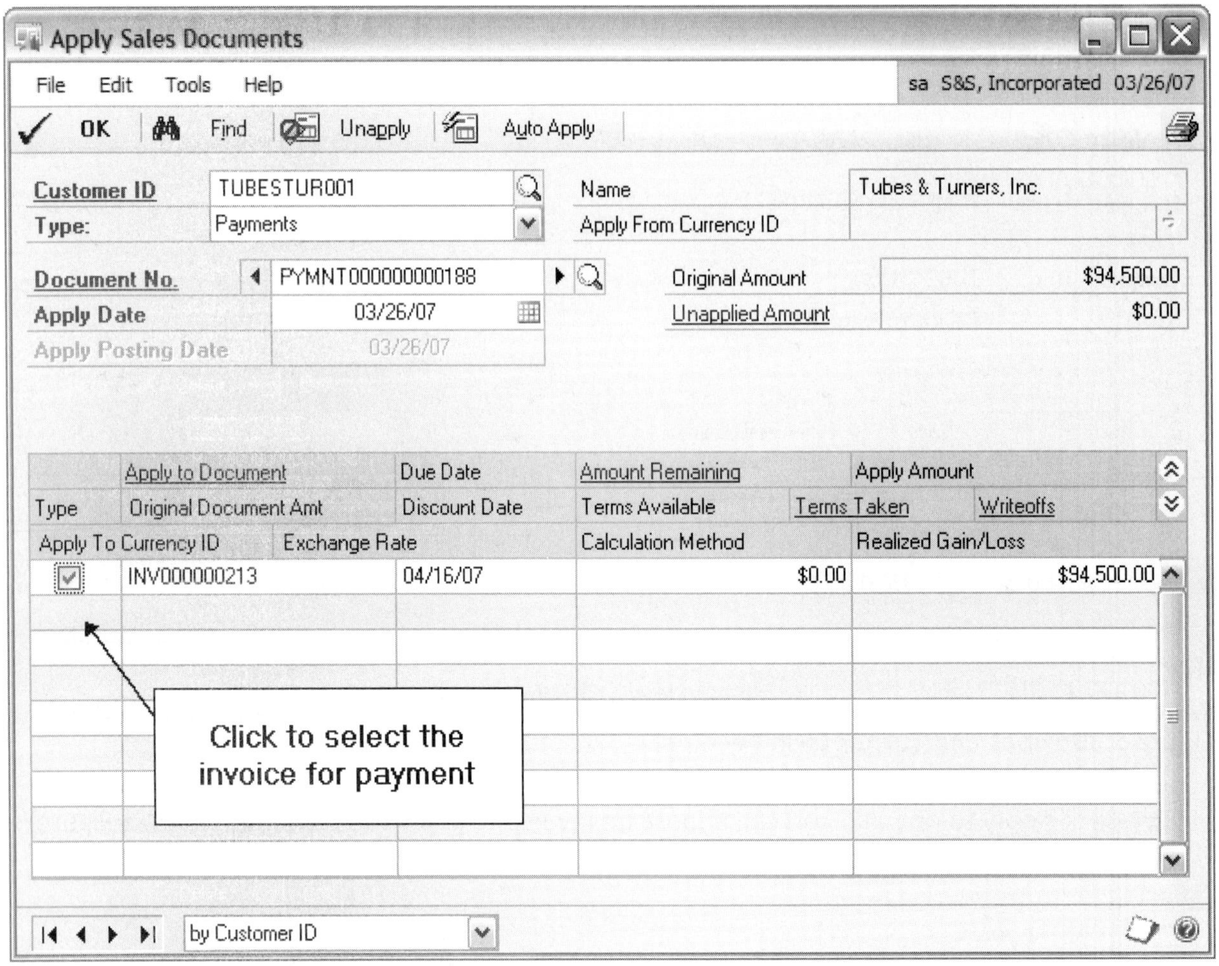

Figure 5:31 Apply the Tubes and Turner Payment

3. Click **OK** to return to the Cash Receipts Entry window. Click **Post**.

4. We next illustrate posting cash receipts with early payment discounts. Enter the cash receipt from **Better Buy** as illustrated. (See Figure 5:32.) Note: Change the transaction date to **March 19, 2007**.

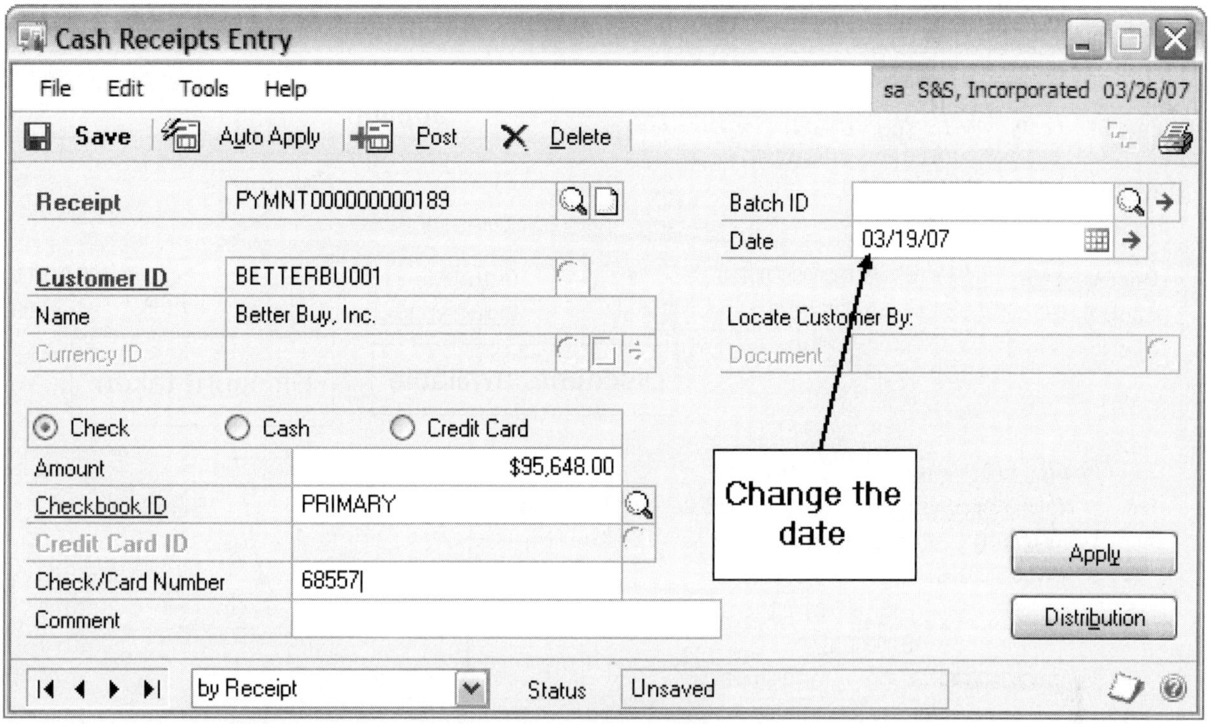

Figure 5:32 Better Buy Cash Receipt Carrying a Discount

5. Click **Apply** and expand the rows. Mark the invoice as shown (Figure 5:33) and notice the discount columns.

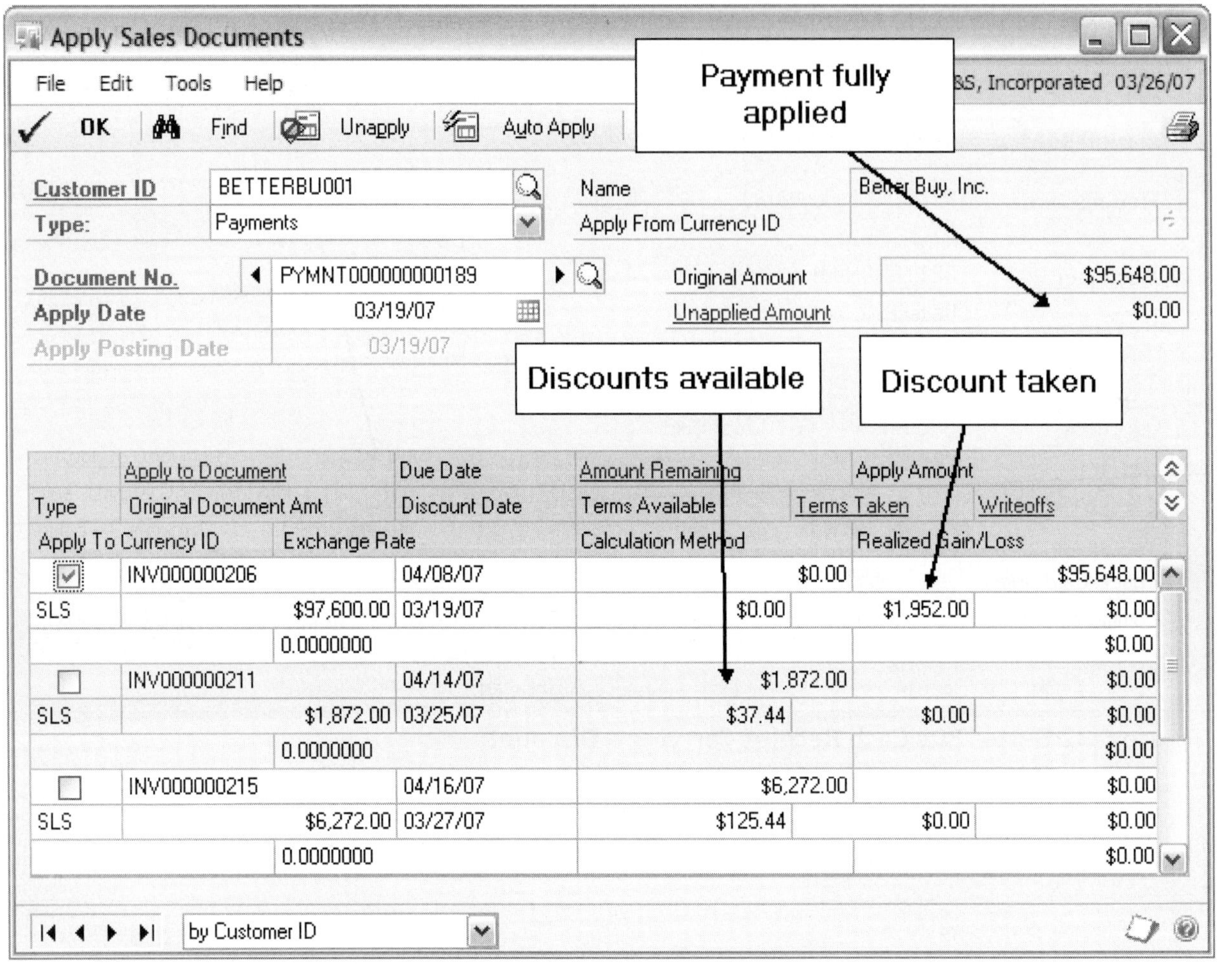

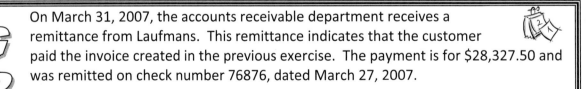

Figure 5:33 Apply Window with a Discount

6. Click **OK** and **Post** the transaction. Close the window so that posting reports print. Notice that the General Posting Journal did not print because these transactions were posted individually. You will need to activate the Financial home page and click Series Post to complete processing. Suspended transactions are prefixed with RMCSH (i.e., receivables management cash).

> On March 31, 2007, the accounts receivable department receives a remittance from Laufmans. This remittance indicates that the customer paid the invoice created in the previous exercise. The payment is for $28,327.50 and was remitted on check number 76876, dated March 27, 2007.
>
> Post this payment against the invoice. Explain how the documents sent from the mailroom serve as a control over cash receipt data entry. What, if any control reports, should be printed prior to posting cash receipts?

E5:5 Cash Receipt from Laufmans

Customer Returns and Credit/Debit Memos

We now look at processing customer returns of inventory and issuing credit memos to customers. Customers may return inventory for a variety of reasons such as damaged items, wrong items, or unwanted items. We explained in our roadmap that returns may be captured by the sales, warehouse, or accounts receivable departments. Furthermore, you can use either the Invoicing or Sales Order Processing Tiers to capture the transaction.

S&S requires the accounts receivable department to enter returns and clerks use the Invoice Processing Tier to perform this task. Complete the next steps to record a return of inventory from Candy Bowl Catalog. This inventory was sold on invoice INV000000172, which remains unpaid.

1. Click **Invoice Entry** and change the document type to **Return**. Select **Candy Bowl Catalog** as the customer.

2. On March 16, 2007, Candy Bowl returned 16 defective receivers for credit. Capture the entry. (See Figure 5:34).

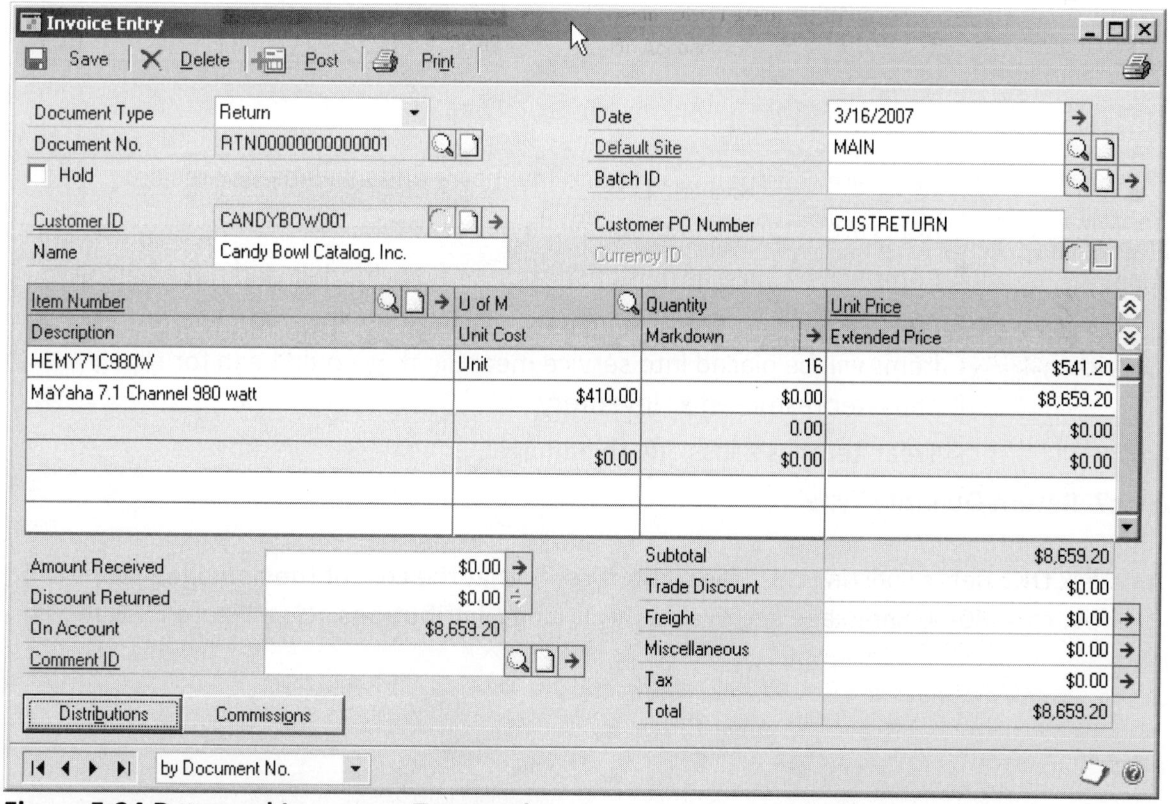

Figure 5:34 Returned Inventory Transaction

3. Upon entering the Quantity, GP prompts as to the disposition of the items. (See Figure 5:35.) Enter 16 as **Damaged** and review the table that follows for information on Return Quantity Type.

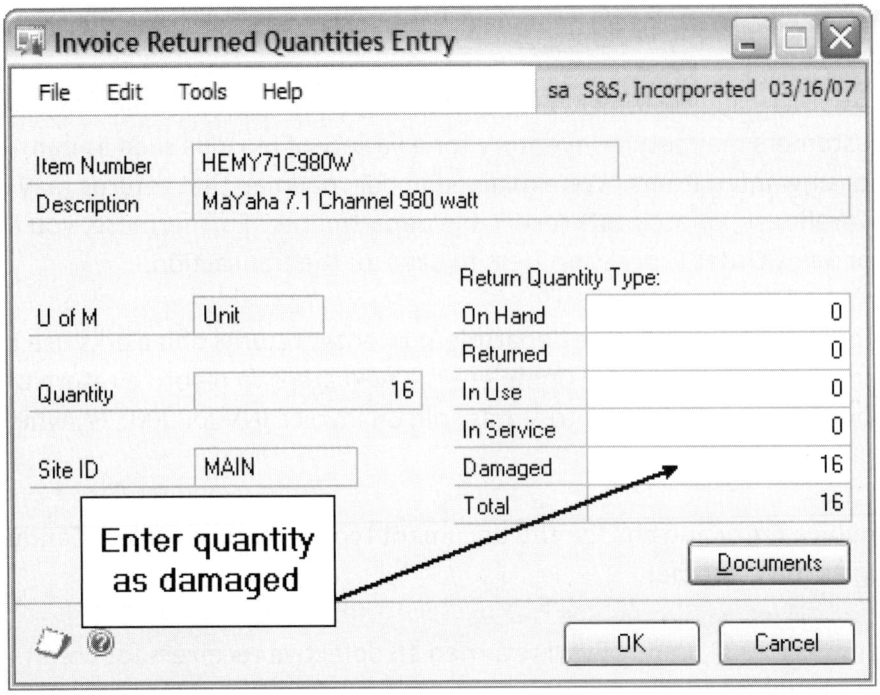

Figure 5:35 Disposition of Returned Inventory

Field	**Purpose**
On Hand	Items are returned to on-hand inventory and available for resale.
Returned	Items are returned and not available for resale.
In Use	Items will be used as demonstration or floor models and not available for resale.
In Service	Items will be placed into service meaning they could be in for repair and later restocked as inventory.
Damaged	Treat items as a loss due to damage.

Table 5:7 Return Quantity Type

4. Click **OK**. Before posting this transaction, verify that the cost of the damaged items will post to 4530-00 Shrinkage and Waste by clicking **Distributions.** (See Figure 5:36.)

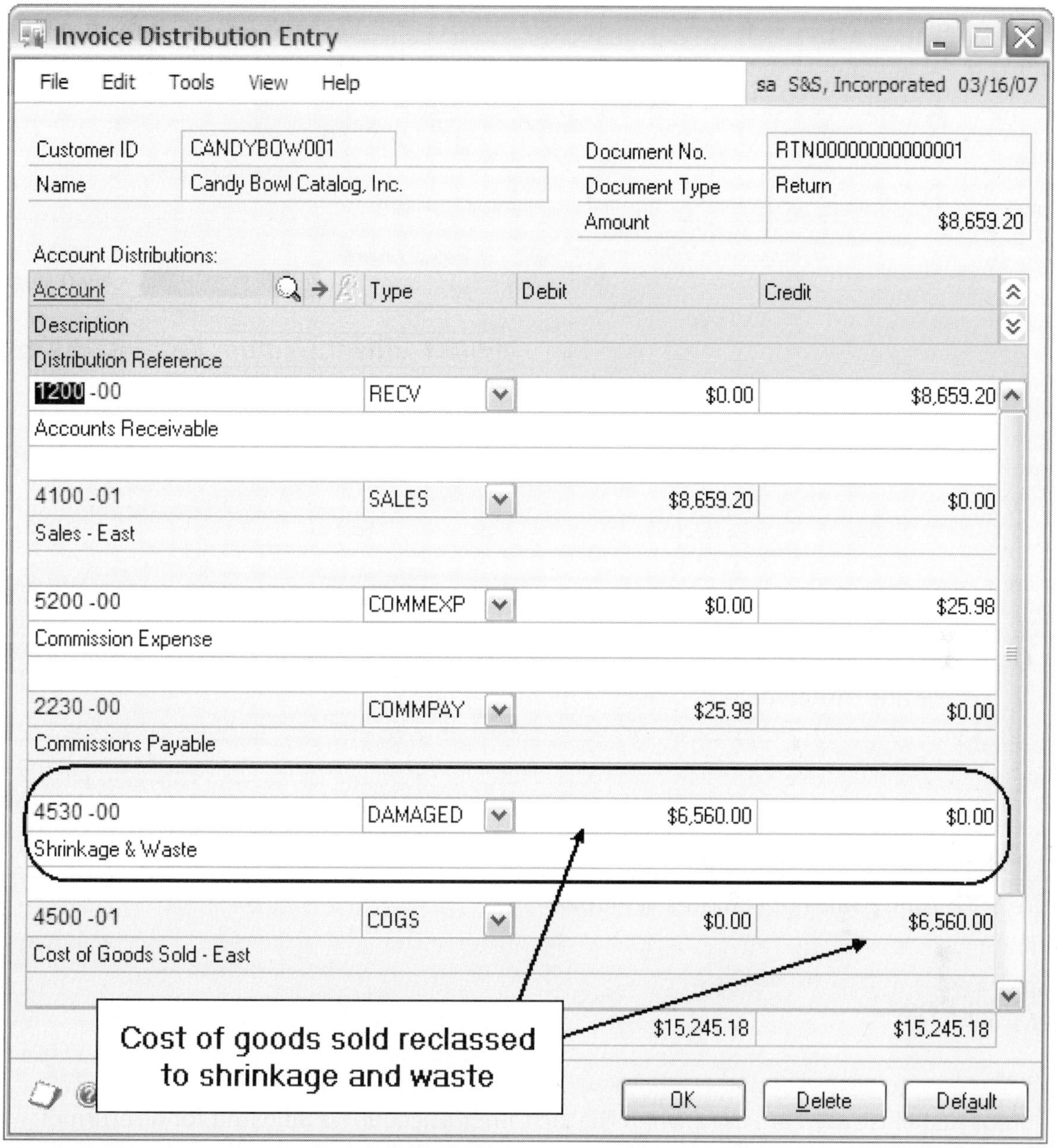

Figure 5:36 General Ledger Distribution for the Return

5. Click **OK** and then **Post** the transaction. Close the window and review the posting reports.

6. You must next apply the return to reduce the unpaid invoice. *(Note: Notice that you could not apply the return during entry.)* Click **Apply Sales Documents**. Look up Candy Bowl and look up the return document. Mark the invoice. (See Figure 5:37.) Note that the Unapplied Amount is zero.

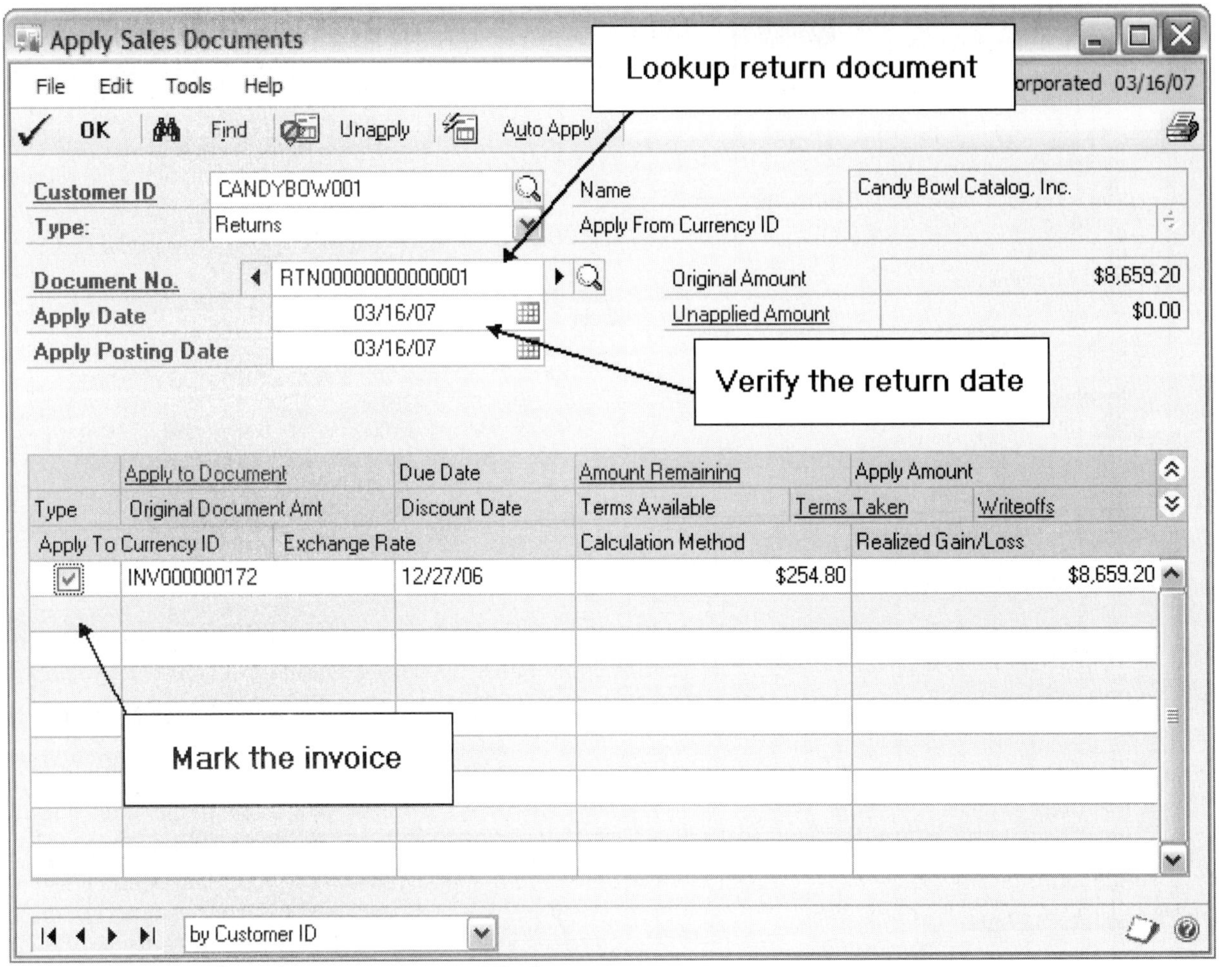

Figure 5:37 Apply Sales Documents Window

7. Click **OK**.

The steps just Illustrated are used when the customer's account is adjusted for a return of inventory. There are other situations that may require adjusting the customer's account balance and for these situations we use a credit memo. This transaction is recorded through the Receivables Processing Tier. Complete the next exercise where we issue a credit to Better Buy to compensate the customer for late delivery of inventory.

1. Click **Transaction Entry** and select **Credit Memos**. *(Note: Credit Memos decrease the customer account balance whereas Debit Memos increase it.)* Look up **Better Buy** and record the following transaction dated March 16, 2007. (See Figure 5:38.)

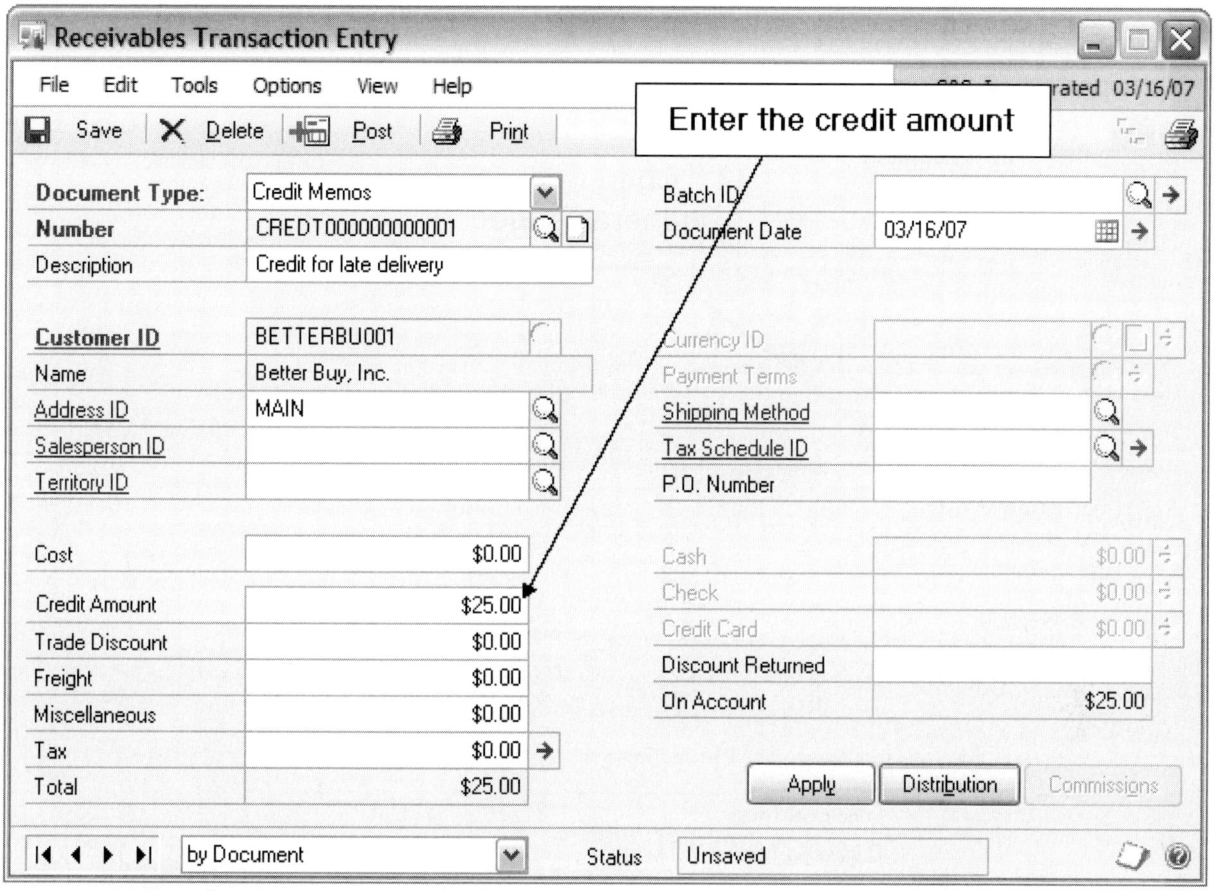

Figure 5:38 Credit Memo Transaction

2. Click **Distributions**, change the sales account to 4400-02 Sales Discounts – MidWest, and click **OK**. (See Figure 5:39.)

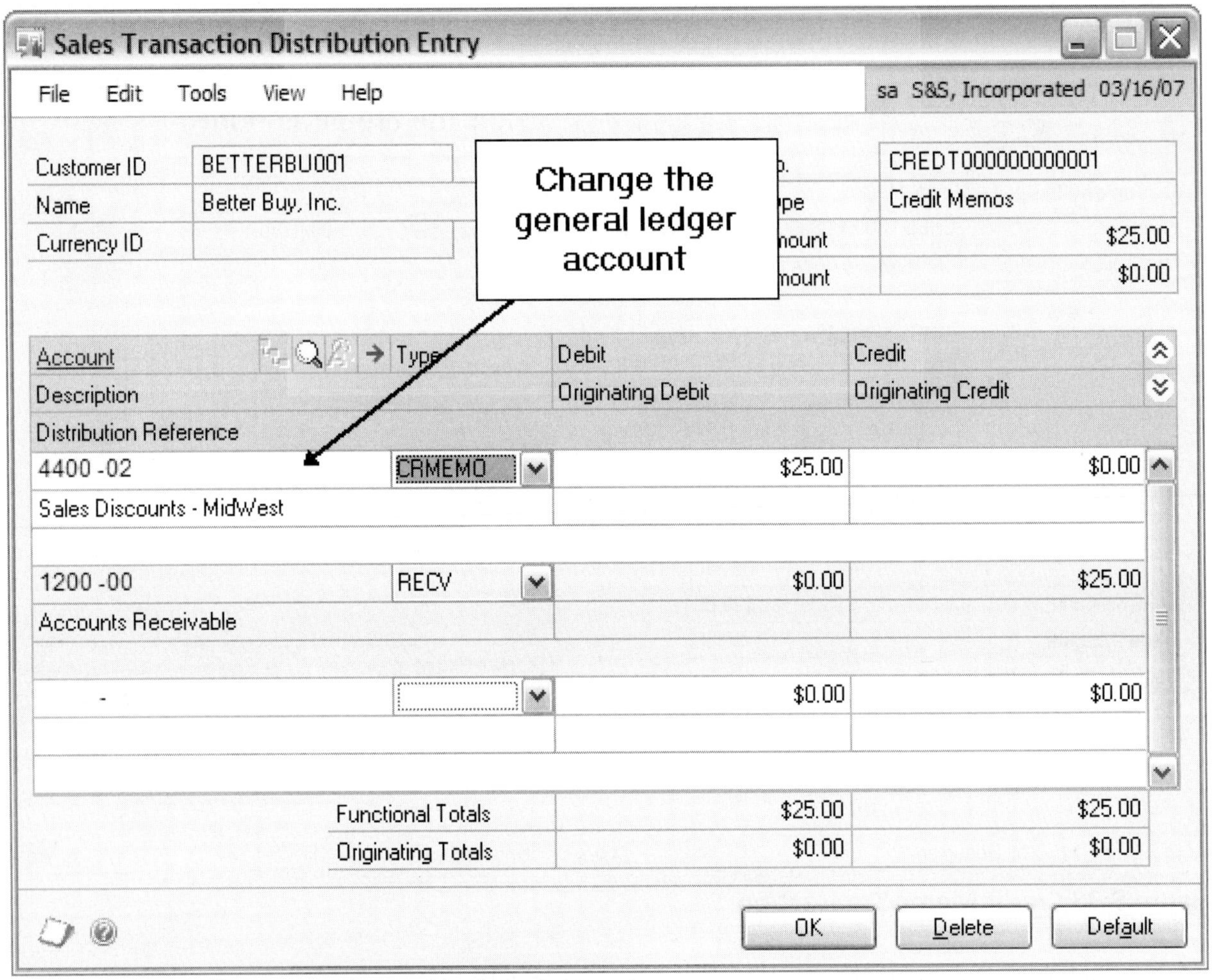

Figure 5:39 Credit Memo General Ledger Accounts

3. You can apply this memo to an invoice during transaction entry. Click **Apply** and mark the invoice illustrated in Figure 5:40. Click **OK** when finished.

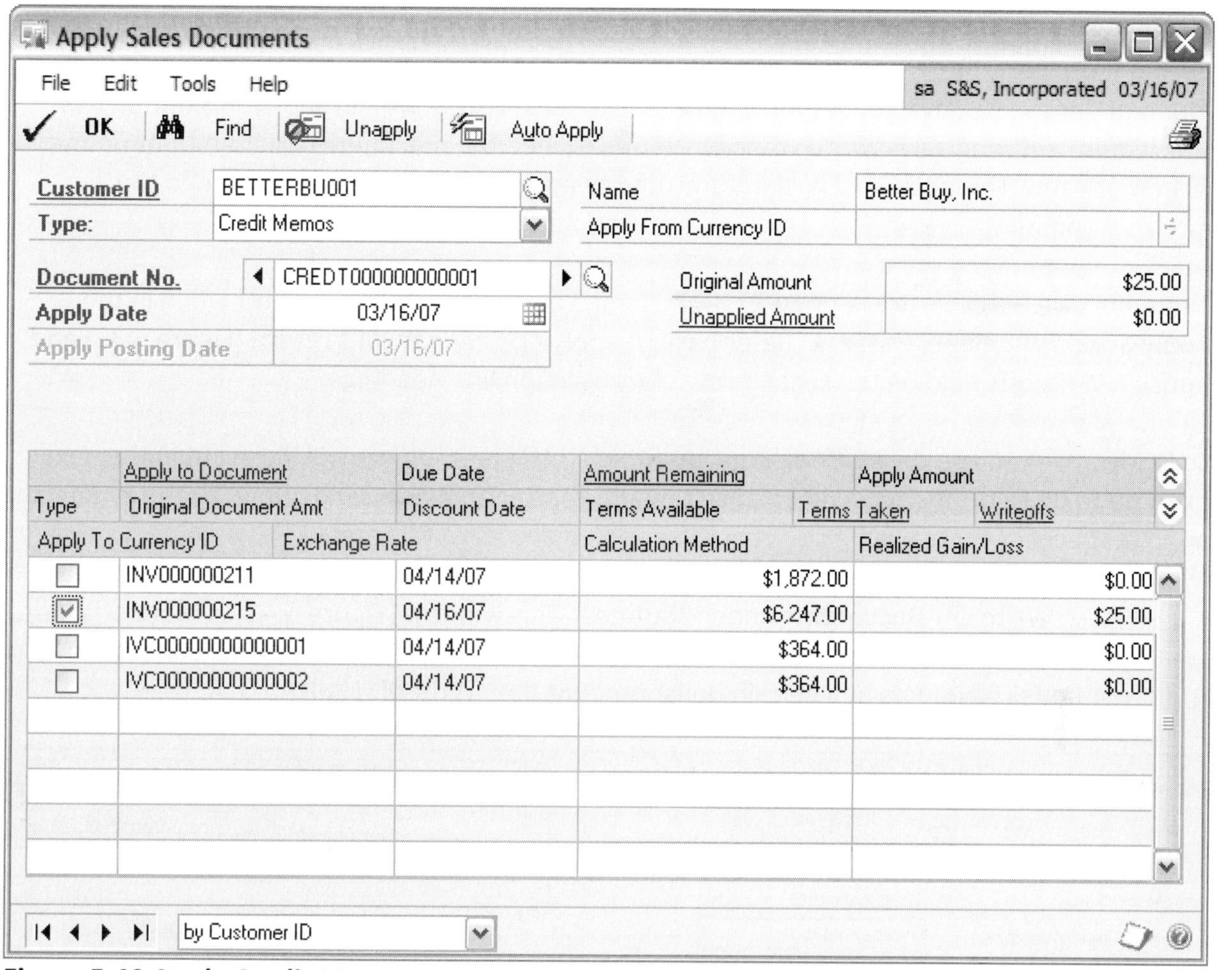

Figure 5:40 Apply Credit Memo

4. Now **Post** the transaction and close the window. Review the posting reports that print.

Two points before leaving this topic. First, internal controls should require approval of customer credits before posting by an accounts receivable clerk. Second, returns, credit memos and debit memos are issued for a variety of reasons so the distribution accounts should be checked prior to posting.

Writing Off Invoices

All invoices carry a threat that customers will fail to pay. If the company implements strong credit authorization controls such situations should infrequently arise; however, procedures cannot guarantee that invoices will not be written off. Write-offs may occur for reasons such as customer over or under payment errors. Regardless, write-offs over a specific dollar amount should be authorized before posting.

GP provides two places for authorizing write-offs. First, recall our topic on customer cards remembering the option to set a maximum write-off dollar amount for each card. Setting a dollar limit here will let accounts receivable clerks perform routine write-offs of over or under payment errors within the authorization limit. The second option for controlling write-offs is found under the Receivables setup window discussed in Level Two. In short, this option lets you require entering a password when write-offs exceed the maximum dollar amount on the customer card. This password is then furnished to employees authorized to exceed the maximum amount.

There are two ways of recording a write-off. First, you can enter the write-off while in the Apply Sales Documents window. Refer back to applying Candy Bowl's return (Figure 5:37) and notice a Writeoffs field on the second row of transaction line headings.

Secondly, you can use the write-off routine, which is the method we will illustrate in the next exercise to write off the $254.80 balance remaining after applying Candy Bowl's return. Keep in mind that accounts receivable clerks may be denied access to this menu.

1. Click **Write Off Documents** under Routines. This window (Figure 5:41) is more efficient when several invoices need to be written off. You can search several accounts for over or under payments of a certain dollar amount (i.e., Writeoff Limit).

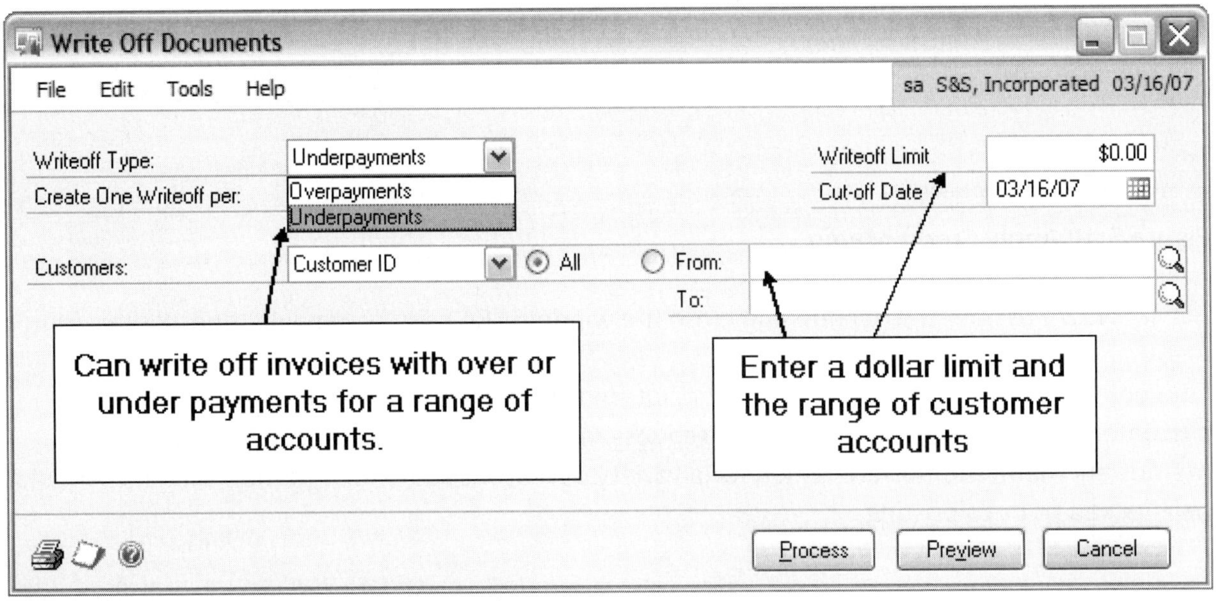

Figure 5:41 Write Off Documents Window

2. Choose **Underpayments**, enter $300.00 as the Writeoff Limit, and search **From** CANDYBOW001 **To** CANDYBOW001. (See Figure 5:42.)

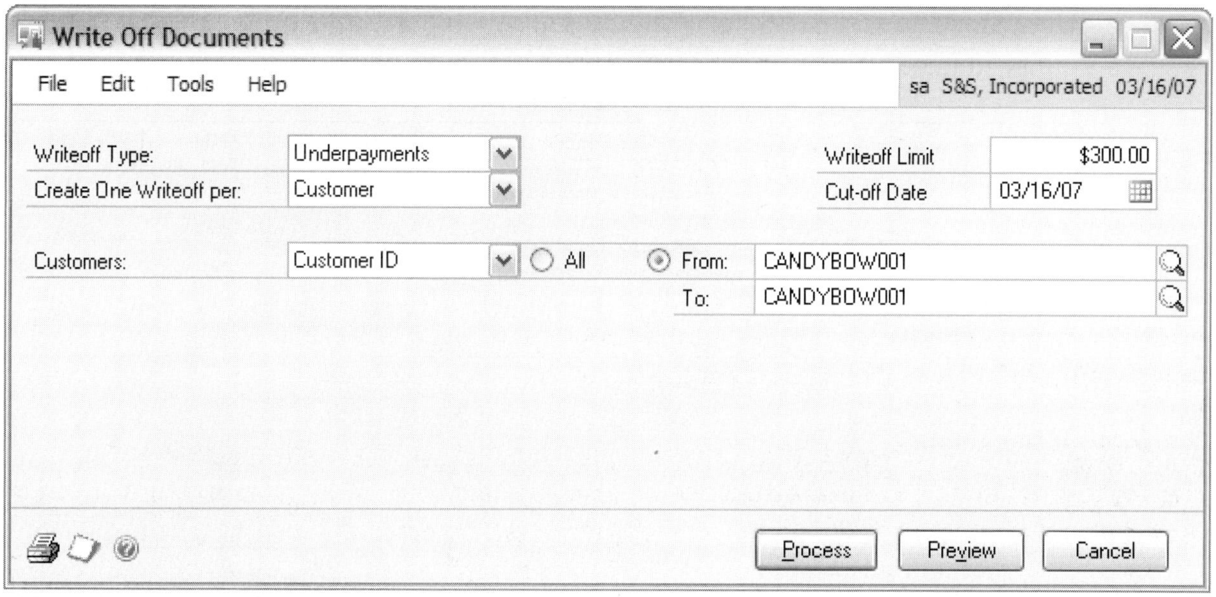

Figure 5:42 Write-off Criteria

3. Click **Preview** and the results are illustrated next. Click **OK**.

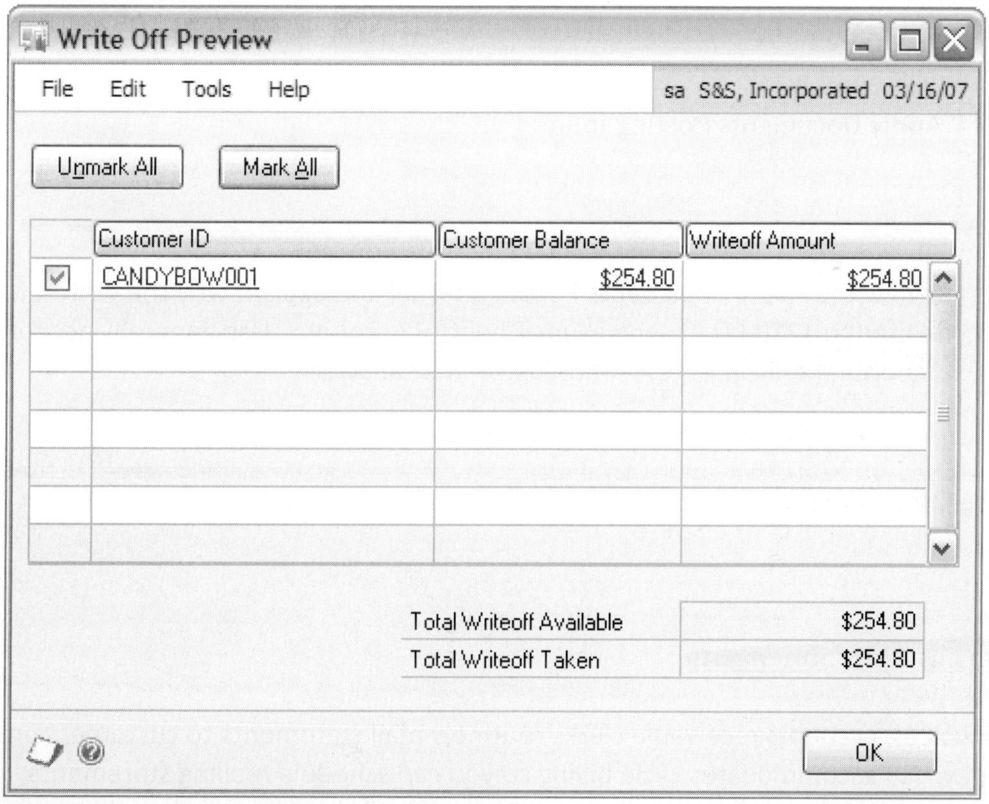

Figure 5:43 Write Off Preview Window

4. Click **Process** to post the write-off. The first posting report is illustrated next. Note the accounts affected. Review remaining reports.

	S&S, Incorporated	Page: 1
User Date: 03/16/07	APPLY DOCUMENTS POSTING JOURNAL	User ID: sa
	Receivables Management	

Audit Trail Code: RMAPY00000002

Batch ID: sa

Batch Origin: Receivables Apply Doc.

Document Number	Type	Customer ID	Name
WCREDT00000000001	CR	CANDYBOW001	Candy Bowl Catalog, Inc.

General Ledger Distributions

Account Number	Account Description	Type	Posting Date	Debit Amount	Credit Amount
1200-00	Accounts Receivable	RECV	03/16/07	0.00	254.80
1210-00	Allowance for Doubtful Account	WRITE	03/16/07	254.80	0.00
				254.80	254.80

Applied Distributions

Document Number	Document Type	Apply Date	Discount	Write off	Amount Applied
INV000000172	SLS	03/16/07	0.00	254.80	0.00
			0.00	254.80	0.00

1 Document(s)

Figure 5:44 Apply Documents Posting Journal

Review the Apply Documents Posting Journal and explain why the write-off was debited to 1210-00 Allowance for Doubtful Accounts. Use generally accepted accounting principles (GAAP) to justify your answer.

E5:7 Write-Off Posting Accounts

Preparing Customer Statements

Besides invoices, accounts receivable clerks routinely mail statements to customers prompting them to pay. GP accommodates cycle billing so you can schedule mailing statements throughout the month to manage cash flow. Cycle billing is implemented on the customer card by entering a statement date such as biweekly, semimonthly, etc. S&S does not use cycle billing so statements are mailed just once a month.

You should age customer accounts and review pending transactions under Series Post on the Sales home page before sending statements. The next exercise illustrates aging accounts and printing statements.

1. Aging customer accounts is very straightforward. Click **Aging** under **Routines** and set the options illustrated in see Figure 5:45. *Note: We will age only a few customers to save time.*

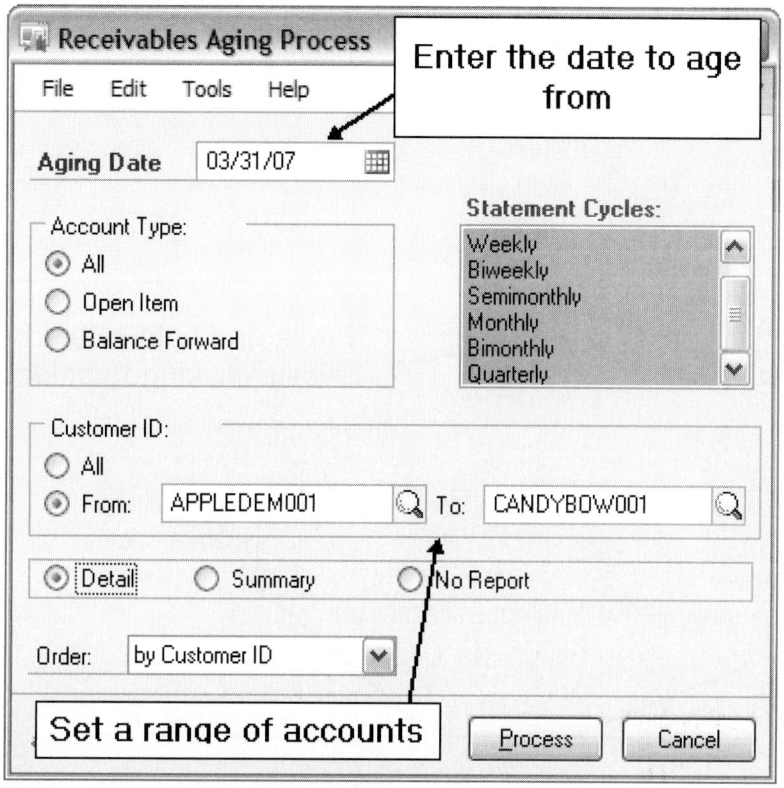

Figure 5:45 Receivables Aging Process Window

2. Click **Process** and print the report to the screen. Close the report.

3. We are now ready to print statements for aged customers. *(Note: We will only print a statement for Barter Bay.)* Click **Statements** under Routines and look up the REGULAR **Statement ID**. Enter the criteria as illustrated next. The table that follows explains statement dates.

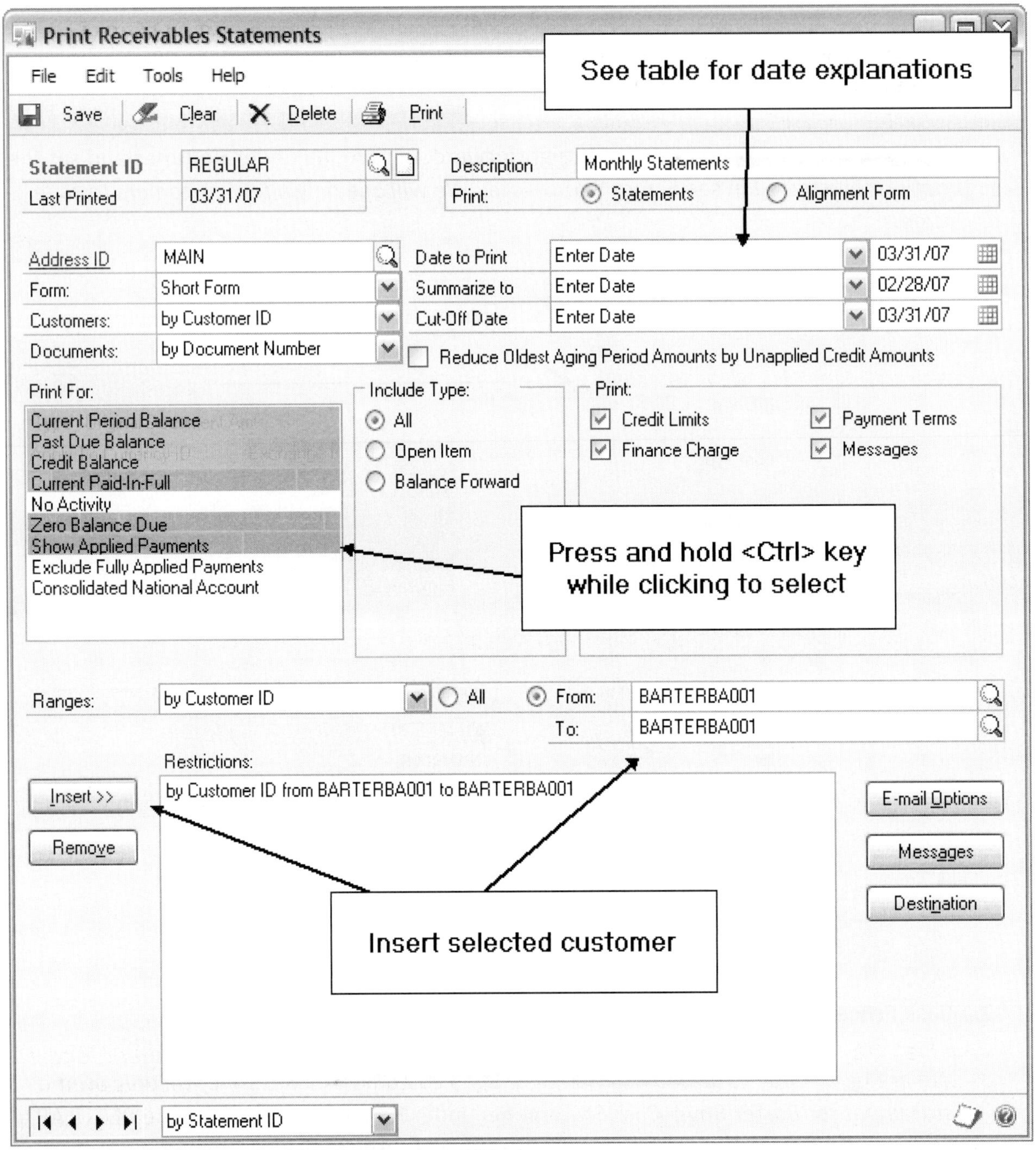

Figure 5:46 Print Receivables Statements Window

Statement Date	Purpose
Date to Print	Date for the printed statement.
Summarize To	Transactions prior to this date are printed as a balance forward.
Cut-Off Date	Do not print transactions after this date.

Table 5:8 Dates in the Statement Window

4. Click **Destination** and set the report to print to the screen. Click **Print** and click **Save** to keep your changes. The statement is illustrated next. S&S prints statements to preprinted forms. Close the statement and the window.

BARTER BAY, INC.
GERALD LEWIS
123 KLEIN ROAD

BOISE ID 87325

Summarized balance forward

Credit Limit: $250,000.00
Payment Terms: Net 30
Finance Charge APR: 12.00%

1

	02/28/07	BBF		$264,440.00	$0.00	$264,440.00
INV000000209	03/14/07	SLS	INV000000209	$69,562.00		$334,002.00

$334,002.00

SLS Sales / Invoices FIN Finance Charges CR Credit Memos
SCH Scheduled Payments SVC Service / Repairs RTN Returns
DR Debit Memos WRN Warranties PMT Payments

$0.00

Current	0-30 Days	31 - 60 Days	61 - 90 Day	91 Days & Over		
$69,562.00	$264,440.00	$0.00	$0.00	$0.00	$0.00	$0.00

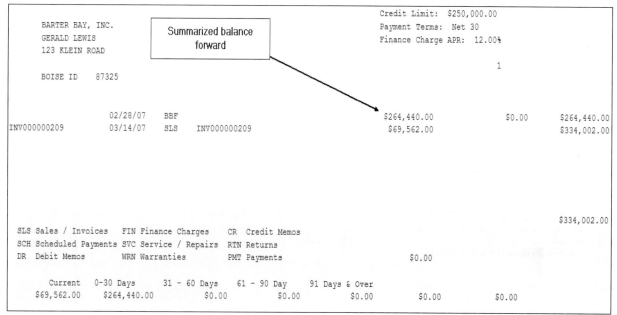

Table 5:9 Barter Bay Statement

This completes tasks performed by the accounts receivable department. We next look at basic reporting for the Sales Series.

Sales Series Reporting

Companies require a variety of analysis, control, and status reports from their general ledger packages. This topic focuses on a few of those reports. Reporting falls into the general categories of Trial Balance, History, Analysis, Posting Journals, Commissions, Setup, and Activity. Trial Balance reports provide information on customer account balances and balance aging. Activity reports are used to monitor Sales Series tasks. History, Commissions, and Analysis reports are used for analyzing sales trends, discounts, gross profit, and salesperson performance. Posting Journals are for reprinting the control reports that print after posting. Finally, Setup reports are used to document internal control options for the series.

We now focus on Trial Balance and Activity reports.

Accounts Receivable Aging Reports

GP provides a variety of trial balance reports on accounts receivable aging. Employees responsible for credit and collection, sales transaction posting, internal controls, and financial statement preparation rely on aging reports. An aging report should be prepared and reviewed at least monthly to identify customer delinquencies.

Aging reports also serve as an internal control tool used to reconcile the Sales Series to the Financial Series. To reconcile these Series, you print the aging report as of a specific date and compare the report total to the total balance on that date in the Accounts Receivable and Sales Discounts Available general ledger accounts.

We will now illustrate this concept.

1. Click **Trial Balance** and choose the **Historical Aged Trial Balance** report. Highlight the existing **Hist AR Aging** report and click **Modify**. The report options (Figure 5:47) are customized to print aged customer balances as of February 28, 2007. Keep these options and click **Print**.

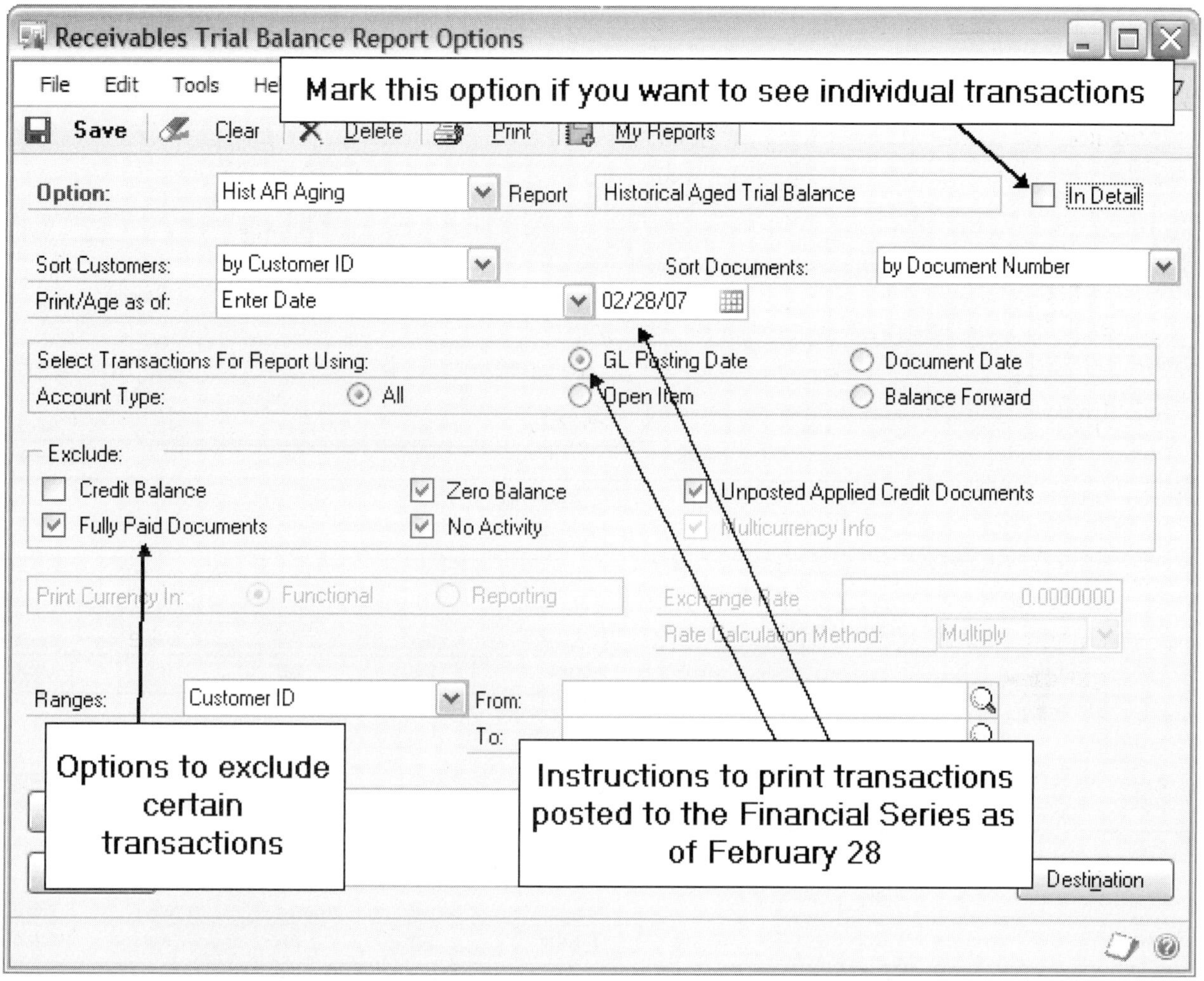

Figure 5:47 Historical Trial Balance Report Options

2. The report is illustrated next. We have noted aging categories and the ending balance for the report.

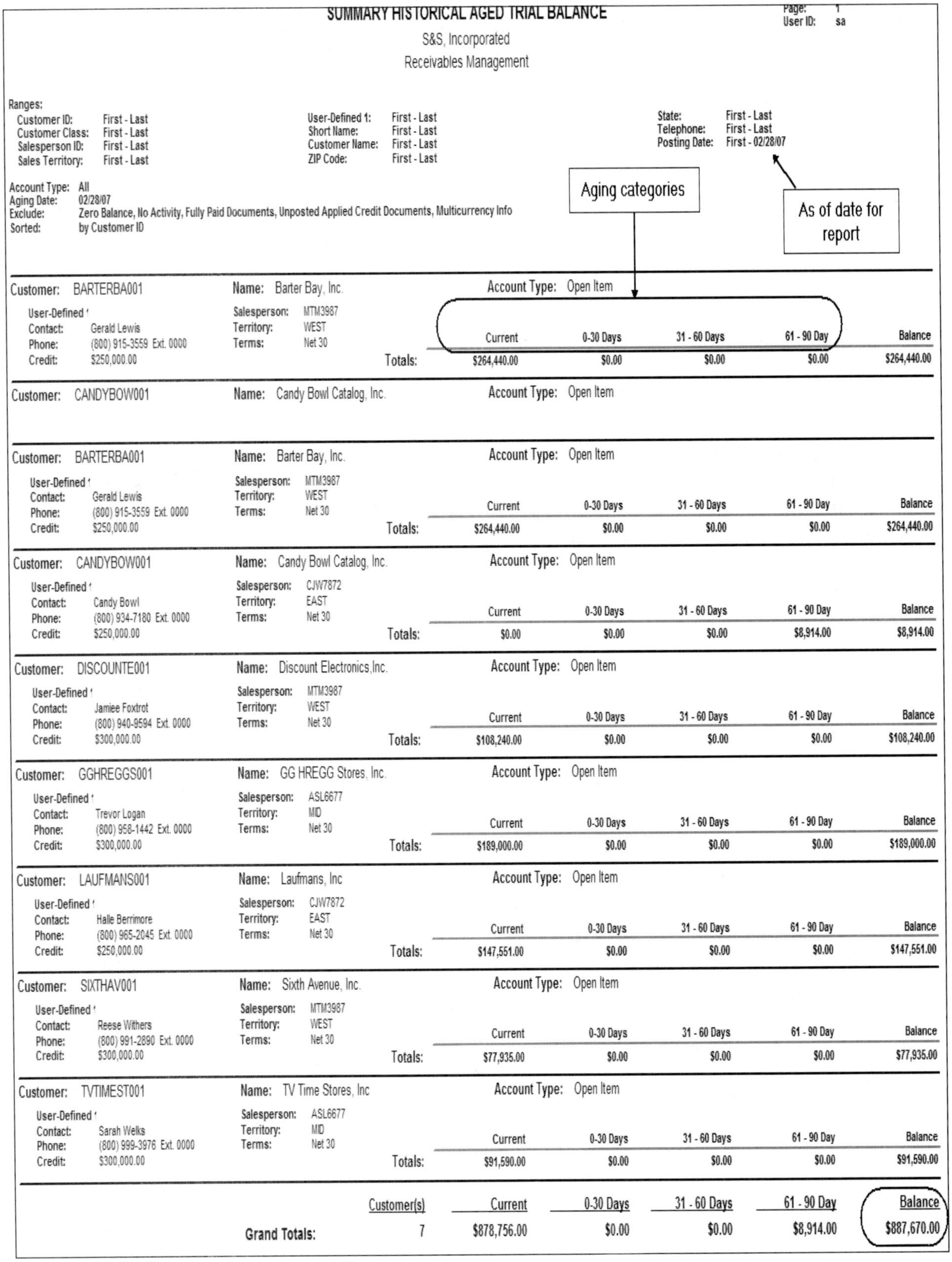

SUMMARY HISTORICAL AGED TRIAL BALANCE

Page: 1
User ID: sa

S&S, Incorporated
Receivables Management

Ranges:

Customer ID:	First - Last	User-Defined 1:	First - Last	State:	First - Last
Customer Class:	First - Last	Short Name:	First - Last	Telephone:	First - Last
Salesperson ID:	First - Last	Customer Name:	First - Last	Posting Date:	First - 02/28/07
Sales Territory:	First - Last	ZIP Code:	First - Last		

Account Type: All
Aging Date: 02/28/07
Exclude: Zero Balance, No Activity, Fully Paid Documents, Unposted Applied Credit Documents, Multicurrency Info
Sorted: by Customer ID

Customer: BARTERBA001 Name: Barter Bay, Inc. Account Type: Open Item
User-Defined 1 | Salesperson: MTM3987
Contact: Gerald Lewis | Territory: WEST
Phone: (800) 915-3559 Ext. 0000 | Terms: Net 30
Credit: $250,000.00

	Current	0-30 Days	31 - 60 Days	61 - 90 Day	Balance
Totals:	$264,440.00	$0.00	$0.00	$0.00	$264,440.00

Customer: CANDYBOW001 Name: Candy Bowl Catalog, Inc. Account Type: Open Item

Customer: BARTERBA001 Name: Barter Bay, Inc. Account Type: Open Item
User-Defined 1 | Salesperson: MTM3987
Contact: Gerald Lewis | Territory: WEST
Phone: (800) 915-3559 Ext. 0000 | Terms: Net 30
Credit: $250,000.00

	Current	0-30 Days	31 - 60 Days	61 - 90 Day	Balance
Totals:	$264,440.00	$0.00	$0.00	$0.00	$264,440.00

Customer: CANDYBOW001 Name: Candy Bowl Catalog, Inc. Account Type: Open Item
User-Defined 1 | Salesperson: CJW7872
Contact: Candy Bowl | Territory: EAST
Phone: (800) 934-7180 Ext. 0000 | Terms: Net 30
Credit: $250,000.00

	Current	0-30 Days	31 - 60 Days	61 - 90 Day	Balance
Totals:	$0.00	$0.00	$0.00	$8,914.00	$8,914.00

Customer: DISCOUNTE001 Name: Discount Electronics,Inc. Account Type: Open Item
User-Defined 1 | Salesperson: MTM3987
Contact: Jamiee Foxtrot | Territory: WEST
Phone: (800) 940-9594 Ext. 0000 | Terms: Net 30
Credit: $300,000.00

	Current	0-30 Days	31 - 60 Days	61 - 90 Day	Balance
Totals:	$108,240.00	$0.00	$0.00	$0.00	$108,240.00

Customer: GGHREGGS001 Name: GG HREGG Stores, Inc. Account Type: Open Item
User-Defined 1 | Salesperson: ASL6677
Contact: Trevor Logan | Territory: MID
Phone: (800) 958-1442 Ext. 0000 | Terms: Net 30
Credit: $300,000.00

	Current	0-30 Days	31 - 60 Days	61 - 90 Day	Balance
Totals:	$189,000.00	$0.00	$0.00	$0.00	$189,000.00

Customer: LAUFMANS001 Name: Laufmans, Inc Account Type: Open Item
User-Defined 1 | Salesperson: CJW7872
Contact: Halle Berrimore | Territory: EAST
Phone: (800) 965-2045 Ext. 0000 | Terms: Net 30
Credit: $250,000.00

	Current	0-30 Days	31 - 60 Days	61 - 90 Day	Balance
Totals:	$147,551.00	$0.00	$0.00	$0.00	$147,551.00

Customer: SIXTHAV001 Name: Sixth Avenue, Inc. Account Type: Open Item
User-Defined 1 | Salesperson: MTM3987
Contact: Reese Withers | Territory: WEST
Phone: (800) 991-2890 Ext. 0000 | Terms: Net 30
Credit: $300,000.00

	Current	0-30 Days	31 - 60 Days	61 - 90 Day	Balance
Totals:	$77,935.00	$0.00	$0.00	$0.00	$77,935.00

Customer: TVTIMEST001 Name: TV Time Stores, Inc Account Type: Open Item
User-Defined 1 | Salesperson: ASL6677
Contact: Sarah Welks | Territory: MID
Phone: (800) 999-3976 Ext. 0000 | Terms: Net 30
Credit: $300,000.00

	Current	0-30 Days	31 - 60 Days	61 - 90 Day	Balance
Totals:	$91,590.00	$0.00	$0.00	$0.00	$91,590.00

	Customer(s)	Current	0-30 Days	31 - 60 Days	61 - 90 Day	Balance
Grand Totals:	7	$878,756.00	$0.00	$0.00	$8,914.00	$887,670.00

Figure 5:48 Historical Aged Trial Balance Report

3. Close the report and the report window. Next compare the report total to the balance in the accounts receivable control accounts. Activate the **Financial** home page and click **Summary** under Inquiry. Look up 1200-00 Accounts Receivable and note that the period balance for February is $887,670.00.

4. Now scroll to 1205-00 Sales Discounts Available and note that its February period balance is zero. (*Note: You must add this account balance to the balance in accounts receivables because S&S tracks potential early payment discount, a feature discussed in Level Two and explained in the following sidebar.)* The total for both accounts agrees to the report balance so the Sales Series reconciles with the Financial Series.

What is the 1205-00, Sales Discounts Available account?

If the option to track discounts available is marked in Sales Series setup, GP tracks potential discounts on invoices that offer early payment terms (i.e., 2%/10, net 30). When posting these invoices, GP posts the potential discount to discounts available and the remaining invoice balance to accounts receivable. Consequently, you must add balances in both accounts to ascertain the total outstanding accounts receivables.

GP handles making appropriate entries to accounts receivable, discounts available, and discounts taken (contra revenue account) when payments for these invoices are posted.

There are times when these Series may become "out of balance." This usually occurs when not following proper procedures for posting or correcting transactions. Therefore, if you find it necessary to correct a posted transaction refer to the instructions found in Appendix C.

The Sales and Financial Series should be reconciled monthly. In Chapter 2 we illustrated using a SmartList to assist in pinpointing transactions that may cause these Series to not reconcile. To underscore the frequency of an out-of-balance condition occurring, we point out that GP has added a new utility feature called Reconcile to help with this process. We will not illustrate this feature.

The point of this discussion is to emphasize that reconciling these Series is an important internal control process that protects the integrity of reported data and customer trust in the company.

Activity Reporting

Activity Reports (Figure 5:49) are import control reports for sales activities. For some companies, these reports replace the documents that trigger activities.

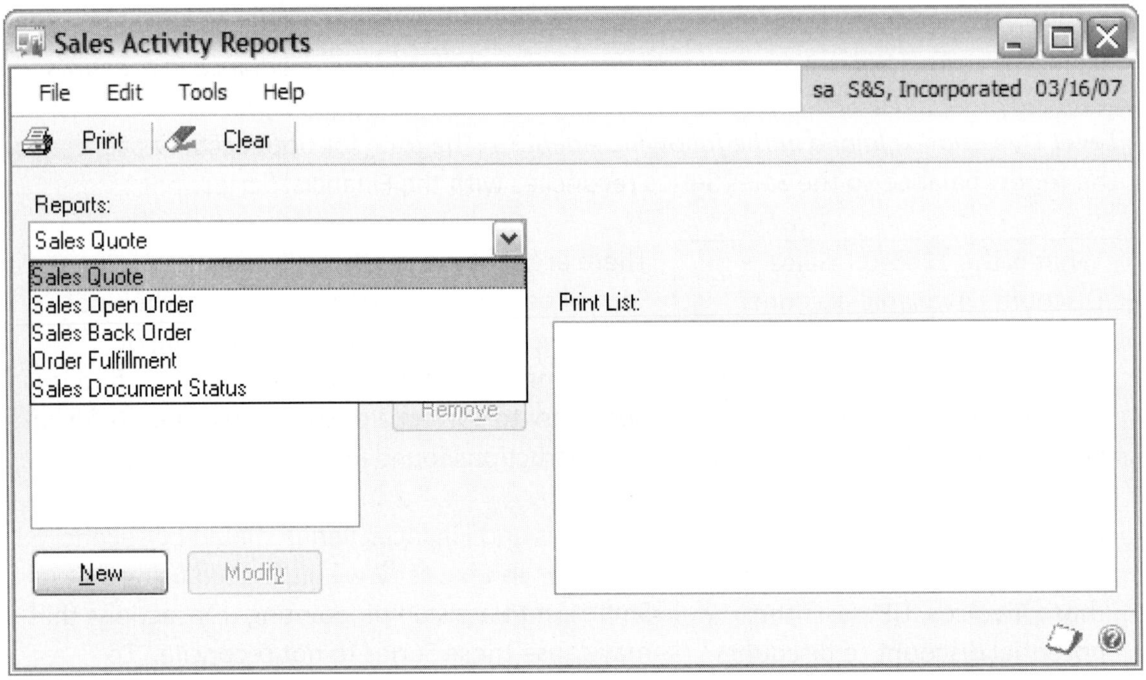

Figure 5:49 Activity Reports

For instance, instead of waiting for a sales order to arrive in the warehouse, the Sales Open Order report (Figure 5:50) prints outstanding orders. These reports can be reviewed by warehouse employees, who can then print picking tickets and immediately pick inventory to fill the order.

```
                                   S&S, Incorporated                                         Page:     1
                                   SALES OPEN ORDER REPORT                                   User ID: sa
                                   Sales Order Processing

Ranges:             From:          To:                                 From:        To:
Customer ID:        First          Last           Master Number:       First        Last
Customer Name:      First          Last           Req. Ship Date:      First        Last
Document Date:      First          Last           Salesperson ID:      First        Last
Document Number:    First          Last           Type ID:             First        Last

Sorted By: by Customer ID                         Print Option: Detailed
Display: Kit Components, User-defined, Serial/Lot Number

^ Drop Ship     # Non-Inventory     + Serial/Lot Numbers Needed     * Allocation Needed

Document Number  Master Number  Type ID      Document Date   Workflow Status   Customer ID     Customer Name
------------------------------------------------------------------------------------------------------------
          Requested Ship Date     Salesperson ID         Deposit Amount      Phone                Repeating
------------------------------------------------------------------------------------------------------------
    Item Number              Item Description          Site     U of M    Qty       Qty       Unit Price Extended Price
                                                                          Ordered   Remaining
------------------------------------------------------------------------------------------------------------

SO000000192            196  STDORDER     03/28/07      Not Activated     CANDYBOW001     Candy Bowl Catalog, Inc.
          03/28/07          CJW7872                          $0.00       (800) 934-7180  Ext. 0000   No
    TVSN34W                 Sunyung 34 Inch Widescreen MAIN     EA             50          50  $2,970.00  $148,500.00
------------------------------------------------------------------------------------------------------------
    Item Number              Item Description          Site     U of M    Qty       Qty       Unit Price Extended Price
                                                                          Ordered   Remaining
------------------------------------------------------------------------------------------------------------

SO000000192            196  STDORDER     03/28/07      Not Activated     CANDYBOW001     Candy Bowl Catalog, Inc.
          03/28/07          CJW7872                          $0.00       (800) 934-7180  Ext. 0000   No
    TVSN34W                 Sunyung 34 Inch Widescreen MAIN     EA             50          50  $2,970.00  $148,500.00

                                 Remaining Subtotal:      $148,500.00     Order Subtotal:        $148,500.00
                                                                          Trade Discount:              $0.00
                                                                          Freight:                     $0.00
                                                                          Misc:                        $0.00
                                                                          Tax:                         $0.00
                                                                          Total:                 $148,500.00

         List 1:                       Text Field 2:                 Date Field 1:
         List 2:                       Text Field 3:                 Date Field 2:
         List 3:                       Text Field 4:
         Text Field 1:                 Text Field 5:

Grand Totals:   Number of Orders       Deposit Total     Remaining Subtotal      Order Subtotal          Order Total
                ------------------------------------------------------------------------------------------------
                               1               $0.00            $148,500.00         $148,500.00          $148,500.00
                ================    ================    ===================   =================   ==================
```

Figure 5:50 Sales Open Order Report

Likewise, the Order Fulfillment report can be printed to trigger shipping and/or account receivable activities.

The Sales Document Status report monitors sales order processing. Daily review of this report can pinpoint order processing delays to improve revenue cycle efficiencies.

> Reprint the posting report that lists the Laufmans invoice created in an earlier exercise.
>
> Use a report to analyze the gross profit on items sold to Better Buy.

E5:6 Sales Series Report Practice

MONTH-ENDING THE SALES SERIES

No discussion on internal controls is complete without looking at Sales Series closing procedures. Closing procedures are steps taken prior to month ending the Sales Series. At month-end our focus is on: (1) Did transactions post to the proper accounting period; (2) Are all transactions for the month finalized and posted in accordance with GAAP; and (3) does the Sales Series reconcile to the Financial Series.

1. Verify that Transactions Posted to the Proper Accounting Period

S&S's accountant, Ashton, has instituted and trained clerks on procedures for posting period-end transactions. The key procedure is controlling transaction processing at the beginning of a month, particularly when considering that S&S set the Sales Series to post to the Financial Series by batch date. Let us illustrate.

At the beginning of March employees will be processing remaining February transactions plus March transactions. Remember that transactions post to the Sales Series using the transaction date but to the Financial Series using the batch date. Thus, to control batch processing, Ashton requires two batches; one dated February and the other dated March. Transactions are then entered into and posted through the appropriate batch. If you commingle transactions, such as combining February with March transactions in a February dated batch, then March transactions will be posted in February.

Furthermore, Ashton sets a cutoff date, which is the last date for posting February transactions. After this date he month-ends the Sales Series as illustrated in Chapter 2. Remember this is done by clicking the GP button to select ***Tools>>Setup>>Company>>Fiscal Periods*** and marking the checkbox for the month under the Series. (See Figure 5:51.)

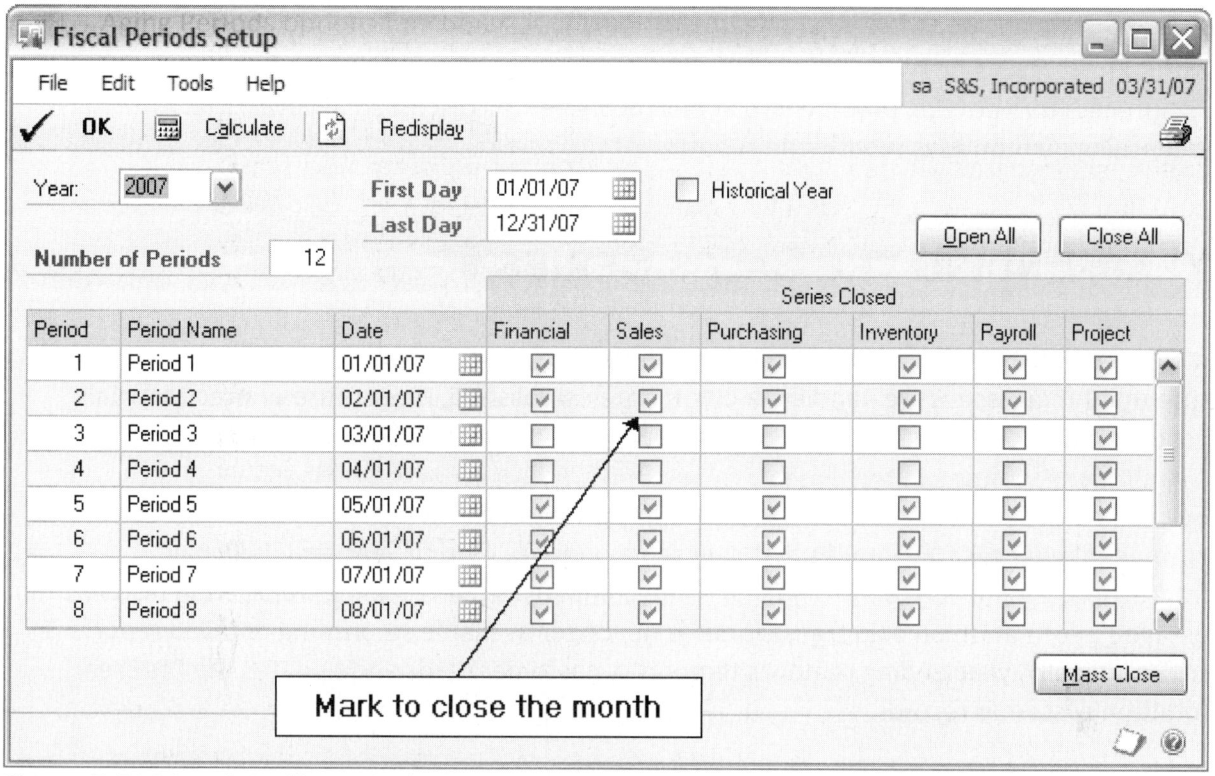

Figure 5:51 Month Ending a Series

If unposted February transactions are later discovered, these are then posted through a March dated batch. The actual February transaction date is retained so that the Sales Series properly ages them. If these transactions are material, Ashton posts a reversing journal entry in the Financial Series to accrue the amount. *(Note: Reversing journal entries are discussed in Chapter 8.)*

2. Verify that all Transactions Finalized and Posted in Accordance with GAAP

Aside from timing concerns, Ashton must verify that all valid February transactions are posted. The first step is to review Sales Series activity reports. For instance, he reviews the Open Orders report looking for old orders that may have been filled but not invoiced. He also reviews the Order Fulfillment report to spot failure to invoice.

He also checks the Sales Series Post window for suspended transactions. Finally, he reviews shipment logs and bills of lading for in-process deliveries. Remember from an earlier invoicing discussion that S&S invoices orders before actual delivery for cash flow reasons. This invoicing procedure is GAAP compliant when the shipping terms are FOB shipping point. However, S&S uses FOB destination point so title does not transfer until actual delivery, which also means that revenue should not be recognized until delivery. Therefore, to comply with GAAP, he posts a reversing journal entry in the Financial Series to adjust revenue and cost of goods sold for in-transit shipments.

3. Verify that the Sales Series Reconciles with the Financial Series

The process for verifying that the two Series reconcile was discussed in Level One. After reconciling, Ashton runs month-end reports.

YEAR-ENDING THE SALES SERIES

At year-end, Ashton follows the same procedures performed when closing a month. He makes sure that timing issues are handled, a cutoff date established, reports are printed, accruals posted, and December closed to future posting.

He then backs up the database. This is very important because year-ending the Series makes permanent changes to data files that cannot be undone. During year-end, fully paid transactions are moved to history files. If the company is not retaining transaction history then detailed information on paid transactions is no longer available so printing detailed reports is critical. Finally, year-ending removes temporary customer cards and updates the Last Year totals on customer records.

The Series should be year-ended before recording transactions for the next year. To year-end, you click **Year End Close** under Routines to open the window illustrated next.

Figure 5:52: Year-End Closing Window

You mark whether to print reports and then choose a Fiscal, Calendar, or All option. For S&S, marking any option operate the same because the company's fiscal year corresponds to the calendar year (i.e., both end in December). If a company's year-end does not occur in December then the Calendar option is marked to year-end as of December.

Level Two

Level Two focuses on Sales Series setup. In the revenue cycle, internal control begins at understanding Sales Series options that assist in meeting internal control objectives. Sales Series options are pervasive controls for all activities performed in this Series.

SALES SERIES SETUP AND INTERNAL CONTROLS

From discussions in Level One you know that Sales Series activities break into sales order processing, invoicing, and receivables. Accordingly, each activity has individual setup options.

Receivables Setup

We begin with Receivables setup options affecting .activities performed in the Receivables Processing Tier. Click **Receivables** under Setup to open the window illustrated next.

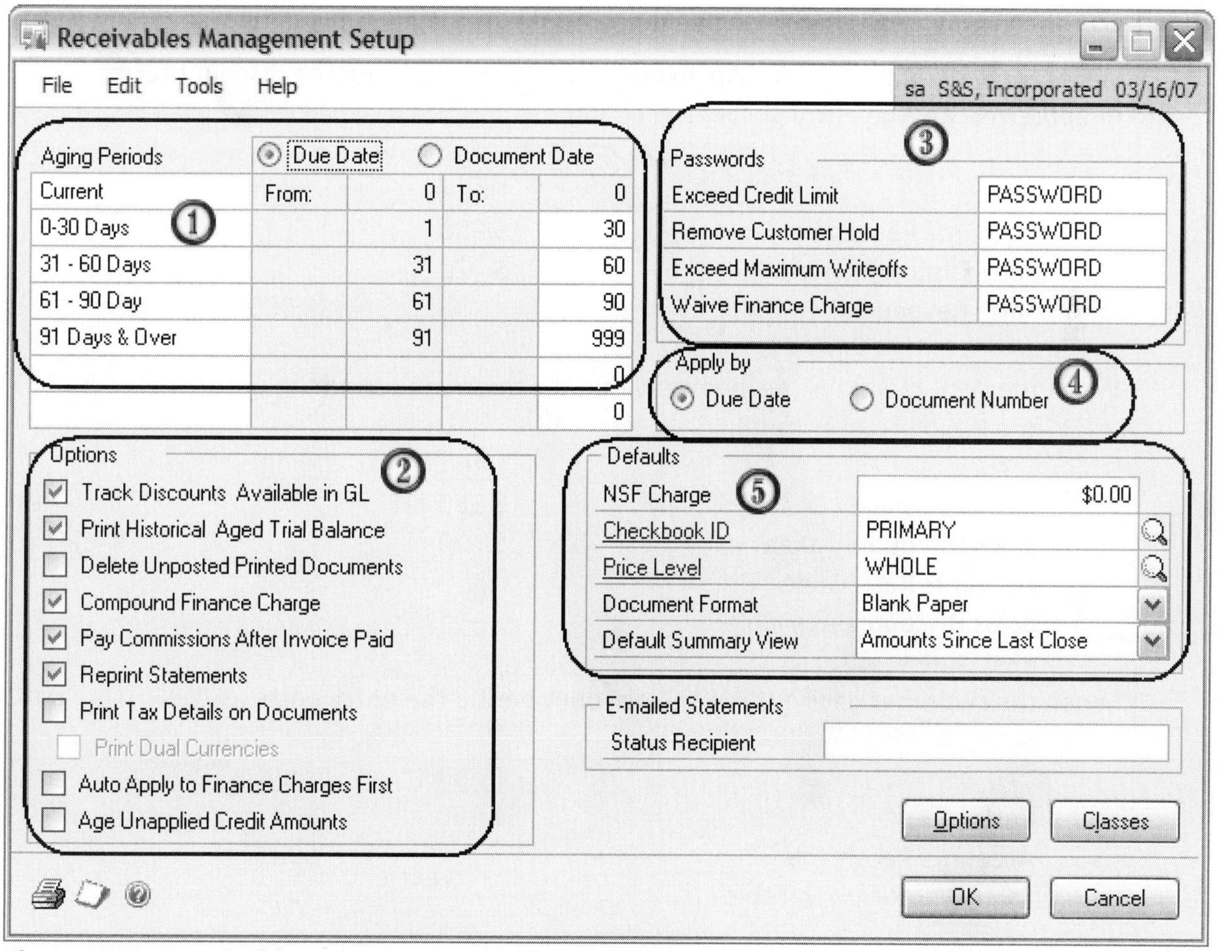

Figure 5:53 Receivables Management Setup Window

Setup controls are divided into five primary sections, namely, Aging Periods, Options, Passwords, Apply by, and Defaults. Explanation on each section follows.

1. **Aging Periods:** These periods set document age brackets for aging reports. Documents include invoices, returns, credit/debit memos, finance charges, and payments. You can choose to age by document date (i.e., transaction date) or by due date and the choice affects aging reports. For instance, assume an invoice dated January 1 that is due on January 31. It is now February 1 and the invoice remains unpaid. If aged by due date then the invoice is 0-30 Days old. If aged by document date then the invoice is 31-60 days old.

2. **Options:** Several of these Options are self-explanatory. We will explain those that are not.

   We begin with the option to **Track Discounts Available in GL**. As discussed in Level One, activating discount tracking instructs GP to post the potential discount amount on an invoice to the discounts available account and the remaining invoice balance to accounts receivable.

   We now provide an example. An invoice posts for $1,000 carrying discount terms of 2/10, Net 30. The entry posts as:

	Debit	Credit
Accounts Receivable	$ 980	
Sales Discounts Available	$ 20	
Sales Revenue		$1,000

   When the customer pays the invoice within the discount period the entry posts as:

	Debit	Credit
Cash	$ 980	
Sales Discounts Taken	$ 20	
Accounts Receivable		$980
Sales Discounts Available		$20

   When the customer pays outside the discount period the entry posts as:

	Debit	Credit
Cash	$1,000	
Accounts Receivable		$980
Sales Discounts Available		$20

Activating the discount option allows companies to analyze the financial effect of offering discount terms.

Print Historical Aged Trial Balance allows companies to regenerate prior period aging reports. However, the company must have also activated options that retain detailed transaction history. These options are found under other Sales Series setup windows as well as on the customer card.

Delete Unposted Printed Documents is an important internal control that means users can only cancel a transaction after printing documents by voiding them. We must assume that printed documents have been released to customers and activating this option enforces document controls by tracking document history.

3. **Passwords:** These are specific authorization controls and are activated by supplying a password for the control. For example, if a write-off exceeds the maximum amount set on the customer card then the clerk cannot post the entry. However, a supervisor with the Exceed Maximum Writeoffs password can permit the entry to post, thus override the control set on the customer card. Notice that we have set all passwords to PASSWORD for simplicity. Of course, this would not be the case in the real world.

4. **Apply By:** These options determine the behavior of the Auto Apply button in the Apply Sales Documents window. If Due Date is selected then the payment is applied to the oldest invoice first. If Document Number is selected then the payment is applied to the earliest document number.

5. **Defaults:** These options determine the default behavior for specific activities performed in the Sales Series. **Checkbook ID** sets a default bank account for posting cash receipts when the customer card fails to assign account. This account also interfaces with bank reconciliation. **Price Level** sets a default price level for sales of inventory when the item card fails to assign a default.

Now click **Options** to view document control numbers. (See Figure 5:54.) These are numbers that GP uses for document numbers in transaction windows. For instance, the next time you post a cash receipt transaction, GP will assign the Next Number illustrated. Also remember that document numbers are part of the audit trail discussed in Chapter 3.

In addition, the window stores the last date certain receivable activities were performed and options for retaining receivables transaction history. Click **OK**.

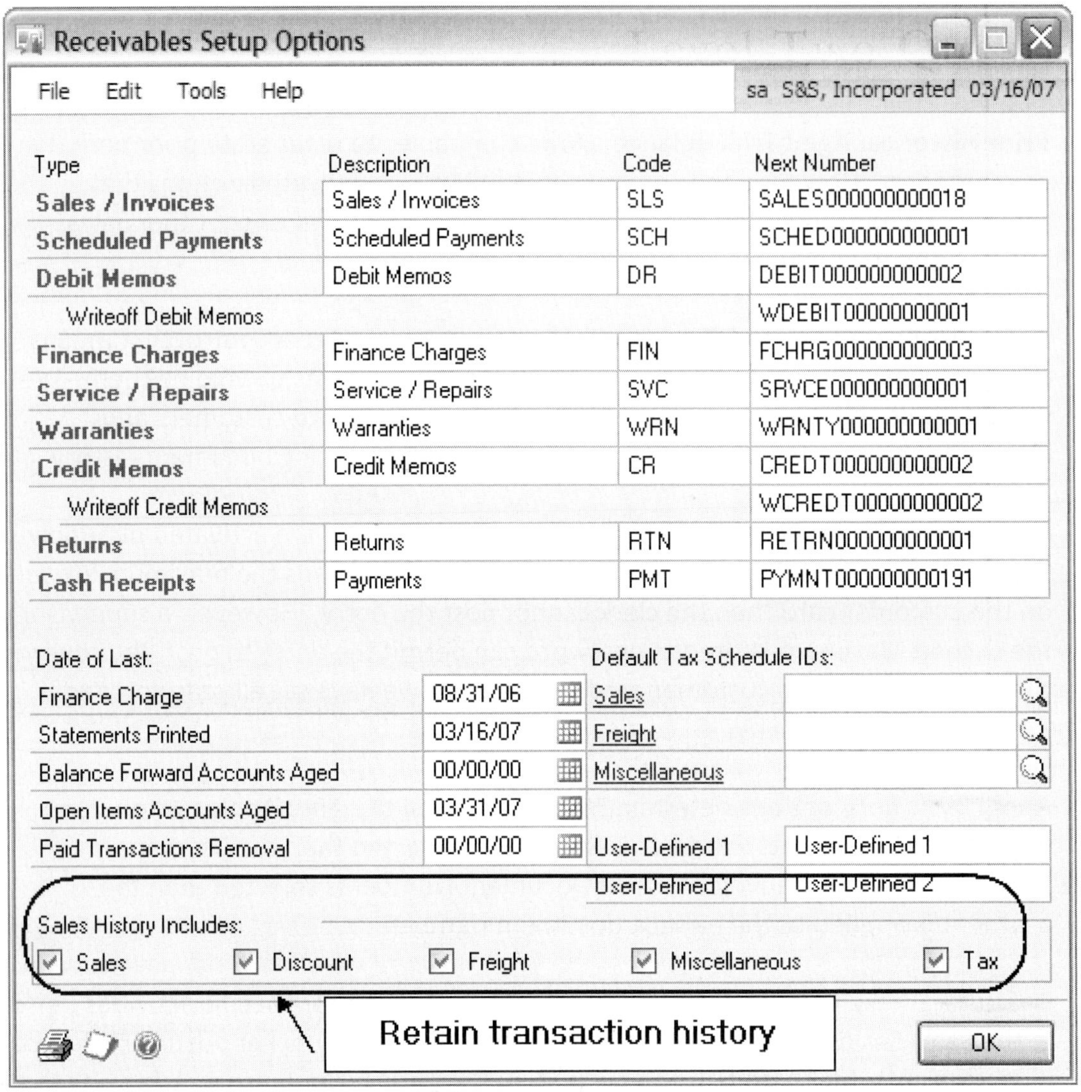

Figure 5:54 Receivables Setup Options

Enter a sales order to Barter Bay for thirty items of TVSN50W. Tab to the next line item and GP prompts to enter a password to exceed Barter's credit limit.

How did GP know Barter's credit limit? How did GP determine that this invoice placed Barter over that credit limit?

Delete the order.

E5:8 Test Receivable Controls

Invoicing Setup

We now discuss control options for tasks performed in the Invoice Processing Tier. These controls are independent of receivable controls.

Click **Invoicing** under setup to open the window illustrated next. Many options are self-explanatory. We will discuss those that are not.

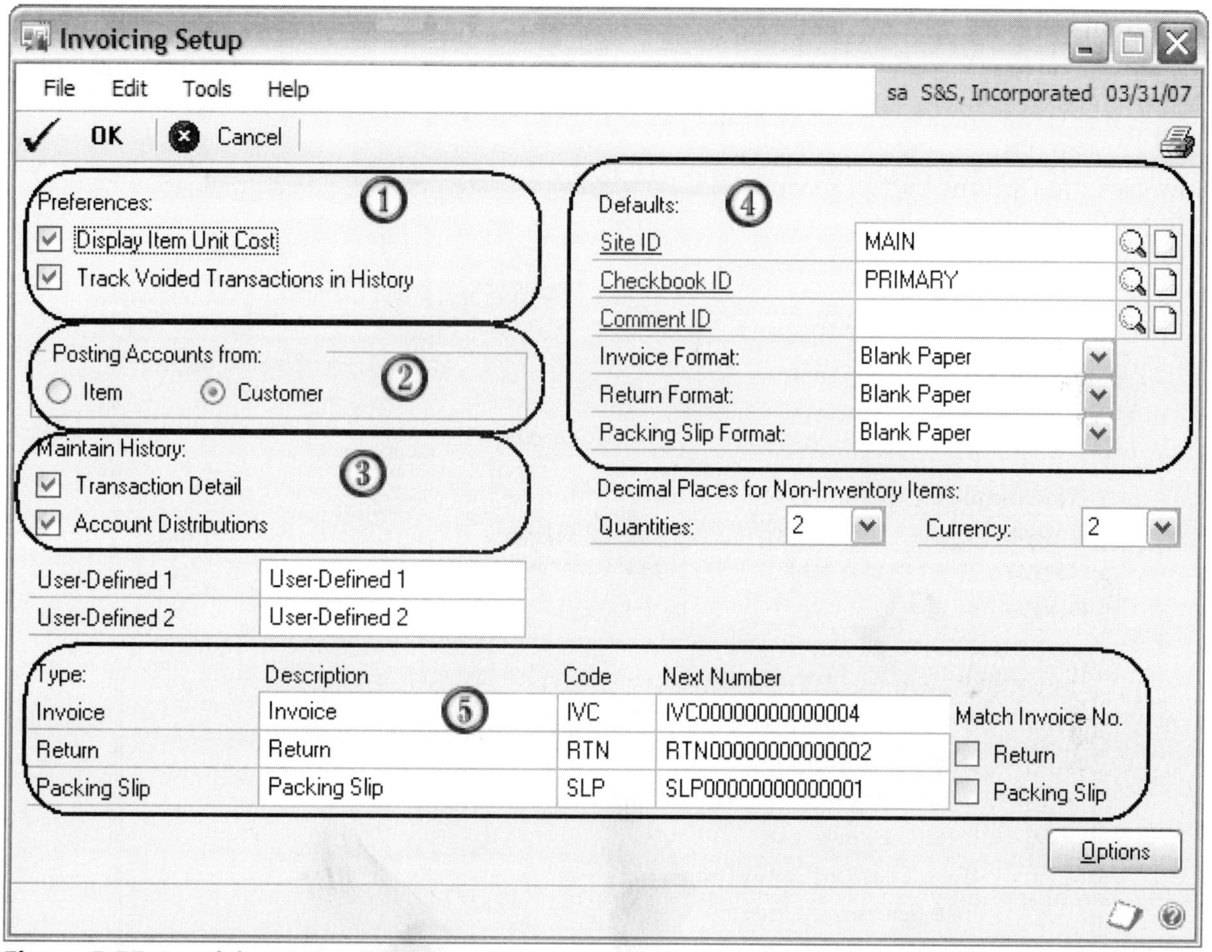

Figure 5:55 Invoicing Setup Window

1. **Preferences** control settings in the Invoice Entry window. **Display Item Unit Cost** causes the unit cost for items to display on line items. **Track Voided Transactions in History** instructs GP to save transaction history for voided invoices. This option combined with the Receivables option that denies deleting printed documents gives companies increased control by retaining history on voided transactions. It also allows companies to monitor sales performance by analyzing the number of voided transactions.

2. **Posting Accounts from** tells GP which general ledger posting accounts to use. In Chapter 3 we accepted the fact that sales invoice transactions post to accounts stored on the customer card and we now see proof.

3. **Maintain History** triggers storing details on historical transactions.

4. **Defaults** are other settings that default for transaction windows.

5. These are default document numbers used by the Invoice Processing Tier, which are different from document numbers used by the Receivables Processing Tier. Each setup window uses distinct audit trail document numbers to identify the transactions originating within the processing tier linked to that setup window. This is a good time to point out that not only must you correct an error by using the Series originating the transaction but also by using the processing tier originating it. Remember that Appendix C covers error correction by Series and transaction type.

Now click the **Options** button to view additional controls over invoicing activities. (See Figure 5:56.)

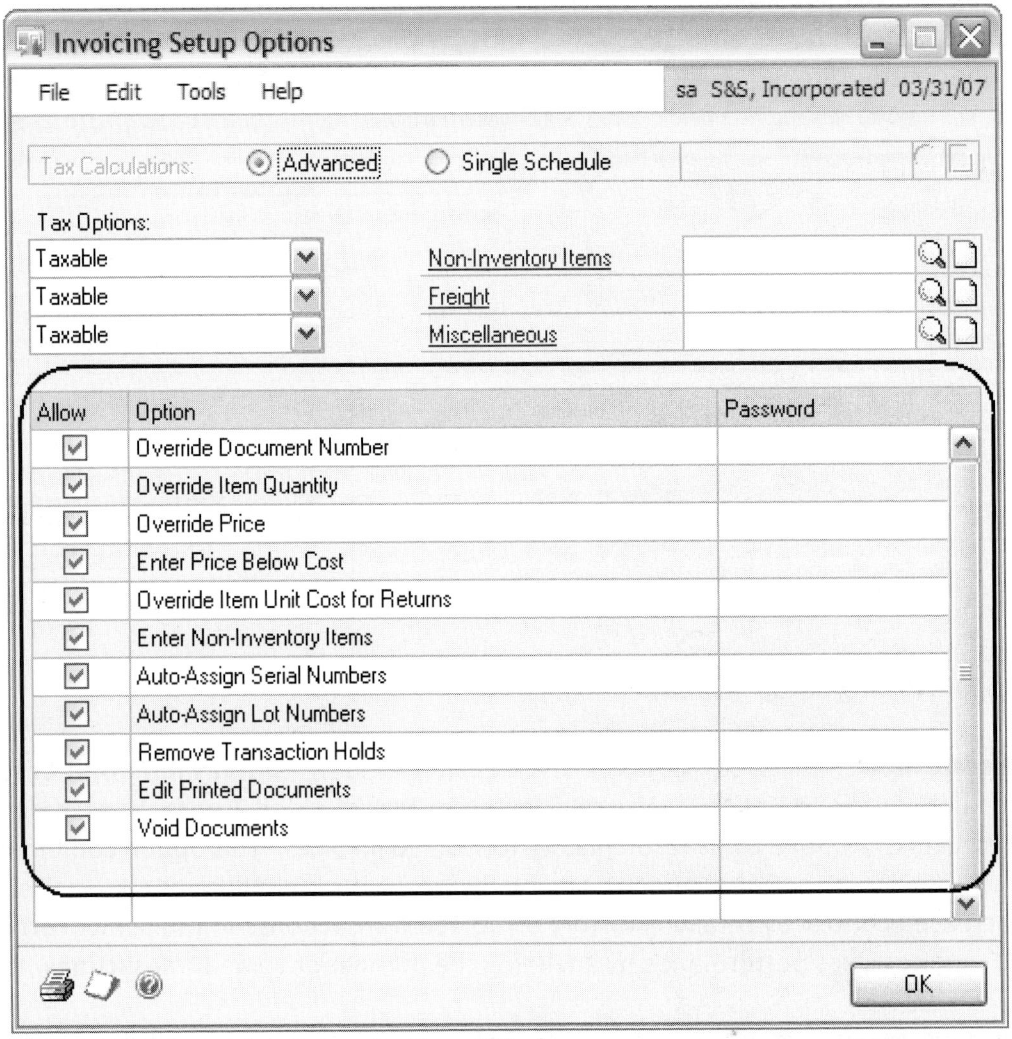

Figure 5:56 Invoicing Setup Options Window

This window enables general and specific authorization over tasks listed at the bottom. General authorization is activated by removing the Allow checkmark. Specific is activated by allowing the task but requiring a password to complete it.

Close all open windows and move to the last setup window.

Sales Order Processing Setup

We now review options that affect sales order processing. Click **Sales Order Processing** under setup to open the window illustrated next.

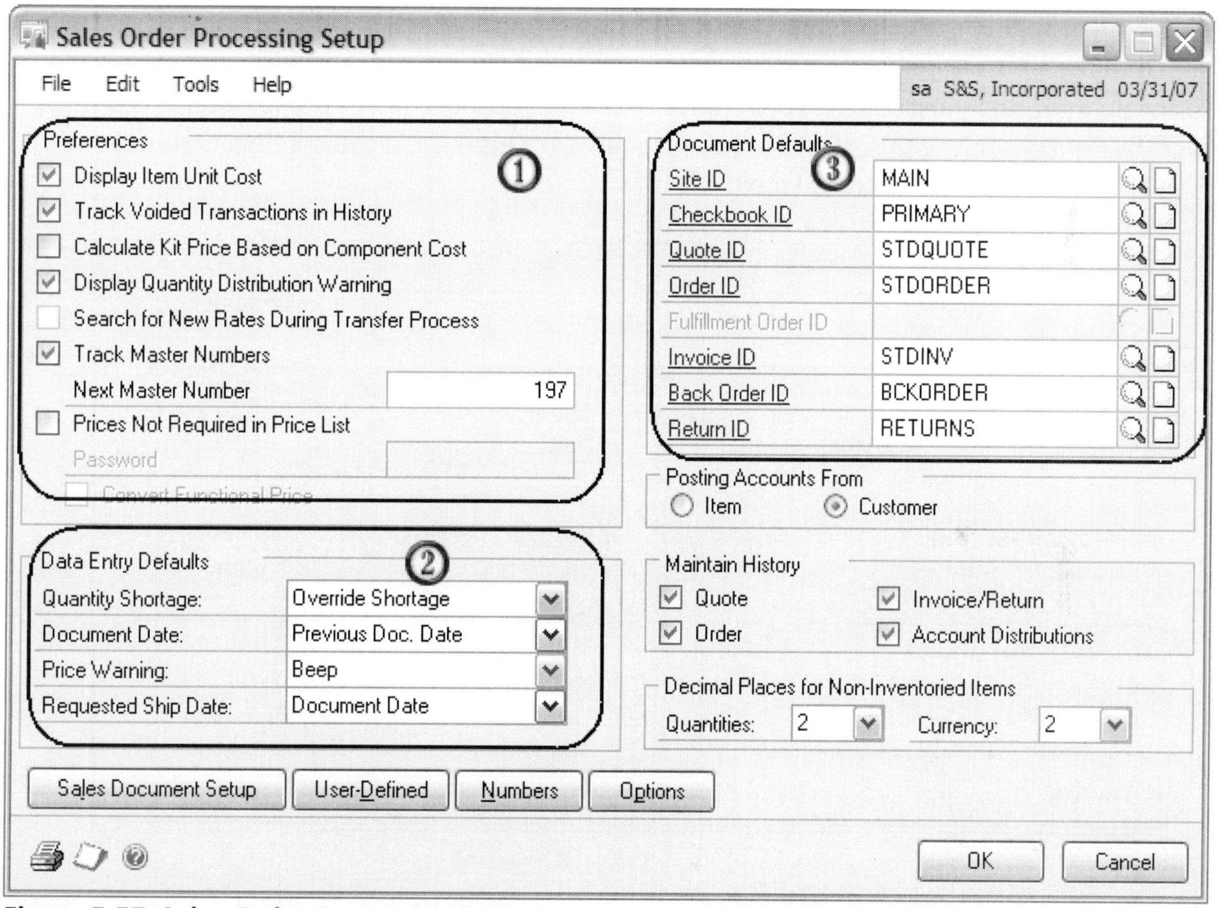

Figure 5:57 Sales Order Processing Setup

Options in this window are similar to those viewed in the Invoice Setup window. We find the familiar Preferences, Posting Accounts From, and Maintain History options. Our discussion will focus on unique options (i.e., those not discussed in Invoice Setup).

1. **Preferences:** The **Prices Not Required in Price List** option controls item pricing. If left unchecked, employees cannot insert a price not appearing in the item price list. Thus, all items must appear and be priced in the Inventory Control Series. Companies customarily

selling non-inventoried or non-priced items will need to activate the preference but may want to assign a password under Options to prevent entering an unauthorized price.

2. **Data Entry Defaults Section:** Defaults to use during data entry. Quantity Shortage is the default instruction for handling inventory allocations discussed in Level 1. Document Date is currently set to use the transaction date on the previous transaction when creating a new transaction. Price Warning is set to beep when changing an item price. Finally, the Requested Ship Date will default from the date on the transaction.

3. **Document Defaults:** Here we find the default forms to use when creating an order, invoice, etc. Forms control the appearance of printed output. Under the current settings, the default form for an order is STDORDER. When the order is transferred to an invoice, the document will transfer to the STDINV form.

Forms do more than just set the appearance of printed output. They also set internal controls over data entry. To see this, click the **Sales Document Setup** button and select **Order**. Look up the STDORDER form as illustrated next.

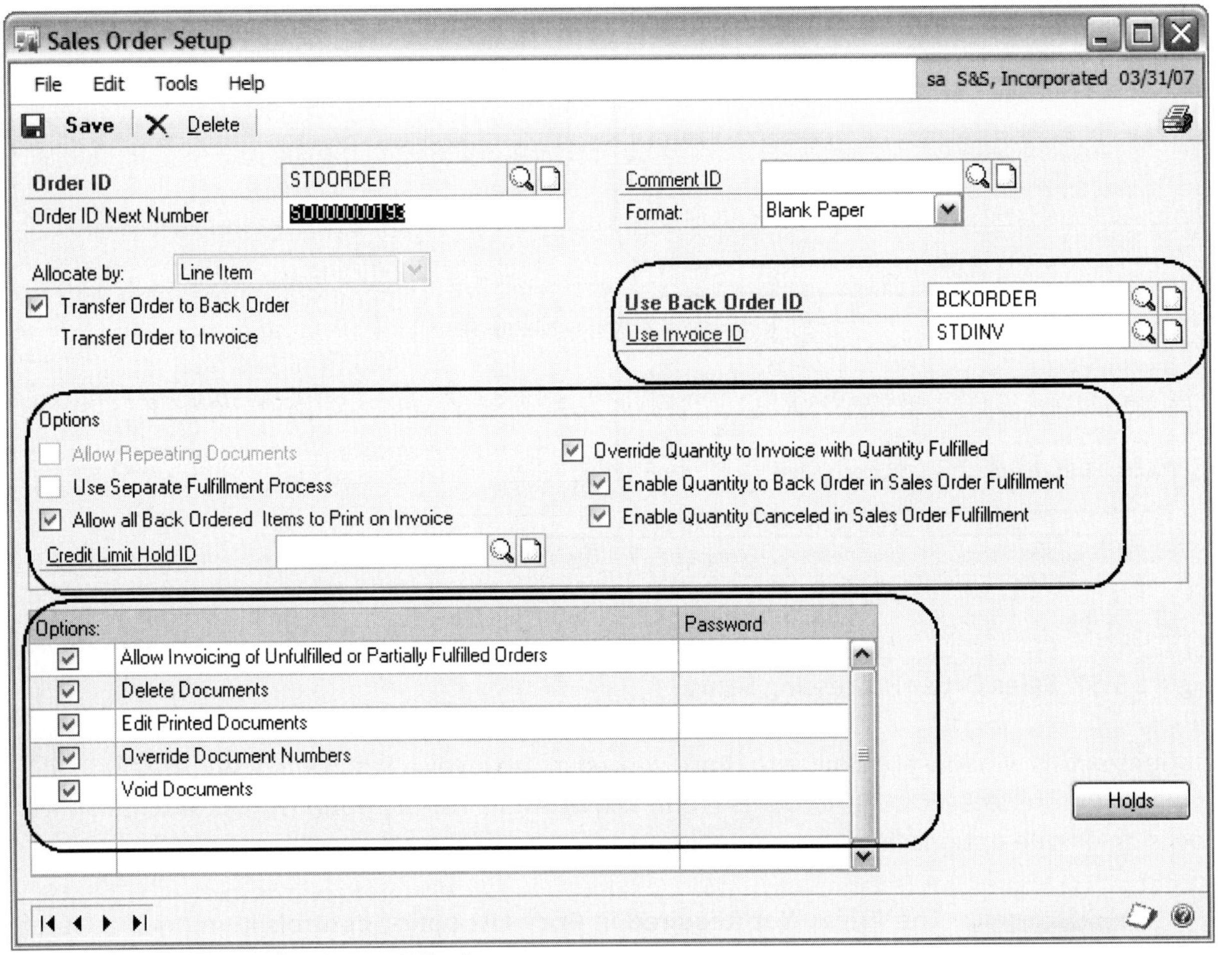

Figure 5:58 Sales Order Setup Window

This form uses the BCKORDER form for back orders and the STDINV form for invoices. We find two Options sections for controlling data entry. You can only perform tasks that are checked. Options at the bottom are used to control general and specific authorization. Marking the option is general authorization whereas supplying a password to complete the task is specific authorization. A couple of controls warrant special mention. The **Edit Printed Documents** option protects output by restricting the edit of printed documents. The **Override Document Numbers** is used to control the edit of source document numbers that form the audit trail.

S&S uses only the STDORDER form; however, companies often create multiple forms types to format output. For instance, a company may use DRPSHP for orders that are drop shipped to the customer. Options must be set for each form.

Close the Sales Order Setup window and take a few minutes to explore other forms under the Sales Document Setup button. You will find similar controls for each form.

Finally, click the familiar **Options** button. (See Figure 5:59.)

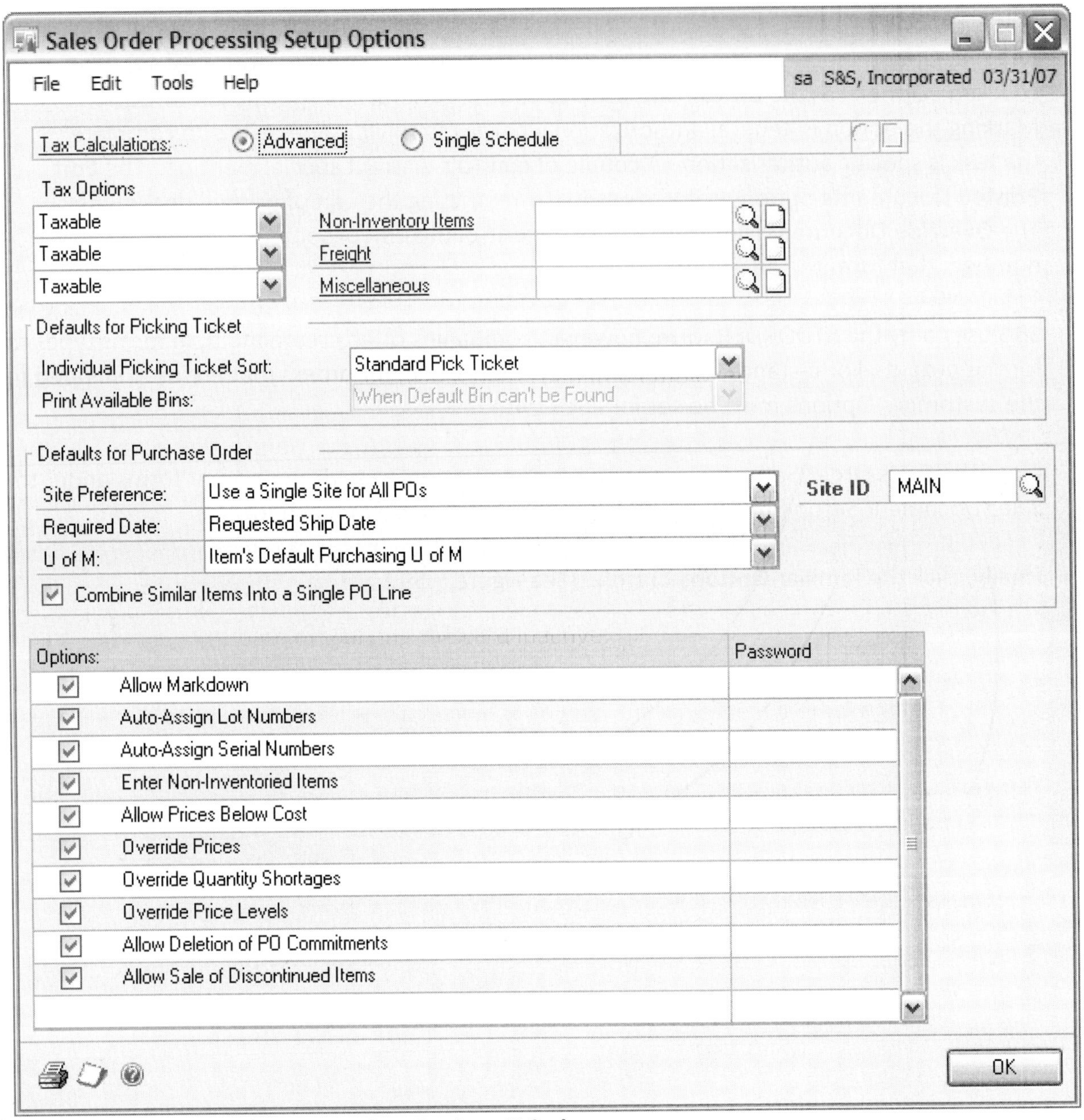

Figure 5:59 Sales Order Processing Options Window

Controls in this window pertain to all data entry in the Sales Order Processing Tier, regardless of the form. Let's say that there is a problem with data entry clerks overriding item prices during invoice entry. You can control this problem by either removing the checkmark from Override Prices or by requiring password entry before overriding a price.

Close all open windows. We next discuss internal controls for customer cards.

Customer Card Internal Controls

In Level One we covered managing customer cards, explaining that these are master records. Internal controls over customer cards come in many forms. First, there are limit controls such as credit limit and maximum writeoff found under Options. (See Figure 5:60.)

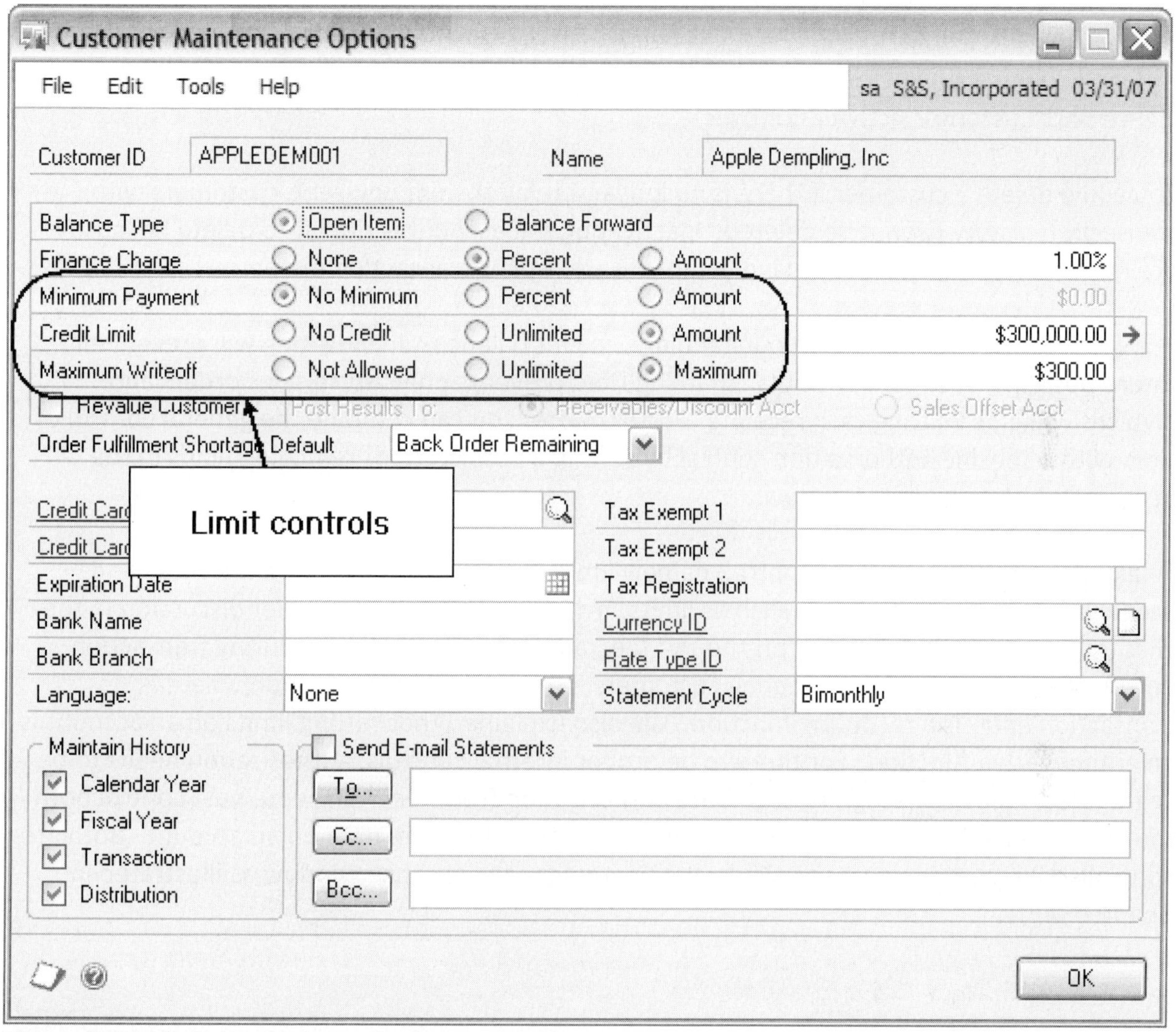

Figure 5:60 Limit Controls on Customer Cards

You can combine general authorization controls on account limits with specific authorization controls on limits by setting passwords in the Receivables Setup window.

Next, customer cards have default general ledger accounts for controlling where entries post. (Not illustrated.) This feature helps to protect the integrity of financial statements.

Companies also need to control future activities for customers. For instance, where the company no longer has a relationship with the customer or the customer fails to remit timely payment on the account. Controls for these situations are found at the top of the Customer Maintenance window, namely **Inactivate** and **Hold**. (See Figure 5:61.)

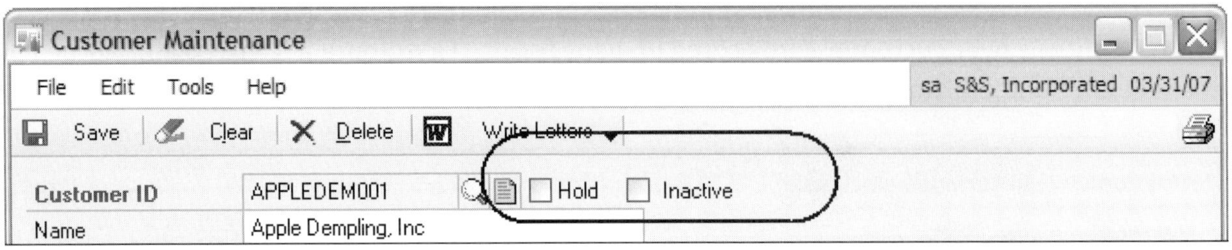

Figure 5:61 Customer Activity Controls

You could delete a customer if there is no longer a relationship; however, customers with transaction history cannot be deleted. Inactivating the account is similar to delete because it prevents future postings of any kind yet inactivate retains transaction history.

But what if the customer has an outstanding account balance? Inactivating will prevent all future postings, even cash receipts. Marking Hold prevents only future sales orders and invoices while permitting cash receipts. Furthermore, you can combine the general control of Hold with a specific authorization control by setting a password for removing holds in the Receivables Management window.

Finally, we reach the ultimate control, namely limiting authorization of new accounts and access to changing control data such as limits. You will remember an earlier discussion in the chapter on creating customers "on-the-fly" (i.e., adding a new customer during transaction entry). We emphasized that creating customers is an authorization function whereas transaction entry is a recording function. We also explained that setting limits on an account is an authorization function. For there to be proper internal controls, authorization needs to be segregated from recording. To segregate authorization from recording you must control both the ability to create customers "on-the-fly" and to access control data on an account. Both are controlled by restricting user access to the Customer Maintenance window as illustrated in Chapter 3

Sales Series Setup Reports

Reporting is an extremely important control tool. In level one we discussed posting reports that validate transaction entry and other reports that monitor activities and analyze data. In this topic we discuss reports that document Sales Series internal controls.

Click **Setup** under Reports and click the dropdown list. (See Figure 5:62.)

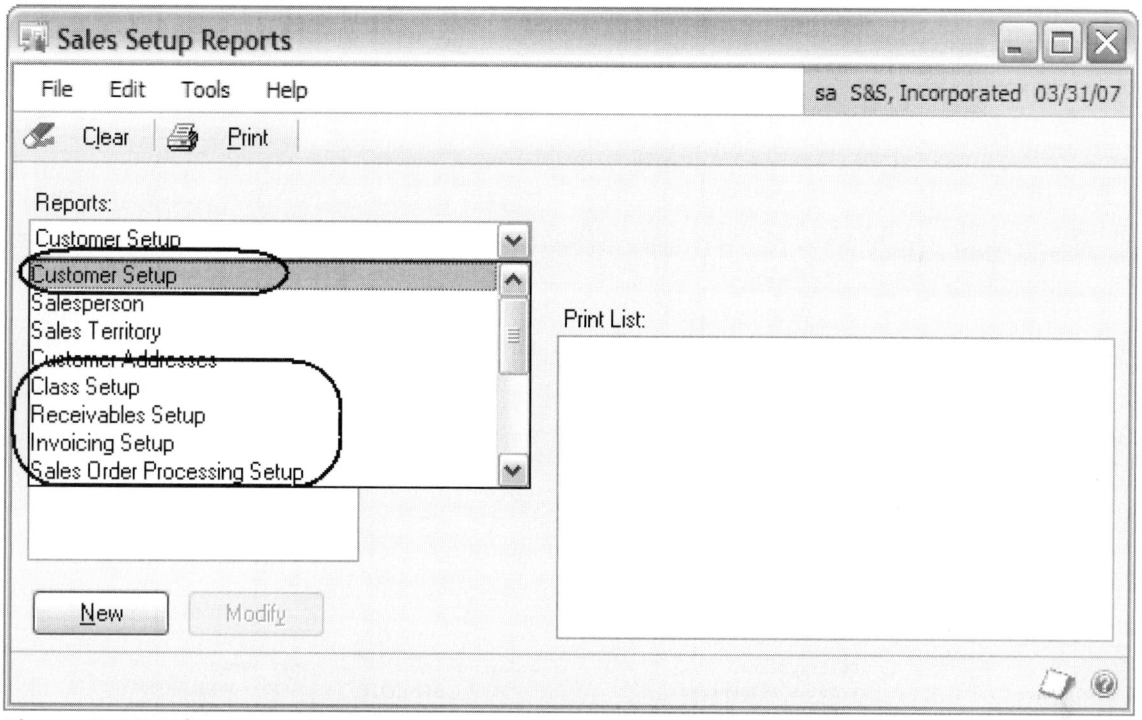

Figure 5:62 Sales Setup Reports

The reports highlighted on this illustration document controls over Sales Series activities and are reviewed for compliance with company internal control policies.

Select **Receivables Setup** and click **New** and name the report **Rec Setup.** Set the **Destination** to the screen and click **Print**. (See Figure 5:63.)

User Date: 03/31/07

S&S, Incorporated
RECEIVABLES SETUP LIST
Receivables Management

Page: 1
User ID: sa

Age By: Due Date

Aging Periods	From:	To:
Current	0	0
0-30 Days	1	30
31 - 60 Days	31	60
61 - 90 Day	61	90
91 Days & Over	91	999

Apply By: Due Date

Options:

Track Discounts Available in GL:	Yes
Compound Finance Charge:	Yes
Print Historical Aged Trial Balance:	Yes
Pay Commissions After Invoice Paid:	Yes
Delete Unposted Printed Documents:	No
Reprint Statements:	Yes
Print Tax Details on Documents:	No
Print Dual Currencies:	No
Auto Apply to Finance Charges First:	No
Age Unapplied Credit Amounts:	No

Passwords

Exceed Credit Limit:	PASSWORD
Remove Customer Hold:	PASSWORD
Exceed Maximum Writeoffs:	PASSWORD
Waive Finance Charge:	PASSWORD

Defaults:

NSF Charge:	$0.00
Checkbook ID:	PRIMARY
Price Level:	WHOLE
Document Format:	Blank Paper
Default Summary View:	Amounts Since Last Close

E-mailed Statements
Status Recipient:

Types:	Description:	Code:	Next Number:
Sales/Invoices	Sales / Invoices	SLS	SALES000000000018
Scheduled Payments	Scheduled Payments	SCH	SCHED000000000001

Figure 5:63 Receivables Setup Report

This report documents controls for the Receivables Management Setup window. Close all open windows. *(Note: You can save the new report.)* Companies should print setup reports so that auditors can review internal controls over sales activities.

This completes our Level 2 discussion. You have also completed the chapter and are ready for the exercises that follow.

Level One Questions

Use the S&S, Inc Project DB database to complete the following tasks.

1. This is a multi-part question.

   a. Create the following customer:

Company Name:	Best Home Electronics
Main Address:	PO Box 174, Kent, OH 44323
Shipping Address:	378 North Main Street, Kent, OH 44323
Co. Contact:	Sue Smith
Phone:	(330) 775-7777
Class:	TRADMID

   b. View the default posting accounts for the new customer. Explain why these accounts are already present.

   c. Set the new customer's credit limit to $70,000. What department(s) could have permission to set this limit?

   d. Print the Sales Series Setup report for customers to document your tasks. Customize the existing Customer Setup report so that it prints a detail report filtered to display only the new customer.

   e. The new customer ordered the following items on March 26, 2007. Create this order and choose Back Order Balance for items with an inventory shortage.

   15 of item TVSN42W
   35 of item TVBT46WPJ

   Print the order and the documents needed to trigger remaining cycle activities. Explain how departments will use these documents. Explain how Back Order Balance works.

   f. The order was filled and shipped on March 27, 2007. Transfer the order to an invoice and create a backorder as well. Print the invoice and backorder remembering to change the date. Print the document used to validate data entry.

   g. Print a statement for the new customer as of March 31, 2007.

   h. On April 6, 2007 the new customer mailed check number 8987 for $46,457.25 as payment in full for the invoice. Post and apply this payment. Print the posting reports.

Level Two Questions

1. Explain how you implement pricing controls in the Sales Series. How does this control minimize threats listed in the Sales Cycle Activities diagram?

2. Why will GP not post a sales order? (Use GAAP to justify your answers.)

3. Explain the features of and steps to implement batch controls over sales invoices.

4. Sales order employees are overriding invoice numbers assigned to transferred sales orders. Explain your solution to the problem, including tests you will make to verify implementing the solution.

5. The owners want to be able to sell an item below cost, but do not want this feature available to employees. Explain how you would provide the owners this flexibility.

6. Explain why strong internal controls deny the ability to edit a printed document. How would you implement this control for sales orders?

7. One of the threats faced by companies is failure to bill customers. Explain specific GP features that detect and minimize this threat.

8. The revenue cycle faces the threat of credit sales to customers with poor or limited credit histories. Explain GP's preventative tool that mitigates this threat.

9. Select a threat listed on the Sales Cycle Activities diagram that has not been asked in a previous question and describe a GP control that addresses the threat.

Chapter 6 EXPENDITURE CYCLE AND GP PURCHASING SERIES

CHAPTER OVERVIEW

With revenue cycle activities under your belt, we move on to the matching side of revenue, namely expenditure cycle activities[22]. This chapter focuses on purchasing activities and using GP's Purchasing Series to perform, report on, and control cycle activities.

- Level One focuses on transaction processing. It begins with our roadmap discussion of activities for the cycle where we review activities, threats, and internal controls by department. We then move to performing these activities. You will also review month-ending and year-ending the Series.

- Level Two focuses on configuring GP's controls over Purchasing Series activities that affect compliance with internal control objectives.

Level One covers:

- The menu structure alongside an expenditure cycle REA diagram
- Managing master records for the Series, namely vendor cards
- Aspects of processing day-to-day expenditure cycle activities such as purchase orders, receipts and returns of inventory, vendor invoices, credit memos, and vendor payments
- Using reports as a control tool and a trigger for activities in the cycle
- Performing Series month-end and year-end closings

Level Two covers:

- Implementing internal controls through Purchasing Series setup

---

[22] For a deeper understanding on expenditure cycle activities, review Romney and Steinbart, *Accounting Information Systems* (11th ed., Pearson Prentice Hall 2009), Chapter 11.

Level One

We first discuss our roadmap for activities in the expenditure cycle. Figure 6:1 illustrates activities, as performed by department, along with threats to these activities and controls that mitigate these threats.

Purchase Orders (POs) initiate expenditure cycle activities. Generally a sales department or warehouse manager enters POs to restock inventory and fill backorders. *(Note: Any department's manager may also enter POs for services and noninventory purchases such as fixed assets).* POs authorize vendor purchases and managers review reports prior to entering a PO to mitigate the threat of overstocking.

Right now you are probably thinking that segregation of duties has been breached because the person recording POs is also authorizing purchases. This is where GP's Purchase Order Enhancements feature enters. With this feature, employees can enter but not print POs. Hence, employees cannot perform the act that authorizes POs, namely printing for release to vendors. We will illustrate PO Enhancements later in the chapter.[23]

PO clerks - auth. function

Purchasing employees review POs in the system to verify compliance with purchasing controls. Employees print PO status reports to confirm that POs for the same vendor are combined; POs are being issued to authorized vendors[24]; and quantities being purchased take advantage of negotiated vendor price breaks. *(Note: S&S's purchasing employees are its owners, Scott Parry and Susan Gonzalez.)* After review, a purchasing employee authorizes the PO by printing and sending a signed copy of it to the vendor. A copy of the PO or an email is also sent to the issuing department to confirm the purchase. As with sales orders, purchase orders do not post.

The next trigger for activities is receipt of a vendor shipment. Warehouse employees receive shipments and must verify that shipments are authorized. To perform this task, they run a daily PO status report with purchasing details and access terminals to look up PO information in GP. After confirming that a shipment is authorized, they inspect items for quality and quantities. Quality inspection confirms that items are not damaged or inferior. Quantity inspection confirms that the correct items and quantities were received. This inspection is performed by comparing package contents to the vendor's packing slip and to the PO or report from GP.

Warehouse employees next enter receipt quantities into GP. Items are placed on shelves and noninventoried goods are sent directly to the ordering department. Back order journals are sent to the sales department as notification of inventory arrivals that fill pending customer orders. Receiving employees then send a receiving report along with vendor packing slips to

---

[23] GP also offers a Purchase Order Generator feature to automatically generate purchase orders for inventory based on stocking requirements. This feature is not included with the student version of the software.

[24] Chapter 4 on inventory has a discussion on assigning vendors to items.

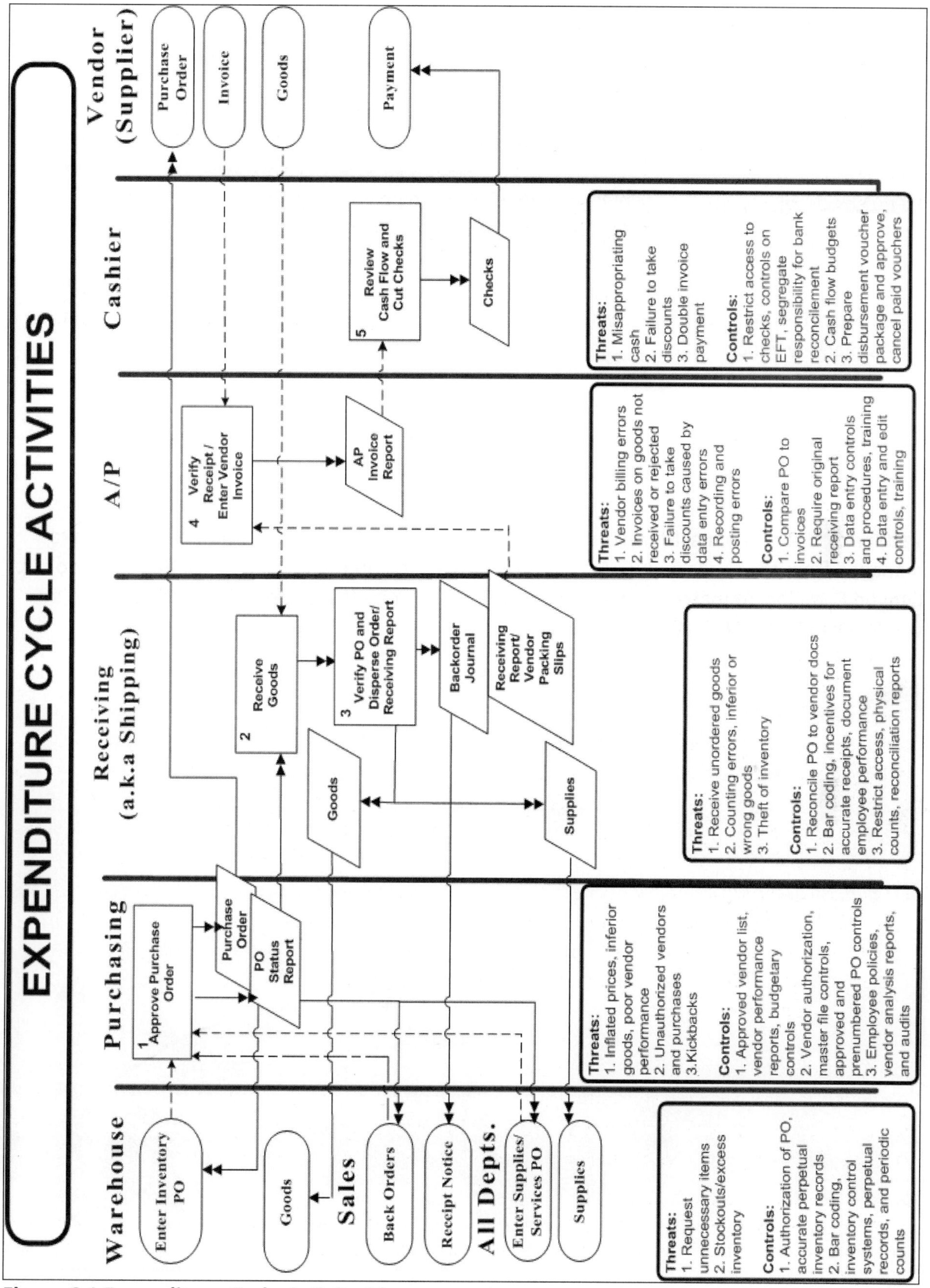

Figure 6:1 Expenditure Cycle Activity Diagram

the accounts payable department. Sometimes vendors enclose the invoice instead of a packing slip. The invoice is also sent to the accounts payable department.

Receipt of a vendor invoice triggers accounts payable department activities. Invoices normally arrive from the mailroom. Employees enter these invoices from the PO receipt in GP. Besides posting invoices, accounts payable employees prepare vendor aging reports to send to the controller and cashier. The cashier reviews S&S's cash position and issues payments to vendors, careful to take advantage of vendor discounts if cash flow permits.

With a basic understanding of expenditure cycle activities we now turn to using GP to perform these activities. As in the sales cycle chapter, we begin with master records for the Purchasing Series, namely vendor cards.

VENDOR CARDS

Vendor cards are the master records for the Purchasing Series. Like customers, vendors are managed from the Cards menu. Activate the **Purchasing** home page and click **Vendor**. Look up Canyon Cam, Inc. to match the next illustration. Remember that a complete listing of S&S's vendors can be found in Appendix B.

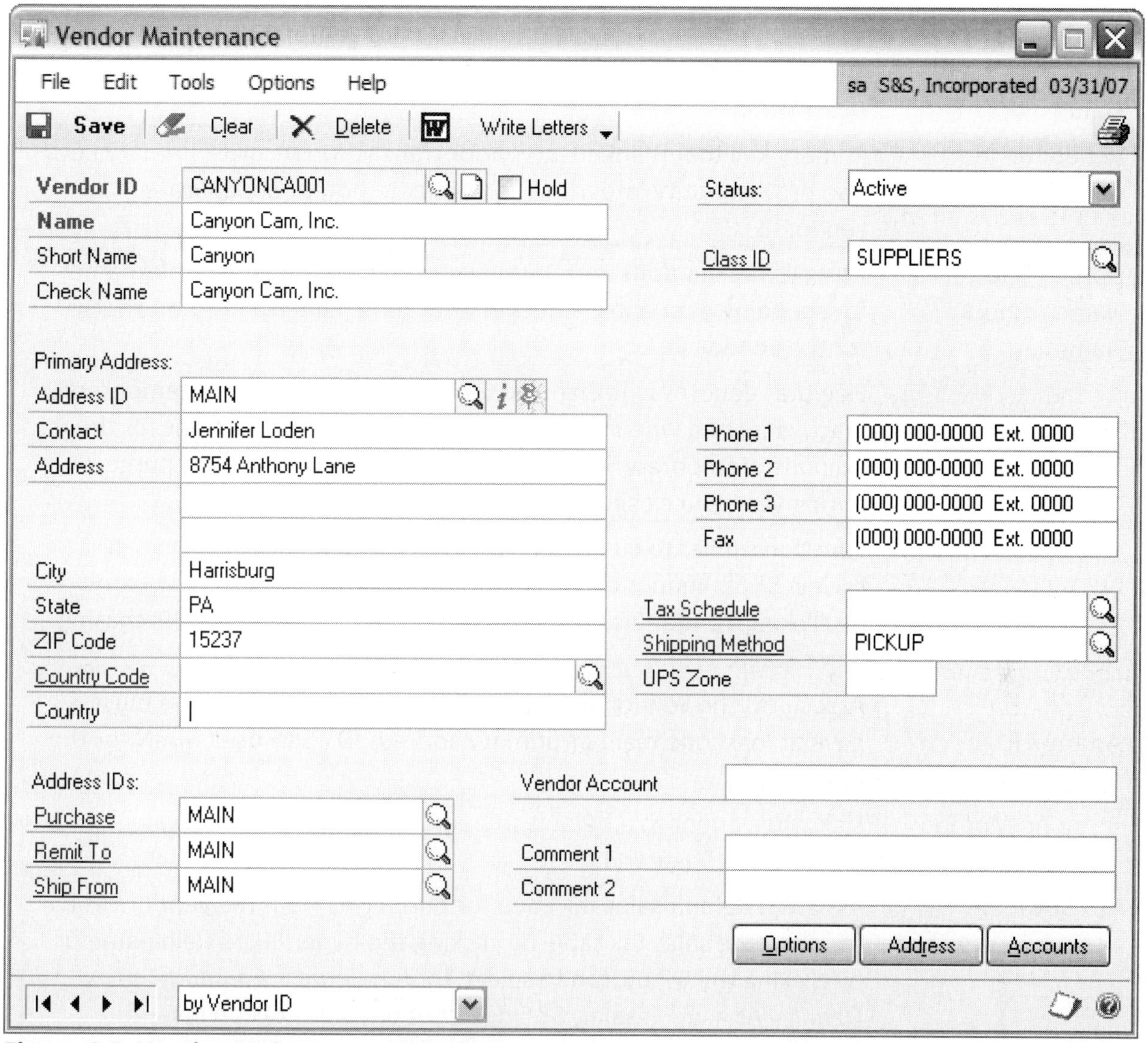

Figure 6:2 Vendor Maintenance Window

S&S assigns Vendor IDs similar to assigning customer IDs (i.e., first eight letters of the name plus a sequentially incremented number.) Remember that access to a Cards menu is an authorization function; therefore, employees recording purchasing transactions should not have access to vendor cards.

The next table provides an explanation of vendor card fields. Remember to explore fields under the Options and Accounts Buttons.

You create and manage vendor cards using the same procedures for creating and managing customer cards discussed in Chapter 4.

Field	**Description**
Vendor ID	Primary key that is linked to vendor transaction records. Primary keys also protect entity integrity, (i.e., mitigate potential duplicate vendors).
Name / Short Name / Check Name	Name is the vendor's legal name. Short Name can store a nickname for speeding data entry. Check Name is the name to print on checks for the vendor.
Status	Flag that denotes whether a vendor is active, inactive, or temporary. Inactive is used when you want to block future transactions for the account. Temporary is used on accounts that you want to purge during year-end closing.
Class ID	Function similar to customer classes in the Sales Series. You can review S&S's vendor classes by clicking the hyperlinked field name or by clicking Vendor Class under the Setup category on the Purchasing home page.
Address ID	Associates the vendor account with an address. All vendors must have at least one main or primary address ID. S&S uses MAIN for the primary ID.
Shipping Method	Links the vendor to a default shipper. The shipping table was discussed in Chapter 4.
Tax Schedule	Assigns a default sales tax code for purchases from the vendor. You can view the sales tax table by clicking the hyperlinked field name or by clicking the GP button to select *Tools>>Setup>>Company>>Tax Details*. As a wholesaler, S&S does not pay sales tax on inventory purchases.
Purchase, Remit To, Ship From	Links to either the main or additional address IDs for the vendor.
Vendor Account	Account number used by the vendor to identify S&S as a customer.
Accounts Button	Default general ledger distribution accounts for posting purchase transactions. These accounts will not used on inventory purchases because accounts on the item card are used.
Address Button	Open a window to create and manage vendor addresses.
Options Button	Access to vendor payment terms, credit limits, and other options, including the option that triggers vendor 1099 tax reporting.

Table 6:1 Vendor Card Fields

Take the time to review other vendor cards and then close the Vendor Maintenance window.

Now is a good time to review default posting accounts for transactions involving inventory. *(Note: Transaction not involving inventory will post to default accounts on the vendor card.)*

GP first looks to Sales Series setup to determine if inventory transactions should post to default accounts on the customer card or item card. In Chapter 4 we explained that S&S instructed GP to use customer card accounts. Consequently, sales revenue, inventory purchases, and inventory expense (i.e., cost of goods sold) will post to accounts on the customer card linked to the transaction.

If the customer card fails to provide accounts, GP next looks at default accounts on the inventory card. If none are present, GP looks at default accounts on the vendor card.

If all the above locations fail to provide accounts, GP looks to accounts default posting accounts. We looked at these in Chapter 3. You can review these accounts by clicking the GP button to select *Tools>>Setup>>Posting>>Posting Accounts*.

Finally, if no default posting account exists, GP shoots and error message during posting and suspends the transaction. This error is corrected using the procedures found in Appendix C.

So how does Ashton verify that transactions posted to customer card accounts? First, remember that S&S posts revenue and expense transactions to departmental accounts, (i.e., accounts with 01, 02, or 03 in the department segment). Consequently, he assigned non-departmental accounts (i.e., accounts with 00 in the department segment) as defaults accounts for item and vendor cards and posting setup. He then reviews monthly postings to determine if a non-departmental account was used. This then tells him to investigate further to determine if a customer card was improperly setup.

GP

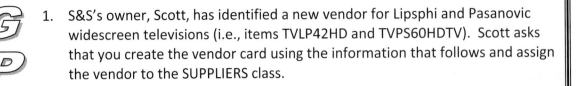

1. S&S's owner, Scott, has identified a new vendor for Lipsphi and Pasanovic widescreen televisions (i.e., items TVLP42HD and TVPS60HDTV). Scott asks that you create the vendor card using the information that follows and assign the vendor to the SUPPLIERS class.

    Bright Electronics Supply
    757 Lakeshore Blvd.
    Cleveland, OH 44107
    Joe Swain, Sales Director
    (216) 754-3216

2. Review the vendor list in Appendix B. SumSang Corporation's Vendor ID does not follow Ashton's primary key assignment rules. Identify the problem and state whether the error can be corrected?

E6:1 Practice with Vendor Cards

Purchasing Series Transactions

With vendor cards under our belt, we now look at Purchasing Series menus for processing transactions. Like the Sales Series, there is a tiered menu structure and this structure is illustrated in Figure 6:3.

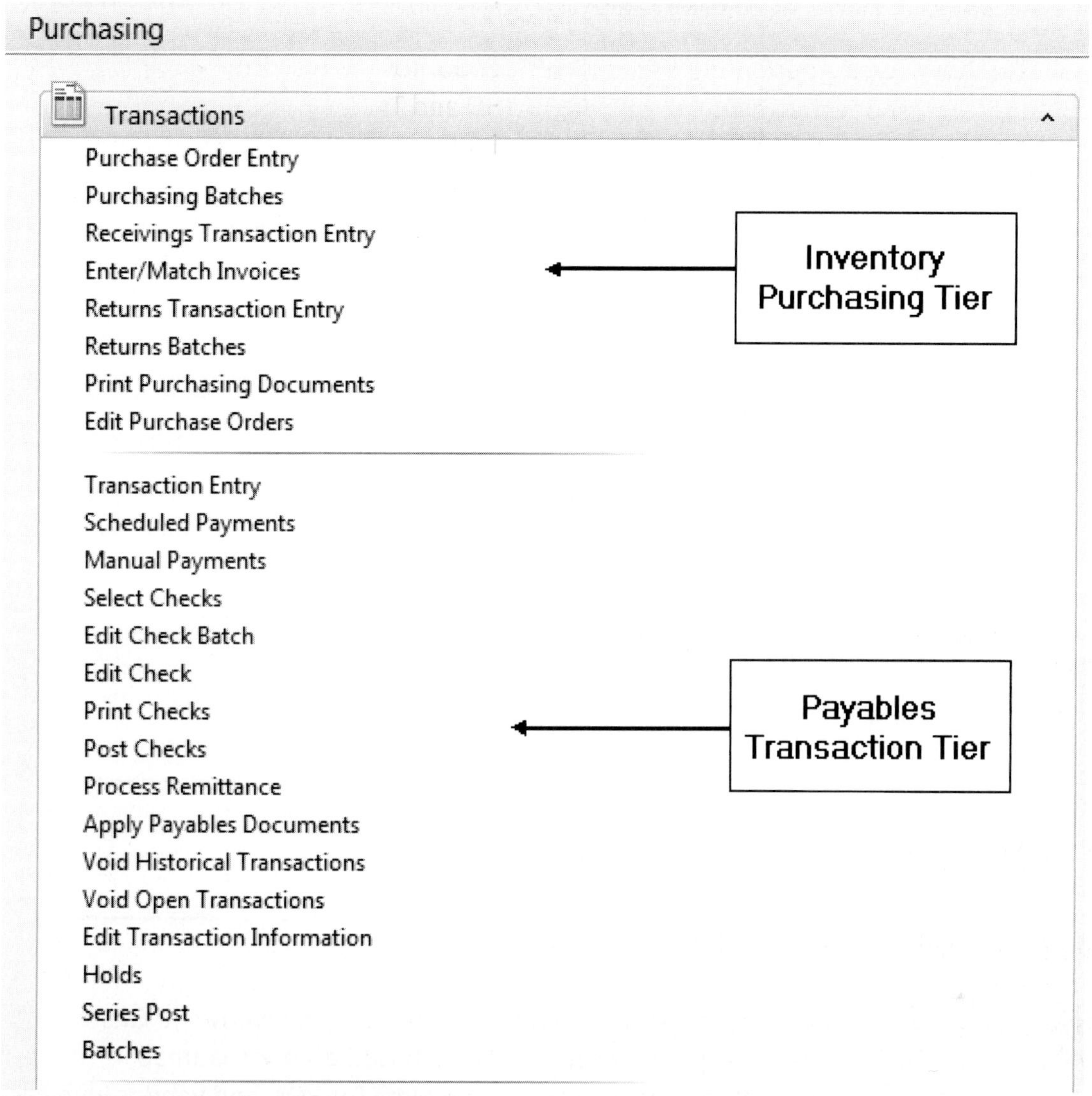

Figure 6:3 Purchasing Series Menus

The first tier initiates transactions that interface with Inventory Control tables. The second processes all remaining Purchasing Series transactions such as noninventory invoices and vendor payments. To understand each tier's interaction with data files review the REA data model that follows.

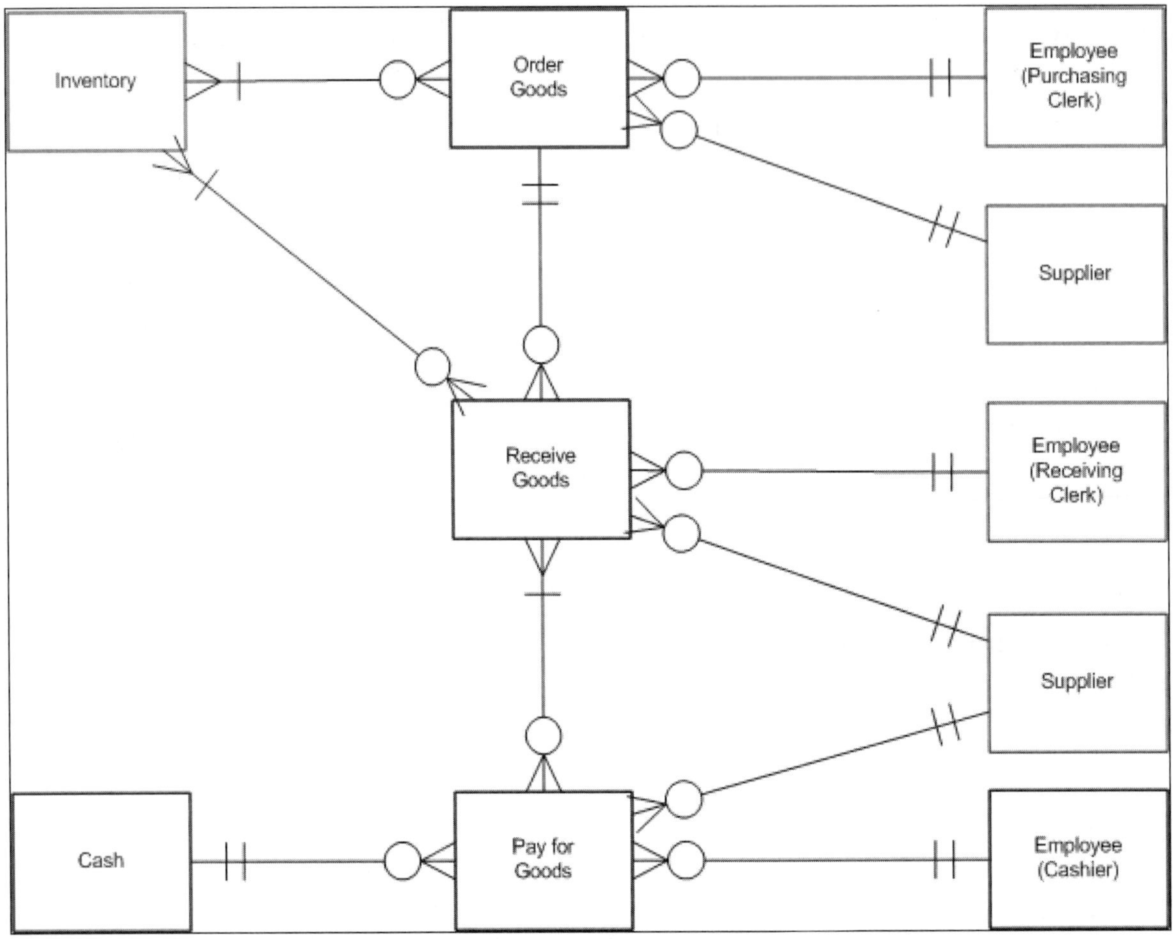

Figure 6:4 REA Data Model for Expenditure Cycle

The diagram shows that Order Goods and Receive Goods interfaces with Inventory. GPs Inventory Purchasing Tier menus correspond to these events. Based on our roadmap discussion, we can safely assume that tasks involving POs, receipts for POs, and vendor invoices for POs are performed through Inventory Purchasing Tier menus.

Next turn your attention to Pay for Goods, which corresponds to GP's Payables Transaction Tier. Notice that this event does not interact with Inventory but does interact with Cash. Thus, tasks such as paying vendors and posting invoices for non-inventory expenses are performed in the Payables Transaction Tier.

PURCHASING AND DEPARTMENTAL ACTIVITIES

We are now ready to perform expenditure cycle activities and begin with the primary triggering event, namely a PO for inventory. S&S will sometimes issues a PO for noninventory purchases such as fixed asset purchases but always issues POs for inventory purchases. A PO is a legal commitment from the buyer to the vendor to pay for the item when received. Given that the financial event does not occur until items are received (i.e., FOB destination point) or shipped (i.e., FOB shipping point), capturing these transactions in GP is purely a database function. In other words, POs are not posted.

GAAP's principles on recognizing assets and liabilities further justify for not posting these transactions. Assets are booked when legal title passes to the buyer. For inventory, title passes per the shipping terms (i.e., FOB shipping or destination point.) Furthermore, liabilities are recognized when incurred or deemed to have been incurred. For inventory, liability arises when you legally have title to the asset.

In the exercise that follows, we illustrate processing a PO.

1. We will issue a PO to Javix Corporation. Click **Purchase Order Entry** and choose **Standard** as the type.

2. Tab past **PO Number** and GP will autofill the document number.

3. Tab to **Date** and enter 3/16/07.

4. Tab to **Vendor ID** and look up Javix Corporation. The top portion of the transaction is illustrated in Figure 6:5. Before continuing, review the next table for information about fields in this window.

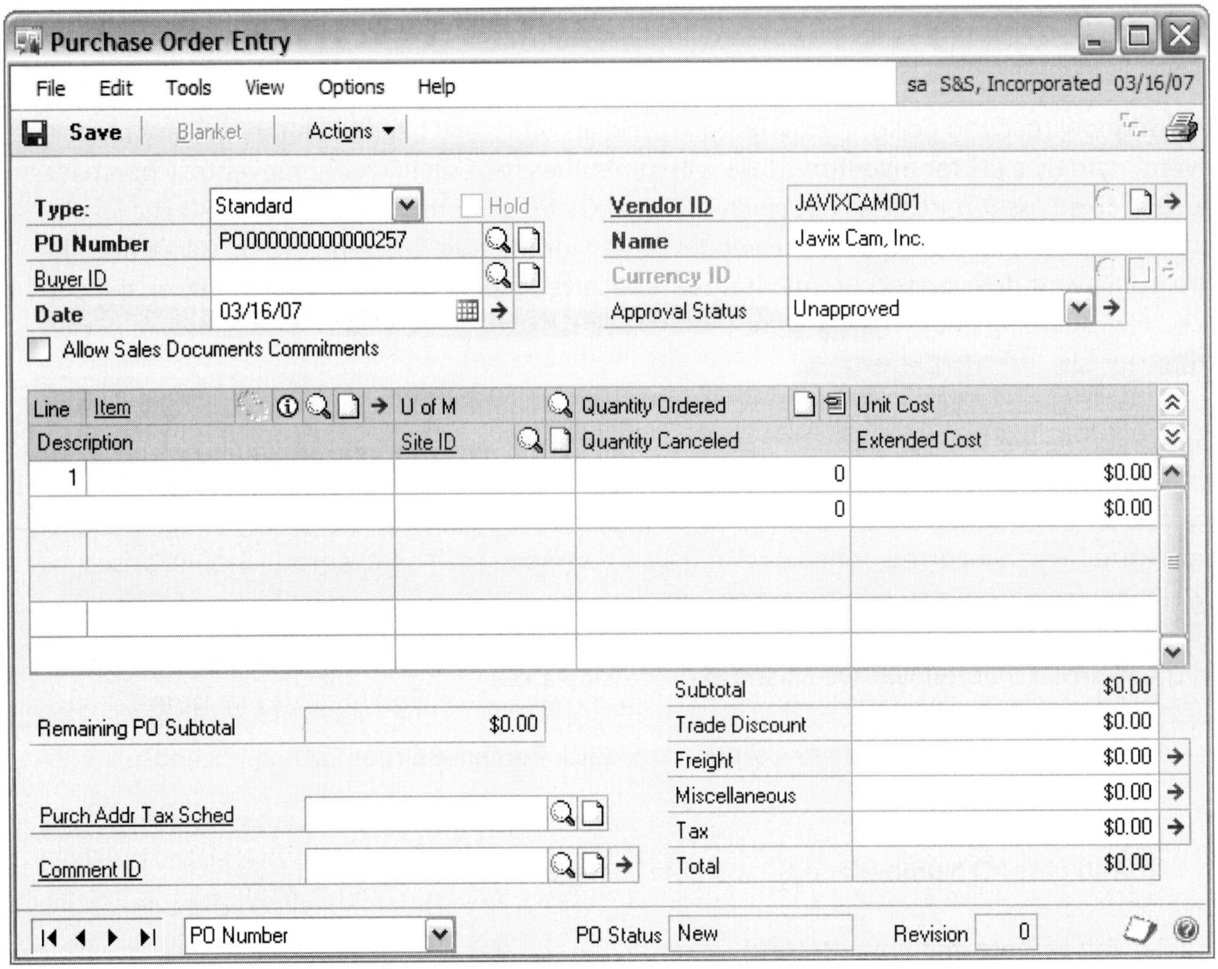

Figure 6:5 Javix Purchase Order

PO Field	Description
Type	Types are Standard, Drop-Ship, Blanket, and Drop-Ship Blanket. **Standard** is used for most POs. **Drop-Ship** orders inventory but instructs the vendor to ship directly to the customer, meaning inventory will never arrive at S&S's warehouse. Drop-Ship is used to speed customer delivery for out-of-stock or nonstocked items. **Blanket** is used to authorize a maximum amount of purchases over a specific time period. After approving the blanket PO, you do not have to authorize individual POs within that limit and GP tracks purchases against the PO.
PO Number	Document control number generated by GP. You should have strong internal controls for tracking PO numbers.
Buyer ID	Links a GP User ID to the transaction, which then interacts with the PO approval process.
Vendor ID	Links the PO to the vendor table. Refer to the REA diagram, noting that transactions in the Order Goods link to master records in the Supplier table. S&S has the same "on the fly" vendor creation issue discussed in Chapter 4 pertaining to customers and prevents vendor creation during PO entry by denying access to the Vendor Maintenance window.
Approval Status	Works with Purchase Order Enhancements to approve POs prior to printing.
Item	This is the first field on line items and links to items in the Inventory table. *(Note: GP also accommodates entering non-inventoried items for purchasing services or fixed assets.)* The lookup window for the item table can be customized in Purchase Order Setup to display only items linked to approved vendors. We explained linking approved vendors to items in Chapter 4.
U of M	Links to the unit of measure table created in the Inventory Control Series and defaults from the item card. S&S purchases most of its inventory by Case 10 or Case 12.
Unit Cost	Defaults from the price last paid the vendor, which is stored on the item card.
Quantity Cancelled	Used to cancel quantities on printed POs. GP assumes that printed POs have been released to vendors and restricts deleting.
Remaining PO Subtotal	When using a blanket PO, the remaining balance on the PO appears in this field.

Table 6:2 Purchase Order Fields

5. We now will assign this transaction to a buyer. Click the lookup icon on Buyer ID to find that S&S has not created any buyers. Close the lookup window.

6. Click the hyperlinked **Buyer ID** field to open the Buyer Maintenance window illustrated next. *(Note: You are accessing a master table.)* This window is used to assign GP User IDs as buyers for the company.

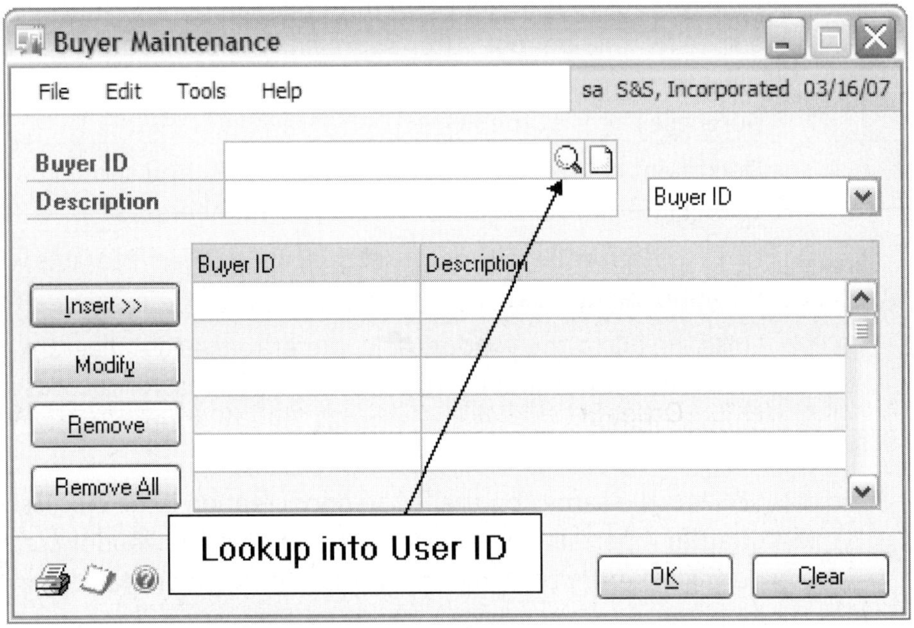

Figure 6:6 Buyer Maintenance Window

7. Click the lookup icon and select **ALevine**. Click **Insert** to link her User ID to the table. Click the lookup icon again to select the **sa** and click **Insert**. You now have the two buyers illustrated next. Click **OK**.

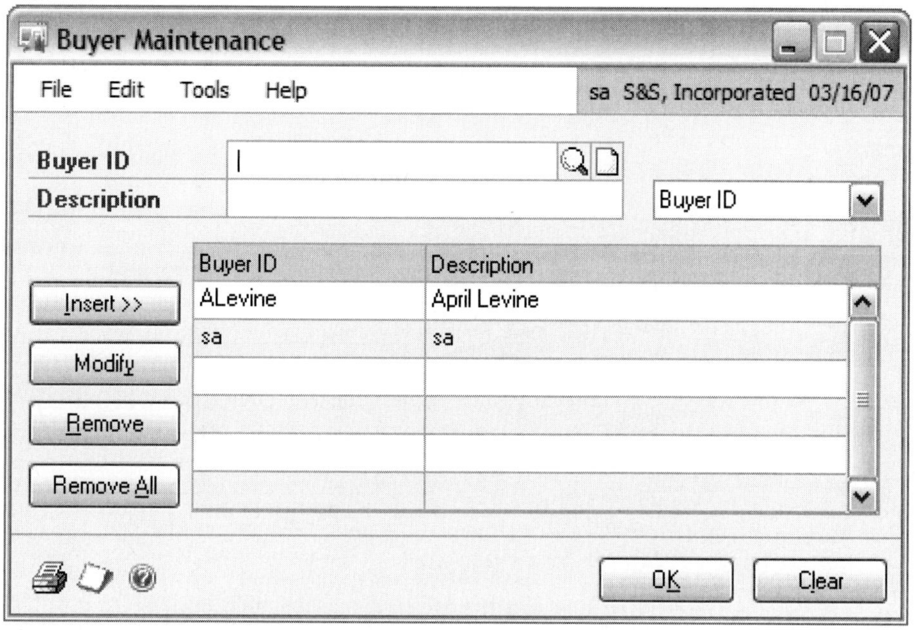

Figure 6:7 User IDs Linked to Buyer Table

8. Return to the Purchase Order Entry window, click the lookup icon on **Buyer ID** and select **ALevine**.

9. Now enter PO line items. Click the lookup icon on **Item**. Remember that you are currently using the default lookup window for items, which sorts by Item Number in ascending order (i.e., lowest value to highest value). (See Figure 6:8.)

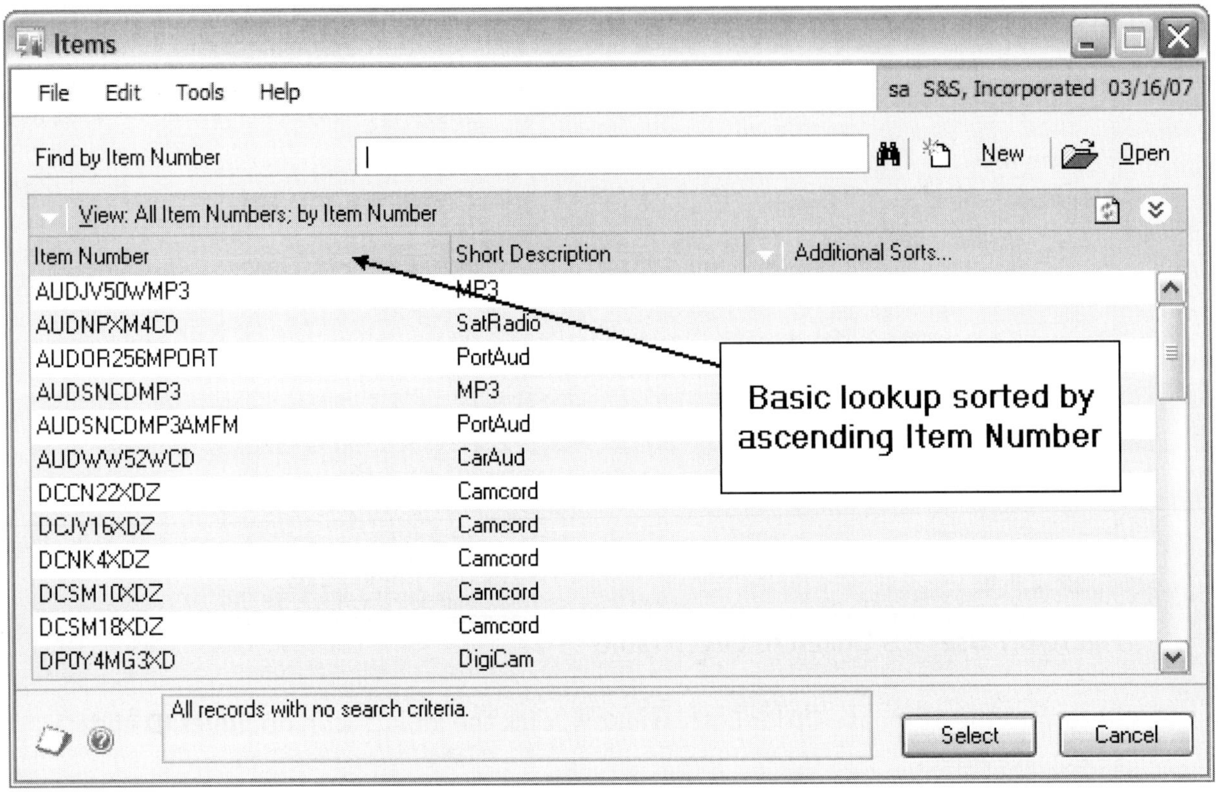

Figure 6:8 Default Item Lookup Window

Click the dropdown on **Additional Sorts** and select **by Description**, changing the sort to item descriptions in ascending order. (See Figure 6:9.) You could click the Description header to resort in descending order.

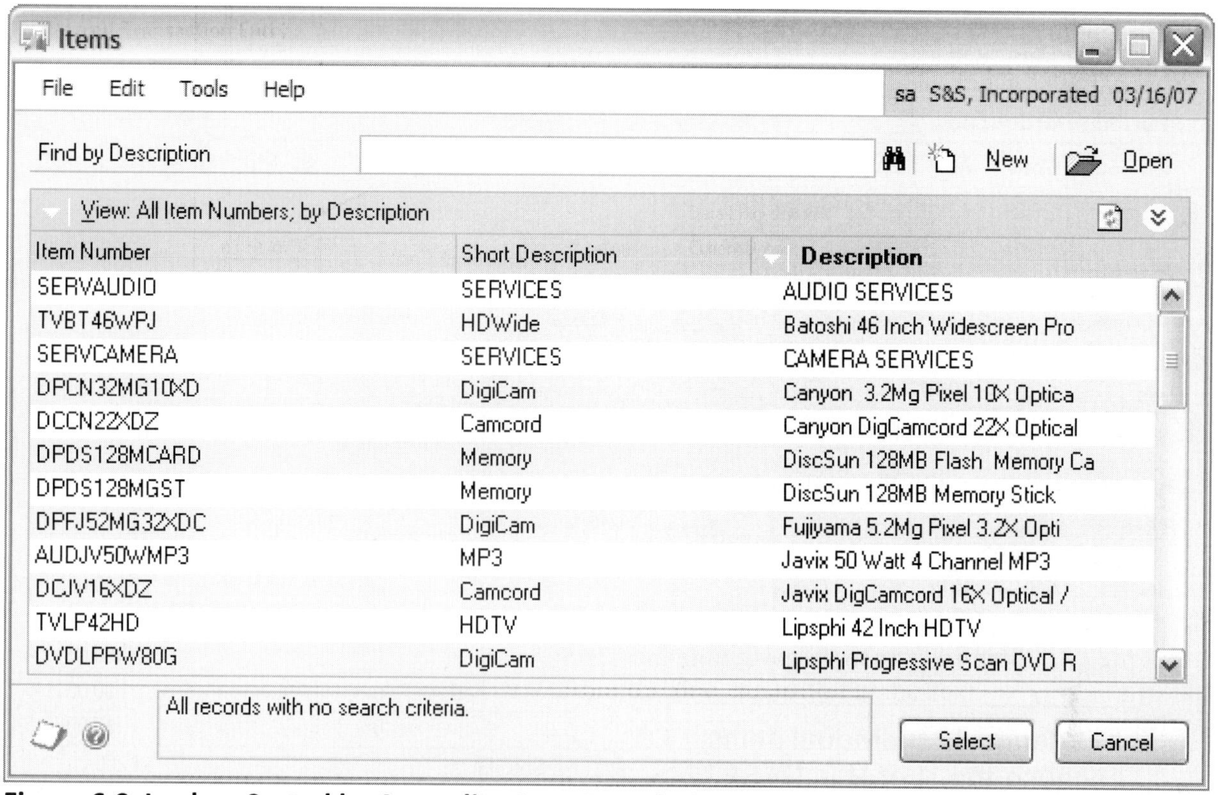

Figure 6:9 Lookup Sorted by Ascending Item Descriptions

Click the **Expansion** icon (Figure 6:10) so you can view description details.

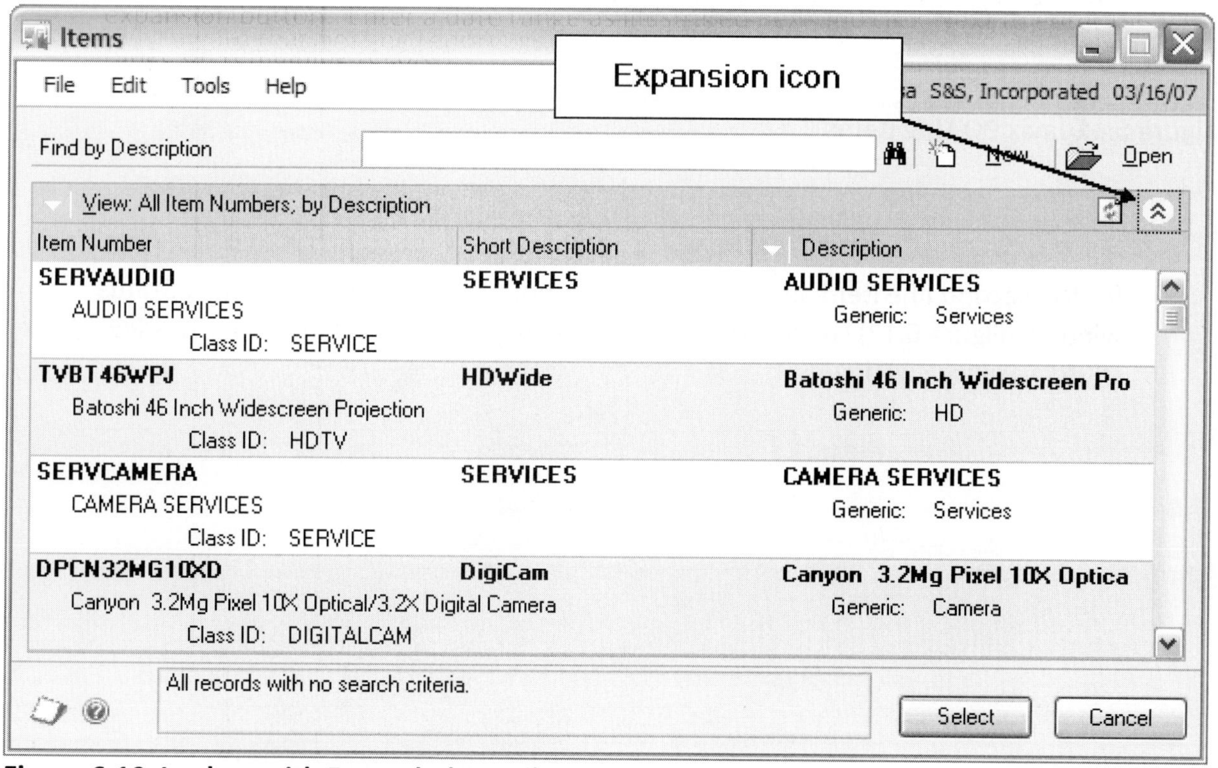

Figure 6:10 Lookup with Expanded Details

10. The Javix PO has two line items. Enter the items shown in Figure 6:11.

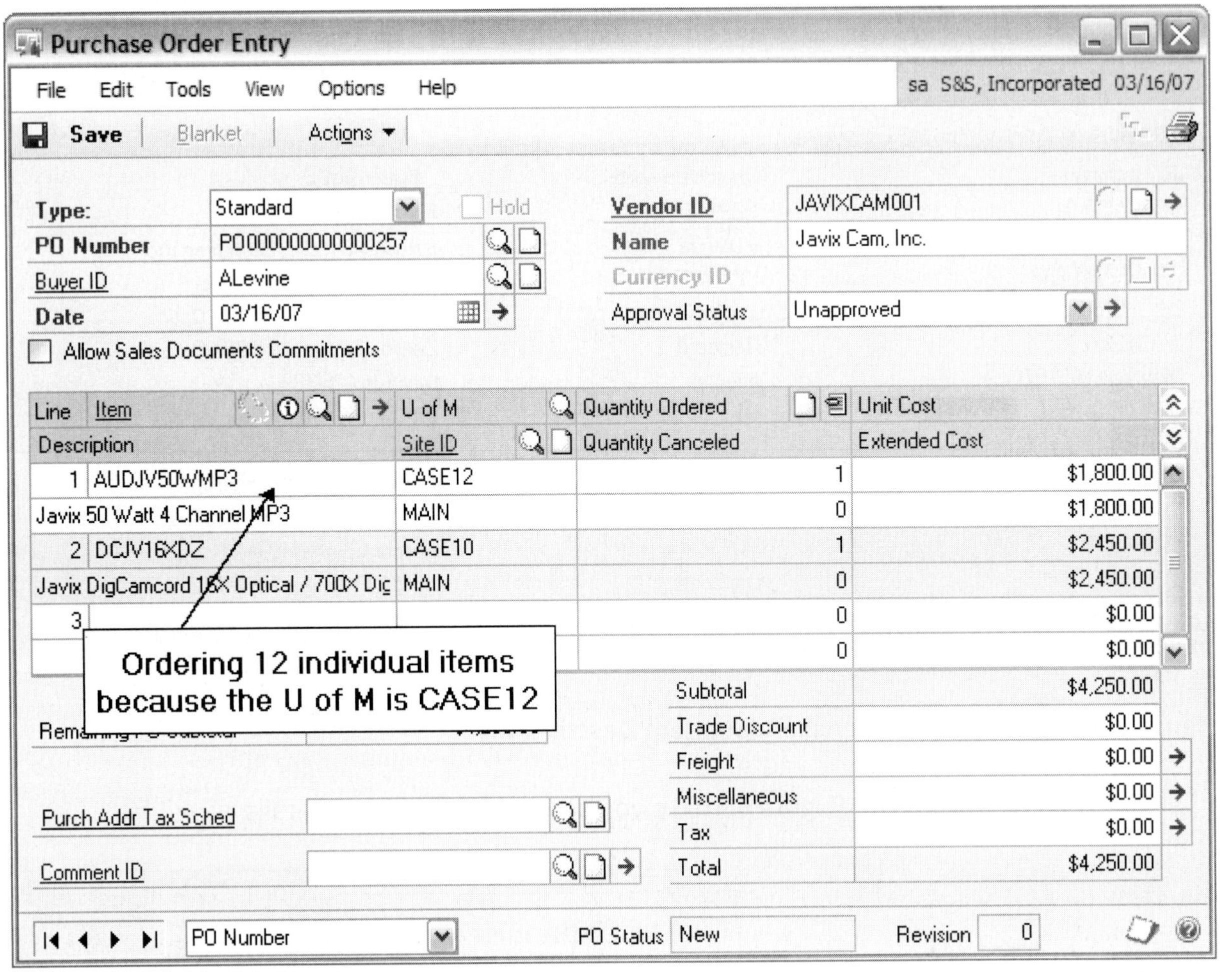

Figure 6:11 Javix PO Line Items

11. Before ordering, you can view item quantity status. Place your cursor in the **Item** field for the **second line item** and click this ⓘ symbol. The Purchasing Quantity Status window (Figure 6:12) shows that the only quantity on order are those for this PO. Click **OK** to close the window.

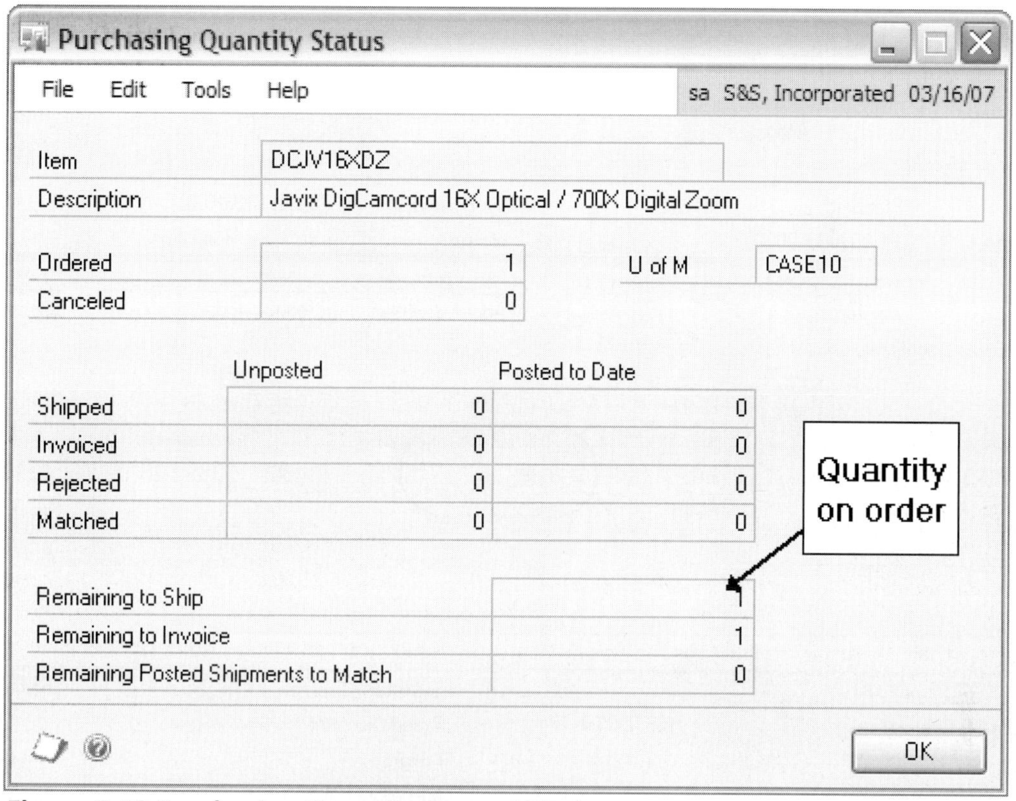

Figure 6:12 Purchasing Quantity Status Window

12. Unlike sales orders, you do not have to save POs to a back so click **Save**.

13. Now look up the PO you created from a sales order in Chapter 5. (See Figure 6:13.) Notice that this  symbol appears in the Quantity Ordered field meaning that some items on the order are committed to filling a sales order

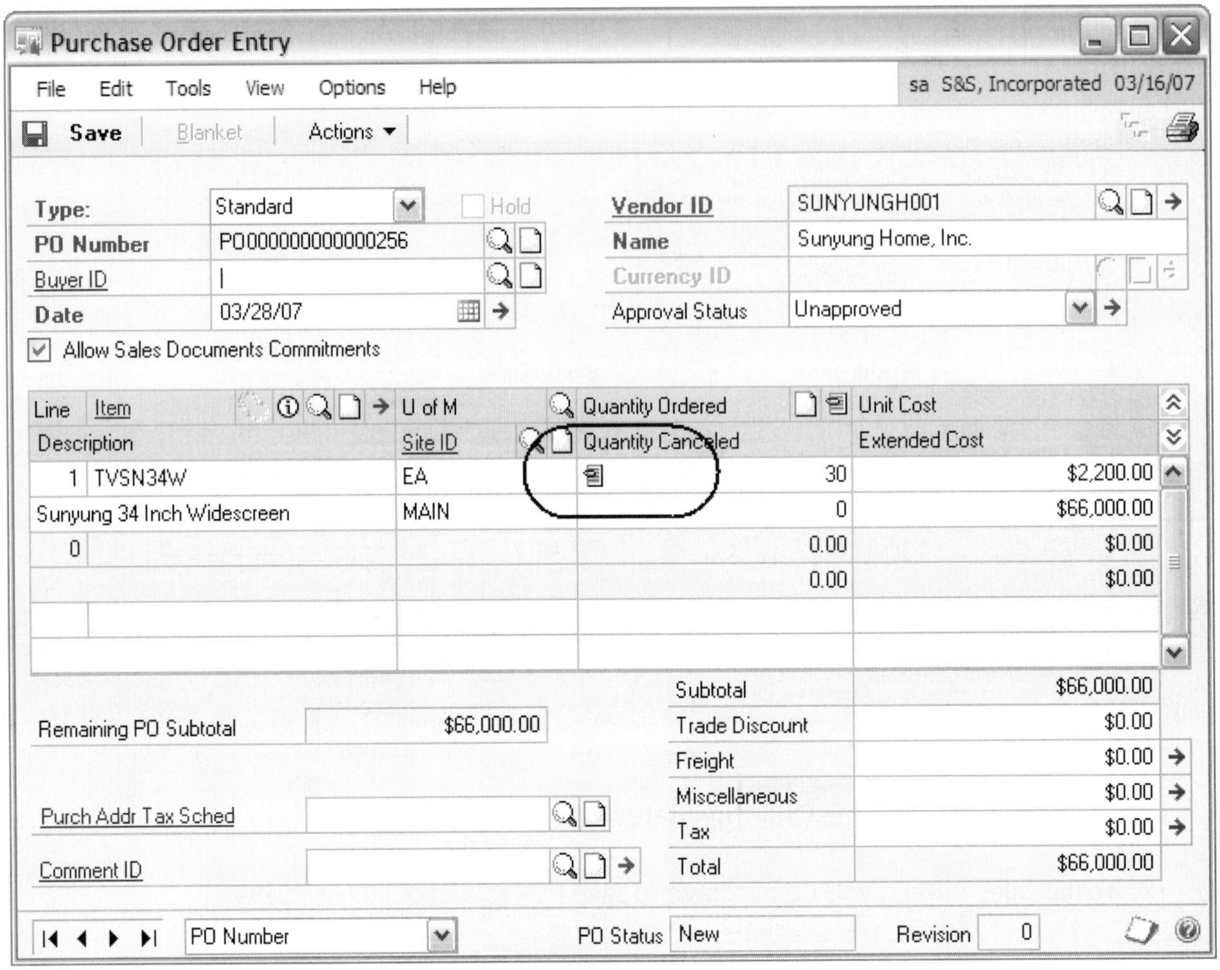

Figure 6:13 PO Quantity Committed to Sales Order

14. Reopen your PO to Javix Cam so it can be printed. Click the **Printer** icon on the window.

15. GP prompts as follows because the Approval Status is Unapproved. Click **OK** to return to the PO.

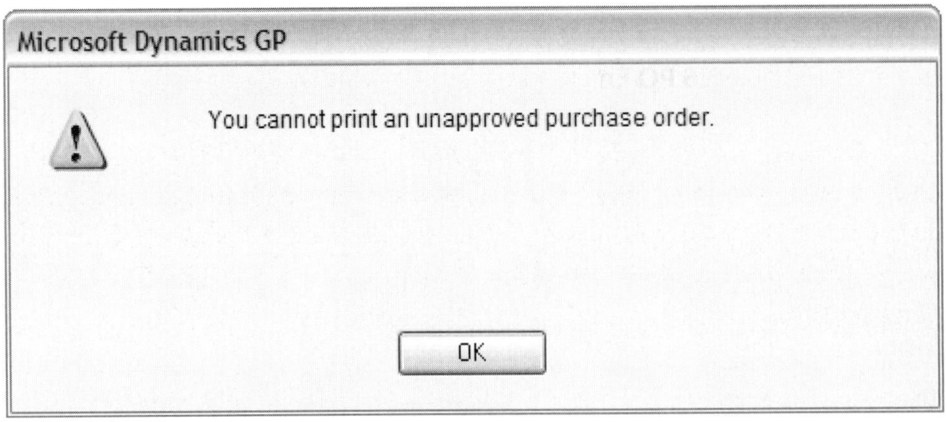

Figure 6:14 Unapproved PO Warning

16. Change the **Approval Status** to **Approved** and GP will prompt as follows, indicating that the buyer is not authorized to issue a PO for this amount. Click **OK**.

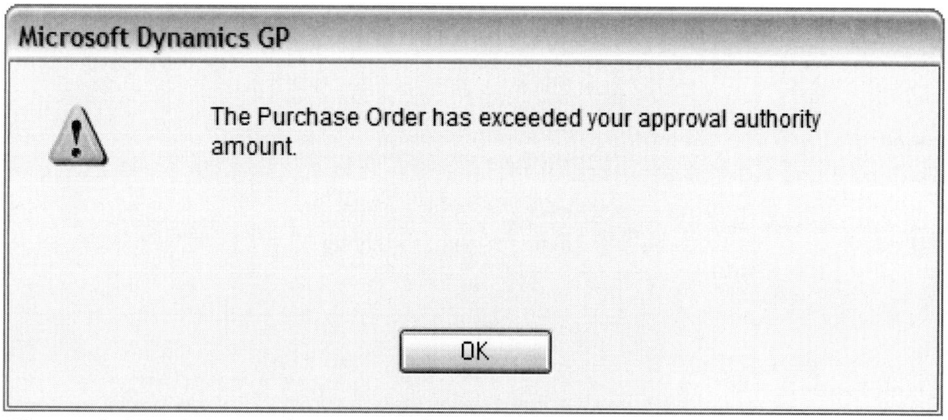

Figure 6:15 PO Exceeds Approval Authority Warning

17. Let us check on the buyer's approval authorization. Close the Purchase Order Entry window. Click **Purchase Orders Enhancements** under Setup on the home page to open the window illustrated next.

Figure 6:16 PO Enhancements Setup Window

18. Click **Approval Setup** and highlight April Levine. On the right (Figure 6:17) we see that she has approval authority up to $5,000 and the PO we are issuing is under this amount. So why are we getting this warning? Recall that the Buyer ID on the PO links to a User ID. You are logged on as **sa** and not April Levine. Entering her ID as the buyer does not override that fact.

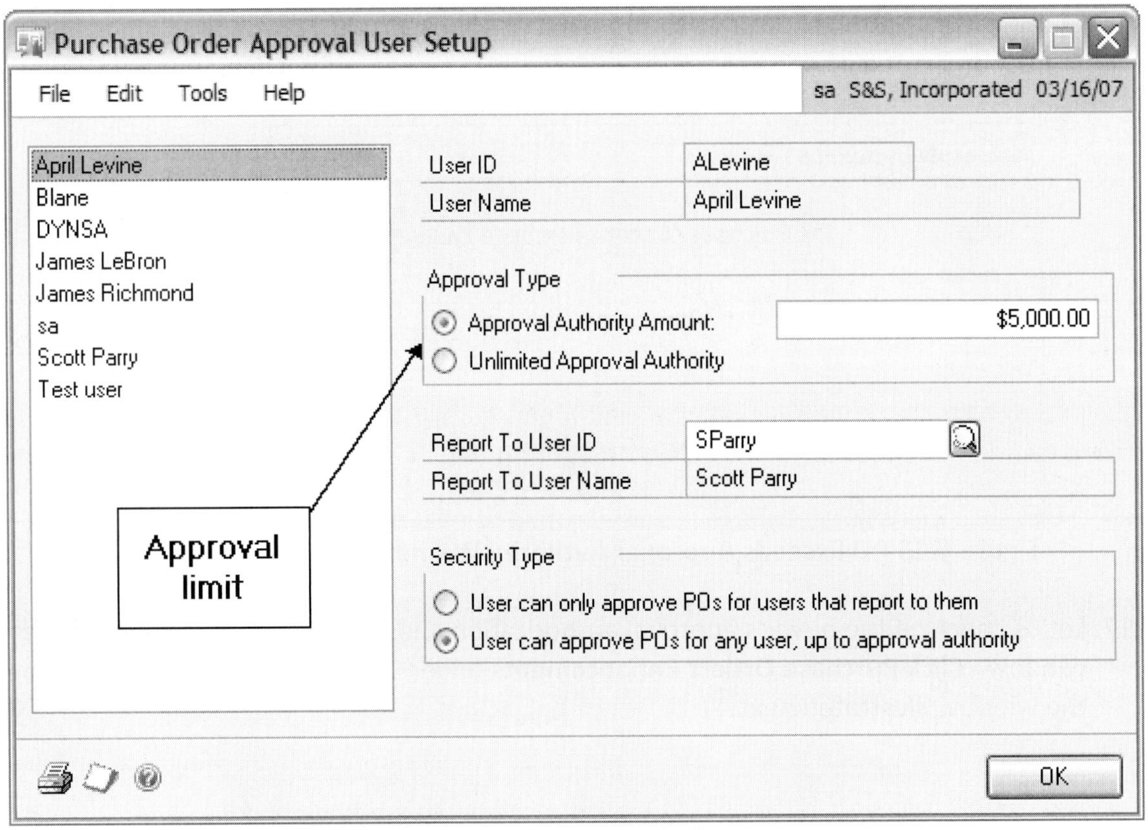

Figure 6:17 Purchase Order Approval User Setup Window

19. Highlight ***sa*** and set the approval status as follows. Click **OK** to save the changes and click **OK** to close the PO Enhancements Setup window.

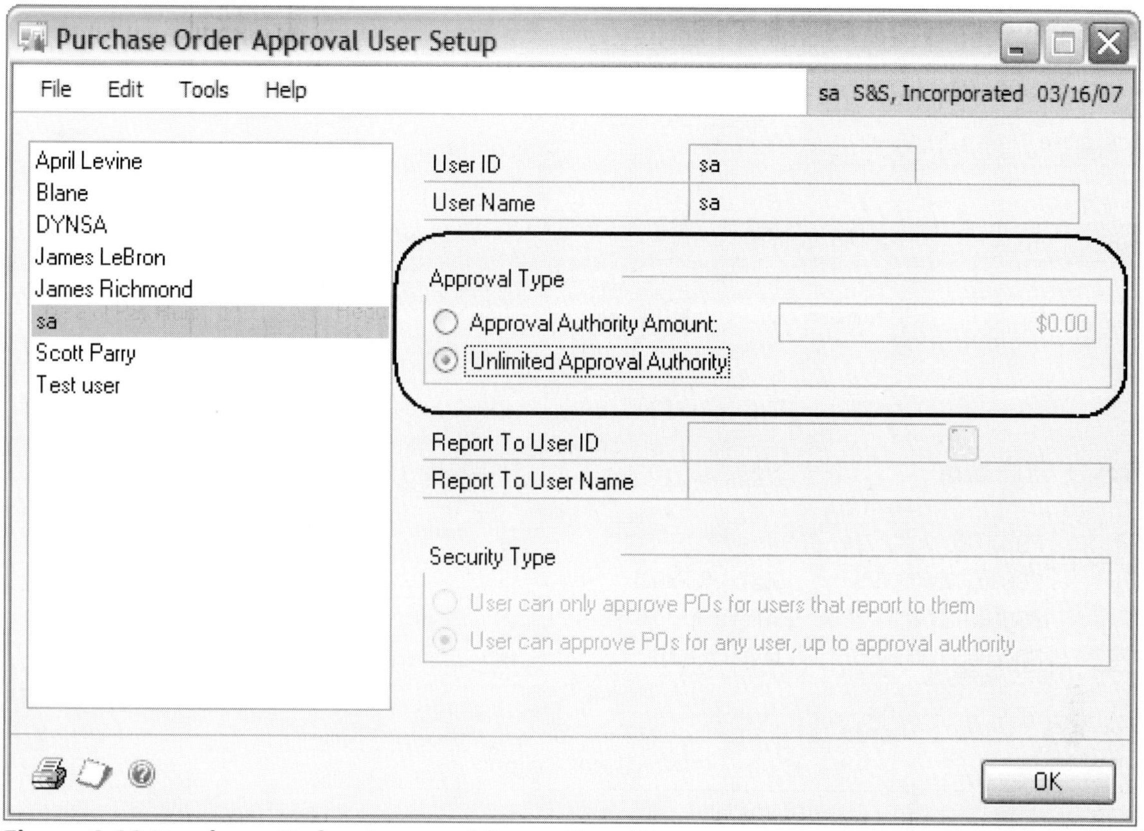

Figure 6:18 Purchase Order Approval for sa User ID

20. We will now approve the PO. Click **Purchase Order Enhancements Entry** under Transactions on the home page. Mark all POs as illustrated next and click **Approve**. Click **X** to close the window and print the reports to the screen.

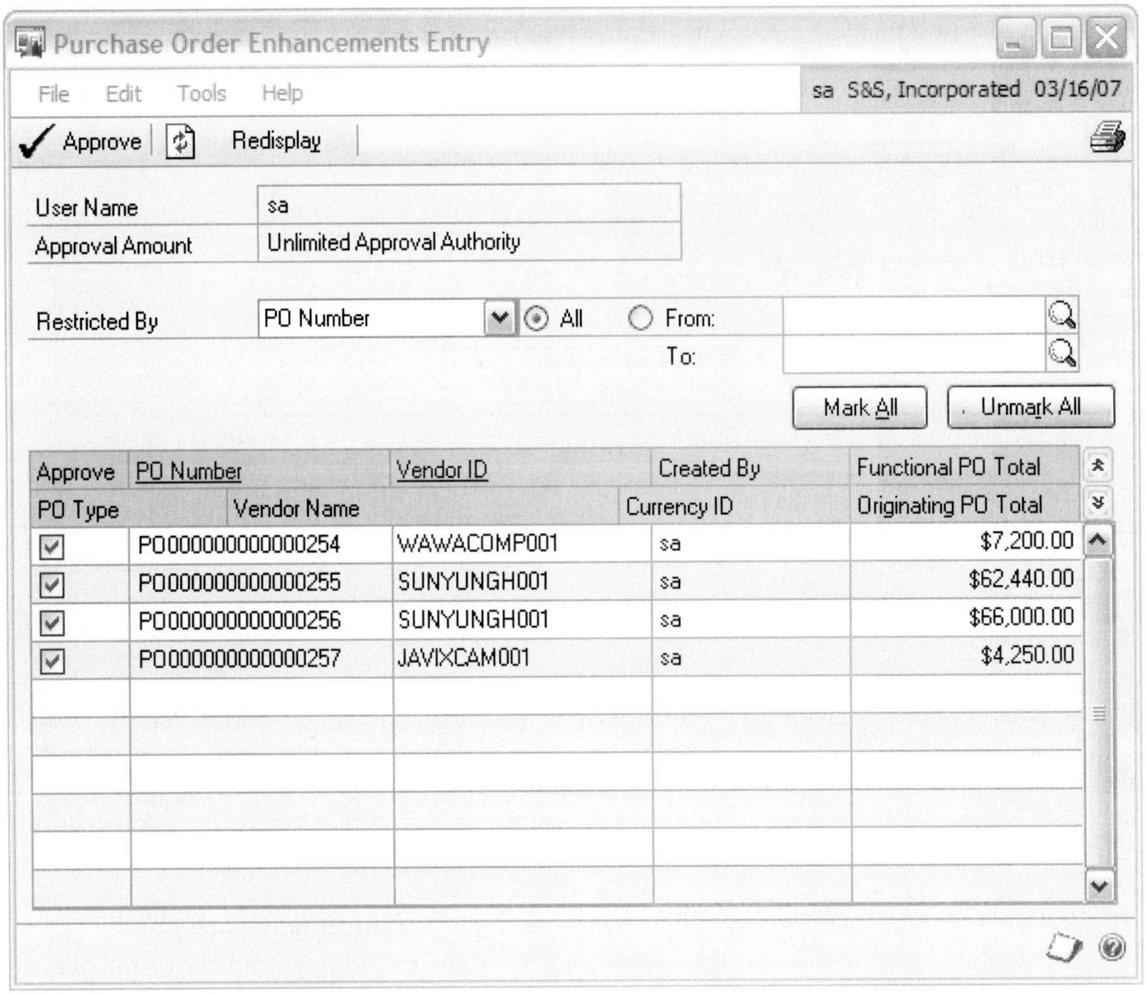

Figure 6:19 Approving POs

21. Now print the approved POs. Click **Print Purchasing Documents** under Transactions and mark the options illustrated next. Click **Print**. Send all output to the screen.

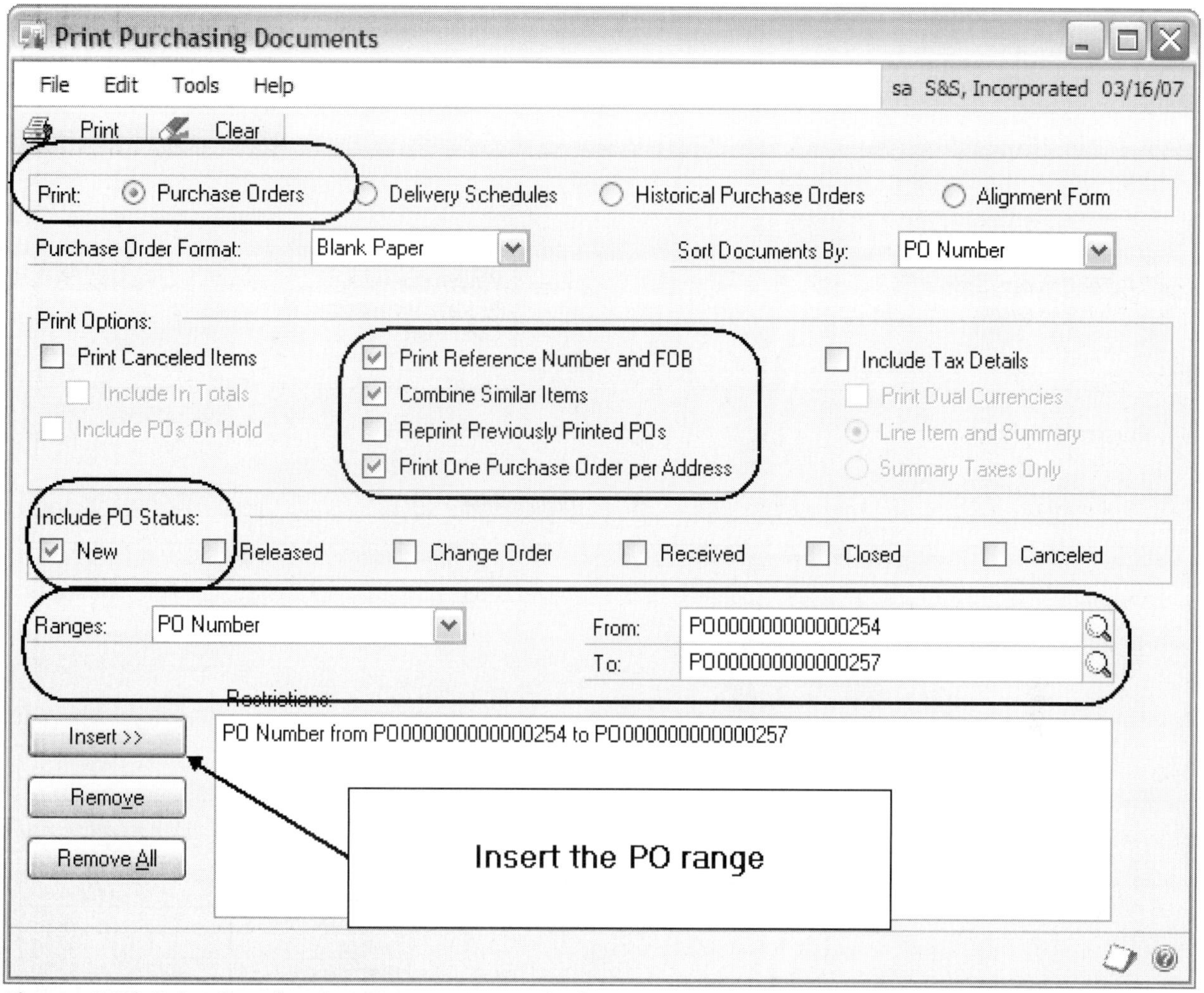

Figure 6:20 Print Purchasing Documents Window

22. The first PO is illustrated next. Notice the signature line for authorizing the PO prior to mailing it to the vendor. Close the POs and then the Print Purchasing Documents window.

S&S Incorporated
382 N. Portage Path
Akron OH 44337

Purchase Order	
Purchase Order No.	PO000000000000254
Date	03/12/07

Vendor:

WAWA Company
87 Maryland Avenue
Canton OH 44323

Ship To:

WAWA Company
87 Maryland Avenue
Canton OH 44323

Contract Number:

* Changed Since the Previous Revision

Shipping Method	Payment Terms	Confirm With	Page
	Net 30		1

L/N	Item / Ship Method	Description / Reference Numbe	Req. Date	U/M	Ordered	Unit Price	Ext. Price
1	WX4CCSCDRRW	WAWA 52 Watt X4 Channel Car Stereo (	03/14/07	CASE12	10	$720.00	$7,200.00
	PICKUP	AUDWW52WCD					

Subtotal	$7,200.00
Trade Discount	$0.00
Freight	$0.00
Miscellaneous	$0.00
Tax	$0.00
Order Total	$7,200.00

Authorized Signature

Figure 6:21 Printed PO

This exercise illustrates PO approval control. Referring back to our roadmap discussion, you now understand that recording a PO is segregated from authorizing (i.e., printing) because GP bases print approval on the User ID logged into the software and not on the Buyer ID linked to the transaction.

What about the discussion in Chapter 4 on associating inventory items to authorized vendors?

Try entering a PO to WAWA Company for item AUDJV50WMP3 and GP prompts to associate this item with the vendor. Level 2 discusses instituting controls over this feature.

Return to the Purchase Order Entry window and look up the Javix PO. After printing, the PO Status at the bottom changes to 

. For internal control reasons, GP places restrictions on modifying released POs. Let us test these restrictions.

1. You cannot delete existing line items. Test this by placing your cursor in a line item and clicking ***Edit>>Delete Row*** on the window menu. You can cancel items by entering a quantity into the Quantity Canceled field.

2. You can add new line items and increase quantities for existing items. Place your cursor in the Quantity Ordered field for the second line item and increase it to 3. Save the PO and reopen it. The PO Status now reads Change Order instead of Release because the PO needs to be reprinted. Close the window.

3. Click **Edit Purchase Order Status** under Transactions and look up the PO to Javix. The window (Figure 6:22) reports two status categories. The first is the status for the entire PO and the second is status by line item. Status types are self-explanatory. Notice that Line Item 2 shows Change Order as a result of the quantity increase. When the order is reprinted, the status will be changed to Released.

   You can use this window to manually change line item statuses; however, it is unnecessary because GP changes statuses as you process the PO. This window is also where you cancel a released PO. This is done by changing the top level status to cancel and clicking Process. Click **X** to close the window,

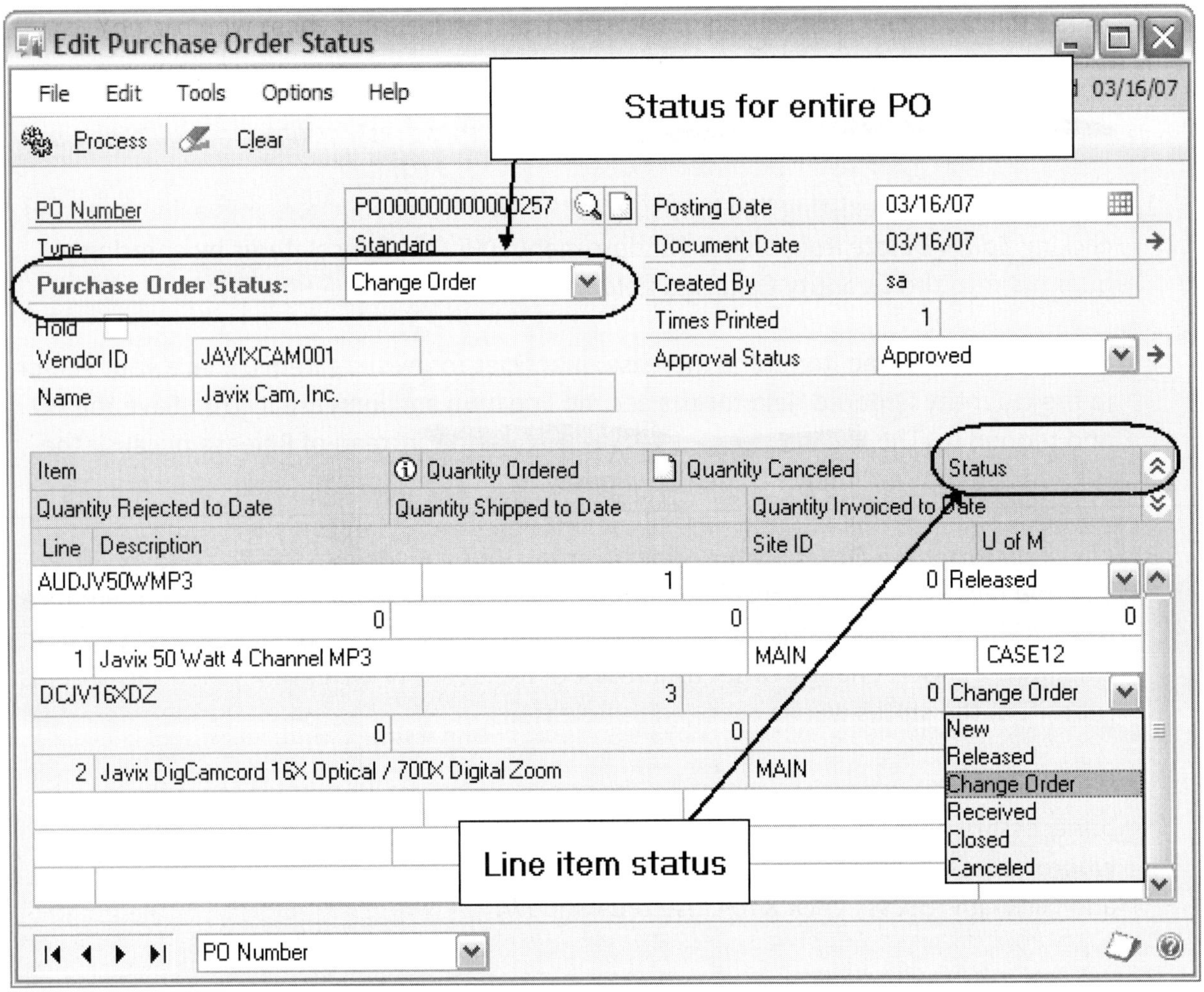

Figure 6:22 Edit Purchase Order Status Window

You should be asking an internal control question at this point. How does S&S ensure that changed POs are reprinted and released to vendors? GP has an answer for that and it is called reporting. Internal controls are often monitored by using reports. Let us review the report that monitors POs.

1. Click **Analysis** under Reports and select the **Purchase Order Status** report.

2. Highlight the existing **PO Status** report and click **Modify**.

3. Set the options to view only **New** and **Changed** statuses and run the report. The report is illustrated next. Close the report and the report window. You can save your changes.

```
                                        S&S, Incorporated                                   Page:    1
User Date:  03/16/07                PURCHASE ORDER STATUS REPORT                            User ID: sa
                                      Purchase Order Processing

Ranges:            From:                          To:                            From:            To:
   Vendor ID       First                          Last                 PO Status First            Last
   Name            First                          Last                 PO Number First            Last
   Document Date First                            Last                 Origin    First            Last
   Buyer ID        First                          Last

Sorted By: Document Date                              Print Option: Detailed
Include PO Line Status: New, Change Order
Include:

# Non-Inventoried Item   & On Hold

PO Number            Type       Doc. Date  Vendor ID         Name                      PO Status         Buyer ID       WF Status
--------------------------------------------------------------------------------------------------------------------------------
   Line  Item                       Item Description                      Vendor Item                 Origin    Line Status
--------------------------------------------------------------------------------------------------------------------------------
    Site ID      U Of M           Qty           Qty          Remaining       Remaining        Unit Cost      Remaining Ext. Cost
                               Ordered       Canceled         to Ship       to Invoice
--------------------------------------------------------------------------------------------------------------------------------
        Receipt No.                Doc. Date          Site ID        U Of M          Qty Shipped     Qty Invoiced     Qty Rejected
--------------------------------------------------------------------------------------------------------------------------------
  PO000000000000257 Standard  03/16/07   JAVIXCAM001       Javix Cam, Inc.           Change Order    ALevine         Not Activated
   2      DCJV16XDZ                Javix DigCamcord 16X Optical / 700X Digita  16xx700xxDCDZ              Manual    Change Order
    MAIN         CASE10              3              0                3             3         $2,450.00                 $7,350.00
                                                                                                                ----------------
                                Original Subtotal:          $7,350.00              Remaining Subtotal:              $7,350.00
                                                                                                                ================

                Grand Totals:       1 Purchase Order(s)
```

Figure 6:23 Purchase Order Status Report

Regardless of the department recording a PO, the purchasing department releases POs to vendors. The requesting department and receiving department need to be notified of release. The old fashioned method of giving notice was to have the purchasing department send a copy of the PO to each department. With GP, these departments can monitor PO status by printing a PO Status report.

> 1. Open the Purchase Order Entry window and identify a weakness other than adding a vendor on-the-fly that fails to segregate recording from authorization. How would you correct this weakness?
>
> 2. When running the PO status report, we selected New and Changed statuses. Why was New included?

E6:2 Working with Purchase Orders

Receiving Department Activities

When inventory arrives from the vendor, receiving (i.e., shipping) department employees follow internal control procedures over accepting the shipment. These procedures include verifying that the receipt is authorized by a PO; the goods are not damaged; and quantities and style of good match the PO. After accepting the shipment, employees then enter received quantities in GP. Vendor packing slips and/or invoices enclosed with the shipment are sent to the accounts payable department.

On March 22, 2007, Javix's shipment for the
PO entered in the previous topic arrives at the dock. The next exercise walks through processing this receipt.

1. Click **Purchasing Batches** and create the batch illustrated next.

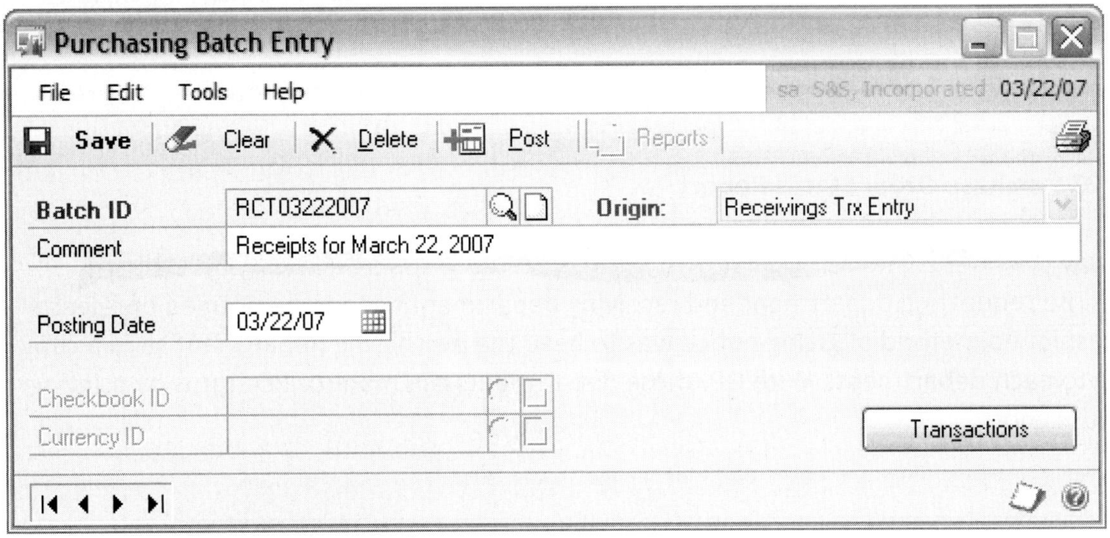

Figure 6:24 Create Receipt Batch

2. Click **Transactions** and then click the dropdown on **Type**. Notice that there are three types of transactions. (See Figure 6:25) **Shipment** is used for processing receipts that are not accompanied by a vendor invoice. **Shipment/Invoice**, is chosen when entering a receipt along with a vendor invoice. **In-Transit Inventory** is used to record shipments between locations (i.e., shipping inventory between multiple company warehouses.)

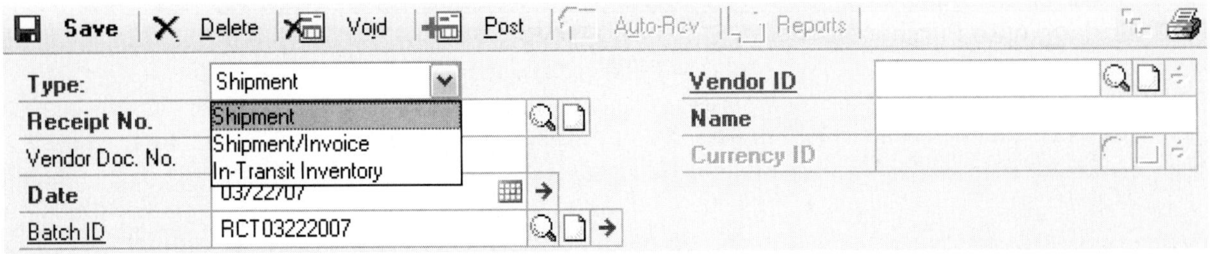

Figure 6:25 Receivings Transactions Types

3. Select **Shipment** to record only a receipt of goods and enter information for the top portion of the window as illustrated next. GP will autofill the Receipt No. after tabbing past the field. Remember that this is a document control number supplied by GP so your number may differ from the one illustrated. Vendor Doc. No. stores the vendor's packing slip number or invoice number when the transaction type is Shipment/Invoice.

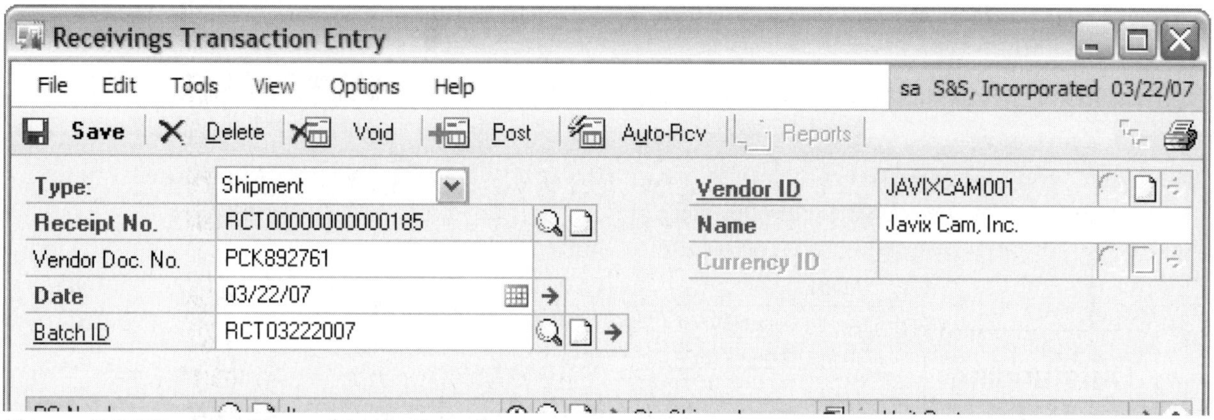

Figure 6:26 Top Section of Javix Receipt

4. We are now ready to record items and quantities received. This task can be performed using one of two methods. First, you can click the lookup icon on PO Number, select a PO, and then tab to the Qty Shipped field for each line item to enter the quantity. Secondly, you can click Auto-Rcv in the toolbar and this is the method we will illustrate.

5. Click **Auto-Rcv** and refer to Figure 6:27 as we explain using this window.

   On the left are outstanding POs to the vendor. On the right are items for these POs. If the vendor name is highlighted and multiple POs exist then the right displays items for all POs. You can highlight individual POs to filter for items on a selected PO.

   You mark items to receive by check marking individual line items or clicking Mark All. After marking, Qty Shipped automatically equals Qty Ordered but can be changed typing a new value into Qty Shipped.

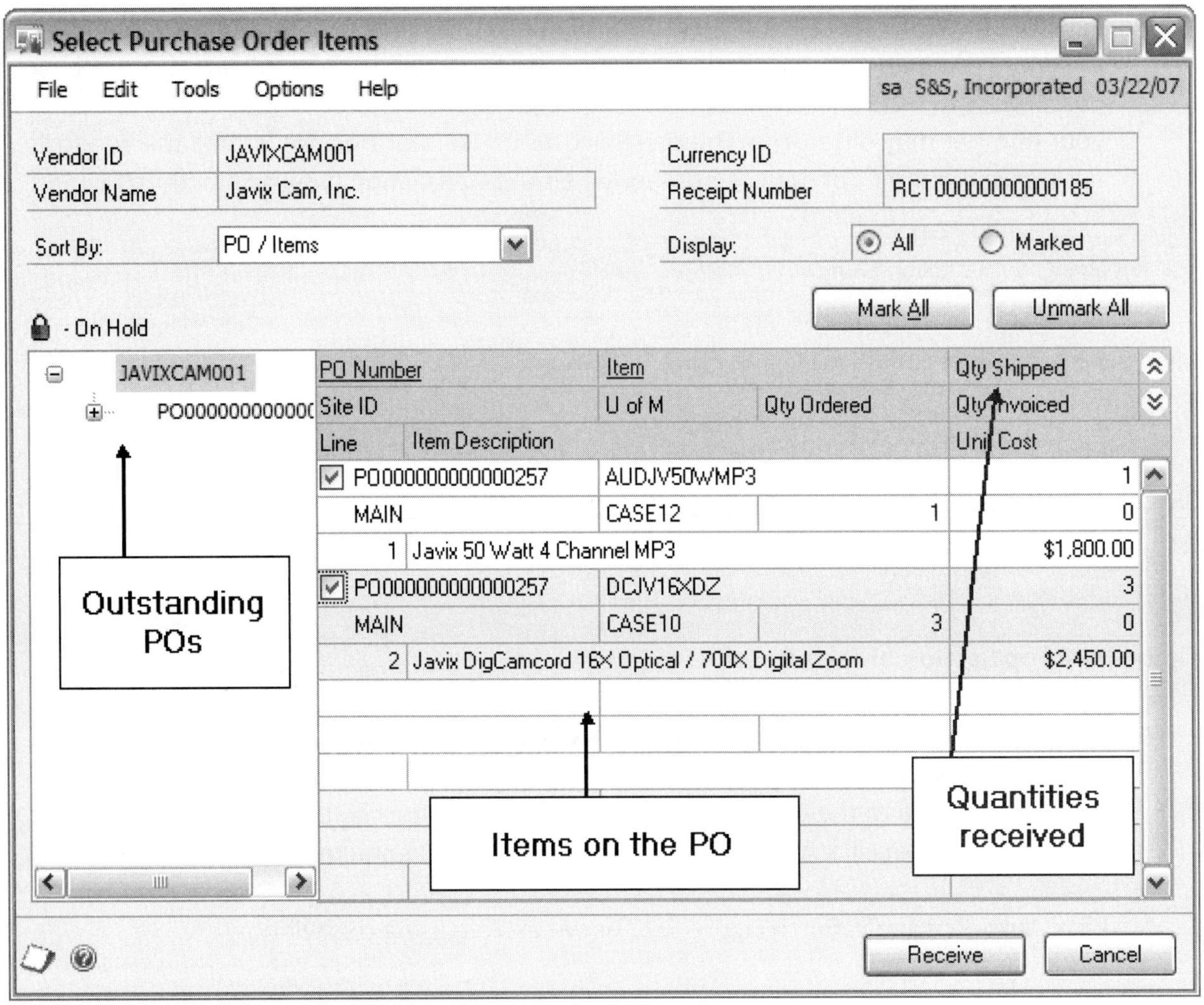

Figure 6:27 Select Purchase Order Items for Javix Receipt

6. Click **Mark All** and then **Receive**.

7. You are returned to the Receivings Transaction Entry window. Click the **Distributions** button and expand the rows. The next illustrations shows general ledger accounts affected when posting. Notice that entries will debit inventory (i.e., asset account) and credit accrued payables (i.e., liability account). Are these entries correct? Let us analyze.

   First, GAAP instructs that liabilities are recognized when incurred. S&S incurred a liability upon receipt of the goods. The liability is accrued until the vendor invoice arrives, wherein it will be reclassified from accrued liabilities to accounts payable. We will see this entry when we post the vendor invoice.

   Next, S&S has received title to an asset. When sold, this asset will be expensed to cost of goods sold. Thus, we have our answer – the entries are correct.

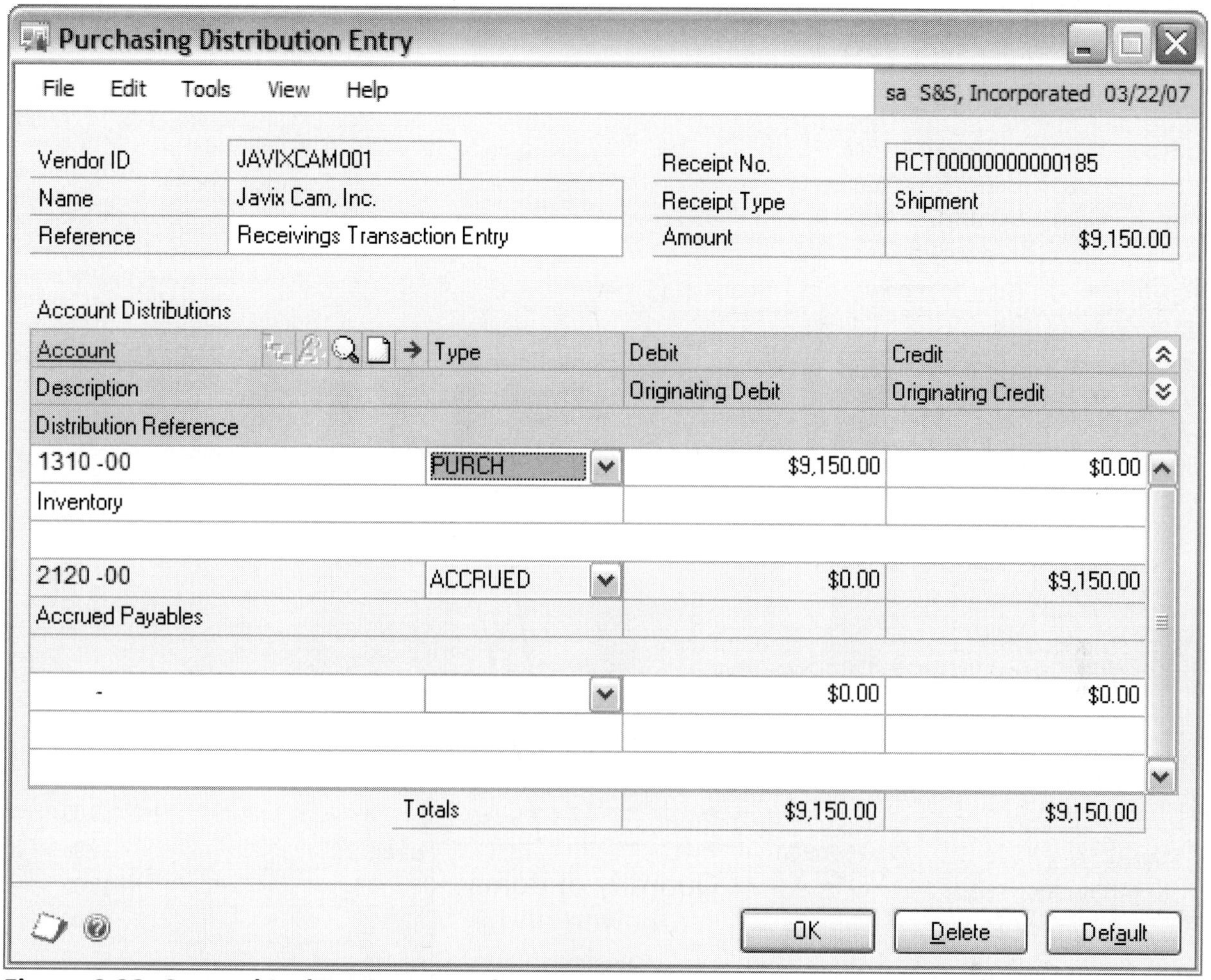

Figure 6:28 General Ledger Accounts for Javix Receipt

8. Click **OK** to return to Receivings Transaction Entry window. Click **Save** and we will enter the next transaction.

9. This time choose **Shipment/Invoice** as the **Type** so we can record an invoice with a receipt. Enter the following transaction to receive all items on the Sunyung Home PO indicated.

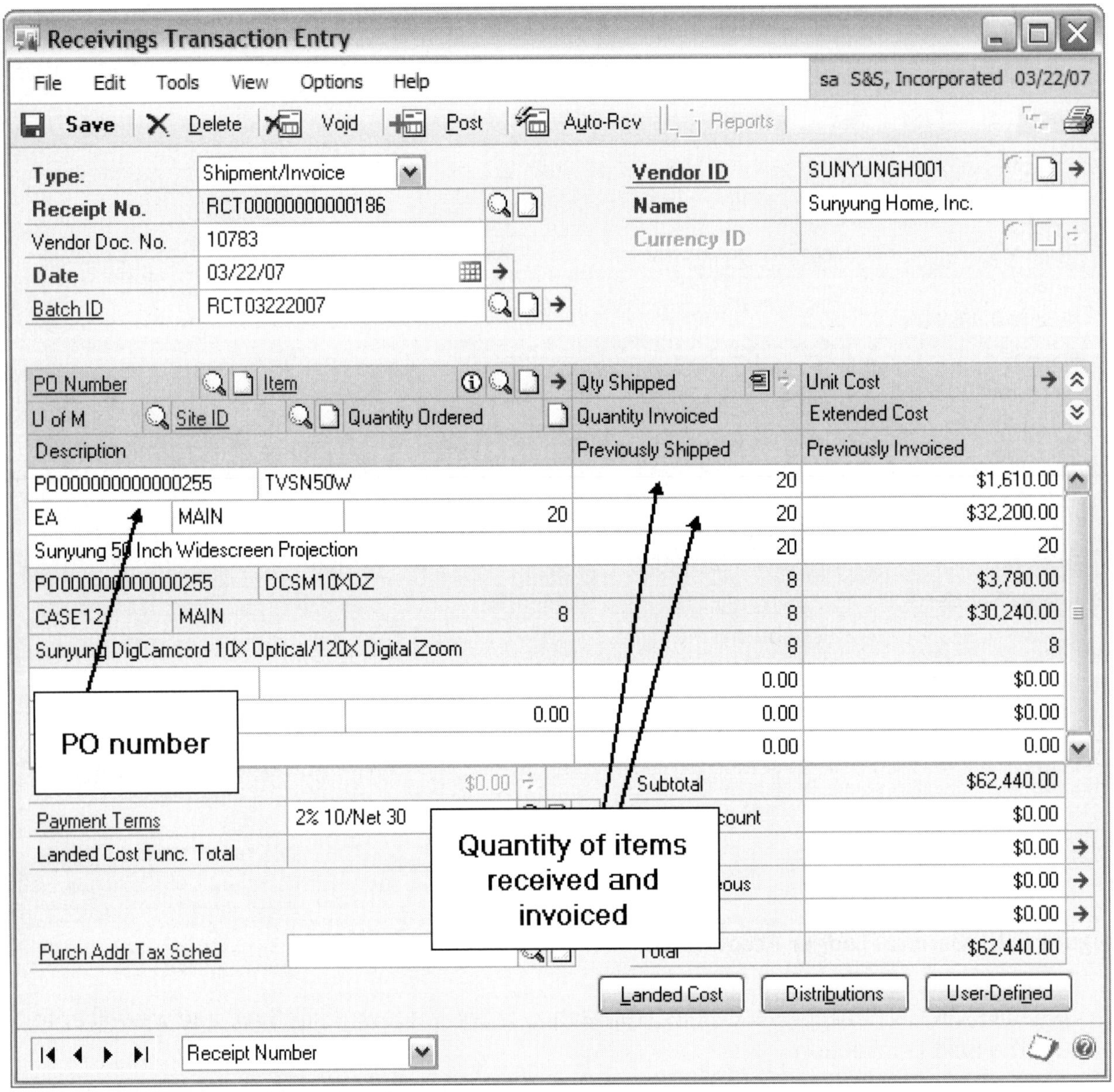

Figure 6:29 Receipt with an Invoice

10. Click **Distributions** and note that this transaction credits accounts payable instead of accrued purchases. This occurs because you are recording both a receipt and a vendor invoice.

    It also credits Purchase Discounts Available (i.e., a contra liability account) because this vendor grants S&S a discount when paying the invoice early. If paid by the discount date, posting the payment transfers the available discount to the discounts taken account. The discounts taken account is a cost of goods sold account. Click **OK**.

11. Save the transaction and close the Receivings Transaction Entry window.

12. Return to the Purchasing Batch Entry window and look up the batch. Click the **Printer** icon and print the Receivings Edit List to the screen. This batch control report should be reviewed for accuracy prior to posting the batch. Close the report.

13. Click **Post** to post the transactions and posting reports to the screen. These are control reports over posting. Close each report and the Purchasing Batch Entry window.

We had you post these transactions for illustrative purposes. In reality, the receiving department only enters and saves transactions. Posting is reserved for the accounts payable department, which is the subject of our next topic.

> On March 27, 2007, the receiving department received a shipment from WAWA Company for 9 items of AUDWW52WCD on PO000000000000254. WAWA will not be shipping the remaining item. Record and post this receipt and then cancel the remaining item on the PO. Packing slip number 7625 was enclosed with the shipment.

E6:3 Practicing Receipts

ACCOUNTS PAYABLE DEPARTMENT ACTIVITIES

The accounts payable department performs several activities, including processing vendor invoices. The steps for processing these invoices depend on whether or not the transaction originated on a PO. In the exercises to follow you will first process invoices for POs and then invoices without a PO.

Vendor Invoices for Transactions Originating on a PO

Thus far, we issued a PO to order items and then recorded the receipt of these items. More importantly, you performed these tasks in the Inventory Purchasing Tier so must now use this tier to process the invoice. Complete the next exercise to process that invoice.

1. On March 28, 2007, invoice number INV23793 from Javix arrives for the item receipt you posted in a previous topic. Set the system date and to 3/28/2007 and click **Purchasing Batches** to create the following batch.

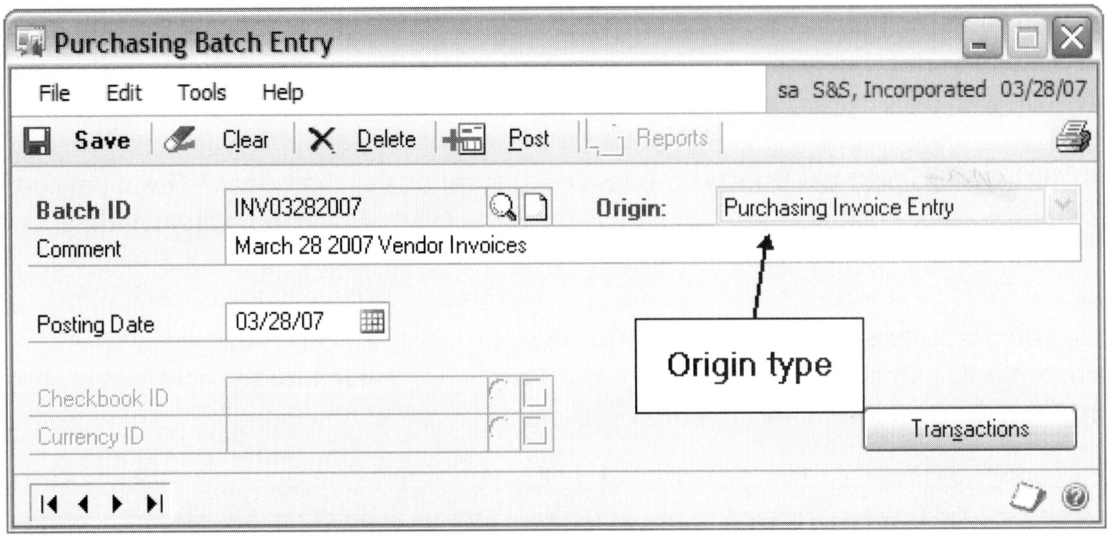

Figure 6:30 Batch for March 28 Vendor Invoices

2. Click **Transactions** to open the next window and complete the top portion as illustrated. Notice that you will date the transaction March 26, 2007 because this is the date on the invoice. It makes sense that you will not receive invoices on the same date as mailed by the vendor. Always set the transaction date to equal the invoice date because the vendor's date, not your processing date, determines when the payment is due.

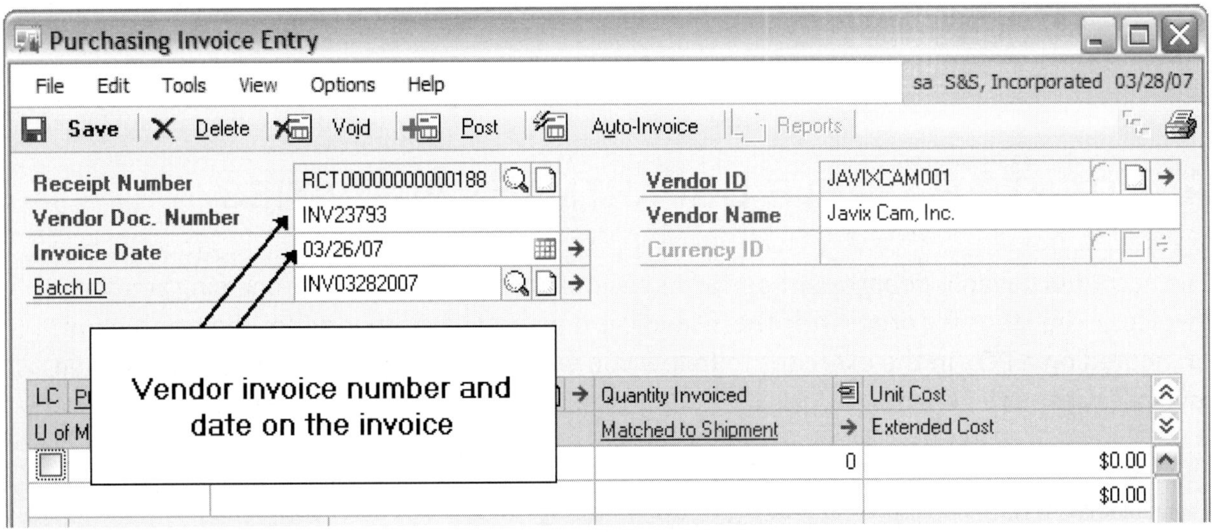

Figure 6:31 Javix Invoice

3. Move to the PO Number field and look up open POs for this vendor. (See Figure 6:32.) POs remain open until you post an invoice against it. Click **Select**.

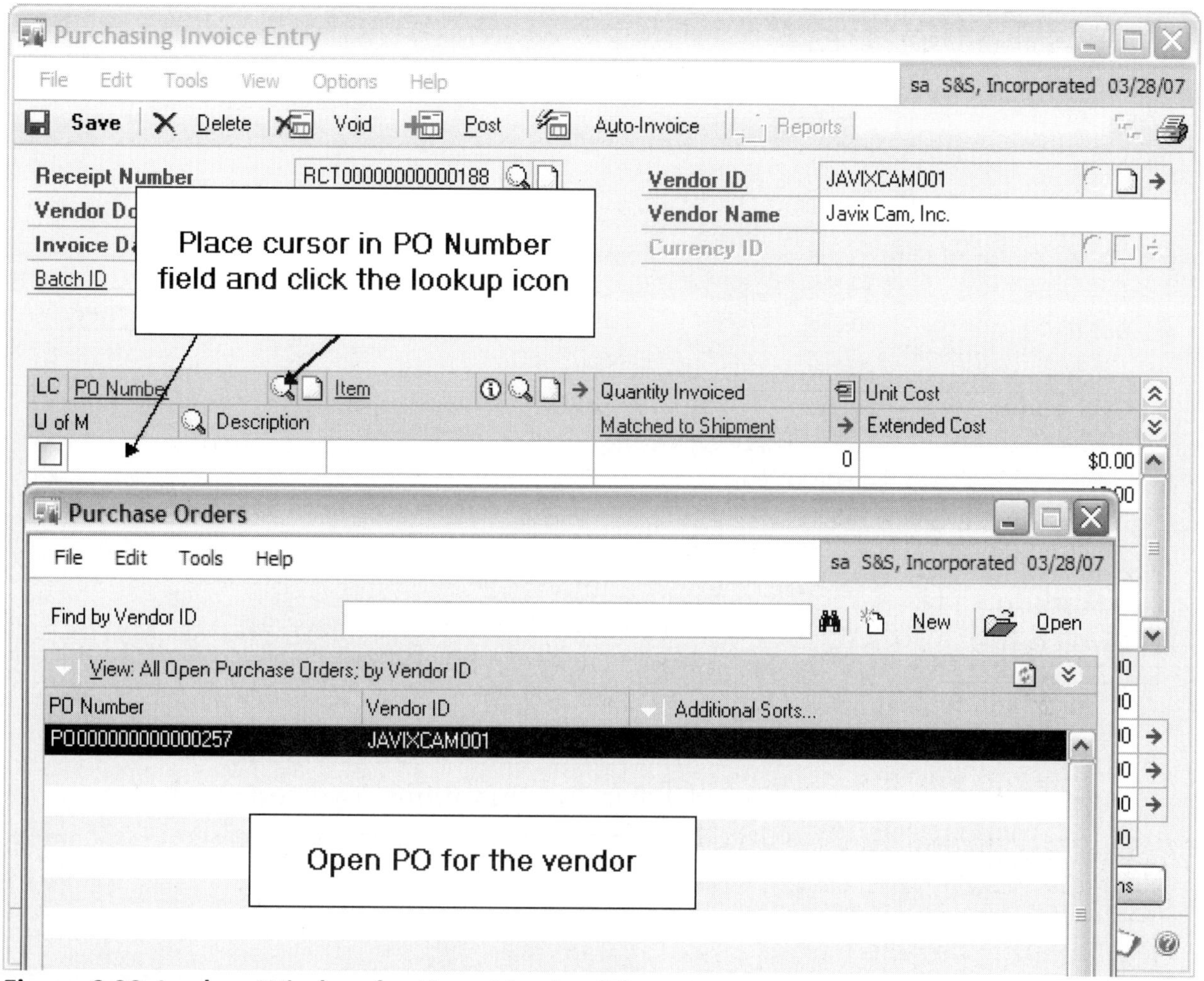

Figure 6:32 Lookup Window for Open Vendor POs

4. You will next enter the quantities invoiced by the vendor. Like receipts, there are two methods for entering these quantities. You can click the lookup icon on Item, select individual line items from the PO, and enter a Quantity Invoiced or click Auto-Invoice to view all line items on the PO, select the line items, and enter quantities. We will illustrate the last method so click **Auto-Invoice** and complete the window as illustrated next. GP autofills the Qty Ordered value as the Qty Invoiced value. You can always change this default by typing in a new value.

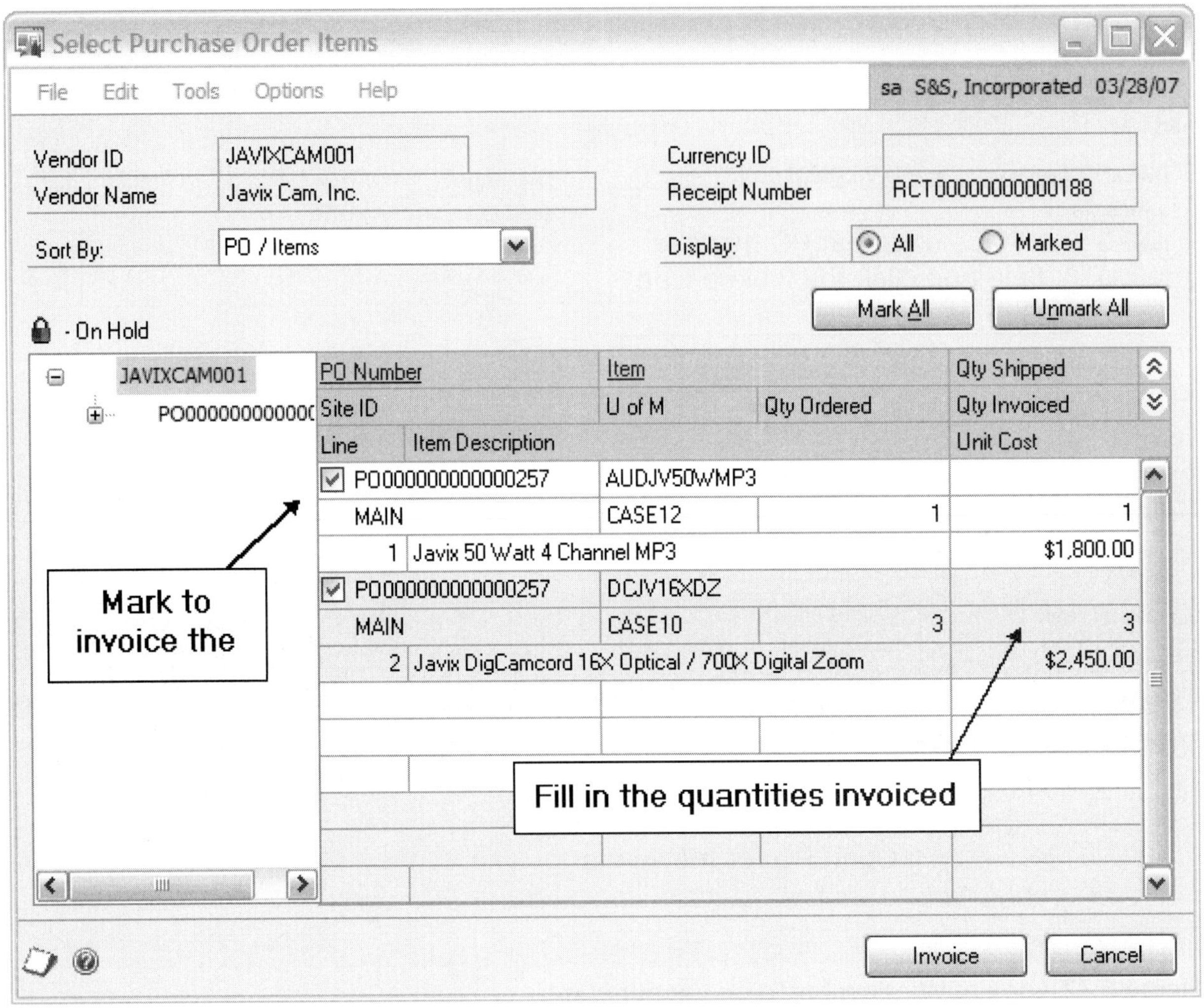

Figure 6:33 Auto Invoice for Javix PO

5. Keep the selections illustrated and click **Invoice**. Return to the Purchasing Invoice Entry window and notice that the receipt number matched to the PO.

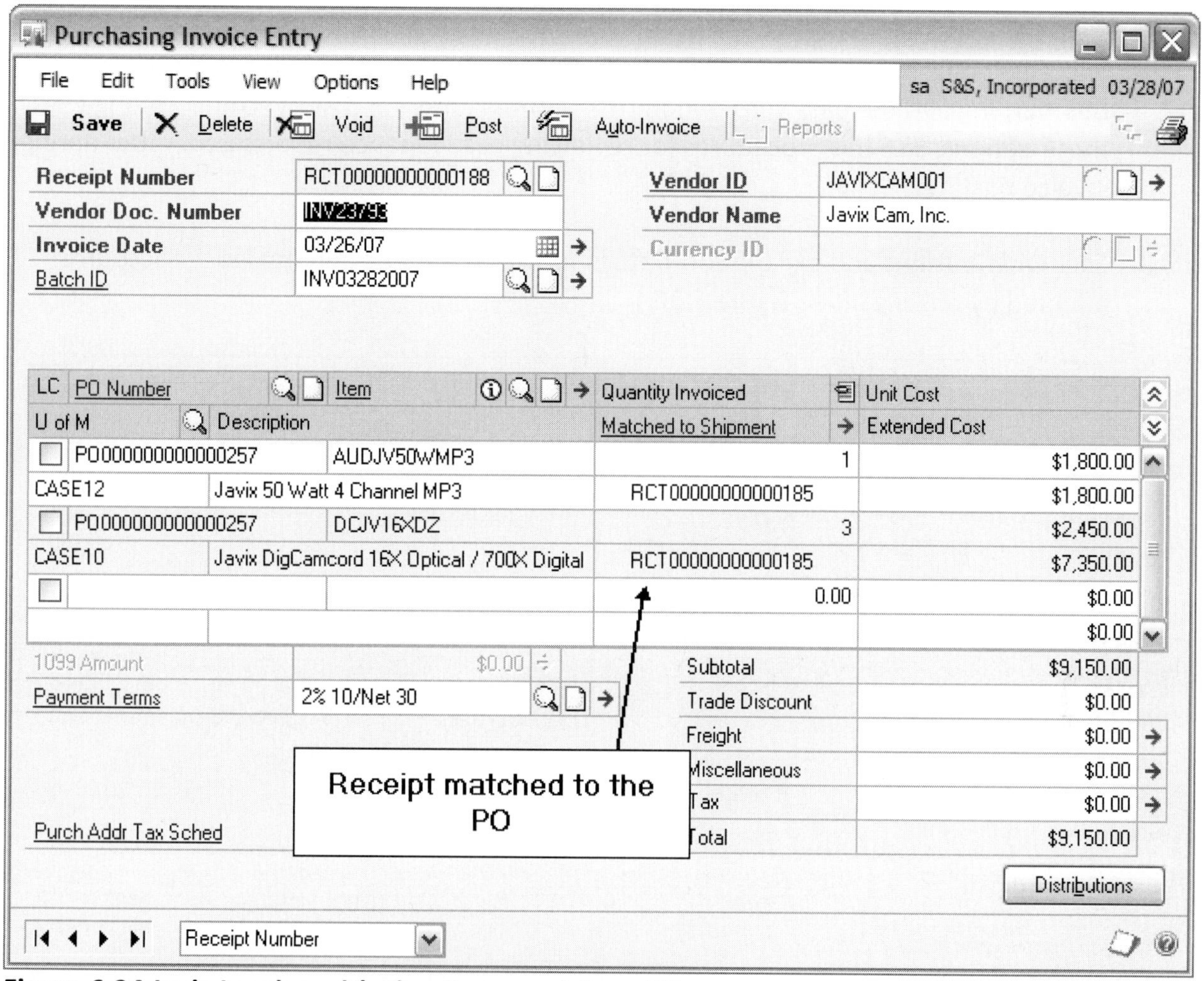

Figure 6:34 Javix Invoice with Line Items and Quantities

6. After matching line items and quantities to the invoice you must next match vendor charges for the items. Notice that the PO displays $1,800 as the cost for the first line item. Javix's invoice shows a different cost. Place your cursor in the **Unit Cost** field for this item and enter **2000.00**. Tab to the next line item and GP issues the following warning to indicate a cost variance from the receipt.

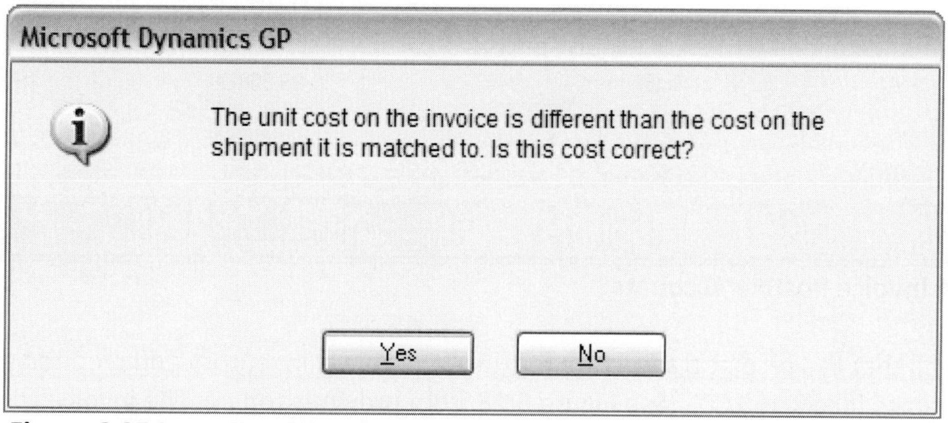

Figure 6:35 Item Cost Warning

7. Click **Yes** to accept the cost override and the first line item now carries this ≠ variance indicator on Unit Cost. In Level Two, we discuss the internal control option triggering this warning and the password option that permits entering cost overrides. Along with these options, S&S has procedures for reviewing cost variance reports generated during invoice posting.

8. Click **Distributions** and expand row details so we can discuss general ledger accounts affected by posting. (See Figure 6:36.)

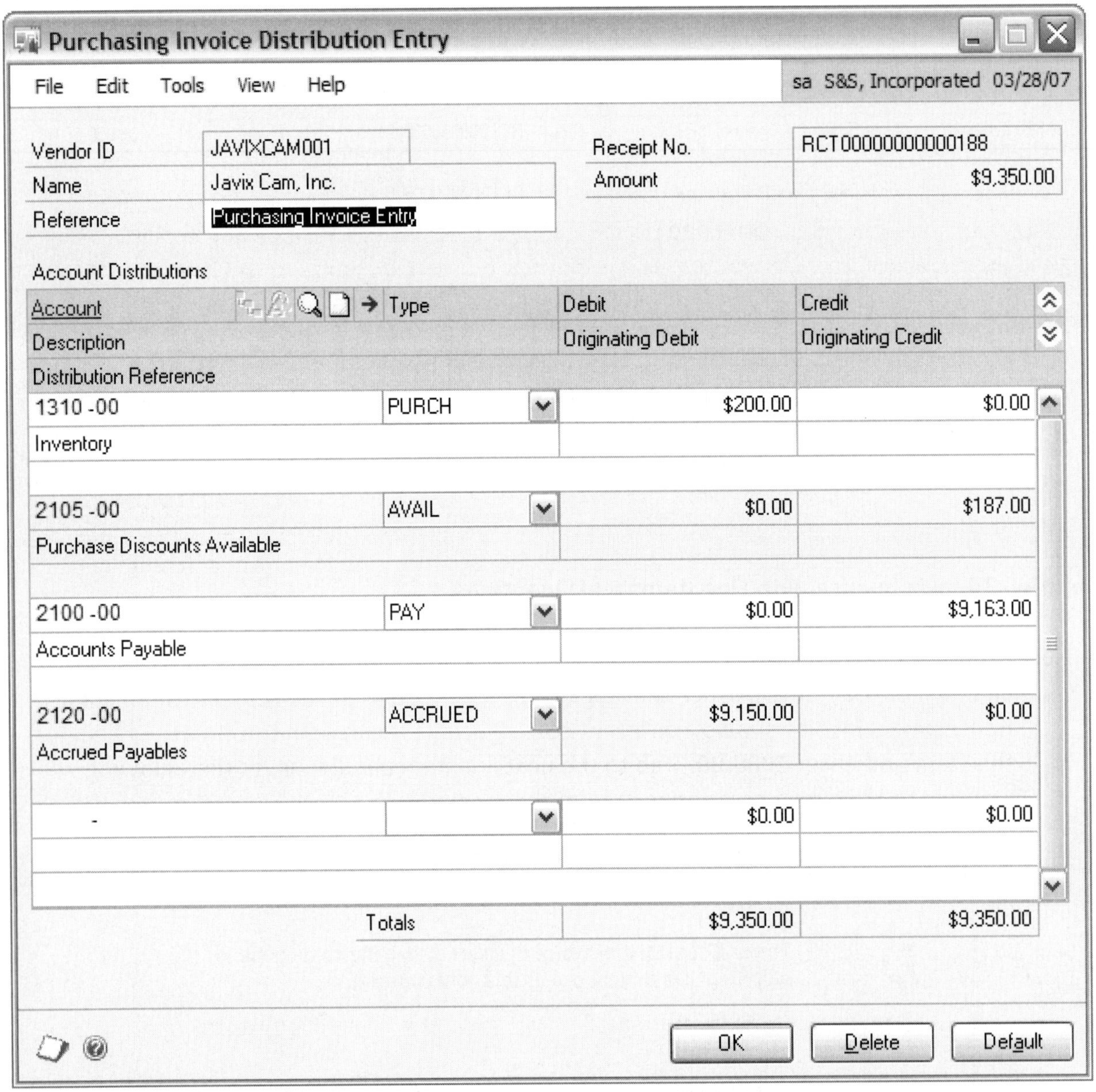

Figure 6:36 Invoice Posting Accounts

Recall that the receipt transaction for this PO debited inventory and credited accrued payables for $9,150.00. (See Figure 6:28 from previous topic.) The invoice transaction will now debit accrued payables for the original amount, thus transferring an accrued liability to an actual liability (i.e., accounts payable).

Furthermore, the invoice carries discount terms and this potential discount will post to purchase discounts available because S&S has chosen the option of tracking available discounts in a separate account. The amount of the discount reduces the entry to accounts payable.

However, we again find an entry debiting inventory. Why did this occur? First, we increased the unit cost for the first line item from $1,800.00 to $2,000.00. Normally this cost variance would post to a cost of goods sold variance account; however, because the value of the variance exceeds the tolerance percentage on the item, it now revalues inventory. Let us review this option.

Click **OK** to close the Purchasing Invoice Distribution Entry window. Keeping the transaction entry window open, activate the **Inventory** home page and click **Item Purchasing Options** under cards. Look up AUDJV50WMP3 and review the next illustration. The options marked function to reprice inventory whenever a cost variance exceeds 5 percent.

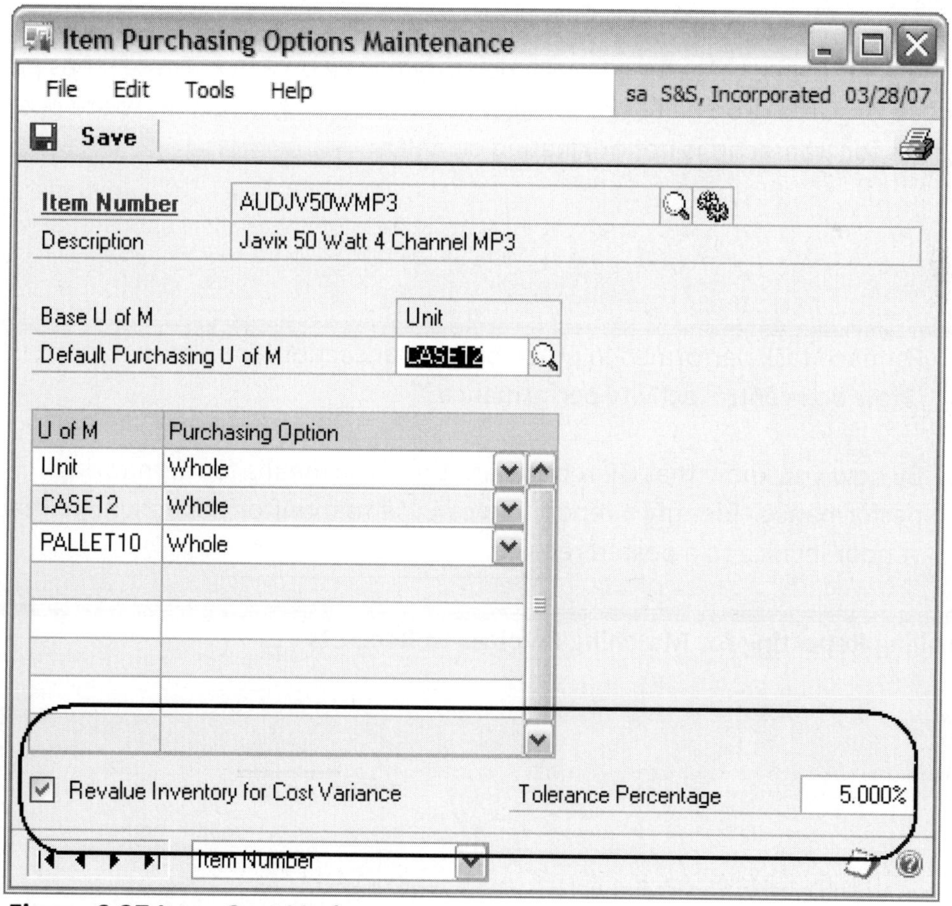

Figure 6:37 Item Cost Variances

So how does this affect inventory sales pricing? Remember from Chapter 4 that S&S calculates item sales prices using a percentage markup on current cost. Consequently, a cost variance that increases inventory cost also raises the sales price. You see the importance of implementing internal controls over cost overrides during vendor invoice entry. Controls can come in the form of implementing batch approval and password protection to authorize cost overrides. These controls will prevent posting until a manager investigates and approves.

9. Close the Item Purchasing Options Maintenance window and activate the Purchasing home page. Return to the Purchasing Invoice Entry window. If needed, you can enter any freight or miscellaneous charges at the bottom of the invoice. Click **Save** and close the window.

10. Return to the Purchasing Batch Entry window, look up the batch, and click **Post.** Print posting reports to the screen. Note that the third report to print is the Invoice Cost Variance Journal, which should be reviewed as a control over posting. Also, remember that the transaction posted in the Purchasing Series as of March 26 (i.e., transaction date) but to the Financial Series as of March 28 (i.e., batch date). Close the batch window.

You have now posted an invoice for a transaction originating on a PO. These steps pertain to any transaction originating on a PO, not just inventory orders. We next illustrate posting vendor invoices for transactions not originating on a PO.

For each task performed in processing a transaction, the accountant must ask: "How do I control activity performance?"

By now you know that GP reports are the basic means for monitoring performance. Identify a report you can use to monitor the activity of matching a vendor invoice to a posted receipt.

E6:4 Controlling Reporting for Matching Invoices to Receipts

Vendor Invoices for Transactions Not Originating on a PO

You use menus on the Payables Transaction Tier to process vendor invoices not originating on a PO. Such invoices include utility, insurance, and rent expenses. Many of these charges recur monthly so saving them in recurring batches saves data entry time.

1. Click **Batches** and look up the **HEALTH** batch. (See Figure 6:38.) This batch is used for posting recurring health insurance invoices. The **Frequency** is Monthly and it one transaction for $6,185.85 is stored in the batch. Click the dropdown list on Frequency to view other choices. We have used Single Use thus far, which instructs GP to remove the batch after posting once. Other options tell GP to save the batch and transactions in the batch for future posting.

   The next date for posting for this batch is 3/12/2007. The batch and transaction will be saved indefinitely after posting because Recurring Posting is 0. If Recurring Posting were set to 12 then the batch and transaction would disappear after posting twelve times. Although not discussed in Chapter 5, this feature is also available for Sales Series batches.

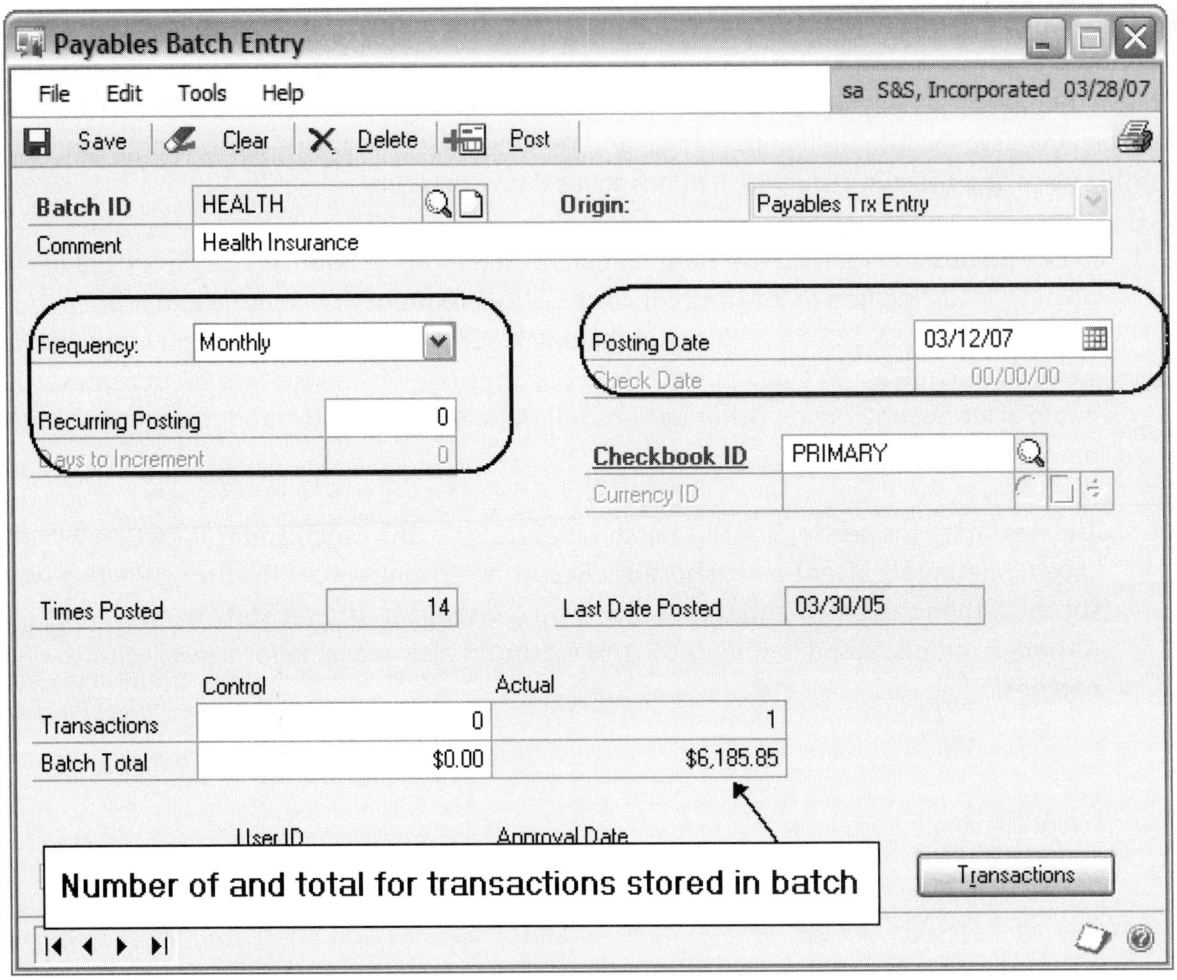

Figure 6:38 Recurring Health Insurance Batch

2. We now review the transaction saved in this batch. Click **Transactions** and look up the following transaction. Recurring batches simplify posting by retaining vendor, amount, and account distributions from previous postings. Even though invoice charges may often change, you can save time because you it takes just a few seconds to modify the saved transaction.

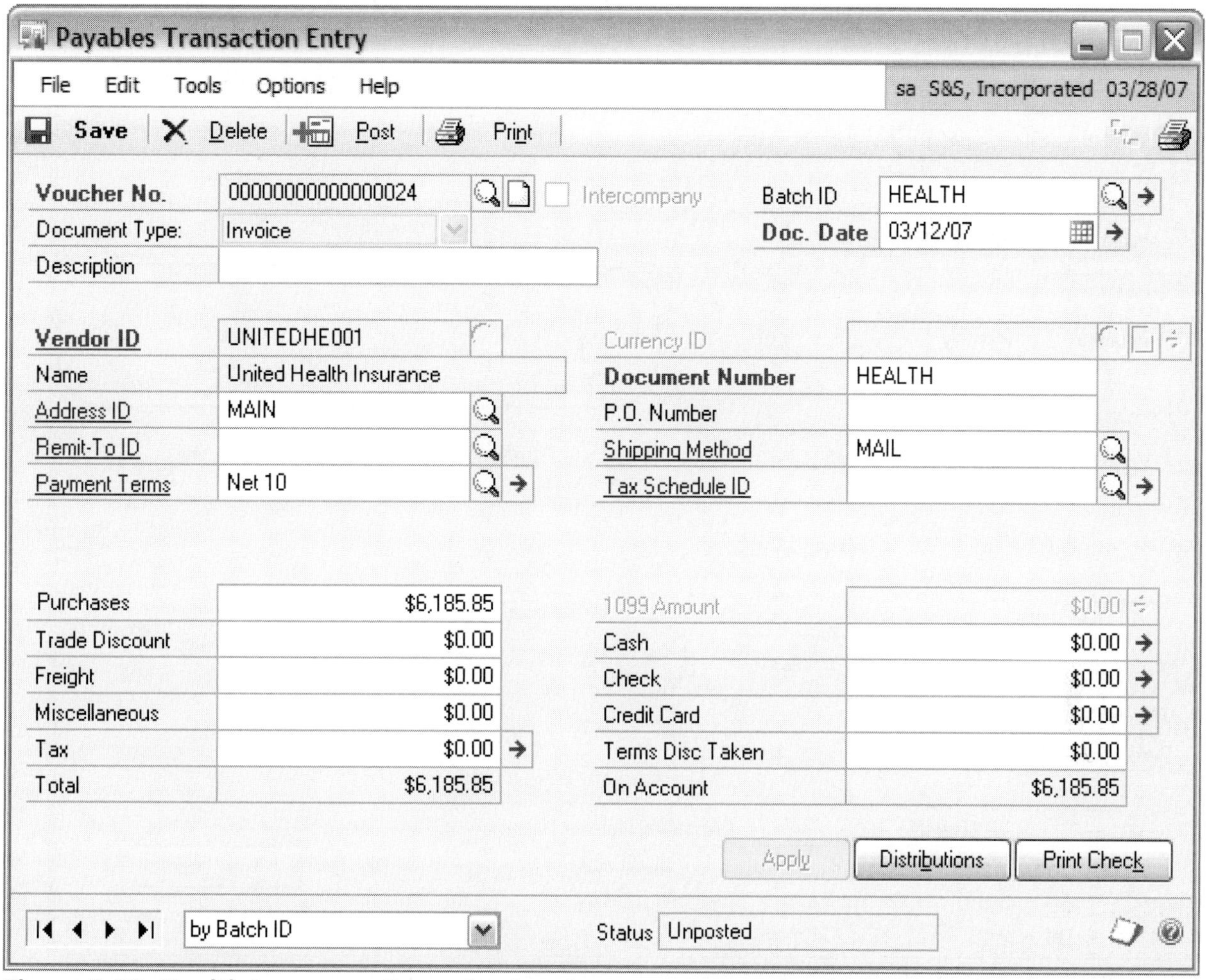

Figure 6:39 Health Insurance Recurring Invoice

3. We next modify the health insurance transaction. The transaction date (i.e., Doc. Date) is the same as the batch date (i.e., 3/12/2007) but this month the invoice date is 3/14/2007 so make this change.

4. There are no other changes so click **Save** and close the transaction window.

5. Return to the Payables Batch Entry window and look up the **INTER** batch. This recurring batch is for posting monthly interest for bank loans. It stores two transactions totaling $12,237.27. The next posting date is 4/5/2007 so March transactions have been posted.

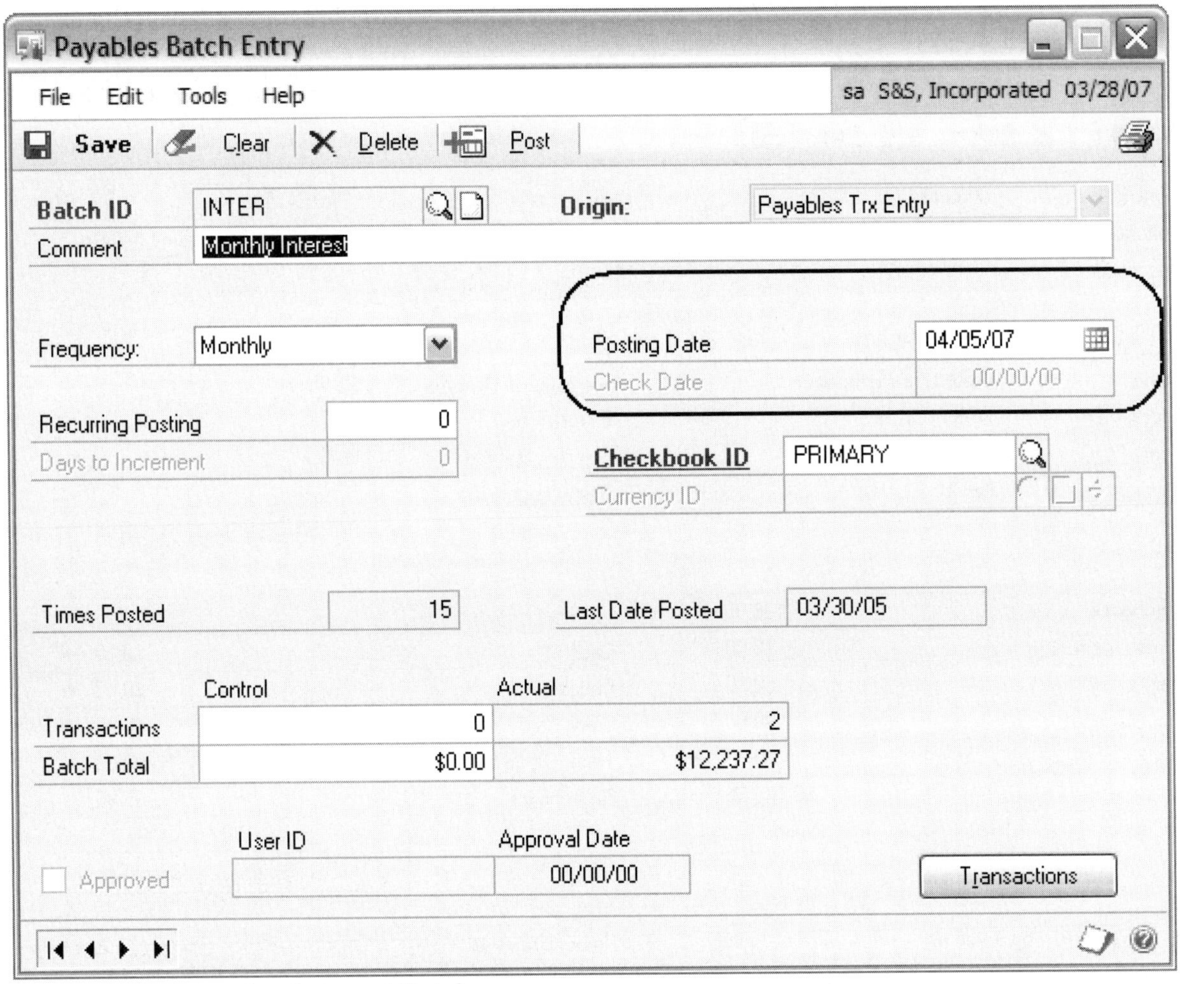

Figure 6:40 Recurring Interest Batch

6. Click **Clear** so we can create a new recurring batch for storing utility invoices. Create the following batch named **UTILITY**. Set **Frequency** to **Monthly** and **Recurring Posting** to **12** so that the batch disappears after posting twelve times. Set **Posting Date** to **3/12/2007**. This date becomes the basis for calculating future dates. After posting this batch, the date will advance to 4/12/2007.

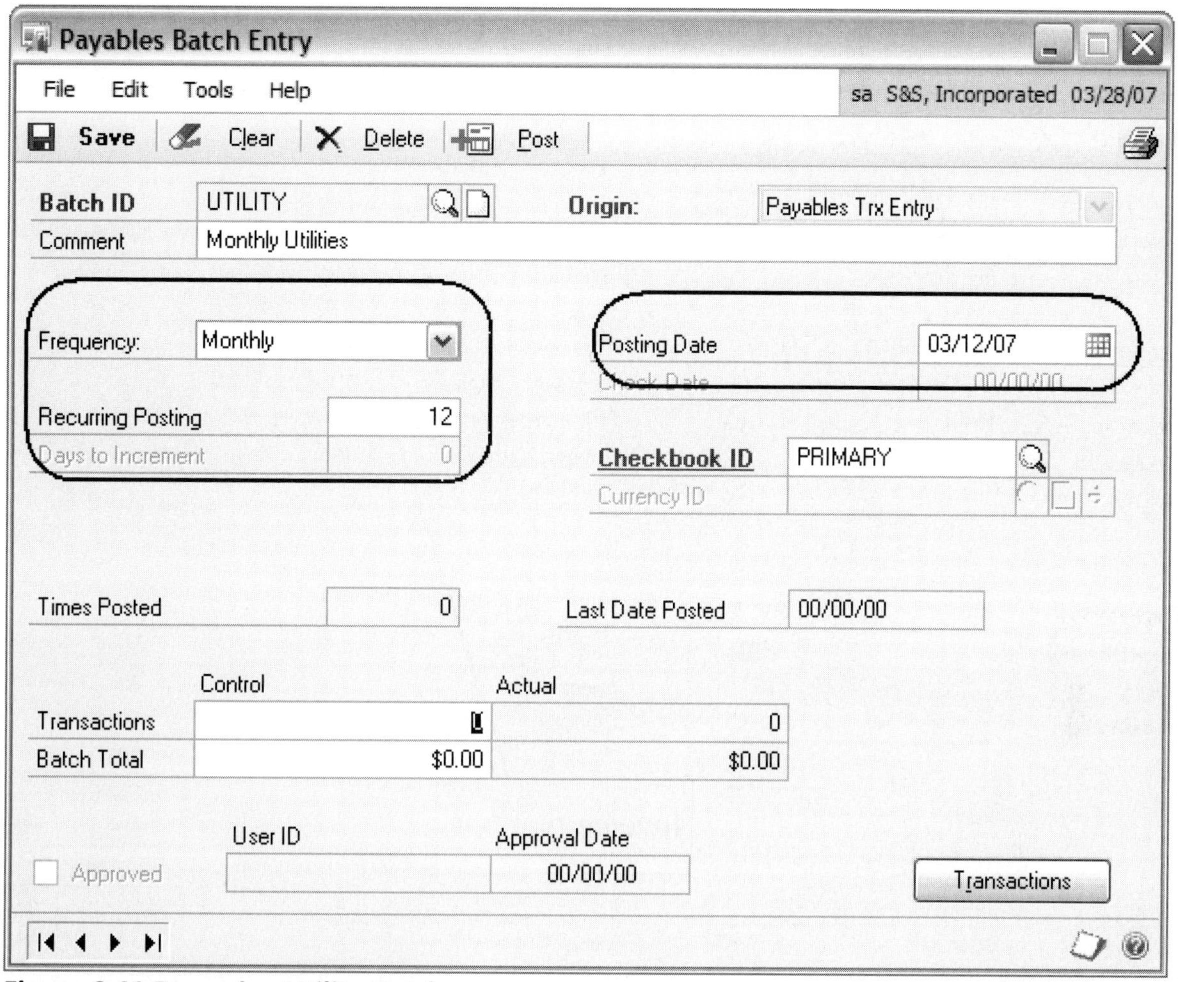

Figure 6:41 Recurring Utility Batch

7. Click **Transactions** and enter the following electric invoice. Pay attention to the Doc Date. Utility bills will not have a vendor invoice number so you must create one. We have created MONTHLYELEC.

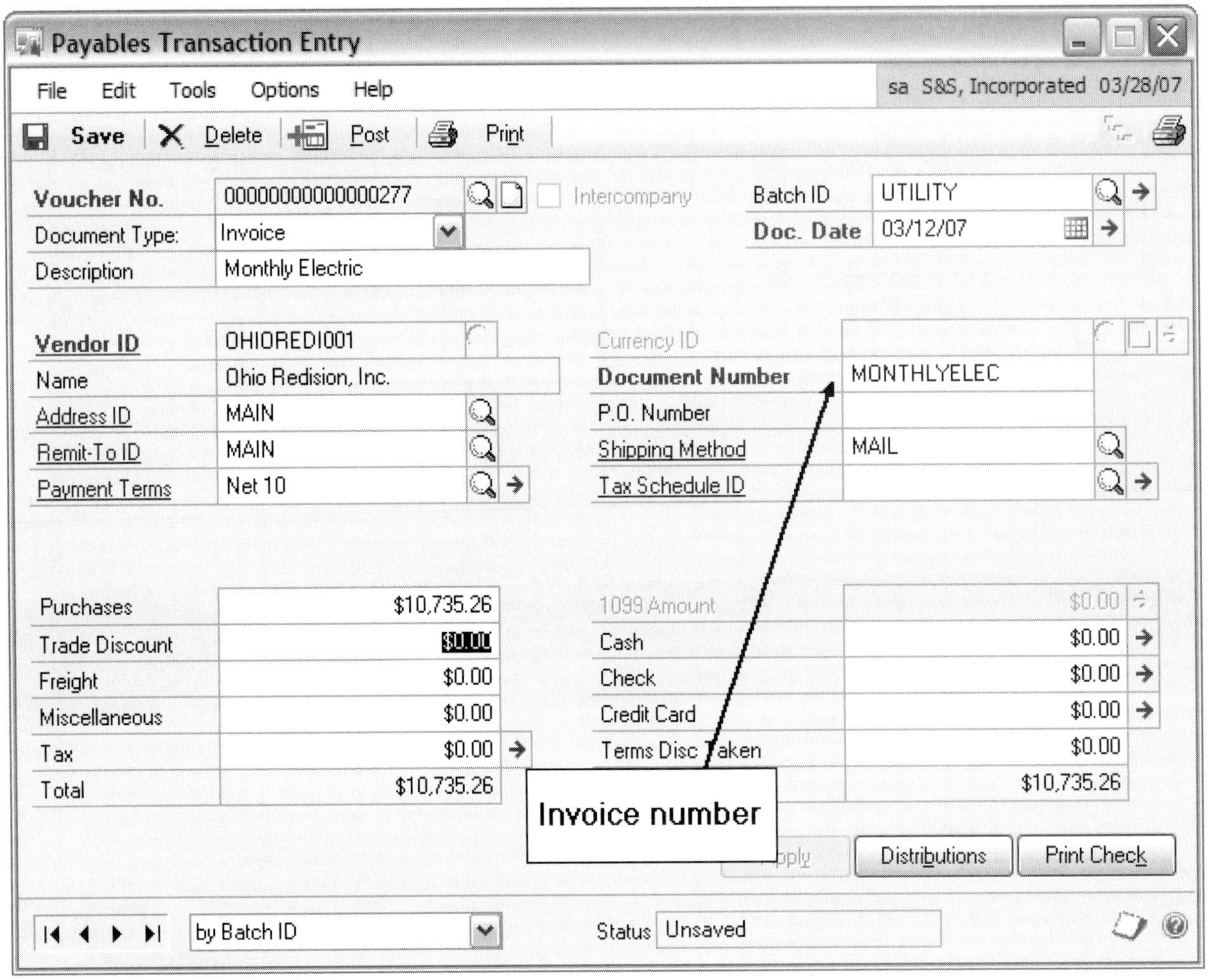

Figure 6:42 Electric Bill

8. Click **Distributions**, noting that this transaction will debit 5610-05 Utilities-Fixed Allocation Account. This account defaulted from the vendor card. Remember that departmental segment 05 identifies allocation accounts discussed in Chapter 2. When posting this invoice, GP allocates the expense to departmental expense accounts using the percentages found on the general ledger account card. *(Note: Remember you can open this card by clicking Fixed Allocation under Cards on the Financial home page.)*

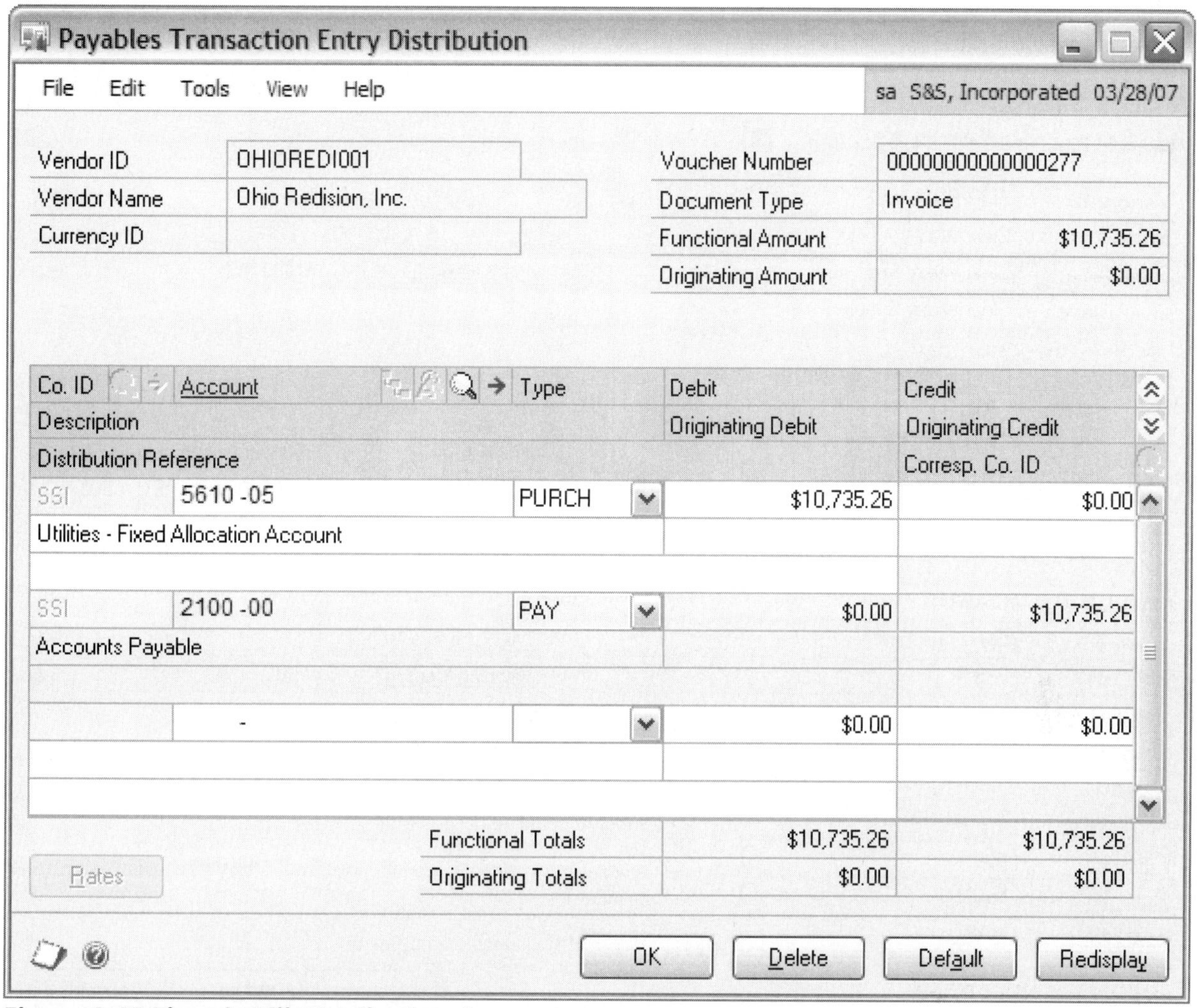

Figure 6:43 Electric Bill Distribution Accounts

9. Click **OK** to close the distribution window. Click **Save** on the transaction.

10. We will now enter the water bill. Enter a **Description** of Monthly Water and tab to **Doc. Date** to enter 3/13/2007.

11. Tab to **Vendor ID**. We will create a new vendor "on-the-fly." Type in CLEARWAT001 and press tab. Click **Add** to create the record and enter the following information for this vendor. Notice that we have chosen the UTILITIES class meaning that general ledger accounts will be assigned from the class record.

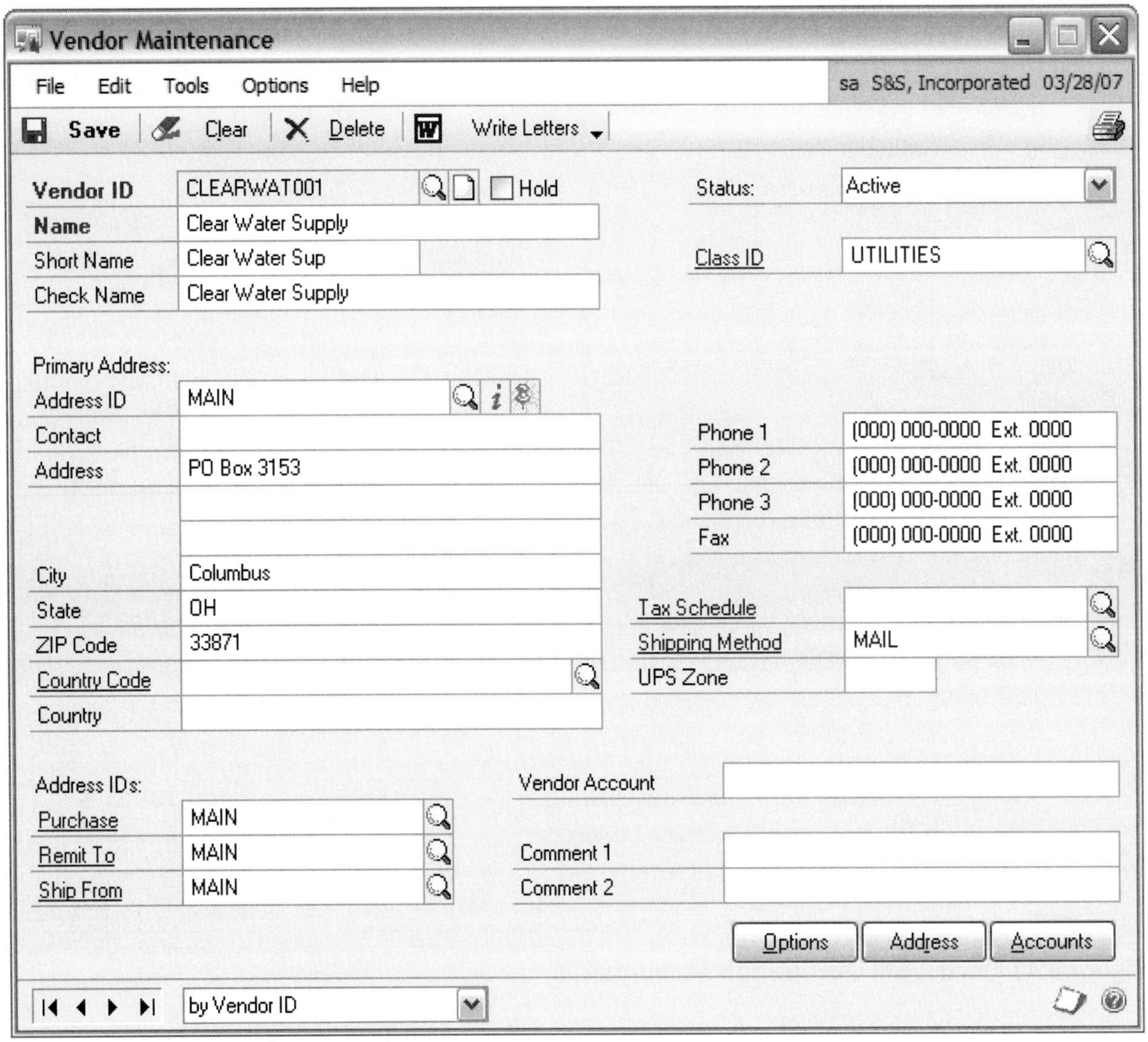

Figure 6:44 New Vendor Account

12. Click **Save** and close the Vendor Maintenance window. Return to the transaction and complete as illustrated next.

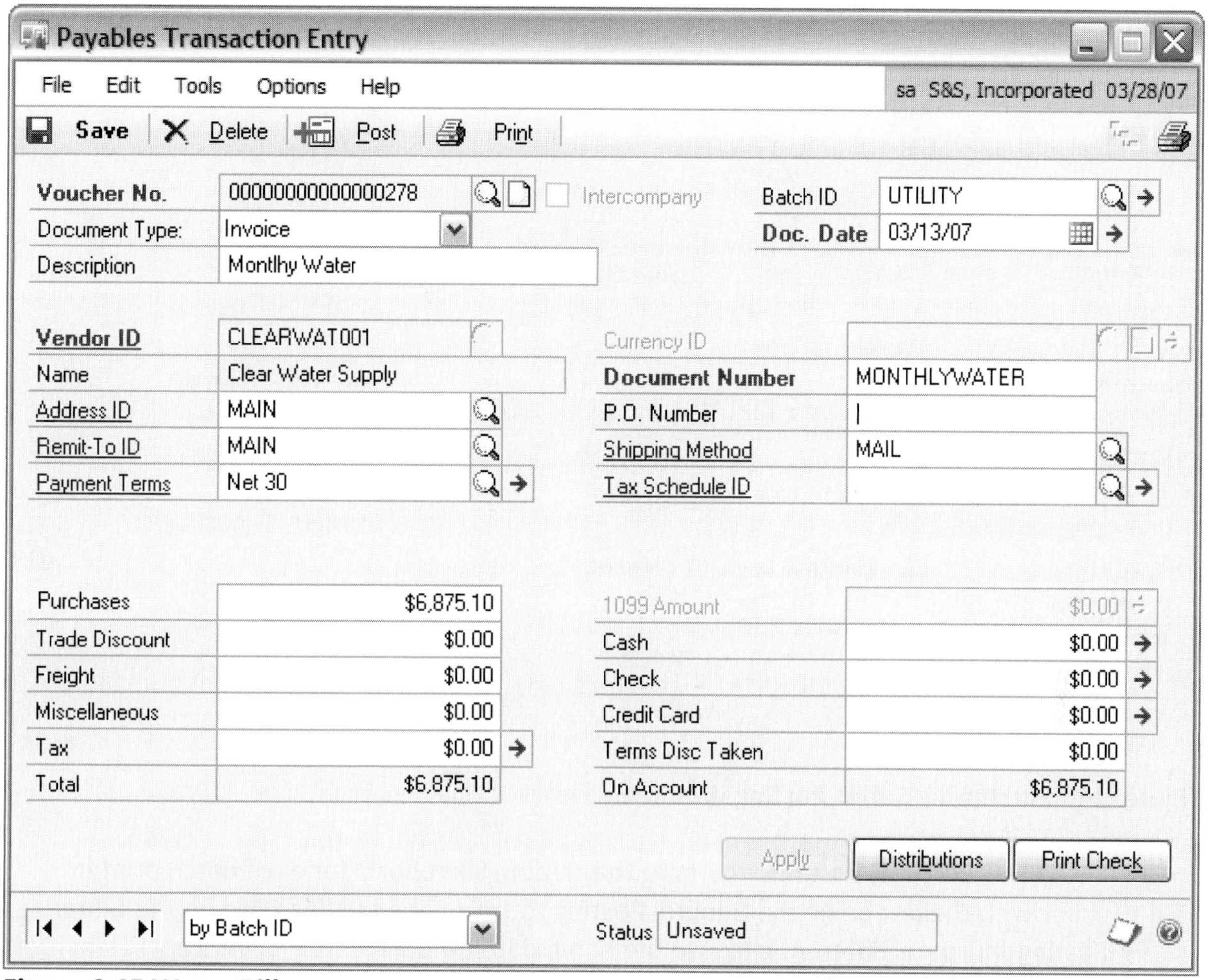

Figure 6:45 Water Bill

13. Save the transaction and close the window.

14. Instead of posting these batches from the batch window, close the payables Batch Entry window so we can post from the Purchasing Series Posting window. Click **Series Post** and mark the batches illustrated in Figure 6:46. Mark the INTER batch because it is the end of March and S&S wants these bills to appear on the aging.

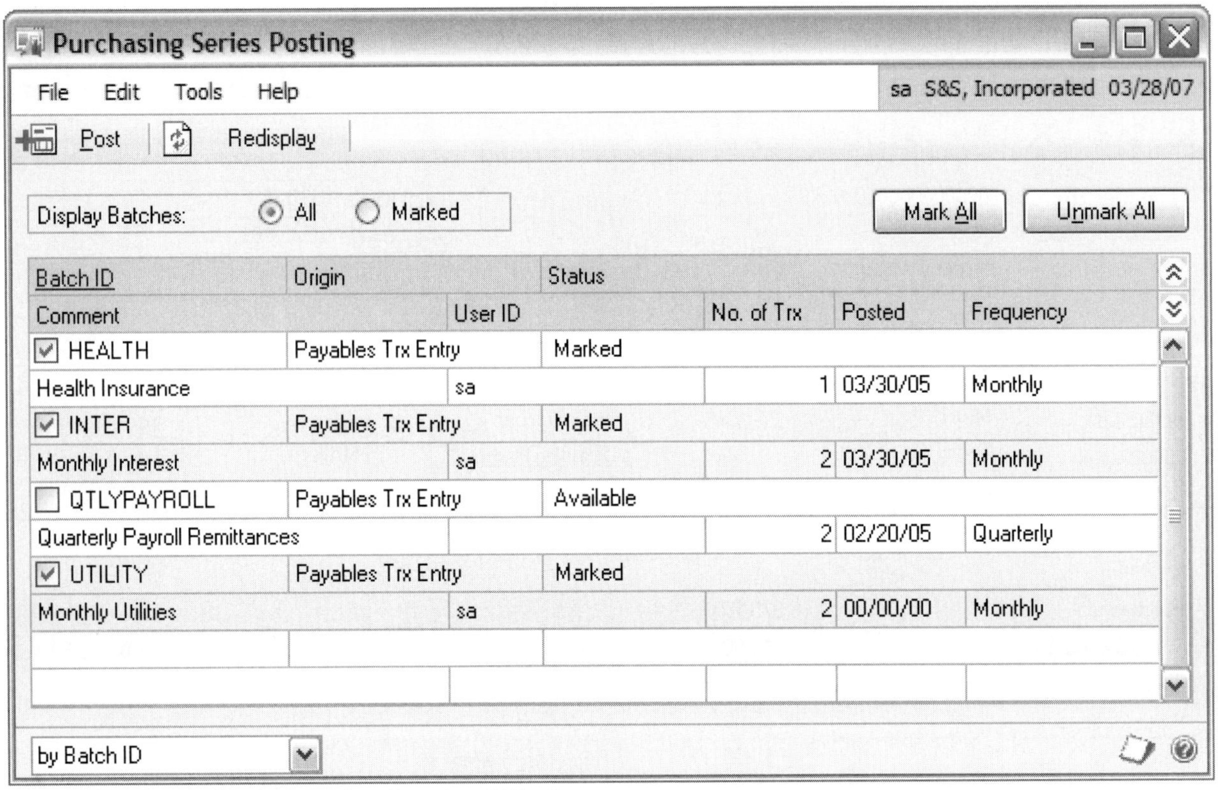

Figure 6:46 Purchasing Series Posting Window

15. Click **Post** and print posting reports to the screen. Six reports for each batch print in order with the last being the General Posting Journal. The posting date on the General Posting Journal is different because the batch date for each batch is different. Hence, despite posting the INTER batch in March, the expense does not appear until April in the general ledger. Be sure to review the General Posting Journal for the utility batch (Figure 6:47) noting that utility costs were spread across departmental expense accounts.

User Date: 03/28/07 — S&S, Incorporated — GENERAL POSTING JOURNAL — General Ledger — Page: 1 — User ID: sa

* Voided Journal Entry

Batch ID: PMTRX00000162
Batch Comment: Monthly Utilities

Approved:	No	Batch Total Actual:	$35,220.72	Batch Total Control:	$0.00
Approved by:		Trx Total Actual:	2	Trx Total Control:	0
Approval Date:					

Journal Entry	Transaction Type	Transaction Date	Reversing Date	Source Document	Transaction Reference	Audit Trail Code	Reversing Audit Trail Code
1,721	Standard	03/12/07		PMTRX	Monthly Electric	GLTRX00000662	

Account	Description	Debit	Credit
5610-01	Utilities - East	$2,898.52	
5610-02	Utilities - MidWest	$2,898.52	
5610-03	Utilities - West	$2,898.52	
5610-04	Utilities - Administrative	$2,039.70	
2100-00	Accounts Payable		$10,735.26
Total Distributions: 5	Totals:	$10,735.26	$10,735.26

Journal Entry	Transaction Type	Transaction Date	Reversing Date	Source Document	Transaction Reference	Audit Trail Code	Reversing Audit Trail Code
1,722	Standard	03/12/07		PMTRX	Montlhy Water	GLTRX00000662	

Figure 6:47 General Journal Posting Journal for Utility Batch

16. Close the Purchasing Series Posting window and reopen the Payables Batch Entry window, look up the UTILITY batch, noting that the Posting Date advanced to 4/12/2007. Close the window.

Although we demonstrated entering vendor invoices through recurring batches, you can still enter them as single post batches. Just remember that all vendor invoices for transactions not originating on a PO are recorded through the Payables Transaction Tier.

We will next look at processing returns of inventory to vendors and credit memos.

S&S has received a vendor invoice from Office Rex Inc. as follows. Post this transaction.

Invoice number 90135 for $1,785.20, dated March 28, 2007
Office supplies, $85.20
New computer, $1,700.00

E6:5 Practice Posting a Vendor Invoice

Return of Vendor Goods

Recall that warehouse employees inspect vendor shipments before entering receipts. Goods may be rejected due to damage, inferior quality, or failure to match items on the PO. If rejected in the warehouse then the quantity is reduced on the receipt transaction and remaining items on the PO can be cancelled.

However, what happens if you return items after posting the receipt or invoice? What happens if the return occurs after paying the invoice? These transactions are entered as returns and the next exercise illustrates this.

Click **Returns Transaction Entry**. *(Note: You can click Returns Batches to process through a batch.)* Click the drop down list on **Type** (Figure 6:48) and review descriptions that follow.

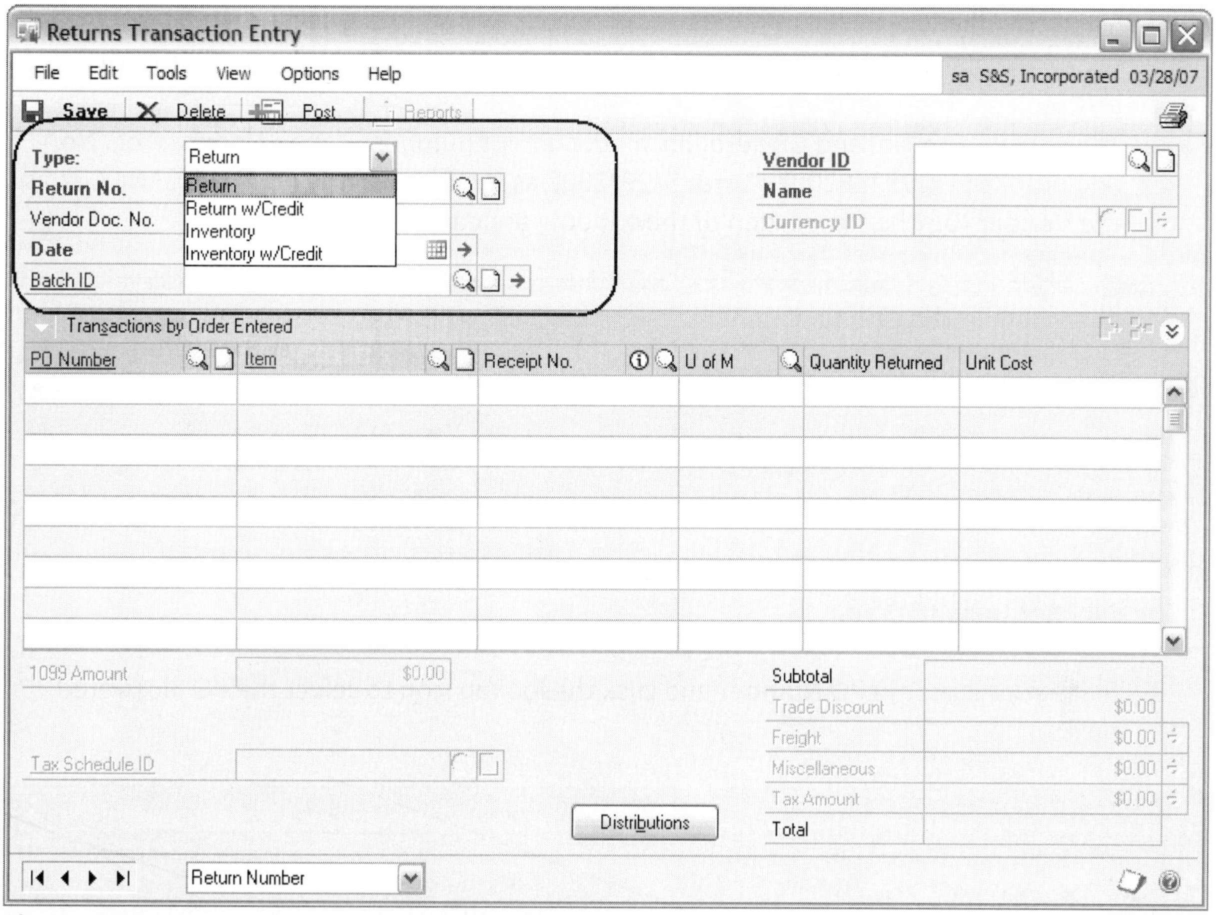

Figure 6:48 Returns Transaction Entry Window

Return is for returning inventory after posting a receipt or but before posting or paying the invoice. This transaction credits inventory and debits accrued payables. On-hand quantities of the item are also reduced. You will then need to verify that the invoice sent by the vendor also reduces the quantities billed.

Return w/Credit is for returns occurring after posting or paying the invoice. The transaction credits inventory and debits accounts payable. On-hand quantities will be reduced. A credit document is also created. This document is then applied to reduce the unpaid invoice or another invoice if the original invoice has been paid.

Inventory and **Inventory w/Credit** is for returns where the vendor is replacing the inventory or replacing plus issuing a credit. If the vendor replaces with a different but similar item then on-hand quantities are adjusted accordingly. The inventory account remains unchanged unless the vendor is issuing a credit.

Let us now practice a return.

1. We will return one of the items on the Javix invoice posted earlier in the chapter. The vendor is issuing a credit to be applied against the open invoice so choose **Return w/Credit** as the Type.
2. Tab past **Return No.** and GP autofills the document number. Tab to **Vendor Doc. No.** and enter RETINV03282007. Enter 3/29/2007 as the **Date** and select JAVIXCAM0001 as the **Vendor ID**. The top portion of the window appears as follows.

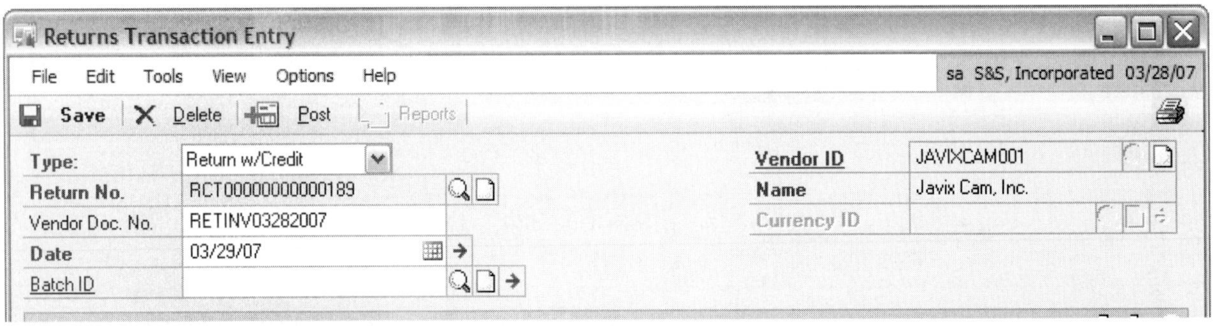

Figure 6:49 Return with Credit

3. Place your cursor in **PO Number** and click the lookup icon to select the PO illustrated next.

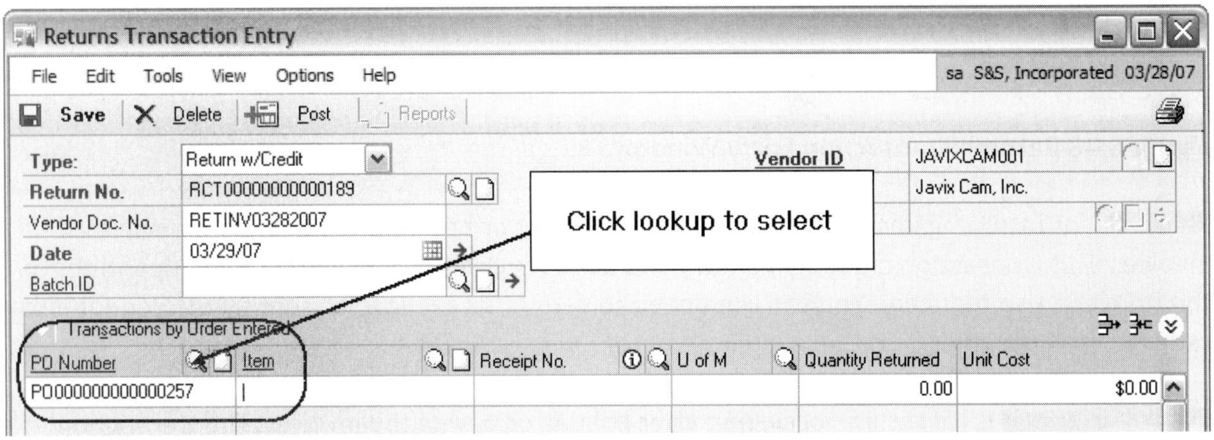

Figure 6:50 Select PO Number

4. Next click the lookup icon on **Item** and highlight DCJV16XDZ. Click **Select.**

5. Click the lookup icon on **Receipt No.** and **Select** the receipt provided.

6. Enter 2 as the quantity returned. The completed return is illustrated next.

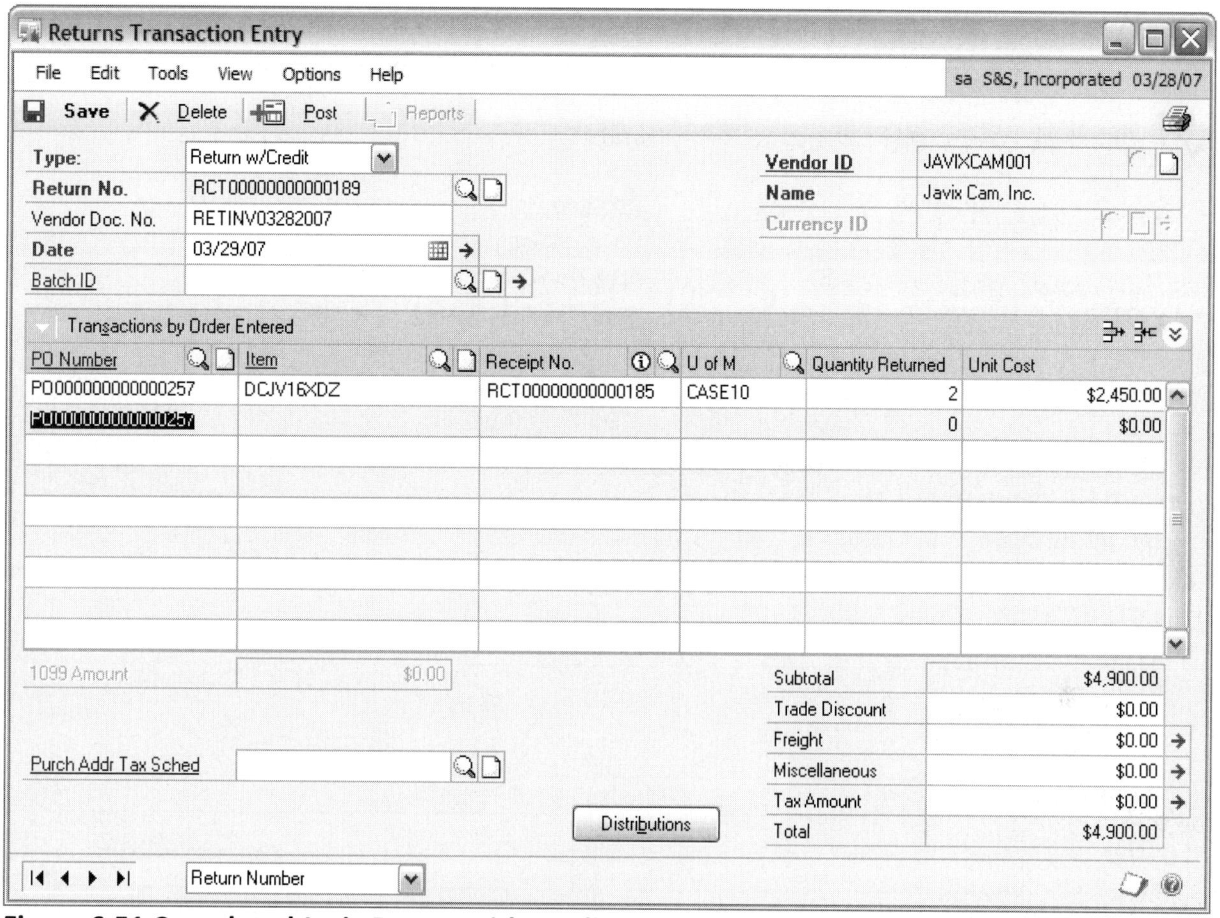

Figure 6:51 Completed Javix Return with Credit

7. Click **Distributions** to view the general ledger accounts, noting that the transaction credits inventory and debits accounts payable. Click **OK**.

8. Click **Post** and close the window. Print posting reports to the screen and review.

9. You must now apply the credit to reduce the invoice. Click **Apply Payables Documents** and look up Javix.

10. Set **Apply Date** to 3/29/2007.

11. Click the lookup icon on **Document No** and select the return.

12. Finally, mark the outstanding invoice as illustrated next.

Figure 6:52 Apply Return to Reduce Invoice

13. Click **OK** to apply the return.

Credit memos

There are other reasons for receiving vendor credit memos that are unrelated to returning inventory. Perhaps the vendor was late on delivery or the invoice was unrelated to purchasing inventory. The credits are posted through the Payables Transaction Tier, which you recall, does not interface with inventory tables. If the credit does reduce inventory costs then you will to post the credit memo as illustrated next and an inventory adjustment transaction through the Inventory Controls Series as illustrated in Chapter 4.

We will now illustrate posting a credit memo.

1. S&S received a credit memo for $300.00 from Channel Oxe for last month's advertising. Click Transaction Entry and enter the transaction as illustrated next.

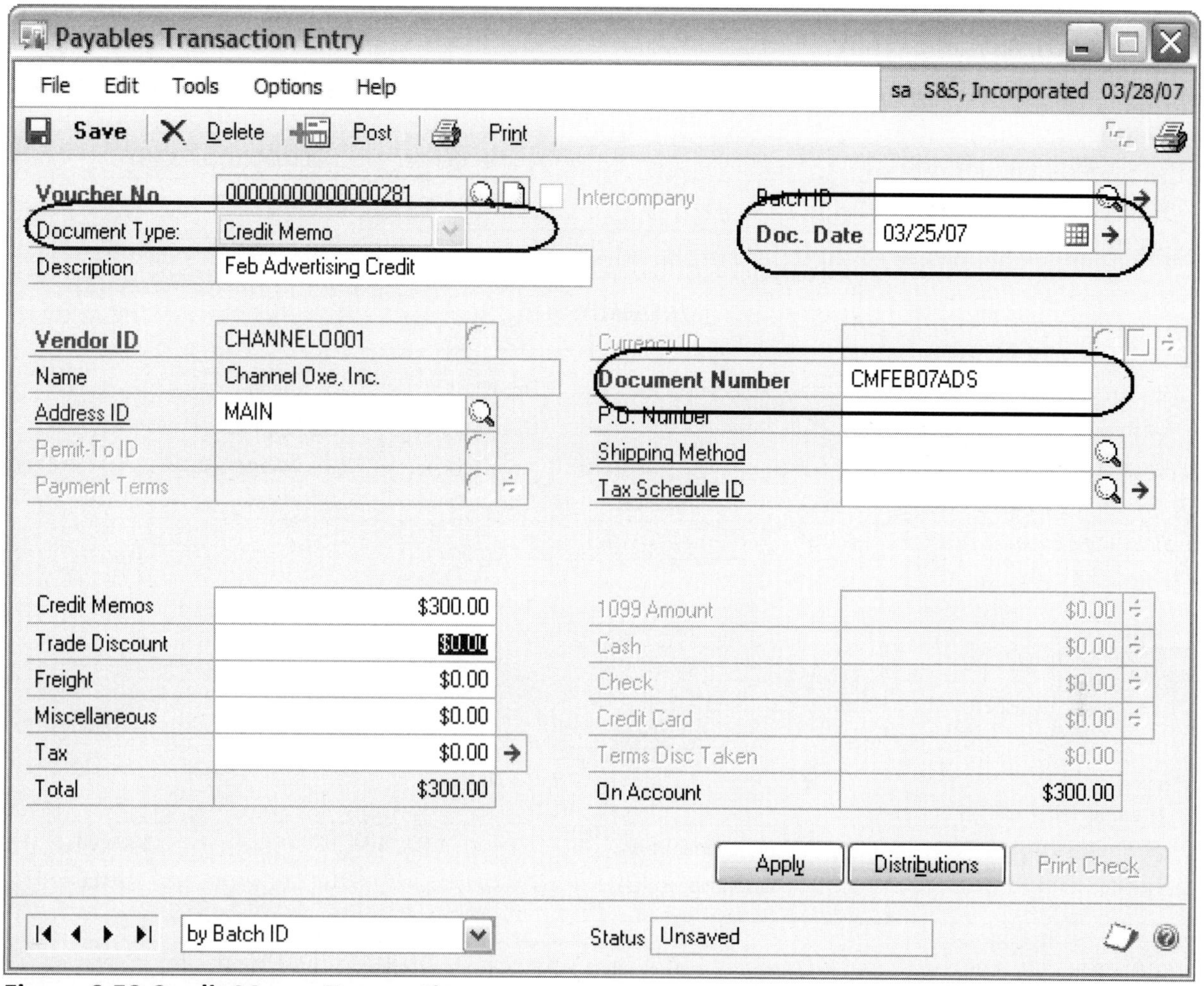

Figure 6:53 Credit Memo Transaction

2. Click **Distributions** so you can reduce advertising expense for the department as illustrated next. Click **OK**.

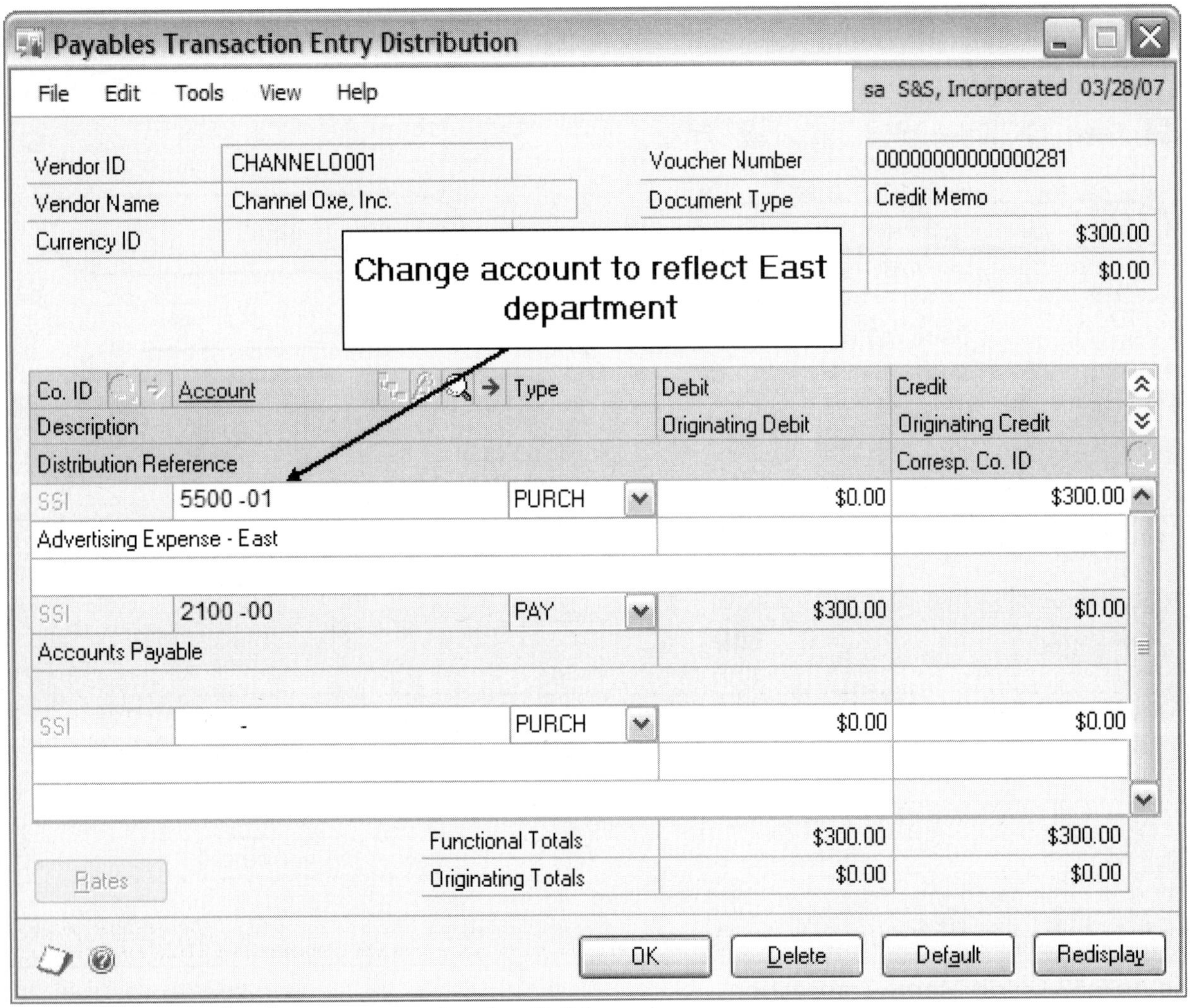

Figure 6:54 Distribution Accounts for Credit Memo

3. You can apply this credit against the invoice before posting the transaction. Click **Apply** and reduce the PAPERADS invoice illustrated next. Click **OK**.

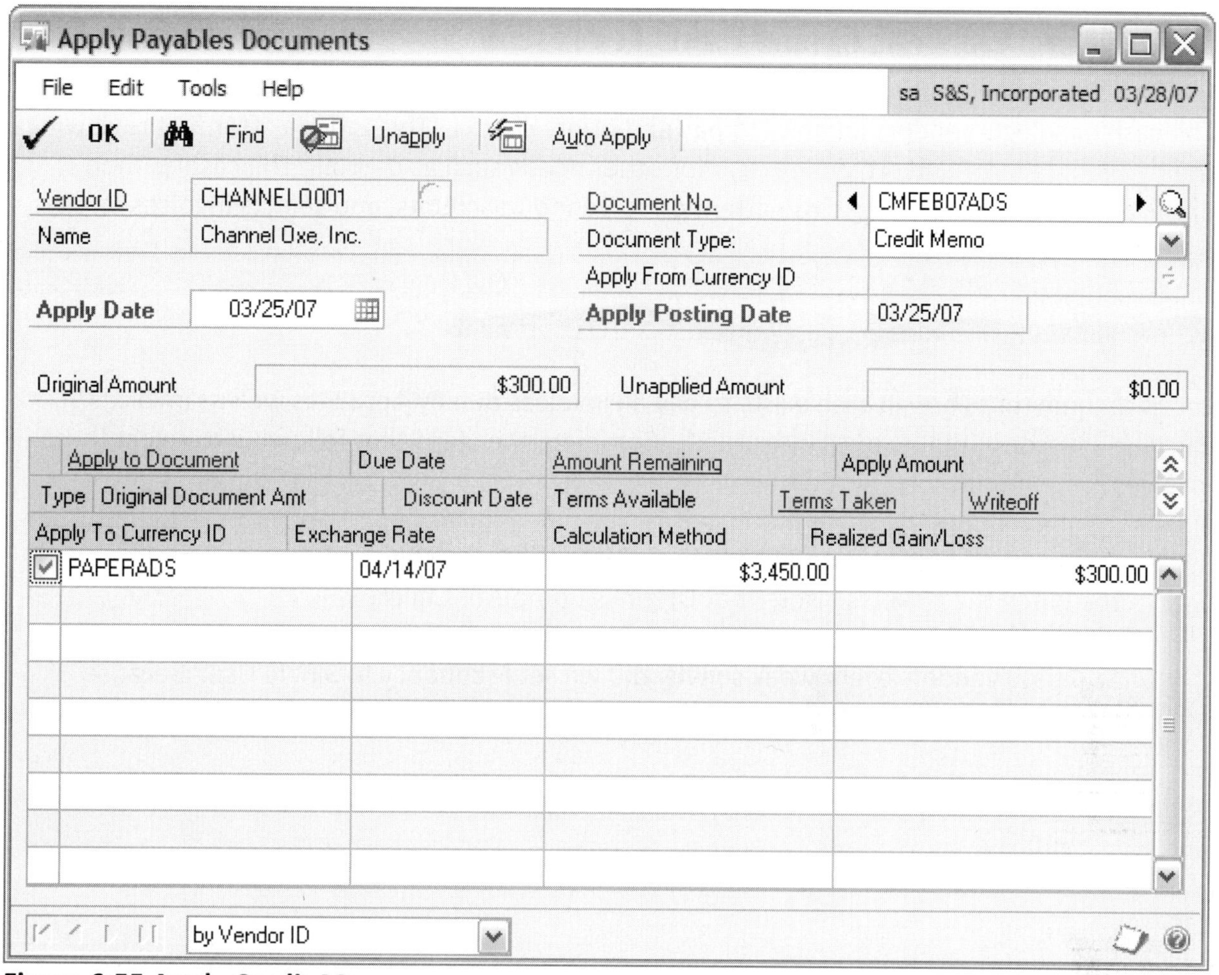

Figure 6:55 Apply Credit Memo

4. Click **Post** and remember to complete posting from the Financial home page.

We now move to paying vendor bills.

CASHIER DEPARTMENT ACTIVITIES

The cashier selects vendors and bills to pay and prints checks. This is done after first reviewing the cash flow report and projecting cash for other needs such as payroll. The cashier then prints an aging report, paying close attention to vendor discounts, and selects invoices to pay before printing the checks.

Selecting Vendor Invoices for Payment and Printing Checks

Let us assume that enough cash exists to pay all invoices due by April 5 as well as invoices carrying a discount that expires by April 11. Complete the steps that following to select these invoices for payment.

1. Change your system date to March 29, 2007. Click **Batches** and create the batch that follows. Note that **Origin** is Computer Check.

   S&S pays vendors every week so why did we set Frequency to Single Use. Because Computer Check batches cannot recur.

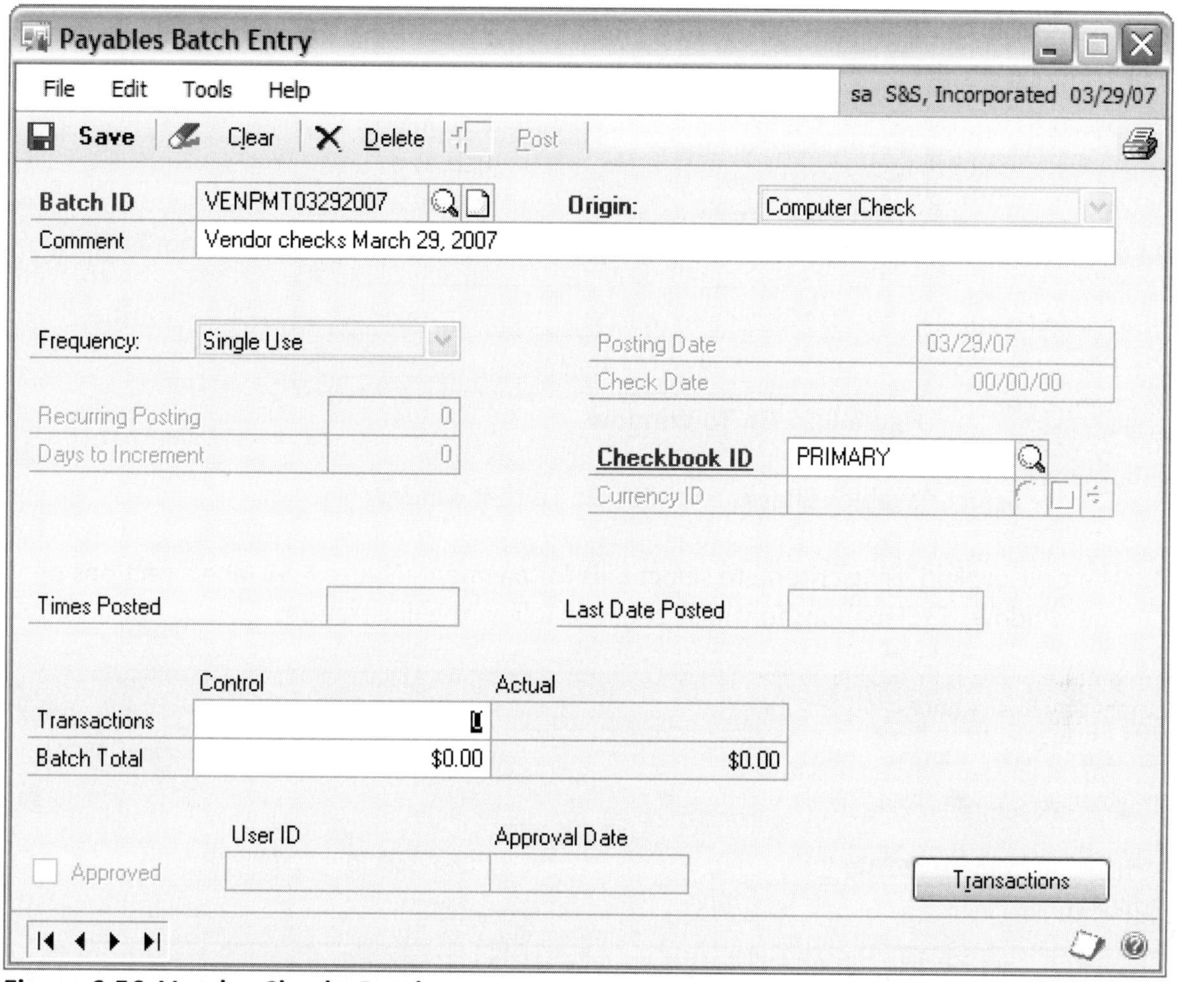

Figure 6:56 Vendor Checks Batch

2. Click **Transactions** and GP prompts as follows. We now explain these choices. *(Note: These choices correspond to individual menus found in the Payables Transaction Tier.)*

Select Payables Checks is used to enter filter criteria that selects invoices to pay.

Edit Payables Check Batch is then used to edit invoice selections for multiple vendors.

Edit Payables Checks is used to edit invoice selections for a single vendor.

Print Payables Checks prints checks to the vendors for the invoices selected.

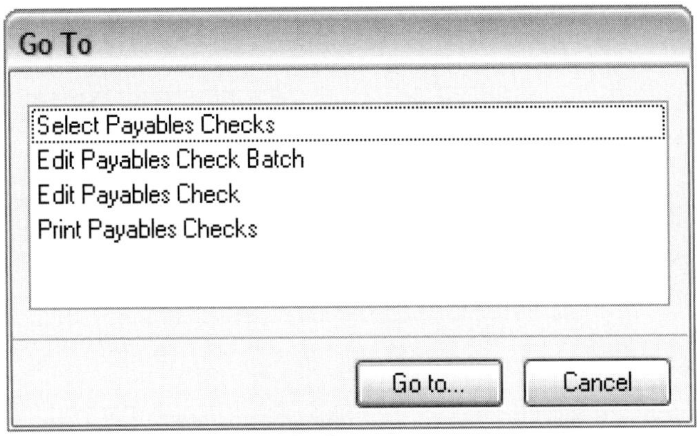

Figure 6:57 Go To Window

3. Choose **Select Payables Checks** and click **Go To** that window.

4. We now explain using criteria to select bills for payment. Figure 6:58 labels sections of the window. Explanations for these sections follow the illustration.

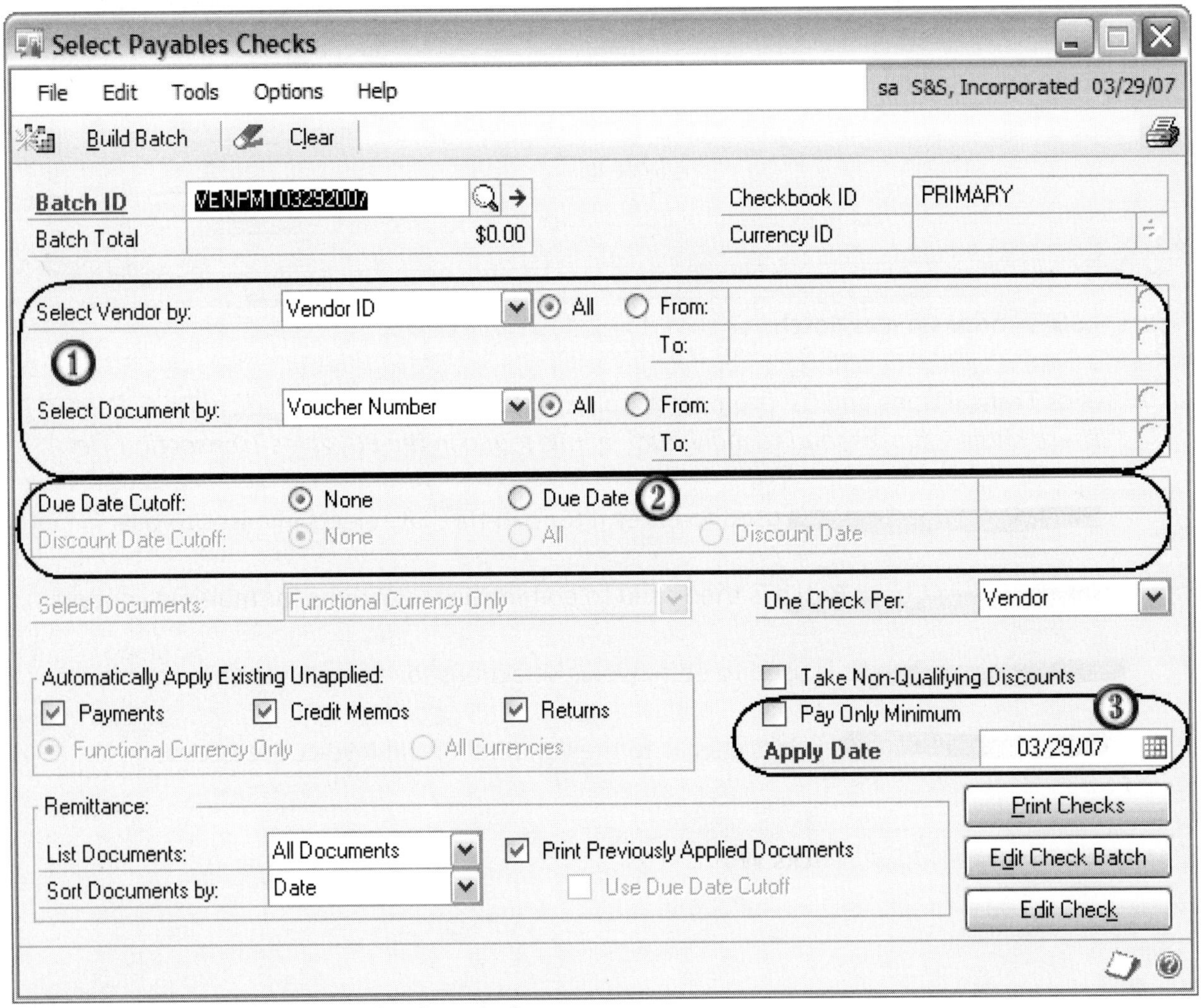

Figure 6:58 Select Payables Checks Window

Section 1: Choosing the From option opens lookup options to the right that allow you to select a single/ range of vendors or single/range of documents to pay.

Section 2: Choosing the Due Date option opens fields to the right for selecting all bills due by a specific date and all bills carrying a discount that expires by a specific date.

Section 3: Sets the date for applying checks to the bills and is normally the date of printing the checks.

5. Remember that we want to pay all invoices due on or before April 5 and all invoices that carry a discount expiring on or before April 11. Enter these criteria as illustrated next.

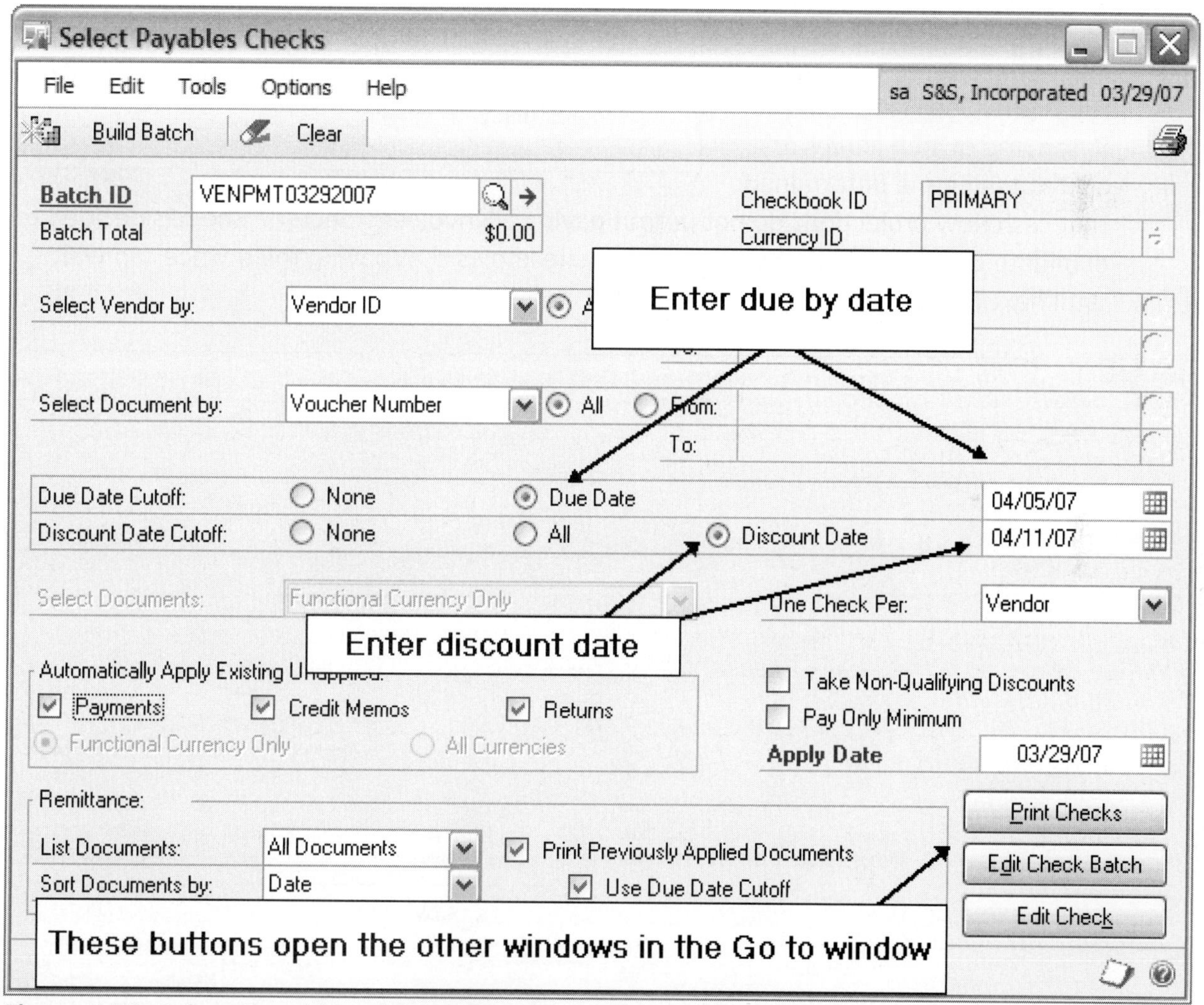

Figure 6:59 Select Payables Checks Window with Screening Criteria

6. Click **Build Batch** and GP queries the database to select invoices to pay. When finished, Batch Total shows invoices totaling $542,620.99 have been selected for payment. *(Note: Your results may differ if you practiced additional transactions or did not complete previous exercises.)* Furthermore, the Build button changes to Add to Batch. If you needed to select additional invoices then entering additional criteria and clicking this button adds invoices to the batch.

7. We next print an edit list to view invoice selections. Click ***File>>Print*** from the window menu and print the report to the screen.

   Scroll down the report and locate the invoice for Ohio Redision. (See Figure 6:60.) Susan, the owner, serves as S&S's cashier and determined that cash flow projections do not permit paying all invoices selected. She has decided to eliminate Ohio Redision's invoice because she knows that paying the invoice can wait until next week.

What about printing the edit list for previous activities?

Although we did not print this list before posting invoices, you should always print the edit list and compare data entry totals to external document control totals to check for accuracy.

Check Number:

Payment Number:	00000000000000490	Terms Disc Available:	$0.00	Check Total:	$10,735.26
Document Date:	03/29/07	Voided:			
Vendor ID:	OHIOREDI001				
Vendor Check Name:	Ohio Redision, Inc.				

Messages:

General Ledger Distributions

Account	Account Description	Account Type	Debit Amount	Credit Amount
1100-00	Cash	CASH	0.00	10,735.26
2100-00	Accounts Payable	PAY	10,735.26	0.00
			10,735.26	10,735.26

Applied to Check

Document Type	Voucher Number	App Date	Discount	Writeoff	Amount Applied
Invoice	00000000000000277001	03/29/07	0.00	0.00	10,735.26
			0.00	0.00	10,735.26

Documents Included on Check

Document Type	Voucher Number	Doc Date	Amount	Amount Paid	Net
Invoice	00000000000000277001	03/12/07	10,735.26	10,735.26	10,735.26
			10,735.26	10,735.26	10,735.26

Figure 6:60 Edit List for Ohio Redision's Invoice

8. Close the report and we will now remove this invoice from the batch. Click **Edit Check Batch** at the bottom of the window. The Edit Payables Check Batch window lists

selected vendors on the left. Clicking a particular vendor displays selected invoices to the right. Scroll down and click OHIOREDI001 on the right to display the selected invoice. (See Figure 6:61.)

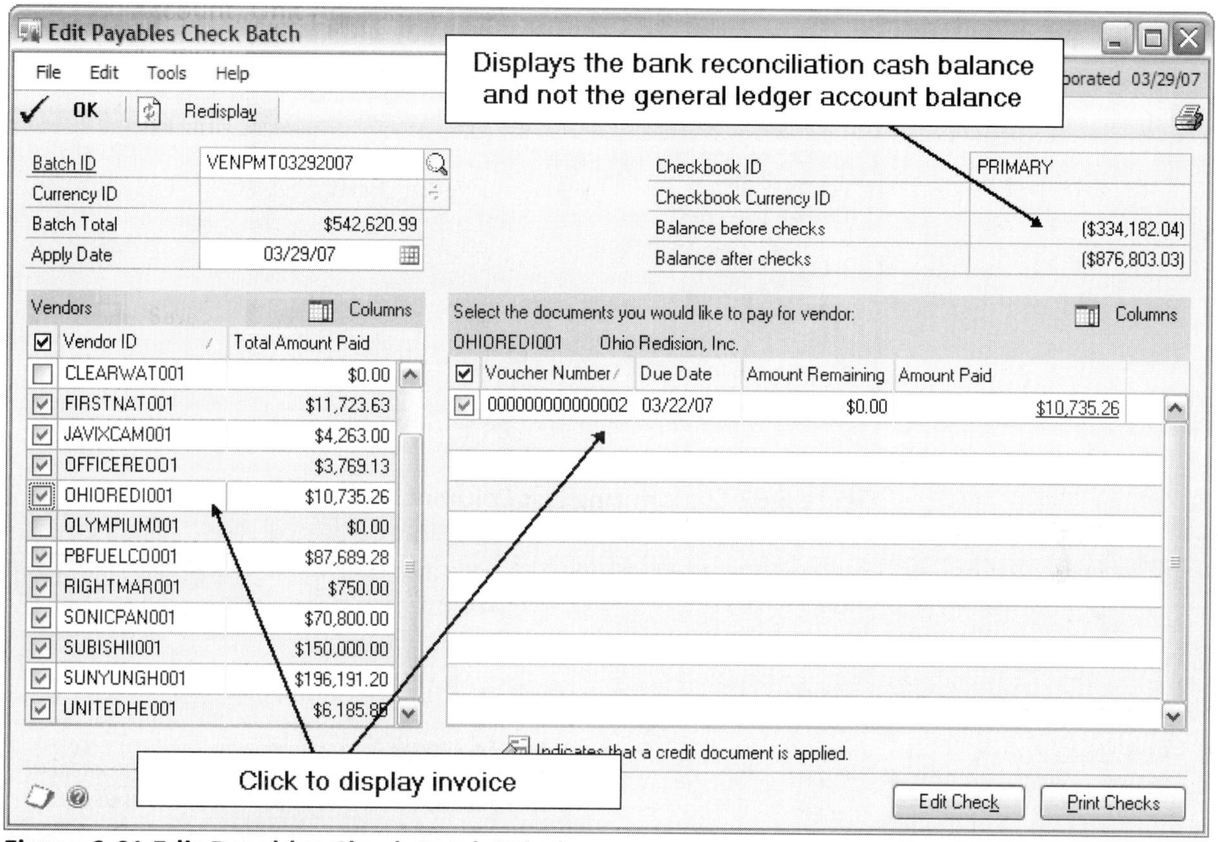

Figure 6:61 Edit Payables Check Batch Window

9. You can customize columns displayed to the right. Click **Columns** to customize as illustrated in Figure 6:62. *(Note: You cannot display more than seven columns.)* Click **OK** and the window appears as illustrated in Figure 6:63.

Figure 6:62 Customizing List Columns

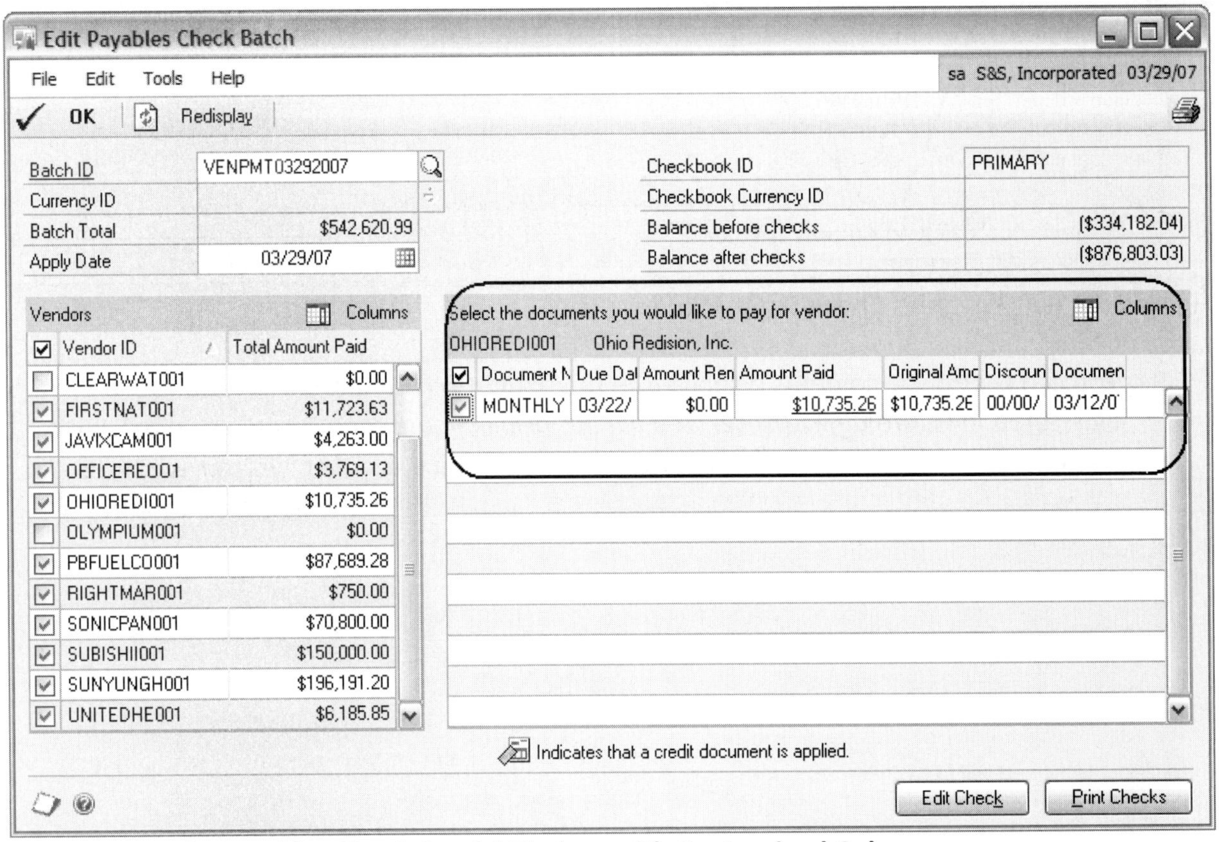

Figure 6:63 Edit Payables Check Batch Window with Customized Columns

10. Before removing Ohio Redision's payment, let us practice reducing the payment. Click **Edit Check** to open the Edit Payables Checks window illustrated next.

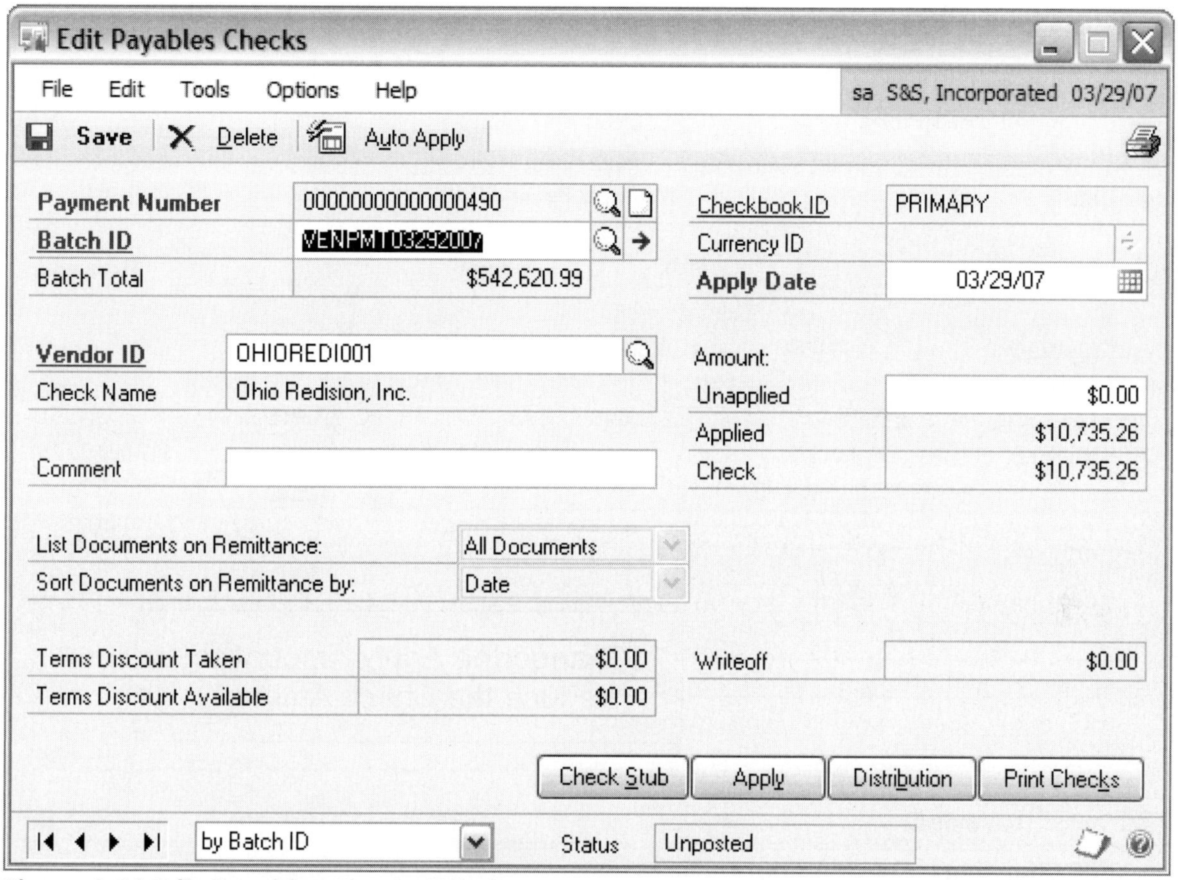

Figure 6:64 Edit Payables Checks Window

11. Click **Apply** and expand the rows. Type 10000.00 into **Apply Amount** and press tab to change the check amount. (See Figure 6:65.) Notice that you can also enter values for Terms Taken and Writeoff. Click **OK** to return to the Edit Payables Checks window. Click **Save** and close the window.

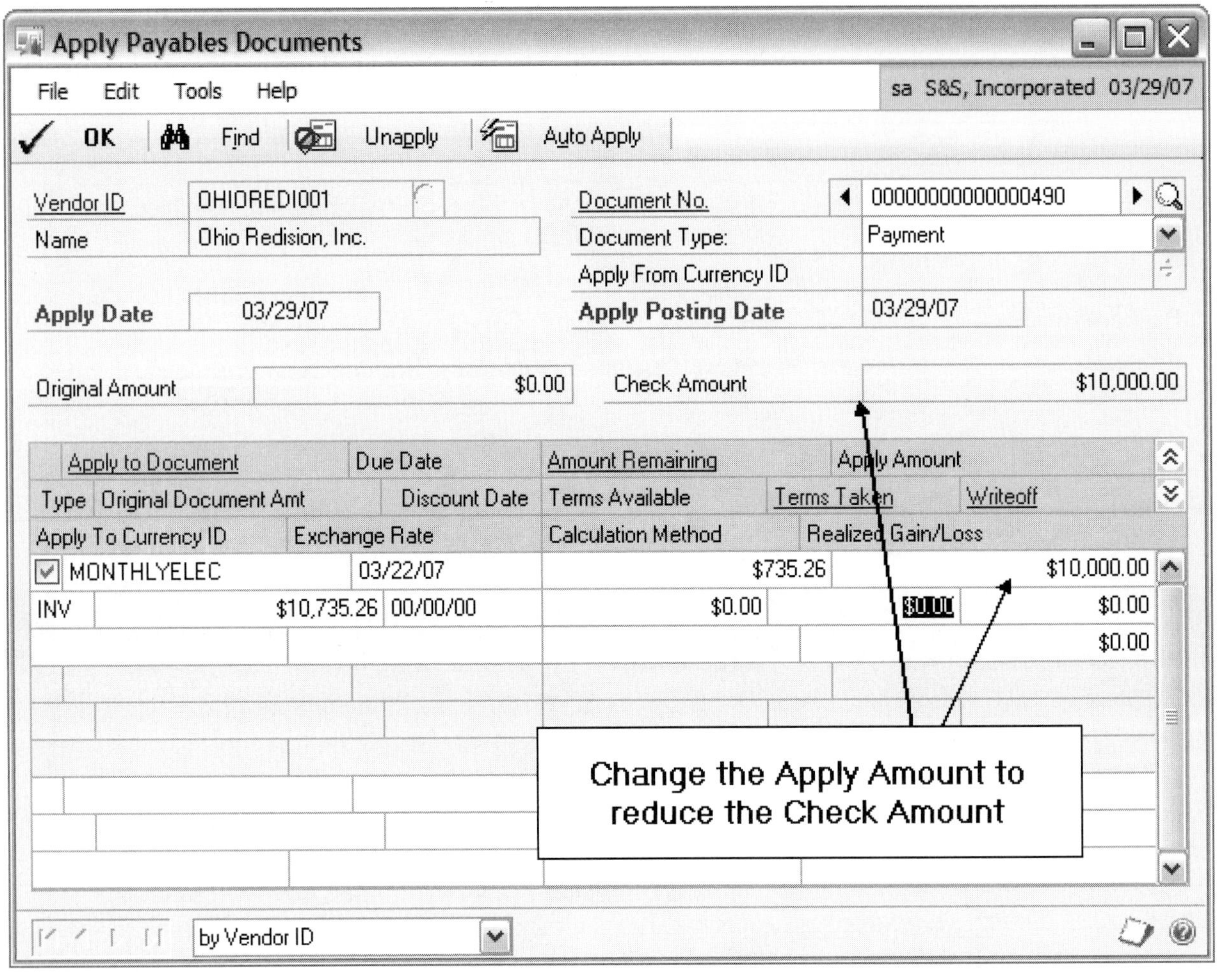

Figure 6:65 Changing a Check Amount

12. Return to the Edit Payables Check Batch window and again click to select OHIOREDI001. Notice that the payment is now $10,000.00. We next remove payment to this vendor. If you want to remove specific invoices for a vendor then clicking the checkbox on the invoice turns off payment for the invoice. Because our vendor has one invoice, click the checkbox for OHIOREDI001 to remove payment to the vendor.

13. You are now ready to print the checks. Click **Print Checks** to open the Print Payables Checks window illustrated next. Before printing, you should review the check number and check date. In the real world, the check number corresponds to the first number on the check stock placed in the printer. Any discrepancy signals an internal control problem in custody over checks.

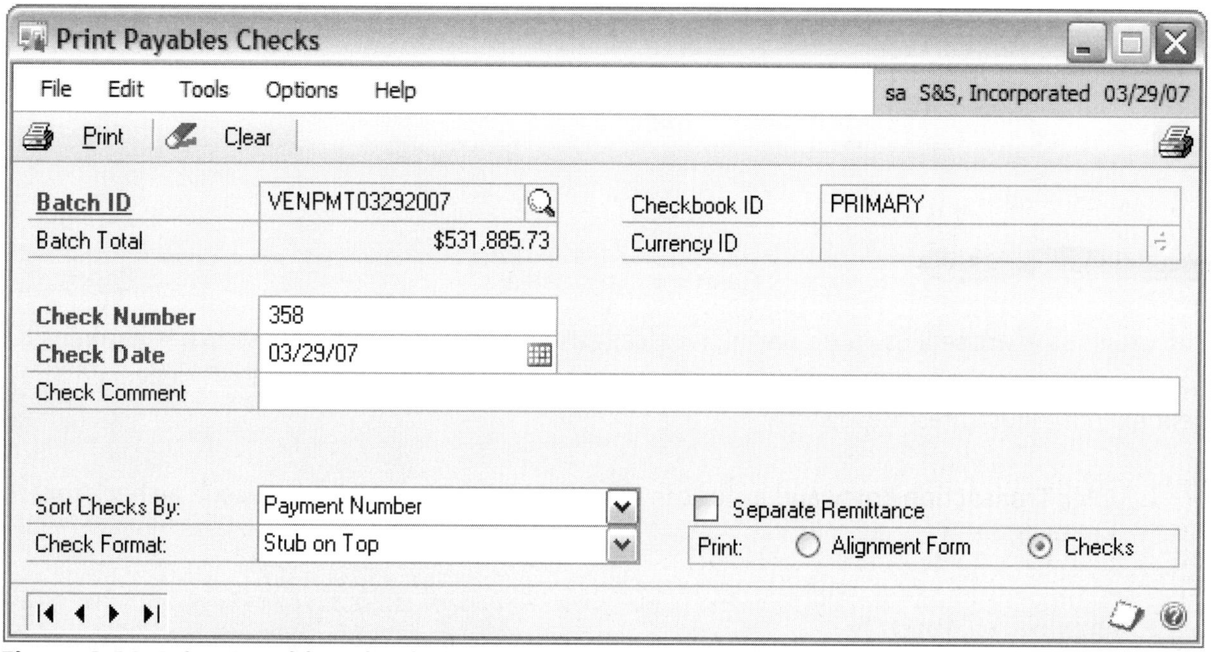

Figure 6:66 Print Payables Checks Window

14. Click **Print** and send the checks to the screen. Close the report. After printing, the Post Payables Checks window appears. Click the dropdown for Process (Figure 6:66) as we explain your choices. Post Checks finalizes check printing by posting entries to the general ledger and applying payments to invoices. Reprint Checks and Void Checks can be used to restart check printing should a printer jam occur.

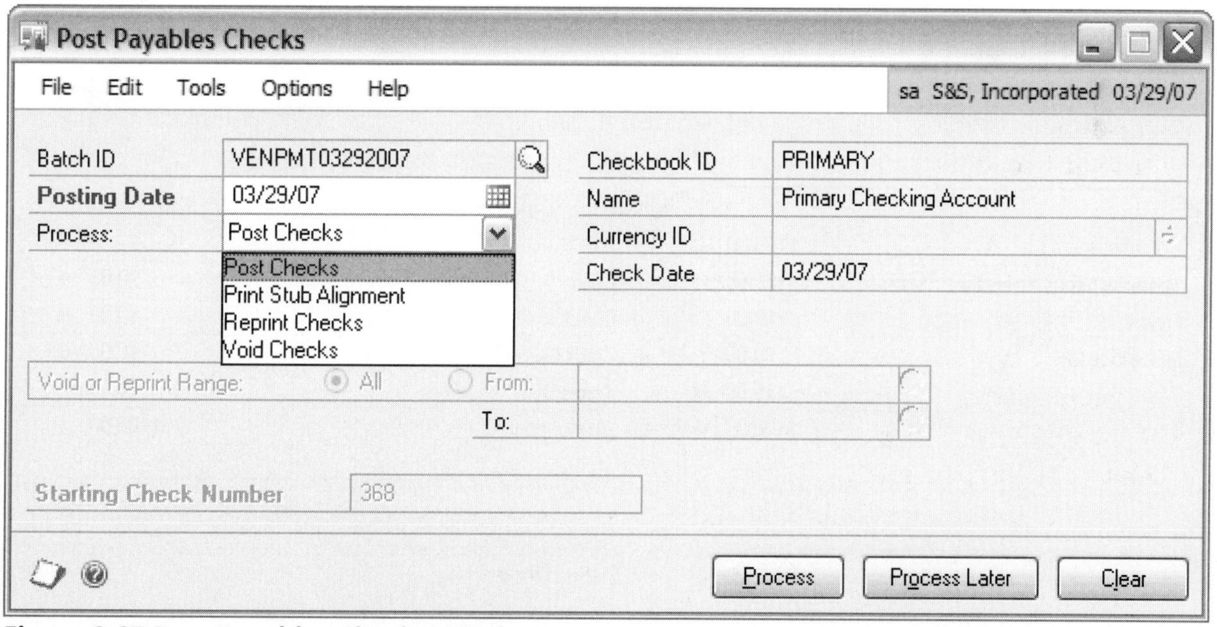

Figure 6:67 Post Payables Checks Window

15. Select **Post Checks** and click **Process**. Print posting reports to the screen and review the Computer Check Register report. This is a control report that identifies checks sent to the vendors. Close all reports and any open windows.

Issuing Manual Checks

The previous exercise illustrated paying invoices already posted to the Series. What happens if you need to write a check for an invoice not posted to the system such as a COD delivery? The next exercise illustrates these steps.

1. Click **Transaction Entry** and enter the information illustrated next to issue a check for postage.

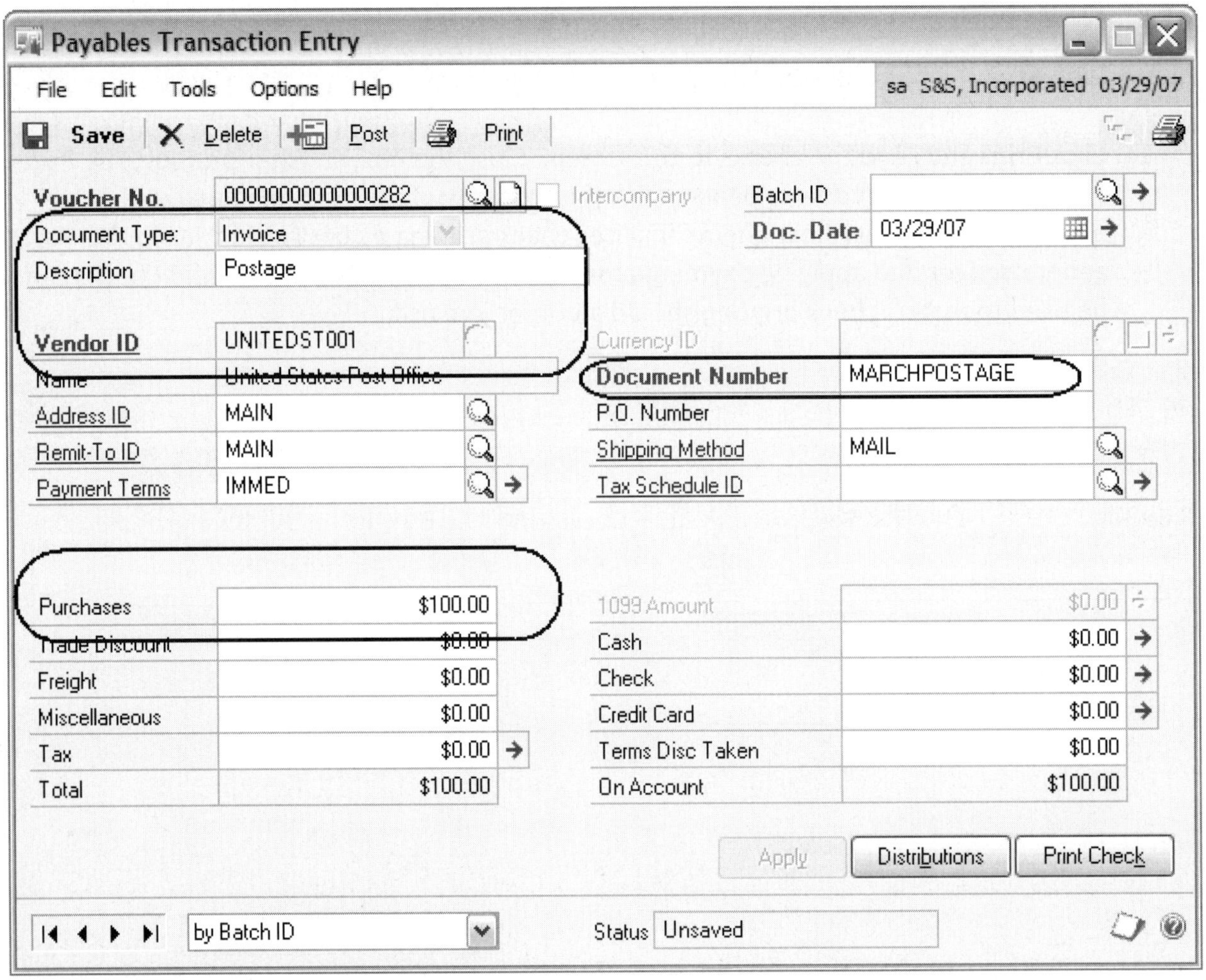

Figure 6:68 Manual Check for Postage

2. Tab to the **Check** field and enter 100.00. The following window opens to select a checkbook and enter a check number. Click **OK**.

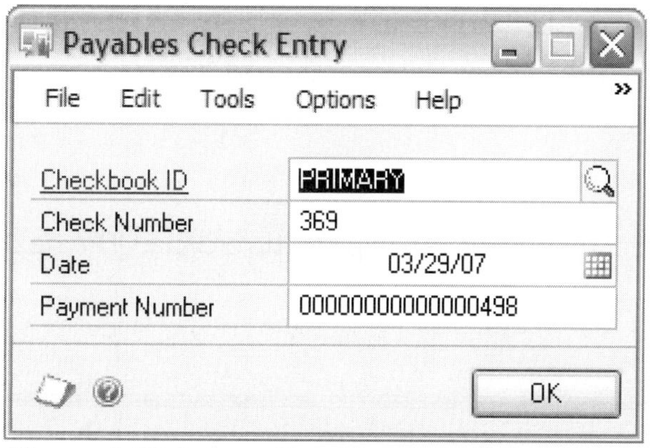

Figure 6:69 Select Checkbook and Supply Check Number

3. Click **Distribution** to find that the transaction posts directly to expense and cash instead of running through expense and accounts payable. (See Figure 6:70.) Click **OK**.

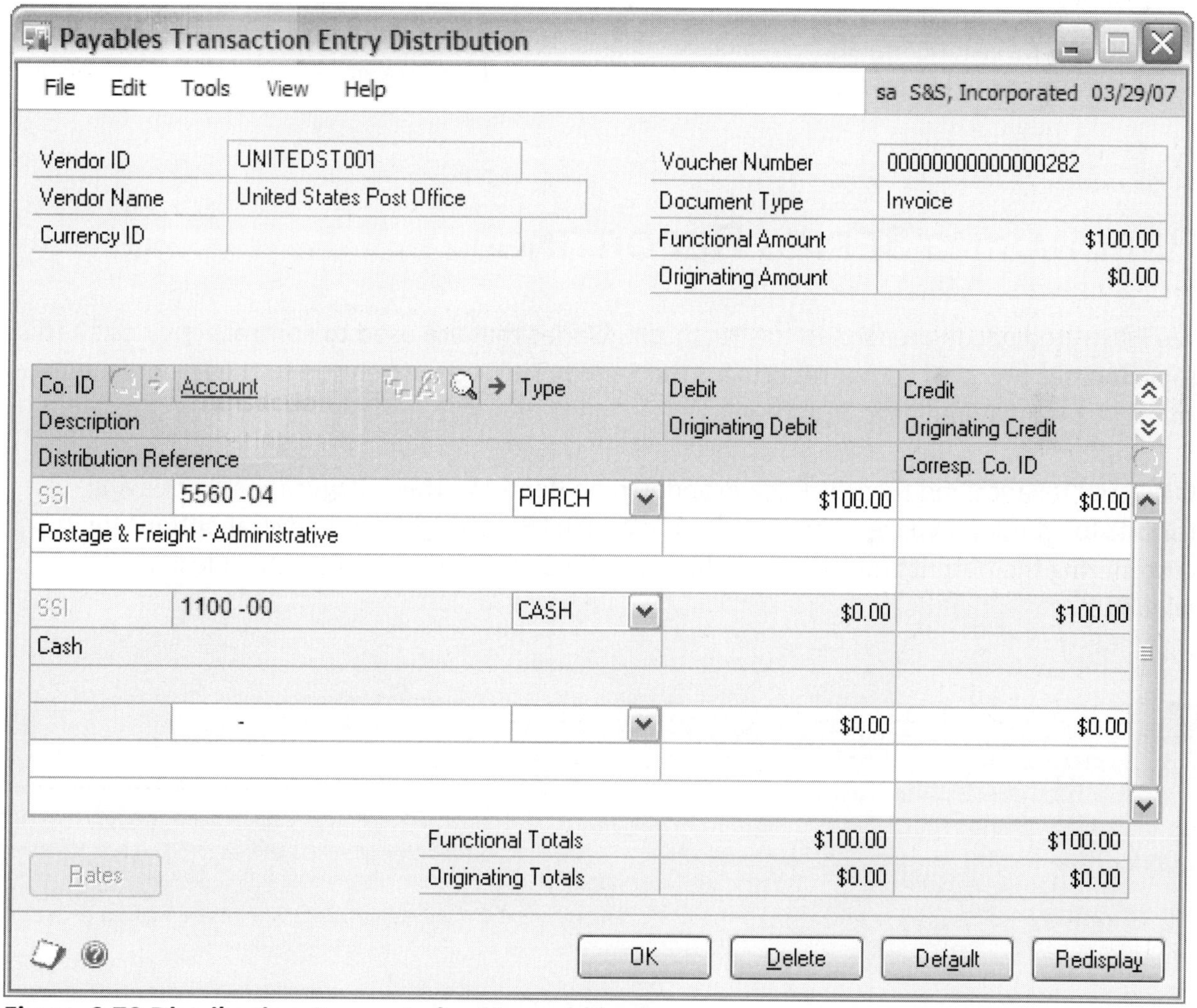

Figure 6:70 Distribution Accounts for Manual Check

4. Click Print Check and then click Print. Send the check to the screen and then close the output.
5. Click **Post** and close the window. Remember to finalize posting from the Financial home page.

You have now completed activities for the expenditure cycle. The next topic reviews Purchasing Series reports.

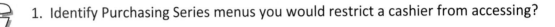

1. Identify Purchasing Series menus you would restrict a cashier from accessing?
2. Identify internal control concerns for the cashier department.

E6:6 Cashier Internal Controls

PURCHASING SERIES REPORTING

We illustrated posting reports in the Purchasing Series that are used to control activities.[25] This topic focuses preparing other reports for the Series. Turn your attention to the Reports category on the home page.

Click **Trial Balance** and then click the dropdown on Reports. These (Figure 6:71) are aging reports for vendor invoices. The Historical Aged Trial Balance provides several options for customizing the output and allows you to run the report as of a specific date. Close the window.

[25] More information on expenditure cycle reporting is available in Romney and Steinbart, *Accounting Information Systems* (11th ed., Pearson Prentice Hall 2009), Chapter 11.

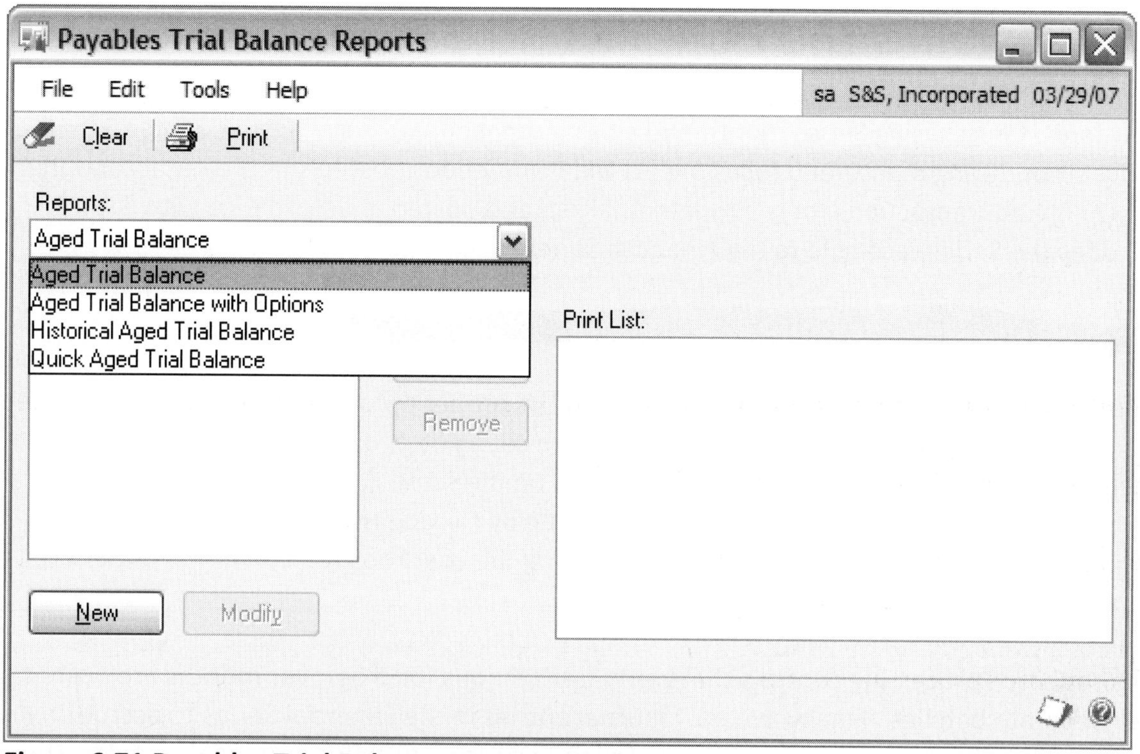

Figure 6:71 Payables Trial Balance Reports Window

Click **History** and then the dropdown on Reports. (Not illustrated). These are reports to print the details for historical transactions in the Series. Close the window.

Click **Analysis** and then the dropdown on Reports. This category contains reports for monitoring activities and many of these were illustrated previously in the chapter. Close the window.

Finally, **Check Information** holds reports that print the check register and detailed information for checks sent to vendors and **Posting Journals** are reports for reprinting the control reports that print after posting. Setup/Lists reports are illustrated in the next level.

As with the Sales Series, you should reconcile the aging report in the Purchasing Series to control accounts in the Financial Series at least monthly. Additionally, auditors may request copies of the check register so it can be reviewed for large payments and out of sequence checks.

MONTH-ENDING THE PURCHASING SERIES

We now look at Purchasing Series month-end closing procedures. Recall from Chapter 5 that these our steps during month-end focus on: (1) Did transactions post to the proper accounting period; (2) Are all transactions for the month finalized and posted in accordance with GAAP; and (3) does the Series reconcile to the Financial Series

1. Verify that Transactions Posted to the Proper Accounting Period

Procedures for verifying that transactions posted to the proper accounting period are the same as those implemented in the revenue cycle. We again set a cutoff date for processing transactions in the prior month. This cutoff date can be the same cutoff date established for sales transactions. We then close the Series to posting by clicking the GP button to select ***Tools>>Setup>>Company>>Fiscal Periods*** and marking the checkbox for the month under the Series. This window was illustrated in Chapter 5.

We also set batch processing controls that verify transactions for crossover months are posted through separate batches. Finally, we post journal entries in the Financial Series to accrue any expenses arising after the cutoff date. Unlike revenue cycle transactions where we control the timing of posting, vendor invoices affecting a period may not always be received before the cutoff date. Expenses like utilities and insurance are often estimated and accrued through reversing journal entries discussed in Chapter 8.

2. Verify that all Transactions Finalized and Posted in Accordance with GAAP

The procedures followed to complete this check are similar to those performed in the revenue cycle. First, purchasing cycle analysis reports are reviewed to spot delays in posting vendor invoices for inventory receipts. Outstanding POs are also reviewed and warehouse records checked to spot delays in posting receipts. If unposted transactions are spotted prior to the cutoff date then these transactions can be posted as normal; otherwise, you must accrue unposted transactions.

Finally, you must always check the Series Post window for pending batches.

Purchasing Series Reconciles with Financial Series

Like the Sales Series, you must reconcile the Purchasing Series to Financial Series control accounts. These procedures were covered in a previous exercise.

YEAR-ENDING THE PURCHASING SERIES

Before closing the year, you perform the procedures for closing a month. As discussed in Chapter 5, year-ending a Series makes permanent changes to the data file; therefore you should always back up your data before closing the year. You should also print reports. It is especially important to print Form 1099. This is an IRS tax form that reports annual payments to a vendor. Year-ending zeroes out this annual payment total and, thereafter, you cannot print the form for the closed year.

When you are ready, the Series is year-ended by clicking Year-End Close under Routines. The window illustrated next looks and functions similar to the year-end closing window for the Sales Series.

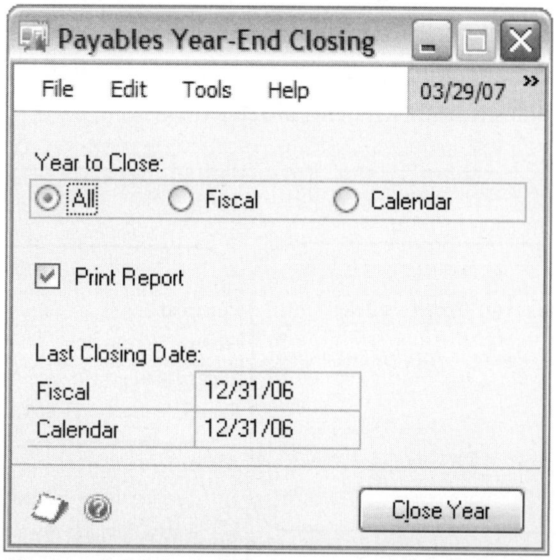

Figure 6:72 Payables Year-End Closing Window

You have now completed this level in the chapter. The next level illustrates implementing internal controls for the Series.

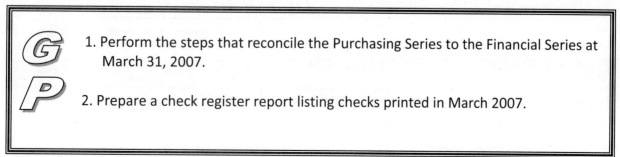

1. Perform the steps that reconcile the Purchasing Series to the Financial Series at March 31, 2007.

2. Prepare a check register report listing checks printed in March 2007.

E6:7 Practice Purchasing Series Reporting

Level Two

This level focuses on setting internal controls for the Purchasing Series. These controls aid with enforcing internal controls over expenditure cycle activities.[26]

Purchasing Series Setup and Internal Controls

Our roadmap at the beginning of the chapter listed threats to the cycle by department. Review the diagram and keep these threats in mind as you complete this topic.

Remember that Purchasing Series transaction menus divide into two tiers. Accordingly, there separate setup menus for each tier. Click **Payables** under Setup. These options control basic activities in the Series. (See Figure 6:73.) We have numbered sections of the window and explain the purpose of each section below the illustration.

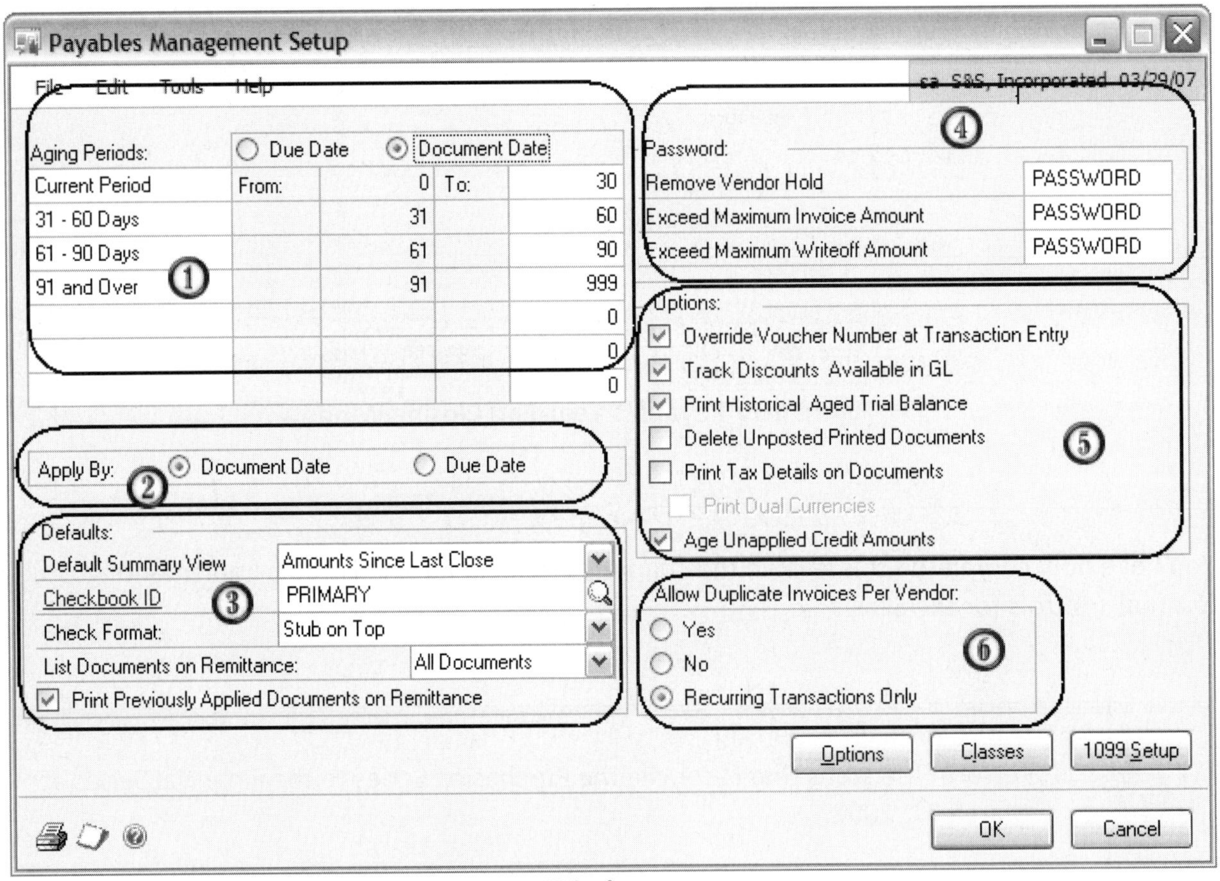

Figure 6:73 Payables Management Setup Window

---

[26] For an in-depth understanding of expenditure cycle control activities, refer to Romney and Steinbart, *Accounting Information Systems* (11th ed., Pearson Prentice Hall 2009), pgs. 433-444.

1. **Aging Periods** options function the same as discussed in the Sales Series by determining the age of invoices on the aging report.

2. **Apply By** provides instructions for using Auto Apply in the Apply window. Under the current settings, auto apply will take a credit memo and apply it to the invoice with the earliest date.

3. **Defaults** autofill selections for transaction windows for the fields indicated.

4. **Passwords** implement specific authorization for the activities indicated. We looked at specific authorization in Level Two of Chapter 5.

5. **Options** are additional controls and features for the Series. Many are self-explanatory. It is here where we find the option to track purchase discounts available in the general ledger. We also see the option that activates printing historical aged trial balance reports. Of course, S&S only has the ability because vendor cards and Purchase Order setup retain transaction history.

6. **Allow Duplicate Invoices Per Vendor** is a control over transaction entry that denies entering a duplicate vendor invoice number.

Click **Options** to view document control numbers and then close the window. (Not illustrated).

Close the Payables Setup Options window and click **Purchase Order Processing**.

This window (Figure 6:74) controls activities performed in the Inventory Purchasing Tier. The discussion that follows explains controls and options we want to focus on.

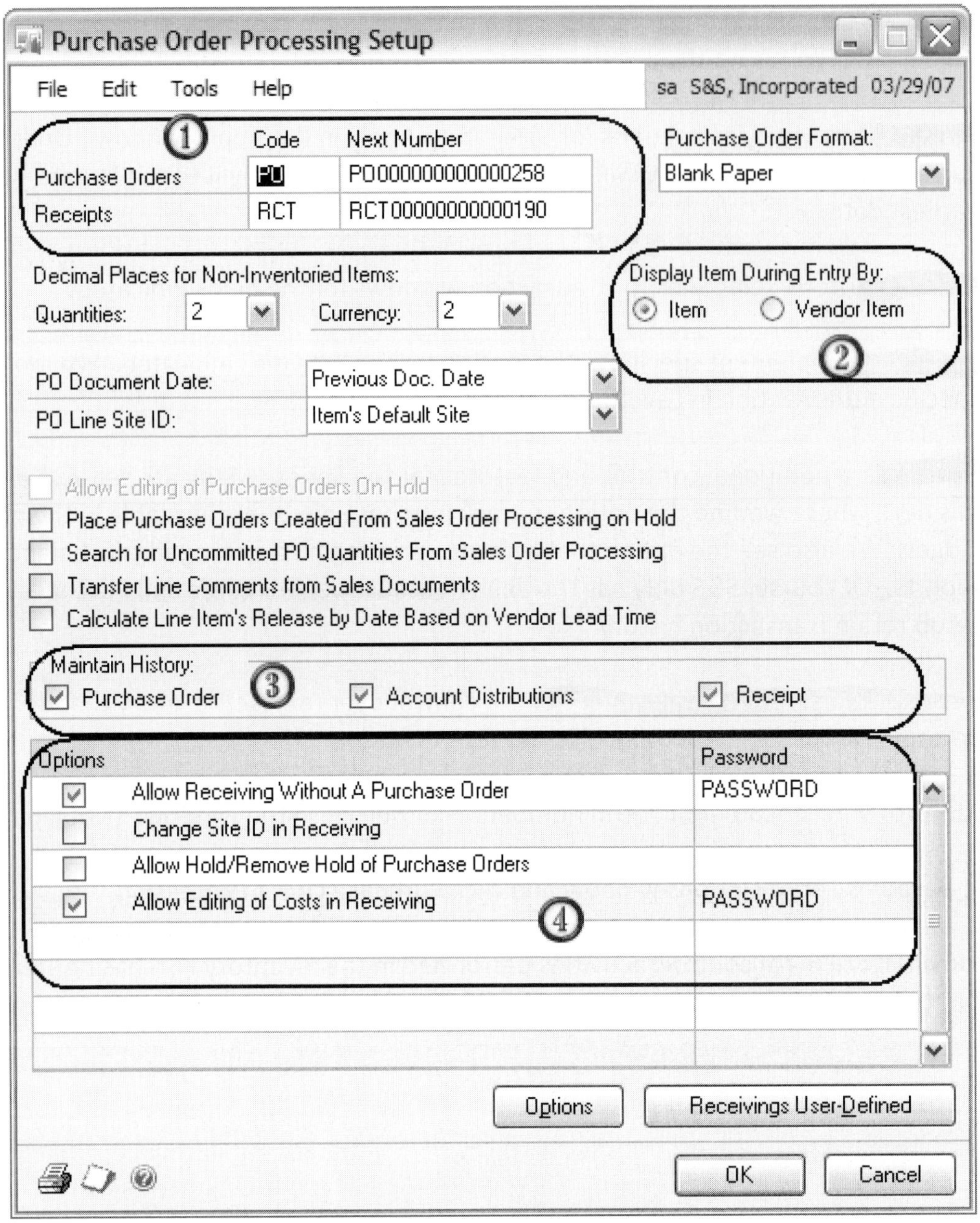

Figure 6:74 Purchase Order Processing Setup Window

1. Document control numbers for Purchase Orders and Receipts.

2. **Display Item During Entry** determines whether the item lookup window displays all items in the inventory table or just items sold by the selected vendor. Marking Item permits users to assign items to vendors, thus overriding assigned vendors on the inventory card. (Note: You can still deny overriding assignment by denying access to inventory cards as illustrated in Chapter 3.)

3. **Maintain History** retains transaction history so you can print historical aging reports.

4. **Options** activate general and specific controls over the activities listed. General controls are implemented by checking or unchecking an activity whereas supplying a password implements specific authorization.

Close the window and complete the next exercise.

> 1. Why would S&S want to password protect the Remove Vendor Hold option?
>
> 2. Explain why S&S activated Allow Duplicate Invoices Per Vendors for recurring transactions.
>
> 3. Explain why S&S provided a password for Allow Receiving Without a Purchase Order.

E6:8 Purchasing Series Controls

PURCHASING SERIES SETUP REPORTS

Level one illustrated posting reports that validate and control transaction entry. Furthermore, recall that Analysis reports monitor activity performance in the cycle. In this topic we focus on reports that document internal control settings for the Series.

Click **Setup/List** and click the dropdown on Reports. (See Figure 6:75.)

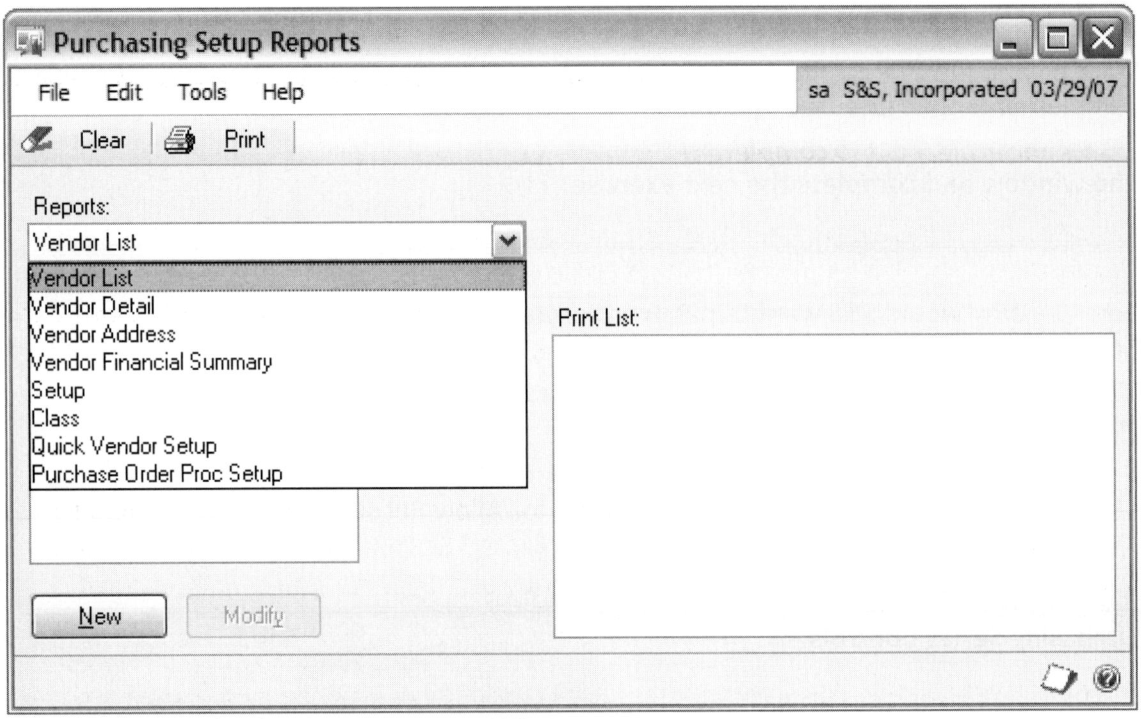

Figure 6:75 Purchasing Setup Reports Window

Setup and Purchase Order Proc Setup reports document internal control options for tasks performed in the Series. These reports should be compared to a company's internal control objectives and reviewed for weaknesses.

Vendor reports list names, addresses, and financial summaries for vendors. Class reports list default options assigned to vendor classes. Remember that these defaults will be assigned to the vendor card by linking the card to a class.

Close the window.

You have now completed the chapter. In the next chapter we look at payroll activities.

Level One Questions

Use the S&S, Inc Project DB to complete these exercises.

1. Using the Inventory Transactions SmartList, gather information for quantities sold for each item in inventory over the time period of February to March of 2007. Export this information into Excel and develop an average quantity sold by item. Compare this average to on-hand quantities at March 31, 2007 and identify any items with on-hand levels insufficient to meet sales trends.

2. Select two inventory items from the previous analysis identified as having insufficient quantities on-hand. Issue POs for these items and complete all activities that process these POs from receipt to invoicing. Record all transactions on March 31, 2007. You can supply your own vendor document numbers. Turn in a copy of the POs and all control reports printed after posting.

3. Post Invoice 76P876, dated March 28, received from Office Rex for a desk costing $1,250.00. Turn in posting reports.

4. As the purchasing manager, prepare a report that analyzes vendor performance?

5. As the accountant, identify reports that aid in analyzing receiving department and accounts payable department performance.

Level Two Questions

1. Review threats listed on the expenditure cycle roadmap diagram. Describe, by department, GP features that control these threats.

2. As the accountant, how would you verify that transactions have posted to the Financial Series before period-ending the Purchasing Series?

3. Explain the significance of monitoring orders received but not invoiced.

4. Describe specific instances of Purchasing Series transaction processing compliance with GAAP.

Chapter 7 PAYROLL CYCLE AND GP PAYROLL SERIES

CHAPTER OVERVIEW

Payroll is the biggest expense for most companies. These expenses include wages, salaries, commissions, payroll taxes and benefits. This chapter focuses on activities performed in the payroll cycle and illustrates using GP's Payroll Series to perform these activities. Along the way, we will discuss controls over activities. The Human Resource Series is included with the Student Edition, but is not covered in this text.

- Level One focuses on using GP Payroll Series to process employee paychecks. After an overview discussion and roadmap diagram of payroll cycle activities, we illustrate managing payroll cards and producing employee wage, commission, and expense checks. We also discuss internal controls over processing payroll and external reporting requirements.

- Level Two focuses on setting pervasive controls for the Payroll Series as well as managing tax, benefit, and deduction codes and payroll posting accounts.

Level One covers:

- Roadmap diagram on and explanation of activities
- Managing payroll master records
- Managing employee, tax withholding, benefits, and deductions
- Routine payroll processing activities, including time entry and paycheck printing
- Month-end, quarter-end, and year-end reporting
- Series closing procedures

Level Two covers:

- Payroll Series setup
- Managing Payroll Series codes
- Reviewing Payroll Series posting accounts

Level One

Payroll is unlike other cycles because the majority of activities are triggered by calendar dates. Employees are paid by a certain pay date and tax remittances are due by dates set by taxing agencies. Taxing agencies also set due dates for filing tax reports. Furthermore, payroll data originate both inside and outside the company. Inside, employees track hours worked and payroll clerks input these hours. Outside, federal, state, and local government agencies revise tax rates and health insurance companies revise premiums.

Our roadmap in Figure 7:1 covers only payroll activities.[27] It does show that the human resources department makes all changes to GP's master tax and withholding tables but the roadmap does not depict other HR activities. We next describe activities for this department.

All changes to Payroll Series master records (i.e., cards) are performed by the HR department to segregate the duty of authorization from recording. This department updates tax records by downloading federal and state tax law changes through GP's online payroll subscription service and manually entering local taxes rates. HR will also manage employee records and changes to benefits and deductions.

S&S's owners function as the HR department. Other duties include hiring and firing employees; performing employee background checks; producing employee handbooks on company policies; training employees; and instituting policies and procedures for complying with federal wage and hour, ERISA, OSHA, and nondiscrimination EEO laws. HR activities do not post transactions but still need to be tracked and monitored in a database such as GP's Human Resource Series. This Series is not illustrated in the text.

Let us now refocus attention to our roadmap. Department managers submit employee time data for hourly paid employees to the payroll office after reviewing and approving. In addition, sales managers submit sales commission and expense data to payroll. Time data is due at the end of each week whereas commission and expense information is due a few days before month-end.

Payroll clerks input time data and run reports to reconcile data entry. Any changes affecting an employee's pay-period status (i.e., new hire or terminated), pay rate, deductions, benefits and tax withholdings must be input by HR prior to processing payroll. The payroll manager verifies that master tables are current before processing payroll. Furthermore, all time must be entered before processing payroll. Hourly employees are paid biweekly; salaried employees paid semimonthly; and salesperson expense and commission paid monthly.

---

[27] For an in-depth discussion on activities in the human resources management/payroll cycle, refer to Romney and Steinbart, *Accounting Information Systems* (11th ed., Pearson Prentice Hall 2009), Chapter 13.

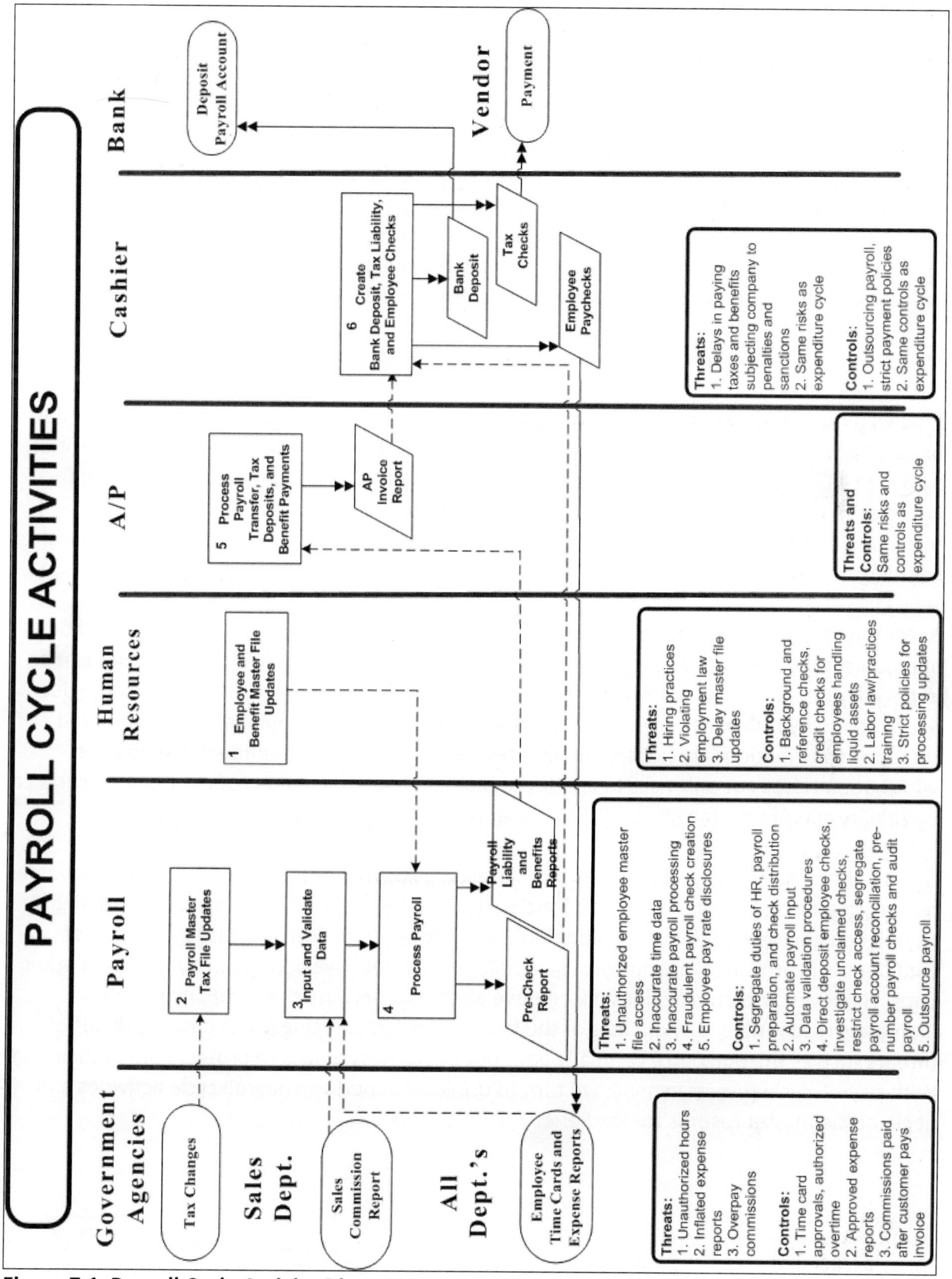

Figure 7:1 Payroll Cycle Activity Diagram

Payroll processing generates a variety of control reports. Payroll employees send payroll liability reports to the accounts payable department immediately after producing paychecks. These reports list tax, benefit, and deduction liabilities for the pay period as well as the dollars needing to be transferred to the payroll checking to cover paychecks. Accounts payable processes these payments and the cashier prints these checks using steps illustrated in Chapter 6.

In the payroll department, paycheck processing stops at the pre-check register. This register is then sent to the cashier for printing paychecks, thus segregating the duty of recording payroll from custody of the checks. After cutting checks, the cashier sends paychecks to department managers for distribution. In addition, the cashier transfers monies to the payroll checking account and prints tax, deduction, and benefit checks by the mandatory remittance date.

This overview appears simple. However, the cycle is fraught with potential errors and risk o disclosing confidential information. As we go through each activity, keep in mind that this cycle is heavily regulated by government agencies. These agencies are not hesitant to impose fines or sanctions for failure to comply with the law. Although this text does not cover HR activities, be aware that these activities face the heaviest regulation. State and federal government agencies sanction companies for practices that discriminate in hiring, promotion, and termination. OSHA regulates employee safety in the workplace and ERISA governs company handling of pension and retirement plans.

As for payroll processing activities, any inefficiencies or delinquencies in performing activities may subject the company to possible fines and/or sanctions by outside agencies. Fines can be imposed for failure to remit tax liabilities, employee withholdings, and tax reports by the due date. Company retirement plans may lose favorable tax status if employee deductions and company contributions are not timely remitted. Failure to protect confidential employee information raises not only risks to employee morale but also violations of the Health Insurance Portability and Accountability Act (HIPAA) that protects the privacy of health data.

Given threats in this cycle, companies often outsource payroll to third parties. Some companies realize greater cost savings by using a third party because of the labor involved in preparing payroll and government filings. In addition, outsourcing payroll can increase protection of confidential payroll information because employees do not have access to pay rates and other data. However, outsourcing does not remove all threats because the company remains ultimately responsible for violations of the law. In fact, outsourcing poses different kinds of threats such as the outsource company goes out of business or fails to protect data at their end. With payroll cycle threats in mind, we turn to using GP to perform payroll cycle activities and begin at the master records for the Series.

PAYROLL SERIES CARDS

Activate the **HR & Payroll** home page and focus on the Cards section. This Series requires more card setup than Series previously discussed. As you know, cards are master records for a Series and payroll has cards for employees, taxes, pay codes, deductions, and benefits.

Click **Employees** and look up April Levine. (See Figure 7:2). Employee cards store basic information about the employee. The table that follows describes fields on this card.

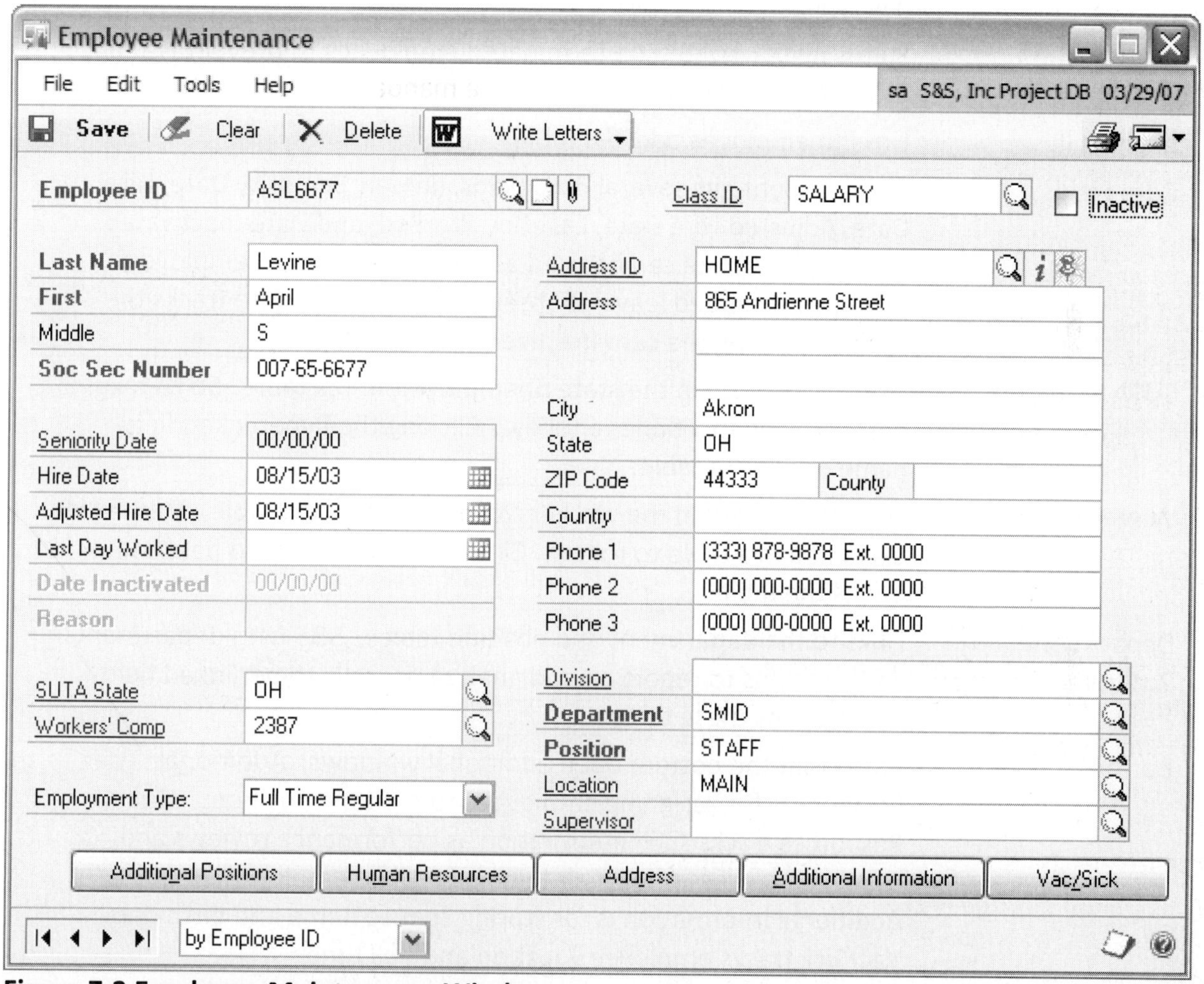

Figure 7:2 Employee Maintenance Window

Field(s)	Description
Employee ID	Primary key for record. S&S uses an employee's initials and last four digits of the social security number.
Name Fields and Soc. Sec. Number	Employee name broken down as Last Name, First, and Middle. This complies with database normalization rules. Soc. Sec. Number is self-explanatory.
Class ID	S&S uses the SALARY and HOURLY classes to group employees by pay type.
Inactive Option	Status field activated on terminated employees to prevent issuing future paychecks.
Address ID	Links to employee address table.
Date Fields	The card contains several date fields, namely Seniority Date, Hire Date, Adjusted Hire Date, Last Day Worked, and Date Inactivated. Adjusted hire date can be used as the rehire date for employees taking an extended leave of absence. Inactivated date tracks the date of marking the card inactive.
SUTA State	Links to a record in the state unemployment tax table. SUTA taxes are explained in a table to follow. Clicking the hyperlinked field name opens the table.
Workers' Comp	Links to a record in the workers' compensation tax table. This tax is explained in a table to follow. Clicking the hyperlinked field name opens the table.
Department and Position	Links to the department and position tables. S&S uses departments and positions to report on and analyze payroll. Hyperlinked field name opens these tables.
Buttons	Buttons at the bottom open additional windows. Additional Positions is for assigning employees to multiple positions. Human Resources tracks such information as performance reviews and training. Address is for maintaining multiple employee addresses. Additional Information is for storing spouse name and birth date. Vac/Sick tracks employee vacation and sick time.

Table 7:1 Employee Card Fields

The employee card does not have an Accounts button so how do I know the default general ledger accounts used during posting? Default posting accounts are stored in the Payroll Accounts window accessed by clicking Payroll Accounts under Setup. This window is discussed in Level Two.

Close the Employee Maintenance window. If you accidentally changed data in the window, click Clear to exit without saving.

We now explain the process of calculating paychecks. First, GP calculates gross pay based on the pay code linked to the employee card. If paid hourly, then gross pay calculates as hours worked in the pay period multiplied by the hourly pay rate. *(Note: Hours exceeding 80 in the biweekly pay period are treated as overtime hours and these hours are multiplied by the overtime rate.)* Salaried employees receive the same gross pay each pay period, calculated as the annual pay rate divided by the number of pay periods. Salaried employees are paid twice per month so pay periods equal 24 (i.e., 12 months times 2 pays per month).

Let us review employee card links to a few of these pay codes.

1. Click **Pay Code** under Cards and look up April's card. Under **Pay Code** look up and select SALARY. The next illustration explains April's gross pay each pay period.

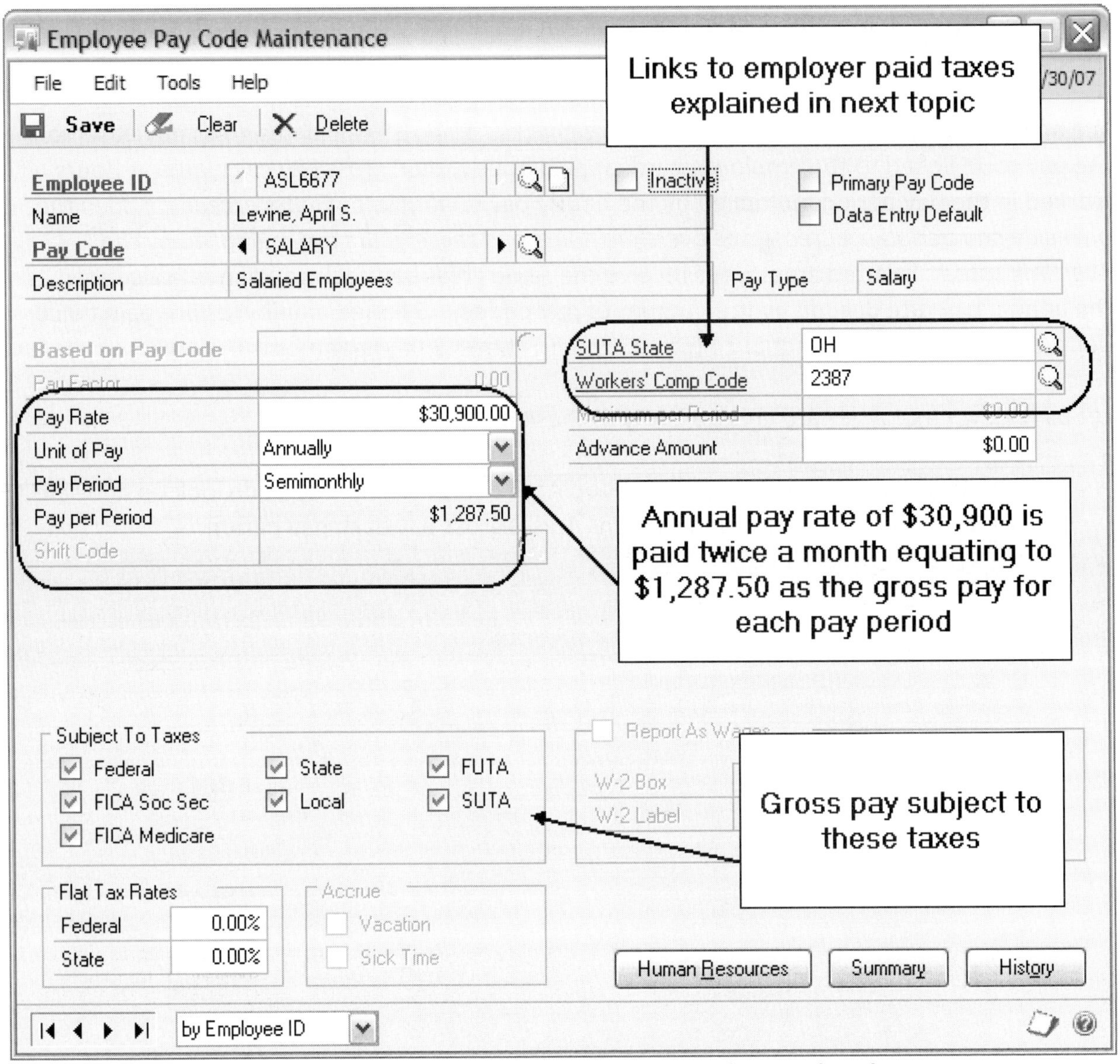

Figure 7:3 Employee Pay Code Maintenance Window for April Levine's Salary

2. April is linked to other pay codes. These codes are for expense reimbursement and sales commissions. Click the right record pointer on Pay Code to open her **TRAVEL** code. (See Figure 7:4.) Notice that expenses are paid once a month and payment is not subject to tax.

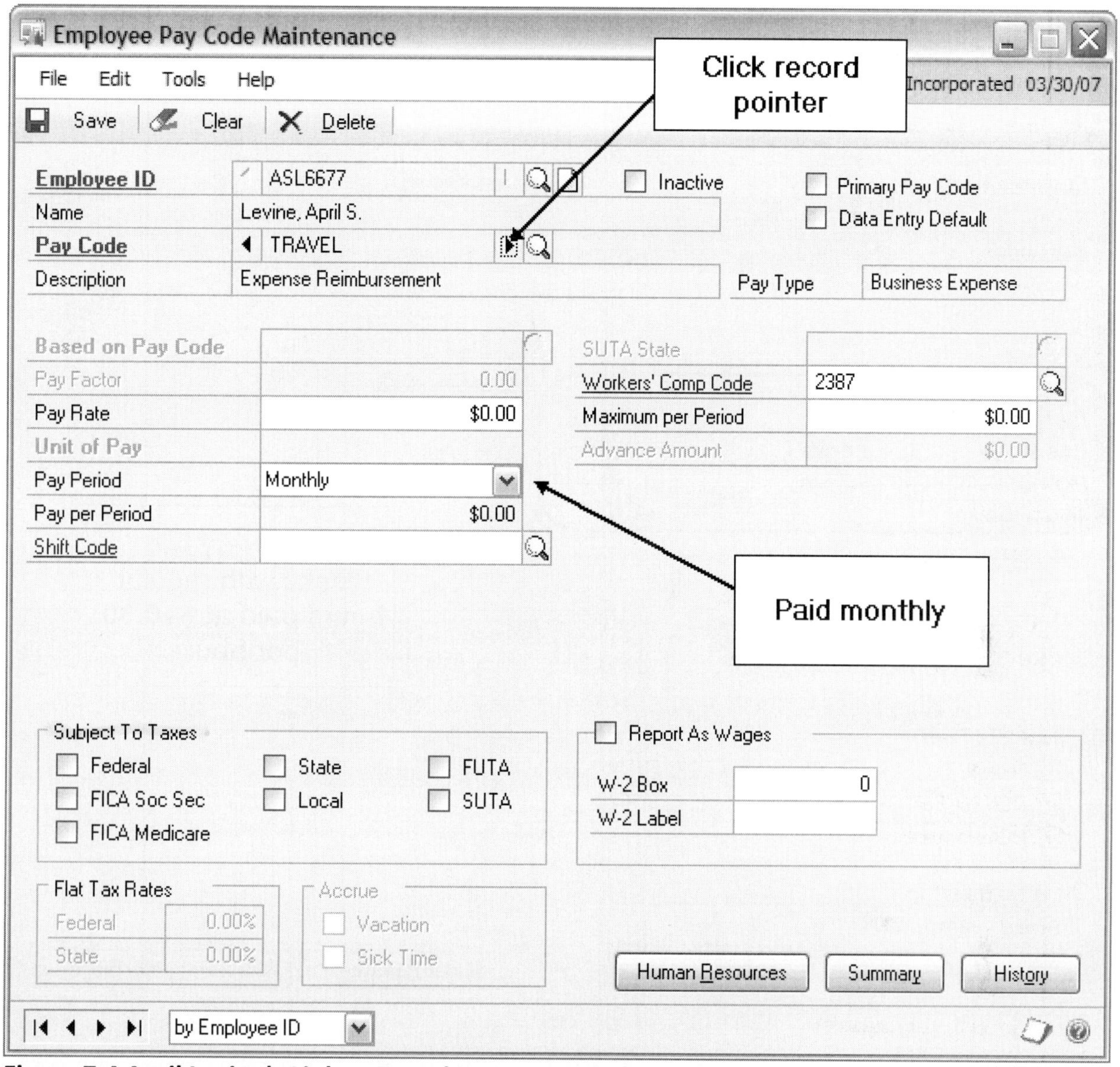

Figure 7:4 April Levine's Link to Travel Expense Reimbursement

3. Click the left record pointer twice to view a link to reimbursement for MEALS and left again for her sales commission (i.e., COMM) link. Note that commissions are subject to tax. (Not illustrated.)

4. Click **Clear** and look up James Richmond. James is paid hourly. Click the right scroll button on Pay Code to see this link. (Figure 7:5.)

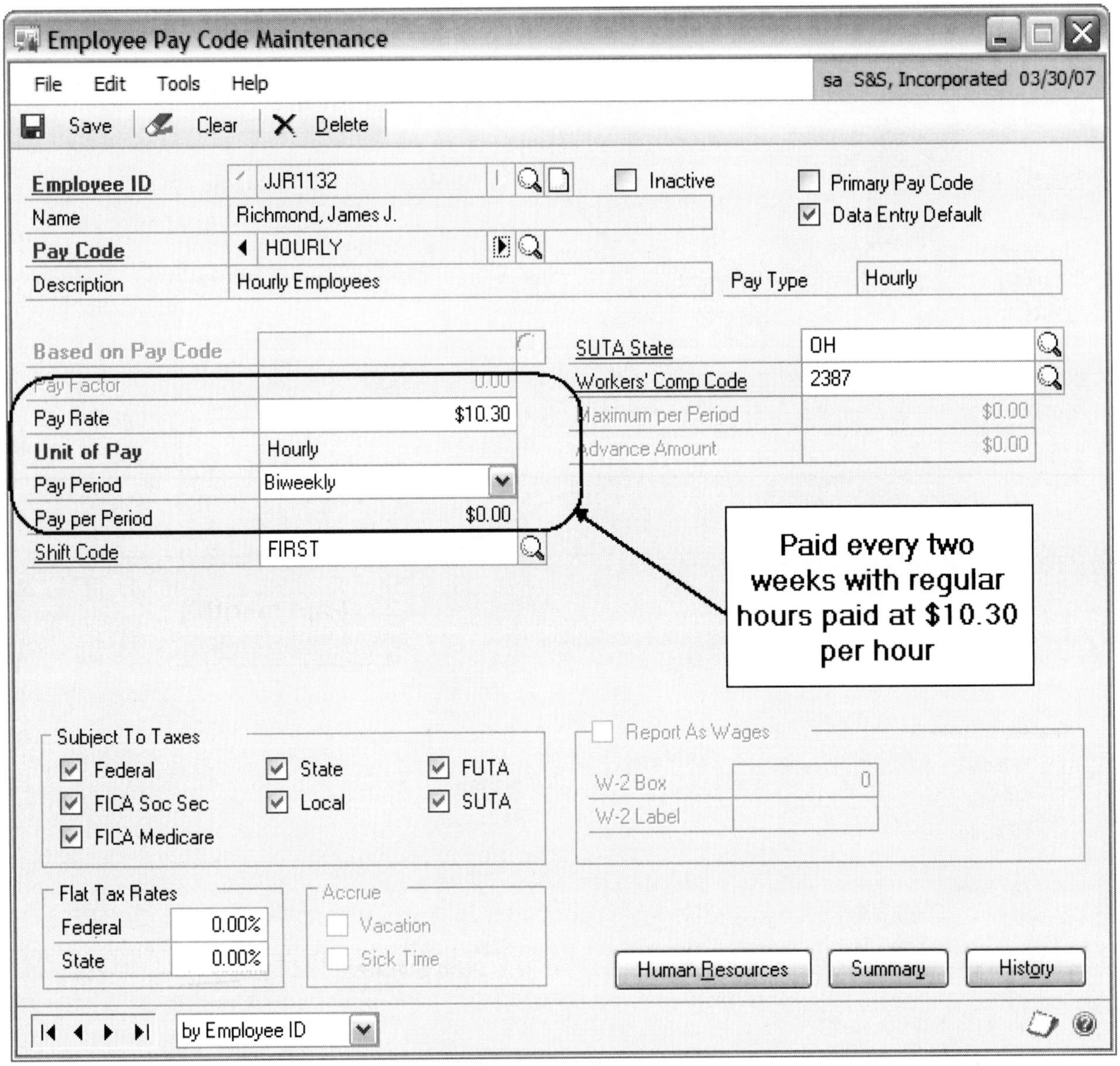

Figure 7:5 James Richmond Link to Hourly Pay Code

5. Click the right scroll button again to view his link for overtime. (See Figure 7:6.)

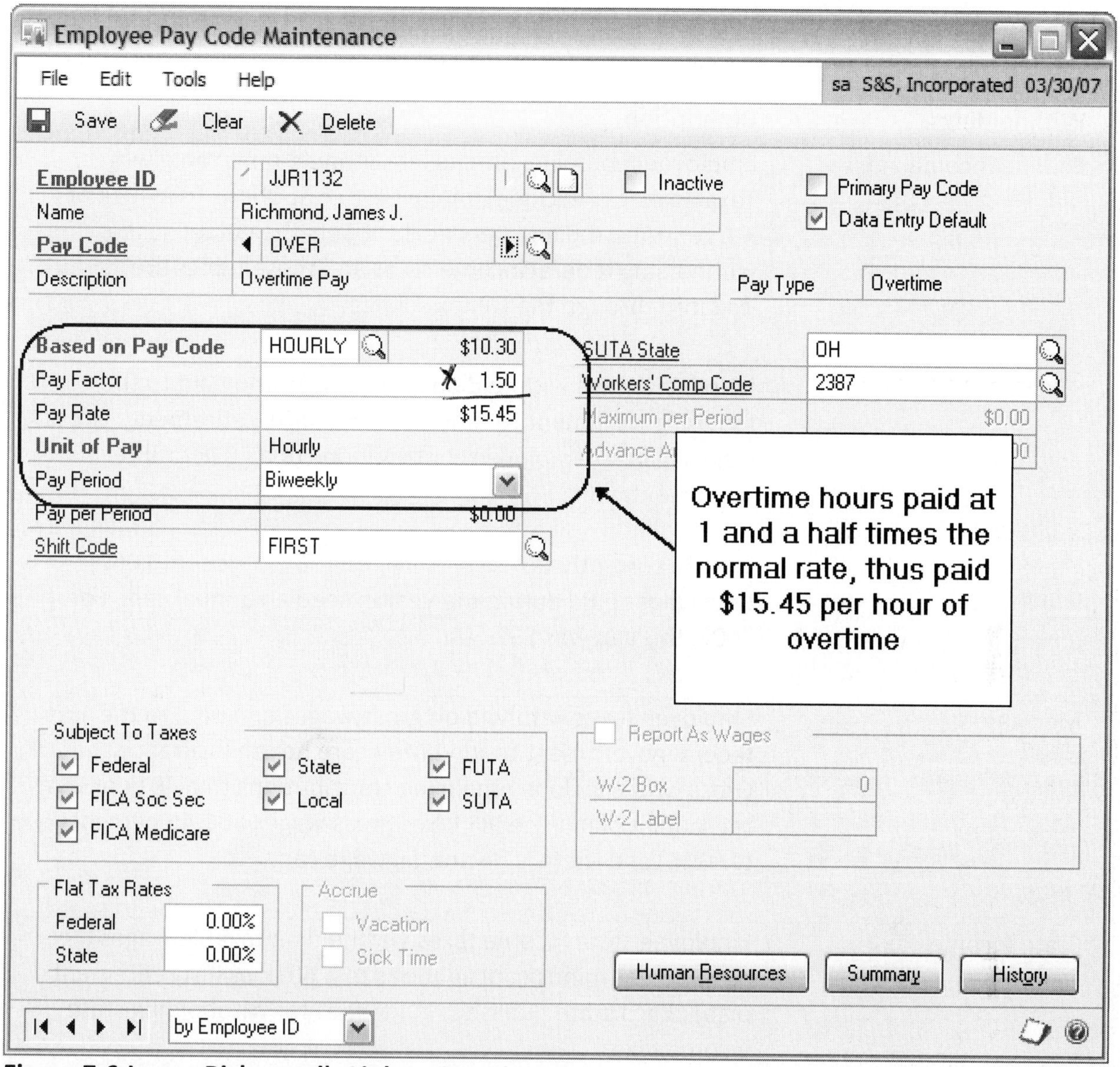

Figure 7:6 James Richmond's Link to Overtime Pay

After calculating gross pay, GP then calculates net pay. Net pay equals gross pay minus total tax withholdings and voluntary deductions. The following tables explain employee tax withholdings and voluntary deductions.

Employee Tax Withholdings	**Description**
Federal Income Tax	Employee federal income taxes withheld on taxable wages. Taxable wages exclude employee contributions to a 401k or IRA retirement plan. IRS Circular E sets the guidelines for withholding federal income taxes and these tables are updated through the GP tax service.
Social Security (FICA)	Employee taxes withheld on gross wages and paid to the federal government to fund Social Security retirement. Gross wages include employee contributions to a 401k or IRA retirement plan. The IRS currently taxes gross wages at 6.2 percent (0.062) until wages paid during the year exceed an annual cap. For 2007, this cap was $97,500.
Medicare	Employee taxes withheld on gross wages and paid to the federal government to fund Medicare health insurance. Gross wages include employee contributions to a 401k or IRA retirement plan. The IRS taxes gross wages at 1.45 percent (0.0145) and there is no annual wage cap.
State Income Tax	Employee state income taxes withheld on taxable wages (i.e., gross wages minus contributions to a 401k or IRA retirement plan). Each state publishes guidelines for withholding state income taxes.

Table 7:2 Employee Payroll Taxes

Employee Voluntary Deductions	Description
Retirement Plans	Employee voluntary contributions to an employer-sponsored retirement plan. Retirement plans include 401k and IRA plans. These contributions are deducted from gross wages to determine federal and state taxable wages.
Health Insurance	Health insurance premiums deducted from net pay when the employer requires its employees to pay for a portion of health insurance costs.
Contributions	Deductions from net pay for charitable contributions made by the employee.

Table 7:3 Employee Voluntary Deductions

S&S also pays taxes on employee compensation plus provides additional benefits such as paying a portion of health insurance costs and matching employee contributions to the company sponsored 401k plan. The next tables explain typical employer tax liabilities and forms of additional employee benefits.

Employer Payroll Taxes	Description
Social Security (FICA) and Medicare	Employer portion of Social Security and Medicare taxes paid on taxable wages. The employer tax equals the tax paid by employees.
Federal Unemployment (FUTA)	Employer tax on gross wages paid to the federal government for subsidizing state unemployment compensation funds. Typically, employers pay 0.08 percent (0.008) on the first $7,000 of annual gross wages to each employee.
State Unemployment (SUTA)	Employer tax on gross wages paid to the state for funding compensation for unemployed workers. Typically the tax rate is based on an employer's unemployment history and/or business type and will be capped after reaching an annual limit on gross wages.
Worker's Compensation	Employer tax paid to the state to fund compensating injured workers. Typically, states set the tax rates based on risk factors in an employee's job.

Table 7:4 Employer Payroll Taxes

Additional Benefits	Description
Retirement Plans	Employer contributions to a company-sponsored 401k or IRA retirement plan. Typically companies match contributions based on the employee's participation in the plan.
Health Insurance	Employer contributions towards health insurance costs. Employers may pay all premiums or require employees to share in this cost.

Table 7:5 Additional Benefits

We will now review April's links to federal, state, and local tax withholdings, benefits, and deductions. This process is complex and omitting any step produces erroneous paychecks. As we go through each step notice that Cards menus are arranged in the order used to link an employee card to withholding, benefit, and deduction cards.

We begin with federal tax withholdings so click **Tax** and look up April's record. (See Figure 7:7.) *(Note: Federal filing statuses and tax rates are downloaded from GP's online payroll tax service.)* We have labeled sections of the window and descriptions for these sections follow.

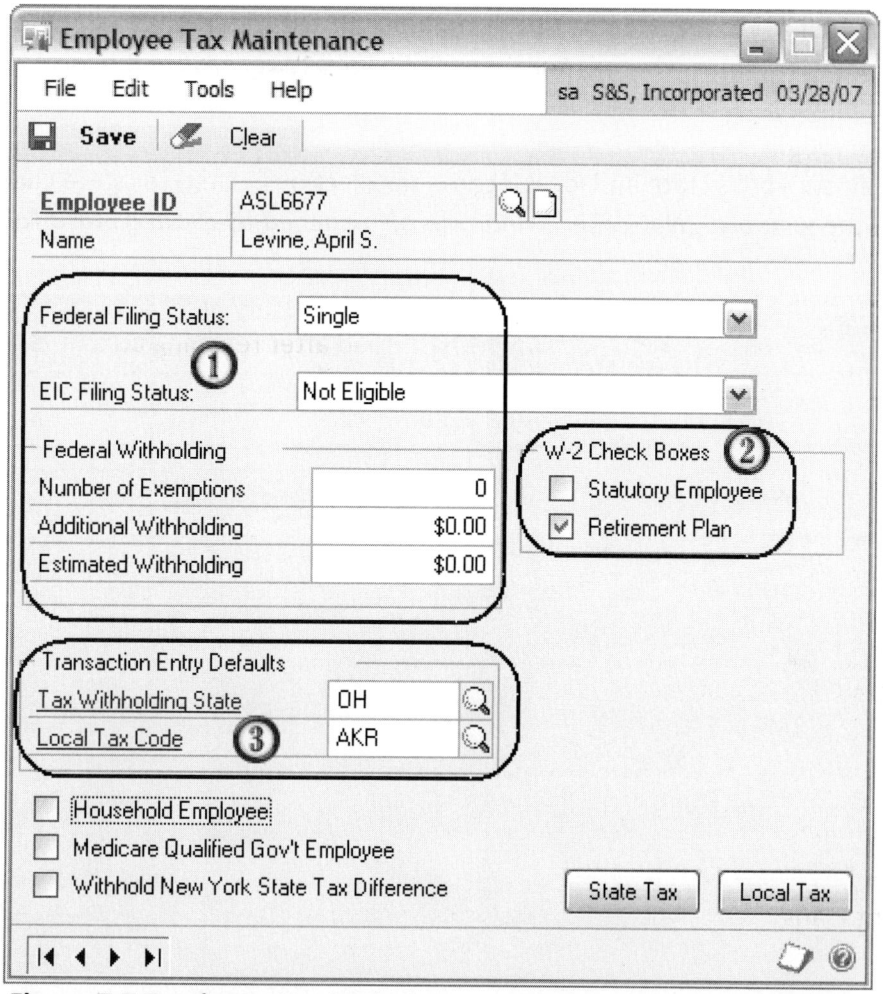

Figure 7:7 Employee Tax Maintenance Window for Federal Taxes

1. **Federal Withholding Elections**: April claims a **Filing Status** of Single with zero in **Number of Exemptions**. These elections determine the amount of federal payroll tax

withheld from each paycheck.[28] April makes these elections by completing IRS Form W-4 and submitting the form to the payroll office.[29]

2. **W-2 Check Boxes**: Additional information to print on W-2 Forms. **Retirement Plan** is checked so April's contributions to the company sponsored 401k retirement plan print on her W-2.

3. **Transaction Entry Defaults**: These are the default tax withholding codes for state and local (i.e., city) income taxes. **Tax Withholding State** links to records in the state withholding tax table whereas **Local Tax Code** links to records in the local income tax withholding table.

We will now review April's state and local income tax elections. First, for state click **State Tax** at the bottom of the window. *(Note: This window is also opened by clicking State Tax under the Cards section of the home page.)*

[28] For more information on federal tax elections and withholding calculations, refer to Circular E available on the IRS website at www.irs.gov.

[29] An example of Form W-4 is available on the IRS website at www.irs.gov. In addition, employees should complete a Department of Immigrations Form I-9, verifying authorization to work in the United States.

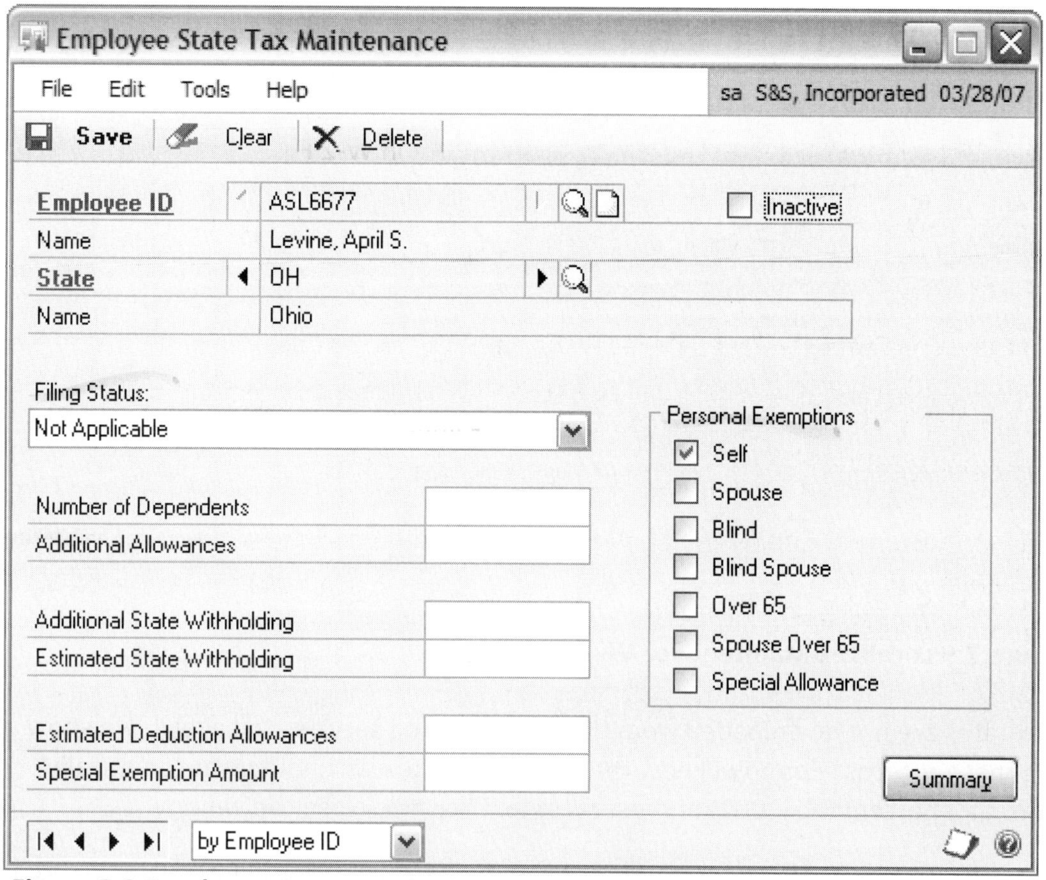

Figure 7:8 Employee State Tax Maintenance Window

Ohio does not use a Filing Status (i.e., Not Applicable) for determining tax withholdings but does allow Personal Exemptions. (Note: These tax rates are also downloaded from GP's online payroll tax service.) April claims only herself and makes this election by completing an Ohio withholding tax form similar to the federal W-4. Click **X** to close this window.

Return to the Employee Tax Maintenance window and click **Local Tax**. *(Note: You can also open this window by clicking Local Tax on the home page.)* Look up AKR for the **Local Code**. (See Figure 7:9.)

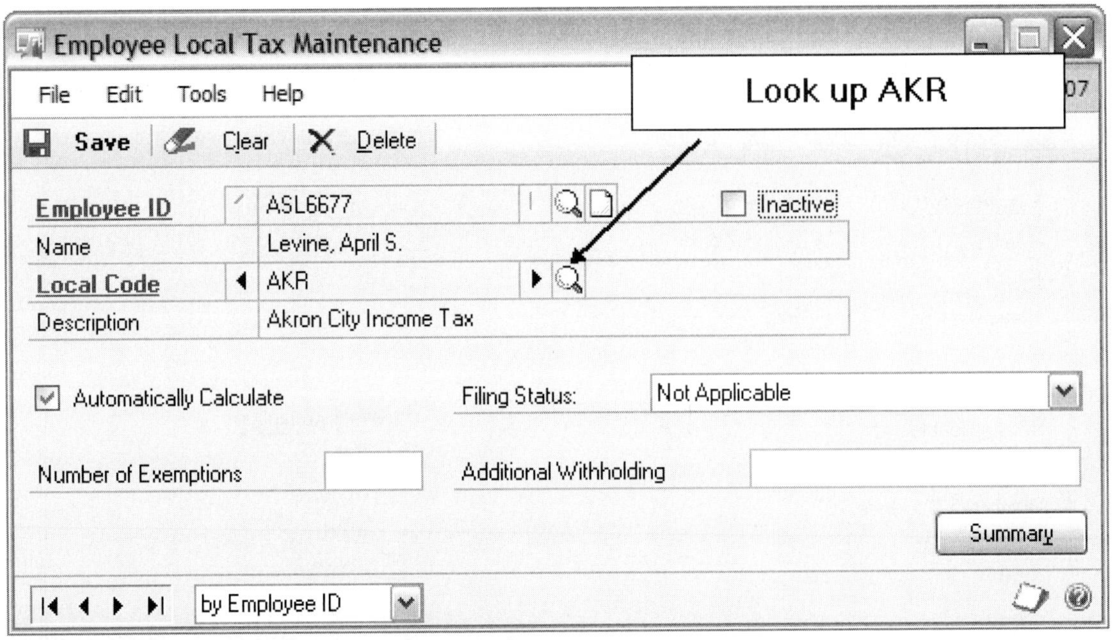

Figure 7:9 Local Tax Maintenance Window

Local tax rates are not downloaded from the online payroll service. In Level 2, we show you creating these records. For now, know that April's local tax withholding automatically calculates at 2 percent (i.e., .002) of gross income. Click <u>**X**</u> to close the window.

You have finished reviewing April's tax withholdings so next we review her pay codes, benefits, and deductions. Windows for these items are opened individually by using the Pay Code, Deduction, and Benefit commands under Cards. We will look at these windows in Level Two where we discuss setting up payroll items. For now, click **Quick Assignment,** look up April, and review the next illustration.

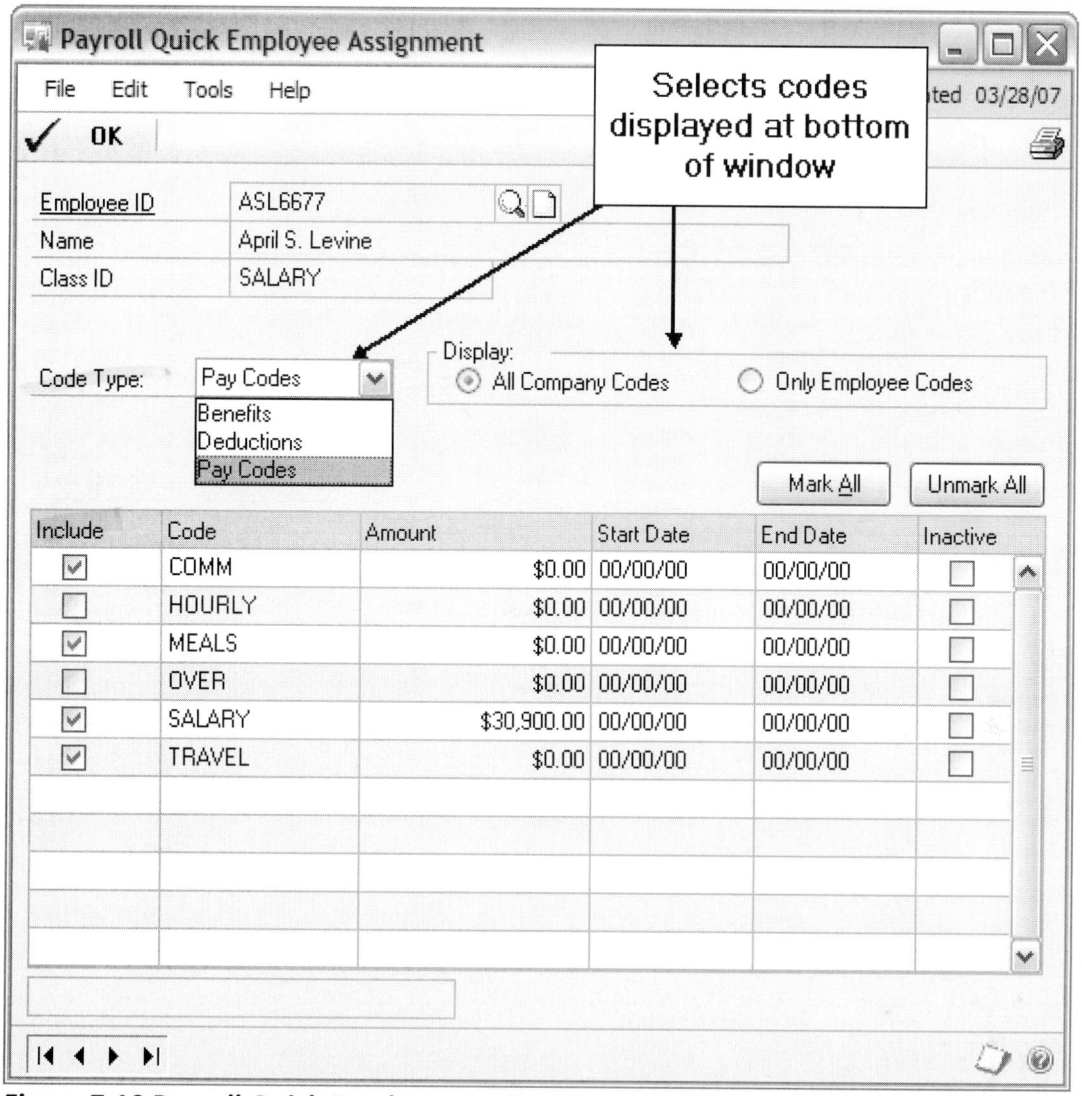

Figure 7:10 Payroll Quick Employee Assignment Window Showing Pay Codes

This window will show pay codes, benefits, and deductions linked to April's employee card. Code Type and Display options determine the code type displaying at the bottom.

We are currently viewing Pay Codes for All Company Codes. If an Include box is marked then that pay code is linked to April's card. We see that April is paid commissions (i.e., COMM), expenses (i.e., MEALS and TRAVEL), and an annual SALARY of $30,900.00.

Click the dropdown list and change Code Type to **Deductions**. (See Figure 7:11.)

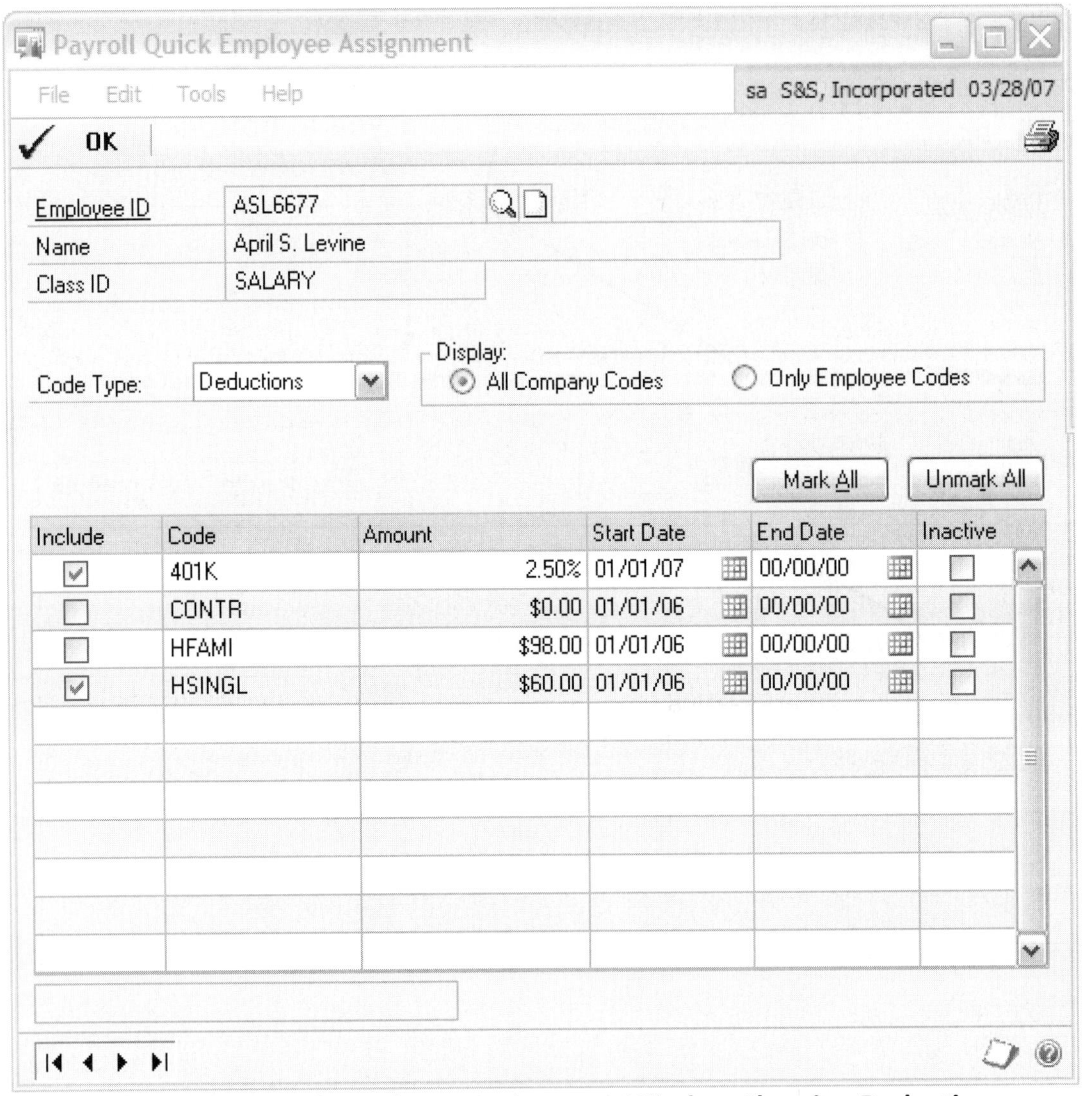

Figure 7:11 Payroll Quick Employee Assignment Window Showing Deductions

The window reveals that April participates in the 401k retirement plan and contributes 2 and one-half percent of her gross pay (i.e., 2.5 %) each pay period. Furthermore, she has taken out health insurance for a single person (i.e., HSINGL) so $60.00 will be deducted from each paycheck.

Change Code Type to **Benefits**, which shows that S&S matches April's 401k contributions fifty percent (i.e., 50.00%). (Not illustrated.) If April contributes $100.00 to her 401k then S&S matches $50.00. Click **OK** to exit the window.

You now understand why we stated earlier that the Payroll Series requires more work on master records (i.e., cards) than any of the Series previously covered. Remember that all changes to employee pay codes, tax withholdings, benefits, and deductions must be entered prior to processing payroll, which is the focus of our next topic.

Use the Quick Assignment window to view Thomas Winchester's pay codes, benefits, and deductions and answer the following questions.

1. How is he paid and what is his pay rate?
2. What voluntary deductions does he make?
3. Does the company provide and benefits? If so, what are those benefits?

E7:1 Practice Identifying Pay Codes, Benefits, and Deductions

PAYROLL SERIES TRANSACTIONS

You are now ready to begin processing payroll. Remember that S&S pays hourly employees biweekly and salaried employees semimonthly. The next pay date for both types of employees just happens to coincide on March 30. Moreover, this date signals the end of the month so employees will also receive sales commission and expense checks.

Complete the next exercise that illustrates paying employees.

Process Hourly Payroll

1. Change the **system date** to March 30, 2007. We begin with processing paychecks for hourly paid employees.
2. Each pay period we need to review transactions in the HOURLY batch and make any adjustments. Click **Batches** and look up **HOURLY**. (See Figure 7:12.) Notice that this is a recurring batch that never expires.

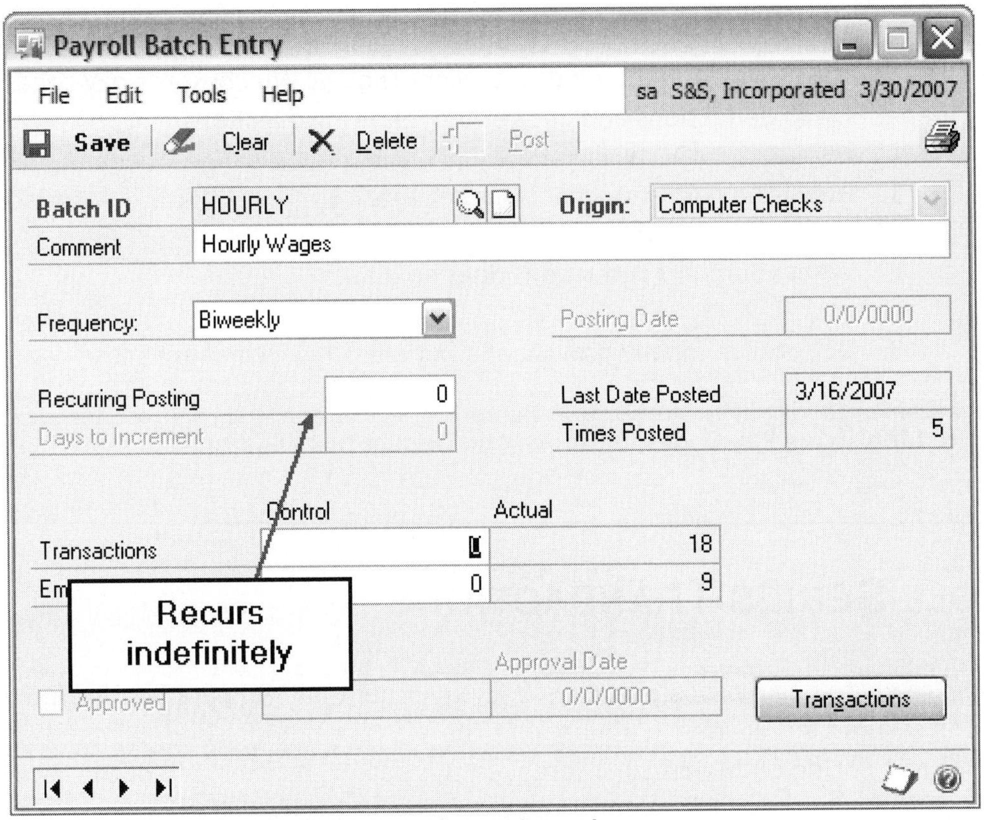

Figure 7:12 Payroll Batch for Hourly-Paid Employees

3. Click **Transactions,** select **Payroll Transaction Entry** (Figure 7:13), and click **Go to.**

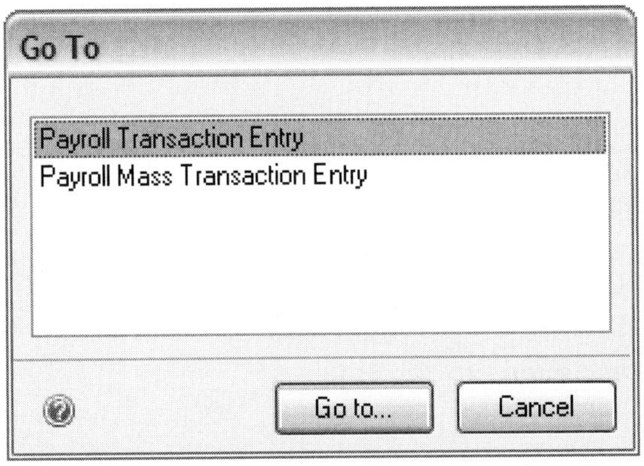

Figure 7:13 Go To Payroll Transaction Entry Window

4. These are paychecks for the current pay period. (See Figure 7:14.) Enter the pay date range, days worked, and weeks worked as illustrated. In the next step we make any adjustments to hours worked in this pay period.

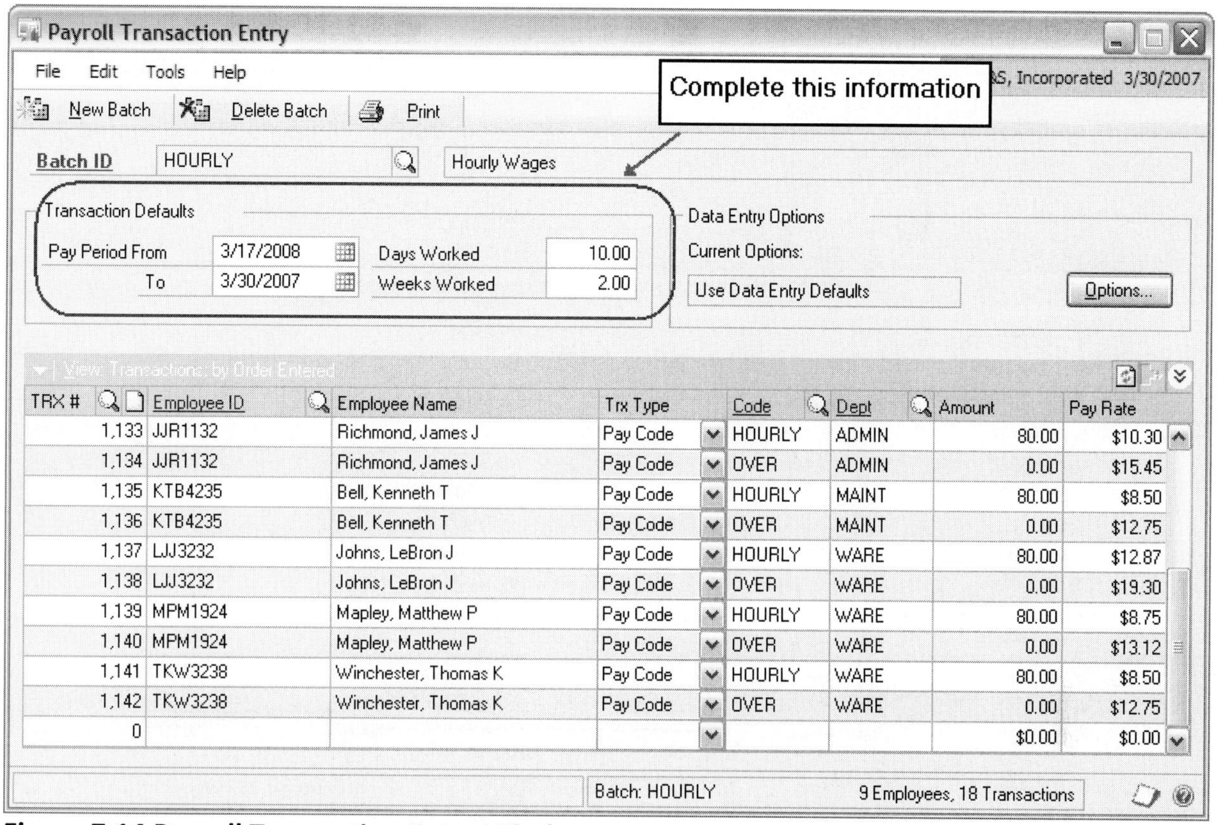

Figure 7:14 Payroll Transaction Entry Window

5. Now focus on **Code** and **Amount** columns because we need to enter hours worked this pay period. Currently all employees have a transaction record for regular hours (i.e., HOURLY code) and overtime hours. Furthermore, each HOURLY record indicates that the employee worked 80.00 during the pay period.

6. **Adam Whitfield** worked less than eighty hours so scroll to the top to locate his HOURLY record. Place your cursor in the **Amount** column and type **78.00**. **James Richmond** worked overtime this pay period so place your cursor in the **Amount** column for his **OVER** record and type **2.00**. These changes are illustrated next.

Amount = worked hours for HOURLY + OVER

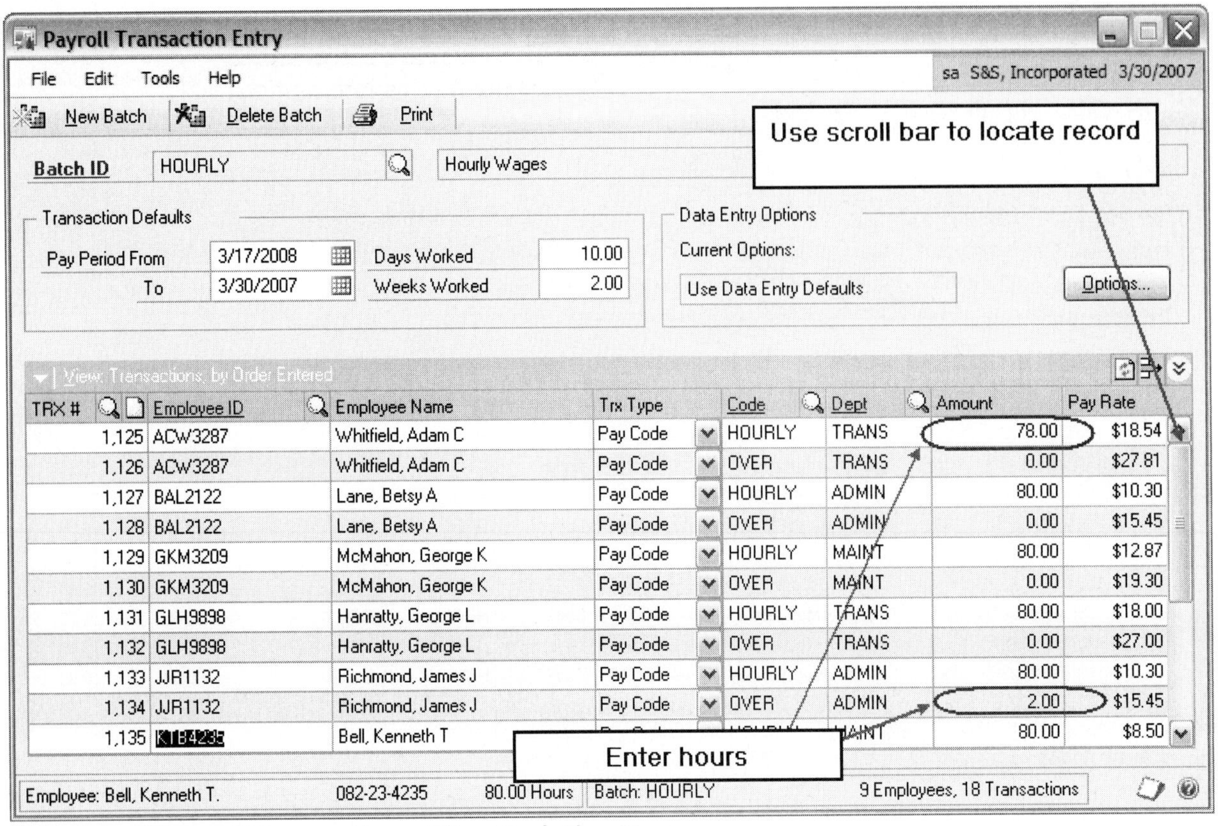

Figure 7:15 Payroll Transactions After Updating Hours

(Note: If needed, you can add employees to new rows at the bottom by looking up the Employee ID, selecting the Code and entering an Amount. You can also remove employees by placing your cursor in the Employee ID and selecting Edit>>Delete Row from the window menu.)

7. You are finished entering hours and ready to print a Payroll Transaction Edit List to document transaction entry. Click **Print** and send output to the screen. Scroll to the last page to locate total hours. (See Figure 7:16.) This report is compared to each employee's time card hours and to total hours. S&S requires a payroll supervisor to initial approval on this report before paychecks are printed. Close the report.

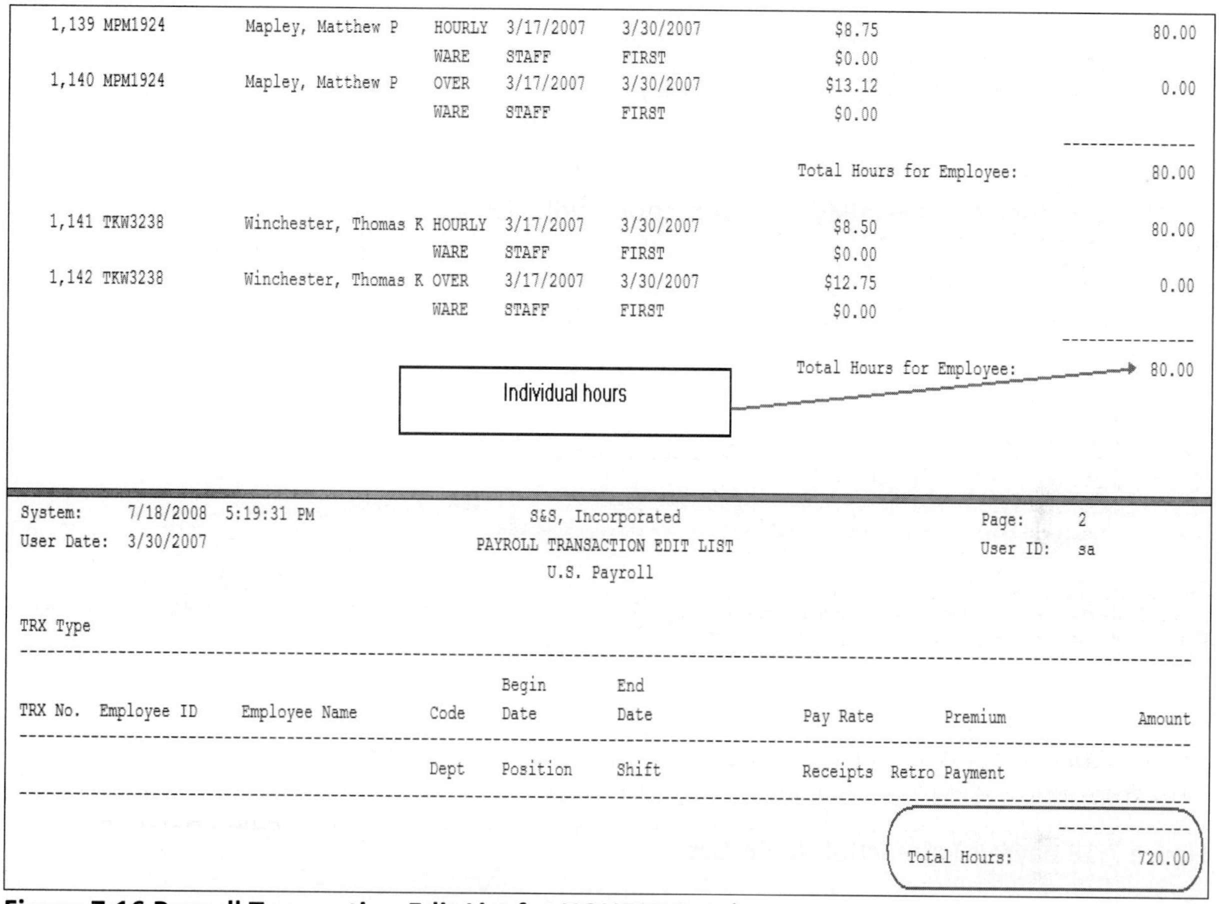

1,139	MPM1924	Mapley, Matthew P	HOURLY	3/17/2007	3/30/2007	$8.75	80.00
			WARE	STAFF	FIRST	$0.00	
1,140	MPM1924	Mapley, Matthew P	OVER	3/17/2007	3/30/2007	$13.12	0.00
			WARE	STAFF	FIRST	$0.00	
						Total Hours for Employee:	80.00
1,141	TKW3238	Winchester, Thomas K	HOURLY	3/17/2007	3/30/2007	$8.50	80.00
			WARE	STAFF	FIRST	$0.00	
1,142	TKW3238	Winchester, Thomas K	OVER	3/17/2007	3/30/2007	$12.75	0.00
			WARE	STAFF	FIRST	$0.00	
						Total Hours for Employee:	80.00

Individual hours

System: 7/18/2008 5:19:31 PM S&S, Incorporated Page: 2
User Date: 3/30/2007 PAYROLL TRANSACTION EDIT LIST User ID: sa
U.S. Payroll

TRX Type

TRX No.	Employee ID	Employee Name	Code	Begin Date	End Date	Pay Rate	Premium	Amount
			Dept	Position	Shift	Receipts	Retro Payment	

Total Hours: 720.00

Figure 7:16 Payroll Transaction Edit List for HOURLY Batch

8. Close the Payroll Transaction Entry window by clicking **X** and GP prompts to print the Payroll Transaction Audit List (Figure 7:17), click **Print** and send output to the screen. The report appears is illustrated in Figure 7:18 and shows changes made to transactions in the batch.

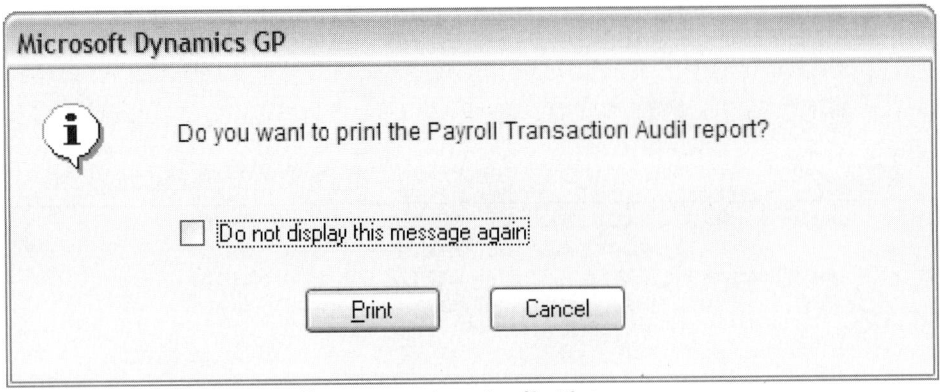

Figure 7:17 Print Payroll Transaction Audit List

S&S, Incorporated
PAYROLL TRANSACTION AUDIT LIST
U.S. Payroll

User Date: 03/30/07

Page: 1
User ID: sa

A = New Transaction O = Modified Old Transaction N = Modified New Transaction
D = Deleted Transaction Z = Zero Units
X = No transaction created; vacation/sick time exceeded. Need password.
M = No transaction created; employee maximum for pay code per period exceeded.

TRX	Employee ID	Batch Number	Code	Date Begin	Date End	Pay Rate	Premium	Amount
O	ACW3287	HOURLY	HOURLY	03/17/07	03/30/07	$18.54		80.00
N	ACW3287	HOURLY	HOURLY	03/17/07	03/30/07	$18.54		78.00
O	JJR1132	HOURLY	OVER	03/17/07	03/30/07	$15.45		0.00
N	JJR1132	HOURLY	OVER	03/17/07	03/30/07	$15.45		2.00

Total Transactions: 4

Figure 7:18 Payroll Transaction Audit List

Close the report and the Payroll Batch Entry window. We next process sales commission and expense reimbursement data for the end of the month.

Process Sales Commission and Expenses

First, we need to gather sales commission information. Remember from Chapter 5 that S&S pays commissions after the customer remits payment. This not only mitigates the threat of paying commissions on uncollectible sales but also reduces motivation for salespeople to make risky sales to earn commissions.

Payroll uses a monthly sales commission report prepared by the sales department to pay commissions so we will prepare this report in the next steps. *(Note: All cash receipts must be posted prior to preparing the report.)*

1. First, verify that your **system date** reads 3/30/2007 and then activate the Sales home page. Click **Transfer Commissions** under Routines to open the window illustrated next. Notice that commissions were last transferred on 2/28/2007.

Figure 7:19 Transfer Sales Commissions Window

2. Verify that the **Detail** option is marked and click **Process.** *(Note: The Detail option means that the report will print in detail.)* Processing commissions actually posts an entry debiting sales commission expense and crediting sales commission liability so a posting journal prints to the screen. (See Figure 7:20.) This report is sent to payroll and used to enter commission data. *(Note: Your numbers may differ from those illustrated if you have practiced more entries in the database.)* The Commission Amount column shows payments due each salesperson. A copy of this report is also sent to the accounting department for posting an adjusting journal entry that is illustrated in Chapter 8.

S&S, Incorporated Page: 1

User Date: 03/30/07 TRANSFERRED COMMISSIONS POSTING JOURNAL DETAIL User ID: sa

Receivables Management

Ranges:

Audit Trail Code: RMCOM00000018 Batch ID: sa

Posting Date: 03/30/07 Batch Origin: Transfer Commission

Sorted: by Salesperson ID

Batch ID: sa Audit Trail Code: RMCOM00000018 Batch Frequency: Single Use Number of TRX: 9

Transfer Date: 03/30/07 Batch Comment: Receivables Transfer Commissions

Salesperson ID Name (Last, First Middle) Territory ID Employee ID

Type	Document Number	Customer ID	Sales Amount	% Sale	Comm %	Commission Amount	Non-Commissioned Amount
ASL6677	Levine, April S		MID		ASL6677		
SLS	INV000000194	GGHREGGS001	$189,000.00	100.00%	0.30%	$567.00	$0.00
SLS	INV000000206	BETTERBU001	$97,600.00	100.00%	0.30%	$292.80	$0.00
		Sub totals:	$286,600.00			$859.80	$0.00
CJW7872	Warner, Curtis J		EAST		CJW7872		
SLS	INV000000172	CANDYBOW001	$118,914.00	100.00%	0.30%	$356.74	$0.00
SLS	INV000000196	LAUFMANS001	$147,551.00	100.00%	0.30%	$442.65	$0.00
SLS	INV000000216	LAUFMANS001	$28,327.50	100.00%	0.30%	$84.99	$0.00
RTN	RTN00000000000001	CANDYBOW001	($8,659.20)	100.00%	0.30%	($25.98)	$0.00
		Sub totals:	$286,133.30			$858.40	$0.00
MTM3987	Murphy, Mary T		WEST		MTM3987		
SLS	INV000000195	DISCOUNTE001	$108,240.00	100.00%	0.30%	$324.72	$0.00
SLS	INV000000197	SIXTHAV001	$77,935.00	100.00%	0.30%	$233.81	$0.00
SLS	INV000000213	TUBESTUR001	$94,500.00	100.00%	0.30%	$283.50	$0.00
		Sub totals:	$280,675.00			$842.03	$0.00
		Totals:	$853,408.30			$2,560.23	$0.00

Figure 7:20 Transferred Commissions Posting Journal in Detail

3. We are now ready to enter commission transactions. Close the report and reactivate the HR & Payroll home page. Click **Batches** and open the **COMMISSIONS** batch.

4. Click **Transactions** and go to **Payroll Transaction Entry**.

5. This time Amount store commission dollars instead of hours worked. The amounts currently in the window are commissions paid last month so we need to enter March commissions as reported under the Commission Amount on the Transferred Commission Posting Journal Detail report.

6. Enter the amounts illustrated next.

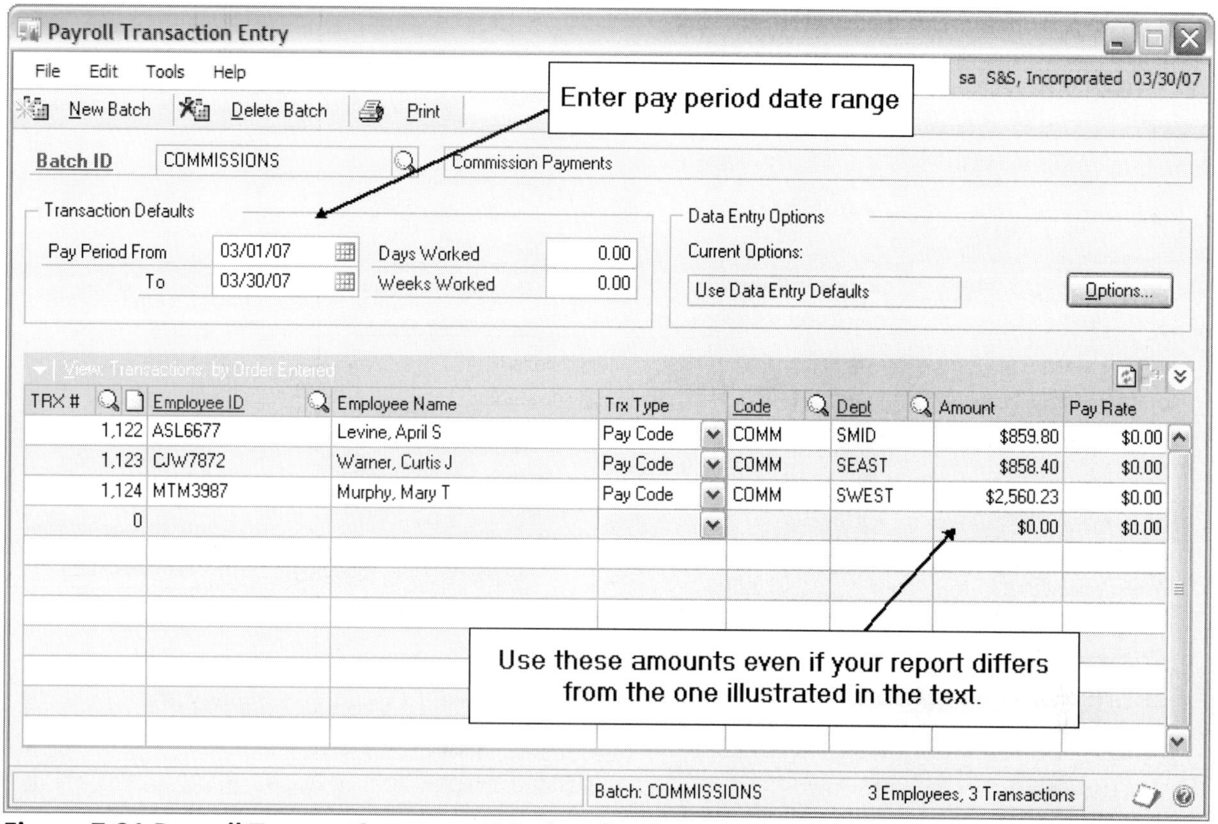

Figure 7:21 Payroll Transaction Entry Window for Commissions

7. Next, place your cursor in the Employee ID field for the first row and click the row expansion button. Enter a date range as illustrated next and click **Next** to enter this range on remaining records.

must do for each record

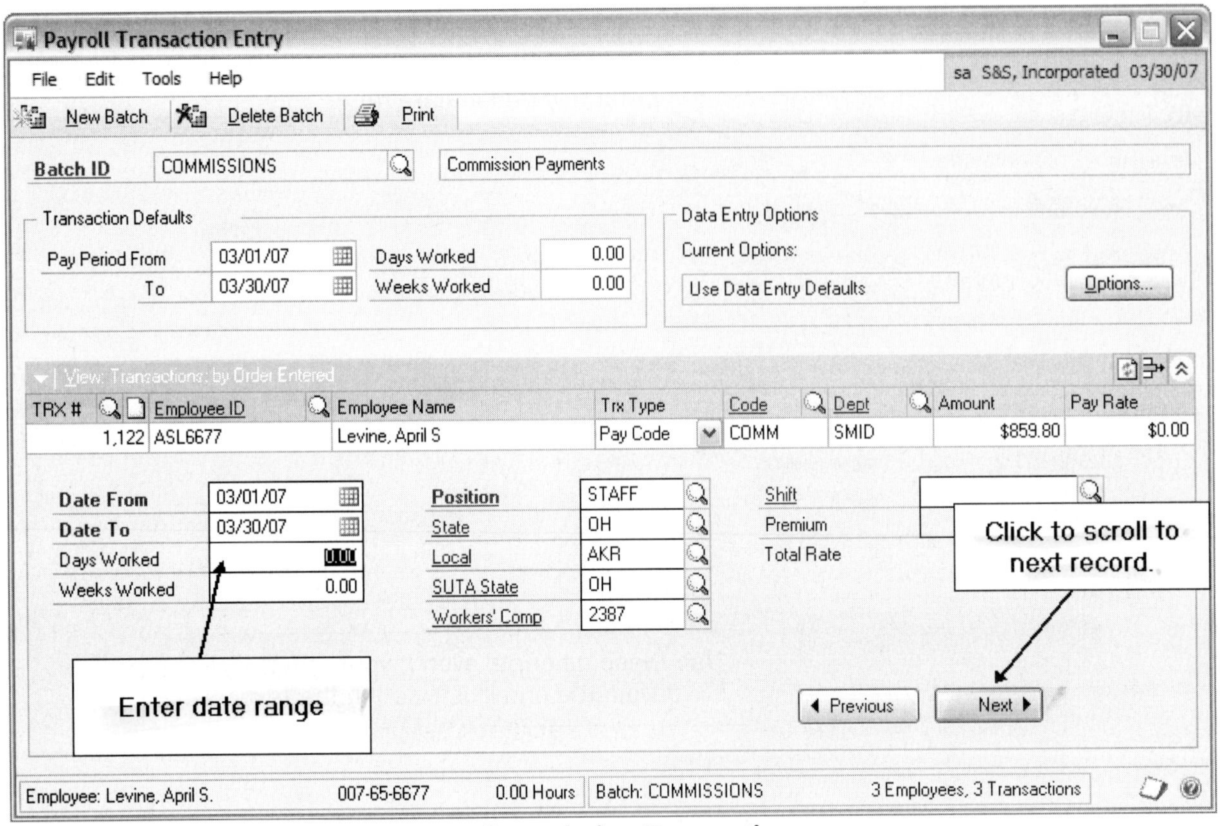

Figure 7:22 Entering Date Ranges on Commission Transactions

8. You will not print an edit list this time but in the real world this report is printed to verify data entry. Click **X** to close the window and print the Payroll Transaction Audit report to the screen.

9. We now enter employee expense reimbursements. Return to the Payroll Batch Entry window and open the **EXPENSES** batch.

10. Click **Transactions** and go to **Payroll Transaction Entry**. Notice that expenses are broken down by meals and travel so that amounts post to correct general ledger accounts. Enter the amounts illustrated next.

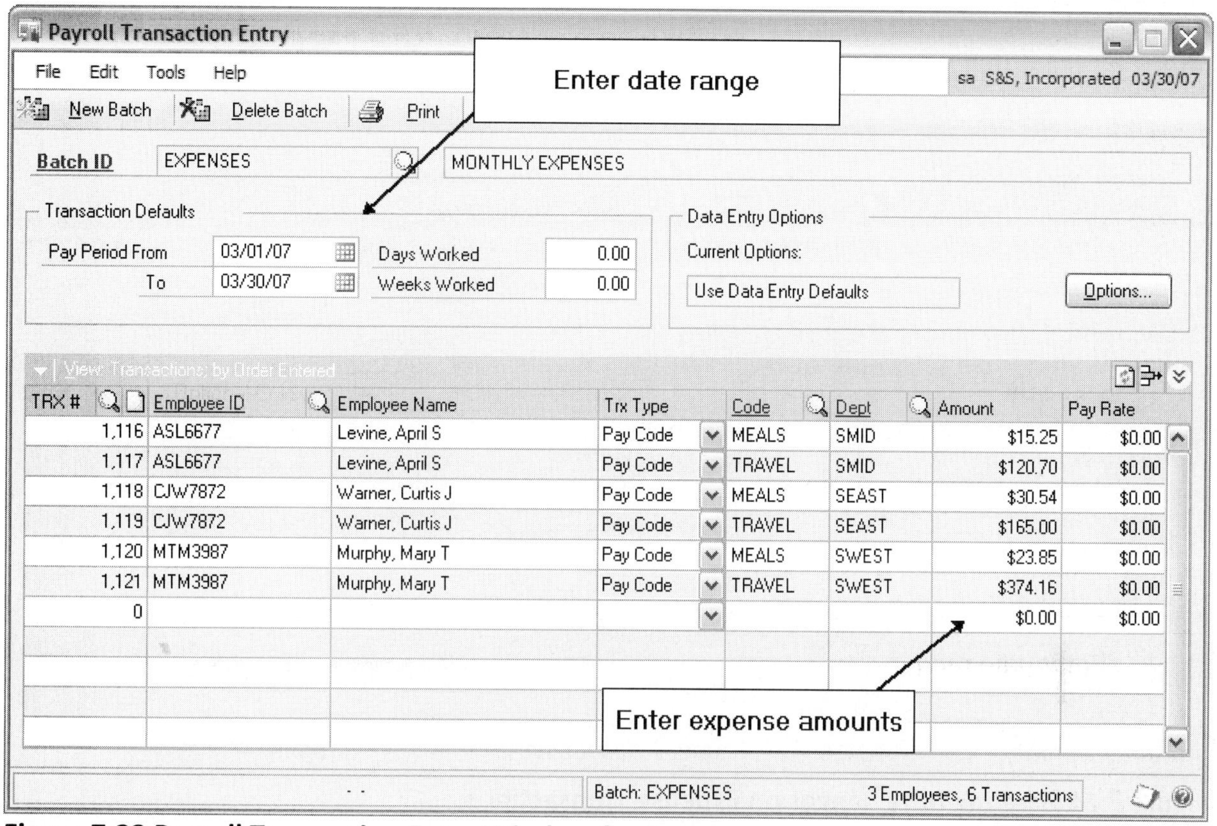

Figure 7:23 Payroll Transaction Entry Window for Expenses

11. Place your cursor in the Employee ID for the first record and expand row details. Enter the date range illustrated next on each transaction record.

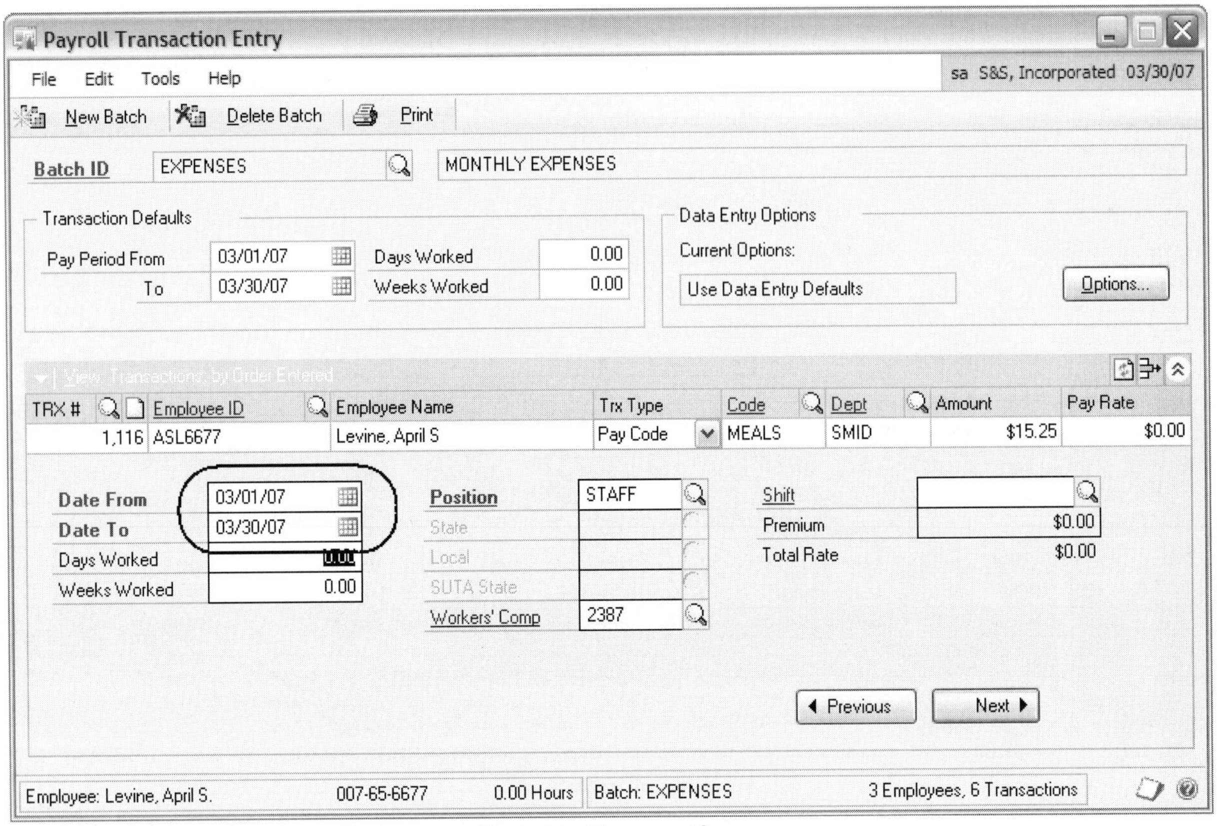

Figure 7:24 Entering Date Ranges on Expense Transactions

12. Click **Print** and send output to the screen to verify your data entry. (See Figure 7:25.)

```
                                              S&S, Incorporated                                    Page:      1
User Date:  03/30/07                      PAYROLL TRANSACTION EDIT LIST                            User ID:   sa
                                                 U.S. Payroll
Ranges:
    Batch:      EXPENSES            MONTHLY EXPENSES
Trx Total Actual:      6        Trx Total Control:      0
Employee Total Actual: 3        Employee Total Control: 0
Approved: No        Approved By:                Approval Date: 00/00/00


TRX Type
-----------------------------------------------------------------------------------------------------------------
                                                   Begin       End
TRX No.  Employee ID     Employee Name     Code    Date        Date             Pay Rate       Premium          Amount
-----------------------------------------------------------------------------------------------------------------
                                           Dept    Position    Shift            Receipts  Retro Payment
-----------------------------------------------------------------------------------------------------------------

TRX Type
-----------------------------------------------------------------------------------------------------------------
                                                   Begin       End
TRX No.  Employee ID     Employee Name     Code    Date        Date             Pay Rate       Premium          Amount
-----------------------------------------------------------------------------------------------------------------
                                           Dept    Position    Shift            Receipts  Retro Payment
-----------------------------------------------------------------------------------------------------------------
Pay Code
   1,116 ASL6677         Levine, April S   MEALS   03/01/07    03/30/07                                         $15.25
                                           SMID    STAFF                          $0.00
   1,117 ASL6677         Levine, April S   TRAVEL  03/01/07    03/30/07                                        $120.70
                                           SMID    STAFF                          $0.00

TRX Type
-----------------------------------------------------------------------------------------------------------------
                                                   Begin       End
TRX No.  Employee ID     Employee Name     Code    Date        Date             Pay Rate       Premium          Amount
-----------------------------------------------------------------------------------------------------------------
                                           Dept    Position    Shift            Receipts  Retro Payment
-----------------------------------------------------------------------------------------------------------------
Pay Code
   1,116 ASL6677         Levine, April S   MEALS   03/01/07    03/30/07                                         $15.25
                                           SMID    STAFF                          $0.00
   1,117 ASL6677         Levine, April S   TRAVEL  03/01/07    03/30/07                                        $120.70
                                           SMID    STAFF                          $0.00
                                                                                                        ---------------
                                                                              Total Hours for Employee:           0.00
-----------------------------------------------------------------------------------------------------------------
                                                   Begin       End
TRX No.  Employee ID     Employee Name     Code    Date        Date             Pay Rate       Premium          Amount
-----------------------------------------------------------------------------------------------------------------
                                           Dept    Position    Shift            Receipts  Retro Payment
-----------------------------------------------------------------------------------------------------------------
Pay Code
   1,116 ASL6677         Levine, April S   MEALS   03/01/07    03/30/07                                         $15.25
                                           SMID    STAFF                          $0.00
   1,117 ASL6677         Levine, April S   TRAVEL  03/01/07    03/30/07                                        $120.70
                                           SMID    STAFF                          $0.00
                                                                                                        ---------------
                                                                              Total Hours for Employee:           0.00

   1,118 CJW7872         Warner, Curtis J  MEALS   03/01/07    03/30/07                                         $30.54
                                           SEAST   STAFF                          $0.00
   1,119 CJW7872         Warner, Curtis J  TRAVEL  03/01/07    03/30/07                                        $165.00
                                           SEAST   STAFF                          $0.00
                                                                                                        ---------------
                                                                              Total Hours for Employee:           0.00

   1,120 MTM3987         Murphy, Mary T    MEALS   03/01/07    03/30/07                                         $23.85
                                           SWEST   STAFF                          $0.00
   1,121 MTM3987         Murphy, Mary T    TRAVEL  03/01/07    03/30/07                                        $374.16
                                           SWEST   STAFF                          $0.00
                                                                                                        ---------------
                                                                              Total Hours for Employee:           0.00
                                                                                                        ---------------
                                                                                   Total Hours                    0.00
```

Figure 7:25 Payroll Transaction Edit List for Expenses

13. Close the report and the transaction window. Close the Payroll Batch Entry window.

You are almost finished entering payroll data. In the next exercise this task is completed by entering pay data for salaried employees.

Process Salaried Payroll

Because salaried employees are paid the same wage each pay period regardless of hours worked, we do not need to create transaction records. You will discover in a later exercise that GP can generate salary transactions while creating paychecks.

Creating Paychecks

You create paychecks by first building a batch and then calculating net pay. Practice this process by completing the next steps.

1. Click **Build Checks** and type **HOURLY** as Default ID. Press tab and click **Add** to create the batch. Enter the following description and click **Save**. Close the window.

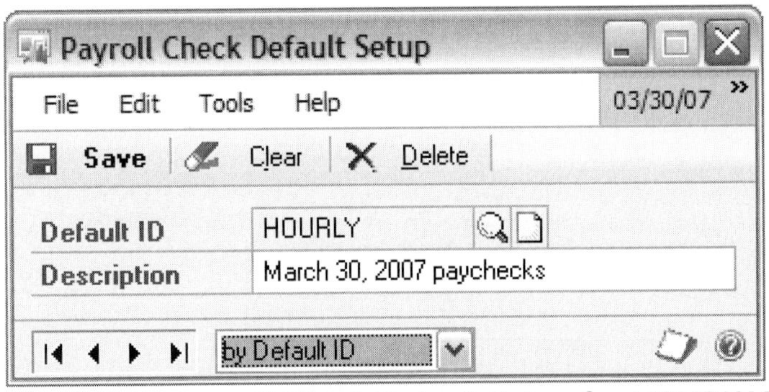

Figure 7:26 Payroll Check Default Setup for HOURLY Batch

2. Enter the following criteria to build paychecks for hourly paid employees. *(Note: In a later exercise you will create commission, expense, and salaried employee paychecks.)*

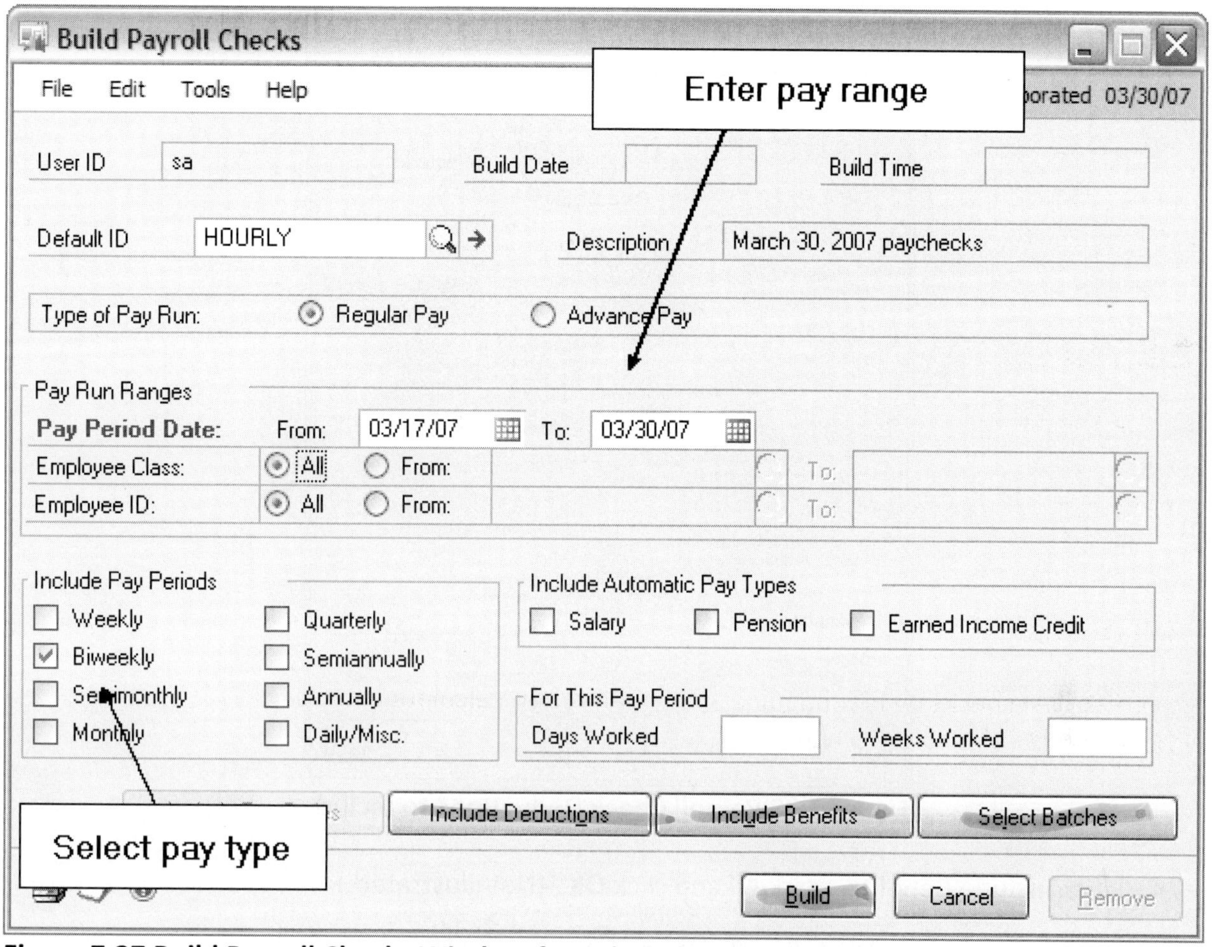

Figure 7:27 Build Payroll Checks Window for Salaried Employees

3. Next, instruct GP to include all deductions and benefits when calculating net pay. Click **Include Deductions** and mark **All**. (See Figure 7:28.) Click **OK**.

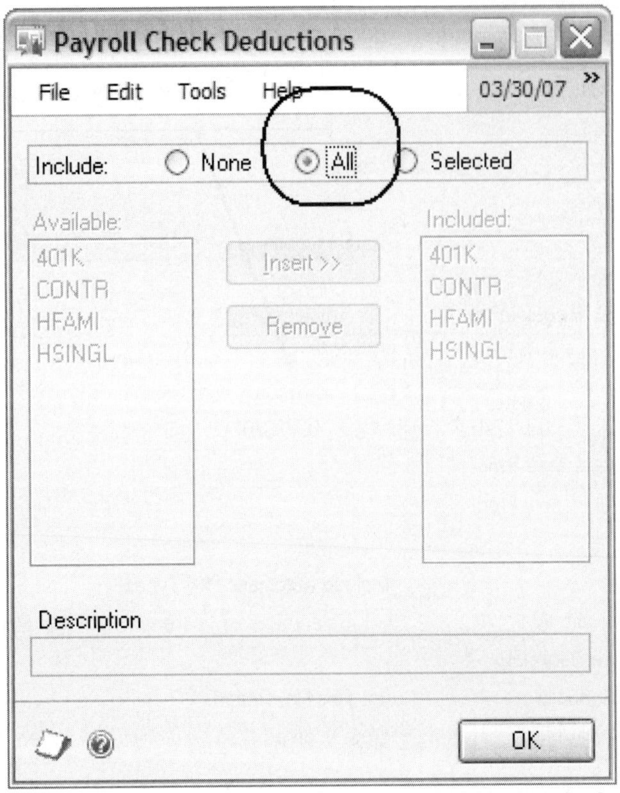

Figure 7:28 Payroll Check Deductions to Include

4. Click **Include Benefits,** mark **All** and click **OK**. (Not illustrated.)

5. You will now add transactions stored in the HOURLY batch. Click **Select Batches** and mark the batch illustrated next. Click **OK**.

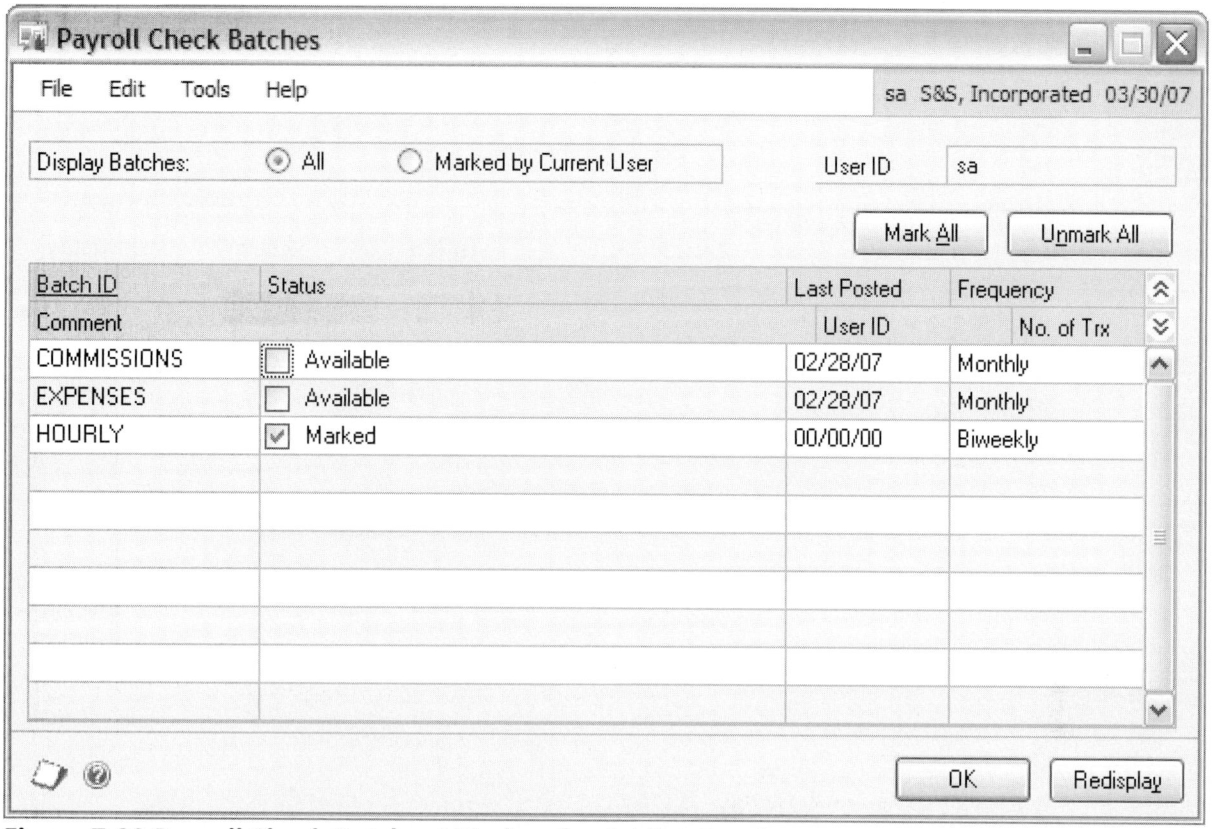

Figure 7:29 Payroll Check Batches Window for Adding Batches

6. You are now ready to build these paychecks. Click **Build** and click **Save** when prompted. Give the system time to build the paycheck transactions. When finished, print the check file report to the screen and confirm your results. (See Figure 7:30.)

```
                                        S&S, Incorporated                              Page:   1
User Date: 03/30/07                     CHECK FILE REPORT                              User ID: sa
                                          U.S. Payroll

Employee ID     Name
------------------------------------------------------------------------------------------------------------
            Code     Description            Dept     Position   Shift          Pay Rate         Premium      Amount/Units
------------------------------------------------------------------------------------------------------------
               State     Local                  W/Comp   SUTA       Weeks    Days              Receipts        Batch ID
------------------------------------------------------------------------------------------------------------
ACW3287         Whitfield, Adam C
  Pay:      HOURLY   Hourly                 TRANS    TRUCK      FIRST          $18.54           $0.00           78.00
               OH        AKR                  9763      OH          2.00     10.00                              HOURLY
  Benefit:  401K     401-K Employer Match                                      50.00% of Deduction
  Deduction: 401K    401-K Employee Contributions                               2.00% of Gross Wages
            CONTR    Contributions                                     $10.00
            HFAMI    Family Health Insurance                          $107.00
  State Tax: OH      Ohio
  Local Tax: AKR     Akron City Income Tax

BAL2122         Lane, Betsy A
  Pay:      HOURLY   Hourly                 ADMIN    APCLER     FIRST          $10.30           $0.00           80.00
               OH        AKR                  2387      OH          2.00     10.00                              HOURLY
  Benefit:  401K     401-K Employer Match                                      50.00% of Deduction
  Deduction: 401K    401-K Employee Contributions                               2.00% of Gross Wages
            HFAMI    Family Health Insurance                          $107.00
  State Tax: OH      Ohio

GKM3209         McMahon, George K
               OH        AKR                  2387      OH          2.00     10.00                              HOURLY
  Benefit:  401K     401-K Employer Match                                      50.00% of Deduction
  Deduction: 401K    401-K Employee Contributions                               2.00% of Gross Wages
            HFAMI    Family Health Insurance                          $107.00
  State Tax: OH      Ohio
  Local Tax: AKR     Akron City Income Tax

GLH9898         Hanratty, George L
  Pay:      HOURLY   Hourly                 TRANS    TRUCK      FIRST          $18.00           $0.00           80.00
               OH        AKR                  9763      OH          2.00     10.00                              HOURLY
  Benefit:  401K     401-K Employer Match                                      50.00% of Deduction
  Deduction: 401K    401-K Employee Contributions                               2.00% of Gross Wages
            HSINGL   Single Health Insurance                           $60.00
  State Tax: OH      Ohio
  Local Tax: AKR     Akron City Income Tax
```

JJR1132	Richmond, James J									
Pay:	HOURLY	Hourly	ADMIN	ARCLER	FIRST		$10.30	$0.00		80.00
	OH	AKR	2387	OH	2.00	10.00			HOURLY	
	OVER	Overtime	ADMIN	ARCLER	FIRST		$15.45	$0.00		2.00
	OH	AKR	2387	OH	0.00	0.00			HOURLY	
Benefit:	401K	401-K Employer Match					50.00% of Deduction			
Deduction:	401K	401-K Employee Contributions					2.00% of Gross Wages			
	HSINGL	Single Health Insurance					$60.00			
State Tax:	OH	Ohio								
Local Tax:	AKR	Akron City Income Tax								
KTB4235	Bell, Kenneth T									
Pay:	HOURLY	Hourly	MAINT	STAFF	FIRST		$8.50	$0.00		80.00
	OH	AKR	8765	OH	2.00	10.00			HOURLY	
Deduction:	HSINGL	Single Health Insurance					$60.00			
State Tax:	OH	Ohio								
Local Tax:	AKR	Akron City Income Tax								
LJJ3232	Johns, LeBron J									
Pay:	HOURLY	Hourly	WARE	SUPR	FIRST		$12.87	$0.00		80.00
	OH	AKR	8765	OH	2.00	10.00			HOURLY	
Benefit:	401K	401-K Employer Match					50.00% of Deduction			
Deduction:	401K	401-K Employee Contributions					2.00% of Gross Wages			
	HSINGL	Single Health Insurance					$60.00			
State Tax:	OH	Ohio								
Local Tax:	AKR	Akron City Income Tax								
MPM1924	Mapley, Matthew P									
Pay:	HOURLY	Hourly	WARE	STAFF	FIRST		$8.75	$0.00		80.00
	OH	AKR	8765	OH	2.00	10.00			HOURLY	
Deduction:	HSINGL	Single Health Insurance					$60.00			
State Tax:	OH	Ohio								
Local Tax:	AKR	Akron City Income Tax								
TKW3238	Winchester, Thomas K									
Pay:	HOURLY	Hourly	WARE	STAFF	FIRST		$8.50	$0.00		80.00
	OH	AKR	8765	OH	2.00	10.00			HOURLY	
Benefit:	401K	401-K Employer Match					50.00% of Deduction			
Deduction:	401K	401-K Employee Contributions					2.00% of Gross Wages			
	HFAMI	Family Health Insurance					$107.00			
State Tax:	OH	Ohio								
Local Tax:	AKR	Akron City Income Tax								
Total Employees:	9									

Figure 7:30 Payroll Check File Report

7. You are now ready to calculate net pay for these paychecks. Click **Calculate Checks** (Figure 7:31) and click **OK**. GP is now deducting tax withholdings and deductions from gross pay to compute net pay. The software is also calculating company benefits. Be patient because the process takes a few minutes.

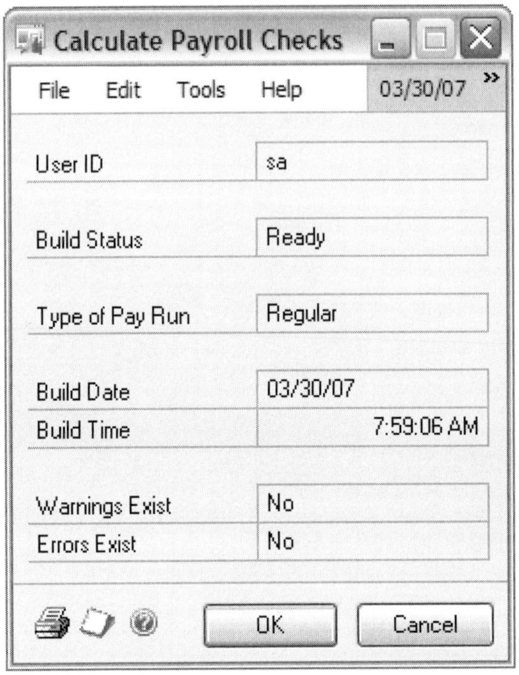

Figure 7:31 Calculate Payroll Checks for Hourly Employees

8. Print the Precheck Report to the screen and review. (See Figure 7:32, showing last page of report.) You should receive no error or warning messages. Errors are most commonly encountered because of missing general ledger account in payroll setup. *(Note: Payroll setup is discussed in Level Two.)* Warnings usually occur because the pay period date range is incorrect. Checks with errors must be corrected before they can be printed. Checks with warnings can be printed; however, paycheck integrity is compromised.

User Date: 03/30/07 S&S, Incorporated Page: 5
CALCULATE CHECKS REPORT User ID: sa
U.S. Payroll

Employee ID Name Soc Sec Number

Code	Pay Type	Dept	Position	Pay Rate	Amount/Units	Gross Wages	Ben/Ded/Tax	Net Wages
				FICA Medicare Withheld			$9.86	
				Federal Withheld			$13.49	
				OH State Withheld			$8.83	
				AKR Local Withheld			$13.60	
							$87.94	
								$471.46

REPORT TOTALS:

WAGES	$8,684.22
BENEFITS	$62.75
DEDUCTIONS	$858.49
TAXES	$1,743.66
NET WAGES	$6,082.07

Figure 7:32 Calculate Checks Report

S&S's internal control policies require the cashier department to print paychecks so you have completed the tasks of preparing paychecks in the payroll department. Payroll department confidentially sends the Calculate Checks Report to the cashier to trigger the final step of paying employees.

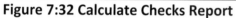

Now that you understand the interaction of codes with employee cards, we need you to make a couple of changes.

1. Thomas Winchester has submitted a new W-4, changing his federal withholding status to single with 2 dependants.

2. April Levine is changing her 401k contribution to 3%. *(Note: Click Yes when prompted to continue after clicking save.)*

Make these changes and name the department you work for.

E7:2 Practice with Employee Cards

Cashier Department Activities

Cashiers use the Calculate Checks Report printed in the previous topic to print paychecks. You will print paychecks for hourly employees in the next steps.

1. Click **Print Checks** and refer to the next illustration. Notice that checks will print from the Payroll Account. Companies often use a separate checking account for payroll to protect confidentiality of payroll data.

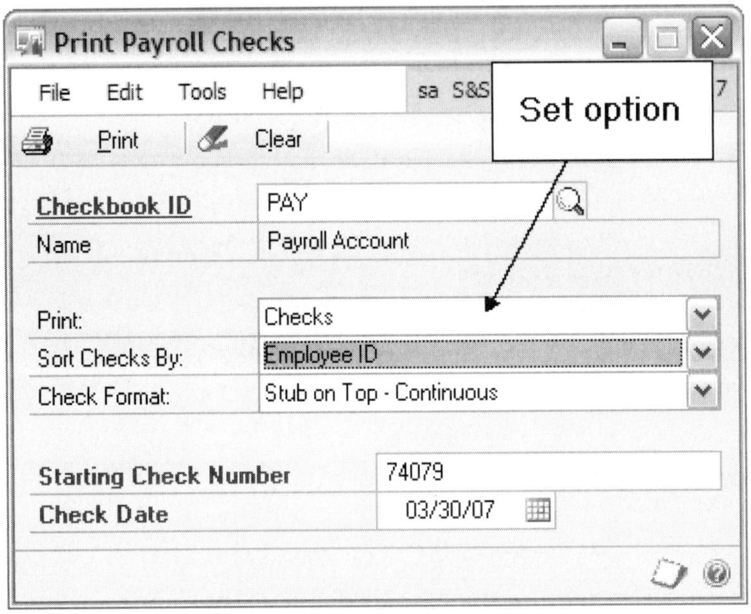

Figure 7:33 Print Payroll Checks Window

2. Change the **Print** option to **Checks** because this option defaults to Alignment, which sends an alignment pattern to the printer.

3. You should always verify the starting check number. In the real world this number is compared to the first check number on check stock placed in the printer. Any discrepancy may indicate missing checks.

4. Click **Print** and send output to the screen. Review the first check and the information that follows. Checks are normally printed to preprinted check stock so that data is labeled.

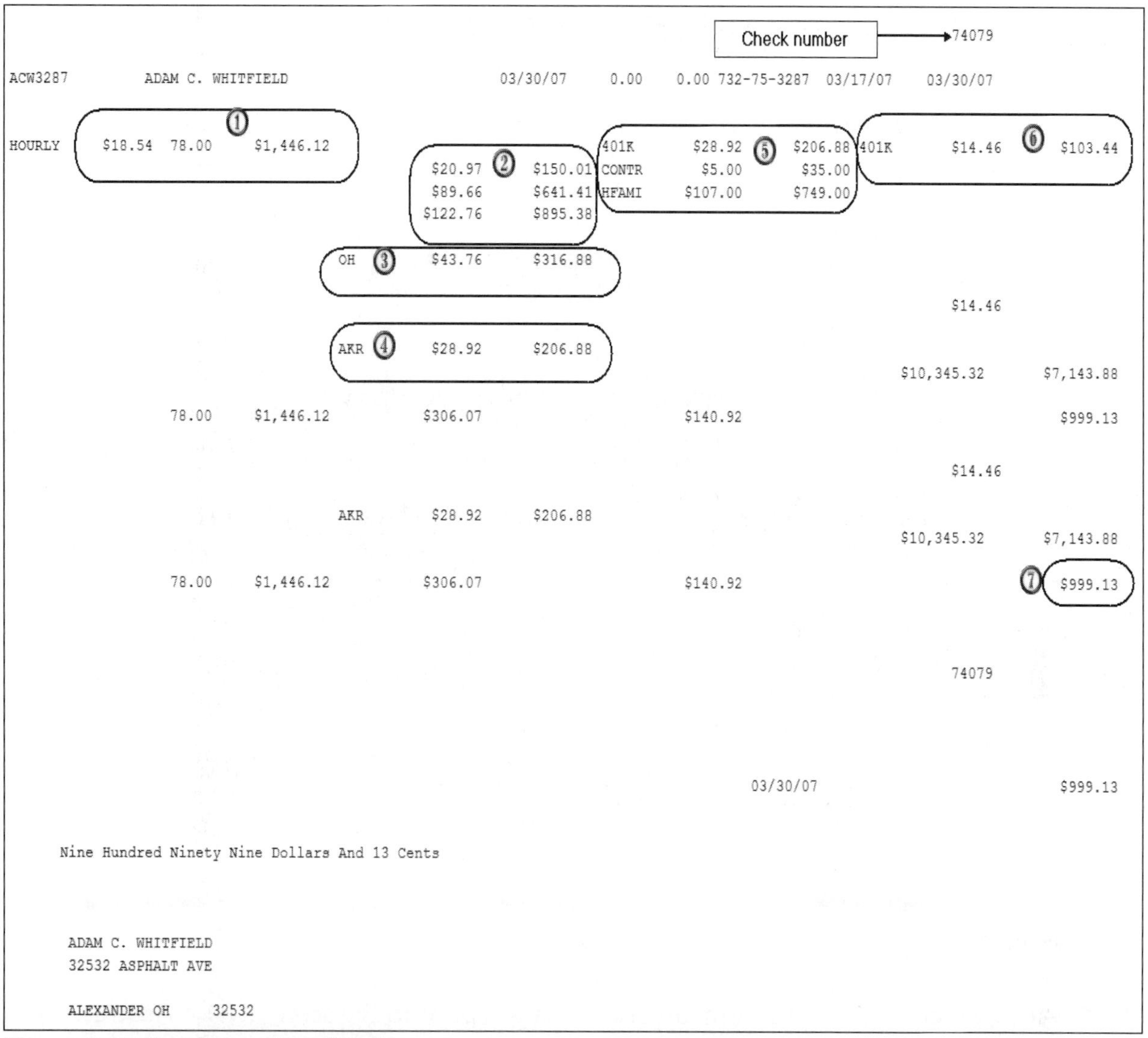

Figure 7:34 Employee Paycheck

Sections	Description
1	Gross pay this pay date along with hourly rate and hours worked
2	Federal tax withholdings this pay and year-to-date
3	State tax withholdings this pay and year-to-date
4	Local tax withholdings this pay and year-to-date
5	Voluntary deductions this pay and year-to-date
6	Company benefits this pay and year-to-day
7	Net pay

5. Close the report and activate the Post Payroll Checks window. This window contains options to void and reprint checks if a printer jam occurred. (See Figure 7:35.)

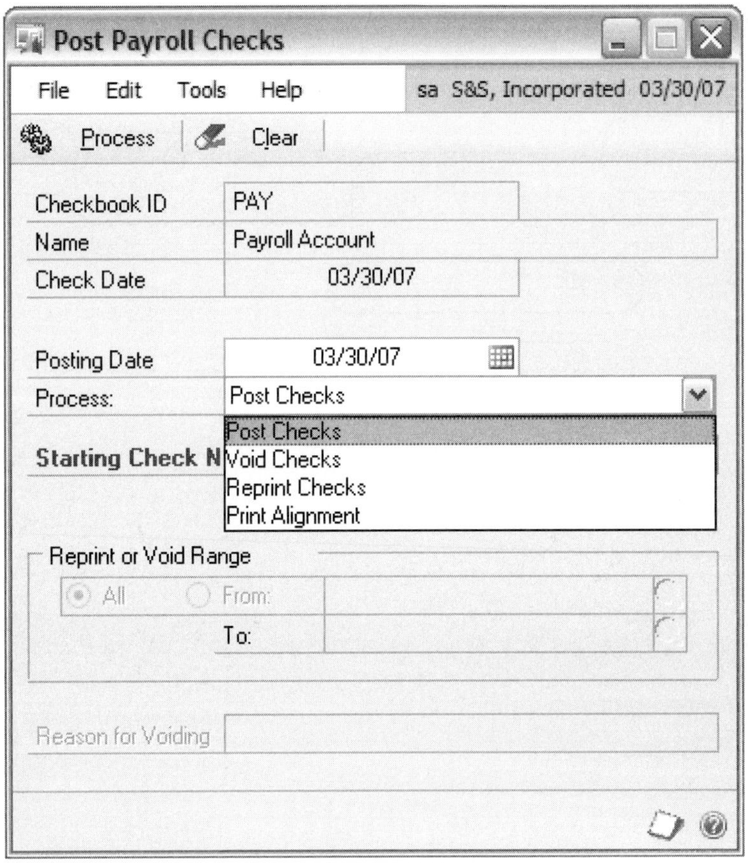

Figure 7:35 Post Payroll Checks Window

6. Keep the **Post Checks** options and click **Process** to post these checks to the general ledger.

The Check Register report and several other reports will print to the screen. (Not illustrated.) Close each report and wait for the General Posting Journal report to appear, signifying completion.

A copy of the check register is filed in the cashier department and a copy is sent to the payroll department as confirmation of check printing. Furthermore, the cashier will use the register to transfer cash from the regular checking account to the payroll checking account to cover paychecks.

Payroll processing does not end at printing paychecks because we still need to print checks remitting payroll liabilities. The next topic illustrates this task.

Using Build Checks, prepare paychecks and commission and expense checks for salaried employees. Modify the existing SALARYPAY default ID and:

1. Enter the pay date range of 3/16/2007 to 3/31/2007;
2. Verify checks are for semimonthly paid employees receiving a salary;
3. Confirm that all deductions and benefits will be calculated into the net pay; and
4. Add the COMMISSIONS and EXPENSES batches.

Print the Check File Report after building the checks.

Remember to calculate these checks after building and print your Calculate Checks report.

Print paychecks to the screen and complete the exercise by posting entries to the general ledger. Print only the General Posting Journal after posting.

E7:3 Practice Building Paychecks

PAYROLL REPORTING: PAY PERIOD AND MONTHLY REPORTS

The payroll department prepares an employee tax withholding and employer tax liability report for each pay period. Payroll also prepares employer benefit and employee voluntary deduction reports at the end of each month. Accounts payable uses these reports to post bills for payroll liabilities and the cashier department prints remits checks by the due date. A table listing due dates for S&S payroll liabilities follows.

Payroll Liability	Payment Due Dates
Employee federal income tax, Social Security, and Medicare withholdings and employer Social Security, and Medicare taxes	Three days after issuing payroll checks
Employee state and local income tax withholdings	Five days after month-end
Employer federal and state unemployment taxes	Five days after the end of a quarter
Employer state workers' compensation taxes	Fifteen days after June 30 and after December 31
Employee 401k deductions and employer matching contributions	Five days after month-end
Employee health insurance deductions	By the due date on the health insurance bill sent by the vendor

Table 7:6 Payroll Liability Due Dates

Failing to remit payroll liabilities by the due date threatens companies to penalty and interest charges imposed by taxing agencies as well as a potential loss of favorable tax treatment for retirement plans. In the payroll department, threats are mitigated by sending liability reports to the accounts payable department immediately after producing paychecks. In the accounts payable department, threats are mitigated by validating through data entry controls that liabilities are posted and also monitoring aging reports. In the cashier department, threats are mitigated by requiring a copy of the check register listing liability payments be sent to the payroll department.

We next illustrate preparing pay period and monthly reports.

1. Click **Period-End** and refer to Figure 7:36. Notice that you can select a Month or Period reporting option.

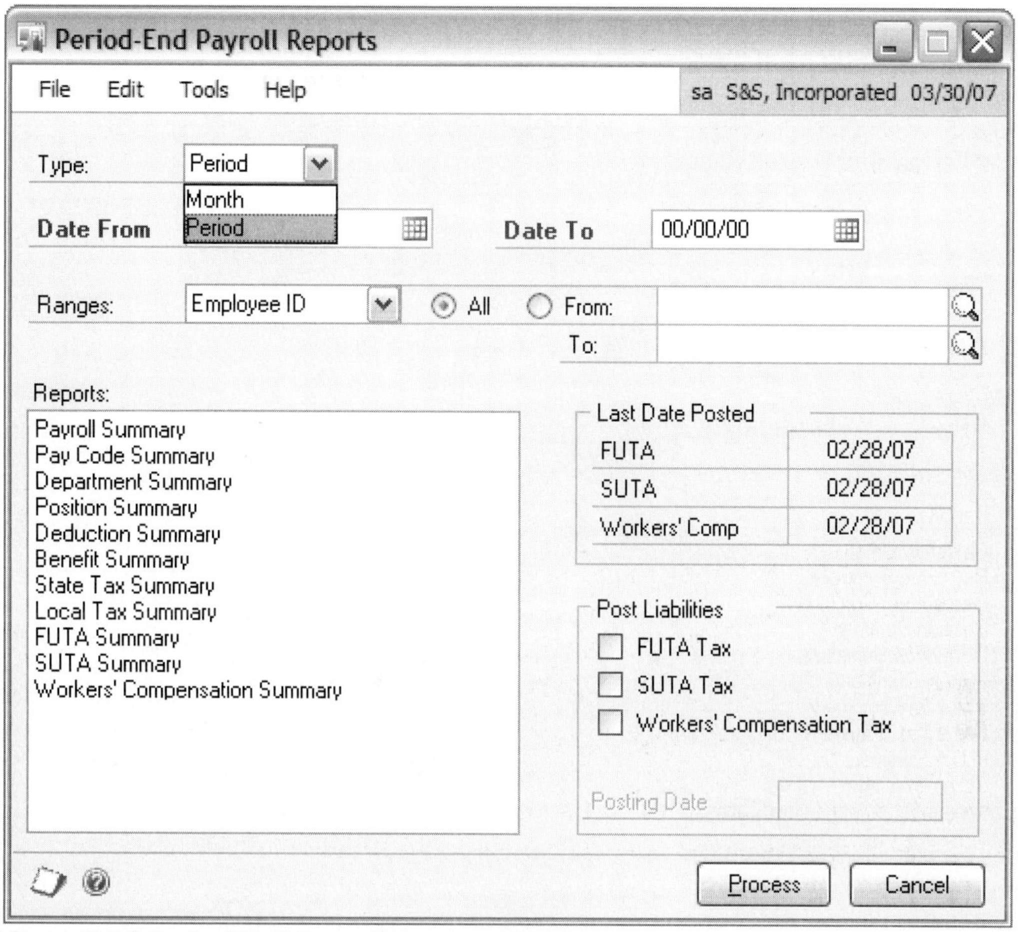

Figure 7:36 Period-End Payroll Reports Window

The next table describes reports printed from this window.

Report Name(s)	Purpose
Payroll Summary	Report employee federal tax, Social Security, and Medicare withholdings and employer Social Security and Medicare tax liabilities.
Pay Code Summary and Position Summary	Report gross wages by pay code or positions.
Deduction Summary	Report employee voluntary deductions.
Benefit Summary	Report employer benefits.
State Tax Summary and Local Tax Summary	Report employee state and local tax withholdings.
FUTA Summary, SUTA Summary, Workers' Compensation Summary	Report employer federal (FUTA) and state (SUTA) unemployment taxes and workers' compensation taxes

Table 7:7 Period-End Payroll Reports

2. Choose **Period** and enter a date range of March 16 to March 31, 2007. Click **Payroll Summary**. (See Figure 7:37.)

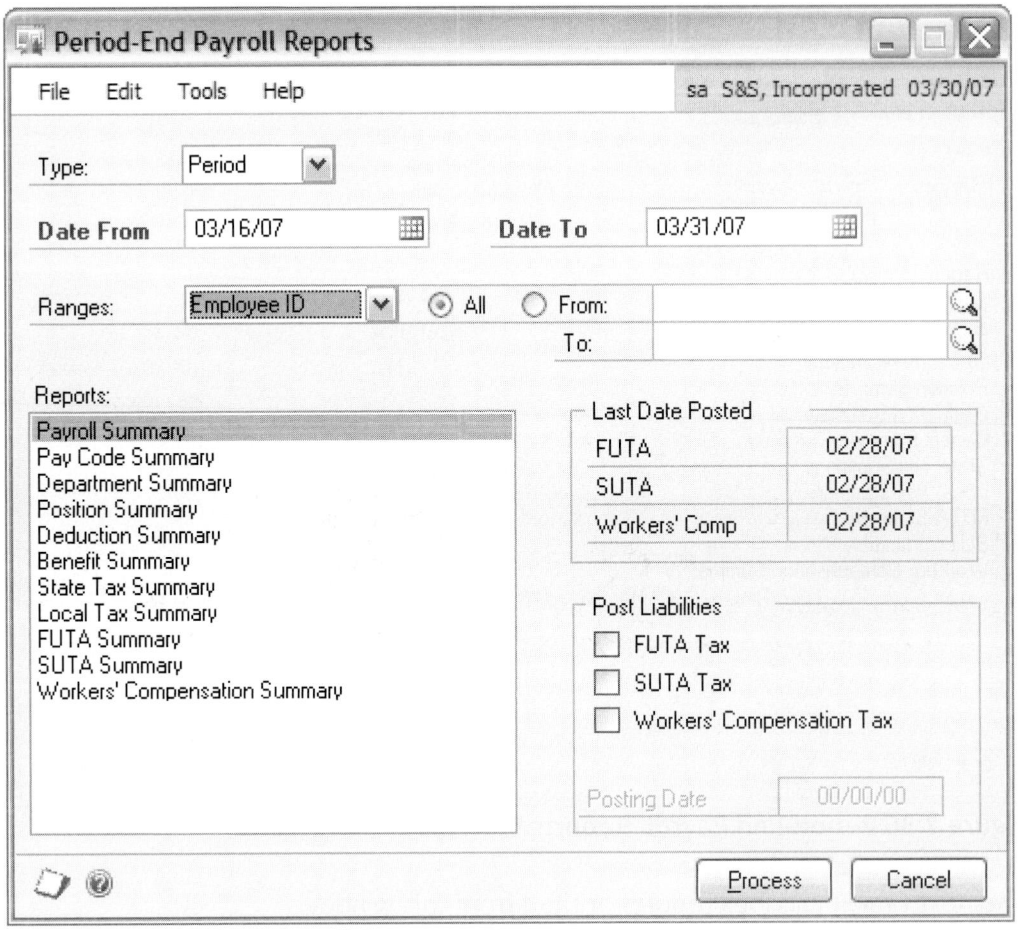

Figure 7:37 Printing Payroll Summary Report

3. Click **Process** and print the following report to the screen listing employee federal tax, Social Security, and Medicare withholdings and employer Social Security and Medicare tax liabilities. Remember that this report is printed each pay period because payment is due three days after the pay date. Close it.

S&S, Incorporated
PAYROLL SUMMARY
Payroll

User Date: 03/30/07
Page: 1
User ID: sa

Ranges:	From:	To:
Employee ID:	First	Last
Class ID:	First	Last
Department:	First	Last
Position:	First	Last

Date From: 03/16/07
Date To: 03/31/07

Description	Total
Gross Wages	$33,472.63
Federal Wages	$30,727.74
Advanced EIC Payments	$0.00
Federal Taxes Withheld	$3,284.79
FICA Soc Sec Wages	$33,472.63
FICA Soc Sec Withheld	$2,075.30
FICA Medicare Wages	$33,472.63
FICA Medicare Withheld	$485.33
Net Wages	$23,886.46
Charged Tips	$0.00
Reported Tips	$0.00
Federal Tax/Tips Withheld	$0.00
FICA Soc Sec Tips	$0.00
FICA Soc Sec Tax/Tips Withheld	$0.00
Uncollected FICA Soc Sec Tax	$0.00
FICA Medicare Tips	$0.00
FICA Medicare Tax/Tips Withheld	$0.00
Uncollected FICA Medicare Tax	$0.00
Charged Receipts	$0.00
Reported Receipts	$0.00
Allocated Tips	$0.00
Federal Tips	$0.00

Figure 7:38 Payroll Summary Report

4. Reopen the Period-End Payroll Reports window. This time we will illustrate printing the monthly report that lists employee state tax withholdings. Select **Month** as the type and choose **March** of **2007**. Click **State Tax Summary.** (See Figure 7:40.)

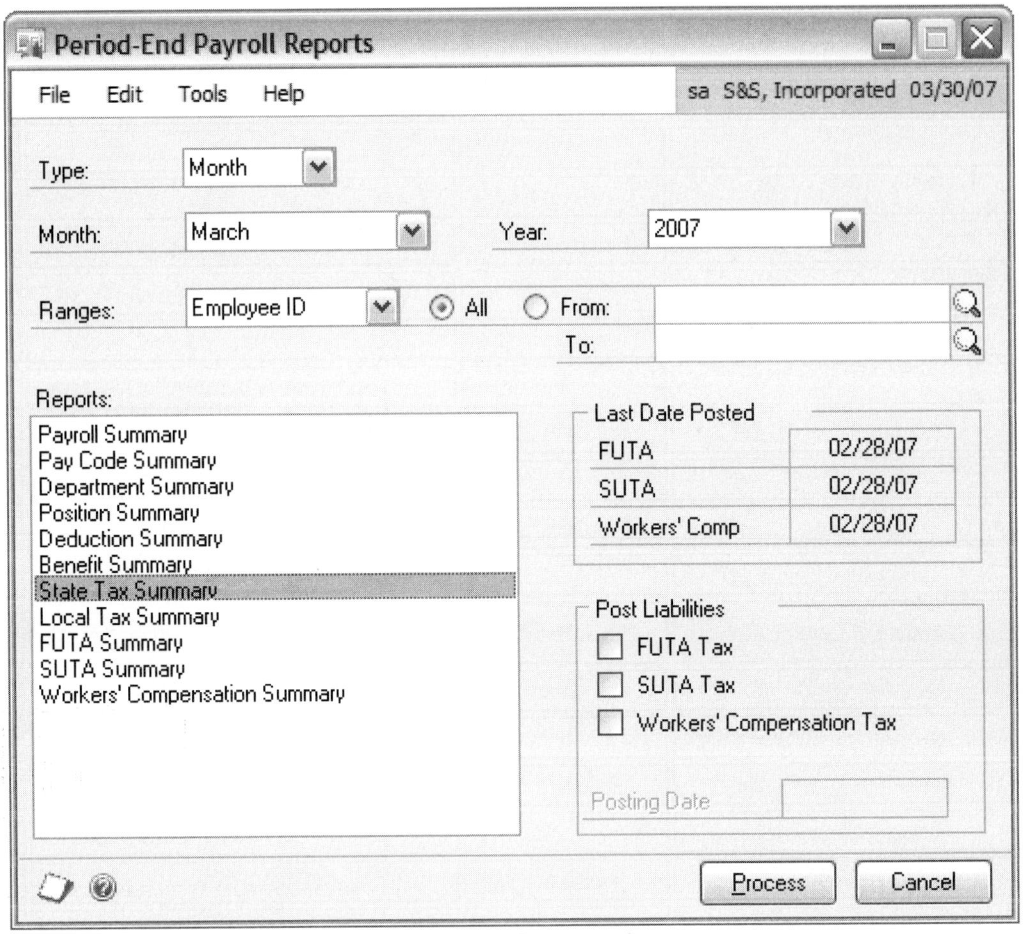

Figure 7:39 Printing State Tax Summary for March

5. Click **Process** and the report prints to the screen as follows. The report shows wages and tax withholdings for the month (i.e., MTD Wages, MTD Tax) along with quarterly and year-to-date wages and tax withholdings. Accounts payable uses the report to remit March withholdings to the taxing agency. Close the report.

User Date: 03/30/07

S&S, Incorporated
STATE TAX SUMMARY
Payroll

Page: 1
User ID: sa

Ranges:	From:	To:
Employee ID:	First	Last
Class ID:	First	Last
Department:	First	Last
Position:	First	Last

Date From: 03/01/07
Date To: 03/31/07

State Code	MTD Wages	MTD Tax	QTD Wages	QTD Tax	YTD Wages	YTD Tax
OH	$49,470.36	$1,624.21	$130,096.37	$4,340.49	$130,096.37	$4,340.49
State Code Totals:	$49,470.36	$1,624.21	$130,096.37	$4,340.49	$130,096.37	$4,340.49

March withholdings due to taxing agency

Figure 7:40 State Tax Summary Report

Accounts payable uses pay period and monthly reports to remit payments using the procedures illustrated in Chapter 6.

GP

1. Print the Deduction Summary report for March 2007. What information is can be obtained from this report?

2. Does the Payroll Summary report list all information accounts payable needs to remit employee tax withholdings? If not, name additional reports that are needed?

3. Print the Pay Code Summary report for March 16 to March 31. What additional information does this report provide that is not available from the Payroll Summary report covering the same time period?

E7:4 Practice Payroll Reporting

PAYROLL REPORTING: QUARTERLY REPORTS

March triggers the end of quarter so the payroll department must send a Form 941 to the IRS. In the next exercise we illustrate producing this report, which reconciles payments federal income, Social Security, and Medicare tax payments to liabilities for the quarter.

1. Click **Quarter-End**, choose the first quarter, and mark the reports illustrated next. (Note: Reports identified as Preparation can be used as working copy reports before printing actual reports.)

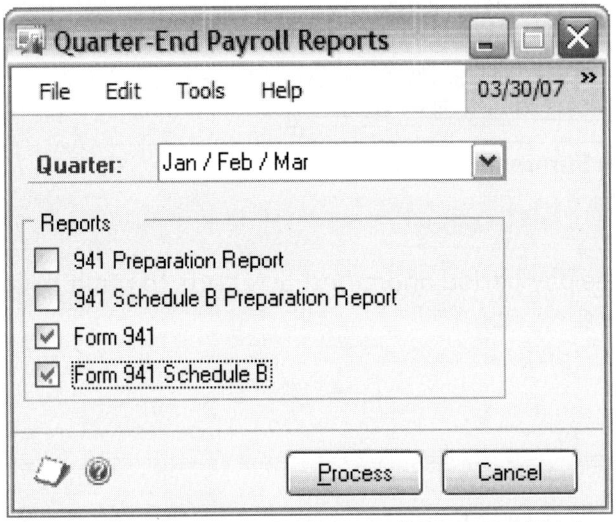

Figure 7:41 Quarter-End Payroll Report Window

2. Click **Process** and choose **Yes** to file Schedule B. Print reports to the screen. These reports are actually printed to IRS preprinted forms and, when printed, appear as illustrated next.

Form **941 for 2007: Employer's QUARTERLY Federal Tax Return** 950108

(Rev. January 2008) Department of the Treasury — Internal Revenue Service OMB No. 1545-0029

(EIN)
Employer identification number ☐☐ – ☐☐☐☐☐☐☐

Name *(not your trade name)* S&S Incorporated

Trade name *(if any)*

Address
Number Street Suite or room number

City State ZIP code

Report for this Quarter of 2008
(Check one.)

- ☑ 1: January, February, March
- ☐ 2: April, May, June
- ☐ 3: July, August, September
- ☐ 4: October, November, December

Read the separate instructions before you fill out this form. Please type or print within the boxes.

Part 1: Answer these questions for this quarter.

1 Number of employees who received wages, tips, or other compensation for the pay period including: *Mar. 12* (Quarter 1), *June 12* (Quarter 2), *Sept. 12* (Quarter 3), *Dec. 12* (Quarter 4)	1	15
2 Wages, tips, and other compensation	2	130,096 . 37
3 Total income tax withheld from wages, tips, and other compensation	3	14,244 . 07
4 If no wages, tips, and other compensation are subject to social security or Medicare tax		☐ Check and go to line 6.

5 Taxable social security and Medicare wages and tips:

	Column 1		Column 2
5a Taxable social security wages	141,840 . 54	× .124 =	17,588 . 23
5b Taxable social security tips	141,840 . 54	× .124 =	4,133 . 38
5c Taxable Medicare wages & tips	.	× .029 =	.

Difference is employee 401k deductions

5d Total social security and Medicare taxes (*Column 2,* lines 5a + 5b + 5c = line 5d)	5d	21,701 . 61
6 Total taxes before adjustments (lines 3 + 5d = line 6)	6	35,945 . 68

7 TAX ADJUSTMENTS (read the instructions for line 7 before completing lines 7a through 7g):

7a Current quarter's fractions of cents	(. 01)
7b Current quarter's sick pay	.
7c Current quarter's adjustments for tips and group-term life insurance	.
7d Current year's income tax withholding (attach Form 941c)	.
7e Prior quarters' social security and Medicare taxes (attach Form 941c)	.
7f Special additions to federal income tax (attach Form 941c)	.
7g Special additions to social security and Medicare (attach Form 941c)	.

7h TOTAL ADJUSTMENTS (combine all amounts: lines 7a through 7g)	7h	(. 01)
8 Total taxes after adjustments (combine lines 6 and 7h)	8	35,945 . 67
9 Advance earned income credit (EIC) payments made to employees	9	.
10 Total taxes after adjustment for advance EIC (line 8 – line 9 = line 10)	10	35,945 . 67
11 Total deposits for this quarter, including overpayment applied from a prior quarter	11	35,945 . 67
12 Balance due (If line 10 is more than line 11, write the difference here.) For information on how to pay, see the instructions.	12	.

13 Overpayment (If line 11 is more than line 10, write the difference here.) . Check one ☐ Apply to next return. ☐ Send a refund.

Figure 7:42 Form 941

Schedule B (Form 941):

Report of Tax Liability for Semiweekly Schedule Depositors

(Rev. January 2006) Department of the Treasury — Internal Revenue Service

Note: Report shows date liability incurred

990306

OMB No. 1545-0029

(EIN) Employer identification number ☐☐ – ☐☐☐☐☐☐☐

Name *(not your trade name)* S&S Incorporated

Calendar year 2 0 0 7 (Also check quarter)

Report for this Quarter ...
(Check one.)

- ☑ 1: January, February, March
- ☐ 2: April, May, June
- ☐ 3: July, August, September
- ☐ 4: October, November, December

Use this schedule to show your TAX LIABILITY for the quarter; DO NOT use it to show your deposits. You must fill out this form and attach it to Form 941 (or Form 941-SS) if you are a semiweekly schedule depositor or became one because your accumulated tax liability on any day was $100,000 or more. Write your daily tax liability on the numbered space that corresponds to the date wages were paid. See Section 11 in *Pub. 15 (Circular E), Employer's Tax Guide,* for details.

Month 1

1	.	9	.	17	.	25	.
2	.	10	.	18	.	26	.
3	.	11	.	19	2,040.28	27	.
4	.	12	.	20	.	28	.
5	2,040.34	13	.	21	.	29	.
6	.	14	.	22	.	30	.
7	.	15	3,116.59.	23	.	31	3,659.44.
8	.	16	.	24	.		

Tax liability for Month 1: 10,856.65

Month 2

1	.	9	.	17	.	25	.
2	2,040.26	10	.	18	.	26	.
3	.	11	.	19	.	27	.
4	.	12	.	20	.	28	4,329.03
5	.	13	.	21	.	29	.
6	.	14	.	22	.	30	.
7	.	15	3,116.55	23	.	31	.
8	.	16	2,040.28	24	.		

Tax liability for Month 2: 11,526.12

Month 3

1	.	9	.	17	.	25	.
2	2,040.32	10	.	18	.	26	.
3	.	11	.	19	.	27	.
4	.	12	.	20	.	28	.
5	.	13	.	21	.	29	.
6	.	14	.	22	.	30	6,365.75
7	.	15	3,116.53	23	.	31	.
8	.	16	2,040.30	24	.		

Tax liability for Month 3: 13,562.90

Fill in your total liability for the quarter (Month 1 + Month 2 + Month 3) = Total tax liability for the quarter ▶

Total must equal line 10 on Form 941 (or line 8 on Form 941-SS).

Total liability for the quarter: 35,945.67

Figure 7:43 Schedule B

3. Close each report.

Payroll may also need to prepare quarterly state and local reports and will use information provided from monthly reports to complete forms sent by these taxing agencies.

PAYROLL REPORTING: YEARLY REPORTS

Payroll employees also print W-2s and a W-3 at the end of the year. Both reports are sent to the Social Security department and W-2s are also passed out to employees. We now illustrate printing these reports.

You will not be able to actually print forms because the Series must be year-ended before printing. However, we can demonstrate options for printing these forms. Click **Print-W-2s** under Routines. You would mark the following options to print W-2s and then print a W-3 summarizing totals for attached W-2s. Close the window.

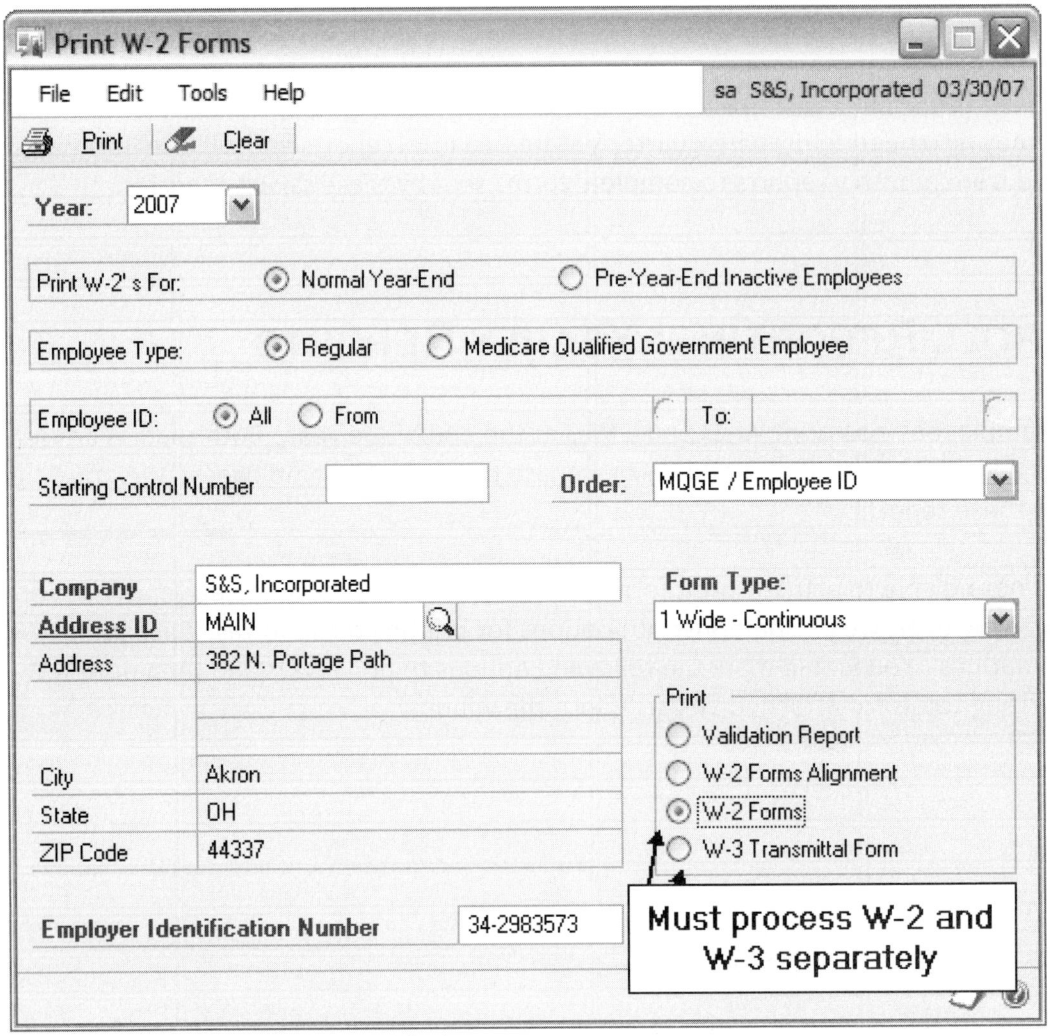

Figure 7:44 Print W-2 Forms Window

You should print a Validation Report prior to printing actual forms. This report is then compared to summary reports illustrated previously and to the Year-End Wage Report printed under Routines. If discrepancies exist then you can click Edit W-2s under Routines to make adjustments.

For more information on these forms, consult the IRS website at www.irs.gov.

MONTH-ENDING THE PAYROLL SERIES

Like other Series, you need to perform steps that close the Payroll Series. Besides printing reports, you need to also post liabilities and expenses for unemployment and workers' compensation taxes because items do not post when printing paychecks.

Let us post these items now.

1. Click **Period-End** under Reports. This time you will print reports along with posting entries. Refer to the next illustration and select the reports illustrated. Mark the **Post Liabilities** options and verify the **Posting Date**. *(Note: In the real world you would print reports and reconcile then return to the window to post.)*

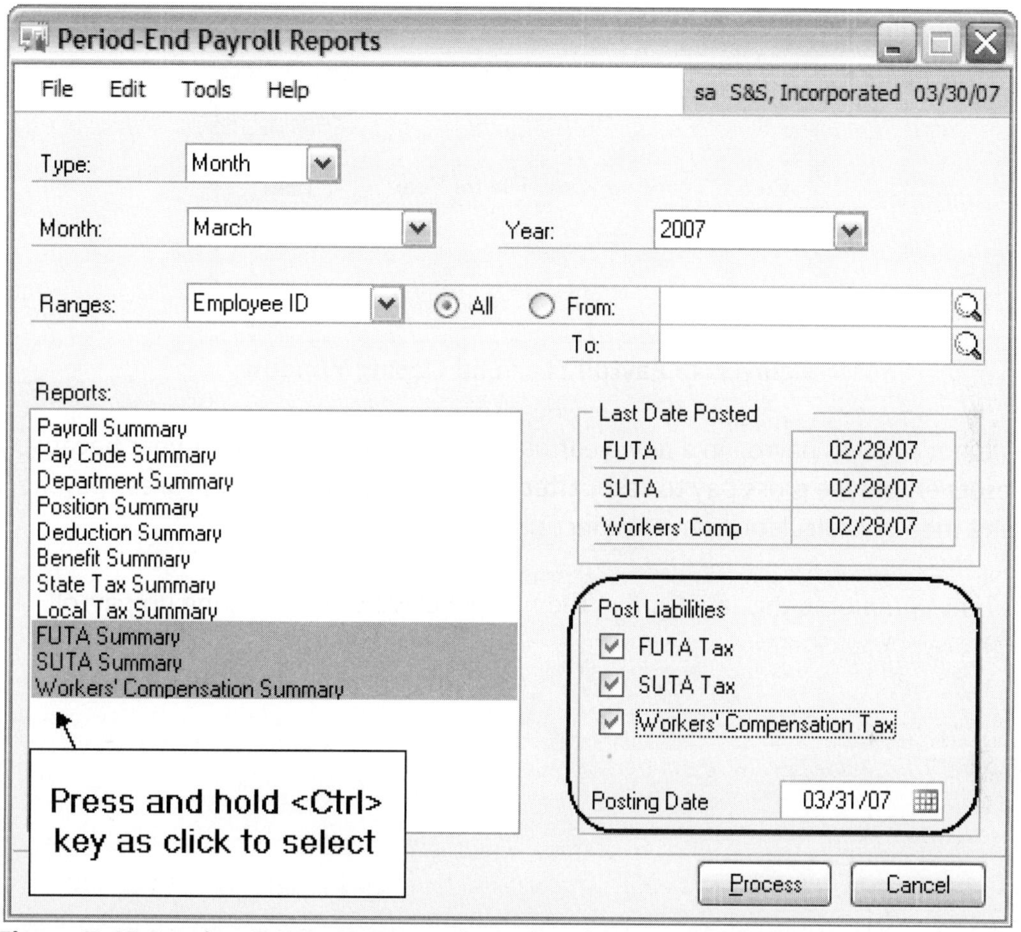

Figure 7:45 Posting FUTA, SUTA, and Workers' Compensation Taxes

2. Click **Process** and print reports to the screen. The FUTA report prints first listing federal unemployment taxes for the month. Close the reports, noting that the General Posting Journal prints last, listing entries made to the general ledger.

Of course, you must mark the month as closed using the Fiscal Periods Setup window illustrated in Chapters 2 and 5. *(Note: This task is performed by clicking the GP button to select Tools>>Setup>>Company>>Fiscal Periods and marking the checkbox for the month under the Series.)*

YEAR-ENDING THE PAYROLL SERIES

Remember that year-ending any Series makes significant changes to data files so you should first complete a back up of the files. Thereafter, you print reports and complete year-ending using the following window. *(Note: This window is opened by clicking Year-End Closing under Routines.)*

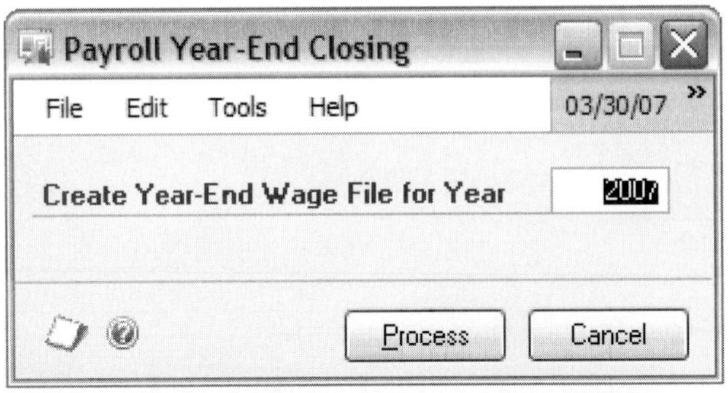

Figure 7:46 Payroll Year-End Closing Window

You should not process payroll in a new year before year-ending the prior year because year-ending resets employee gross pay to zero, affecting tax brackets. If you process paychecks prior to resetting then tax calculations may be incorrect.

You have now completed this level and in the next level we discuss setting up payroll.

Level Two

In this level we focus on Payroll Series setup. First we look at controls over the Series.[30] Then we discuss managing payroll codes such as pay type and conclude with reviewing the posting accounts for payroll transactions.

PAYROLL SERIES SETUP AND INTERNAL CONTROLS

Click **Payroll** under Setup to review default settings and review the next illustration.

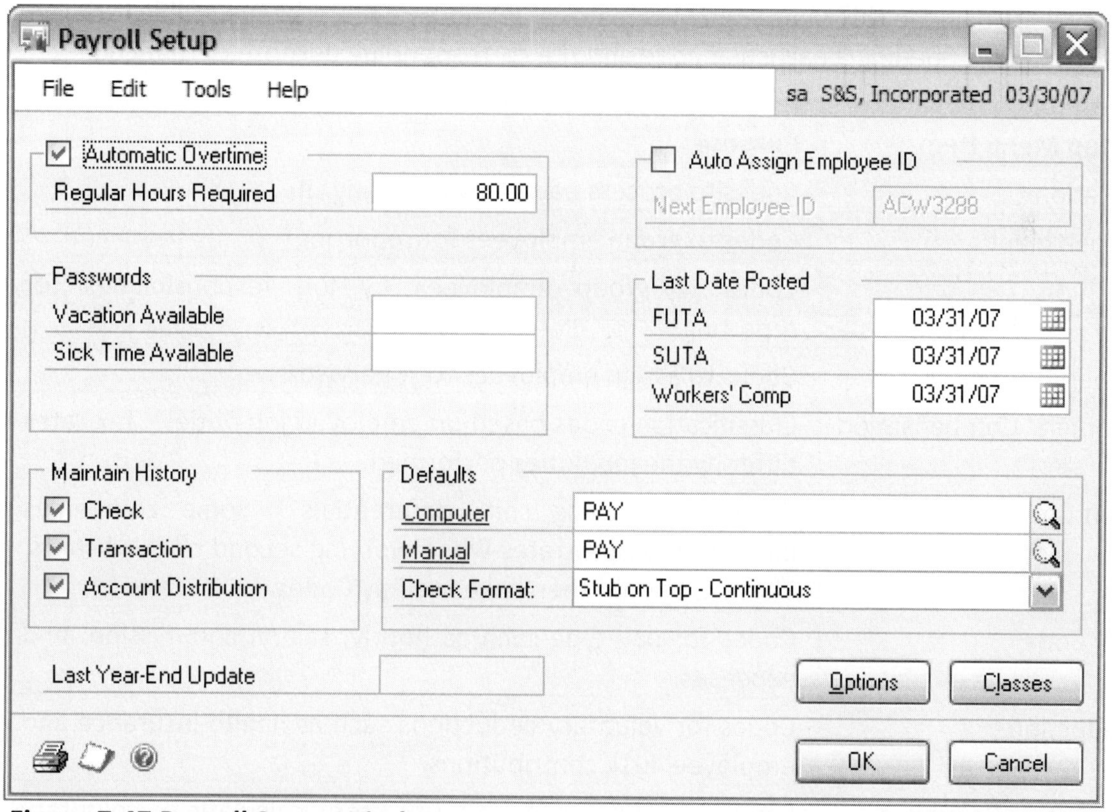

Figure 7:47 Payroll Setup Window

We find the usual options for maintaining history. Notice that payroll tax tables were last updated in 2004 (i.e., Last Year-End Update) so your copy of tax tables is outdated.

Automatic Overtime holds instructions for calculating overtime hours. If hourly paid employees work more than 80 hours in the bi-weekly pay period then excess hours are to be treated as

[30] Before reading this section, students are benefited by referring to payroll and human resource internal control topics in Romney and Steinbart, *Accounting Information Systems* (11th ed., Pearson Prentice Hall 2009), pgs. 510-515.

overtime. Of course, this is an automatic calculation that can be changed during payroll entry to accommodate overtime if an employee works 42 hours one week and 38 the next week.

Under **Options** you will find options for tracking additional information and document control numbers.

Close this window and we next look at managing codes.

PAY TYPE, TAX, DEDUCTION, AND BENEFIT CODES

In Level One, we illustrated linking pay types, taxes, benefits, and deduction codes to the employee card and in this topic we discuss setting up those codes. The next table lists menus under Setup for opening a particular code and the corresponding purpose of that code.

Setup Menu Item	Purpose
Location	Codes to process payroll by company site.
Department	Codes to group employees for reporting.
Position	Codes to group employees by job responsibilities for reporting.
Supervisor	Codes to assign employees to supervisors.
Workers' Compensation	Classification codes based on employee job duties. Tax rates differ by the job duties performed.
Shift Code	Codes establishing shift differentials. Some companies increase base pay rates when working second or third shifts. These codes are then linked to Pay Codes.
Pay Code	Codes for pay type such as hourly, salary, commission, and expenses.
Deduction	Codes for voluntary deductions such as health insurance and employee 401k contributions.
Deduction Sequence	Sequence sets the priority for calculating voluntary deductions. For instance, if an employee has wage attachments or child support deductions, these should be subtracted from gross pay prior to deducting charitable contributions.
Benefit	Code for the employer provided benefits such as matching 401k contributions.
Local Tax	Codes for local taxes and the related tax rate.
Unemployment Tax	Codes for unemployment taxes and the related tax rate.

Table 7:8 Payroll Series Codes

We next look at a few of these codes.

1. Click **Pay Code** under Setup and look up **HOURLY**. (See Figure 7:48.) This window stores defaults that are assigned to hourly paid employees linked to the card. Notice that Pay Type and Unit of Pay are hourly. The Pay Period is Biweekly, meaning paid every two weeks. Finally, all pay received under this code is subject to the taxes marked.

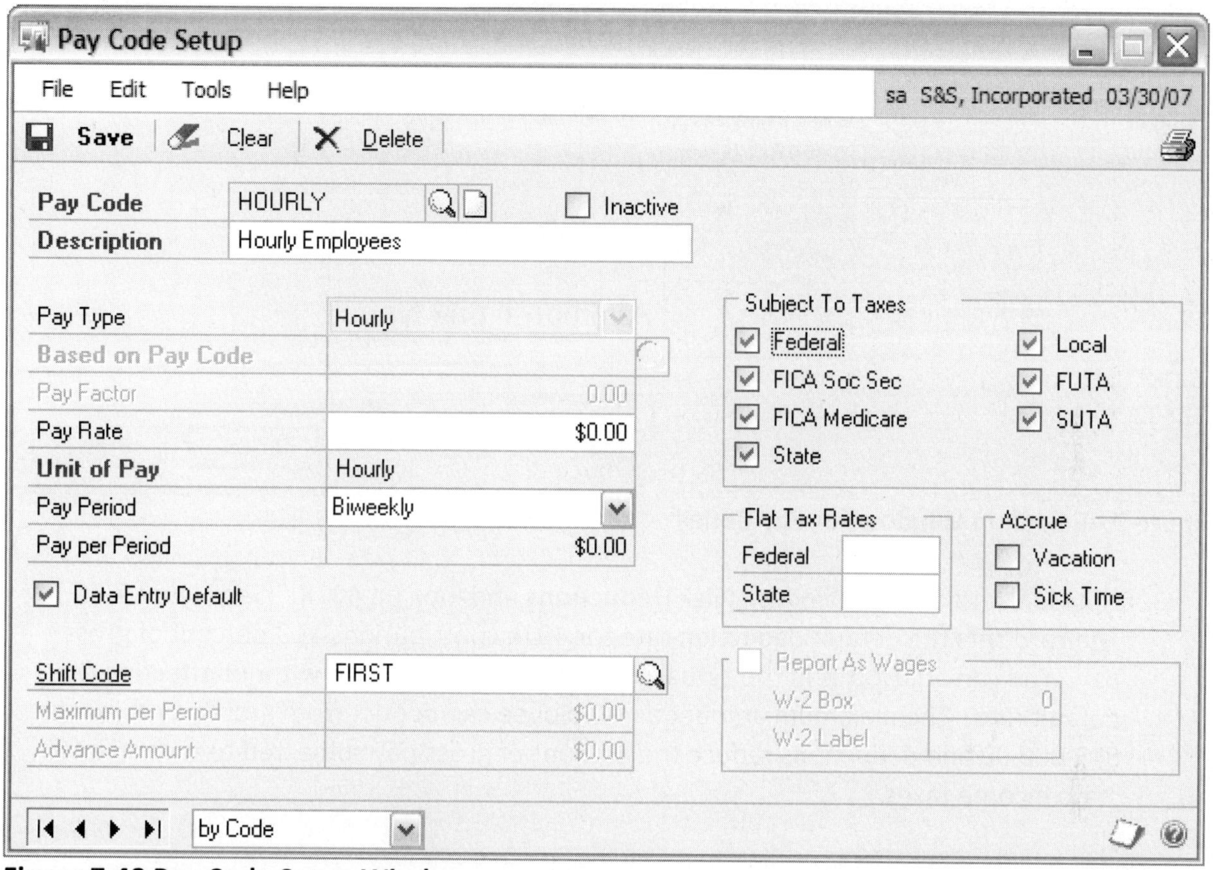

Figure 7:48 Pay Code Setup Window

2. The lookup window for Pay Code reveals that this window is used to manage all the pay types illustrated in this chapter. (See Figure 7:49.) Close the Pay Code Setup window

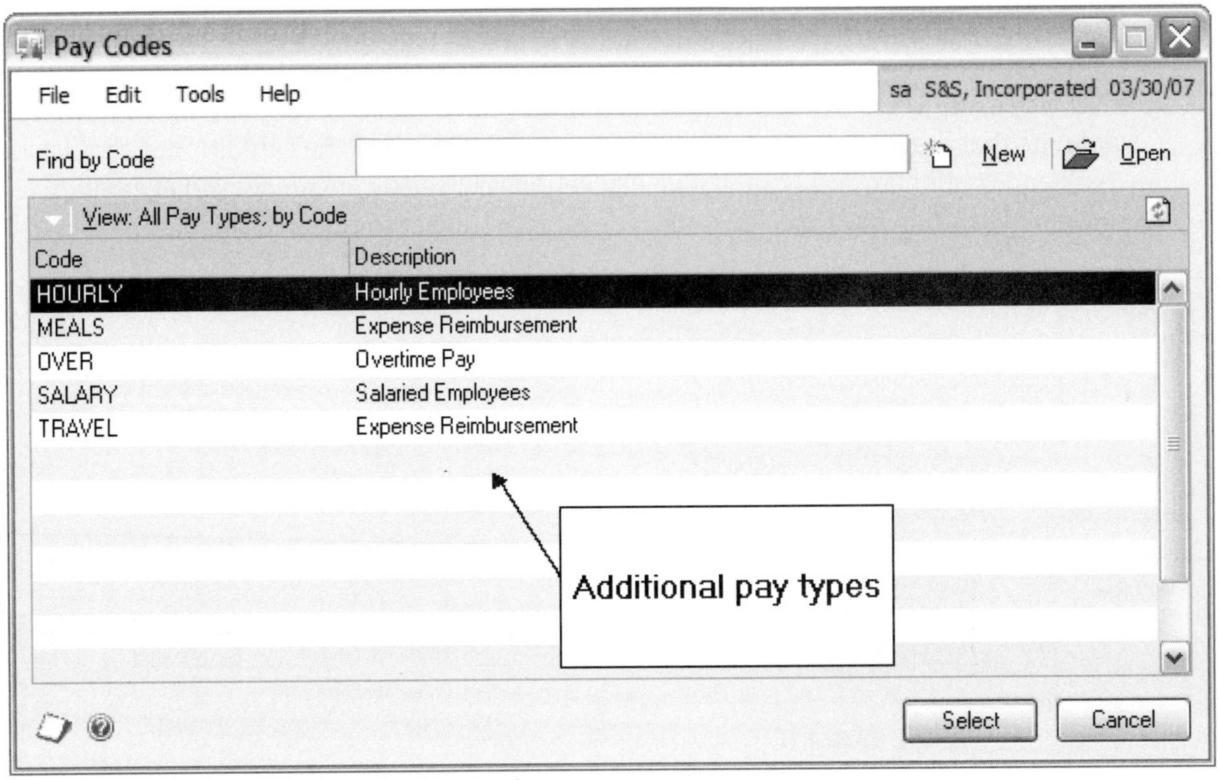

Figure 7:49 Lookup Window for Pay Codes

3. Now look at deduction codes. Click **Deductions** and look up **401K**. (See Figure 7:50.) The card sets the default deduction rate for 401k contributions at 3 percent of gross pay. You can adjust this in the actual link to the employee card without affecting the default rate. The maximum amount an employee can deduct from gross pay a year is $13,000.00 and deductions reduce the amount of gross pay subjected to federal and state income taxes.

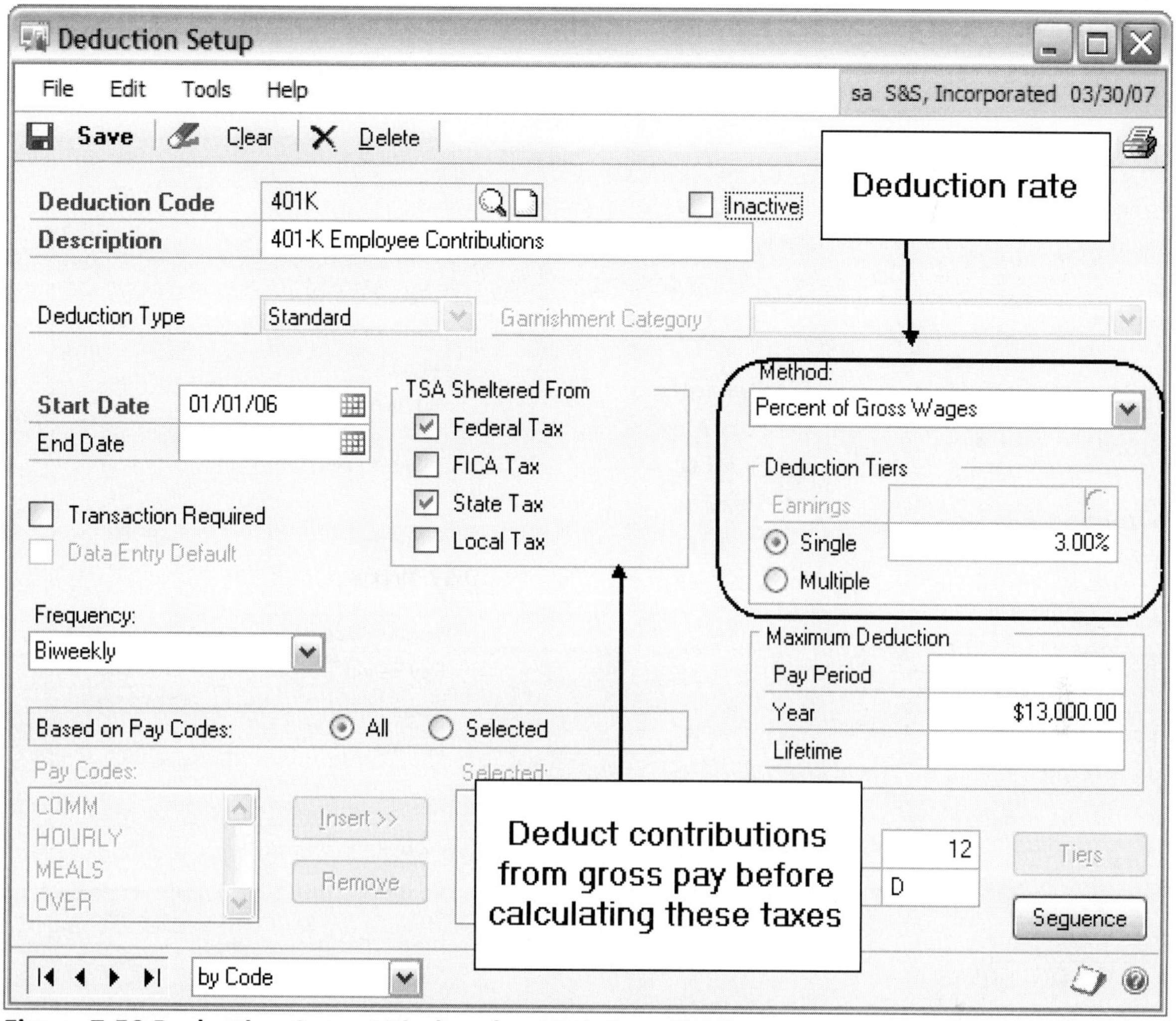

Figure 7:50 Deduction Setup Window for 401k Contributions

4. Now look up the **HFAMI** code because it works differently. (See Figure 7:51.) This code deducts a fixed amount of $98.00 from each paycheck if the employee elects family health insurance coverage. Again, gross pay is reduced by these deductions before calculating federal and state tax withholdings. Close the window.

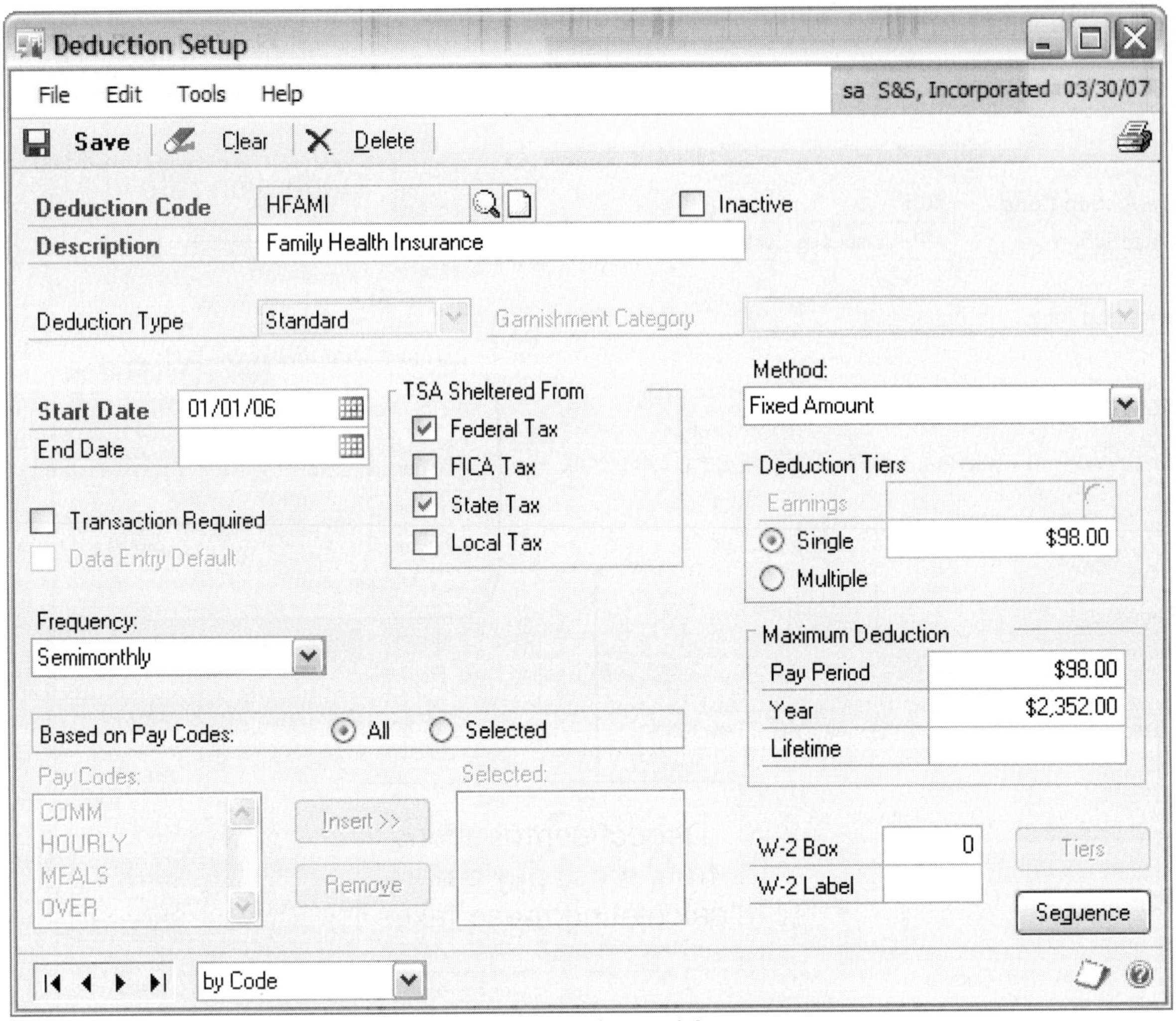

Figure 7:51 Deduction Setup Window for Family Health Insurance

5. Let us now look at benefits. Click **Benefit** and look up 401K. (Figure 7:52.) This is the card for employer matching contributions to the 401k retirement plan. We see that S&S matches employee contributions at 50 percent of their deductions, up to a maximum of $5,000.00 per year. The employer match is not subject to tax and is made once a month. Close the window.

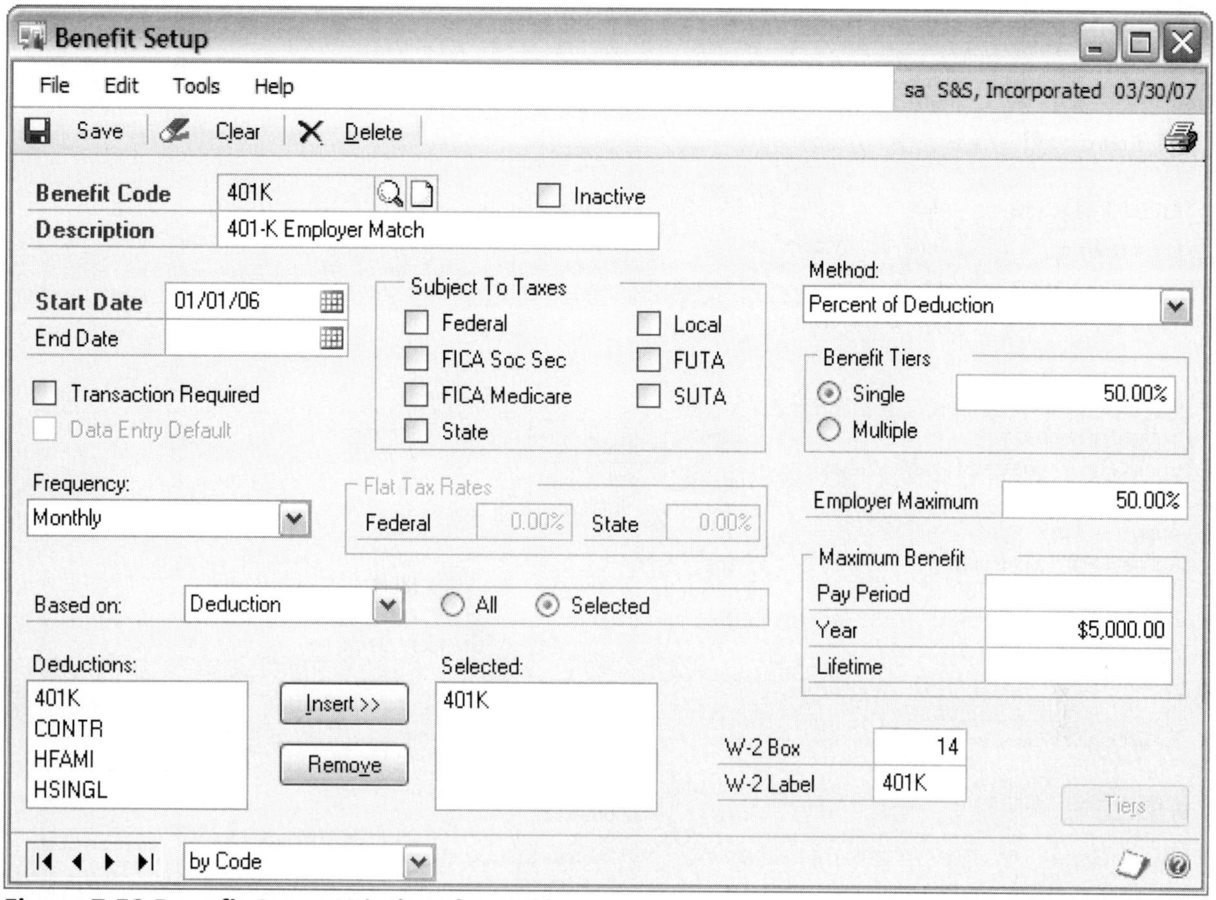

Figure 7:52 Benefit Setup Window for 401k

6. Next click **Local Tax** and look up AKR. (Figure 7:53.) This is city tax code that instructs GP to withhold 2 percent of gross pay from employee paychecks. Close the window.

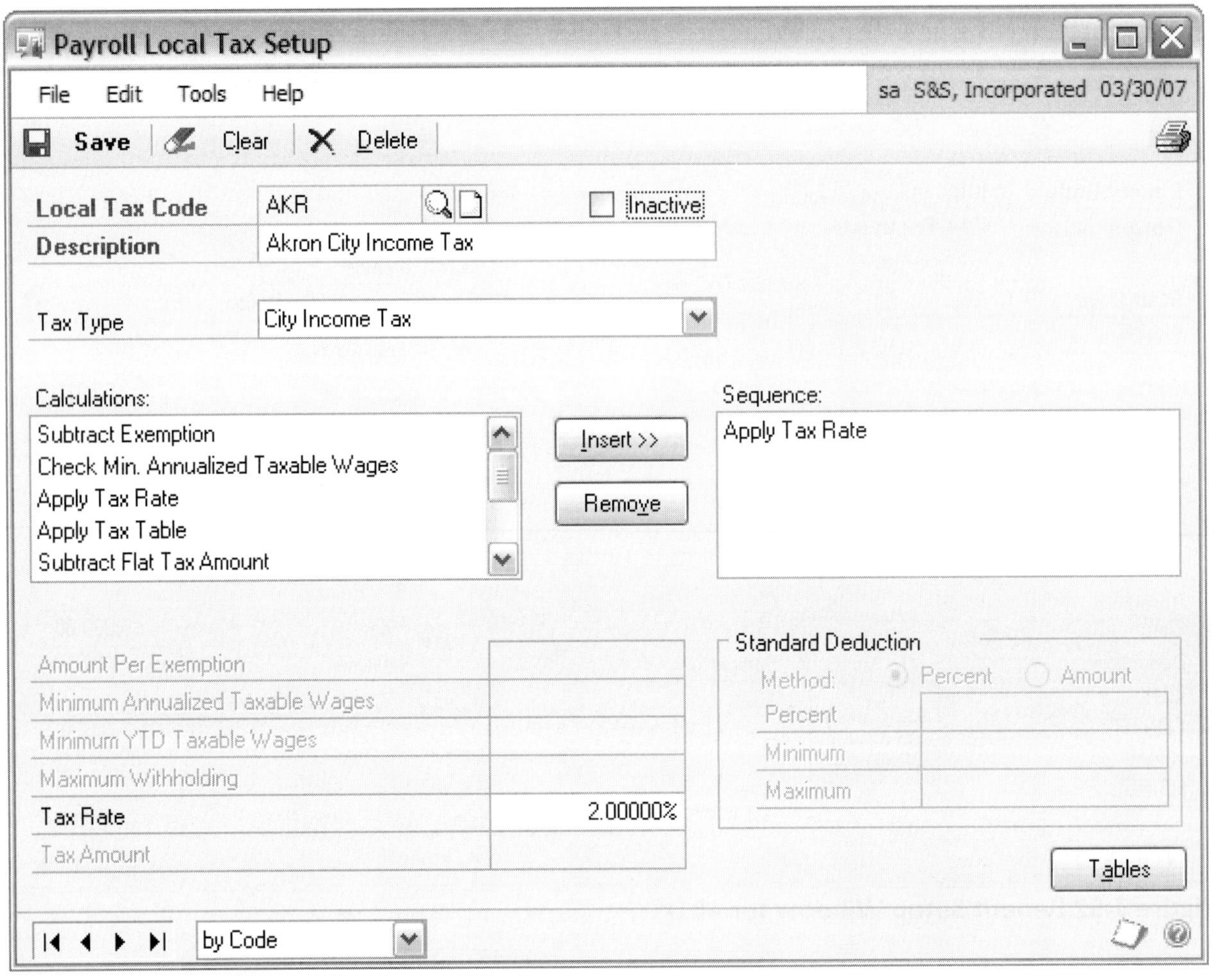

Figure 7:53 Payroll Local Tax Setup Window

7. Click **Unemployment Tax** and look up **OH.** (See Figure 7:54.) This is the card for state unemployment taxes (i.e., SUTA) paid by the employer. S&S pays a 1.9 percent (i.e., .019) tax on annual gross wages up to $9,000.00. Close the window.

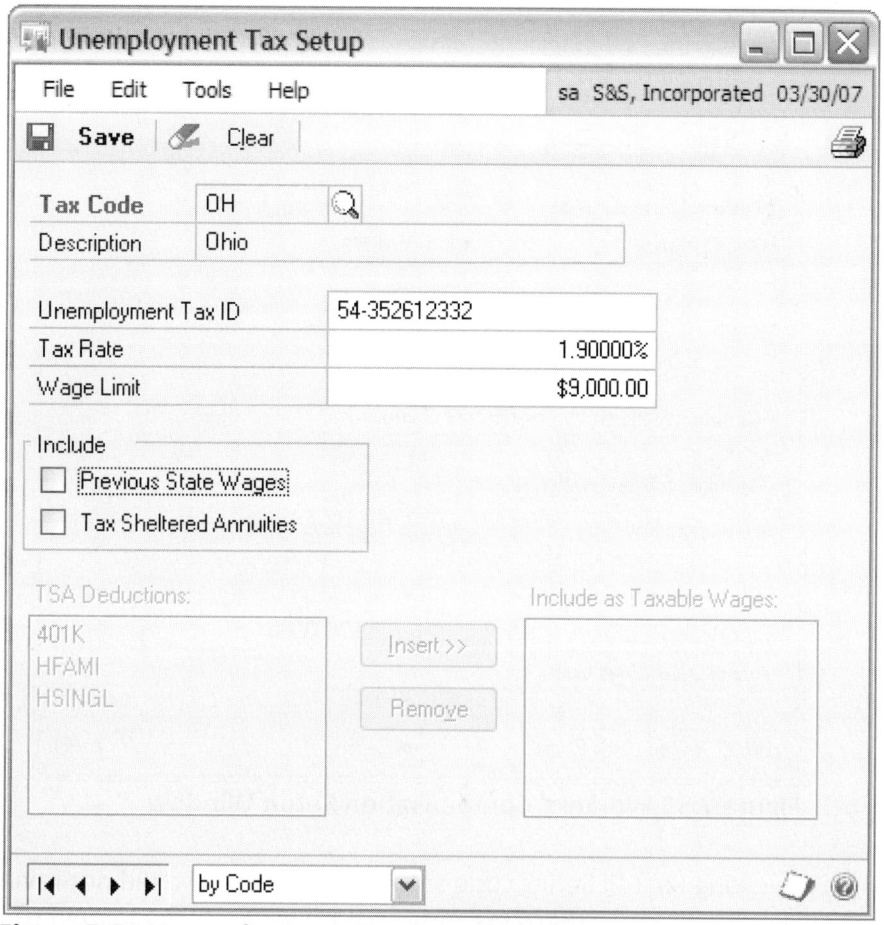

Figure 7:54 Unemployment Tax Setup Window

8. Finally, click Workers' Compensation and look up 2387. (See Figure 7:55.) This is the tax rate S&S pays for office workers. S&S will pay the state .7 percent (i.e., .007) of these workers' gross pay. Close the window.

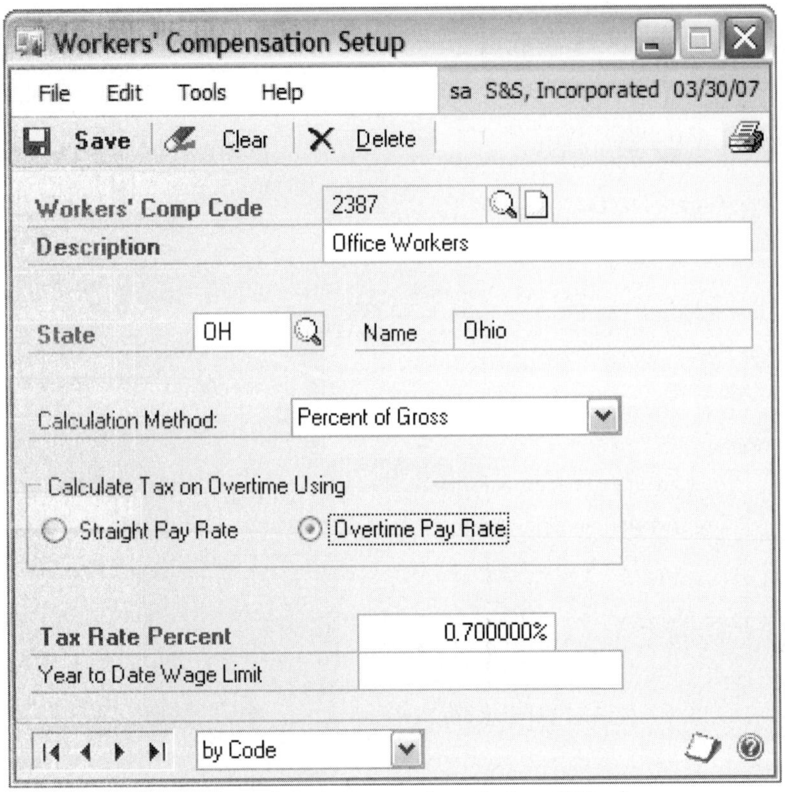

Figure 7:55 Workers' Compensation Setup Window

You have finished reviewing Payroll Series code setup. Notice that we did not review federal and income state tax codes because these tax rates and tables are downloaded from the online payroll tax service. In the next topic we look at establishing the general ledger accounts used when posting Payroll Series transactions.

GP

S&S received notice of a wage garnishment for George Hanratty. Implement this deduction. *(Note: Click Yes when prompted to bypass Human Resource Series.)*

1. Add a new deduction code named GARN. The deduction is not sheltered from taxes and the amount is $10.00 each pay period with a lifetime maximum of $620.00.

2. Link this deduction to the employee's card. *(Note: Click Default when prompted.)*

E7:5 Practice Managing Codes

PAYROLL POSTING ACCOUNT SETUP

Codes in the Payroll Series present complicated issues for posting. Transactions need to post to multiple general ledger accounts so GP provides a separate window for designating those accounts. The next exercise illustrates this window.

1. Click the GP button and select ***Tools>>Setup>>Posting>>Payroll Accounts***. The window (Figure 7:56) assigns posting accounts by Payroll Account Type, as illustrated in the dropdown list. Accounts assigned to a type are pervasive, meaning there is no opportunity to change an account during transaction entry.

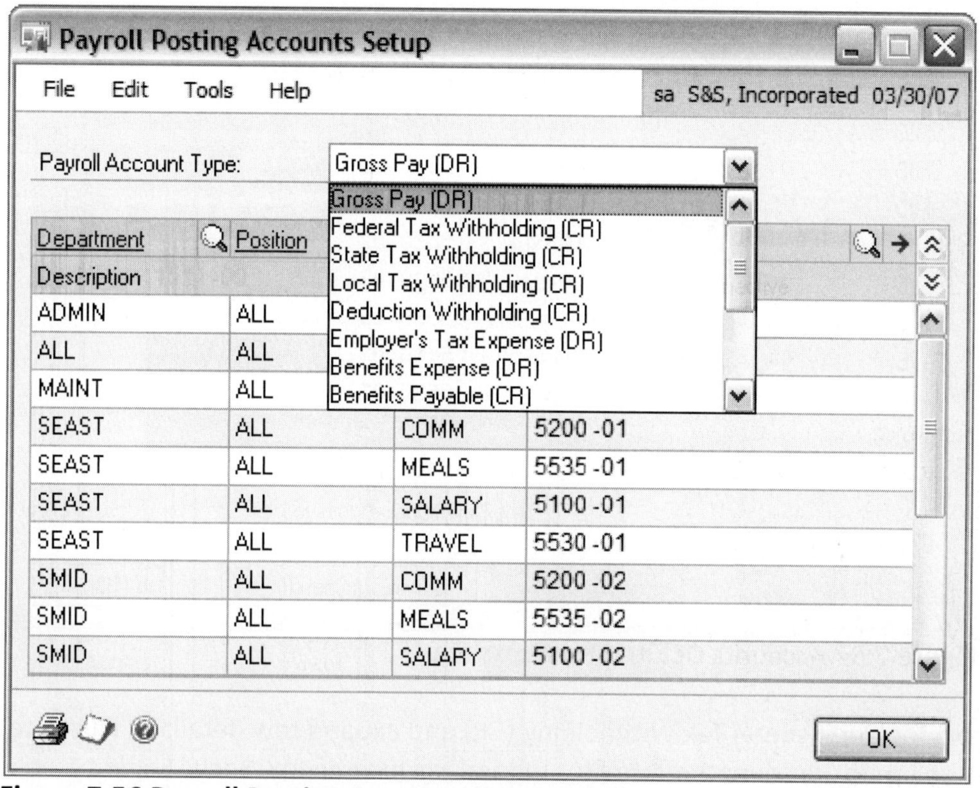

Figure 7:56 Payroll Posting Accounts Setup Window

2. Choose Gross Pay (DR) as illustrated next to view expense accounts debited for gross pay. Accounts are assigned by department and pay type codes. If an employee working in the SEAST department receives commission pay then expense account 5200-01 is debited for that commission expense. Notice that gross pay for employees working in the transportation (i.e., TRANS) and warehouse (i.e., WARE) departments posts to a fixed allocation account (i.e., account with 05 as the department segment) so that expense will be allocated across departments.

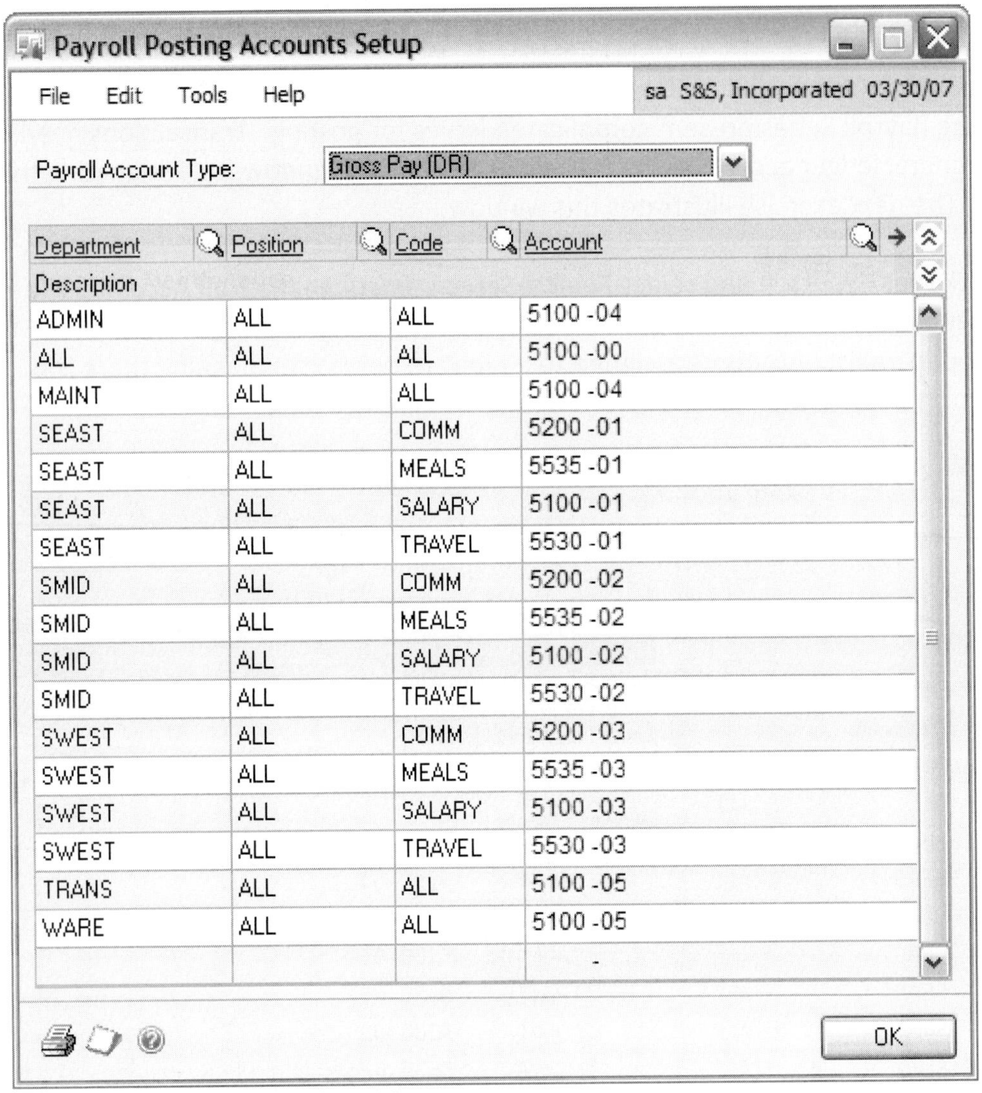

Department	Position	Code	Account
ADMIN	ALL	ALL	5100 -04
ALL	ALL	ALL	5100 -00
MAINT	ALL	ALL	5100 -04
SEAST	ALL	COMM	5200 -01
SEAST	ALL	MEALS	5535 -01
SEAST	ALL	SALARY	5100 -01
SEAST	ALL	TRAVEL	5530 -01
SMID	ALL	COMM	5200 -02
SMID	ALL	MEALS	5535 -02
SMID	ALL	SALARY	5100 -02
SMID	ALL	TRAVEL	5530 -02
SWEST	ALL	COMM	5200 -03
SWEST	ALL	MEALS	5535 -03
SWEST	ALL	SALARY	5100 -03
SWEST	ALL	TRAVEL	5530 -03
TRANS	ALL	ALL	5100 -05
WARE	ALL	ALL	5100 -05
			-

Figure 7:57 Accounts Debited for Gross Pay

3. Next, look up Federal Tax Withholding (CR) and expand row details as illustrated next. These are the accounts credited for federal tax income tax, Social Security, and Medicare withholdings.

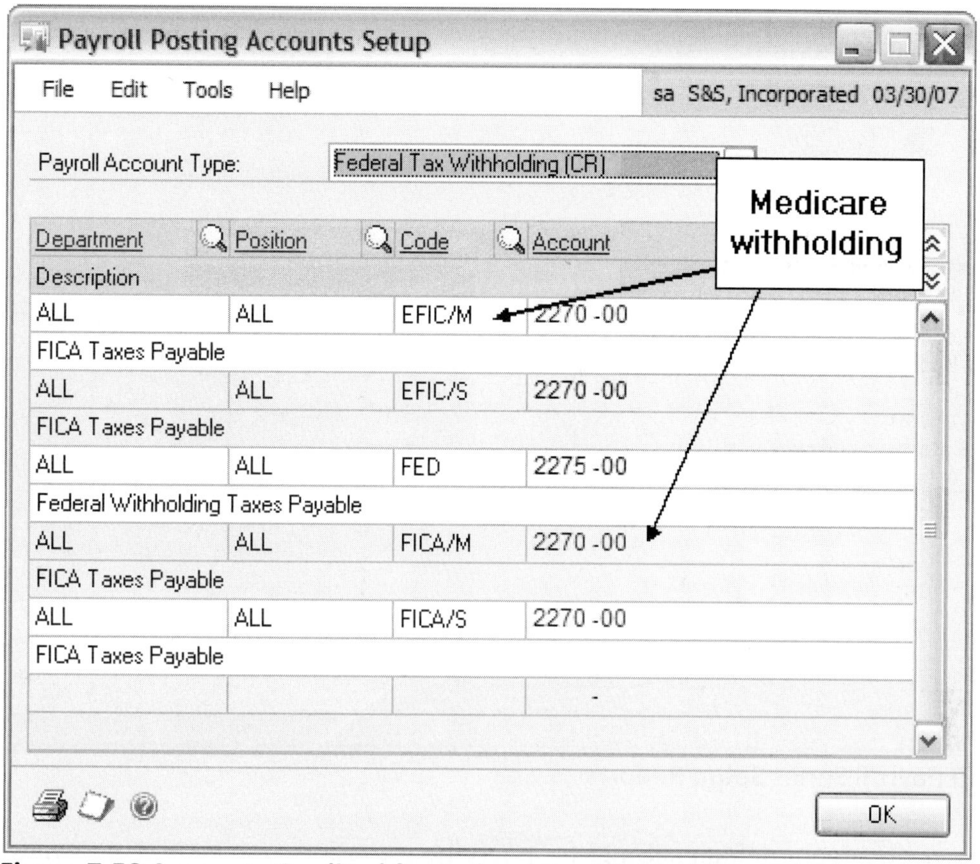

Figure 7:58 Accounts Credited for Federal Tax Withholdings

4. Take the time to review other types and then close the window.

PAYROLL SERIES SETUP REPORTS

You know that posting reports are used to monitor and control payroll transactions. Furthermore, pay period, monthly, quarterly, and yearly reports monitor task performance and compliance with external reporting requirements. This topic focuses on reviewing internal control settings for the Series to document compliance with internal control objectives.

Click **Setup** under Reports and click the dropdown list as illustrated next.

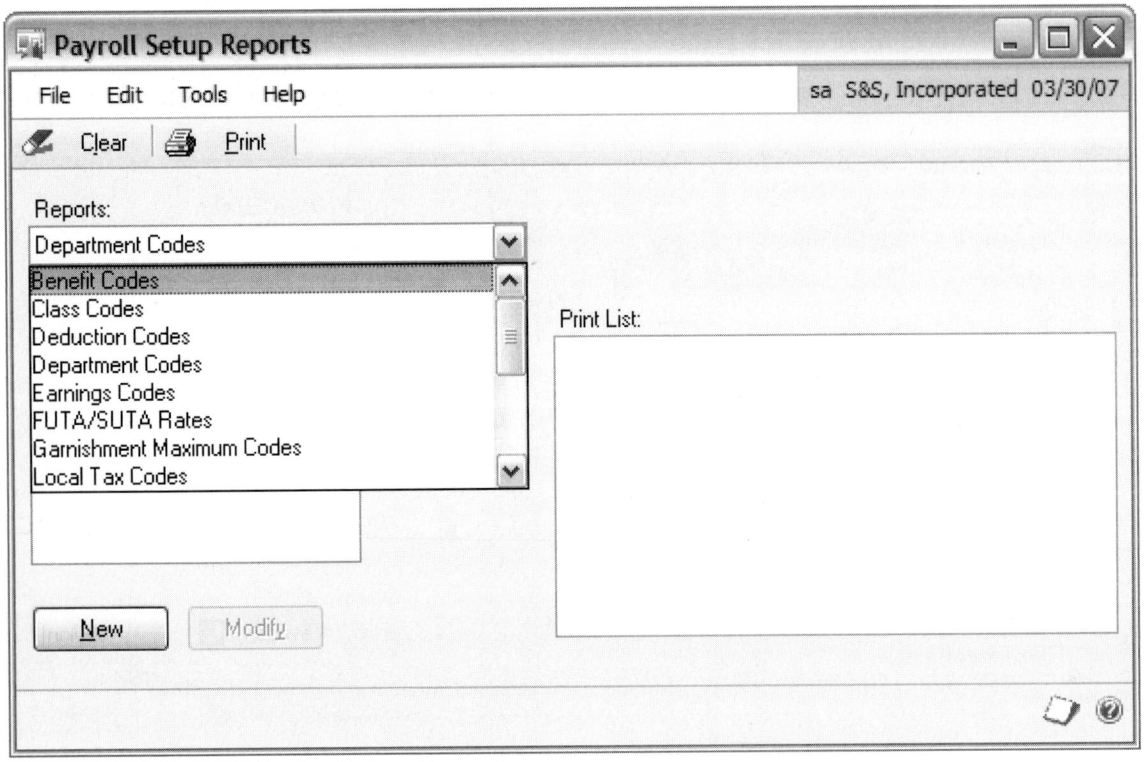

Figure 7:59 Payroll Series Setup Reports

These reports document default settings for payroll transactions and should be reviewed for compliance with company internal control policies.

You have now completed the chapter. In the next chapter, we wrap up the March accounting period by performing tasks in the Financial Series that close the period.

Level One Questions

1. An employee requests a pay advance and the owners grant the request. Review the Build Payroll Checks window to determine if GP can accommodate this transaction so that it is controlled in the Payroll Series.

2. How does GP treat the 401k benefit code differently from the 401k deduction code when calculating net pay?

3. Name the report you would validate prior to processing paychecks. Explain how this report is validated.

4. Explain what could happen if you fail to link an employee card to a Payroll Series code. Provide a specific example.

5. Describe human resource activities and analyze controlling threats in this department.

6. What is the difference between running a Payroll Summary report for the month of March and the same report for the period covering March 1, 2007 to March 31, 2007?

7. Do you know why expense reimbursement for meals and travel are posted to separate expense accounts? You can research your answer on the IRS website at www.IRS.gov.

Level Two Questions

1. Make recommendations for monitoring and controlling overtime pay.

2. Analyze payroll cycle threats listed on the activity diagram at the beginning of the chapter. Explain GP controls you could use to mitigate threats.

3. What report will document that FUTA and SUTA taxes are properly setup?

4. Review the Payroll Posting Accounts Setup window to identify the following payroll account types. State whether these are employee or employer taxes, the nature of the tax, and the effect on general ledger accounts.

   a. W/Comp Tax Payable (CR)
   b. W/Comp Tax Expense (DR)
   b. Employer's Tax Expense (DR)

5. Explain what can happen if you fail to year-end the Payroll Series.

Chapter 8 FINANCIAL REPORTING AND GP FINANCIAL SERIES

CHAPTER OVERVIEW

Preceding chapters always began with a diagram illustrating cycle activities by department before illustrating performing those activities. However, financial reporting is not a cycle. Instead, it involves a series of tasks the close the accounting period, including reviewing general ledger postings from other cycles and making adjusting and/or correcting entries prior to producing financial statements. [31] Therefore, you will review closing checklists of tasks performed in the Financial Series by the accounting department. When completed, the accounting department closes the accounting period to prevent future postings and issues financial reports. With this background in mind, we introduce accounting department activities as follows:

- Level One focuses on completing tasks described in the accounting period closing checklist prior to issuing financial statements. Tasks include reviewing general ledger posting, making adjusting and correcting entries and preparing bank reconciliations.

- Level Two focuses on advanced reporting.

Level One covers:
- Closing checklists for the expenditure cycle and accounting period
- Reviewing posted transactions using the general ledger detail trial balance
- Posting journal entries to correct errors and adjust account balances
- Recording banking transactions and preparing bank reconciliations
- Producing financial reports
- Closing the Financial Series

Level Two covers:
- Creating basic financial statements
- Using advanced financials to customize statements

[31] Before reading this chapter, students are benefited by reading financial reporting topics in Romney and Steinbart, *Accounting Information Systems* (11th ed., Pearson Prentice Hall 2009) Chapter 14.

Level One

The accounting period for March 31, 2007 has ended so the controller, Ashton, begins his preclosing procedures. First, he updates cycle closing checklists that establish Series posting cutoff dates for processing March activities and due dates for completing other tasks. Ashton's cycle closing checklist for the expenditure cycle is illustrated next. He prepares similar cycle closing checklists for each cycle and sends to department managers. Managers complete their assigned tasks and return an updated checklist to Ashton.

S&S, Incorporated
Expenditure Cycle Closing Checklist
For Period Ended March 30, 2007

Cutoff Date: 4/5/2007

Activity	Due Date	Status	Date	Notes
Purchasing Manager				
Review receiving logs and compare to outstanding POs and receiving reports.	4/2/2007	Completed	4/2/2007	
Post all vendor invoices by cutoff date.	4/5/2007	Completed	4/5/2007	
Review vendor invoice and payment posting journals for posting errors.	4/5/2007	Completed	4/5/2007	Reclassify $1,250 posted to office expense for a desk purchased on Office Rex invoice number 17650, dated 3/01/2007.
Review Series Posting window and post pending batches	4/5/2007	Completed	4/5/2007	
Review vendor aging report for missing invoices.	4/6/2007	Completed	4/6/2007	Water bill not received.
Prepare Purchase Series reports	4/6/2007	Completed	4/6/2007	
Controller's Office				
Close the Series	4/5/2007	Completed	4/5/2007	
Reconcile the Series	4/5/2007	Completed	4/5/2007	
Review Financial Series Posting window to finalize Purchase Series Postings	4/6/2007			
Post entries listed by purchasing manager	4/6/2007			

Figure 8:1 Closing Checklist for Expenditure Cycle

On April 6, Ashton reviews the expenditure cycle closing checklist updated by the purchasing manager to confirm tasks are complete. The purchasing manager will note any correcting entries that need to be posted and lists bill that have were not received by the cutoff date. Aston will post entries in the Financial Series for any items noted before issuing financial statements.

Ashton also prepares a closing checklist for the accounting period with tasks to be performed by the accounting department. This checklist is illustrated next.

S&S, Incorporated
Accounting Period Closing Checklist
For Period Ended March 30, 2007

Cutoff Date: 4/6/2007

Activity	Due Date	Status	Date	Notes
Journal Entries				
Post Savings Account Interest	4/3/2007			Statement arrives on the 3rd
Reclassify Commission Transfer	4/4/2007			Total commission transferred on March 30 was $2,560.23
Post Depreciation	4/4/2007			Add accounting department desk purchased from Office Rex for $1,250 on 3/01/2007
Accrue Wages	4/4/2007			Accrue 7 days of average monthly wages for hourly employees
Adjust Prepaid Insurance	4/5/2007			
Post correcting and adjusting entries from cycle closing checklists	4/6/2007			
Accrue Bank Note Interest	4/6/2007			
Accrue Income Taxes	4/9/2007			
Reviewing				
Review Detail General Ledger Report	4/5/2007			
Confirm owners reconciled bank statements	4/5/2007			Statements arrive on the 3rd
Reporting				
Preliminary review of Financial Statements	4/6/2007			
Print Final Copy of Financial Statements	4/9/2007			
Print Management Reports	4/9/2007			
Close Financial Series	4/9/2007			

Figure 8:2 Closing Checklist for Accounting Department

Closing checklists form the basis for illustrations at this level. In topics to follow, you complete remaining tasks on these checklists so please take the time to understand these documents.

FINANCIAL CARDS

As with previous chapters, we begin by reviewing master records for the Series (i.e., cards). We reviewed Account, Unit Account, Variable Allocation, and Fixed Allocation windows in Chapter 2 so this topic should be a refresher.

Click **Account** and look up the cash card illustrated next.

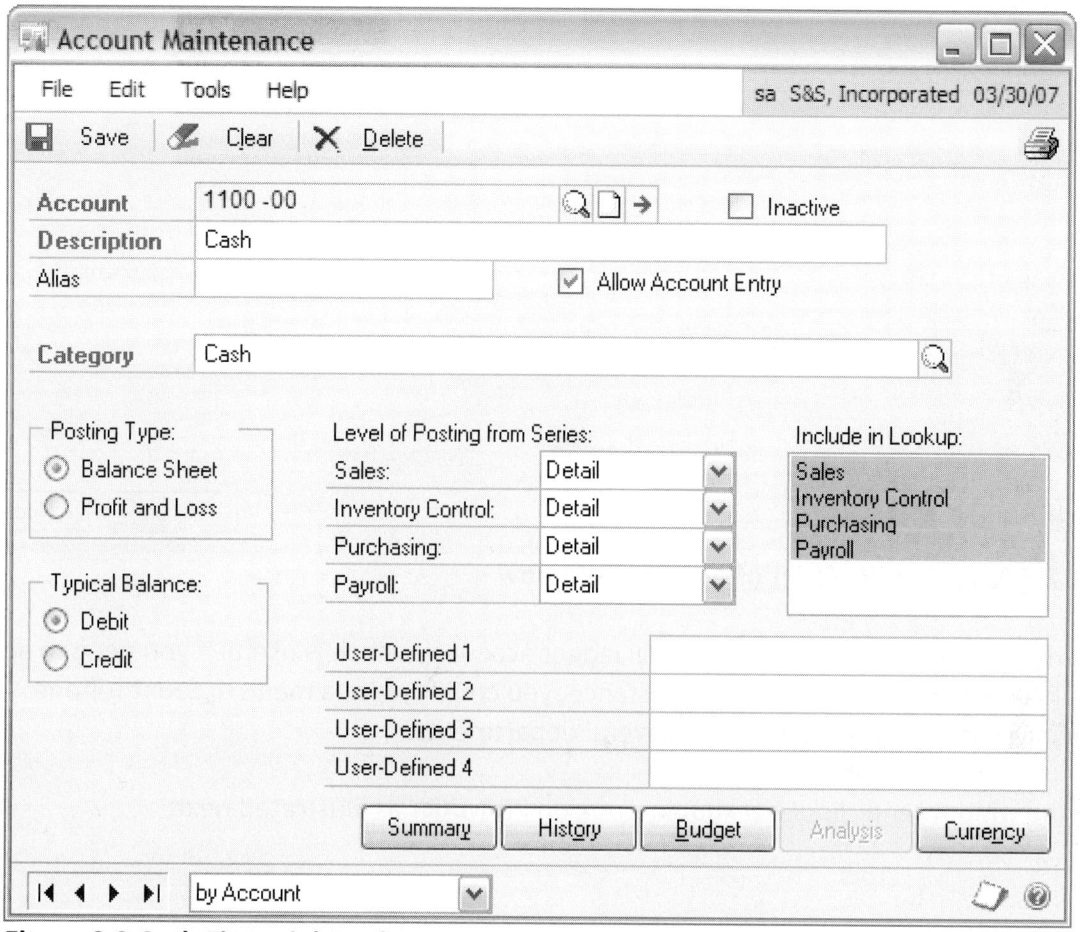

Figure 8:3 Cash Financial Card

The **Summary** button displays the account balances by period for the current year whereas the **History** button shows this same information for prior years (i.e., closed years). The **Budget** button displays budget data for the account. GP offers Excel Based Budgeting so you can import budget data from an Excel spreadsheet.

Close the window and click **Mass Modify**. The Mass Modify Chart of Accounts window (Figure 8:4) is a quick way of managing accounts.

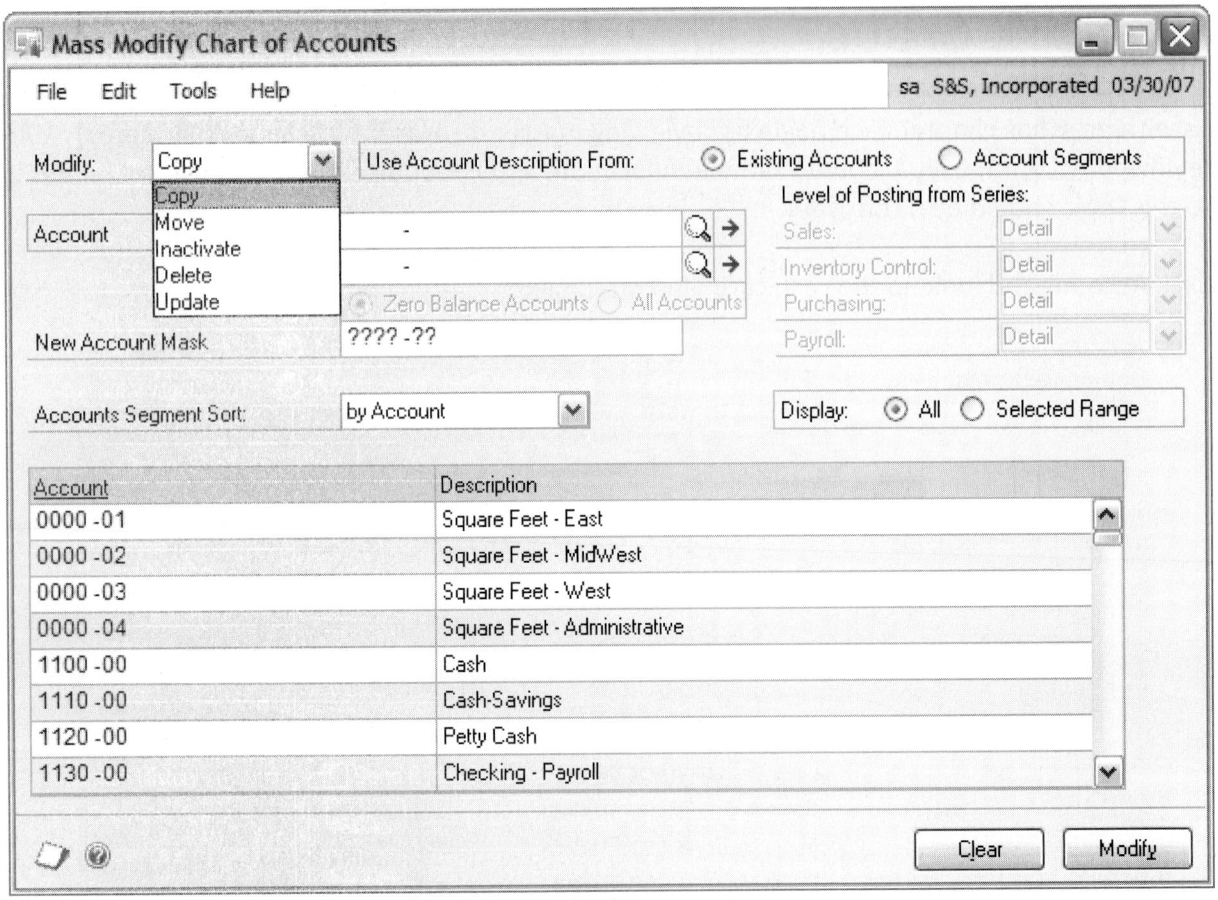

Figure 8:4 Mass Modify Chart of Accounts Window

Notice that this window will copy general ledger accounts, which is useful if you need to add multiple departmental accounts. For instance, you could create a meals account for one department and copy this account to several departments.

Close the window and click **Checkbook**. Look up **PRIMARY** as illustrated next.

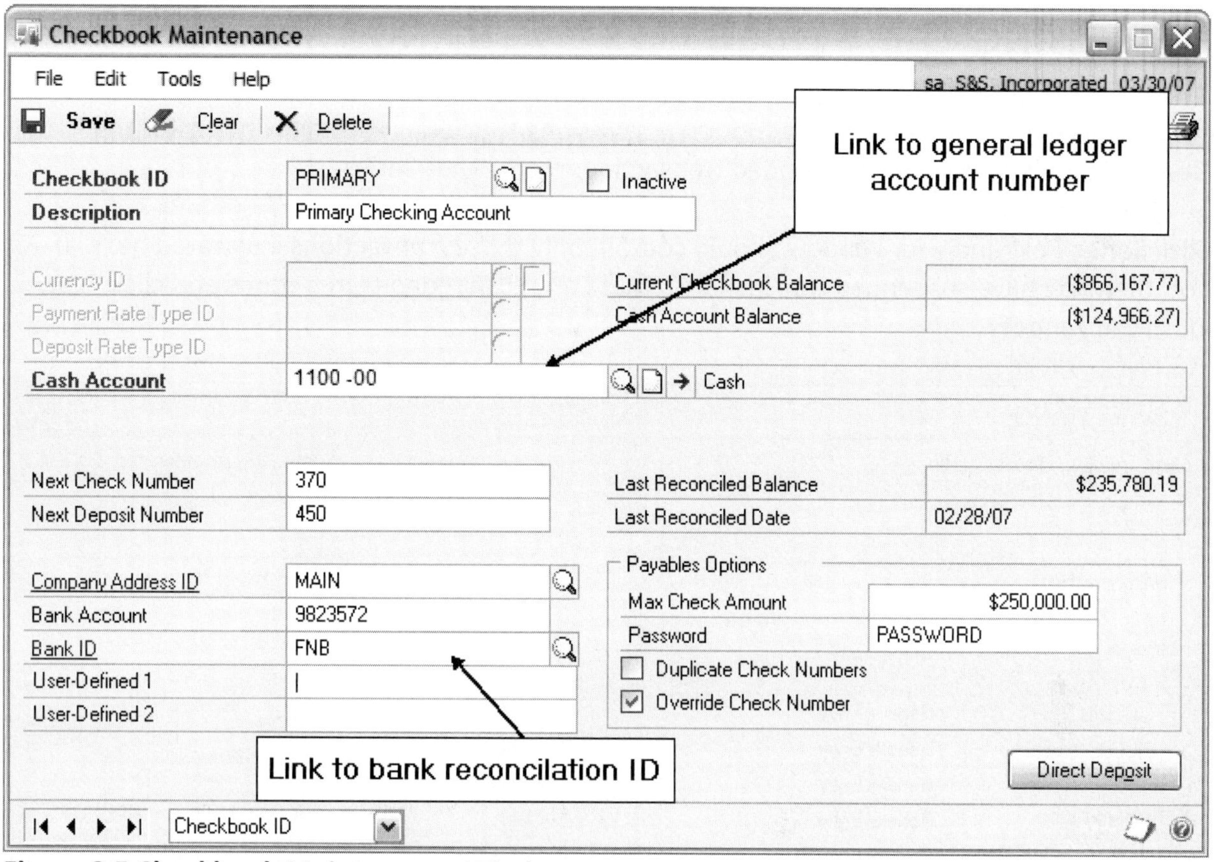

Figure 8:5 Checkbook Maintenance Window

This window manages links to general ledger cash accounts and GP's bank reconciliation feature. There are also general controls for limiting the maximum check amount and controlling duplicate check numbers and check number overrides. Finally, you see a specific authorization password that can permit overriding the maximum check limit.

Did you notice that the Current Checkbook Balance and Cash Account Balance are negative? Current Checkbook Balance comes from the balance in the bank reconciliation window and will be adjusted when you reconcile the bank statement. Cash Account Balance comes from the March 30 period-end balance in the general ledger account and will be adjusted when you record banking transactions.

Close the window. You are now ready to complete activities on the closing checklists previously illustrated.

REVIEWING THE SERIES POSTING WINDOW

The first step in closing the account period is reviewing the Series Posting window for the Financial Series to post any suspended transactions from other Series.

Click **Series Post** and your window should contain only those transactions illustrated next. If not, then you have suspended transactions. Mark any suspended transactions and click Post. Close the window.

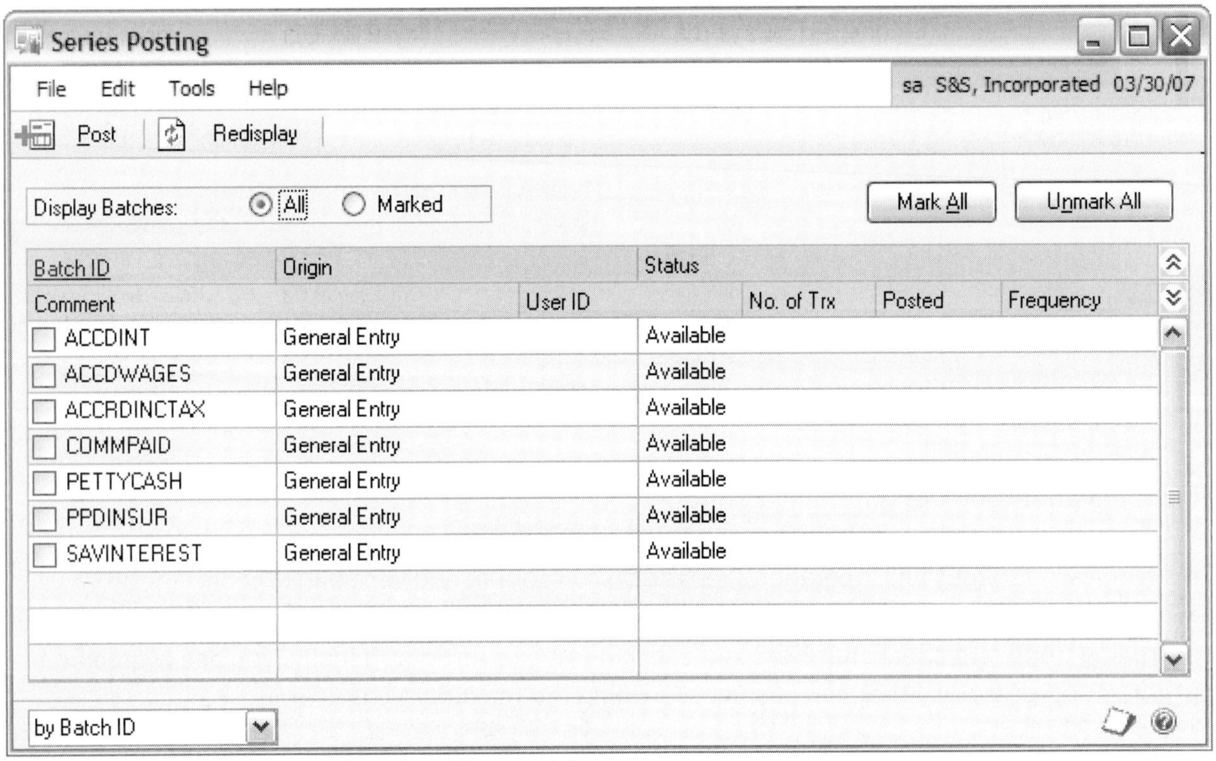

Figure 8:6 Series Post Window for Financial Series

We are now ready to complete tasks that close the accounting period and start by reviewing transactions posted in March.

REVIEWING THE DETAILED TRIAL BALANCE REPORT

The next step in closing the accounting period is performing a review of entries listed on the detailed trial balance report. This report was illustrated in Chapter 2 and is printed from the Trial Balance menu under Reports.

You review the report to identify missing transactions such as depreciation entries and adjustments to prepaid expense accounts. Furthermore, you want to note any unusual entries that may indicate a posting error.

Ashton has reviewed this report and found missing entries and a posting error. You will record these entries in the next topic.

JOURNAL ENTRIES

You are now ready to post entries that correct posting errors and adjust account balances.

Correcting Entries

Correcting entries reclassify posting errors such as posting a debit as a credit or posting an entry to the wrong general ledger account. Correcting entries cannot fix posting errors such as selling the wrong item to the wrong customer or posting a bill to the wrong vendor. Instead, you must correct these errors in the Series originating the transaction (i.e., Sales Series, Purchasing Series).

The purchasing manager indicated that the Office Rex invoice posted to the wrong general ledger account. You will now correct this entry. The next steps illustrate using a journal entry to correct the vendor bill posting for a desk purchase by reclassifying the purchase amount from office expense to a fixed asset accounts.

1. Click **General** under Transactions. Before recording this entry, expand row details for the window and review the next illustration and table that follows.

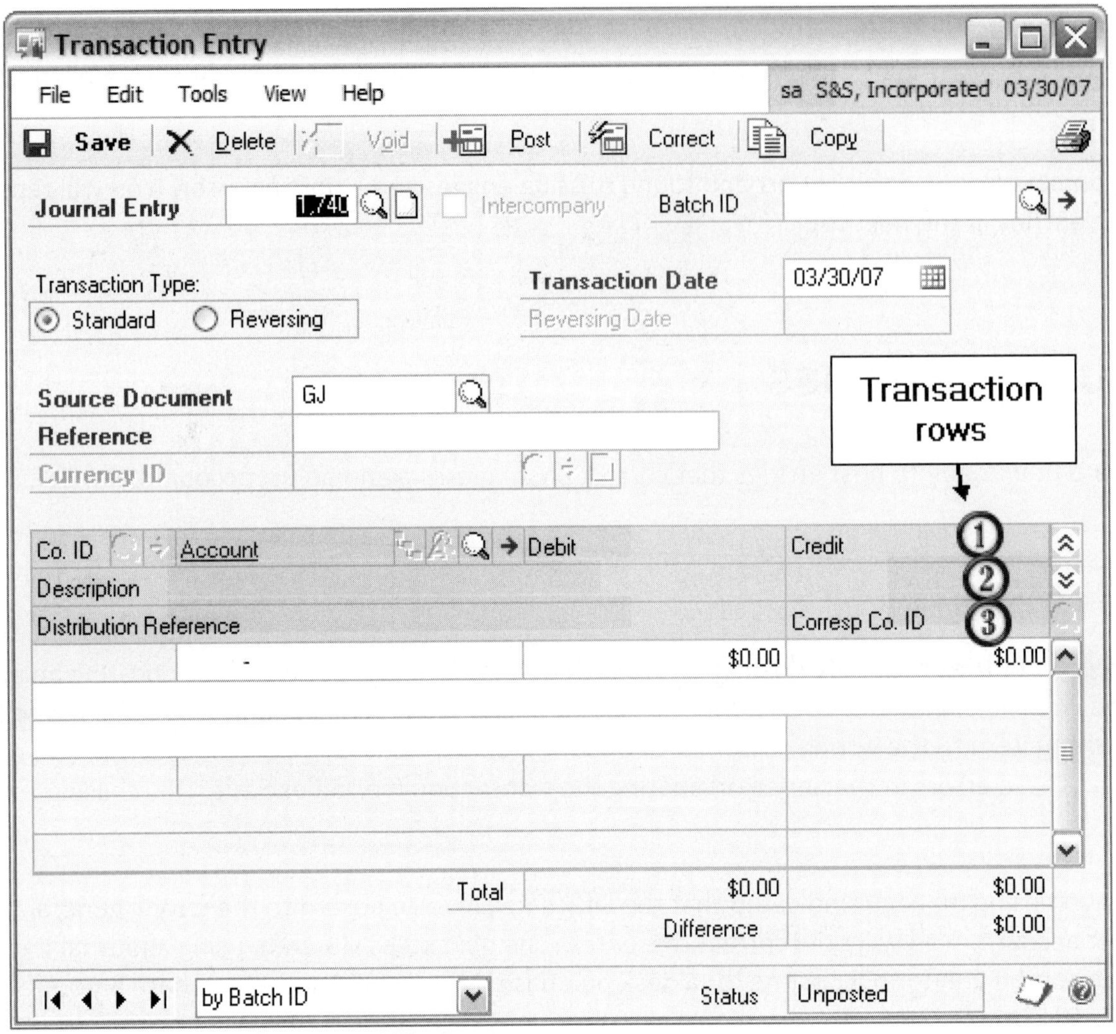

Figure 8:7 Transaction Entry Window

Field Name	Description
Journal Entry	Audit trail document number that is sequentially updated by GP.
Batch ID	Assign to a batch created through the Batches menu.
Transaction Type	Options to indicate if a standard or reversing journal entry. Reversing means to post the transaction on one date and post a transaction reversing the entry on another date. If marked, then the Reversing Date field activates.
Transaction Date / Reversing Date	Entries post to general ledger accounts on the Transaction Date and, if reversing, post that entry on the Reversing Date.
Source Document	Audit trail source document code discussed in Chapter 2.
Reference	Brief description of the transaction that appears in the account inquiry window and journal reports.
Transaction Row 1	**Account** links to the general ledger account number. **Debit** or **Credit** field stores the financial amount. *(Note: Co ID is used with the Intercompany Series and is not covered in this text.)*
Transaction Row 2	**Description** displays the description on the general ledger account number selected in the Account field.
Transaction Row 3	**Distribution Reference** stores additional text to describe the transaction on the general ledger detail report because the Reference description does not display on this report.

Table 8:1 Description for Transaction Entry Fields

2. Tab to **Transaction Date** and enter 3/1/2007. Notice that this date corresponds to the original posting date in the Purchasing Series. When correcting transactions, you should use the original posting date, if possible, to simplify tracing entries on the detailed trial balance report; however, you will not be able to use the original date if the error was discovered after closing the accounting period.

3. Refer to the next illustration to complete the window. Notice that Reference and Distribution Reference describe reasons for making this entry.

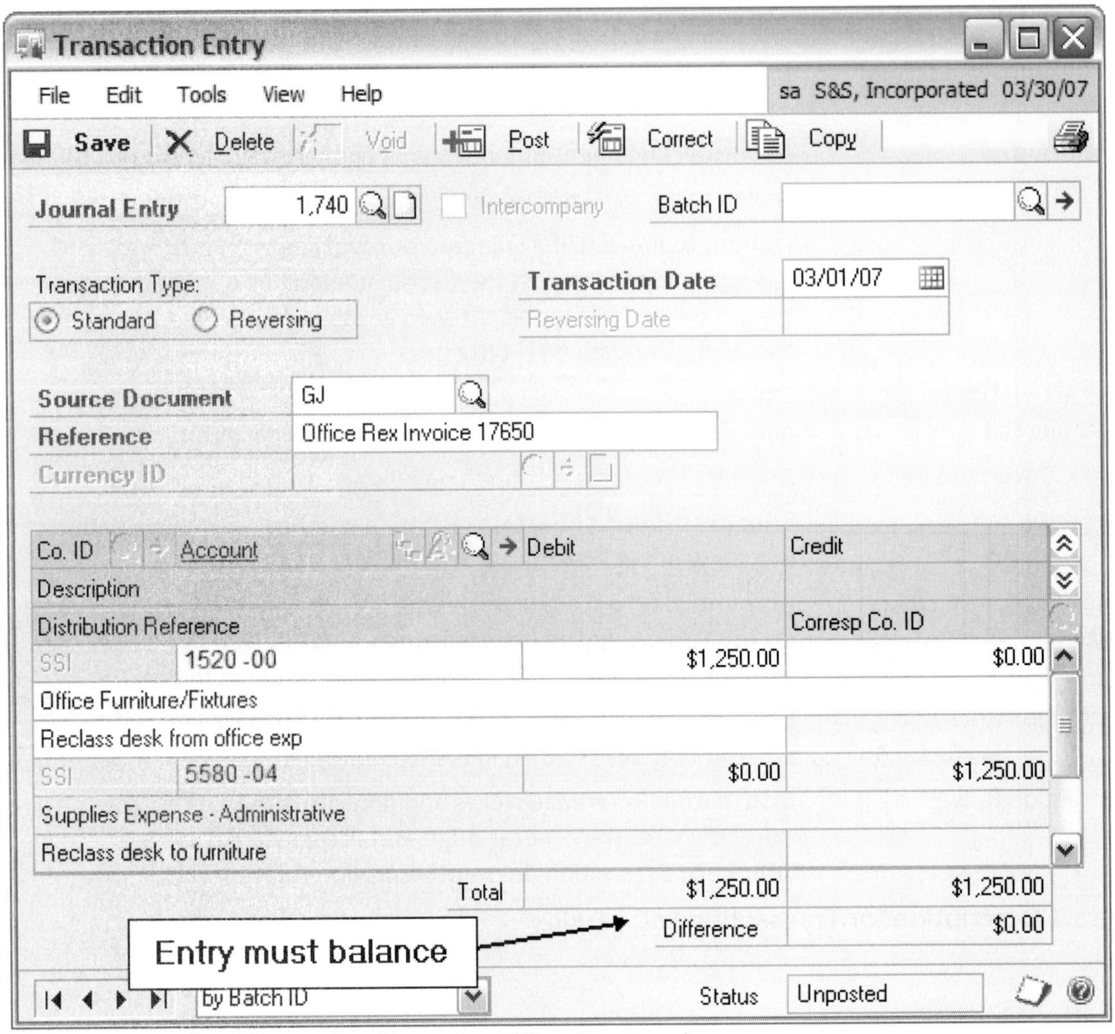

Figure 8:8 Reclassify Posting Error on Office Rex Invoice

4. Verify that the entry balances and click **Post.** Close the window and the General Posting Journal prints. Financial Series transactions always finalize to the general ledger regardless of whether you post a transaction in a batch or post individually. In other words, these transactions never suspend.

5. Now review your posting. Click **Detail** under Inquiry and look up the office furniture account. (See Figure 8:9.) We have produced a Detailed Trial Balance Report for this transaction. (See Figure 8:10.) Notice that the Reference description appears in the inquiry window whereas the Distribution Reference description appears on the report. This helps to understand documenting journal entry transactions.

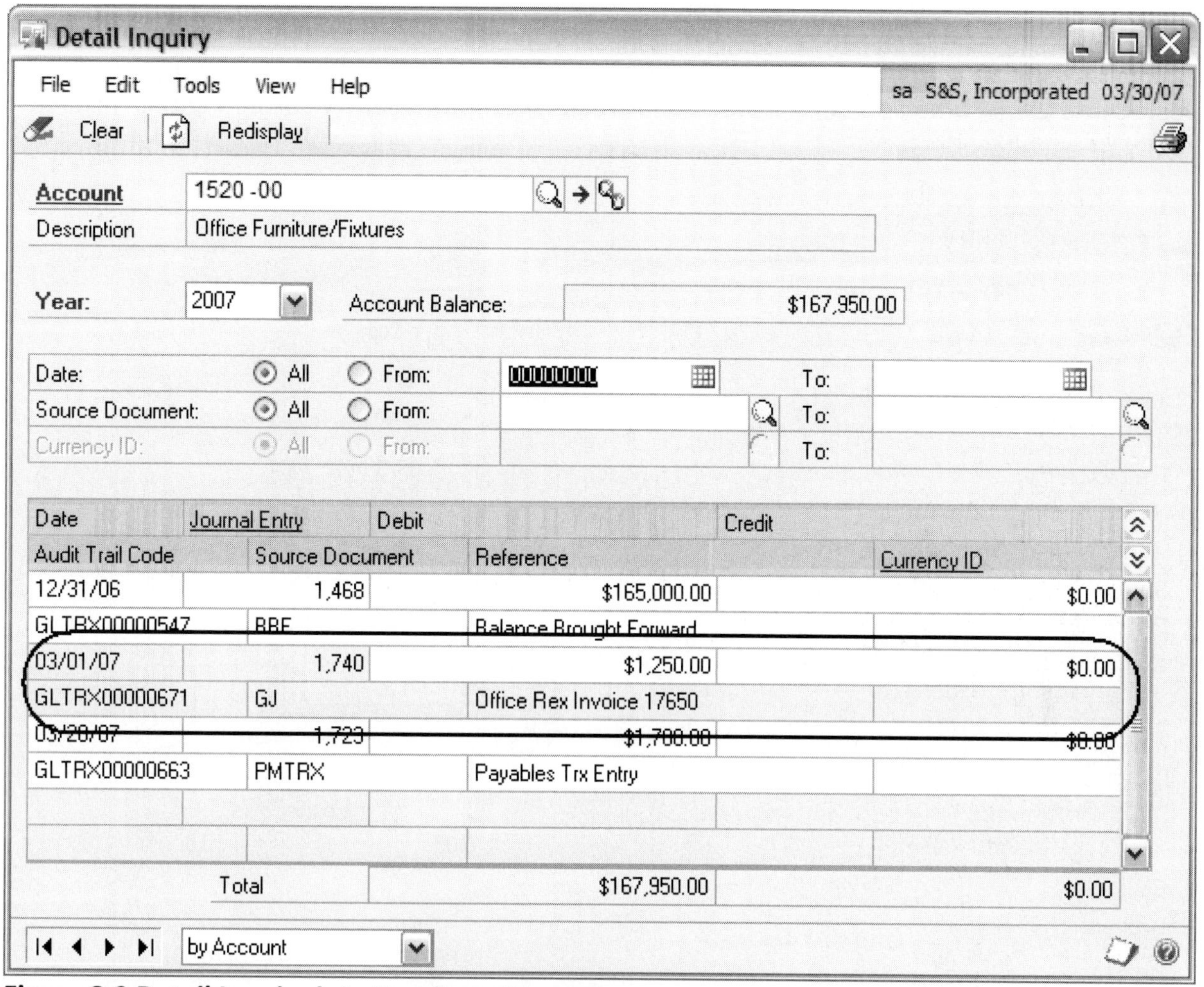

Figure 8:9 Detail Inquiry into Furniture Account

03/30/07

DETAILED TRIAL BALANCE FOR 2007

S&S, Incorporated

General Ledger

Page: 1
User ID: sa

From: 03/01/07, 1520-00 — To: 03/31/07, 1520-00

Subtotal By: No Subtotals
Sorted By: Main

Include: Posting, Unit

1520-00 — Description: Office Furniture/Fixtures — Beginning Balance: $165,000.00

Jrnl No.	Orig. Audit Trail	Distribution Reference	Orig. Master Number	Orig. Master Name	Debit	Credit
1,740	GLTRX00000671	Reclass desk from office exp			$1,250.00	
1,723	PMTRX00000163	New computer	90135	Office Rex, Inc.	$1,700.00	

Account		Net Change	Ending Balance	Debit	Credit
1520-00	Totals:	$2,950.00	$167,950.00	$2,950.00	$0.00

	Accounts	Beginning Balance	Net Change	Ending Balance	Debit	Credit
Grand Totals:	1	$165,000.00	$2,950.00	$167,950.00	$2,950.00	$0.00

Figure 8:10 Detailed Trial Balance Report for Furniture Account

One final point. If correcting a debit entry that should have been a credit entry or vice versa, post the journal entry so that you can later trace the correction. For instance, assume we posted interest income as a debit instead of a credit. The journal entry correcting this mistake would be as follows.

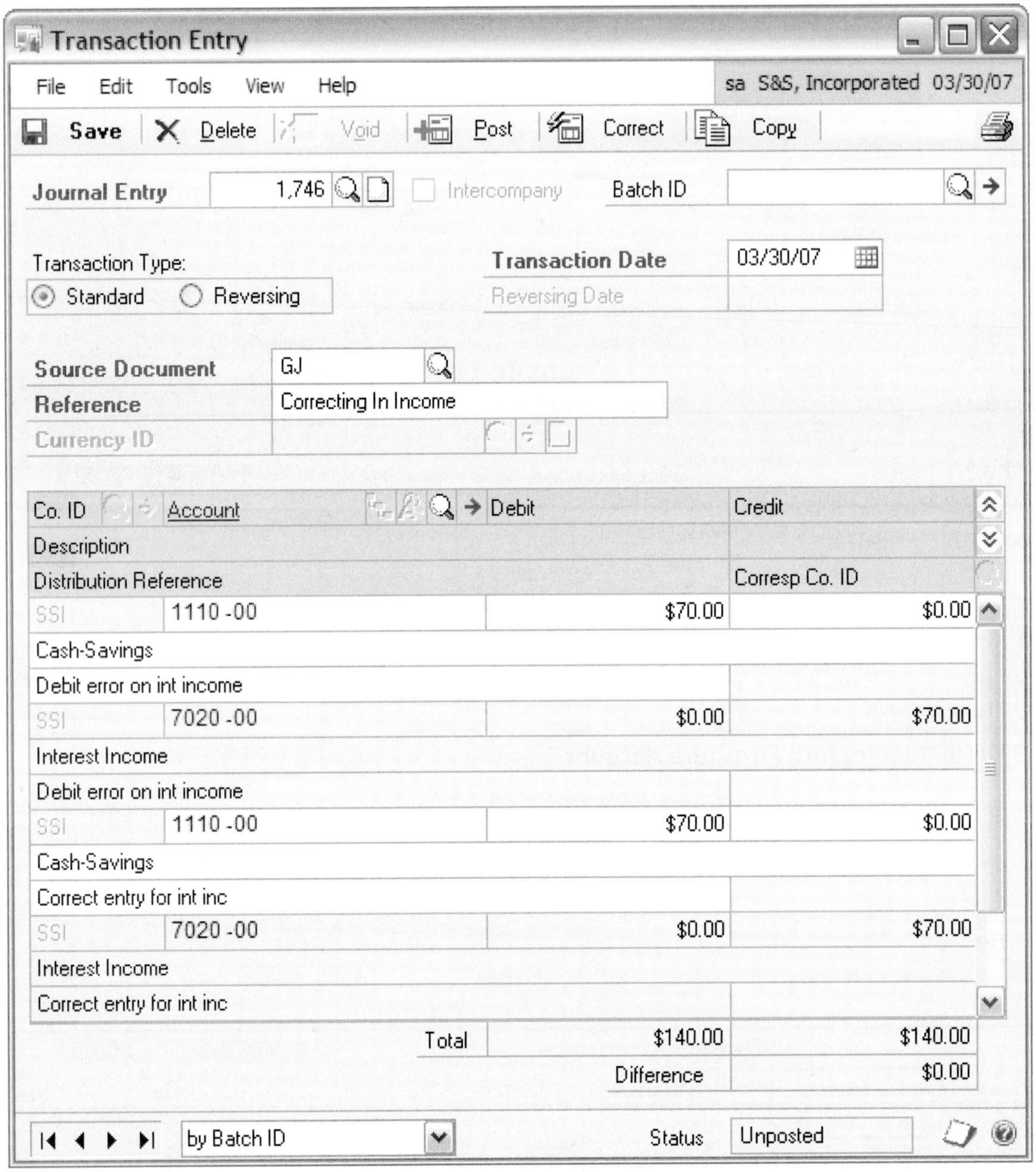

Figure 8:11 Example of Correcting Posting Error for Interest Income

Using this procedure, you can later trace the reason for correction.

Adjusting Entries

Adjusting entries are used to make adjustments to account balances for entries not posted through other cycle activities. Adjusting entries include booking depreciation expense, accruing expenses, deferring revenue, and expensing prepaid expenses. Adjusting entries often repeat so Ashton has stored these transactions in recurring batches.

1. Click **Batches** and view the lookup window for saved batches. (See Figure 8:12.) Note that these batches recur monthly.

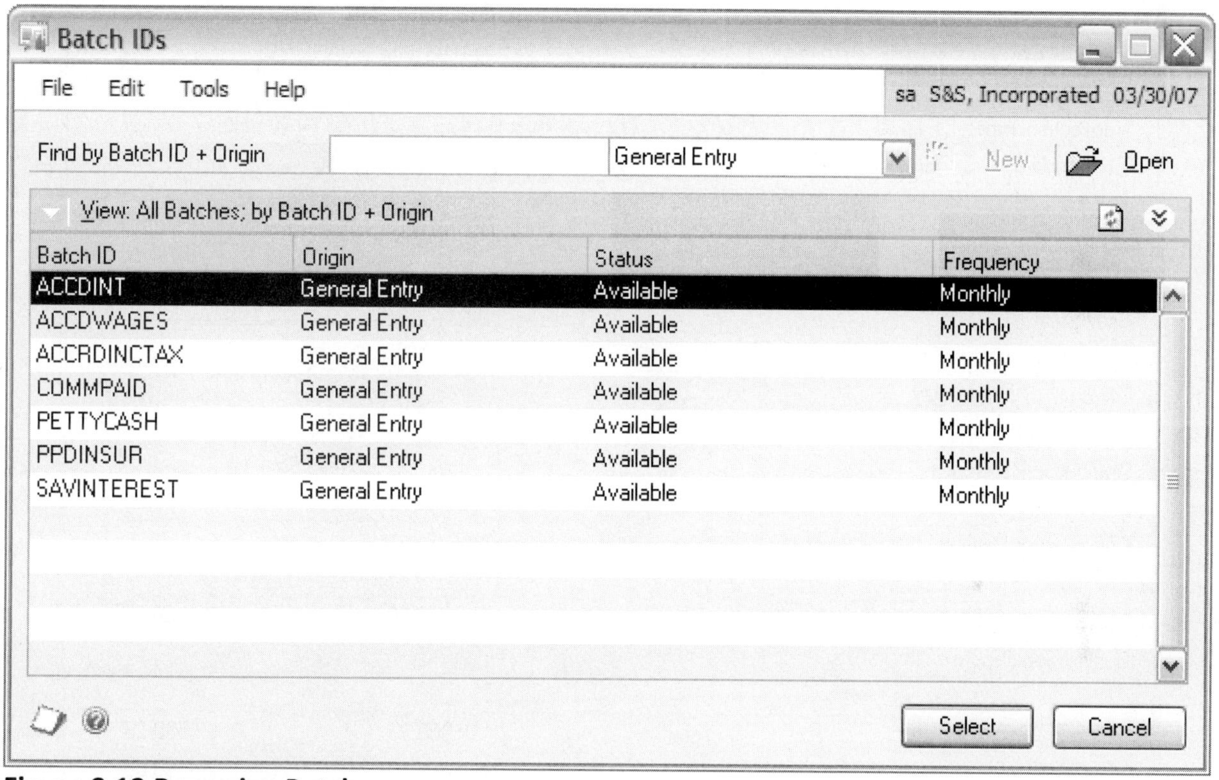

Figure 8:12 Recurring Batches

2. Select **COMMPAID**.

3. Click **Transactions** and, in **Journal Entry**, look up the transaction stored in the COMMPAID batch. This transaction adjusts Sales Series commission expense entries. Sales Series posting accounts can only debit one expense account so S&S set this series to debit 5200-00 Commissions Expense and credit 2230-00 Commissions Payable when posting a sales invoice. However, S&S wants commission expense reported by department so set Payroll Series posting accounts to debit departmental commission expense accounts instead of commission payable. We now have commission expense booked twice and this entry takes the payroll amount out of 5200-00 Commissions Expense and 2230-00 Commission Payable. So why didn't Ashton just post commission expense to an allocation account to spreads costs across department? Commissions are

not allocable through a fixed amount or variable percentage because commission expense corresponds to actual sales made by a salesperson in that department.

4. Enter the transaction as follows. The adjustment corresponds to the commissions transferred on March 30, which also corresponds to the amounts paid to salespeople on March 30.

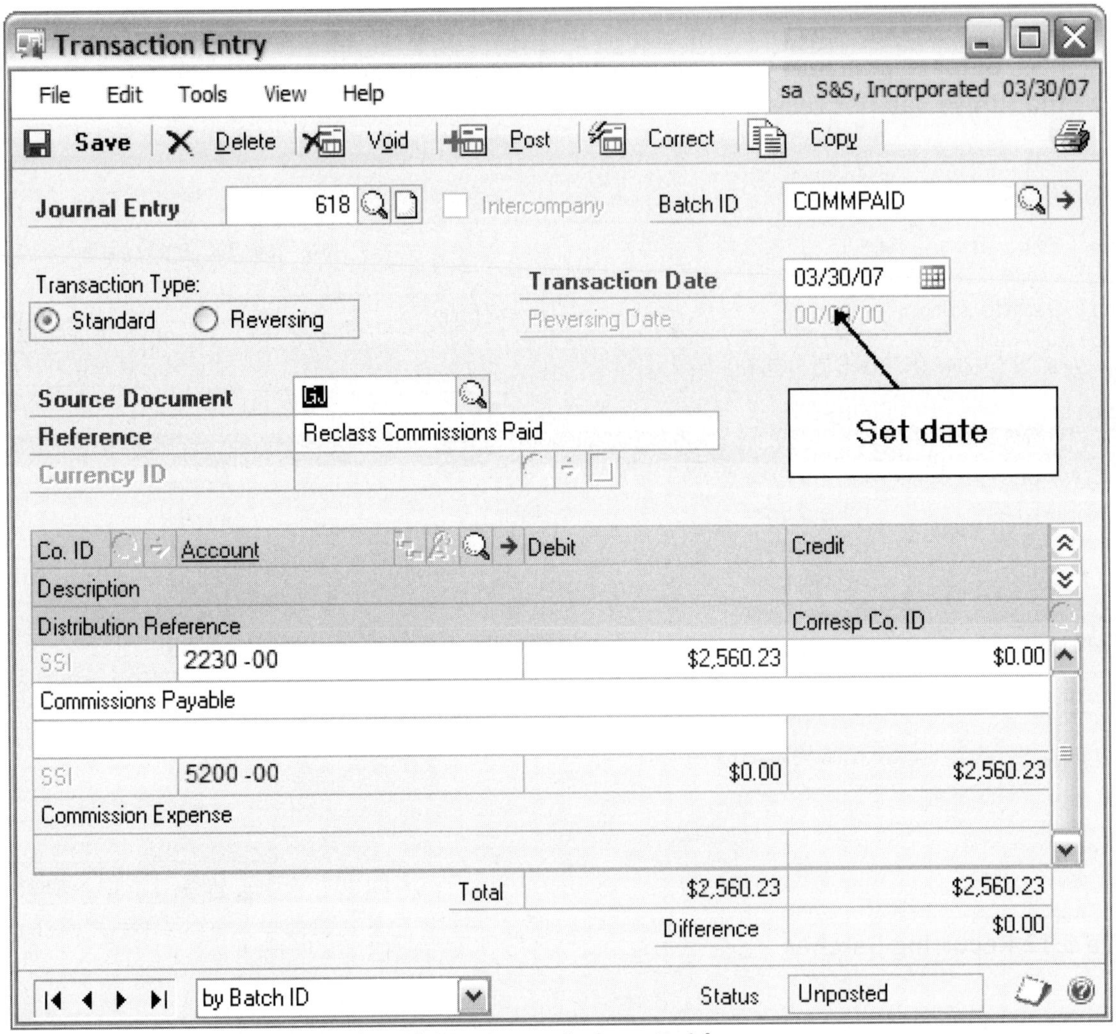

Figure 8:13 Transaction Reclassifying Commissions Paid

5. Save the transaction. You will post it later.

6. Next post accrued wages. Look up the Journal Entry stored in the **ACCDWAGES** batch and change the Transaction date to 3/30/2007 as illustrated next.

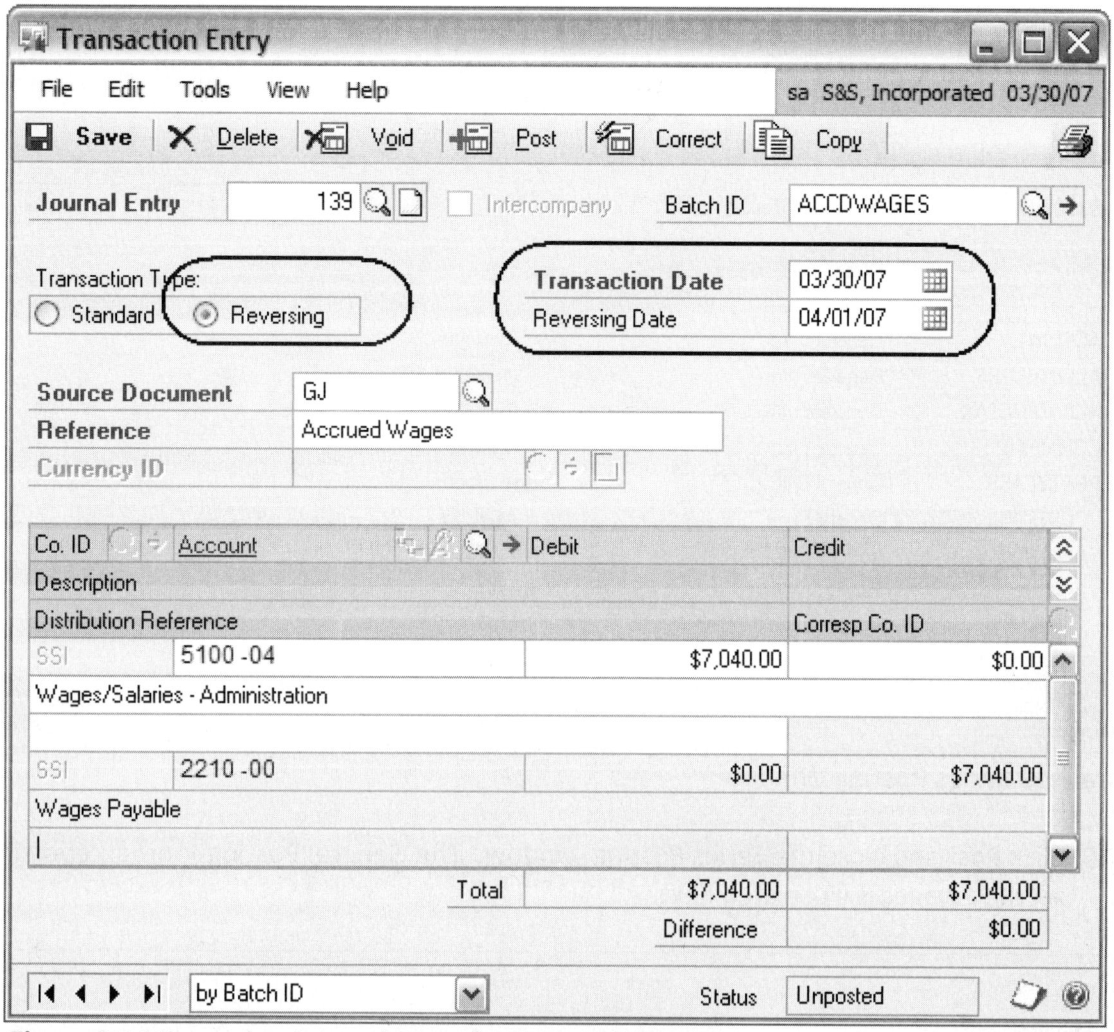

Figure 8:14 Reversing Journal Entry for Accrued Wages

7. Notice that this is a reversing journal entry debiting 5100-04 Wages/Salaries – Administration and crediting 2210-00 Wages Payable on March 30, 2007. It will also credit 5100-04 Wages/Salaries-Administration and debit 2210-00 Wages Payable on April 1, 2007.

8. Click **Save** and close the Transaction Entry and the Batch windows.

9. You will now post these batches. Click **Series Post** and mark the batches illustrated next.

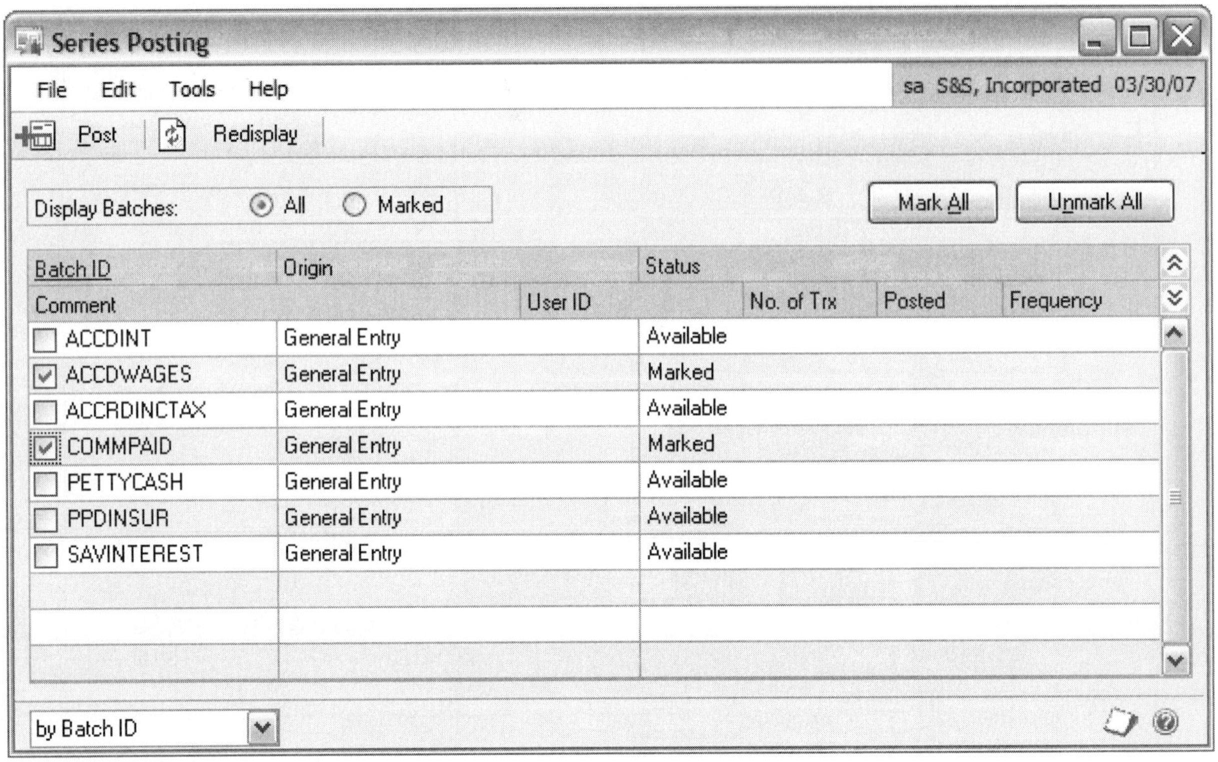

Figure 8:15 Series Posting Window

10. Click **Post** and close the Series Posting window. The General Posting Journal report for accrued wages is illustrated next.

```
                                    S&S, Incorporated                          Page:    1
User Date:  03/30/07              GENERAL POSTING JOURNAL                      User ID: sa
                                      General Ledger

* Voided Journal Entry


Batch ID:       ACCDWAGES
Batch Comment:  Accrued Wages


Approved:       No          Batch Total Actual:       $14,080.00     Batch Total Control:           $0.00
Approved by:                Trx Total Actual:                  1     Trx Total Control:                 0
Approval Date:


    Journal    Transaction  Transaction  Reversing   Source    Transaction              Audit Trail    Reversing Audit
    Entry      Type         Date         Date        Document  Reference                Code           Trail Code
--------------------------------------------------------------------------------------------------------------------
         139   Reversing    03/30/07     04/01/07    GJ        Accrued Wages            GLTRX00000672  GLREV00000672

               Account                 Description                              Debit                Credit
               ----------------------  ---------------------------------------  -------------------  -------------------
03/30/07       5100-04                 Wages/Salaries - Administration           $7,040.00
03/30/07       2210-00                 Wages Payable                                                    $7,040.00
04/01/07       5100-04                 Wages/Salaries - Administration                                  $7,040.00
04/01/07       2210-00                 Wages Payable                             $7,040.00
                                                                                -------------------  -------------------
          Total Distributions:       4                            Totals:      $14,080.00            $14,080.00


       Total Journal Entries:        1
```

Figure 8:16 General Posting Journal for Accrued Wages

Depreciation Entries

Ashton uses an Excel spreadsheet to calculate monthly depreciation expense. *(Note: The Fixed Asset Series is included with your software but is not covered in this text. This Series integrates fixed asset transactions and depreciation entries to the Financial Series.)* Figure 8:17 is the summary sheet used to post depreciation expense. This spreadsheet also tracks detailed asset information on separate worksheets that are not illustrated.

S&S Straight Line Depreciation FYE 12/31/2007						
Asset Class	**Estimated Useful Life (Years)**	**Prior Year Cost**	**Deletion Cost**	**Acquisition Cost**	**Current Year Cost**	**Monthly Depreciation**
Buildings	50	$765,000			$ 765,000	$ 1,275.00
Office Furniture and Fixtures	7	$165,000			$ 165,000	$ 1,979.17
Vehicles	5	$367,876			$ 367,876	$ 6,131.27
Computer Hardware	4	$165,000			$ 165,000	$ 3,437.50
Computer Software	3	$ 67,000			$ 67,000	$ 1,861.11
Total						**$ 14,684.05**

Figure 8:17 Excel Depreciation Worksheet

Ashton has not created a recurring batch for depreciation expense so you will do that in the next practice exercise.

GP

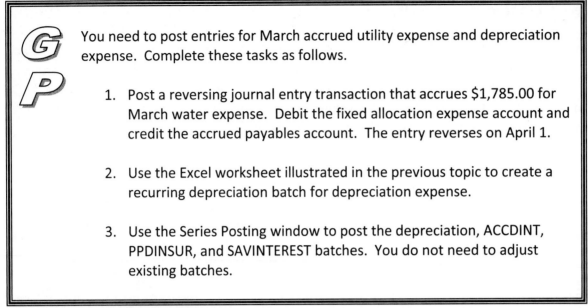

You need to post entries for March accrued utility expense and depreciation expense. Complete these tasks as follows.

1. Post a reversing journal entry transaction that accrues $1,785.00 for March water expense. Debit the fixed allocation expense account and credit the accrued payables account. The entry reverses on April 1.

2. Use the Excel worksheet illustrated in the previous topic to create a recurring depreciation batch for depreciation expense.

3. Use the Series Posting window to post the depreciation, ACCDINT, PPDINSUR, and SAVINTEREST batches. You do not need to adjust existing batches.

E8:1 Practice Adjusting Entries

Banking Transactions

Ashton's review of the trial balance report discloses that entries for a bank transfer to payroll and an advance on the line of credit are missing. You will post these entries next.

1. Click **Bank Transactions** and enter the following receipt from the line of credit.

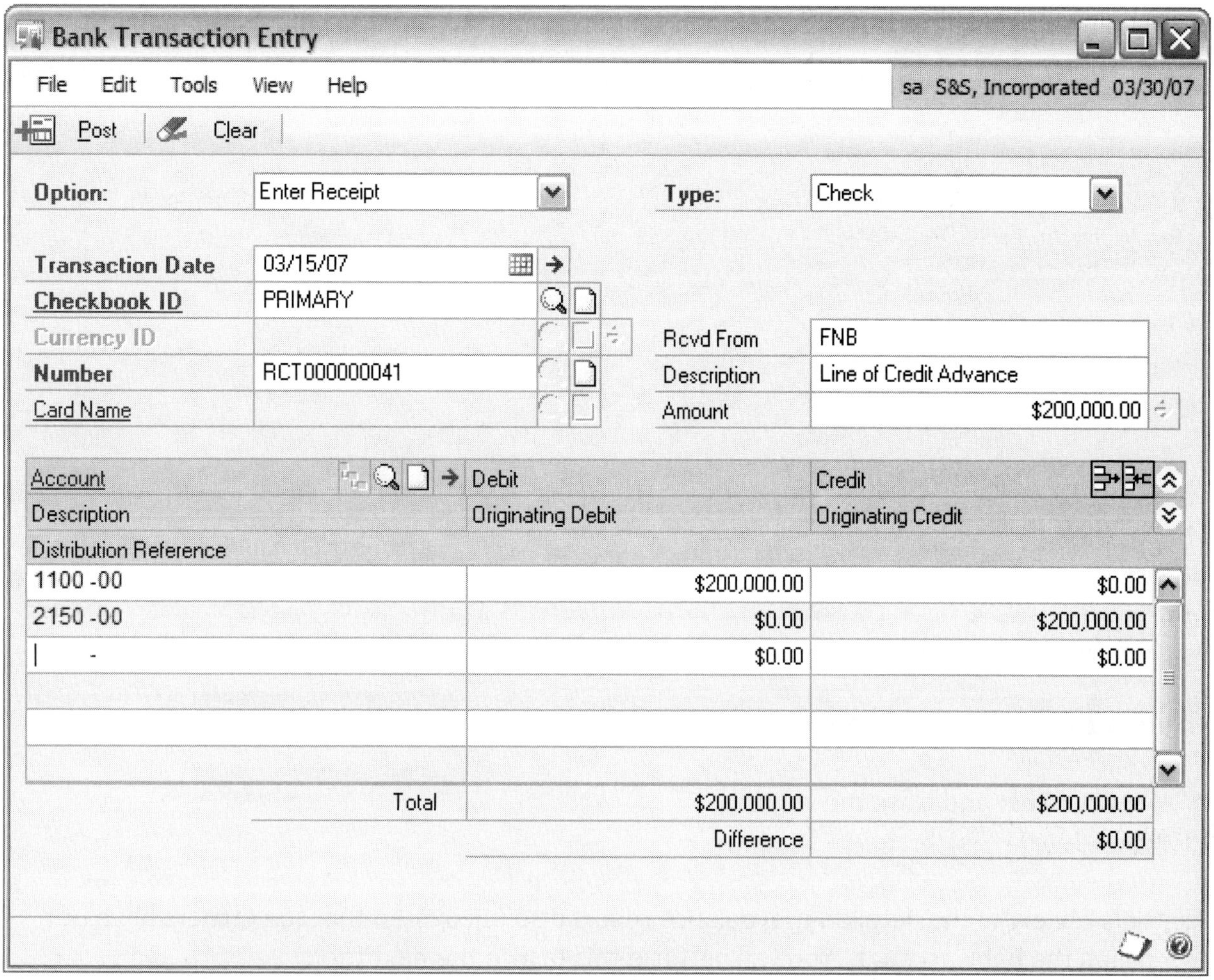

Figure 8:18 Bank Transaction Entry

2. Click **Post** and close the window.

3. Now record the transfer from the regular checking account to the payroll checking account. Click **Bank Transfer** and enter the following transaction.

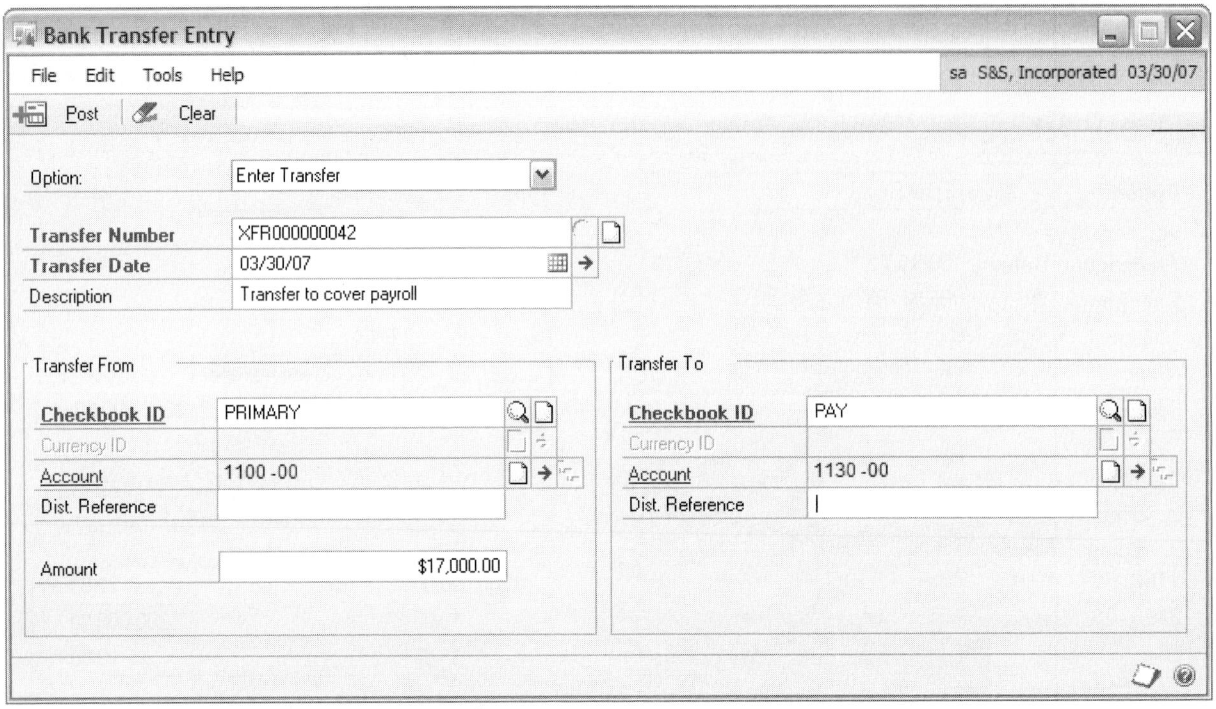

Figure 8:19 Bank Transfer Entry Window

4. Click **Post** and close the window.

Ashton's review of the detailed trial balance report also uncovered that the owners have not reconciled the bank account. You will perform this task in the next topic.

BANK RECONCILIATION

S&S received the following bank statement for the regular checking account. This topic illustrates reconciling that statement in GP.

S&S, Incorporated
Bank Statement Date: March 31, 2007

Beginning Balance from February Statement				$ 235,780.19
March Deposits				
	Mar 2, 2007		189,000.00	
	Mar 9, 2007		108,240.00	
	Mar 13, 2007		147,551.00	
	Mar 15, 2007		277,935.00	
	Mar 19, 2007		95,648.00	
	Mar 26, 2007		94,500.00	
	Mar 27, 2007		28,327.50	
Total Deposits for March				941,201.50
March Checks Cleared				
	Mar 2, 2007	331	6,369.31	
	Mar 2, 2007	335	37,050.00	
	Mar 2, 2007	339	90.00	
	Mar 19, 2007	340	513.64	
	Mar 19, 2007	341	11,767.36	
	Mar 19, 2007	342	396.00	
	Mar 19, 2007	343	11,723.63	
	Mar 19, 2007	344	7,107.15	
	Mar 19, 2007	345	765.00	
	Mar 21, 2007	346	55,200.00	
	Mar 21, 2007	347	11,878.97	
	Mar 21, 2007	348	380.00	
	Mar 21, 2007	349	1,278.91	
	Mar 21, 2007	350	135.00	
	Mar 21, 2007	351	11,891.31	
	Mar 26, 2007	352	3,750.00	
	Mar 26, 2007	353	69,000.00	
	Mar 26, 2007	354	2,303.15	
	Mar 26, 2007	355	95,250.00	
	Mar 29, 2007	356	96,202.80	
	Mar 29, 2007	357	126,910.00	
Total Cleared Checks for March				549,962.23
Less Bank Transfers				
	Mar 16, 2007		20,000.00	
	Mar 30, 2007		17,000.00	
Total March Transfers				37,000.00
March Service Charges				65.70
Ending Bank Balance March 31, 2007				$ 589,953.76

Figure 8:20 S&S Bank Statement for March

Bank Deposits

You begin the process of reconciling bank statements by posting bank deposits to the reconciliation window.

1. Click **Bank Deposits** and enter the following information at the top of the window.

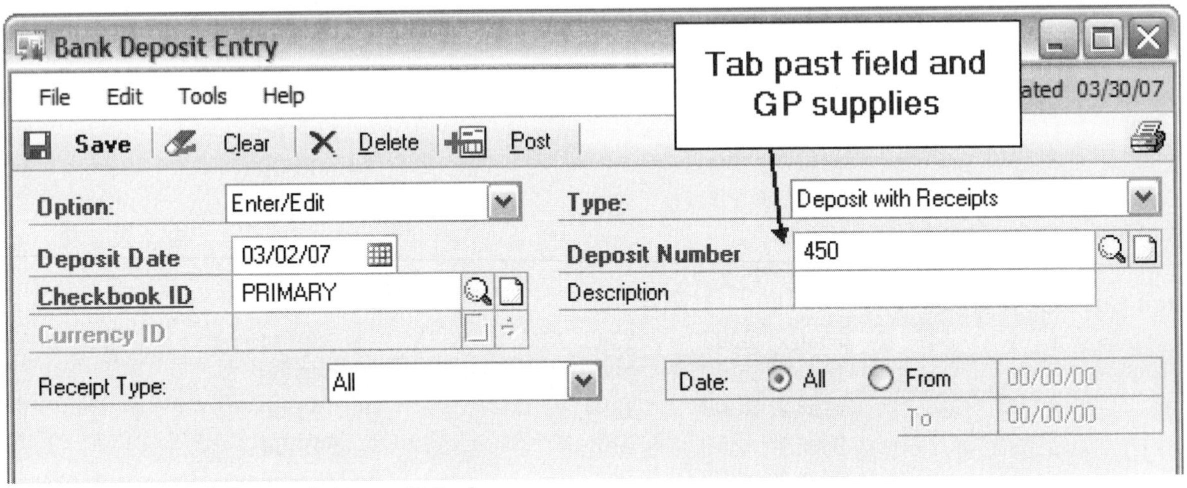

Figure 8:21 Bank Deposit Entry Window

2. Mark the deposit made on 03/02/2007 as illustrated next. Note that Deposit Amount agrees to the amount listed on the bank statement.

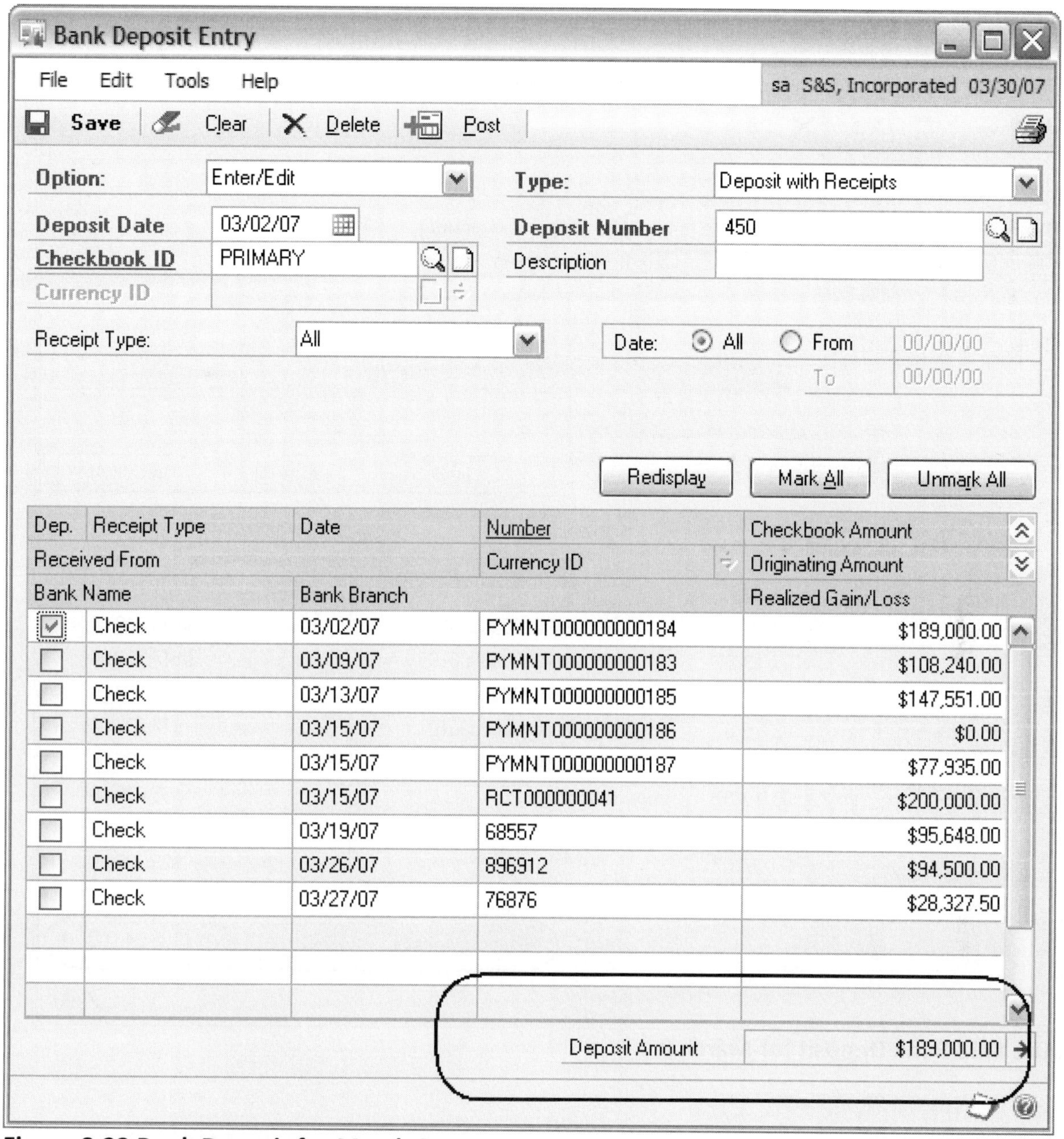

Figure 8:22 Bank Deposit for March 2

3. Click **Post**. This action does not post financial entries to the general ledger. Instead, you are posting bank deposit to the bank reconciliation window.

4. You need to continue posting bank deposits to this window. Complete this task by referring to the next series of illustrations. Remember to click **Post** after each deposit and these deposits match the bank statement.

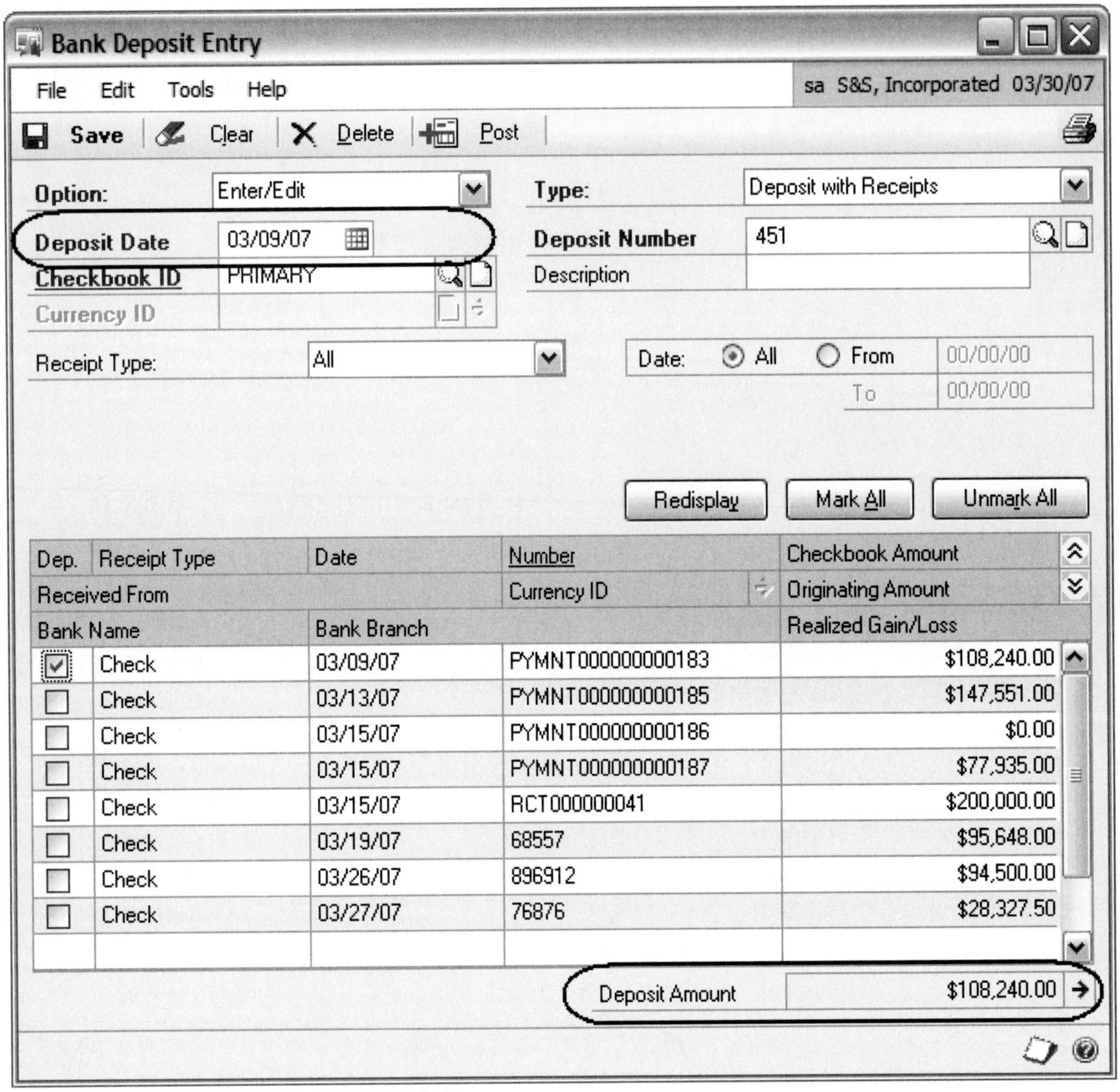
Bank Deposit Entry
File Edit Tools Help
sa S&S, Incorporated 03/30/07
Save Clear Delete Post
Option: Enter/Edit
Type: Deposit with Receipts
Deposit Date 03/09/07
Deposit Number 451
Checkbook ID PRIMARY
Description
Currency ID
Receipt Type: All
Date: All From 00/00/00
To 00/00/00
Redisplay
Mark All
Unmark All
Dep. Receipt Type Date Number Checkbook Amount
Received From Currency ID Originating Amount
Bank Name Bank Branch Realized Gain/Loss
Check 03/09/07 PYMNT000000000183 $108,240.00
Check 03/13/07 PYMNT000000000185 $147,551.00
Check 03/15/07 PYMNT000000000186 $0.00
Check 03/15/07 PYMNT000000000187 $77,935.00
Check 03/15/07 RCT000000041 $200,000.00
Check 03/19/07 68557 $95,648.00
Check 03/26/07 896912 $94,500.00
Check 03/27/07 76876 $28,327.50
Deposit Amount $108,240.00

Figure 8:23 Bank Deposit for March 9

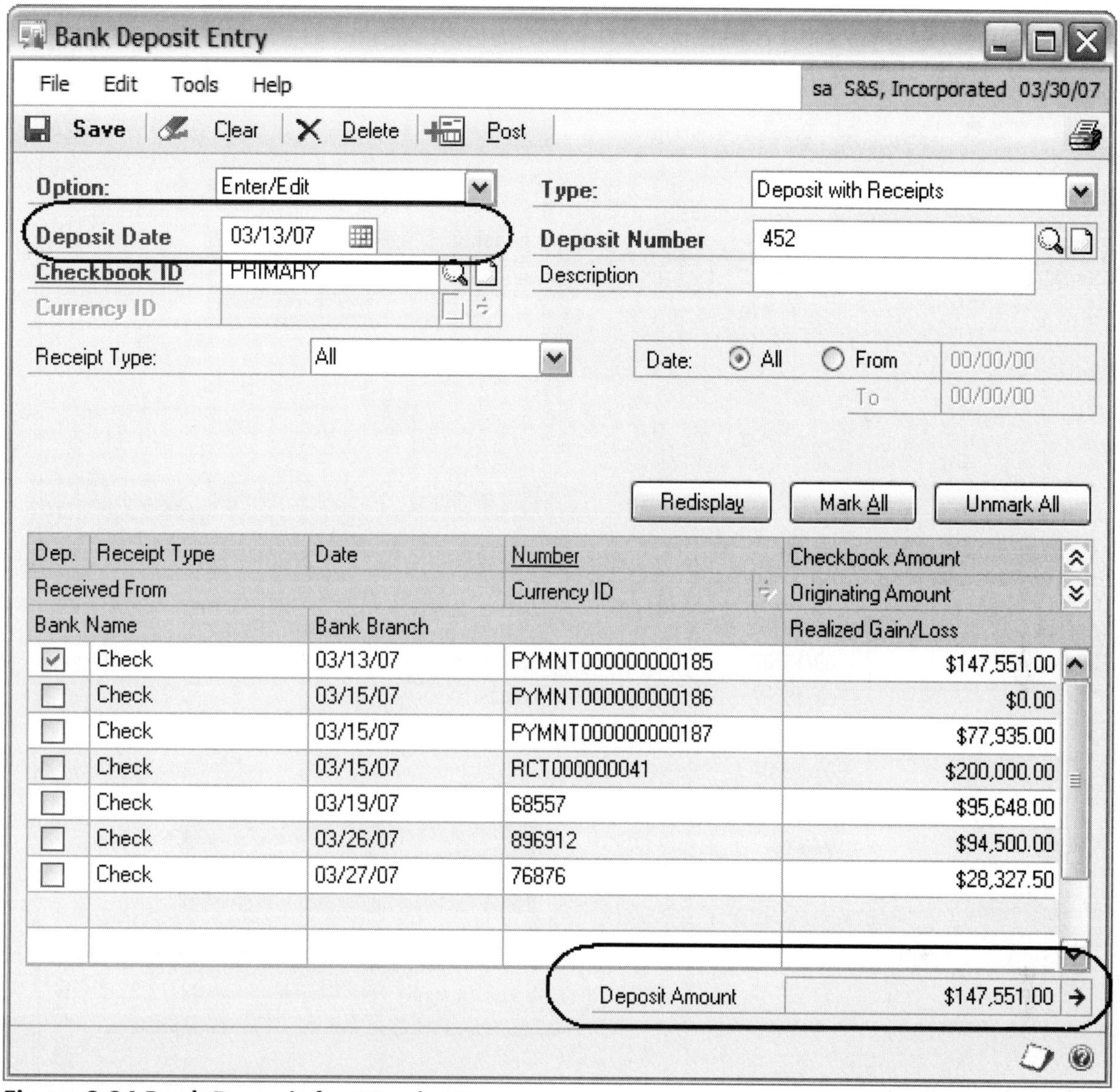

Figure 8:24 Bank Deposit for March 13

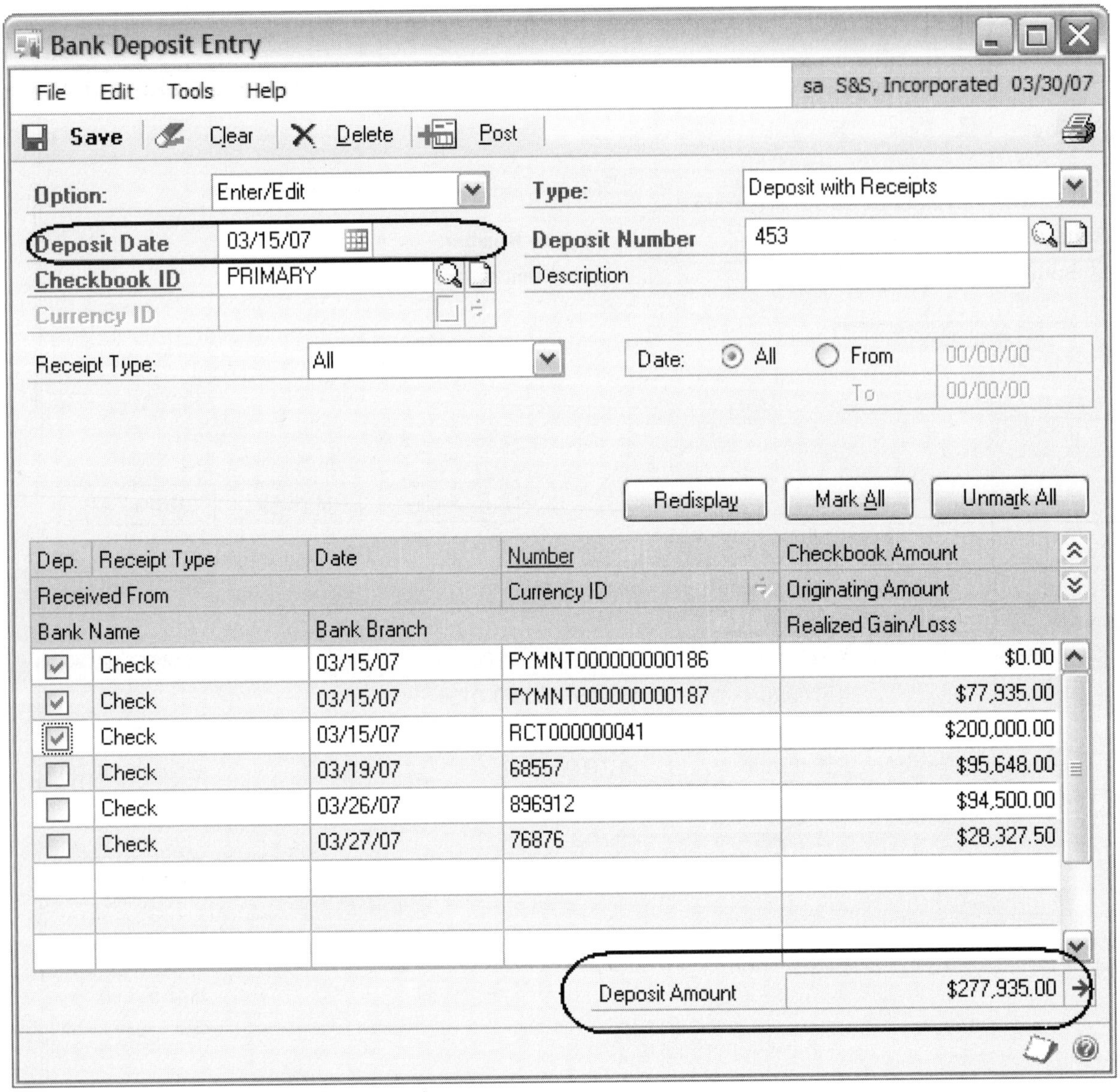

Figure 8:25 Bank Deposit for March 15

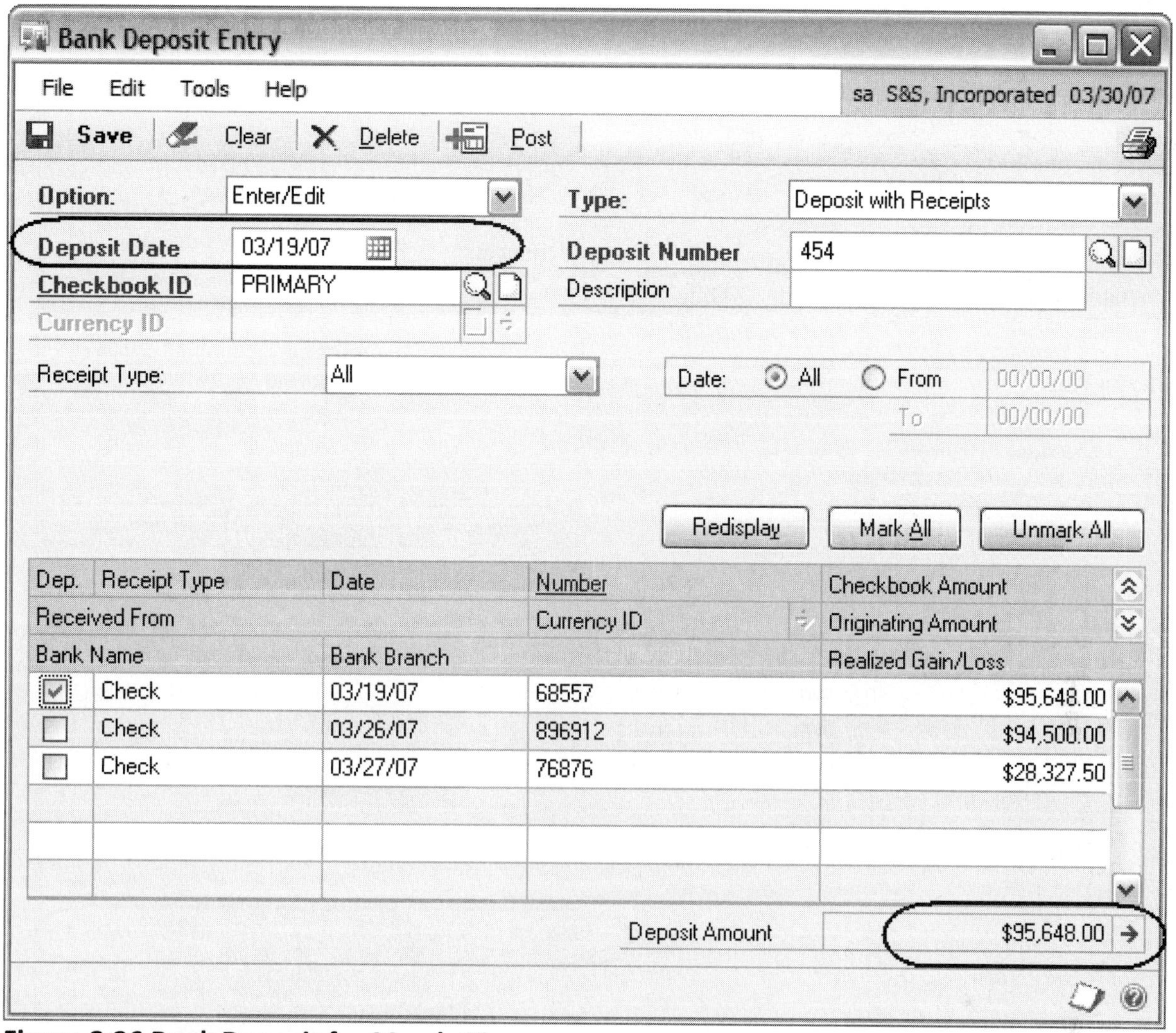

Figure 8:26 Bank Deposit for March 19

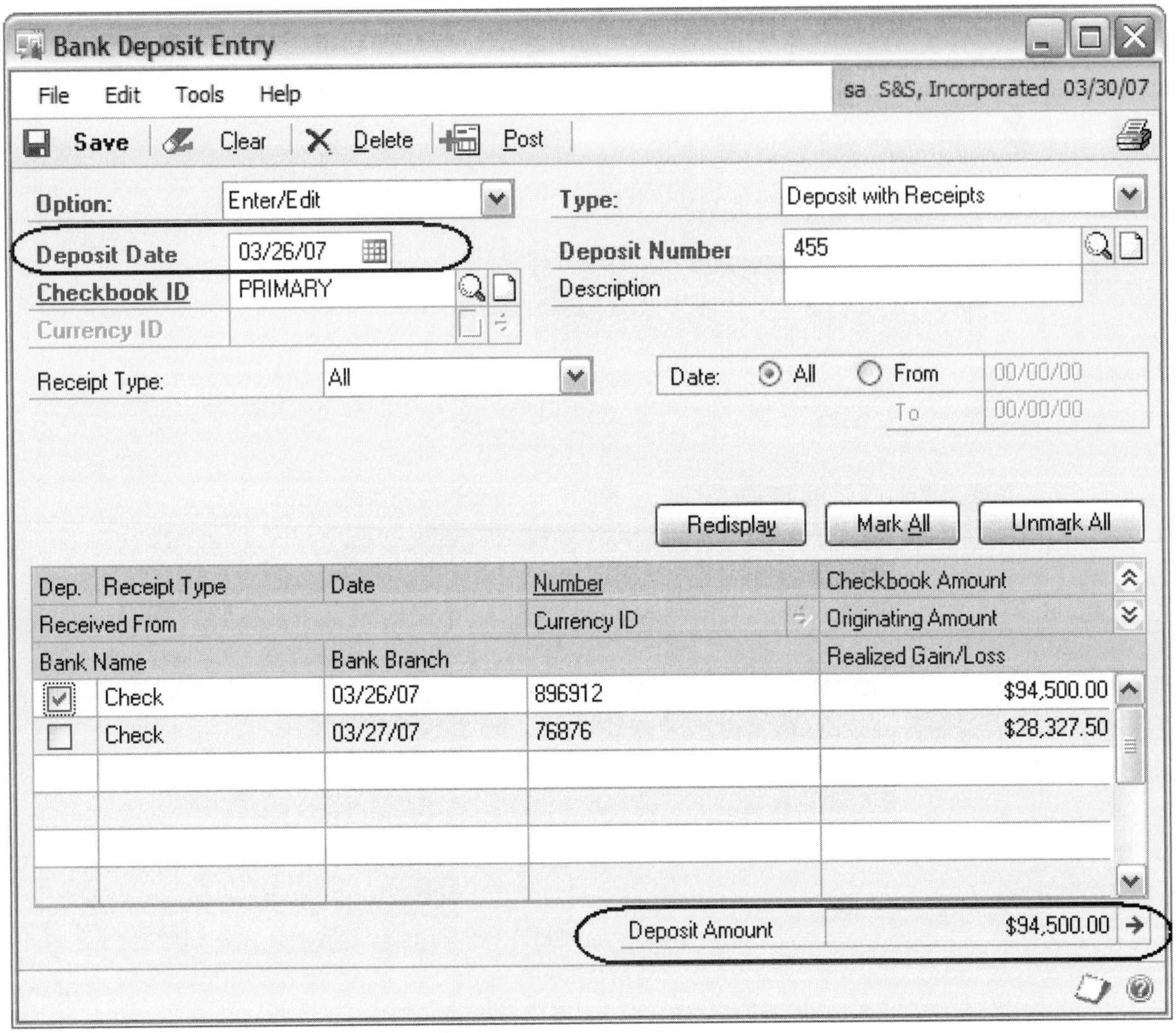

Figure 8:27 Bank Deposit for March 26

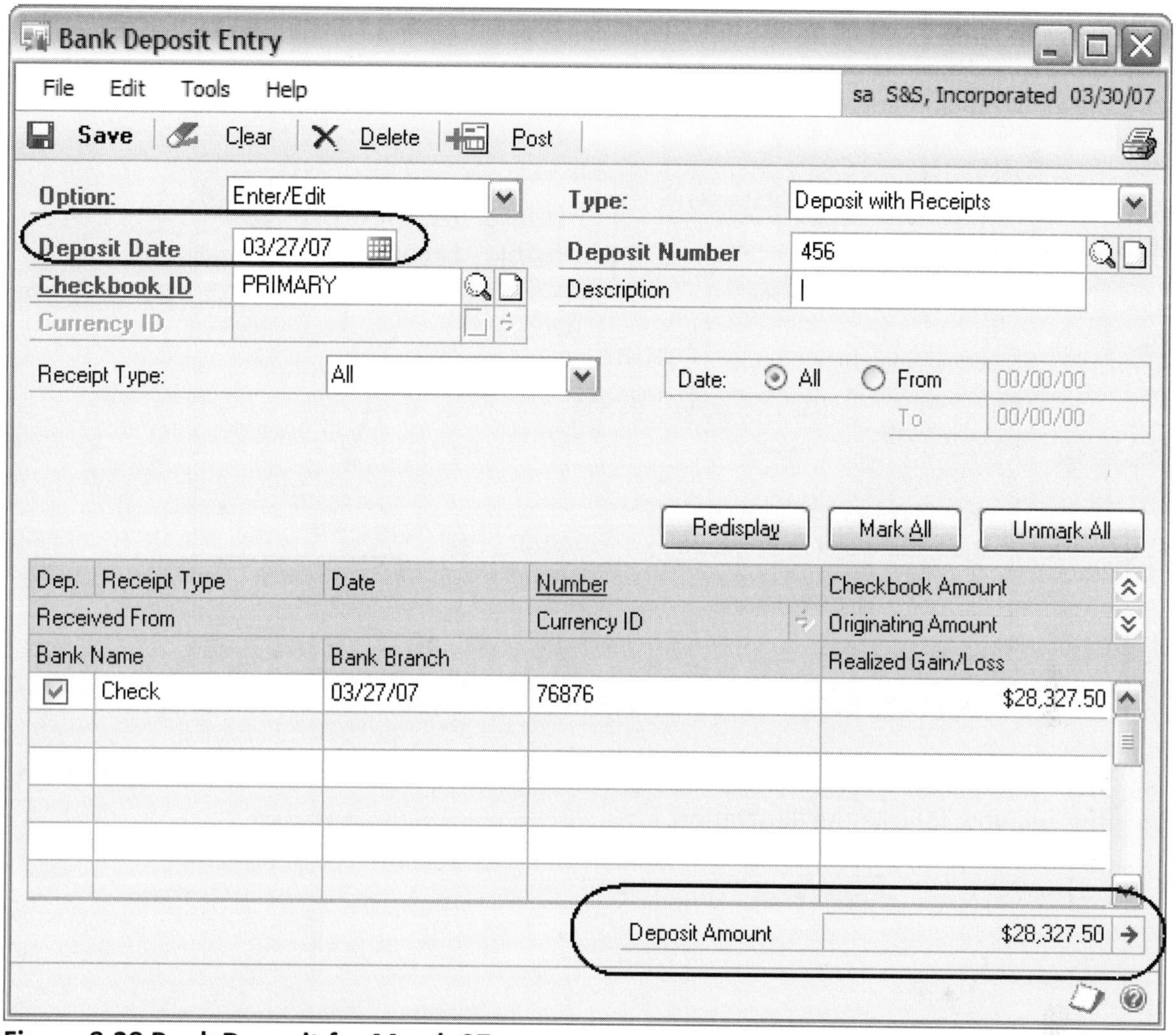

Figure 8:28 Bank Deposit for March 27

5. Click **X** to close the window and the Bank Deposit Report prints to the screen. Close it.

You are now ready to prepare the March 30 bank reconciliation for this account using the following steps.

Reconciling the Bank Statement

1. Click **Reconcile Bank Statement** and enter the information illustrated next.

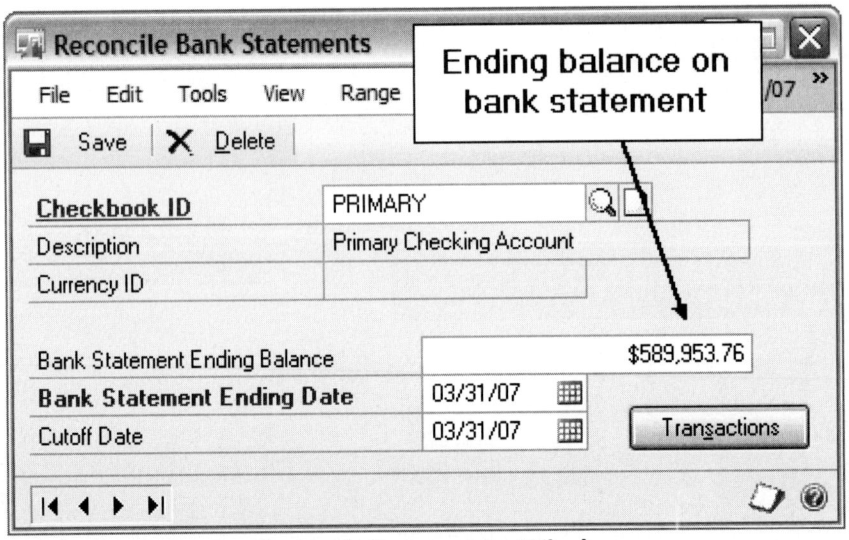

Figure 8:29 Reconcile Bank Statements Window

2. Click **Transactions** and refer to the next illustration. An explanation on clearing items in this window follows the illustration.

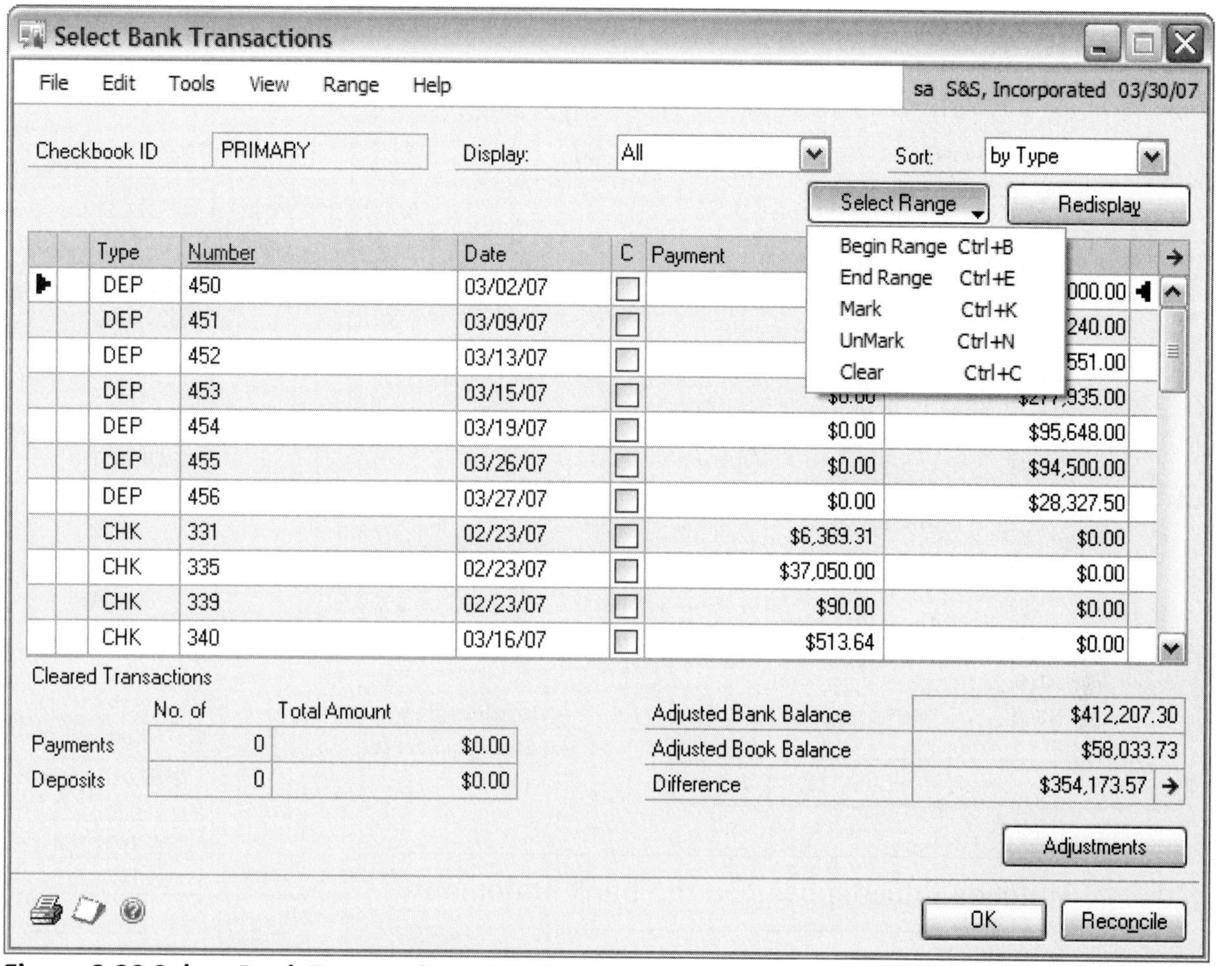

Figure 8:30 Select Bank Transactions Window

Sort Option: The window currently lists items in order of type (i.e., deposit, check, bank transfer). You can resort by Date by selecting this option and clicking Redisplay.

Select Range Button: Used to clear a range of items. First, click the beginning row in the range and choose Begin Range. Next, click ending row in the range and choose End Range. Finally, choose Mark to clear items in the range.

3. First, clear deposits in the window that are listed on the bank statement. DEP in the Type column identifies deposit transactions.

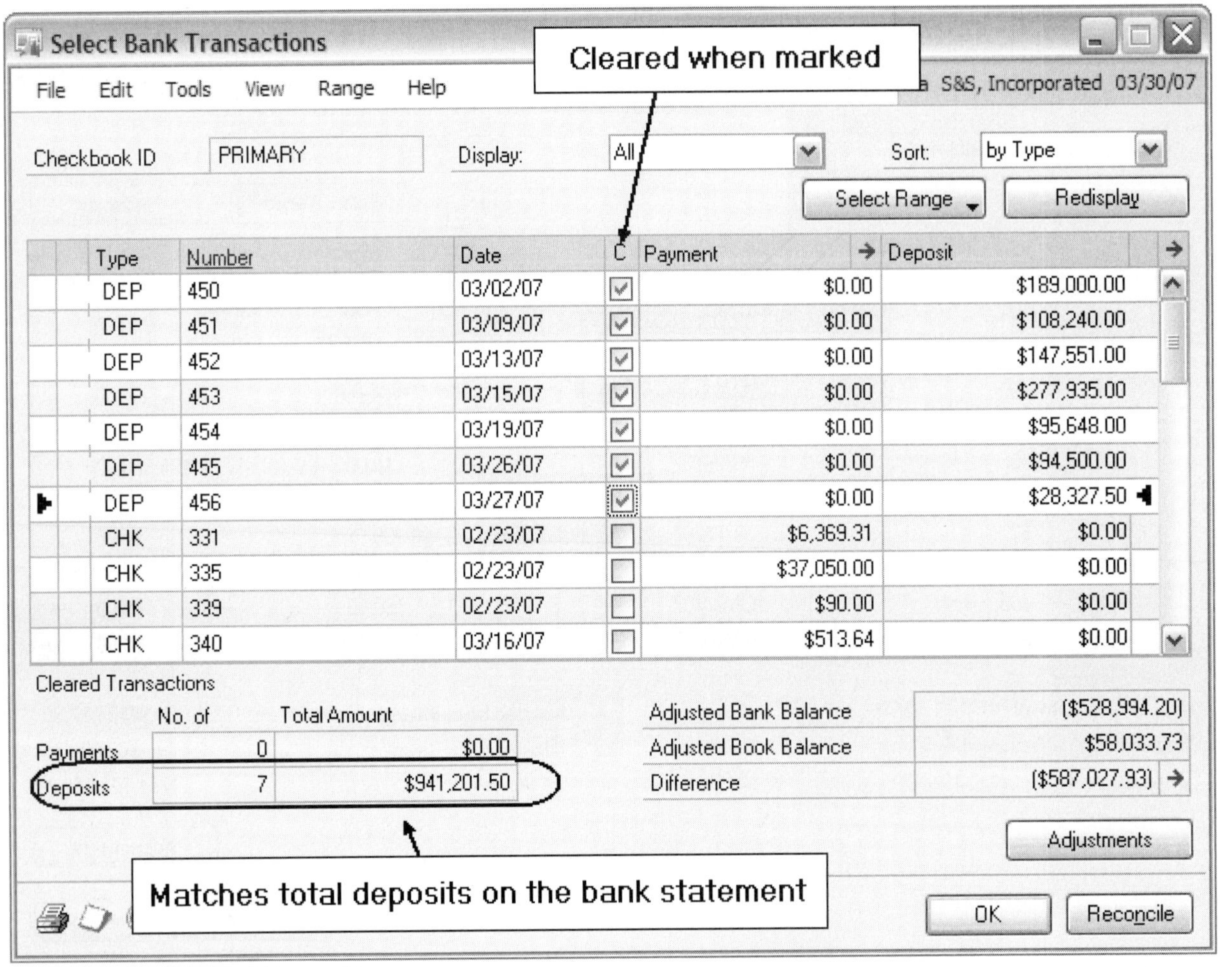

Figure 8:31 Cleared Deposits

4. Next, clear checks (i.e., CHK) listed on the bank statement.

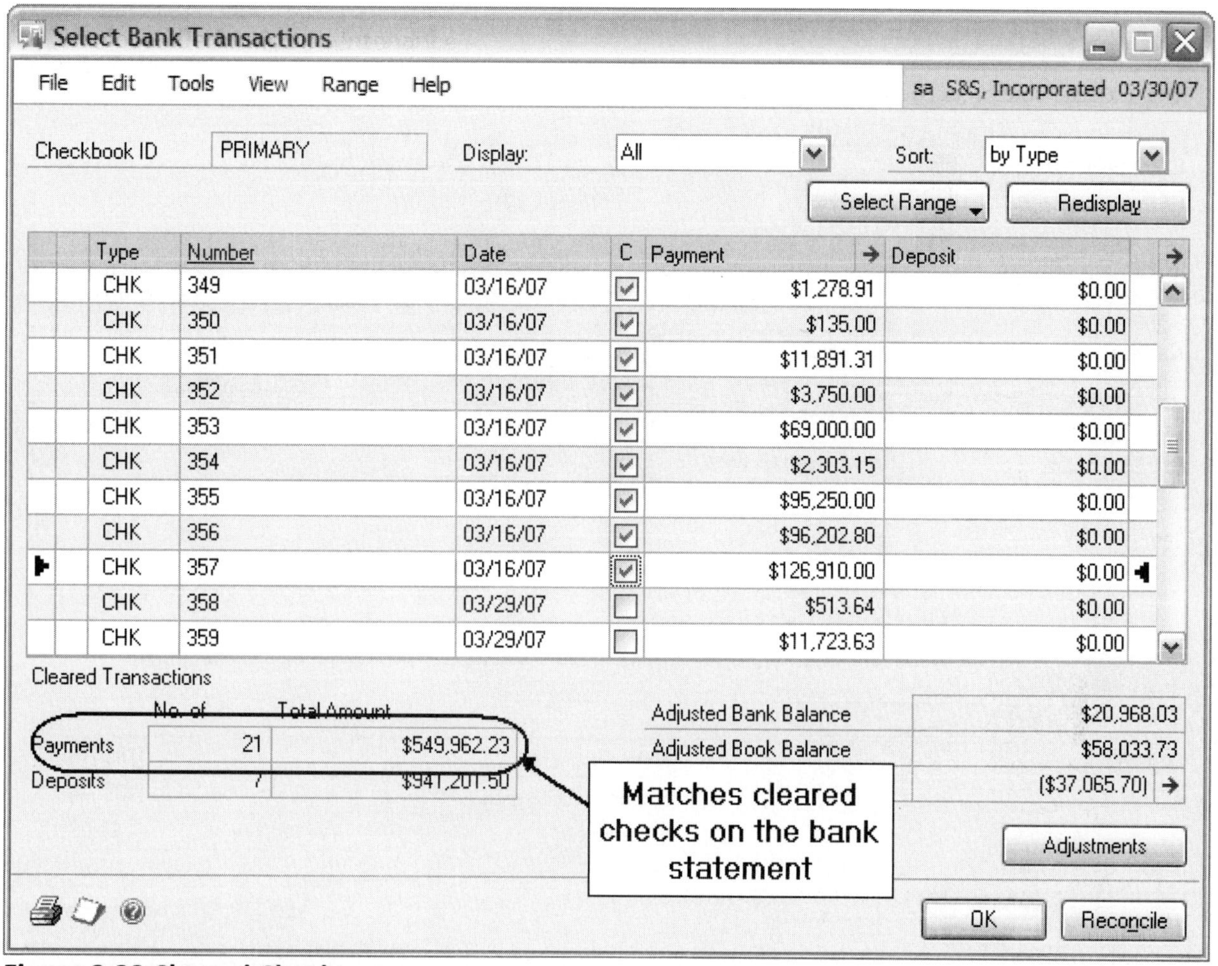

Figure 8:32 Cleared Checks

5. Scroll to the last two items and clear the bank transfers (i.e., XFR). (Not illustrated.)

6. Finally, you need to enter bank charges for this month. Click **Adjustments** and enter these charges as follows.

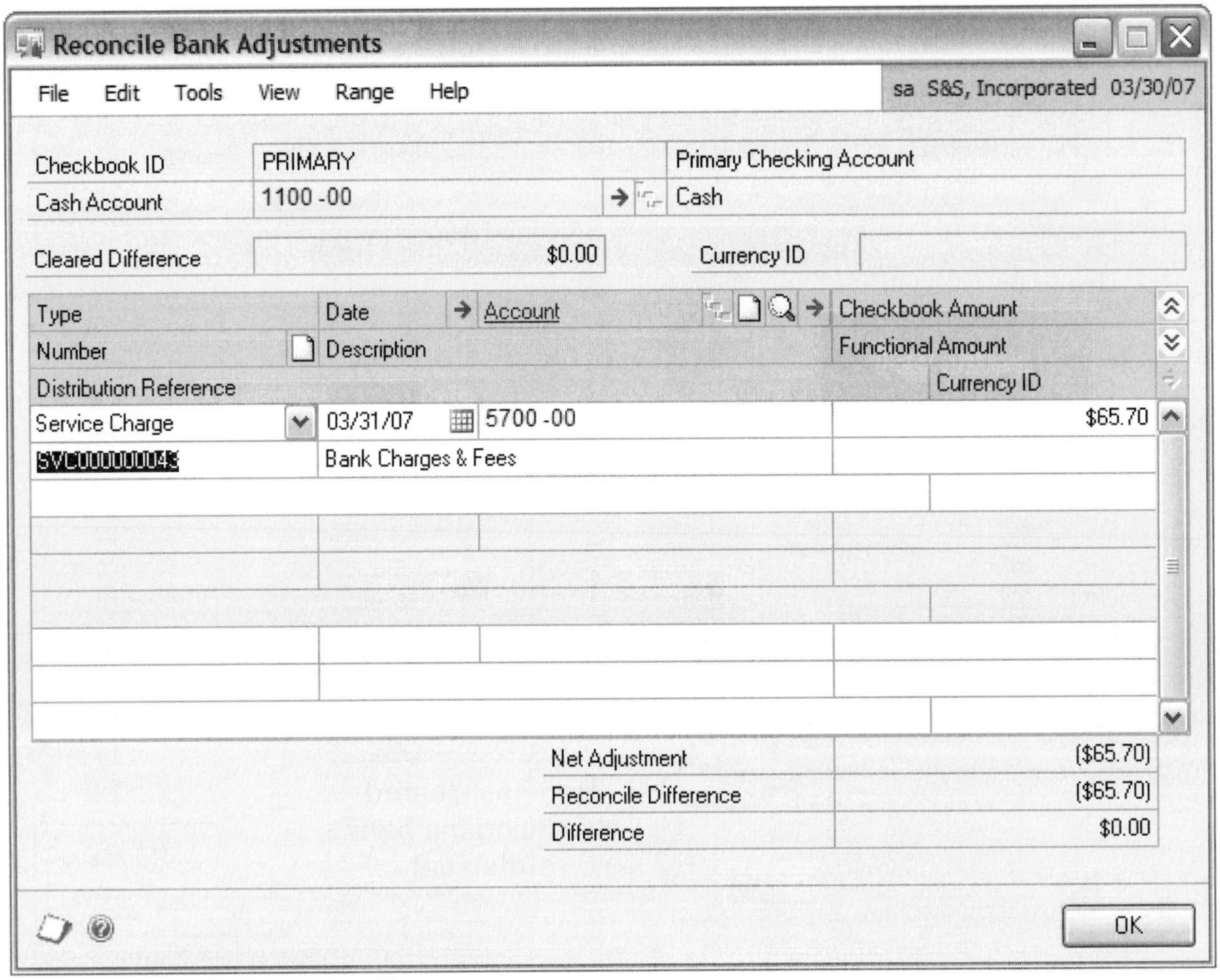

Figure 8:33 Bank Statement Charges

7. Click **OK** and return to the Select Bank Transactions window. The bank account is reconciled when the Difference is zero.

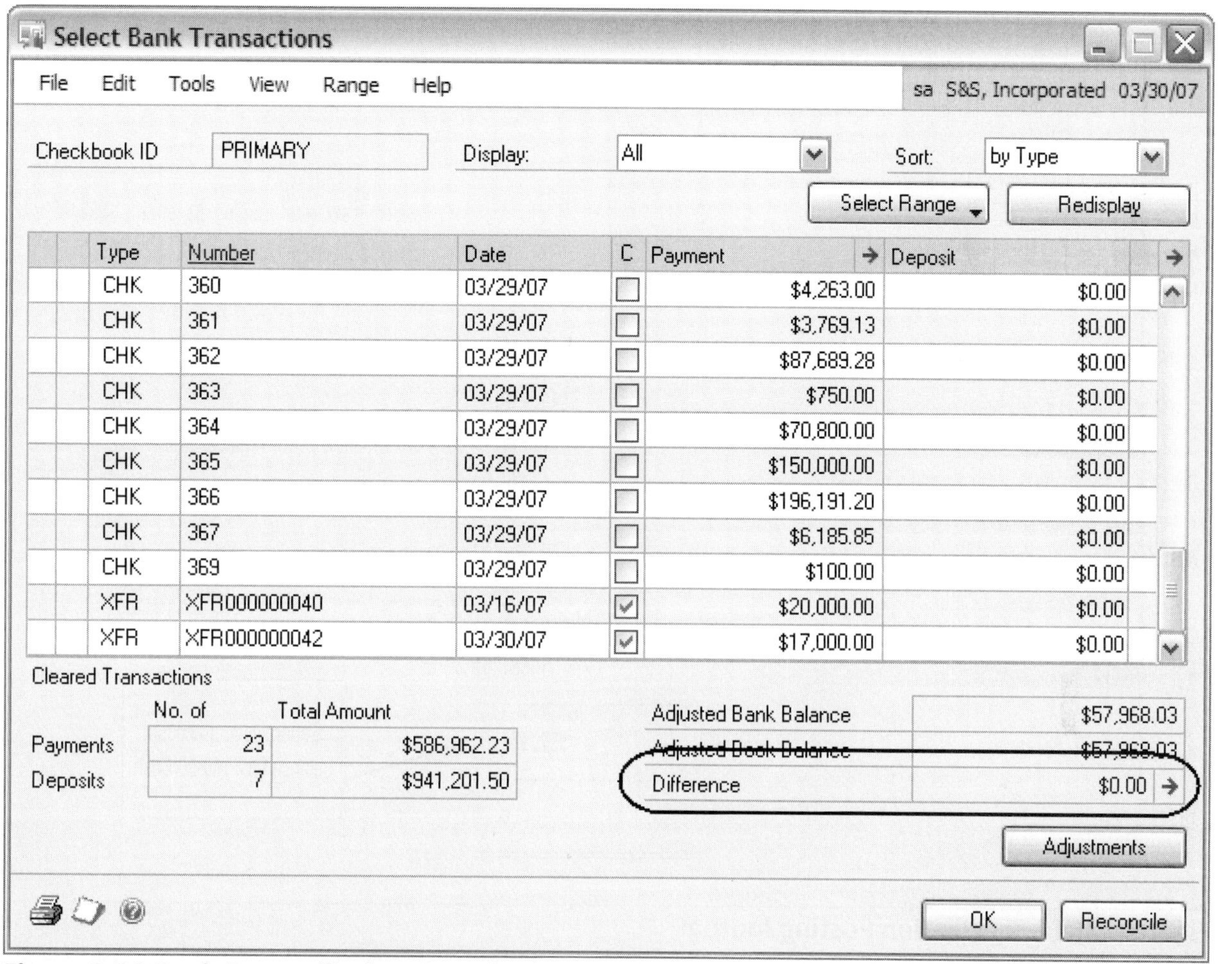

Select Bank Transactions
File Edit Tools View Range Help
sa S&S, Incorporated 03/30/07
Checkbook ID PRIMARY
Display: All
Sort: by Type
Select Range
Redisplay
Type Number Date C Payment Deposit
CHK 360 03/29/07 $4,263.00 $0.00
CHK 361 03/29/07 $3,769.13 $0.00
CHK 362 03/29/07 $87,689.28 $0.00
CHK 363 03/29/07 $750.00 $0.00
CHK 364 03/29/07 $70,800.00 $0.00
CHK 365 03/29/07 $150,000.00 $0.00
CHK 366 03/29/07 $196,191.20 $0.00
CHK 367 03/29/07 $6,185.85 $0.00
CHK 369 03/29/07 $100.00 $0.00
XFR XFR000000040 03/16/07 $20,000.00 $0.00
XFR XFR000000042 03/30/07 $17,000.00 $0.00
Cleared Transactions
No. of Total Amount
Payments 23 $586,962.23
Deposits 7 $941,201.50
Adjusted Bank Balance $57,968.03
Adjusted Book Balance $57,968.03
Difference $0.00
Adjustments
OK
Reconcile

Figure 8:34 Bank Reconciliation Complete

8. Click **Reconcile.** GP prompts to print an Outstanding Transactions Report that lists transactions not clearing the March statement. Print this report to the screen. *(Note: It does not actually print until after printing other reports.)*

9. The Reconciliation Posting Journal prints first. (See Figure 8:35.) The Adjusted Book Balance on this report should agree to the March 31 ending balance in 1100-00 Cash. Close the report.

S&S, Incorporated
Page: 1

User Date: 03/30/07
RECONCILIATION POSTING JOURNAL
User ID: sa

Bank Reconciliation

Audit Trail Code: CMADJ00000026
Checkbook ID: PRIMARY
Description: Primary Checking Account

Bank Statement Ending Balance: $589,953.76
Bank Statement Ending Date: 03/31/07
Cutoff Date: 03/31/07

Statement Ending Balance	$589,953.76
Outstanding Checks (-)	$531,985.73
Deposits in Transit (+)	$0.00
Adjusted Bank Balance	$57,968.03
Checkbook Balance as of Cutoff	$58,033.73
Adjustments	($65.70)
Adjusted Book Balance	$57,968.03
Difference	$0.00

General ledger account balance for 1100-00 Cash

Figure 8:35 Reconciliation Posting Journal

10. The Bank Adjustments Posting Journal prints next, showing the bank fee transaction. Close it. GP also prints the Cleared Transactions Journal listing transactions clearing the statement and the Outstanding Transactions report. Close these reports.

11. Finally the General Posting Journal prints to document posting bank charges to the general ledger account. Close this report.

We will now check the March 31 balance in 1100-00. Click **Summary** under Inquiry and look up this account. Compare the ending balance to the Reconciliation Posting Journal. Close the window when finished.

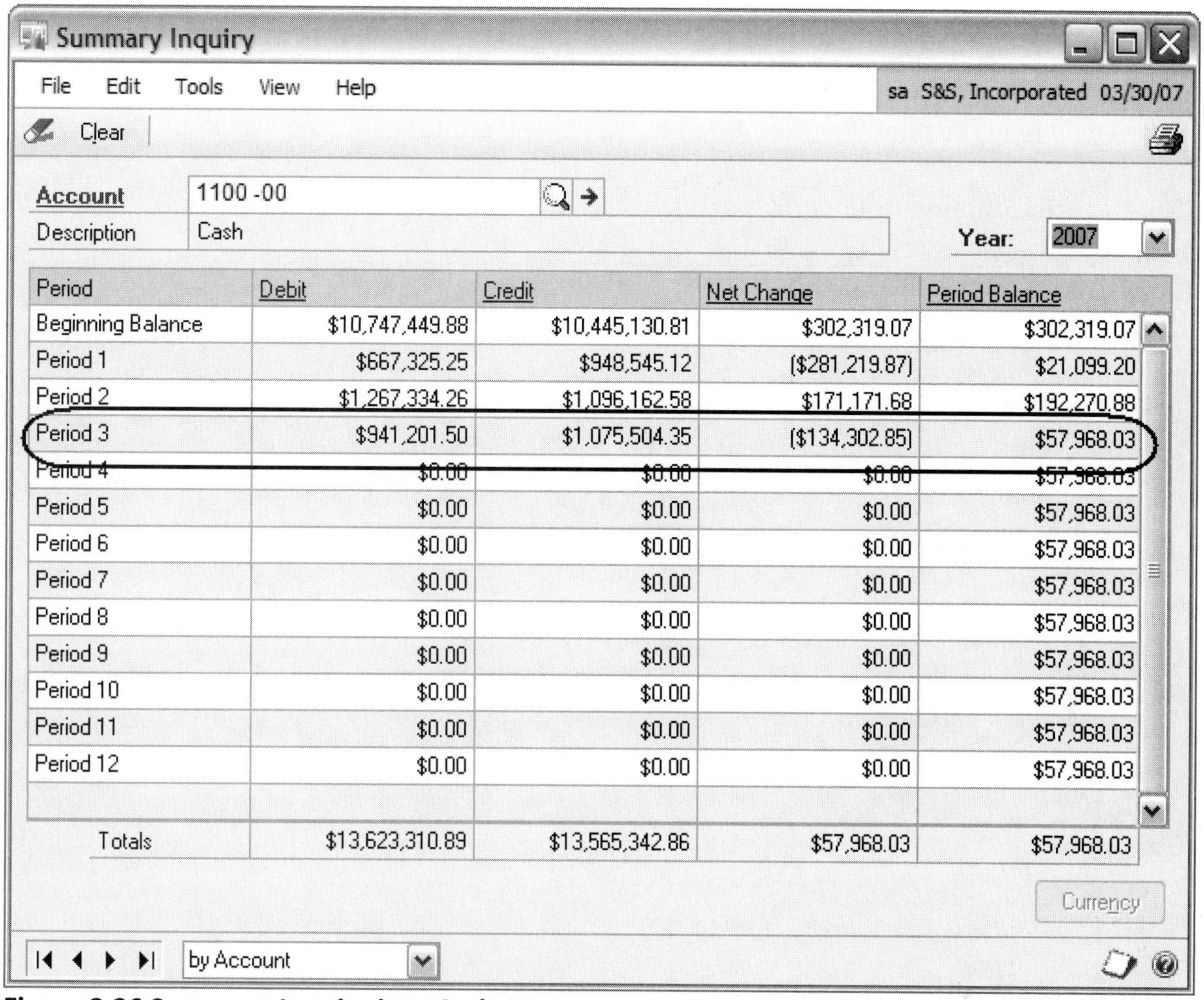

Period	Debit	Credit	Net Change	Period Balance
Beginning Balance	$10,747,449.88	$10,445,130.81	$302,319.07	$302,319.07
Period 1	$667,325.25	$948,545.12	($281,219.87)	$21,099.20
Period 2	$1,267,334.26	$1,096,162.58	$171,171.68	$192,270.88
Period 3	$941,201.50	$1,075,504.35	($134,302.85)	$57,968.03
Period 4	$0.00	$0.00	$0.00	$57,968.03
Period 5	$0.00	$0.00	$0.00	$57,968.03
Period 6	$0.00	$0.00	$0.00	$57,968.03
Period 7	$0.00	$0.00	$0.00	$57,968.03
Period 8	$0.00	$0.00	$0.00	$57,968.03
Period 9	$0.00	$0.00	$0.00	$57,968.03
Period 10	$0.00	$0.00	$0.00	$57,968.03
Period 11	$0.00	$0.00	$0.00	$57,968.03
Period 12	$0.00	$0.00	$0.00	$57,968.03
Totals	$13,623,310.89	$13,565,342.86	$57,968.03	$57,968.03

Figure 8:36 Summary Inquiry into Cash Account

You have completed the accounting department's closing checklist. In the real world you would print a trial balance and perform one last review of account balances. Thereafter, you are ready to print financial statements.

FINANCIAL STATEMENTS

We are now ready to print financial statements. We will print the Income Statement first.

Click **Financial Statements** under Reports and click the lookup icon. (See Figure 8:37.)

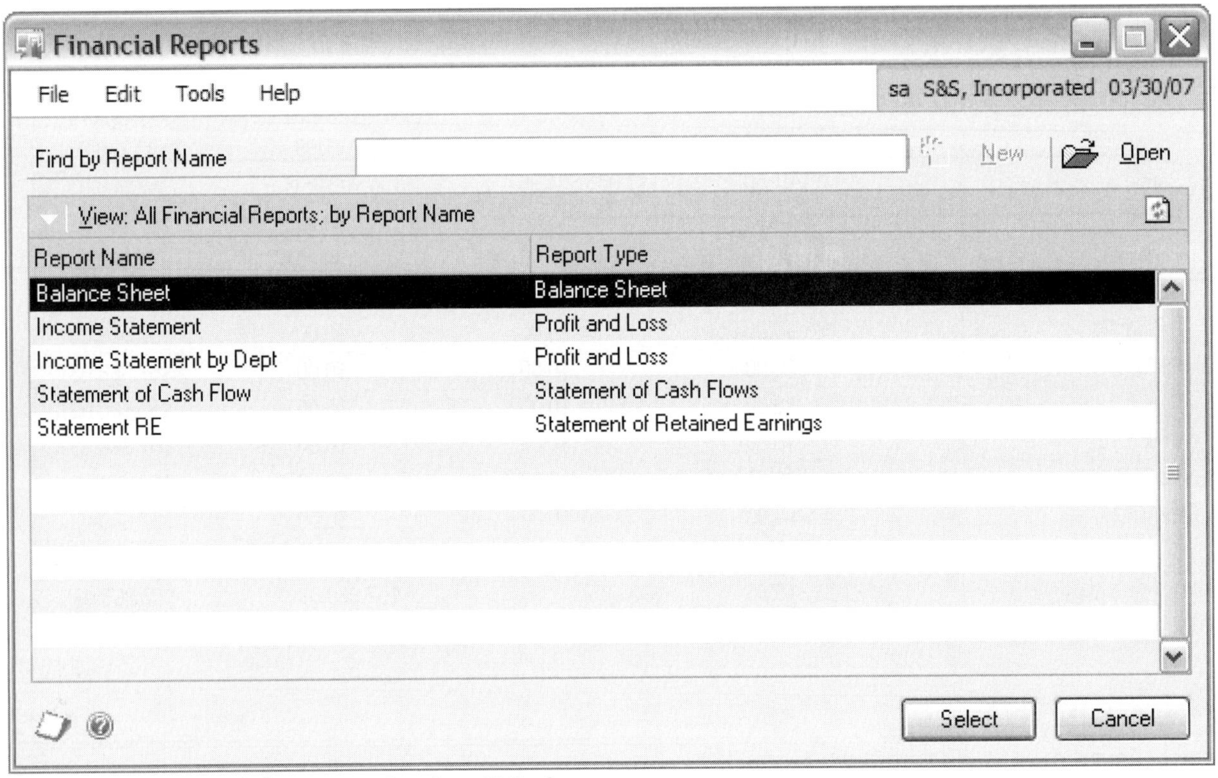

Figure 8:37 Financial Reports Lookup Window

Ashton designed the reports listed in this window and in Level Two we illustrate the process. There are two income statements, one for consolidated income and the other for departmental income, a balance sheet, and a statement of cash flow, and a statement of retained earnings. Let us print the income statement.

1. Choose **Income Statement**. Notice that GP's report type is Profit and Loss.

2. Verify that your system date is 3/31/2007 because GP uses the system date as the report date.

3. Highlight the report under Options and click **Insert** to the print list. Click **Print**. The report is illustrated next.

S&S, Incorporated
Income Statement
For 01/01/07 To 03/31/07
For All Mains
For All Departments

Page: 1

	Current Period	Current YTD	Prior YTD
Sales	$1,098,088.10	$3,248,851.25	$2,095,603.01
Sales Returns and Discounts	1,977.00	6,649.89	4,804.91
Net Sales	$1,096,111.10	$3,242,201.36	$2,090,798.10
Cost of Goods Sold	$818,018.20	$2,567,450.63	$1,604,958.50
Gross Profit On Sales	$278,092.90	$674,750.73	$485,839.60
Operating Expenses			
Selling Expenses	$19,889.75	$93,026.96	$107,436.60
Administrative Expense	$7,314.16	$39,735.28	$70,310.49
Salaries Expense	$61,015.74	$164,274.89	$130,291.77
Other Employee Expenses	$2,633.42	$8,491.87	$9,253.51
Depreciation & Amortization Expense	$14,684.05	$14,684.05	$44,007.51
Total Operating Expenses	$105,537.12	$320,213.05	$361,299.88
Net Operating Income	$172,555.78	$354,537.68	$124,539.72
Other Income and Expense			
Other Income	$436.27	$1,393.51	$9,652.05
Interest Expense	$12,237.27	$37,691.86	$38,334.03
Total Other Income And Expenses	($11,801.00)	($36,298.35)	($28,681.98)
Net Income Before Taxes	$160,754.78	$318,239.33	$95,857.74
Income Tax Expense	$0.00	$49,000.00	$21,360.00
Net Income	$160,754.78	$269,239.33	$74,497.74

Figure 8:38 Income Statement

4. You next print the balance sheet. Close the income statement and change Report to **Balance Sheet**. Remove the income statement from the Print List and insert the balance sheet report under Options into the Print List. Click **Print**. The balance sheet is illustrated next. Review the report and close it.

S&S, Incorporated
Balance Sheet
As Of 03/31/07

Page: 1

	Current YTD	Prior YTD
Assets		
Current Assets		
Cash		
Cash	$57,968.03	$112,899.70
Cash-Savings	122,301.62	95,028.17
Petty Cash	1,325.80	125.00
Checking - Payroll	1,006.90	2,897.24
Total Cash	$182,602.35	$210,950.11
Short-Term Investments		
Total Short-Term Investments	$0.00	$0.00
Accounts Receivable		
Accounts Receivable	$1,242,147.36	$659,079.68
Sales Discounts Available	177.44	0.00
Allowance for Doubtful Accounts	19,727.20	10,000.00
Total Accounts Receivable	$1,222,597.60	$649,079.68
Notes Receivable		
Total Notes Receivable	$0.00	$0.00
Inventory		
Inventory	$1,009,758.01	$940,988.00
Total Inventory	$1,009,758.01	$940,988.00
Prepaid Expenses		
Prepaid Insurance	$9,300.00	$8,780.00
Total Prepaid Expenses	$9,300.00	$8,780.00
Total Current Assets	$2,424,257.96	$1,809,797.79

S&S, Incorporated
Balance Sheet
As Of 03/31/07

Page: 2

	Current YTD	Prior YTD
Long-Term Investments		
Total Long-Term Investments	$0.00	$0.00
Property, Plant and Equipment		
Land	$120,000.00	$120,000.00
Buildings	765,000.00	765,000.00
Office Furniture/Fixtures	167,950.00	165,000.00
Vehicles	367,876.00	367,876.00
Computer Hardware	175,790.22	165,000.00
Computer Software	67,000.00	67,000.00
Total Property, Plant and Equipment	$1,663,616.22	$1,649,876.00
Accumulated Depreciation		
Accum Depr - Buildings	$22,950.00	$10,200.00
Accum Depr - Office Furn/Fixtures	35,372.10	15,714.32
Accum Depr - Vehicles	110,362.86	49,050.16
Accum Depr - Computer Hardware	62,594.36	27,500.00
Amortization - Computer Software	33,499.98	14,888.88
Total Accumulated Depreciation	$264,779.30	$117,353.36
Other Assets		
Total Other Assets	$0.00	$0.00
Total Assets	$3,823,094.88	$3,342,320.43

S&S, Incorporated
Balance Sheet
As Of 03/31/07

Page: 3

	Current YTD	Prior YTD
Liabilities and Equity		
Current Liabilities		
Accounts Payable		
Accounts Payable	$79,819.44	$380,520.21
Accrued Payables	42,765.00	0.00
Total Accounts Payable	$122,584.44	$380,520.21
Notes Payable		
Notes Payable	$300,000.00	$200,000.00
Total Notes Payable	$300,000.00	$200,000.00
Current Maturities of Long-Term Debt		
Total Current Maturities of Long-Term Debt	$0.00	$0.00
Taxes Payable		
FUTA Taxes Payable	$800.03	$0.00
SUTA Taxes Payable	2,052.07	0.00
FICA Taxes Payable	3,791.62	0.00
Federal Withholding Taxes Payable	2,574.13	0.00
State Withholding Taxes Payable	1,624.21	0.00
City Withholding Taxes Payable	1,079.64	0.00
Worker's Comp Payable	1,257.15	0.00
Accrued Income Taxes	95,600.00	21,360.00
Total Taxes Payable	$108,778.85	$21,360.00
Interest Payable		
Interest Payable	$14,200.00	$12,600.00
Total Interest Payable	$14,200.00	$12,600.00

S&S, Incorporated Balance Sheet As Of 03/31/07	Current YTD	Page: 4 Prior YTD
Total Dividends Payable	$0.00	$0.00
Other Current Liabilities		
Wages Payable	$7,040.00	$3,100.00
Commissions Payable	6,301.47	(2,656.91)
Deductions Payable	95.00	0.00
401-K Payable	1,866.44	0.00
Total Other Current Liabilities	$15,302.91	$443.09
Total Current Liabilities	$560,866.20	$614,923.30
Long-Term Debt		
Notes Payable - Long Term	$2,000,000.00	$2,000,000.00
Total Long-Term Debt	$2,000,000.00	$2,000,000.00
Total Liabilities	$2,560,866.20	$2,614,923.30
Common Stock		
Common Stock	$10,000.00	$10,000.00
Total Common Stock	$10,000.00	$10,000.00
Additional Paid-in Capital - Common		
Additional Paid In Capital	$300,000.00	$300,000.00
Total Additional Paid-in Capital - Common	$300,000.00	$300,000.00
Common Dividends		
Total Common Dividends	$0.00	$0.00
Retained Earnings		
Retained Earnings	$682,989.35	$342,899.39
Total Retained Earnings	$682,989.35	$342,899.39
Net Profit/(Loss)	$269,239.33	$74,497.74
Total Equity	$1,262,228.68	$727,397.13
Total Liabilities and Equity	$3,823,094.88	$3,342,320.43

Figure 8:39 Balance Sheet

5. Close the Financial Statement Report window.

As illustrated, preparing financial reports is easy. It is all the steps leading up to printing that are difficult. In the real world you would also print the cash flow statement and perhaps other management reports such a performance report that compares actual financial results to budgeted projections. *(Note: The sample data does not include budget numbers; therefore, these reports are not illustrated.)*

With financial reporting complete, you are ready to close the March accounting period.

MONTH-ENDING THE FINANCIAL SERIES

As in other Series, you month-end the Financial Series by clicking the GP button to select ***Tools>>Setup>>Company>>Fiscal Periods*** and making the month closed. Ashton performs this step after printing financial statements and management reports to block posting to a closed period.

YEAR-ENDING THE FINANCIAL SERIES

Each January Ashton completes the steps that close December and then year-ends the Financial Series. Remembering that year-ending significantly alters data tables, he first performs a backup of the database.

Click **Year-End Closing** under Routines to view the window used to close this Series. (See Figure 8:40.)

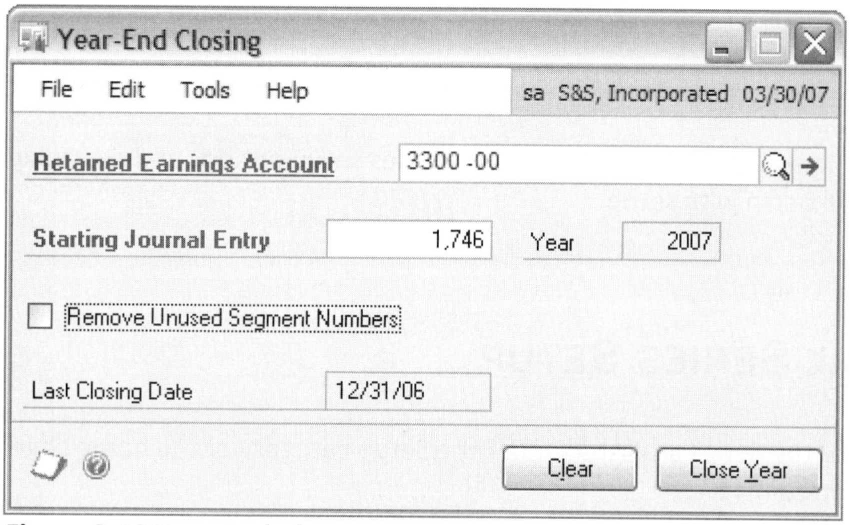

Figure 8:40 Year-End Closing Window

The window shows that closing the year posts net income/loss for the year to 3300-00 Retained Earnings. GP posts this entry by recording a closing entry zeroing out revenue and expense account balances to retained earnings.

GP also posts beginning account balances for asset, liability, and equity accounts when year-ending the Series. Because of this, you will not be able to prepare a balance sheet for the new year until the prior year is closed.

Click **X** to close this window. You have now completed this level. The next level looks at setup options for the Series and designing financial statements.

Level Two

In this level we look at setting up the Financial Series setup options and designing financial reports. We will begin with setup.

FINANCIAL SERIES SETUP

Setup menus for the Series are listed under the Setup category of the home page. Click **General Ledger**. (See Figure 8:41.)

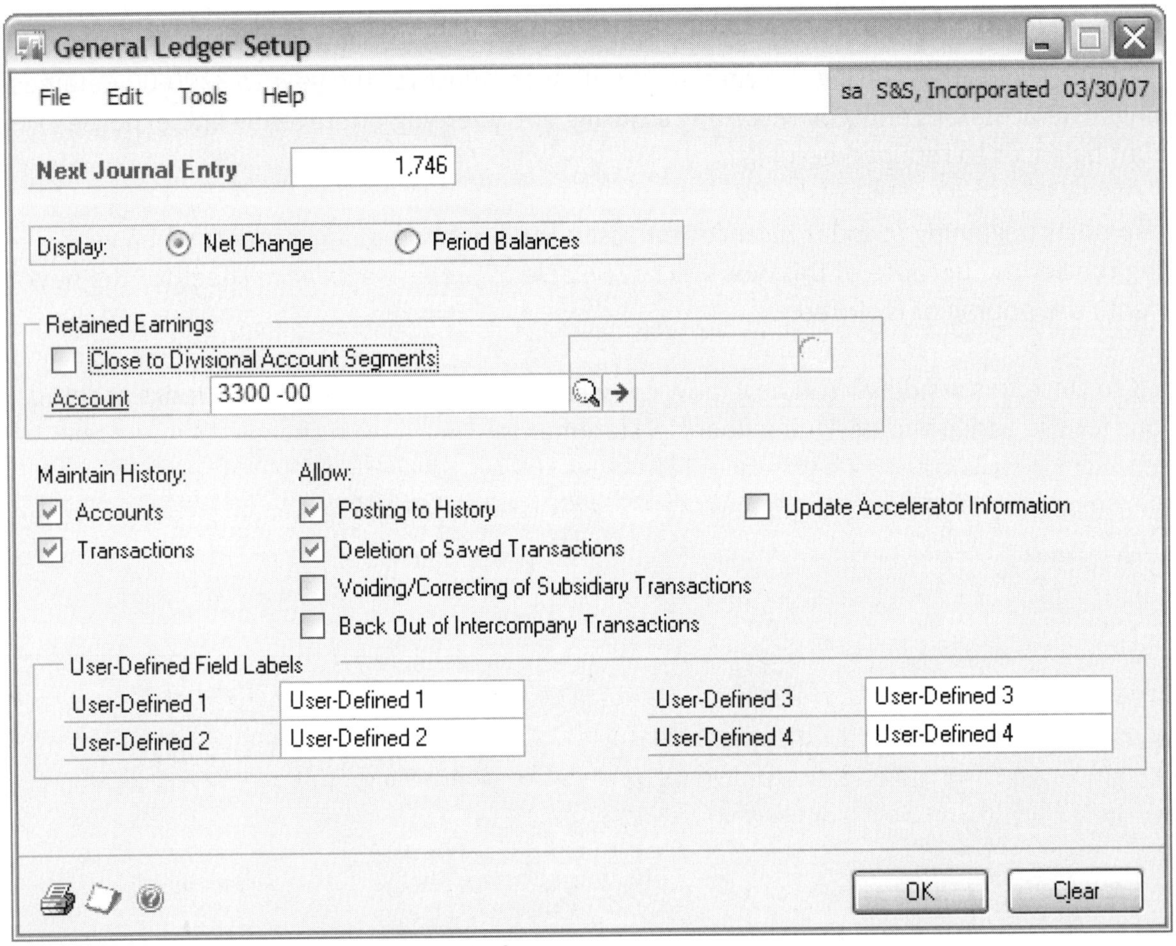

Figure 8:41 General Ledger Setup Window

This window lists the document number for the journal entry transactions. It also shows that transaction history is maintained and closing entries post to 3300-00 Retained Earnings.

Click **X** to close the window.

Now click **Category** to view the window illustrated next.

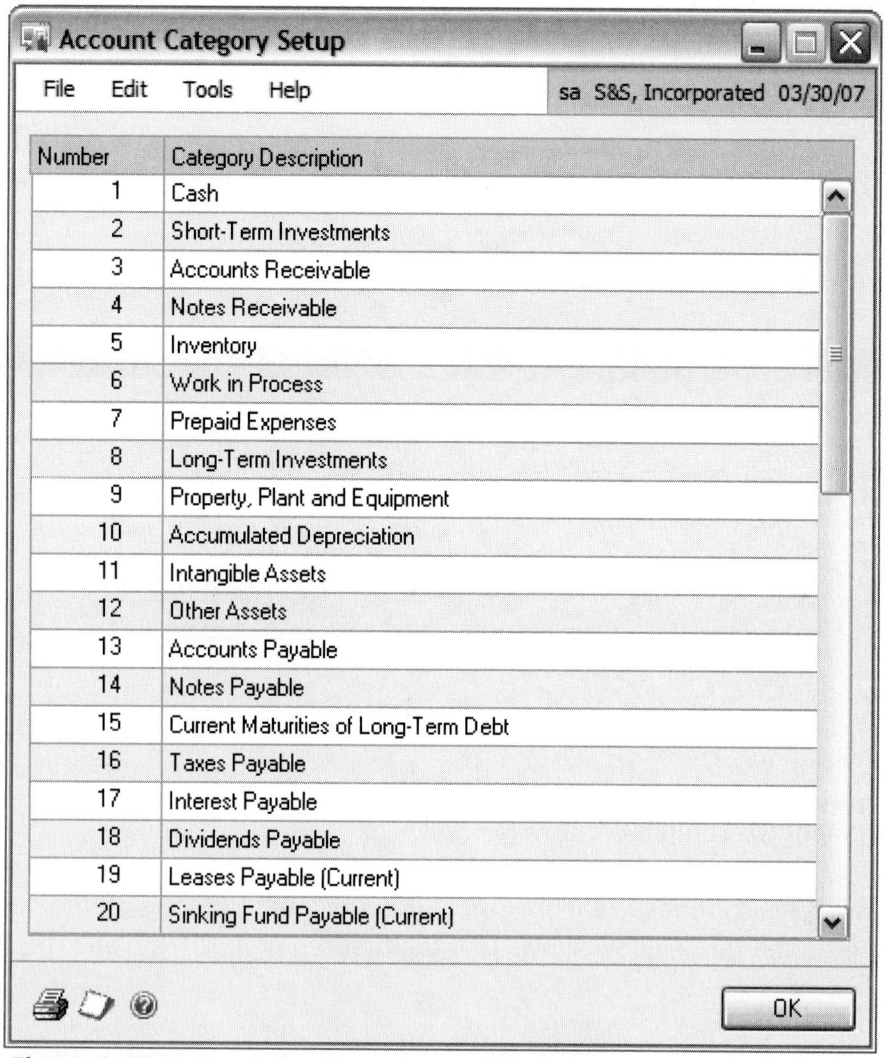
Account Category Setup
File Edit Tools Help
sa S&S, Incorporated 03/30/07
Number Category Description
1 Cash
2 Short-Term Investments
3 Accounts Receivable
4 Notes Receivable
5 Inventory
6 Work in Process
7 Prepaid Expenses
8 Long-Term Investments
9 Property, Plant and Equipment
10 Accumulated Depreciation
11 Intangible Assets
12 Other Assets
13 Accounts Payable
14 Notes Payable
15 Current Maturities of Long-Term Debt
16 Taxes Payable
17 Interest Payable
18 Dividends Payable
19 Leases Payable (Current)
20 Sinking Fund Payable (Current)
OK

Figure 8:42 Account Category Setup Window

As illustrated in Chapter 2, you must assign a category to each general ledger account. These categories are then used to determine placement of the account on financial statements. For instance, all general ledger accounts in the category of Accounts Receivable will be reported under the Accounts Receivable heading of the balance sheet.

GP provides forty-eight predefined categories. You can change a category's descriptions but cannot add additional categories.

Close the window.

Next, click **Segment**, click the lookup icon on Segment ID, and scroll to the top. (See Figure 8:43.)

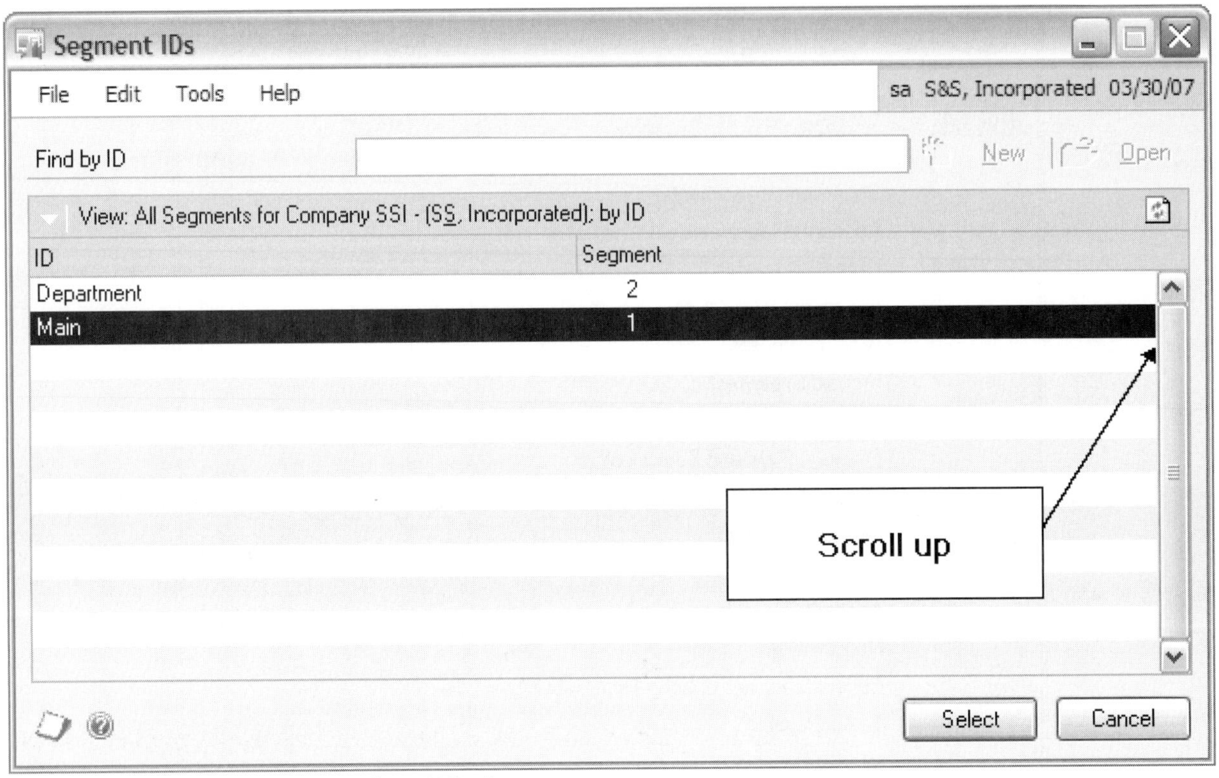

Figure 8:43 Segment IDs Lookup Window

Segment IDs assign descriptions to each segment in an account number. Remember that S&S uses two segments and this window shows that the first segment is Main and the second is Department.

Click **Cancel** to close the lookup window and then close the Account Segment Setup window.

You have completed reviewing Financial Series setup windows. We next discuss report design.

FINANCIAL SERIES SETUP REPORTS

As you know, setup reports document default settings and control options for a Series. Click **Setup** under Reports and click the dropdown list as illustrated next.

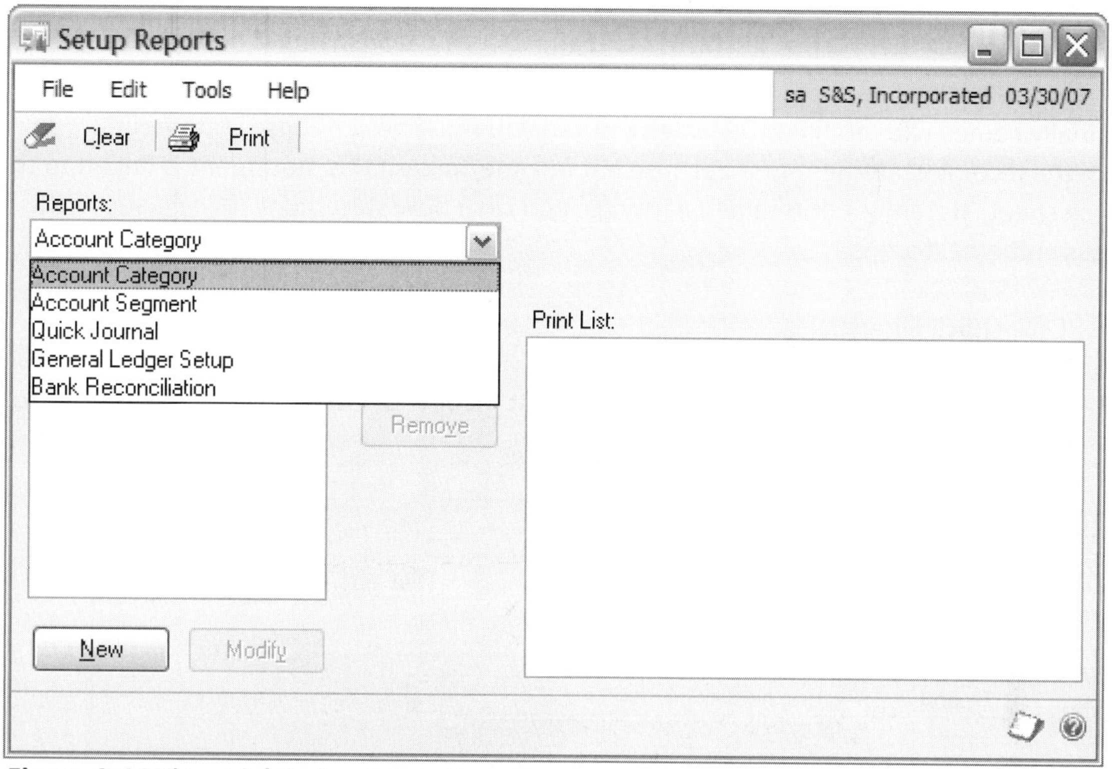

Figure 8:44 Financial Series Setup Reports

This list shows reports you can print to document Financial Series settings but these reports are not all that is needed.

You are well aware that posting reports in the Financial Series and other Series document transaction entry. Additionally, Financial Series audit trail reports under Cross-Reference document user activity in the software and Administration home page reports document user security for the software.

But did you also know that posting journal entries is a popular method of concealing fraud? [32] This is why S&S requires signed documentation supporting journal entries before these entries are posted. It is also why access to the Financial Series is restricted to accounting department personnel only.

Besides these measures, you can review detailed trial balance reports to identify unusual entries that may indicate fraud. Preparing account analysis reports may show trends indicating fraud. Finally, printing financial statement reports comparing actual to budgeted results and analyzing variances is another method of detecting fraud.

---

[32] Refer to Romney and Steinbart, *Accounting Information Systems* (11th ed., Pearson Prentice Hall 2009) pgs. 539-543.

Designing Basic Financial Statements

GP initially comes with no financial statements so you must design these statements. You design the income statement first because net income/loss on this statement is linked to the balance sheet, statement of retained earnings, and cash flow statement. We illustrate this process in the next steps.

1. Click **Quick Financial**.

2. We will design a new statement so type **Test Income Stmt** for Report and select **Profit and Loss** for the Type. (See Figure 8:45.)

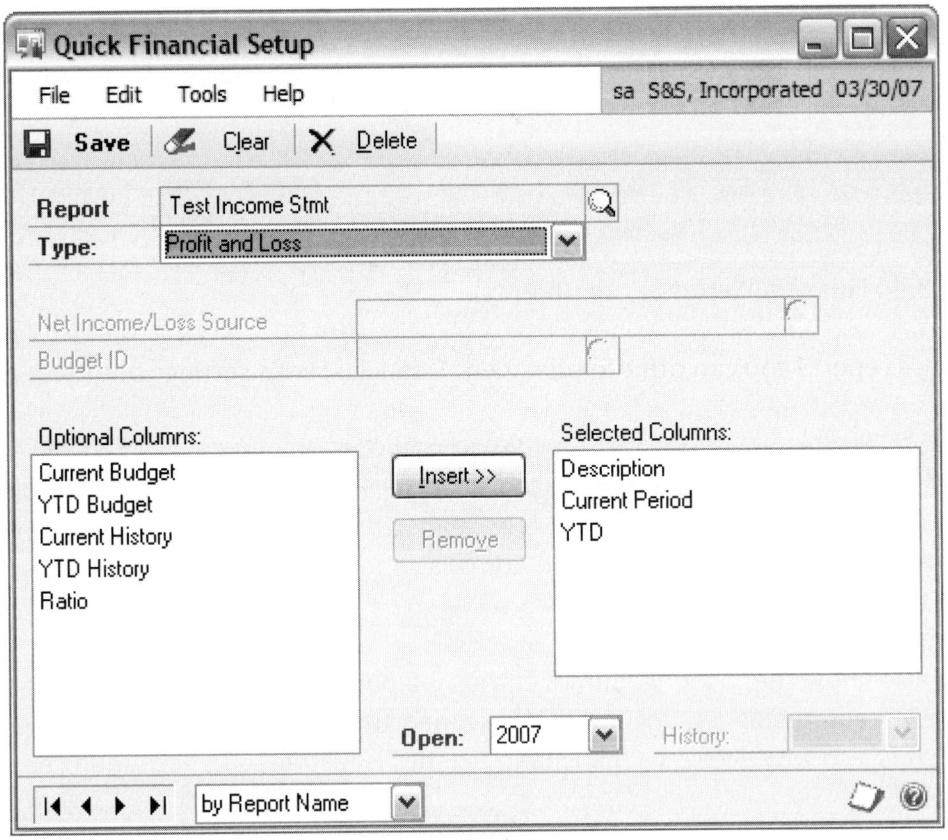

Figure 8:45 Quick Financial Setup Window

3. Highlight **YTD History** under Optional Columns and click **Insert**. Now set the **History** option to **2006** as illustrated next.

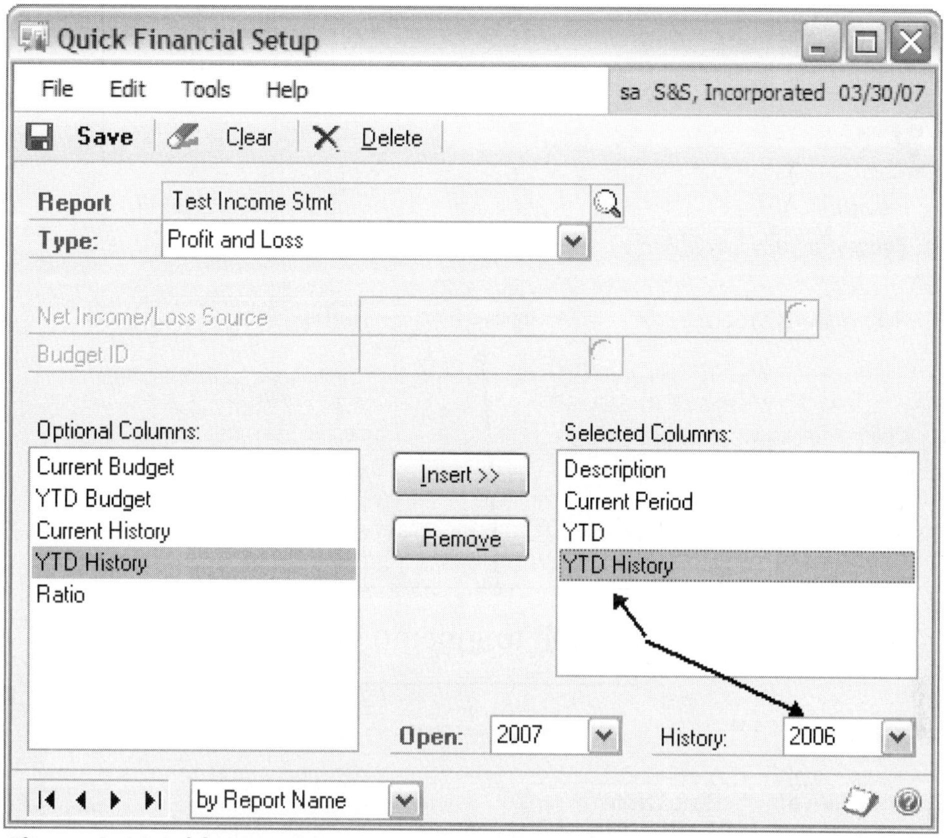

Figure 8:46 Add YTD History to Income Statement

4. Click **Save**. Now create a balance sheet. Type **Test Bal Sheet** and select **Balance Sheet**. For **Net Income/Loss Source**, look up and select **Test Inc Stmt**. (See Figure 8:47.)

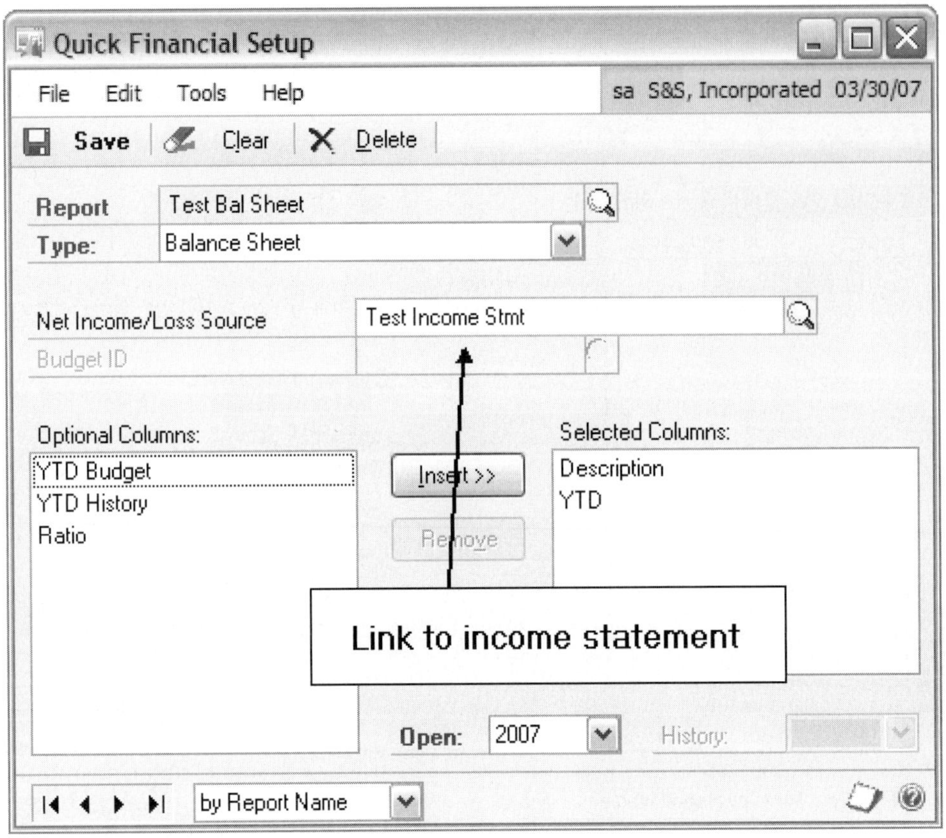

Figure 8:47 Designing Balance Sheet

5. Click **Save** and close the window.

6. Now click **Financial Statements** and click the lookup icon on Report. The window (Figure 8:48) lists your newly created statements.

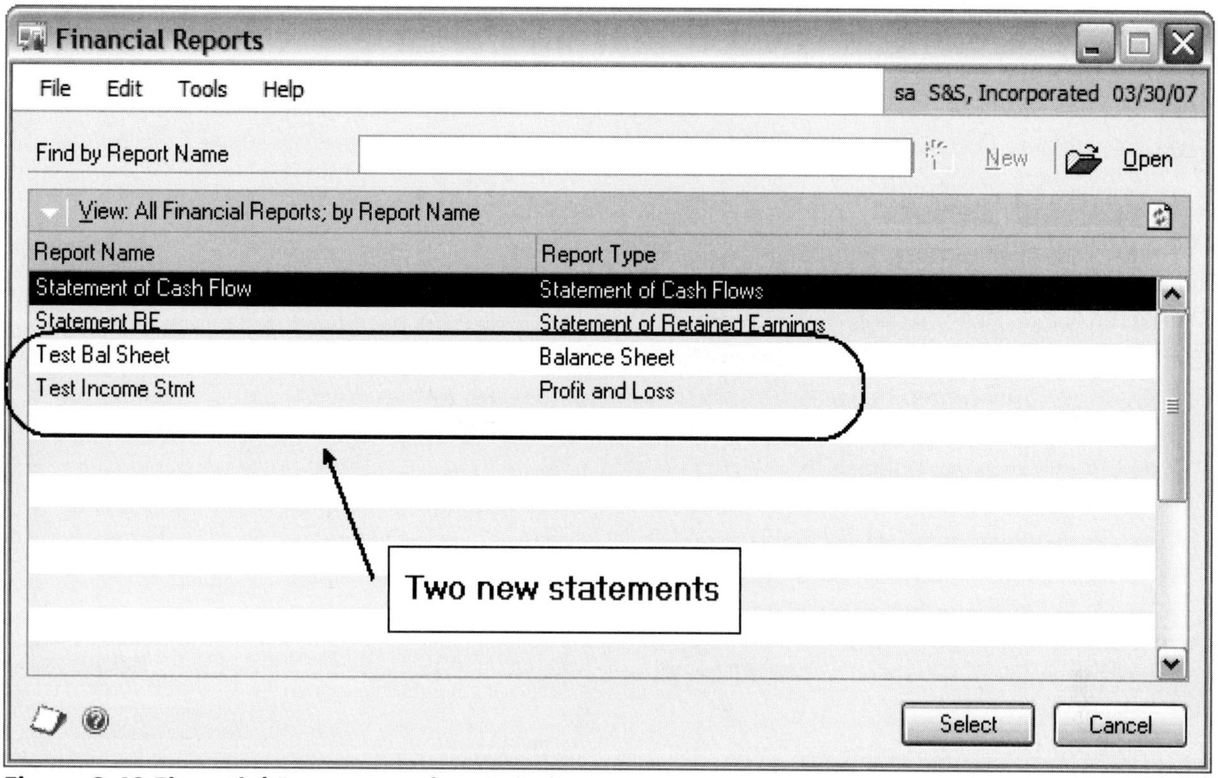

Figure 8:48 Financial Reports Lookup Window

7. Select **Test Bal Sheet**. Click **New** and enter the following information.

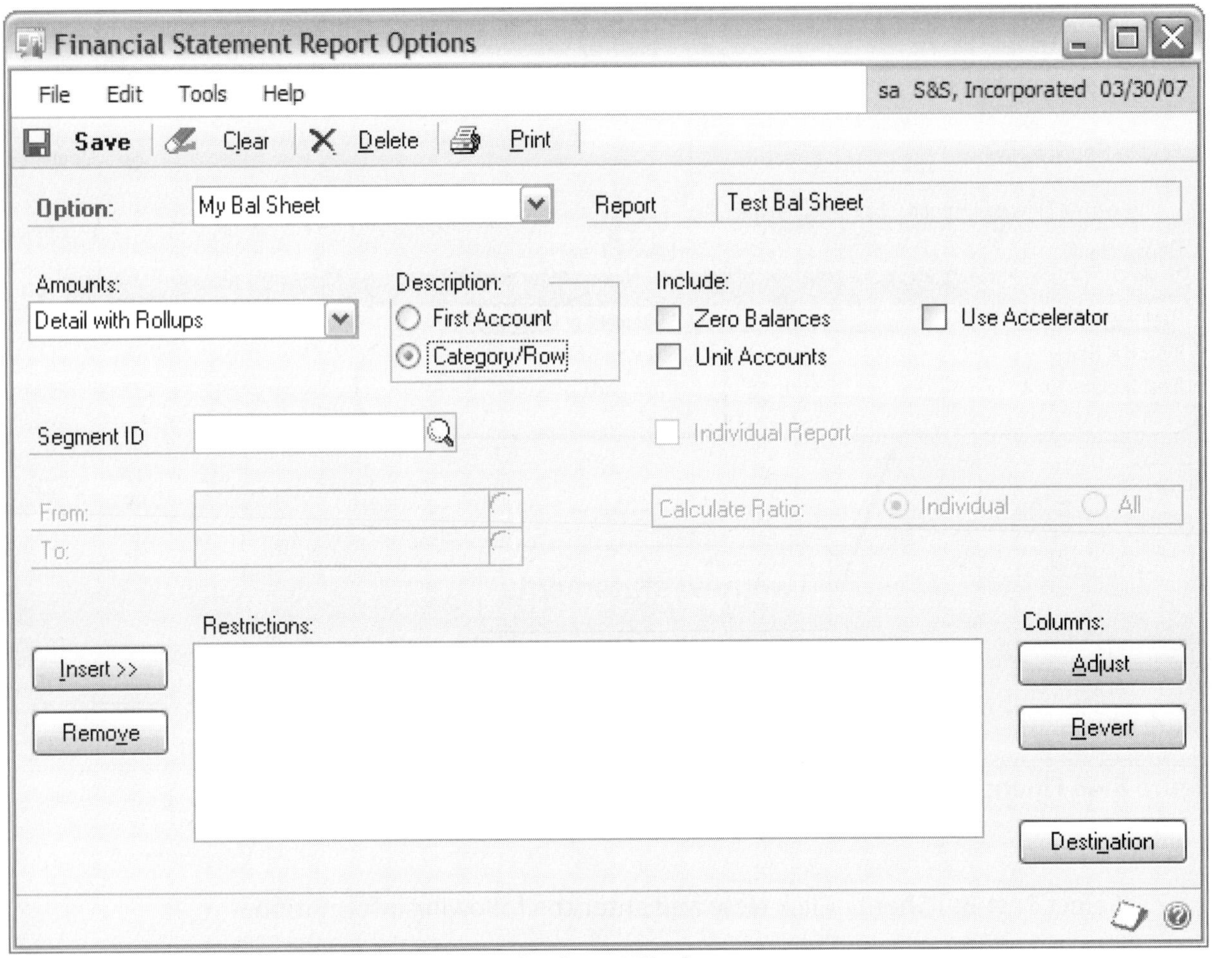

Figure 8:49 Financial Statement Report Options Window

8. Selecting **Detail with Rollups** means the statement will list individual accounts and then a subtotal. For instance, it will list Cash and Payroll Checking with a subtotal for all cash accounts.

9. Selecting **Category/Row** means that statement sections will use the description on the category instead of the description of the first account number in that section. For instance, if there is an Accounts Receivable Other and an Accounts Receivable Main with both accounts assigned to the Accounts Receivable category, the balance sheet section will state Accounts Receivable instead of the account name.

10. Click **Save** and close any open windows.

Quick financials are nice when you need standard statements. Remember that these statements are created by referring to the category assigned to the general ledger account. However, what if you want to print information in a different format such as matching each fixed asset account with a corresponding accumulated depreciation account and then subtotaling each? That is when you designed advanced financial reports, which is the subject of our next topic.

ADVANCED FINANCIAL STATEMENTS

Ashton was not satisfied with the layout of the basic income statement, so he decided to customize this report. We next illustrated customizing quick financial reports.

1. Click **Advanced Financial** and highlight your **Test Income Stmt** created in the previous topic as illustrated next.

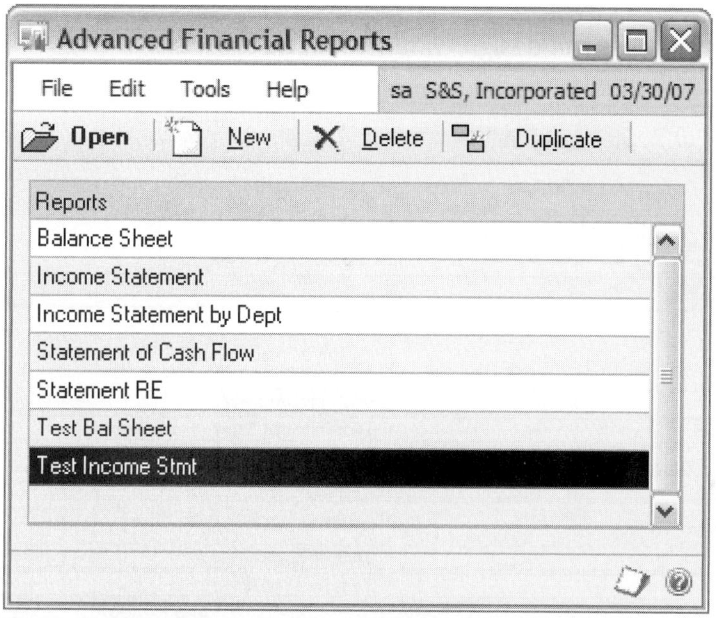

Figure 8:50 Advanced Financial Reports Window

2. Click **Open** to access the report definition window illustrated next.

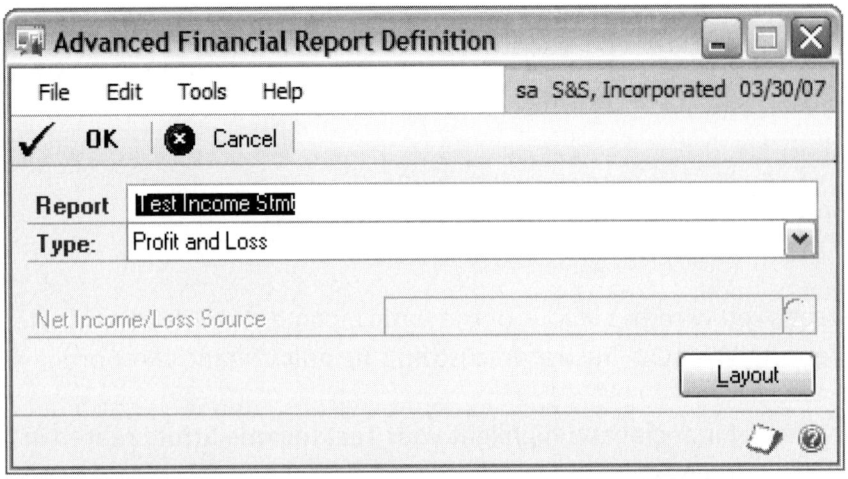

Figure 8:51 Advanced Financial Report Definition Window

3. Click **Layout** to access the design window illustrated next.

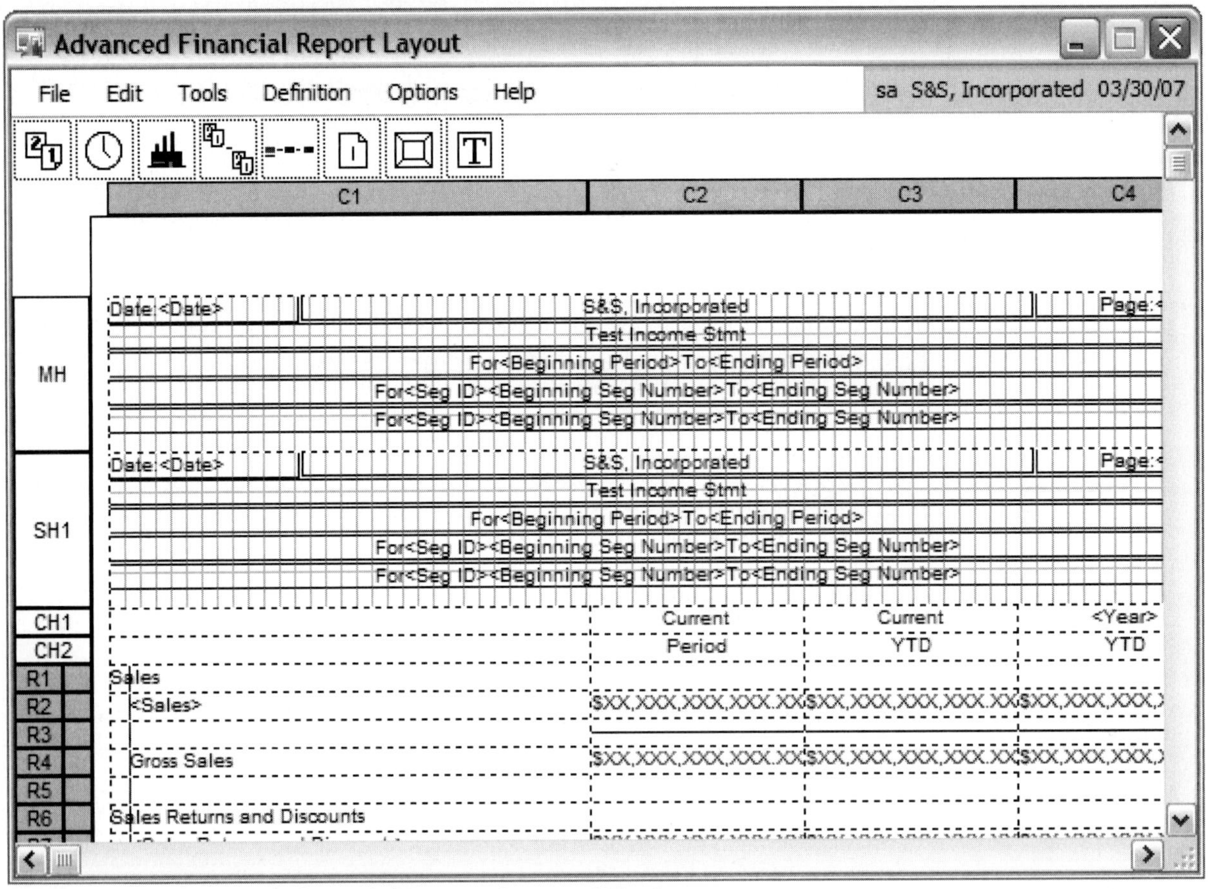

Figure 8:52 Advanced Financial Report Layout Window

4. You manipulate the layout by double clicking row numbers and column labels. Double click the column labeled **C2** to open its Financial Column Definition window illustrated next.

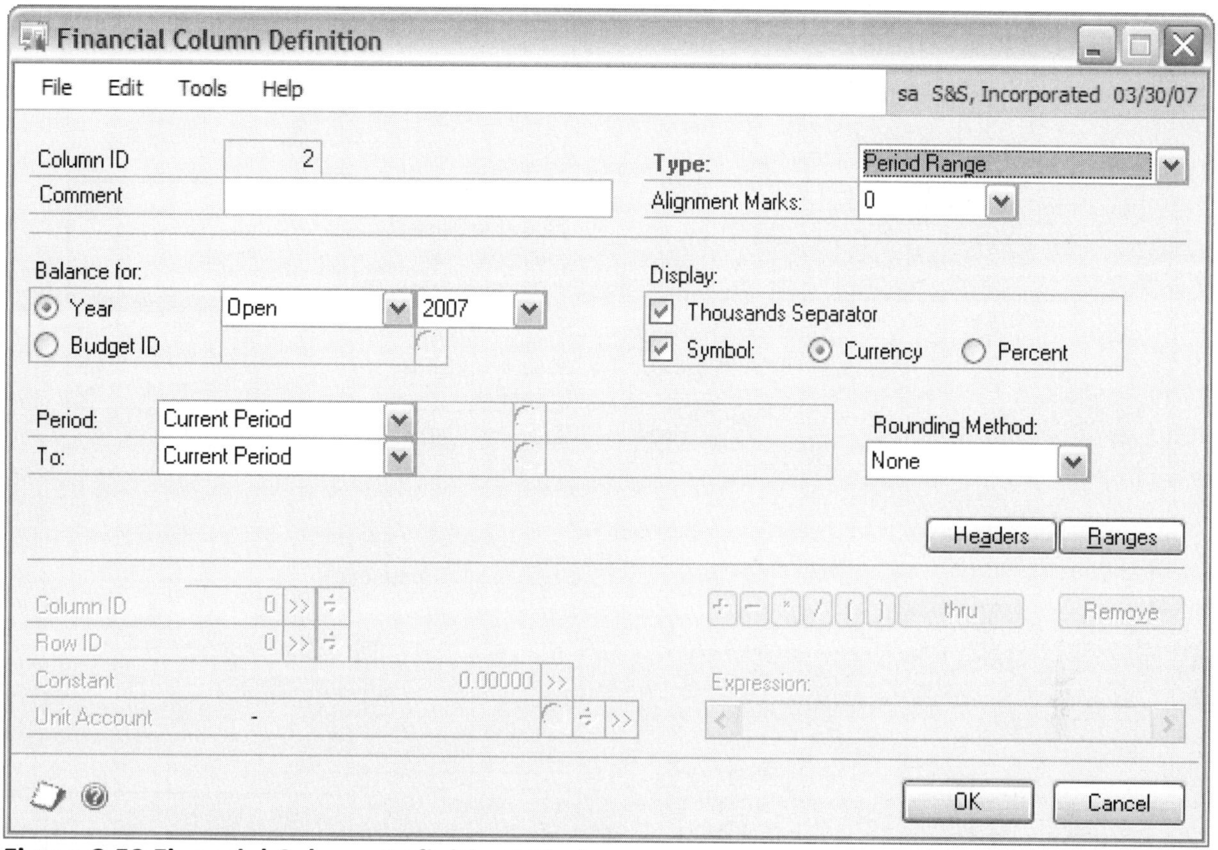

Figure 8:53 Financial Column Definition Window

5. The window shows that this column reports income and expense in the current period for the open year of 2007. The current period is determined by your system date. Click **OK**.

6. Now double click column **C3** and note that this column reports year-to-date income and expense for the current year. Click **OK**.

7. Open column **C4** and note that it reports year-to-date income and expense for 2006. Click **OK**.

8. Now that we viewed columns, let us look at rows. Double click **Row 1** to open the Financial Row Definition window illustrated next.

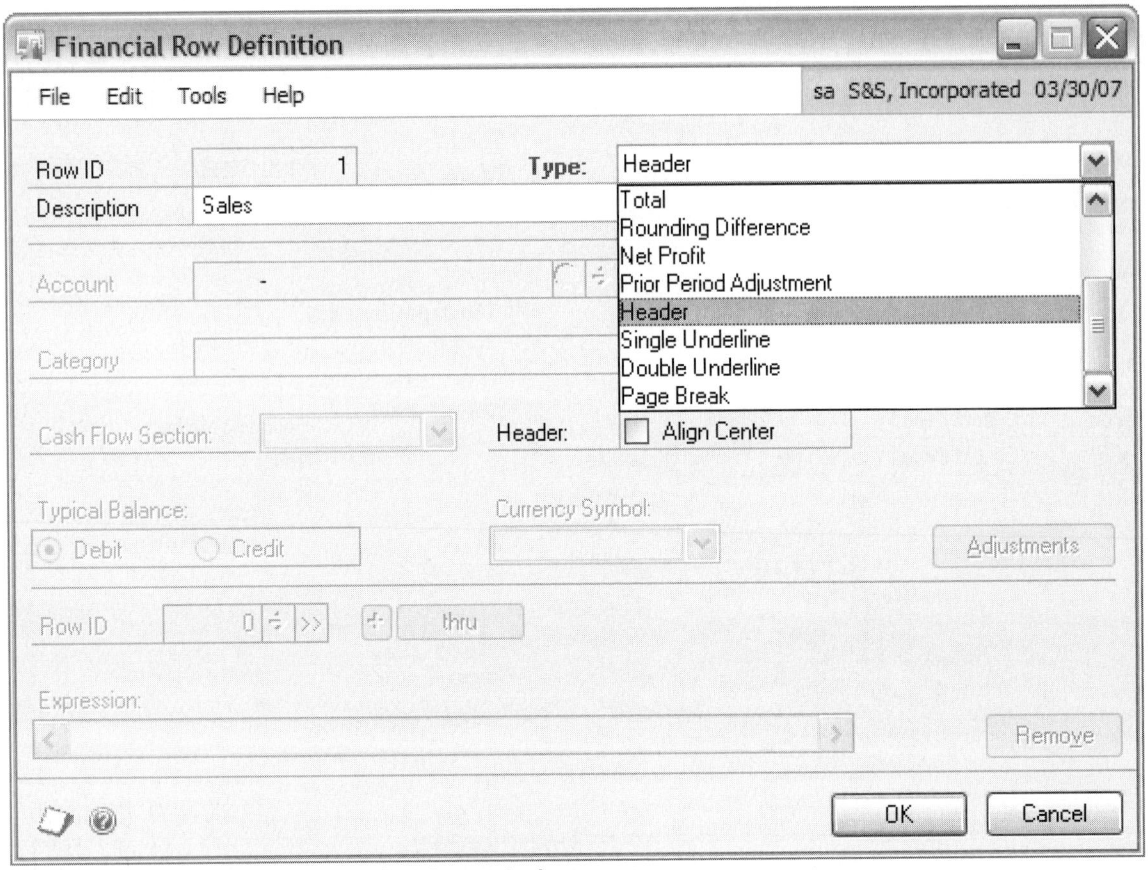

Figure 8:54 Financial Row Definition Window

9. This is a Header row meaning it provides a heading for the accounts grouped under it. Notice that the Description for the heading is Sales. Click OK.

10. Open **Row 2.** (See Figure 8:55.) This row reports account balances by Account Category meaning that it will list the account balances for general ledger accounts assigned to the Sales category. If you wanted to instead list a specific range of accounts then change the Type to Account Range and insert an account range as illustrated in Figure 8:56. Click **OK**.

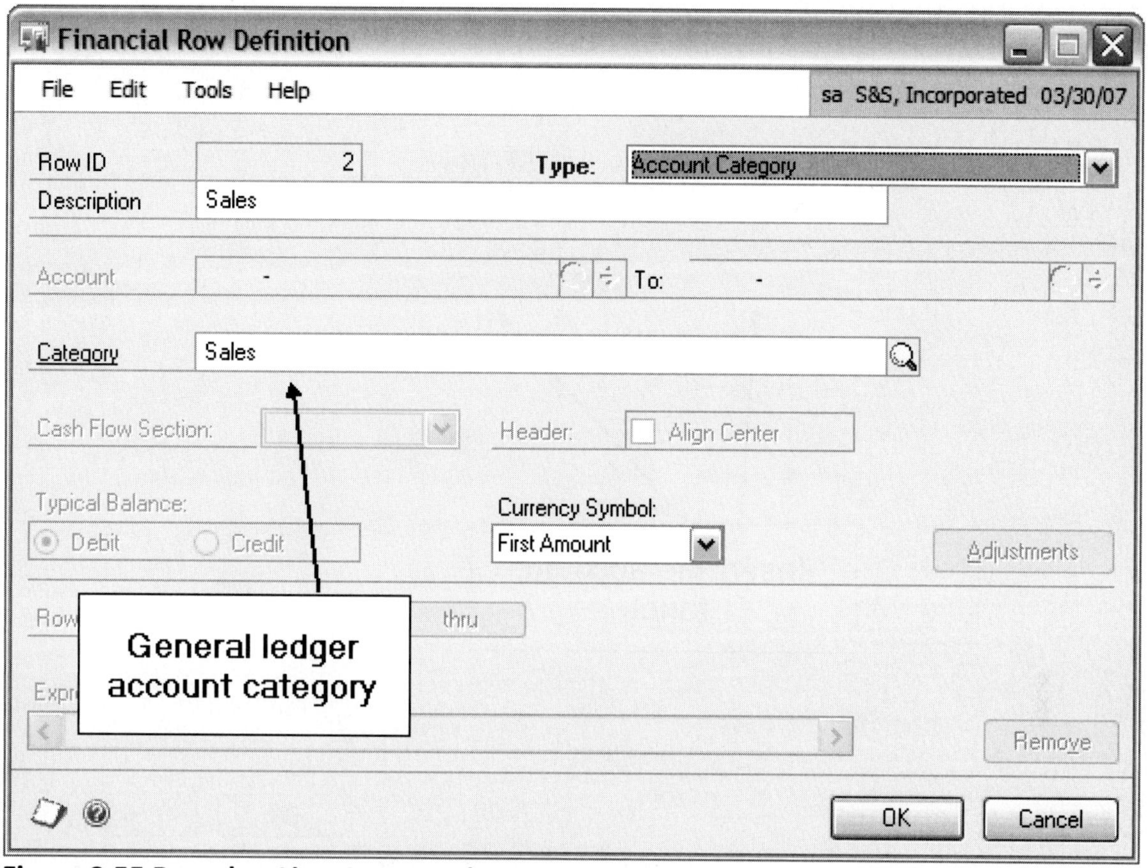

Figure 8:55 Row that Lists Accounts by Category

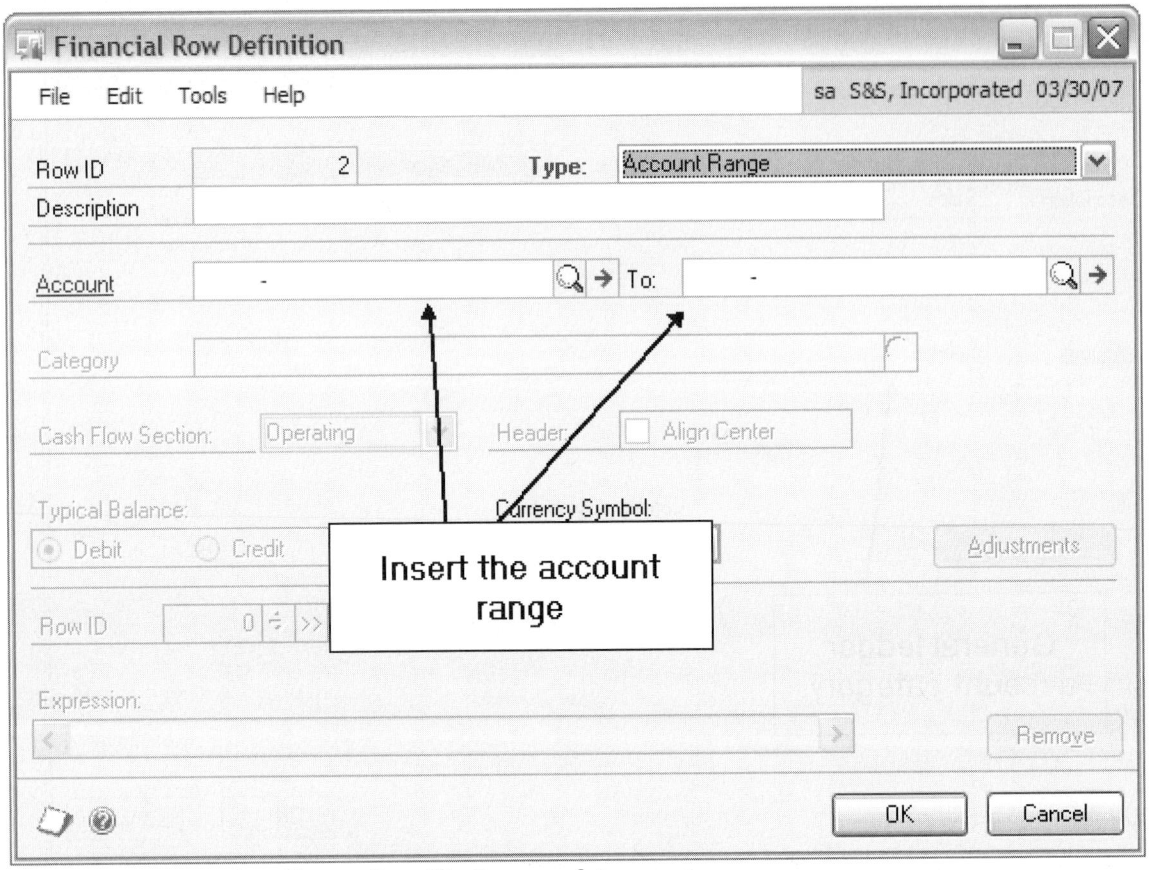

Figure 8:56 Row that Lists a Specific Range of Accounts

11. Open **Row 3** to see that it formats by placing a single underline. Click **OK**.

12. Open **Row 4**. (See Figure 8:57.) This is a total row that adds amounts reported on Row 2 (i.e., R2). Hence, it will report the total for Sales accounts. Click **OK**.

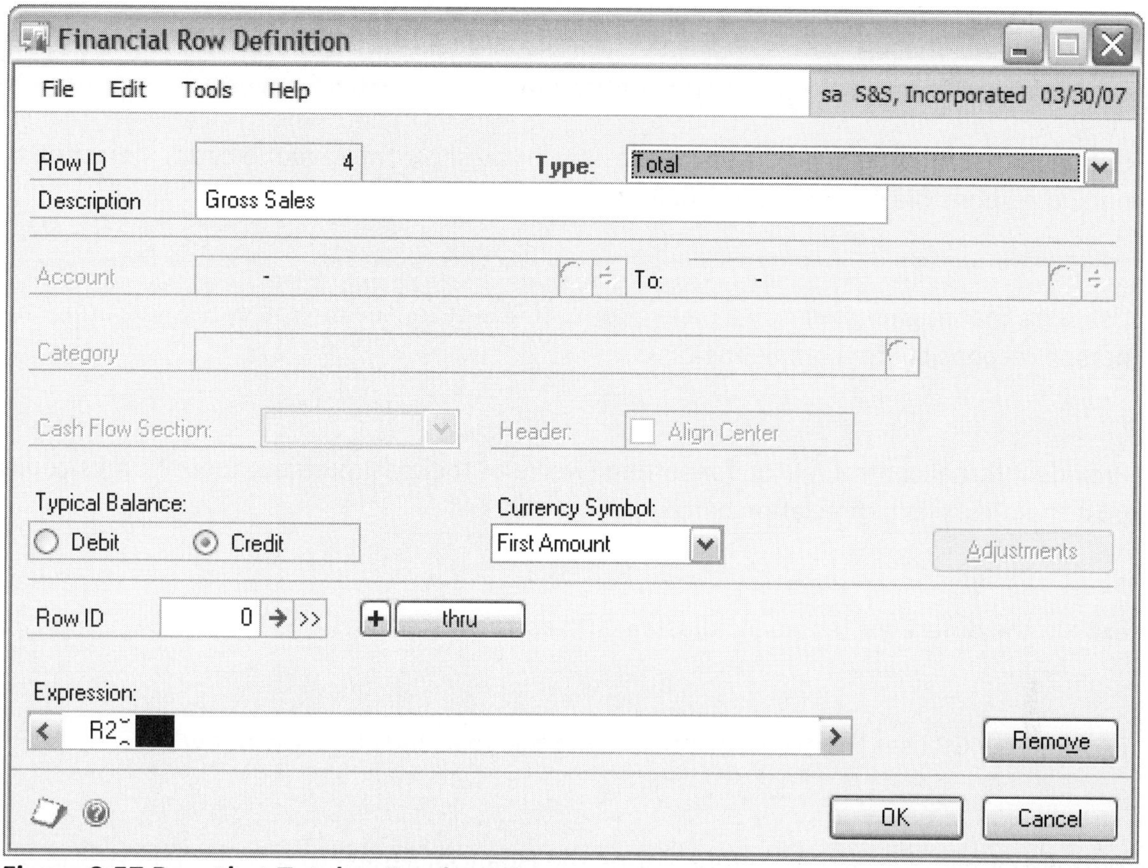

Figure 8:57 Row that Totals a Previous Row

13. To view a more complicated formula, open Row 61 showing that this row adds together balances from several previous rows. (Not illustrated.)

Take the time to look through some of the other rows on the report. You delete and add rows by clicking a row and selecting File on the menu and choosing either Delete or Insert. Rows will be inserted above the row selected. You use the same procedures if adding or deleting a column.

Click **X** to close the layout window, discarding any changes made to the report. Click X to close remaining windows.

Congratulations on completing this text! You now have a solid background on using GP. You can post transactions for the Sales, Inventory, Purchasing, Payroll, and Financial Series. But your skills go beyond just posting. You understand the importance of implementing strong internal controls over accounting activities. You know the options in each Series that implement internal controls for a cycle and the reports that document these controls. Moreover, you know the reports that analyze company performance and evaluate cycle efficiencies.

Level One Questions

1. List tasks that might appear on a cycle closing checklist for the revenue cycle, indicating the person responsible for completing tasks.

2. List tasks that might appear on a cycle closing checklist for the payroll cycle, indicating the person responsible for completing tasks.

3. Provide internal control reason for setting twelve as the maximum number of times you can post the recurring depreciation batch.

4. Explain the difference between adjusting and correcting entries.

5. Explain how GP uses the account appearing in the year-end closing window.

6. Why are other Series closed before closing the Financial Series?

Level Two Questions

1. Analyze threats in the Financial Series. Describe controls that will mitigate these threats. Did S&S implement any of your controls?

2. How might you use a cross-reference report to reduce threats to financial data?

3. How does the income statement interact with the balance sheet?

4. External auditors arrive next week. What reports will you prepare for their arrival?

Appendix A DATA BACKUP / RESTORE PROCEDURES AND ERROR MESSAGES

BACKING UP AND RESTORING DATABASES

After using GP, perform a backup of your databases by clicking the GP menu to select ***File>>Backup***.

GP prompts for a system password and this password is ***sa***. The figure below illustrates the Database Backup Window and files to back up. Backup procedures should be performed on companies worked on during the GP session and the System Database.

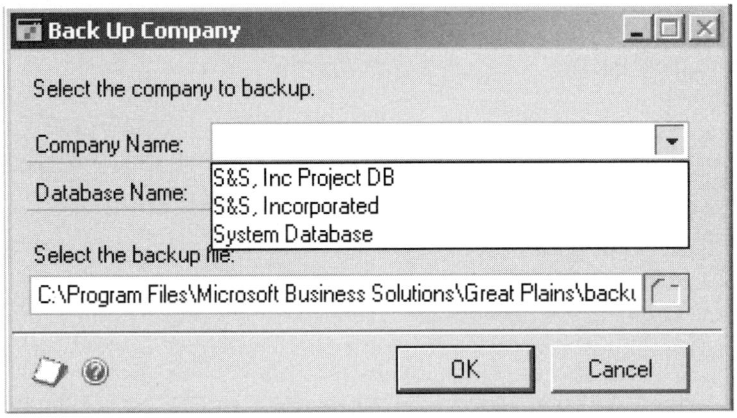

Remember to click the folder icon to select a backup location and name the backup file. Clicking OK will save backup files to the location shown in the path. *(Note: The first time you choose a location, click OK for GP to create the backup path.)*

To restore data files, return to the GP button and select ***File>>Restore***. A window appears similar to the above illustration. Choosing a company database activates the folder icon to browse and select the backup file to restore. GP exits the software to restore the database. This process takes time, so be patient and do not close any windows.

Remember that **IF YOU HAVE NOT BACKED UP YOUR WORK YOU CANNOT RESTORE YOUR WORK**, but you can always return to the Student CD and recopy the original databases to your computer as illustrated in Chapter 1.

GP Error Messages

User Already Logged In Message

If your system crashes or GP abruptly closes, your user ID will remain logged into GP. Upon returning, the number for Current Users and Users Allowed will equal below are the same.

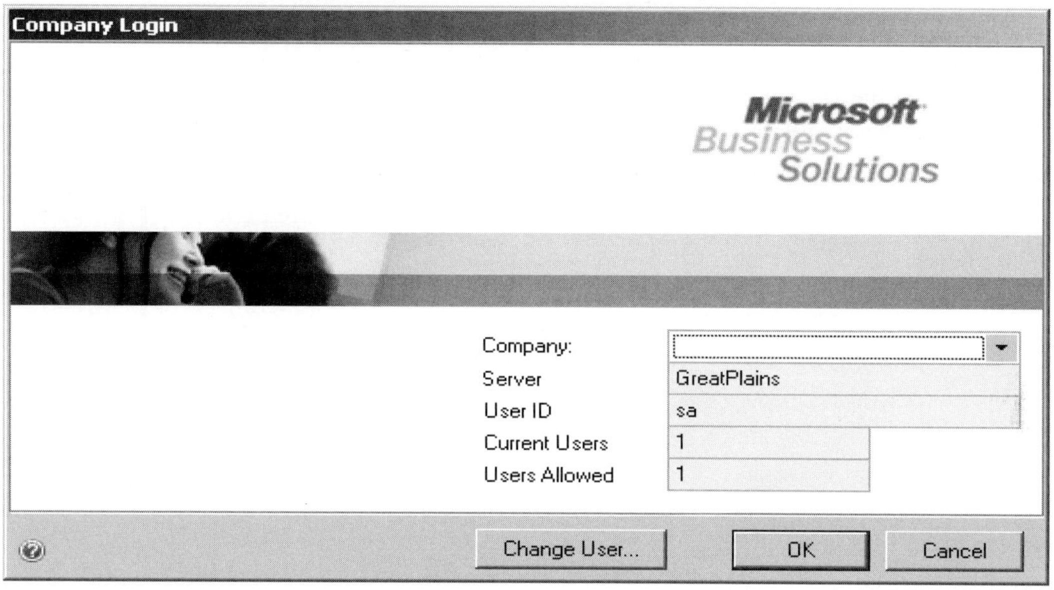

Select the company name you were using when the system was interrupted. GP sends a message that the *sa* account is already logged in. Answer Yes when prompted to view the current login.

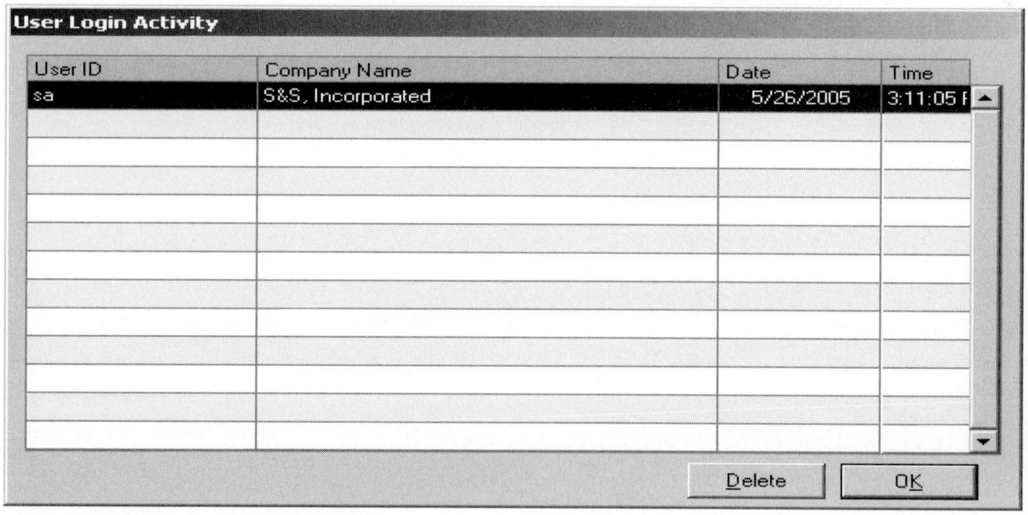

Highlight the *sa* account and click Delete. This action returns you to the GP login screen where the Current Users field contains a zero. You can now select any company for login.

OLE Pathname Error

Databases do not store the local pathname for notes so you may receive the following message if you click the notes icon in a window. Clicking the folder icon and selecting a path will correct this error.

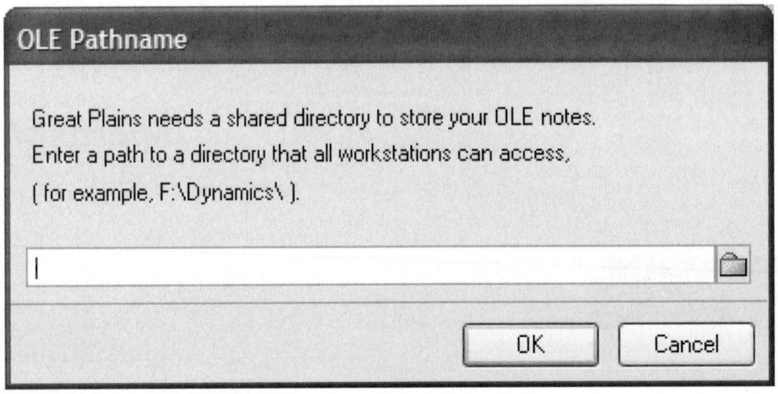

Appendix B COMPANY SPECIFICS

S&S CHART OF ACCOUNTS

Account Number	Account Description	Posting Type	Account Category
0000-01	Square Feet – East	Unit Account	
0000-02	Square Feet – MidWest	Unit Account	
0000-03	Square Feet – West	Unit Account	
0000-04	Square Feet - Administrative	Unit Account	
1100-00	Cash	Balance Sheet	Cash
1110-00	Cash-Savings	Balance Sheet	Cash
1120-00	Petty Cash	Balance Sheet	Cash
1130-00	Checking - Payroll	Balance Sheet	Cash
1200-00	Accounts Receivable	Balance Sheet	Accounts Receivable
1205-00	Sales Discounts Available	Balance Sheet	Accounts Receivable
1210-00	Allowance for Doubtful Accounts	Balance Sheet	Accounts Receivable
1270-00	Marketable Securities	Balance Sheet	Short-Term Investments
1310-00	Inventory	Balance Sheet	Inventory
1410-00	Prepaid Insurance	Balance Sheet	Prepaid Expenses
1430-00	Prepaid - Other	Balance Sheet	Prepaid Expenses
1500-00	Land	Balance Sheet	Property, Plant and Equipment
1510-00	Buildings	Balance Sheet	Property, Plant and Equipment
1515-00	Accum Depr - Buildings	Balance Sheet	Accumulated Depreciation
1520-00	Office Furniture/Fixtures	Balance Sheet	Property, Plant and Equipment
1525-00	Accum Depr - Office Furn/Fixtures	Balance Sheet	Accumulated Depreciation
1530-00	Vehicles	Balance Sheet	Property, Plant and Equipment
1535-00	Accum Depr - Vehicles	Balance Sheet	Accumulated Depreciation
1540-00	Computer Hardware	Balance Sheet	Property, Plant and Equipment
1545-00	Accum Depr - Computer Hardware	Balance Sheet	Accumulated Depreciation
1550-00	Computer Software	Balance Sheet	Property, Plant and Equipment
1555-00	Amortization - Computer Software	Balance Sheet	Accumulated Depreciation
2100-00	Accounts Payable	Balance Sheet	Accounts Payable
2105-00	Purchase Discounts Available	Balance Sheet	Accounts Payable

Account Number	Account Description	Posting Type	Account Category
2120-00	Accrued Payables	Balance Sheet	Accounts Payable
2150-00	Notes Payable	Balance Sheet	Notes Payable
2160-00	Current Maturities Long Term Debt	Balance Sheet	Current Maturities of Long-Term Debt
2170-00	Interest Payable	Balance Sheet	Interest Payable
2210-00	Wages Payable	Balance Sheet	Other Current Liabilities
2230-00	Commissions Payable	Balance Sheet	Other Current Liabilities
2260-00	FUTA Taxes Payable	Balance Sheet	Taxes Payable
2265-00	SUTA Taxes Payable	Balance Sheet	Taxes Payable
2270-00	FICA Taxes Payable	Balance Sheet	Taxes Payable
2275-00	Federal Withholding Taxes Payable	Balance Sheet	Taxes Payable
2280-00	State Withholding Taxes Payable	Balance Sheet	Taxes Payable
2285-00	City Withholding Taxes Payable	Balance Sheet	Taxes Payable
2290-00	Sales Taxes Payable	Balance Sheet	Taxes Payable
2295-00	Worker's Comp Payable	Balance Sheet	Taxes Payable
2310-00	Deductions Payable	Balance Sheet	Other Current Liabilities
2320-00	401-K Payable	Balance Sheet	Other Current Liabilities
2330-00	Unearned Revenue	Balance Sheet	Other Current Liabilities
2340-00	Dividends Payable	Balance Sheet	Other Current Liabilities
2350-00	Accrued Income Taxes	Balance Sheet	Taxes Payable
2410-00	Notes Payable - Long Term	Balance Sheet	Long-Term Debt
2420-00	Mortgage Payable	Balance Sheet	Long-Term Debt
3000-00	Common Stock	Balance Sheet	Common Stock
3100-00	Additional Paid In Capital	Balance Sheet	Additional Paid-in Capital - Common
3300-00	Retained Earnings	Balance Sheet	Retained Earnings
4100-00	Sales	Profit and Loss	Sales
4100-01	Sales - East	Profit and Loss	Sales
4100-02	Sales - MidWest	Profit and Loss	Sales
4100-03	Sales - West	Profit and Loss	Sales
4300-00	Sales Returns	Profit and Loss	Sales Returns and Discounts
4300-01	Sales Returns - East	Profit and Loss	Sales Returns and Discounts
4300-02	Sales Returns - MidWest	Profit and Loss	Sales Returns and Discounts
4300-03	Sales Returns - West	Profit and Loss	Sales Returns and Discounts
4400-00	Sales Discounts	Profit and Loss	Sales Returns and Discounts
4400-01	Sales Discounts - East	Profit and Loss	Sales Returns and Discounts

Account Number	Account Description	Posting Type	Account Category
4400-02	Sales Discounts - MidWest	Profit and Loss	Sales Returns and Discounts
4400-03	Sales Discounts - West	Profit and Loss	Sales Returns and Discounts
4500-00	Cost of Goods Sold	Profit and Loss	Cost of Goods Sold
4500-01	Cost of Goods Sold - East	Profit and Loss	Cost of Goods Sold
4500-02	Cost of Goods Sold - MidWest	Profit and Loss	Cost of Goods Sold
4500-03	Cost of Goods Sold - West	Profit and Loss	Cost of Goods Sold
4510-00	Purchases Variance	Profit and Loss	Cost of Goods Sold
4520-00	Freight Charges	Profit and Loss	Cost of Goods Sold
4530-00	Shrinkage & Waste	Profit and Loss	Cost of Goods Sold
4540-00	Transportation Expense	Profit and Loss	Cost of Goods Sold
4600-00	Purchase Discounts Taken	Profit and Loss	Cost of Goods Sold
5100-00	Wages/Salaries Expense	Profit and Loss	Salaries Expense
5100-01	Wages/Salaries - East	Profit and Loss	Salaries Expense
5100-02	Wages/Salaries - MidWest	Profit and Loss	Salaries Expense
5100-03	Wages/Salaries - West	Profit and Loss	Salaries Expense
5100-04	Wages/Salaries - Administration	Profit and Loss	Salaries Expense
5100-05	Wages - Warehouse/Truckers	Allocation	
5200-00	Commission Expense	Profit and Loss	Salaries Expense
5200-01	Commission Expense - East	Profit and Loss	Salaries Expense
5200-02	Commission Expense - MidWest	Profit and Loss	Salaries Expense
5200-03	Commission Expense - West	Profit and Loss	Salaries Expense
5300-00	Payroll Tax Expense	Profit and Loss	Salaries Expense
5310-01	FICA Tax Expense - East	Profit and Loss	Salaries Expense
5310-02	FICA Tax Expense - MidWest	Profit and Loss	Salaries Expense
5310-03	FICA Tax Expense - West	Profit and Loss	Salaries Expense
5310-04	FICA Tax Expense - Administration	Profit and Loss	Salaries Expense
5310-05	FICA - Warehouse/Truckers	Allocation	
5320-01	FUTA Tax Expense - East	Profit and Loss	Salaries Expense
5320-02	FUTA Tax Expense - MidWest	Profit and Loss	Salaries Expense
5320-03	FUTA Tax Expense - West	Profit and Loss	Salaries Expense
5320-04	FUTA Tax Expense - Administration	Profit and Loss	Salaries Expense
5320-05	FUTA - Warehouse/Truckers	Allocation	
5330-01	SUTA Tax Expense - East	Profit and Loss	Salaries Expense
5330-02	SUTA Tax Expense - MidWest	Profit and Loss	Salaries Expense
5330-03	SUTA Tax Expense - West	Profit and Loss	Salaries Expense

Account Number	Account Description	Posting Type	Account Category
5330-04	SUTA Tax Expense - Administration	Profit and Loss	Salaries Expense
5330-05	SUTA - Warehouse/Truckers	Allocation	
5340-01	Workers Comp Expense - East	Profit and Loss	Salaries Expense
5340-02	Workers Comp Expense - MidWest	Profit and Loss	Salaries Expense
5340-03	Workers Comp Expense - West	Profit and Loss	Salaries Expense
5340-04	Workers Comp Expense - Administration	Profit and Loss	Salaries Expense
5340-05	Workers Comp - Warehouse/Truckers	Allocation	
5400-00	Employee Benefits	Profit and Loss	Other Employee Expenses
5410-01	Health Insurance Expense - East	Profit and Loss	Other Employee Expenses
5410-02	Health Insurance Expense - MidWest	Profit and Loss	Other Employee Expenses
5410-03	Health Insurance Expense - West	Profit and Loss	Other Employee Expenses
5410-04	Health Insurance Expense - Administration	Profit and Loss	Other Employee Expenses
5410-05	Health Insur - Warehouse/Truckers	Allocation	
5420-01	401-K Expense - East	Profit and Loss	Other Employee Expenses
5420-02	401-K Expense - MidWest	Profit and Loss	Other Employee Expenses
5420-03	401-K Expense - West	Profit and Loss	Other Employee Expenses
5420-04	401-K Expense - Administration	Profit and Loss	Other Employee Expenses
5420-05	401-K Expense - Warehouse/Truckers	Allocation	
5500-00	Advertising Expense	Profit and Loss	Selling Expense
5500-01	Advertising Expense - East	Profit and Loss	Selling Expense
5500-02	Advertising Expense - MidWest	Profit and Loss	Selling Expense
5500-03	Advertising Expense - West	Profit and Loss	Selling Expense
5510-00	Contracted Labor	Profit and Loss	Administrative Expense
5510-04	Contracted Labor - Administrative	Profit and Loss	Administrative Expense
5520-00	Repairs & Maintenance - Building	Profit and Loss	Administrative Expense
5520-01	Repairs & Maintenance - East	Profit and Loss	Selling Expense
5520-04	Repairs & Maintenance - Administrative	Profit and Loss	Administrative Expense
5530-00	Travel	Profit and Loss	Administrative Expense
5530-01	Travel - East	Profit and Loss	Selling Expense
5530-02	Travel - MidWest	Profit and Loss	Selling Expense
5530-03	Travel - West	Profit and Loss	Selling Expense
5530-04	Travel - Administrative	Profit and Loss	Selling Expense
5535-00	Meals & Entertainment	Profit and Loss	Selling Expense

Account Number	Account Description	Posting Type	Account Category
5535-01	Meals & Entertainment - East	Profit and Loss	Selling Expense
5535-02	Meals & Entertainment - MidWest	Profit and Loss	Selling Expense
5535-03	Meals & Entertainment - West	Profit and Loss	Selling Expense
5535-04	Meals & Entertainment - Administrative	Profit and Loss	Administrative Expense
5540-00	Rent - Equipment	Profit and Loss	Administrative Expense
5540-01	Rent - Equipment - East	Profit and Loss	Selling Expense
5540-02	Rent - Equipment - Mid	Profit and Loss	Selling Expense
5540-03	Rent - Equipment - West	Profit and Loss	Selling Expense
5540-04	Rent - Equipment - Administrative	Profit and Loss	Administrative Expense
5560-00	Postage & Freight	Profit and Loss	Administrative Expense
5560-04	Postage & Freight - Administrative	Profit and Loss	Administrative Expense
5580-00	Supplies Expense	Profit and Loss	Administrative Expense
5580-01	Supplies Expense - East	Profit and Loss	Selling Expense
5580-02	Supplies Expense - Mid	Profit and Loss	Selling Expense
5580-03	Supplies Expense - West	Profit and Loss	Selling Expense
5580-04	Supplies Expense - Administrative	Profit and Loss	Administrative Expense
5600-00	Telephone Expense	Profit and Loss	Selling Expense
5600-01	Telephone Expense - East	Profit and Loss	Selling Expense
5600-02	Telephone Expense - MidWest	Profit and Loss	Selling Expense
5600-03	Telephone Expense - West	Profit and Loss	Selling Expense
5600-04	Telephone Expense - Administration	Profit and Loss	Administrative Expense
5600-05	Telephone Fixed Allocation Account	Allocation	
5610-00	Utilities	Profit and Loss	Selling Expense
5610-01	Utilities - East	Profit and Loss	Selling Expense
5610-02	Utilities - MidWest	Profit and Loss	Selling Expense
5610-03	Utilities - West	Profit and Loss	Selling Expense
5610-04	Utilities - Administrative	Profit and Loss	Administrative Expense
5610-05	Utilities - Fixed Allocation Account	Allocation	
5620-00	Insurance Expense	Profit and Loss	Administrative Expense
5620-04	Insurance Expense - Administration	Profit and Loss	Administrative Expense
5700-00	Bank Charges & Fees	Profit and Loss	Administrative Expense
5710-00	Bad Debt Expense	Profit and Loss	Administrative Expense
5810-00	Depreciation Expense	Profit and Loss	Depreciation & Amortization Expense
5820-00	Amortization Expense	Profit and Loss	Depreciation & Amortization Expense

Account Number	Account Description	Posting Type	Account Category
7010-00	Finance Charge Income	Profit and Loss	Other Income
7020-00	Interest Income	Profit and Loss	Other Income
7030-00	Miscellaneous Income	Profit and Loss	Other Income
7040-00	Gain on Disposal of Assets	Profit and Loss	Gain/Loss on Asset Disposal
8010-00	Interest Expense	Profit and Loss	Interest Expense
8030-00	Miscellaneous Expense	Profit and Loss	Other Expenses
8040-00	Loss on Disposal of Assets	Profit and Loss	Gain/Loss on Asset Disposal
9010-00	Income Tax Expense	Profit and Loss	Income Tax Expense
9999-00	Suspense	Profit and Loss	Nonfinancial Accounts

S&S Inventory Items

Item Number	Item Description	Short Name	Current Cost
AUDJV50WMP3	Javix 50 Watt 4 Channel MP3	MP3	$150.00
AUDNPXM4CD	NeerPio XM Ready 4 Channel CD R/RW	SatRadio	$102.00
AUDOR256MPORT	ORI 256MG Portable Digital Audio Player	PortAud	$85.00
AUDSNCDMP3	Sunyung CD/MP3/ATRAC3	MP3	$36.00
AUDSNCDMP3AMFM	Sunyung Portable CD/MP3/AM/FM/TV	PortAud	$50.00
AUDWW52WCD	WAWA 52 Watt X4 Channel Car Stereo CD-R/RW	CarAud	$60.00
DCCN22XDZ	Canyon DigCamcord 22X Optical / 440X Digital Zoom	Camcord	$280.00
DCJV16XDZ	Javix DigCamcord 16X Optical / 700X Digital Zoom	Camcord	$245.00
DCNK4XDZ	Nikki DigiCamcord 8Mg Pixel 4X Digital Zoom	Camcord	$460.00
DCSM10XDZ	Sunyung DigCamcord 10X Optical/120X Digital Zoom	Camcord	$315.00
DCSM18XDZ	Sumsang DigCamcord 18X Optical / 900X Digital Zoom	Camcord	$191.67
DPOY4MG3XD	Olympium 4Mg Pixel 3XOptical 4XDigital Camera	DigiCam	$127.00
DPCN32MG10XD	Canyon 3.2Mg Pixel 10X Optical/3.2X Digital Camera	DigiCam	$284.00
DPDS128MCARD	DiscSun 128MB Flash Memory Card	Memory	$26.00
DPDS128MGST	DiscSun 128MB Memory Stick	Memory	$30.00
DPFJ52MG32XDC	Fujiyama 5.2Mg Pixel 3.2X Optical/3.9X Digital Camera	DigiCam	$173.00
DPSN51MG3XDC	Sunyung 5.1Mg Pixel 3X Optical/2X Digital Camera	DigiCam	$200.00
DVDLPRW80G	Lipsphi Progressive Scan DVD R/RW 80G	DigiCam	$300.00
DVDNTPHFVCR	Nithze Progressive DVD HiFi VCR	DVDCombo	$150.00
DVDNVPCD	Navox Progressive DVD/CD	DVDCombo	$25.00
DVDRD7PORT	Roidlop 7 Inch Portable DVD	DVD	$100.00
DVDSMCD	Sumsang DVD/CD Near HD	DVDCombo	$105.00
DVDVNVHS	Vania DVD/VHS	DVDCombo	$42.00
DVDVX8PORT	VoxAudi 8 Inch Portable DVD	DVD	$195.00
DVRVT40	Vito 40 HR DVR	DVR	$56.67
DVRVT80	Vito 80 HR DVR	DVR	$72.00
HEMY71C980W	MaYaha 7.1 Channel 980 watt	Stereo	$410.00
HESB51DVD	SEBO 38 DVD 5.1 Home Entertainment	HomeEnt	$1,350.00
HESB6SPKR	SEBO 6 Speaker System	Stereo	$360.00
HESN51DVDVCR	Sunyung 5.1 Home Entertainment Combo DVD/VCR	HomeEnt	$435.00
SERVAUDIO	AUDIO SERVICES	SERVICES	$0.00
SERVCAMERA	CAMERA SERVICES	SERVICES	$0.00

Item Number	Item Description	Short Name	Current Cost
SERVVIDEO	VIDEO SERVICES	SERVICES	$0.00
VBT46WPJ	Batoshi 46 Inch Widescreen Projection	HDWide	$690.00
TVLP42HD	Lipsphi 42 Inch HDTV	HDTV	$560.00
TVPS60HDTV	Pasanovic 60 Inch Widescreen HDTV	HDWide	$1,905.00
TVSB52W	Subishi 52 Inch Widescreen DLP	Widescreen	$1,860.00
TVSN34W	Sunyung 34 Inch Widescreen	Widescreen	$2,200.00
TVSN42W	Sunyung 42 Inch Widescreen Projection	Projection	$1,365.00
TVSN50W	Sunyung 50 Inch Widescreen Projection	Projection	$1,610.00
TVSP37P	SonicPan 37 Inch Plasma	Plasma	$1,070.00

S&S Customer Accounts

Customer Number	Customer Name	Sales Territory	Payment Terms ID
APPLEDEM001	Apple Dempling, Inc	EAST	Net 30
BAMAZON001	Bamozon, Inc.	WEST	Net 30
BARTERBA001	Barter Bay, Inc.	WEST	Net 30
BETTERBU001	Better Buy, Inc.	MID	2% 10/Net 30
BOOKBUYE001	Book Buy Earnest, Inc.	EAST	Net 30
CANDYBOW001	Candy Bowl Catalog, Inc.	EAST	Net 30
DANMAYLO001	Dan Maylor, Inc.	WEST	Net 30
DISCOUNTE001	Discount Electronics, Inc.	WEST	Net 30
ELECTRON001	Electronic Town, Inc.	MID	Net 30
ETRADERS001	E-Traders Market, Inc	MID	Net 30
FILLARDS001	Fillards, Inc.	MID	Net 30
GGHREGGS001	GG HREGG Stores, Inc.	MID	Net 30
GIGGLEPL001	Giggle Place, Inc.	MID	Net 30
JANEDYAN001	Jane Dyant, Inc.	EAST	Net 30
KDPENNYS001	KD Penny's, Inc.	MID	Net 30
KOLLISTE001	Kollister's, Inc.	MID	Net 30
LAUFMANS001	Laufmans, Inc	EAST	Net 30
LERNEERS001	Lerneers & Lowers, Inc.	WEST	Net 30
MARKETPL001	Market Place, Inc.	MID	Net 30
PINKHOUS001	Pink House Electronics ,Inc.	WEST	Net 30
PRECISEM001	Precise Markets, Inc	MID	Net 30
RICKSSPO001	Rick's Specialty Goods, Inc.	EAST	Net 30
SIXTHAV001	Sixth Avenue, Inc.	WEST	Net 30
SMALLSCR001	Small Screen Sales, Inc.	EAST	Net 30
STEPHANI001	Stephanie's Discount, Inc.	MID	Net 30
TEDDIGO001	Teddi Gower, Inc.	WEST	Net 30
TELEVISI001	Television World, Inc.	EAST	Net 30
TIFFANYS001	Tiffany's Bargains, Inc.	EAST	Net 30
TRADERST001	Traders Table, Inc.	MID	Net 30
TRADESRU001	Trades R Us, Inc.	EAST	Net 30
TUBESTUR001	Tubes & Turners, Inc.	WEST	Net 30
TVTIMEST001	TV Time Stores, Inc	MID	Net 30
WORLDOFC001	World of Circuits, Inc.	MID	Net 30
ZEARSSTO001	Zears Stores, Inc.	EAST	2% 10/Net 30

S&S Vendor Accounts

Vendor ID	Vendor Name	Payment Terms ID	Vendor Class ID
AKRONCIT001	Akron City Tax	IMMED	PAY/ADM
BANKAMER001	Bank Amerex	IMMED	PAY/ADM
BRIGHTEL001	Bright Electric, Inc.	Net 30	R&M
CANYONCA001	Canyon Cam, Inc.	2% 10/Net 30	SUPPLIERS
CBSPHONE001	CBS Phone Company, Inc.	Net 10	UTILITIES
CELLULAR001	Cellular America	Net 30	MARKETING
CHANNELO001	Channel Oxe, Inc.	Net 30	MARKETING
CHEXPAYI001	Chexpay, Inc.	Net 30	PAY/ADM
COOLEYSA001	Cooley's AC Repair, Inc	Net 30	R&M
CUPSNPAP001	Cups N Paper Stuff, Inc.	Net 30	OTHER
EMARKETI001	E-Marketing Company, Inc.	Net 30	MARKETING
FEDERALXP001	Federal Xpert	Net 30	PAY/ADM
FIRSTNAT001	First National Bank	IMMED	PAY/ADM
FLIPFLOP001	Flipflop Travel Agency, Inc	Net 30	PAY/ADM
INTERNAL001	Internal Revenue Services	IMMED	PAY/ADM
JAVIXCAM001	Javix Cam, Inc.	2% 10/Net 30	SUPPLIERS
LAWNGREE001	Lawn Green, Inc.	Net 30	R&M
LOAINTER001	LOA Internet, Inc.	Net 10	UTILITIES
MUTUALHE001	Mutual Health Insurance, Inc.	Net 10	PAY/ADM
NEERPIOI001	Neer Pio, Inc.	Net 30	OTHER
NIKKICAM001	Nikki Cam, Inc.	Net 30	SUPPLIERS
OFFICEREO01	Office Rex, Inc.	Net 30	OTHER
OHIODEPT001	Ohio Department Unemployment	IMMED	PAY/ADM
OHIOREDI001	Ohio Redision, Inc.	Net 10	UTILITIES
OHIOTAXD001	Ohio Tax Department	IMMED	PAY/ADM
OHIOWORK001	Ohio Workers Comp	Check	PAY/ADM
OLYMPIUM001	Olympium Pic, Inc.	Net 30	SUPPLIERS
ORICORPO0001	Ori Corporation	Net 30	SUPPLIERS
OSCARDIS001	Oscar Disposal, Inc.	Net 10	R&M
PASANOVI001	Pasanovic, Inc.	Net 30	SUPPLIERS
PAYDAYPR001	Payday Processing, Inc.	Net 30	PAY/ADM
PBFUELCO001	PB Fuel Company	Net 30	OTHER
PETTYCAS001	Petty Cash	IMMED	PAY/ADM
RADIOWKR001	Radio WKRP, Inc.	Net 30	MARKETING
RETIREME001	Retirement Benefits	IMMED	PAY/ADM
RIGHTMAR001	Right Marketing, Inc.	Net 30	MARKETING
ROOTROTE001	Root Roter Plumbing, Inc.	Net 30	R&M
RYANDANG001	Ryan Dan Group, Inc.	Net 30	MARKETING

Vendor ID	Vendor Name	Payment Terms ID	Vendor Class ID
SHELLYST001	Shelly's Temp Service	Net 30	PAY/ADM
SOFTWARE001	Software People, Inc.	Net 30	PAY/ADM
SONICPAN001	Sonic Pan, Inc.	Net 30	SUPPLIERS
SUBISHII001	Subishi, Inc.	Net 30	SUPPLIERS
SUMSANGCO001	SumSang Corporation	Net 30	SUPPLIERS
SUNYUNGH001	Sunyung Home, Inc.	2% 10/Net 30	SUPPLIERS
TRAVELOR001	Travelor's Business	Net 30	PAY/ADM
TRUCKSUP001	Truck Supplies, Inc.	Net 30	R&M
UNITEDHE001	United Health Insurance	Net 10	PAY/ADM
UNITEDPA001	United Parcel Service	Net 30	PAY/ADM
UNITEDST001	United States Post Office	IMMED	PAY/ADM
UNITEDWA001	United Way	IMMED	PAY/ADM
WATERCLE001	Water Clear, Inc.	Net 10	UTILITIES
WAWACOMP001	WAWA Company	Net 30	SUPPLIERS
WENERTIM001	Wener Time Cable, Inc.	Net 10	UTILITIES
WESTDOMI001	West Dominion Gas, Inc.	Net 10	UTILITIES
ZEARSSTO001	Zears Stores, Inc.	Net 30	SUPPLIERS
ZELLCOMP001	Zell Computer Repair, Inc.	Net 30	R&M

S&S Employees Accounts

Employee ID	Last Name	First Name	Employee Class	Department	Job Title
KTB4235	Bell	Kenneth	HOURLY	MAINT	STAFF
APF3232	Fleming	Ashton	SALARY	ADMIN	ACCT
SMG4255	Gonzalez	Susan	SALARY	ADMIN	OWNER
GLH9898	Hanratty	George	HOURLY	TRANS	TRUCK
LJJ3232	Johns	LeBron	HOURLY	WARE	SUPR
BAL2122	Lane	Betsy	HOURLY	ADMIN	APCLER
ASL6677	Levine	April	SALARY	SMID	STAFF
MPM1924	Mapley	Matthew	HOURLY	WARE	STAFF
GKM3209	McMahon	George	HOURLY	MAINT	SUPR
MTM3987	Murphy	Mary	SALARY	SWEST	STAFF
SJP5132	Parry	Scott	SALARY	ADMIN	OWNER
JJR1132	Richmond	James	HOURLY	ADMIN	ARCLER
CJW7872	Warner	Curtis	SALARY	SEAST	STAFF
ACW3287	Whitfield	Adam	HOURLY	TRANS	TRUCK
TKW3238	Winchester	Thomas	HOURLY	WARE	STAFF

Appendix C CORRECTING TRANSACTIONS

POSTING ERRORS

Distribution Account Missing Error or Posting to a Closed Period Error

If a distribution account is missing from the Distributions window or the posting date for a batch is to a closed accounting period then GP suspends posting and issues the following message.

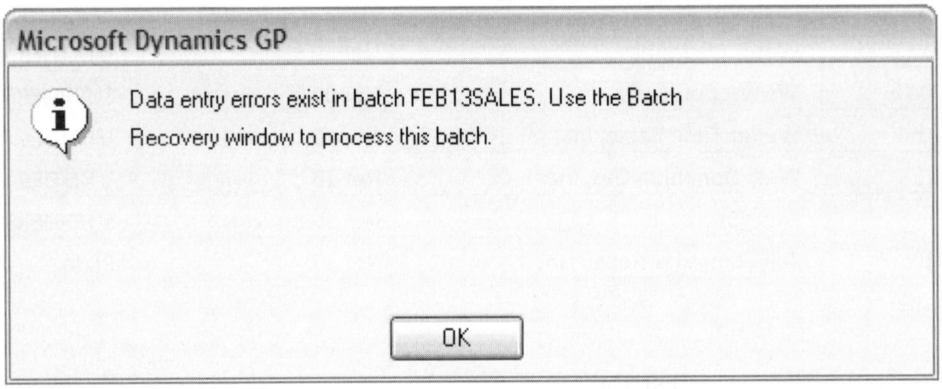
Microsoft Dynamics GP
Data entry errors exist in batch FEB13SALES. Use the Batch Recovery window to process this batch.
OK

To correct, you must first recover the suspended transaction using the Batch Recovery window illustrated next. This window is opened by clicking the GP button to select ***Tools>>Routines>> Batch Recovery.***

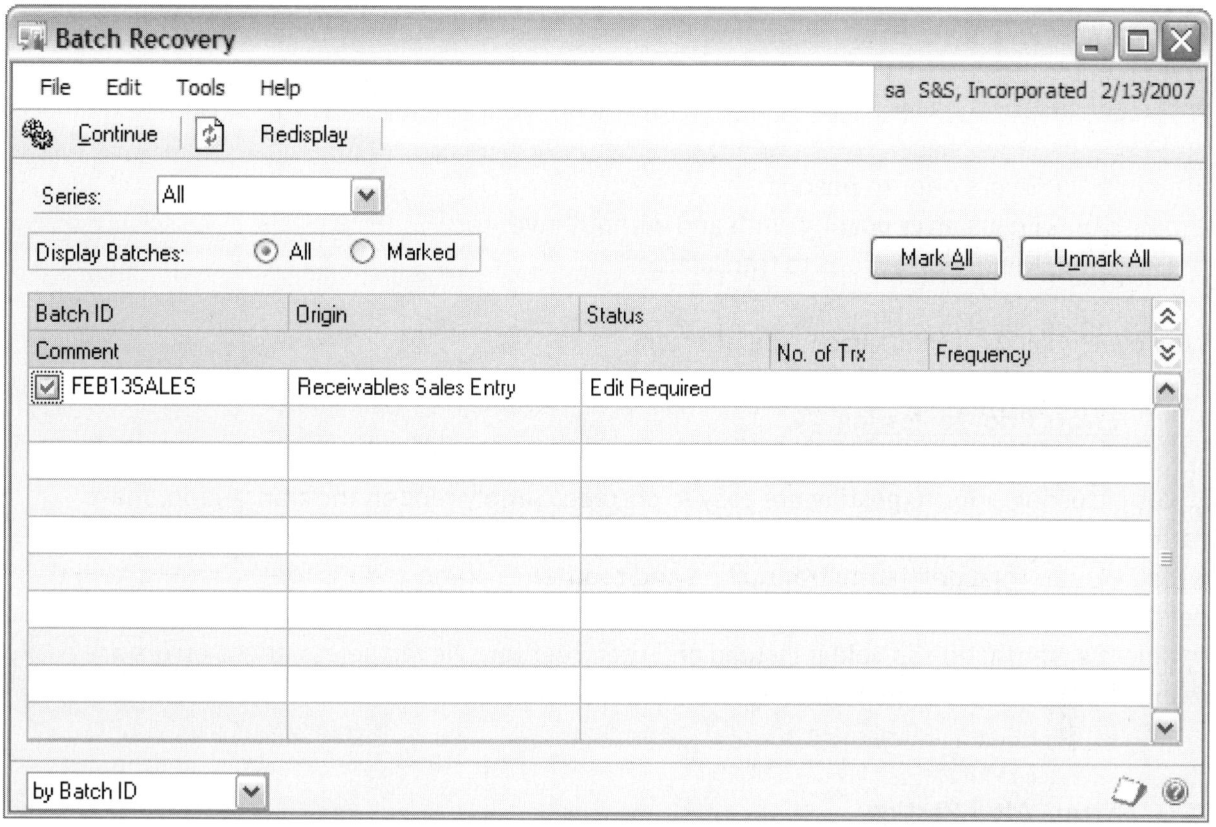

Mark the batch and click **Continue** to release it. Then return to the original transaction and change the date or open the Distributions window to supply any missing account number.

CORRECTION PROCEDURES

We all make posting errors so do not panic if, just as you hit that post button, you remember that you forgot to change something. Thus, proper error correction procedures are vital to maintaining data integrity.

In Chapter 4, we illustrated adjusting entries for the Inventory Control Series and these are the steps you would use to correct errors in item quantities. Additionally, correcting posting errors in the Financial Series were illustrated under correcting journal entries in Chapter 8. What follows are instructions for correcting errors made in the Sales, Purchasing, and Payroll Series.

Sales Series Posting Errors

Posting errors for the Sales Series come in several forms. For simplicity, we categorize them as:

1. Errors prior to posting
2. Errors after posting: with and without inventory
3. Minor corrections to transactions

We now explain correcting each type of error.

1. Errors Prior to Posting

Errors occurring prior to posting are easy to correct. Simply reopen the transaction, make corrections, and resave. If the error involves a sale to the wrong customer or an invoice for the wrong vendor then delete the transaction and reenter it. If the error is for the wrong item then delete the line item and reenter it. Depending on Series control settings, you may not be able to delete a transaction so void it instead and then reenter. Nevertheless, these errors are easily resolved because permanent posting has not occurred.

2. Errors After Posting

Errors Involving Inventory

These are errors on transactions posted in either the Sales Order Processing or Invoice Processing Tiers so errors have permanently interfaced with the customer and inventory tables. You correct these errors by posting a transaction returning inventory and then posting a new invoice.

Example: An invoice for inventory was posted to the wrong customer or for the wrong item. The entry is corrected by: *(Note: Use the original transaction date if the Series is still open for that date.)*

- Issuing a return of inventory for the incorrect customer or a return for the wrong item, noting error in the description field as the reason for return. Remember to apply the return to the invoice. *(Note: Returns are illustrated in Chapter 5.)*

- Issuing an new invoice to the correct customer.

Errors Not Involving Inventory

These are errors on transactions posted in the Receivables Processing tier so are only interfaced with the customer table and are simpler to correct.

Example: A credit memo posted to the wrong customer. To correct, click Posted Transactions to open the window illustrated next.

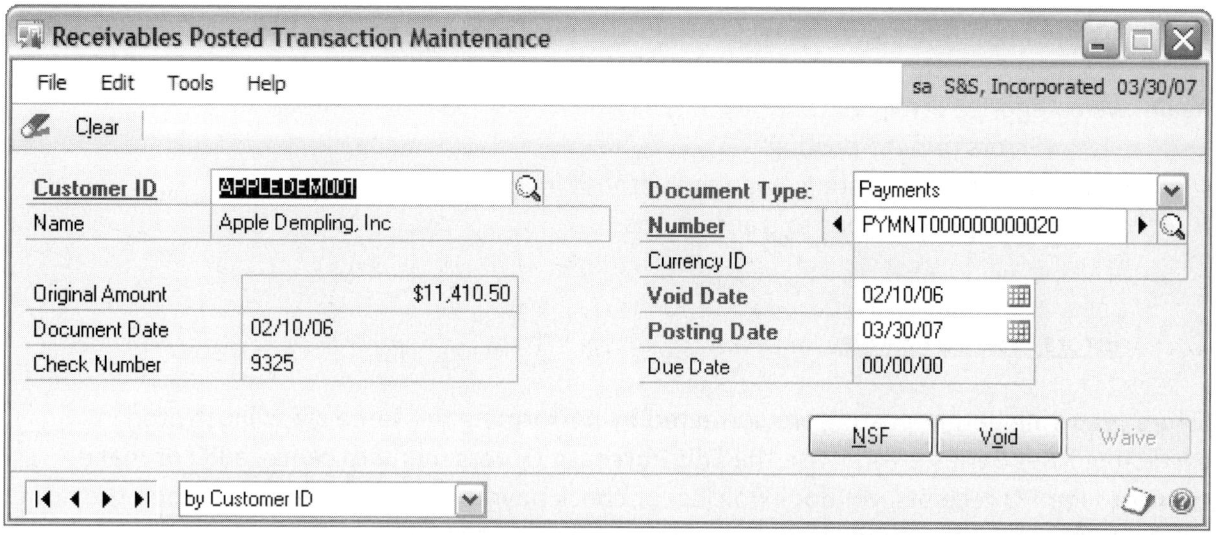

Look up the customer and document number and click **Void**. Close the window to post and print the posting reports. You can now reenter the correct transaction.

3. Minor Corrections to Transactions

You can also make minor corrections to posted transactions by clicking **Edit Transaction Information** to open the window illustrated next. This window allows changes to fields that are not grayed out and fields you can change varying by document type.

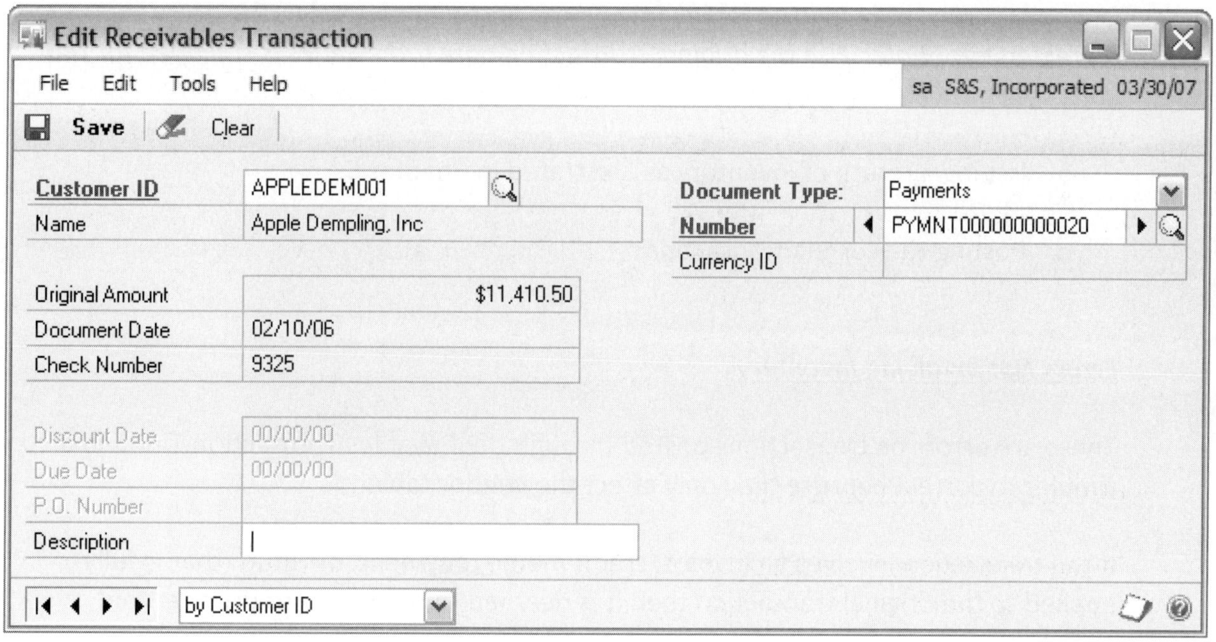

Purchasing Series Error Corrections

Error correction procedures for vendors are similar to those for Sales Series transactions. Errors include invoices posted to the wrong vendor or for the wrong item and vendor check errors. Such errors are a normal part of doing business.

Again, we categorize errors as:

1. Errors prior to posting
2. Errors after posting: with and without inventory
3. Minor corrections to transactions

1. Errors Prior to Posting

Errors occurring before posting are corrected by performing the same steps illustrated in correcting Sales Series errors. Use the **Edit Purchase Orders** menu to cancel a PO or make changes. For PO receipts, vendor invoicing, or check payment batches, simply reopen the transaction, make corrections by deleting or changing, and resave.

2. Errors After Posting

Errors Involving Inventory

These are errors posted through the Inventory Purchasing Tier that have permanently interfaced with the vendor and inventory table. Correct these errors using the following steps.

Example: A receipt or invoice for inventory was posted incorrectly. The entry is corrected by: *(Note: Use the original transaction date if the Series is still open for that date.)*

- Issuing a return of inventory as illustrated in Chapter 6.
- Posting the correct transaction.

Errors Not Involving Inventory

These are errors on transactions posted through the Payables Transaction Tier and are simpler to correct because they only affect the vendor table.

If the transaction involves an invoice, credit memo, payment, or return that is fully applied to the original transaction then it is deemed to be history so use the **Void**

Historical Payables Transaction menu to look up the transaction and void it. Otherwise, use the **Void Open Transactions** menu to void it. *(Note: You cannot use these procedures to void invoices involving inventory.)*

If the transaction is partially applied then use the Apply Payables Documents window to remove its application before voiding the transaction.

Be sure to check the Posting Date before voiding. If possible, use the original date on the transaction. If the original date is in a closed accounting period then select a date in the open period.

3. <u>**Minor Corrections**</u>

As in the Sales Series, you can make minor changes to posted transactions using the **Edit Transaction Information** menu. Once again, you can change fields that are not grayed out and fields that can be changed vary by document type.

Payroll Series Error Correction Procedures

You have to be very careful correcting payroll errors because corrections affect employee W-2's and withholding calculations as well as company tax calculations and reporting.

You make corrections by clicking **Void Checks** on the Payroll home page and selecting **PAY** under **Checkbook ID**. You then enter criteria that looks up the transaction and click Redisplay. On the next illustration, we have looked up check number 74083.

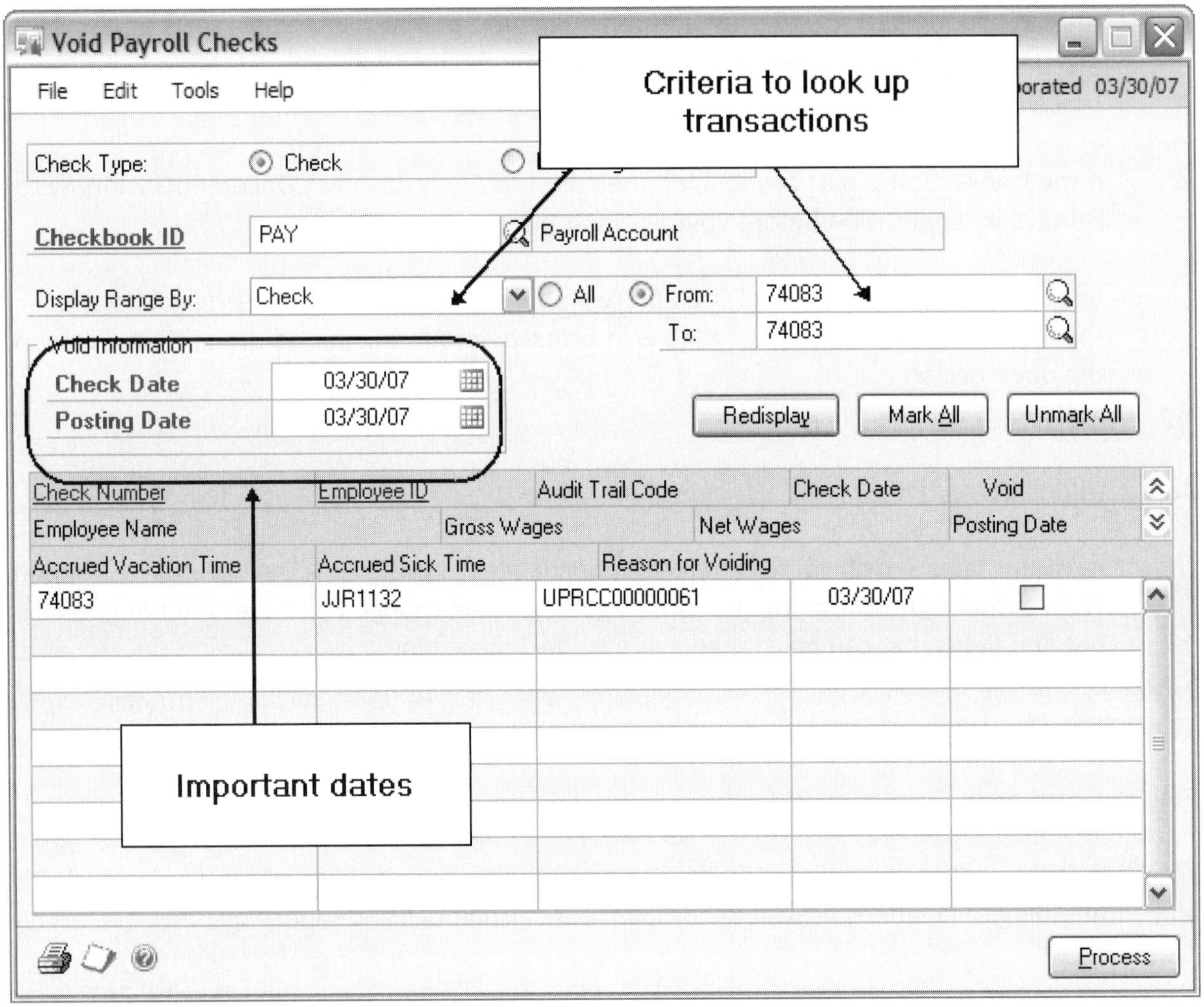

We have highlighted important dates. **Check Date** must always be the original date on the paycheck because this interacts with employee and employer tax calculations and employer tax reporting. **Posting Date** is the effective date in the Financial Series and will be either the original date on the paycheck or a date in the open period.

To void a paycheck, mark the **Void** option and click **Process**.

Appendix D EXERCISE SOLUTIONS

CHAPTER 1 EXERCISES

E1:1 Practice Using Lookup Windows and Hyperlinks

First select account 4100-01 Sales – East. *Note: You can type 4100 into the Account field before launching the lookup window and GP advances the lookup list to revenue accounts.* Highlight the transaction posted on January 25, 2007 and click the Journal Entry hyperlink.

In the Transaction Entry Zoom window, click the Source Document hyperlink to open the details illustrated below. The information you were asked to provide is marked on the illustration.

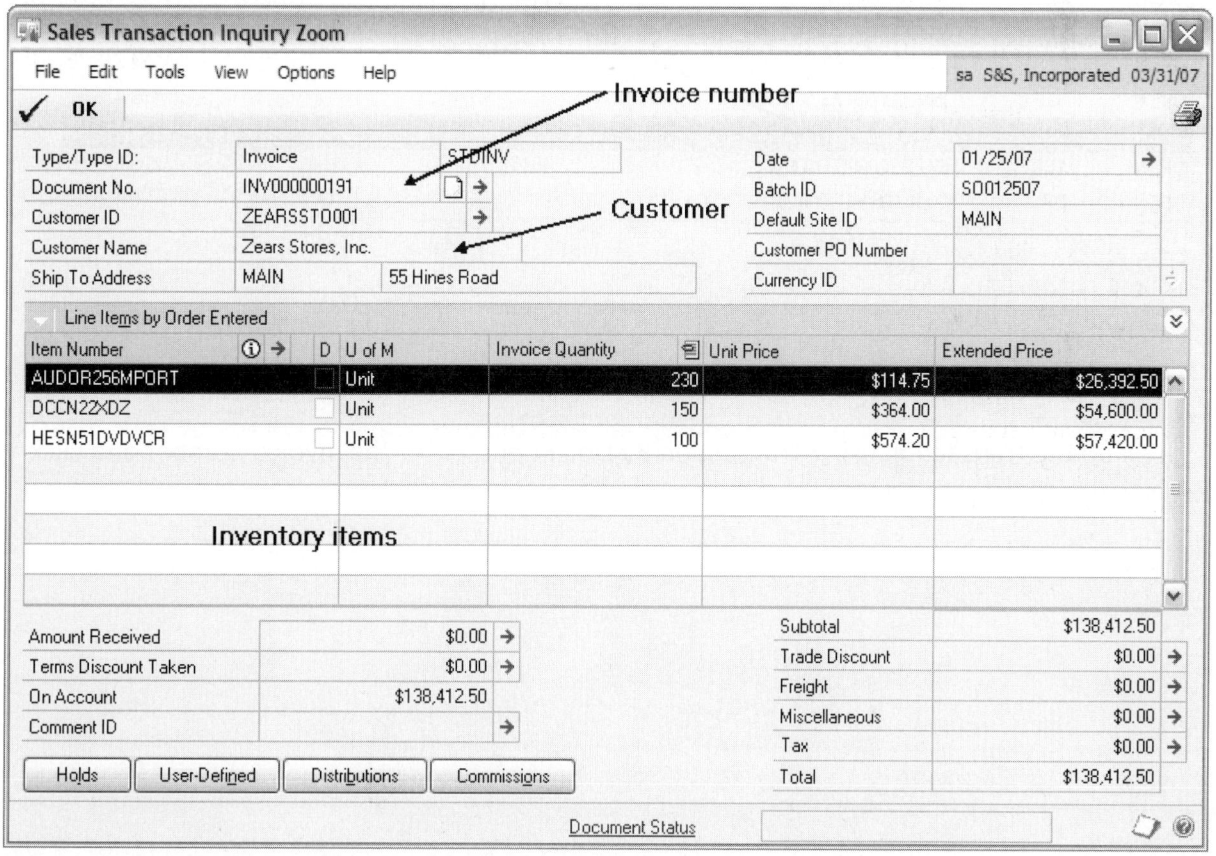

You can look up the same data using Transaction by Customer. Look up Zears Stores, Inc. in the Receivables Transaction Inquiry - Customer window, highlight the invoice and click the Document Number hyperlink.

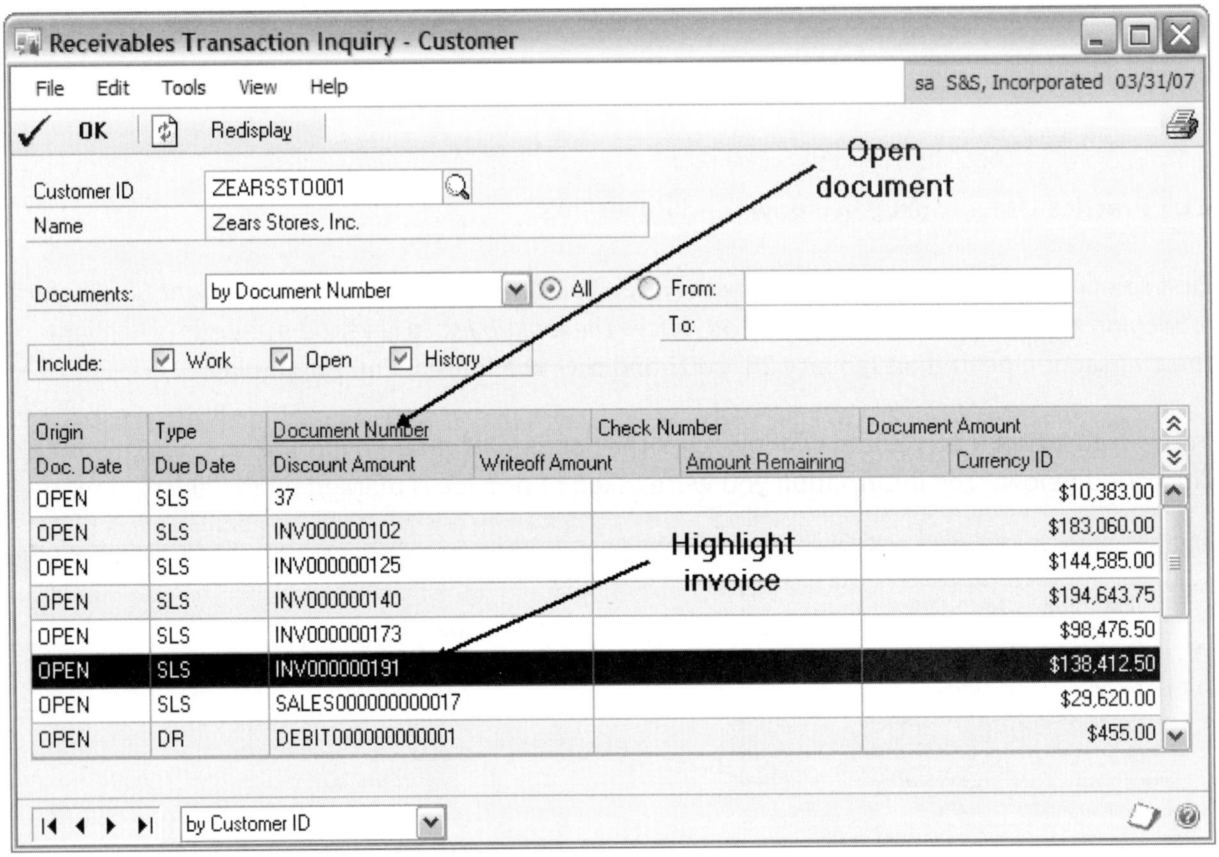

To look up the transaction using Transaction By Document, enter the invoice number and click Redisplay as illustrated next.

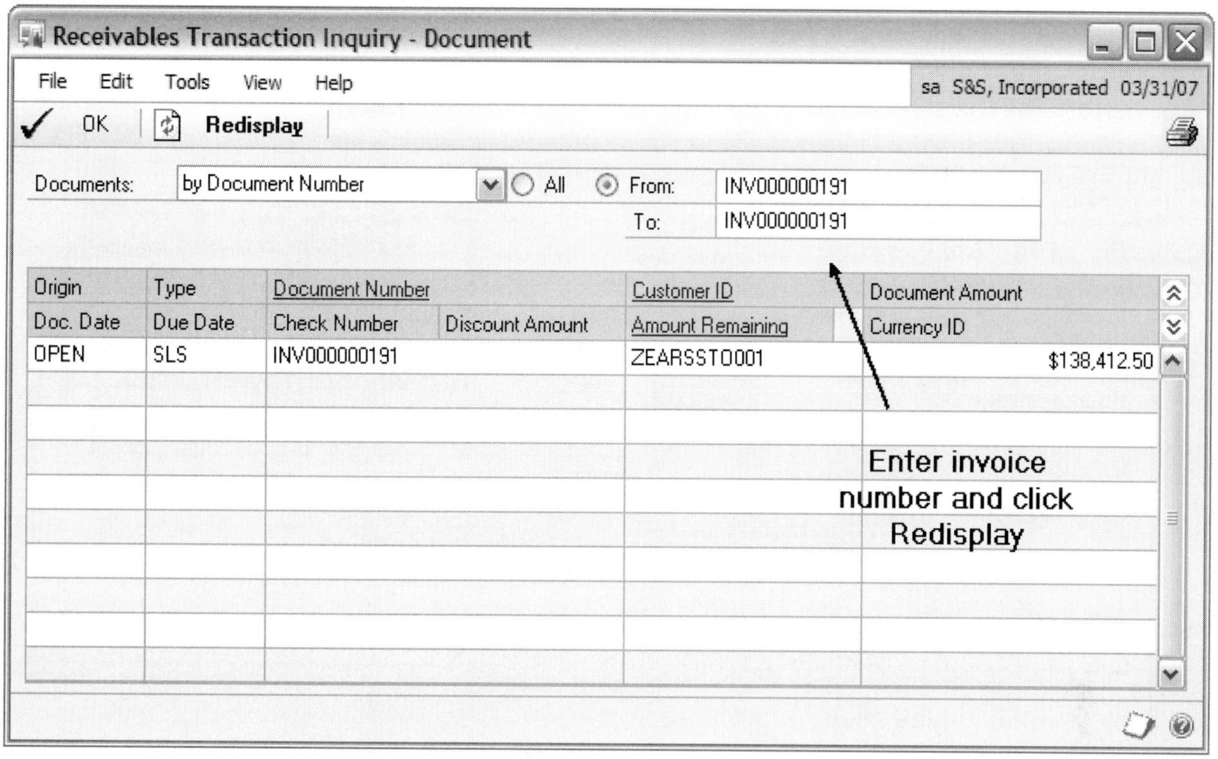
Receivables Transaction Inquiry - Document
File
Edit
Tools
View
Help
sa S&S, Incorporated 03/31/07
OK
Redisplay
Documents:
by Document Number
All
From:
INV000000191
To:
INV000000191
Origin
Type
Document Number
Customer ID
Document Amount
Doc. Date
Due Date
Check Number
Discount Amount
Amount Remaining
Currency ID
OPEN
SLS
INV000000191
ZEARSST0001
$138,412.50
Enter invoice number and click Redisplay

E1:2 Practice Printing Multiple Reports

After performing the steps listed in the exercise, the report window appears as illustrated next.

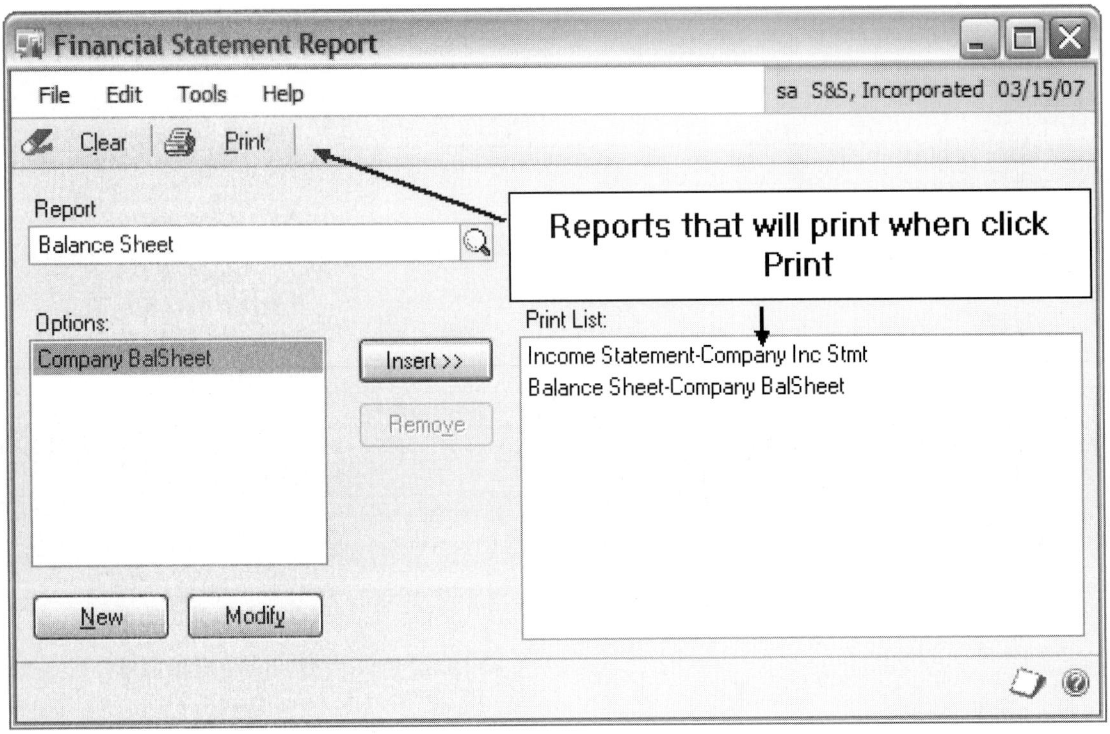

CHAPTER 2 EXERCISES

E2:1 Create and Delete General Ledger Posting Accounts

You have to determine the account number first. By referring to our tables for creating accounts, we know that a fixed asset account begins with the numbers of "15". You can then refer to existing accounts to see that Buildings is already numbered 1510-00 so the next sequential number for buildings results in assigning 1511-00 as the new account number.

You must also verify that this is a Balance Sheet account, increased by a debit and then assign the account to appear under the Property, Plant, and Equipment category on the Balance Sheet. *(Note: You can obtain the category by referring to the 1510-00 Building account.)*

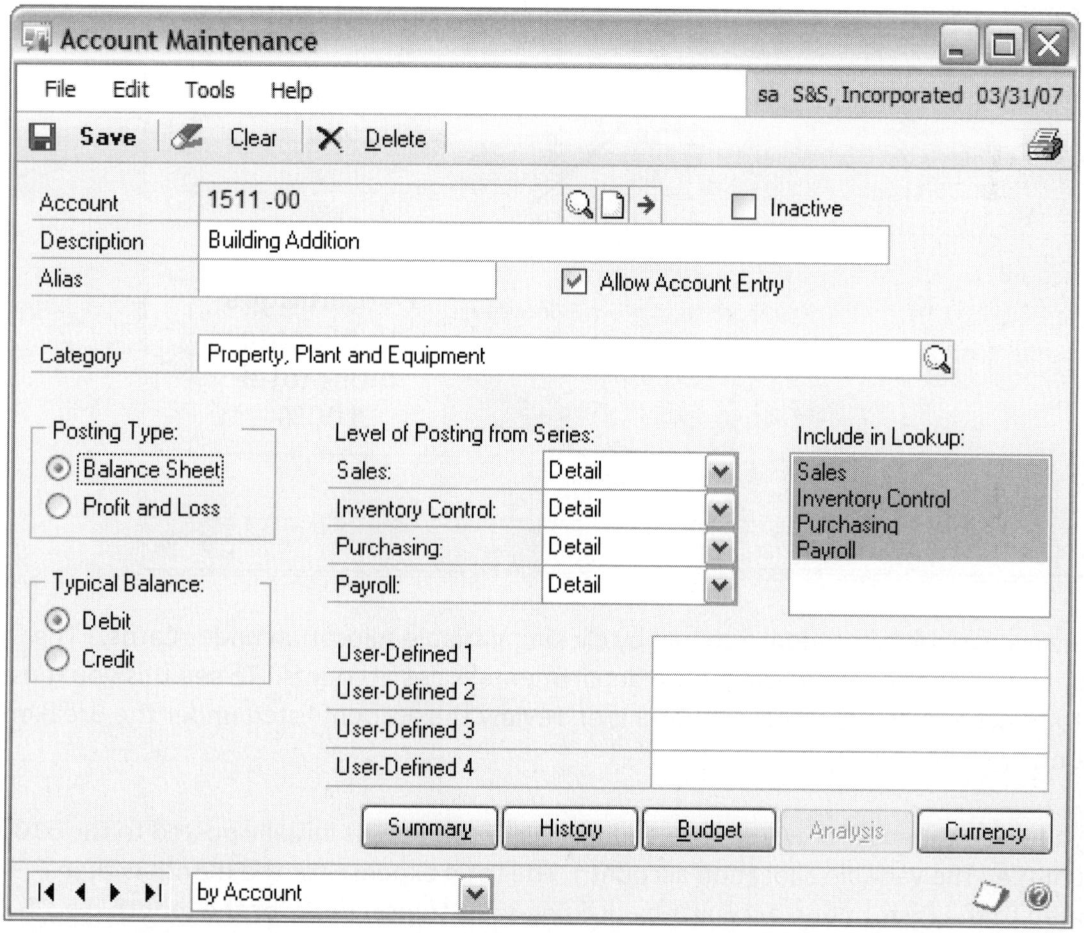

E2:2 Variable and Fixed Allocation Accounts

You review fixed allocation accounts by clicking Fixed Allocation under Cards. Thus, all utilities are initially posted to the fixed allocation account of 5610-05. GP then distributes the expense to the accounts listed under Distribution Account using the percentages provided.

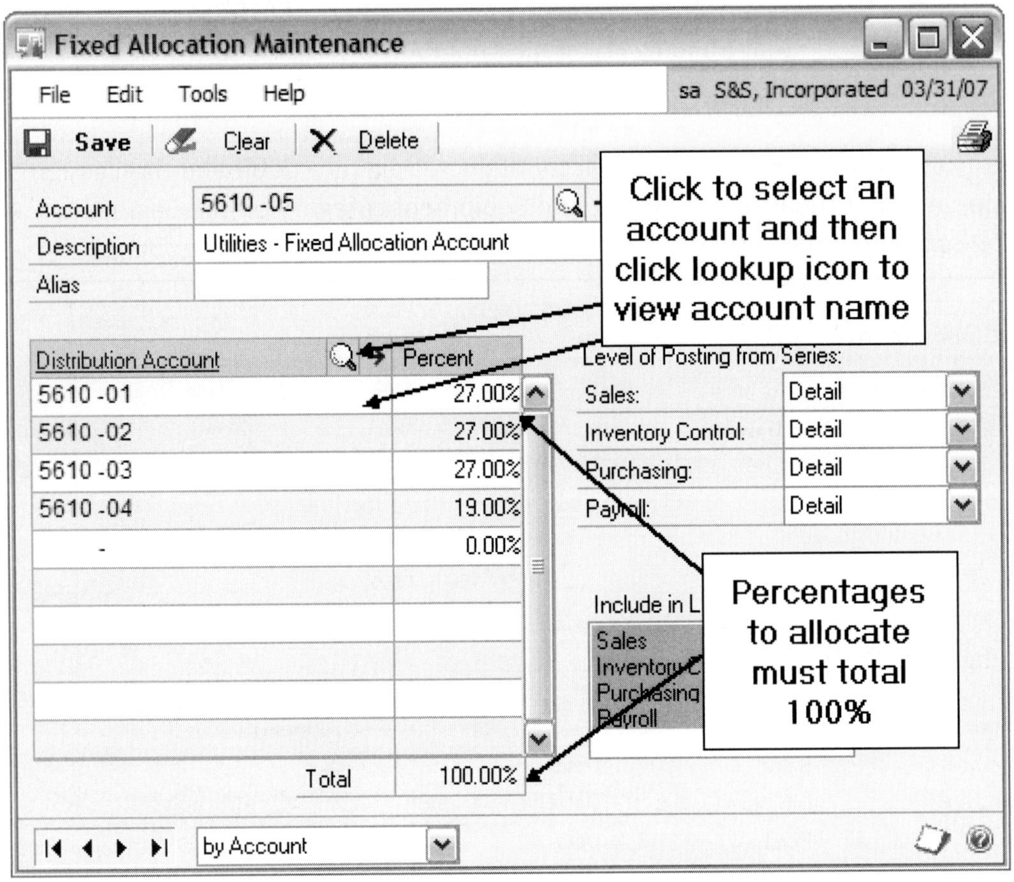

You review variable allocation accounts by clicking Variable Allocation under Cards. The accounts used to breakdown wages are departmental sales accounts. To see this you must first click to select a Distribution Account and then review the account listed under the Breakdown Account.

Thus, all wage expense for warehouse and trucker employees is initially posted to the 5100-05 account (i.e., the variable allocation account.) The total expense for the month is then allocated to the Distribution Accounts by dividing sales transactions for the month (i.e., Trx Period) in the Breakdown Account by the total sales transactions for the month for all Breakdown Accounts.

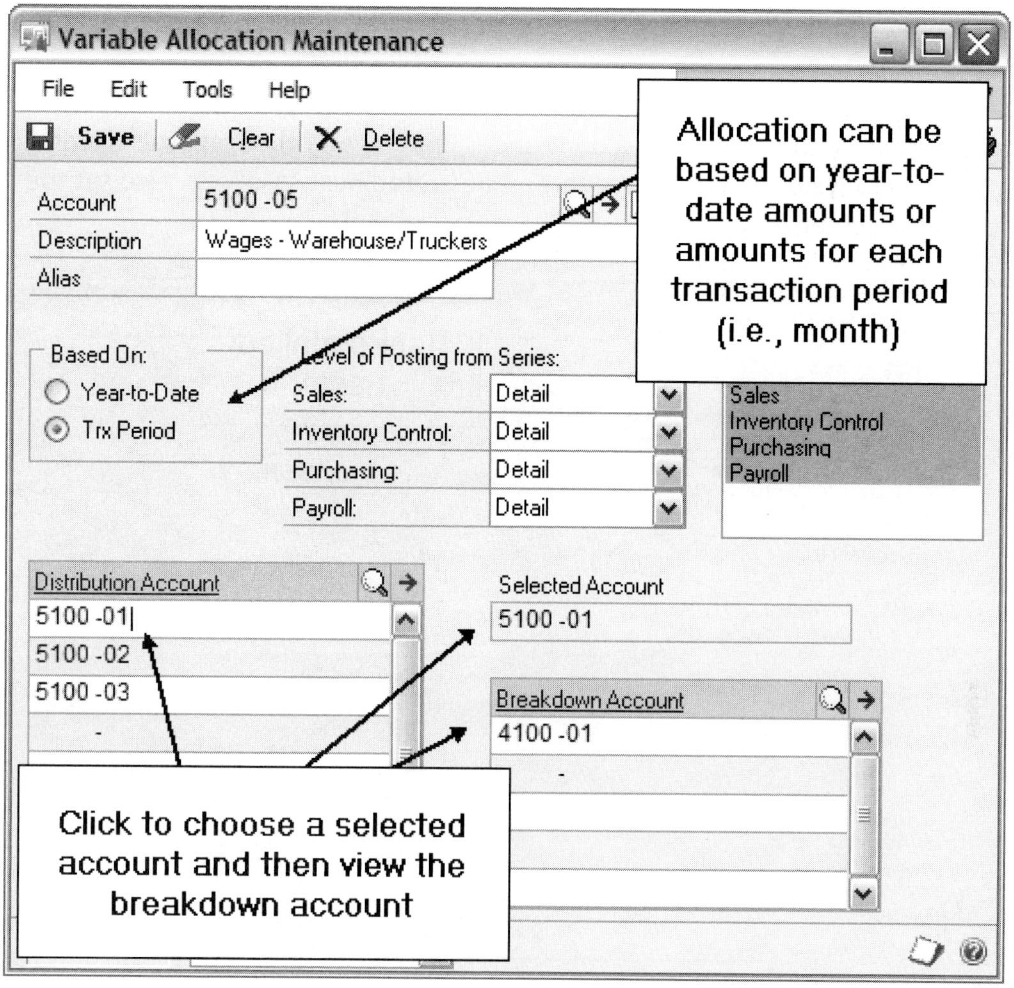
Variable Allocation Maintenance
File Edit Tools Help
Save Clear Delete
Account 5100 -05
Description Wages - Warehouse/Truckers
Alias
Allocation can be based on year-to-date amounts or amounts for each transaction period (i.e., month)
Based On:
Year-to-Date
Trx Period
Level of Posting from Series:
Sales: Detail
Inventory Control: Detail
Purchasing: Detail
Payroll: Detail
Sales
Inventory Control
Purchasing
Payroll
Distribution Account
5100 -01
5100 -02
5100 -03
Selected Account
5100 -01
Breakdown Account
4100 -01
Click to choose a selected account and then view the breakdown account

E2:3 Generate COA Report

The report is first created by clicking Account under Reports and choosing the Fixed Allocation category. Next, click New and create a report as illustrated next. Make sure to set the Destination to the screen.

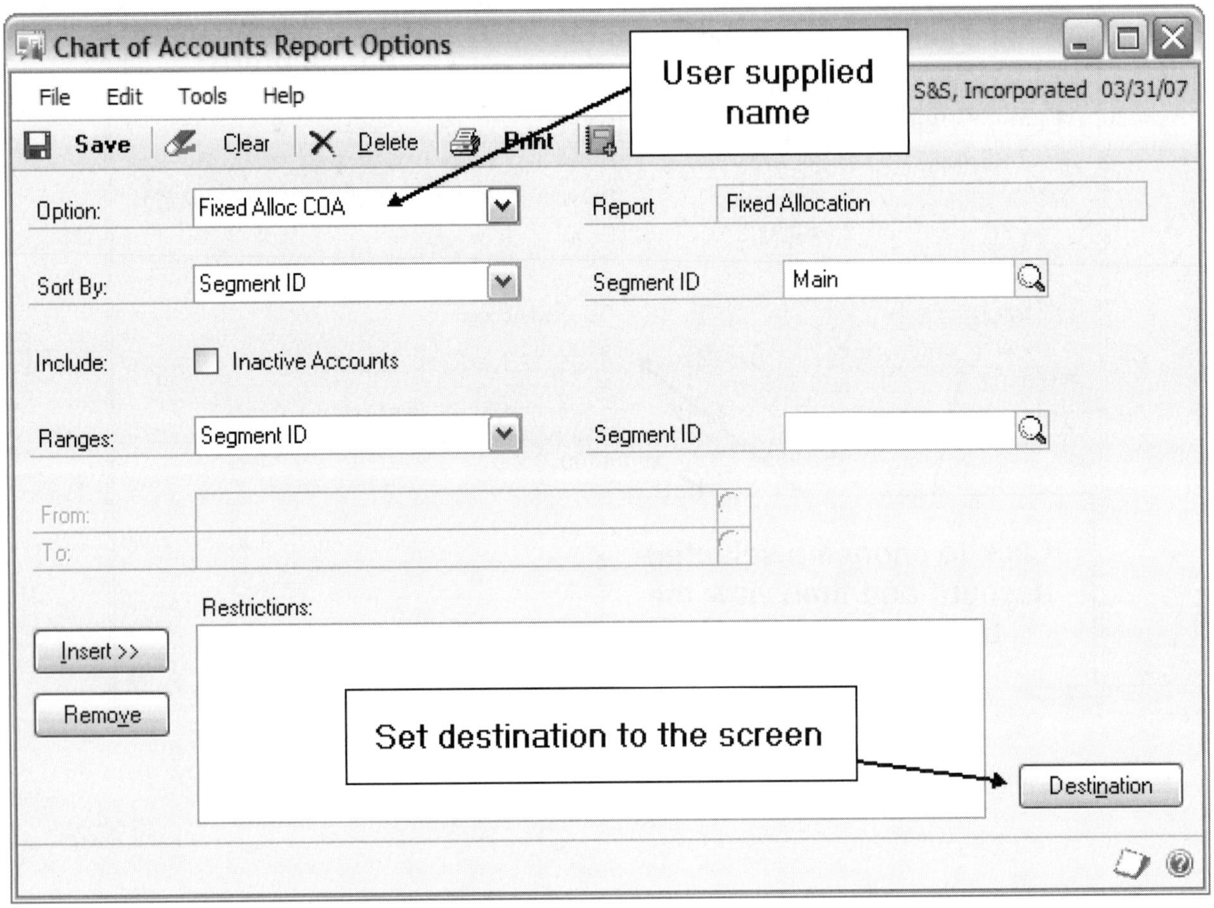

The printed report appears next. After printing, close the report options window and click Save to save the new report.

User Date: 03/31/07	S&S, Incorporated FIXED ALLOCATION ACCOUNTS LIST General Ledger		Page: 1 User ID: sa

Ranges: From: To:
Account First Last
Account Description First Last

Sorted By: Main Include:

Allocation Account	Description	Alias	Active	Distribution Account	Percentage
5600-05	Telephone Fixed Allocation Account		Yes		
				5600-01	27.00%
				5600-02	27.00%
				5600-03	27.00%
				5600-04	19.00%
				Total Distribution Percentage:	100.00%
5610-05	Utilities - Fixed Allocation Account		Yes		
				5610-01	27.00%
				5610-02	27.00%
				5610-03	27.00%
				5610-04	19.00%
				Total Distribution Percentage:	100.00%

Total Fixed Allocation Accounts: 2

Chapter 4 Exercises

E4:1 Test an Item's Sales Price

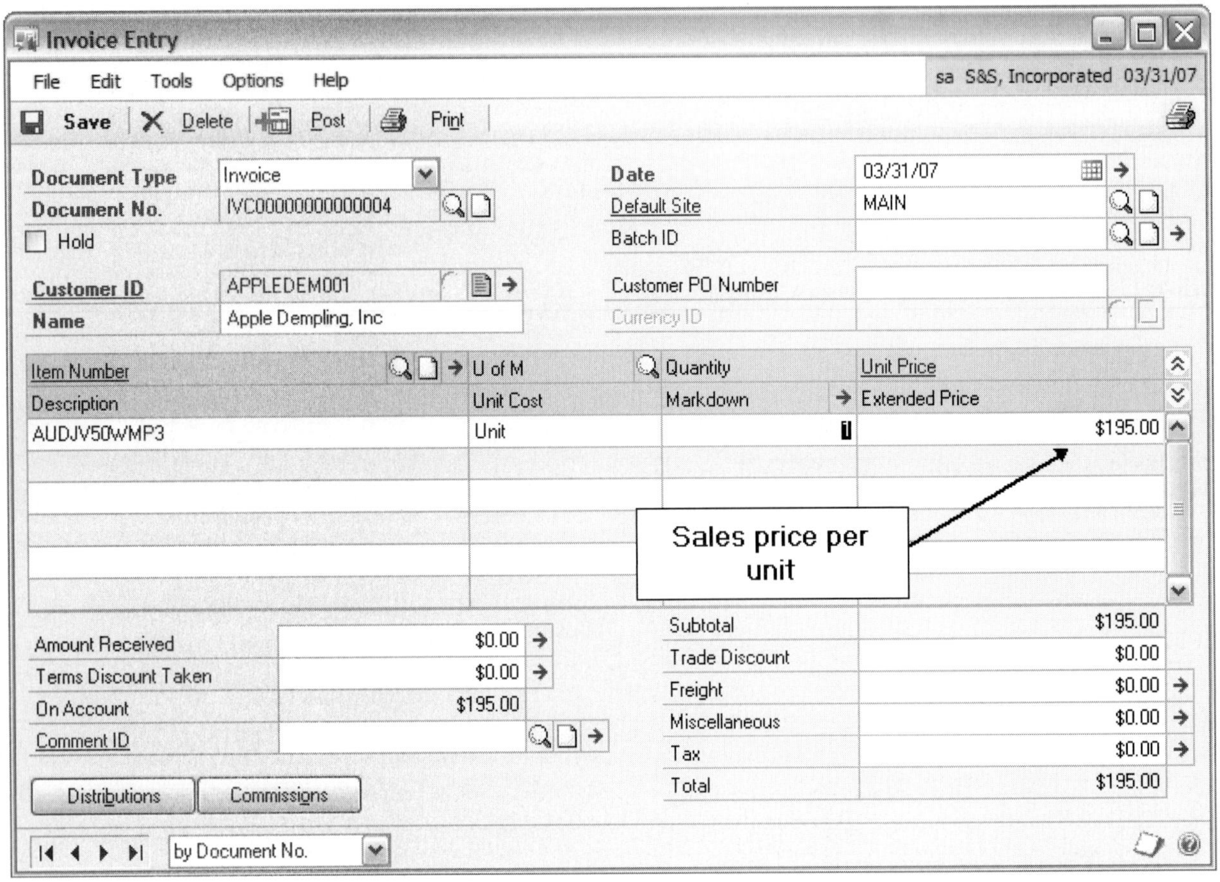

E4:2 Practice Assigning Vendors

To assign Nikki Cam as the preferred vendor for DPD128MCARD, click Quantities/Site and perform the following. Save the record when finished. *(Note: GP automatically links the vendor to the item.)*

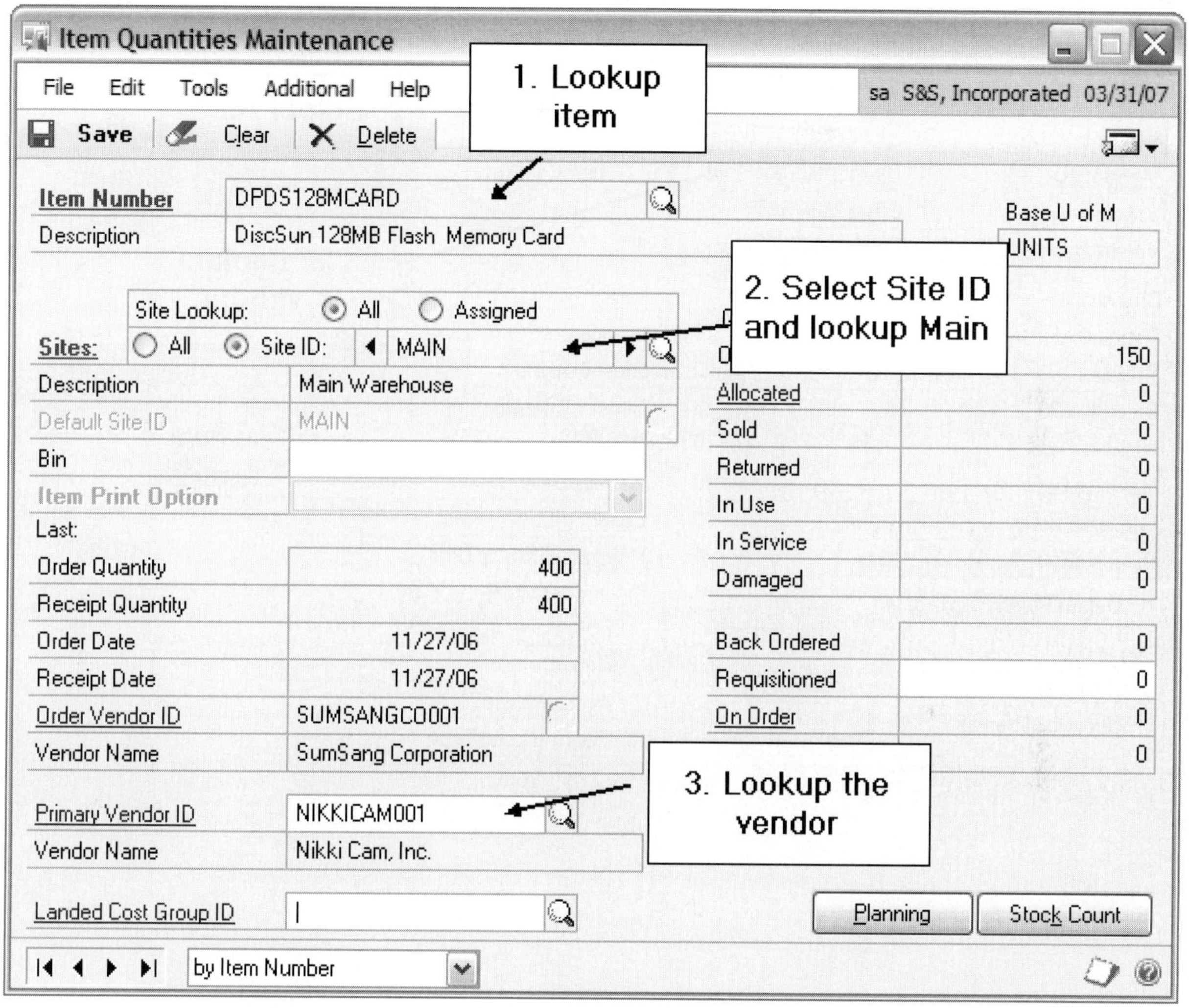

To link Nikki as a vendor selling item DPDS128MGST, click Vendors and follow the instructions on the next illustration. Click Save when finished.

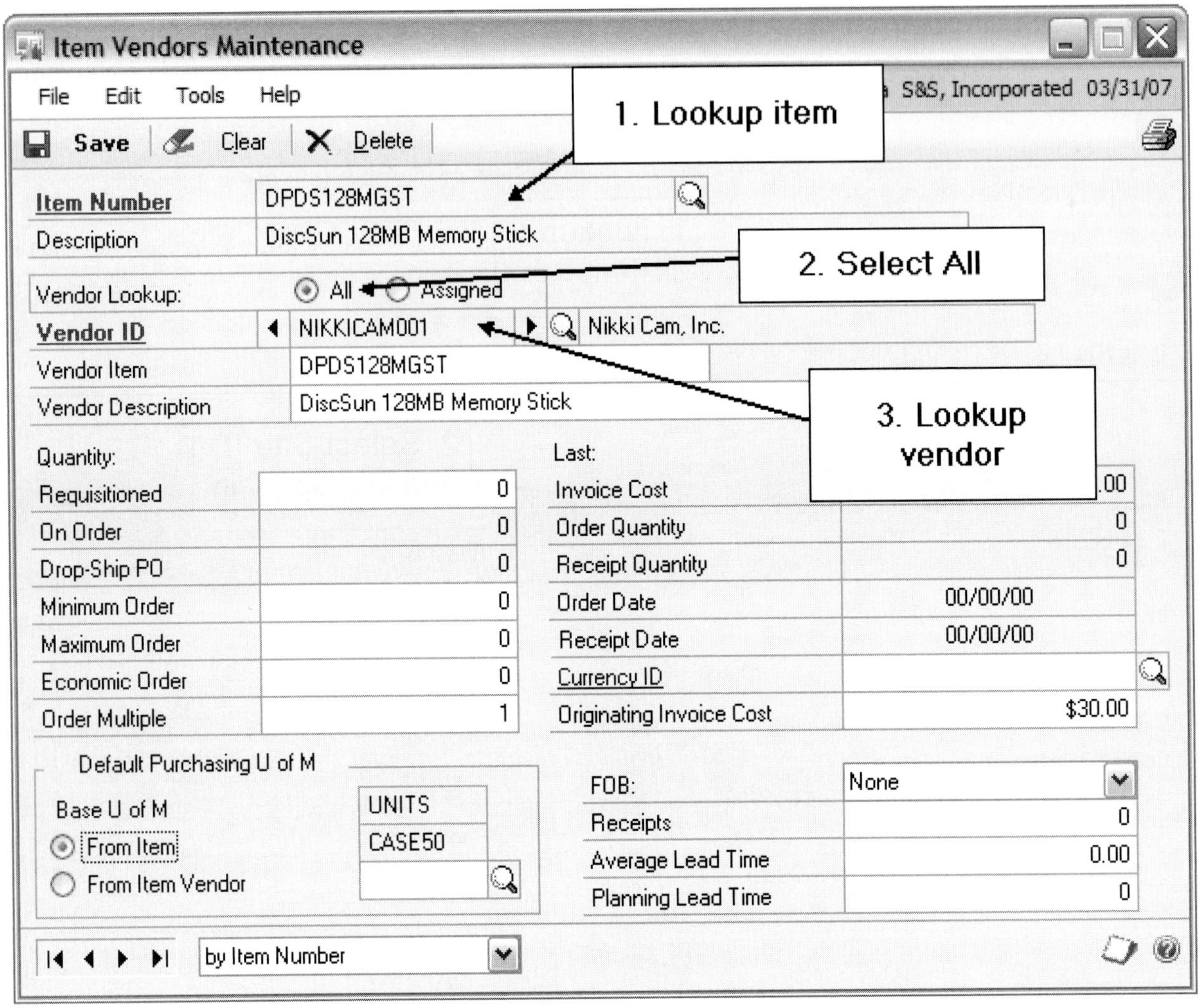

E4:3 Practice Recording Inventory Variance

Click Transaction Entry and enter the transaction as illustrated next. The unit cost is not entered because GP supplies this amount based on inventory valuation. Click Post and posting reports print.

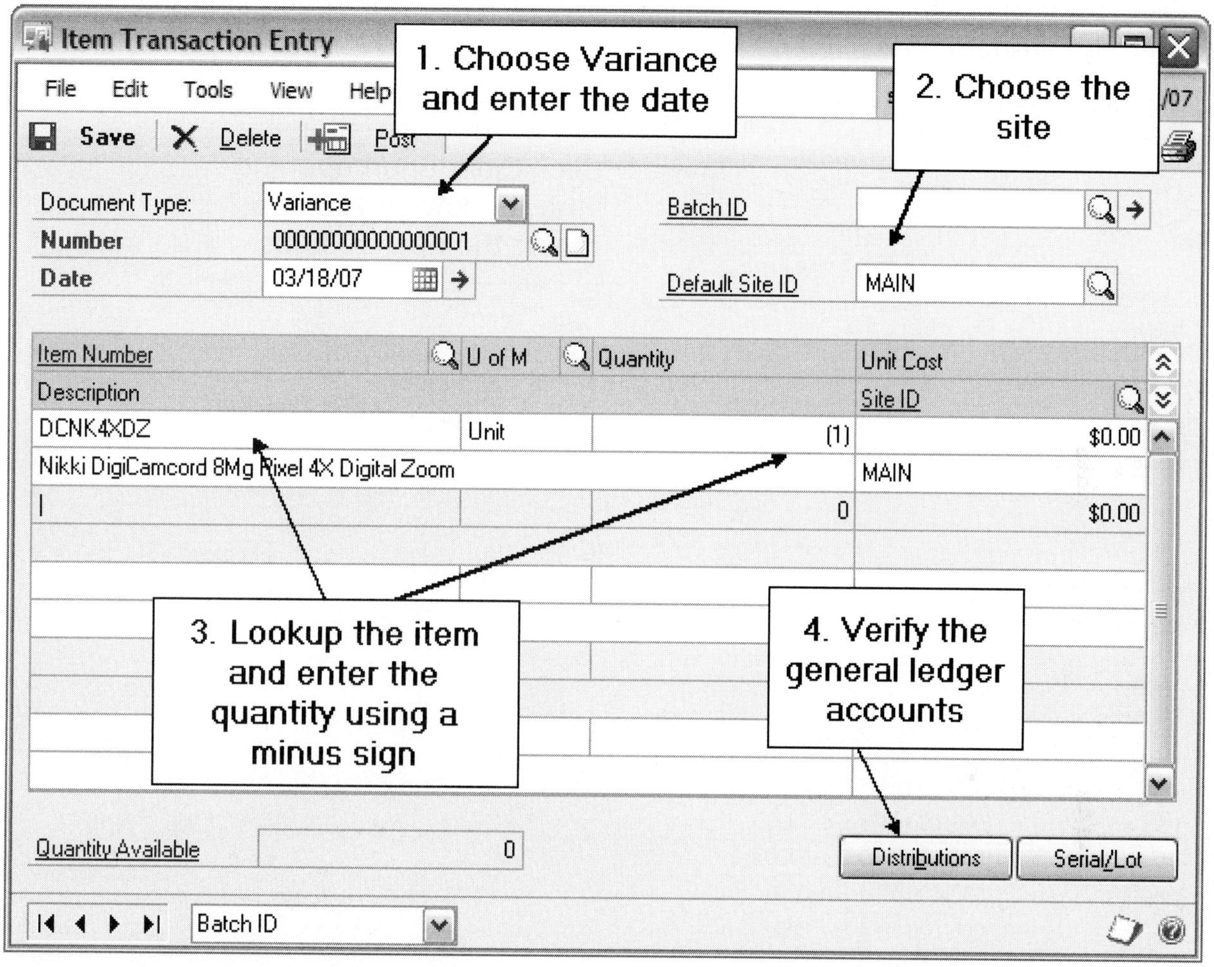

The posting reports that printed were chosen using the ***Tools>>Setup>>Posting>>Posting*** menu and selecting the Inventory Series with Transaction Entry Origin. Remember that you just posted an individual transaction (i.e., not in a batch); therefore, the transaction remains suspended in the Financial Series. *(Note: The General Posting Journal did not print, which is an indicator that the transaction did not finalize in the Financial Series.)*

The reports that printed listed the Audit Trail Code as prefixed by IVADJ. Activate the Financial home page and click Series Post under Transactions. Mark the transaction prefixed with IVADJ and click Post.

Chapter 5 Exercises

E5:1 Practice Managing Customer Cards

1. Click Customer under Cards and open Giggle Place. Click the Address button to enter the information illustrated next.

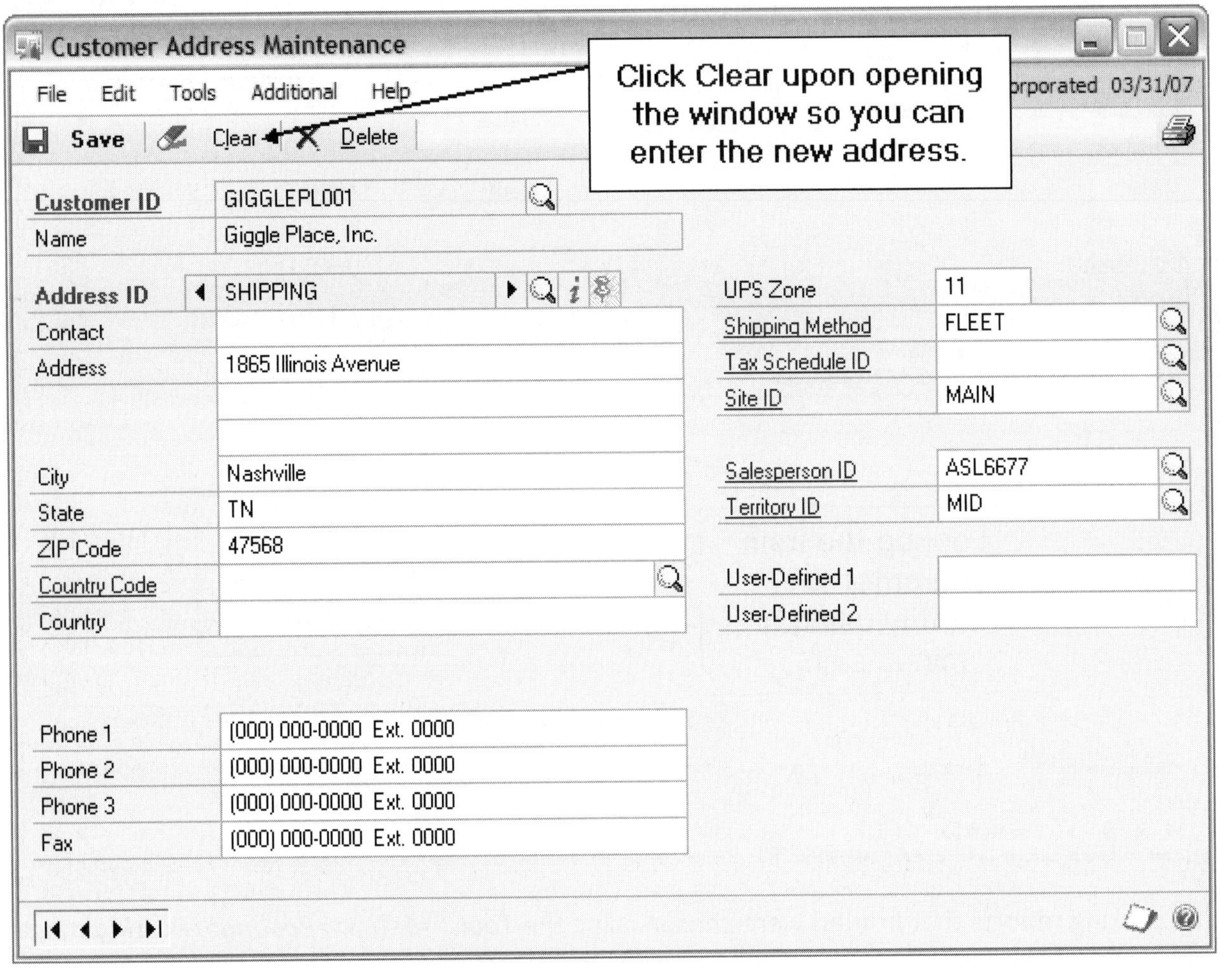

After saving, you link the new Address ID as illustrated next.

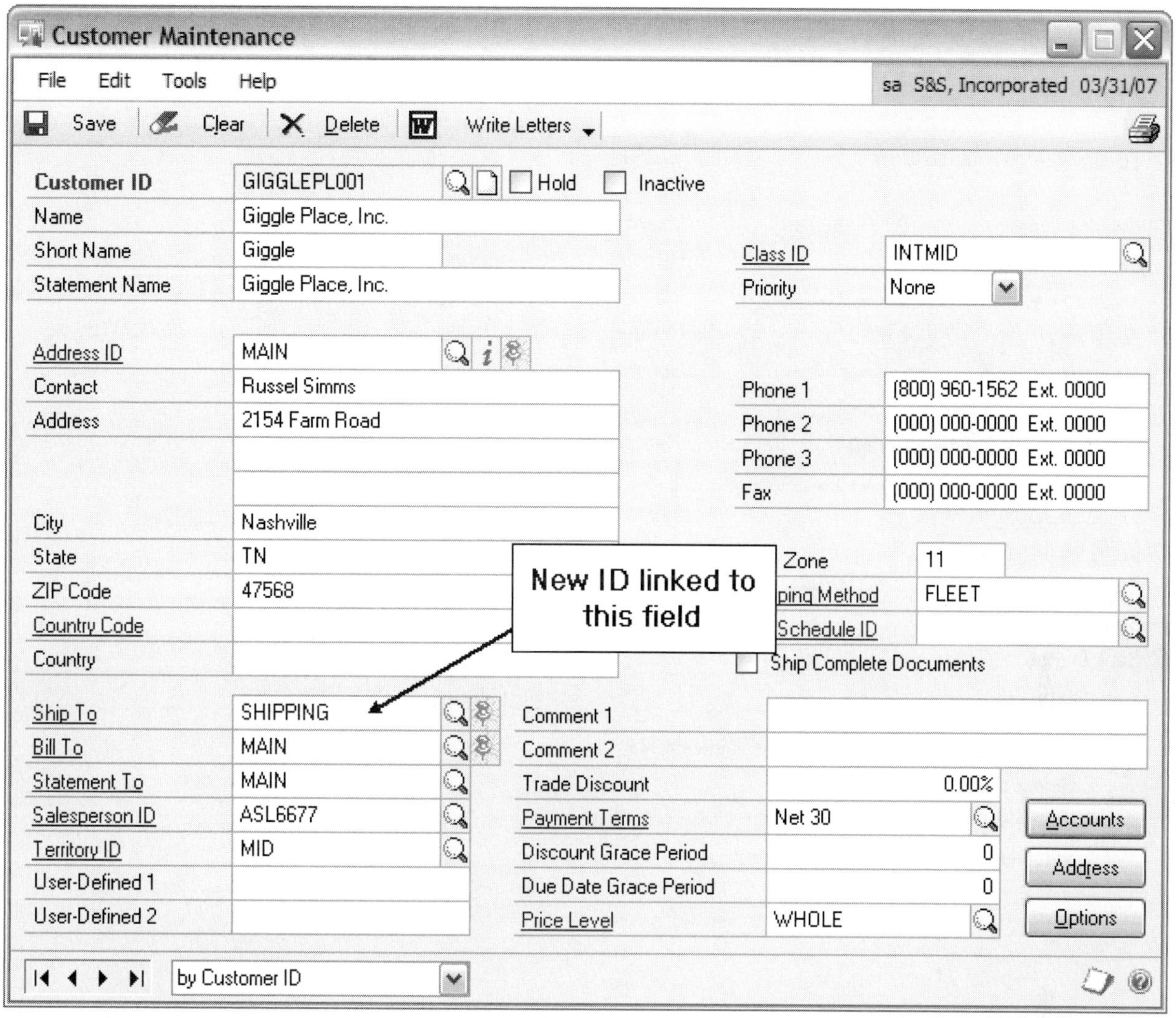

2. To increase Fillard's credit limit, look up the customer and click the Options button. Change the credit limit field as illustrated next.

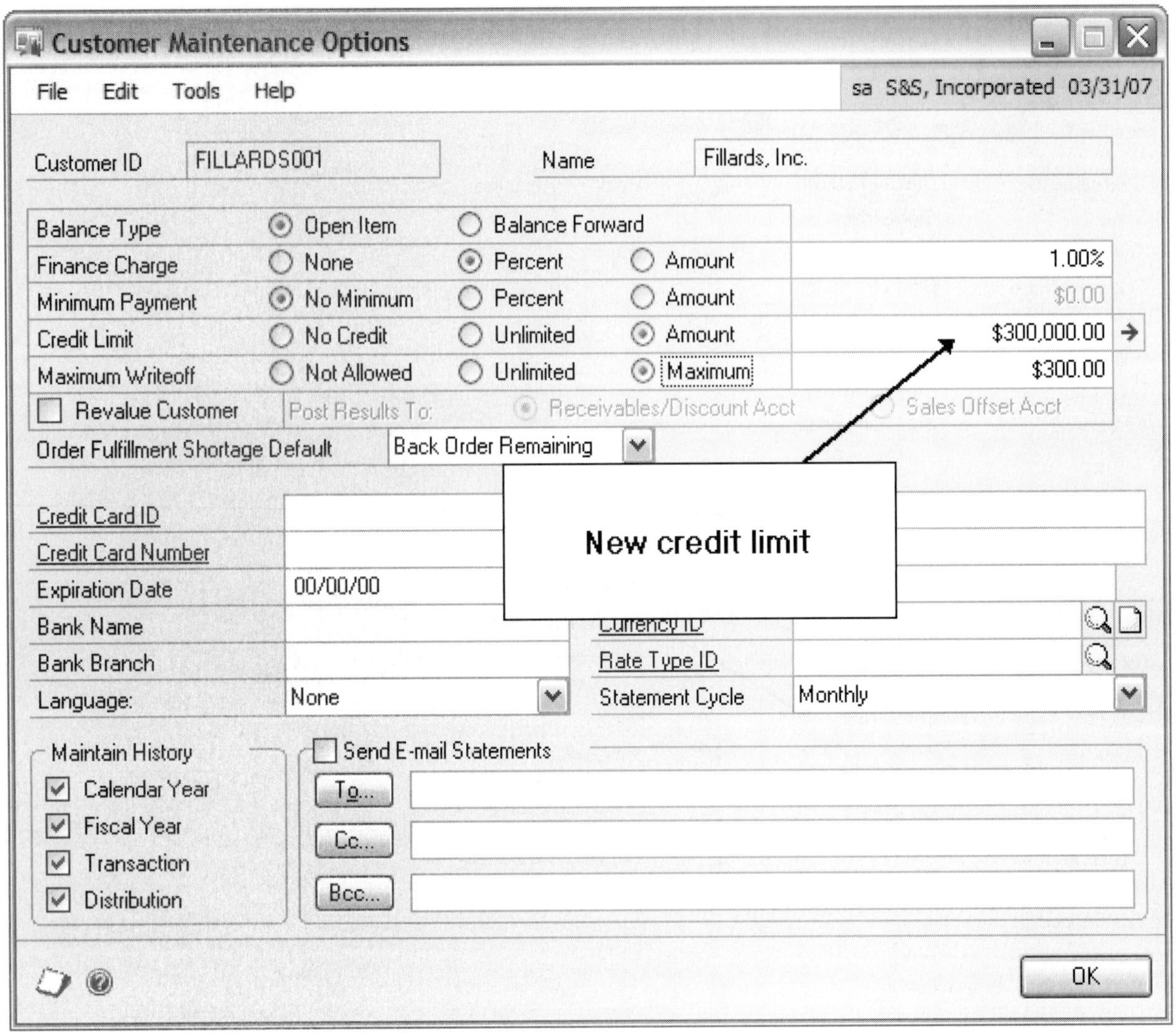

Changes to payment terms are illustrated next.

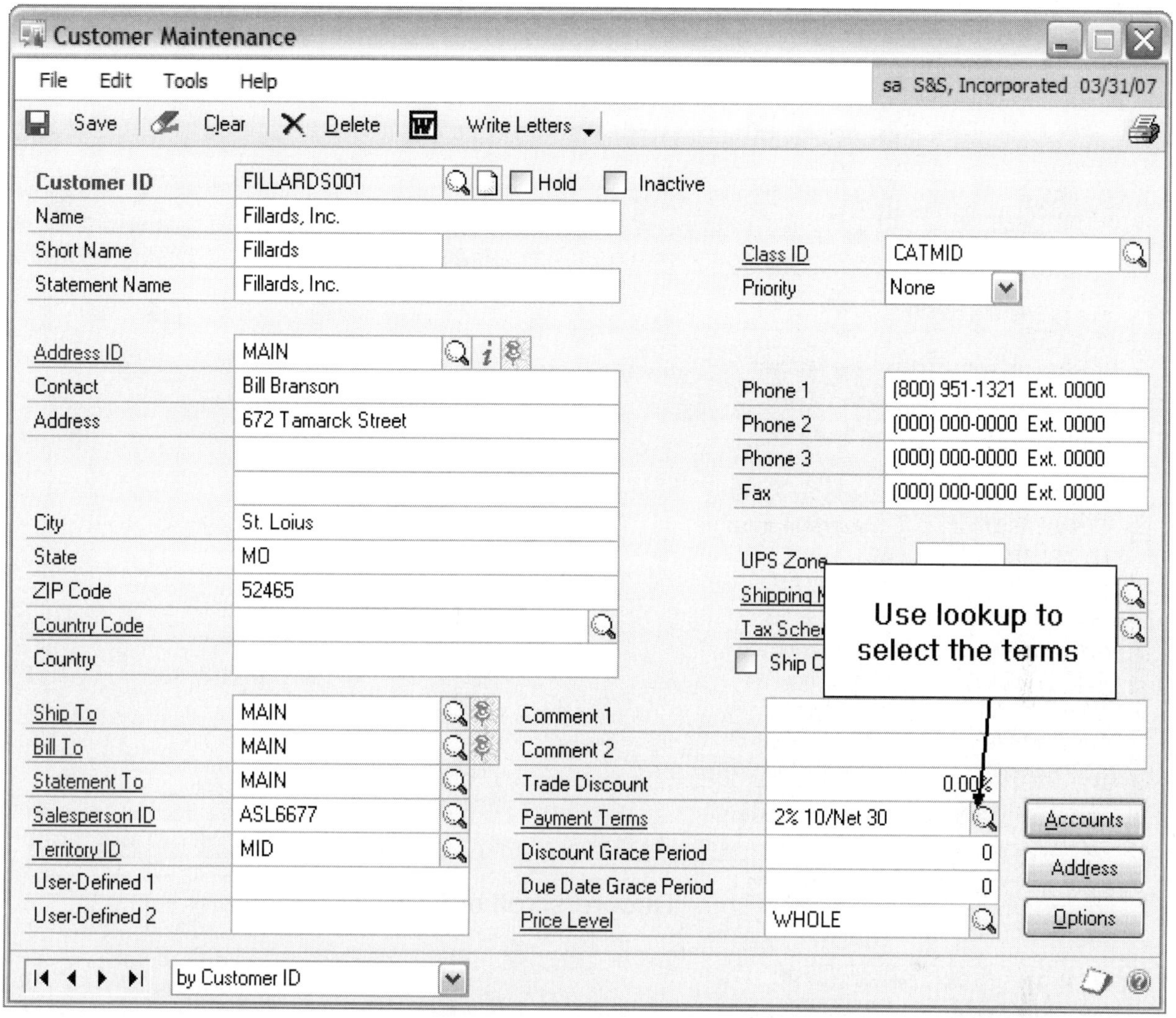

3. To view customers assigned to the MID (i.e., Midwest) territory, change the record scroll option to by Sales Territory ID and click open the lookup window as shown in the next illustration.

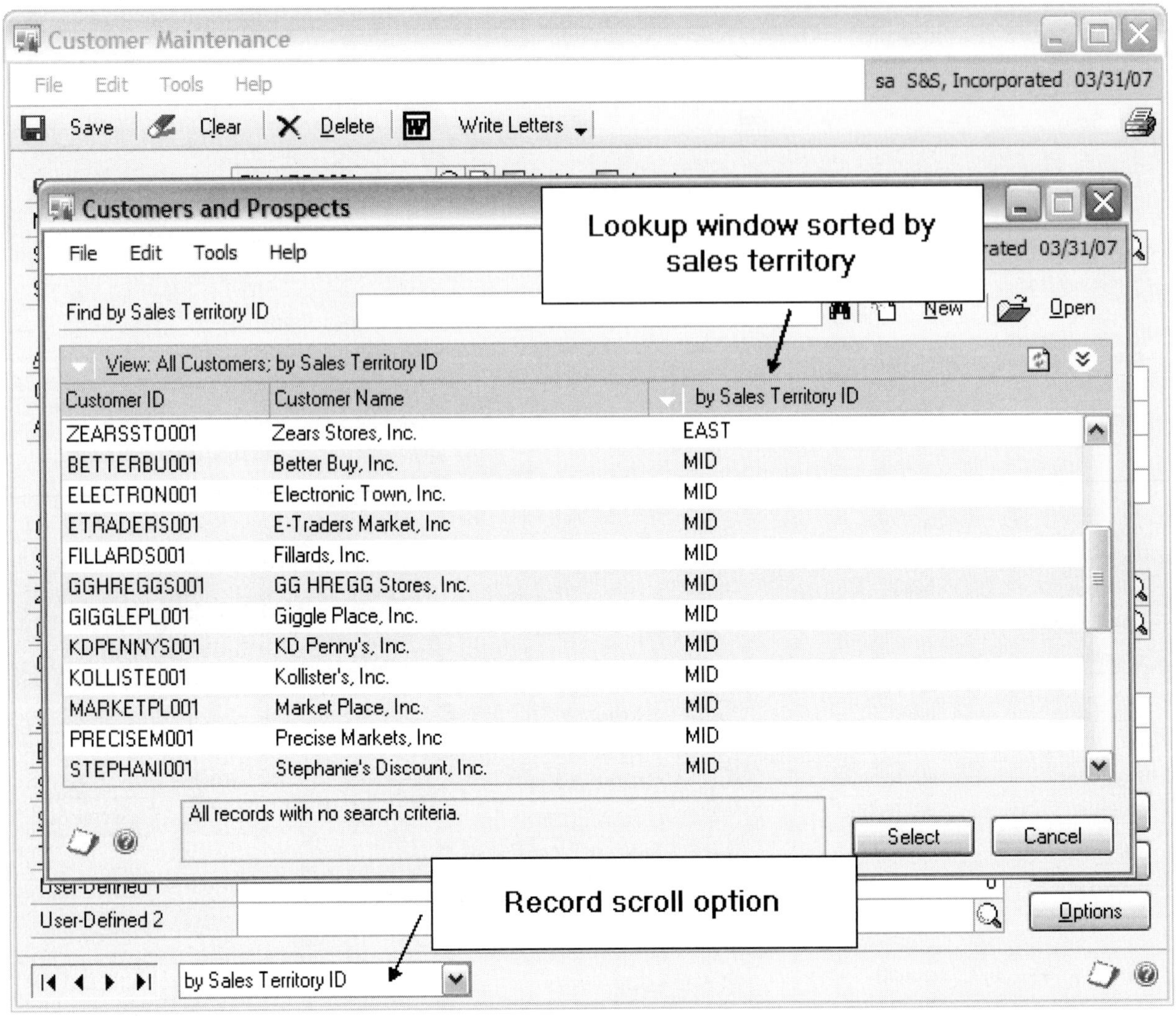

To view the name of the salesperson for this territory, open a record for a MID customer and click the lookup icon on Salesperson ID. You can also open any record and click the hyperlinked field name. The salesperson is April Levine.

4. The credit department should authorize new customers and establish other critical controls such as credit limits and payment terms. At smaller companies, like S&S, where a credit department does not exist, this responsibility can fall to the owners, Susan and Scott.

5. Sales and Accounts Receivable department employees can be granted permission to change noncritical customer information. GP provides the Address menu for managing this data.

E5:2 Practice Adding a New Customer

Open the Customer Maintenance window and complete the window as illustrated.

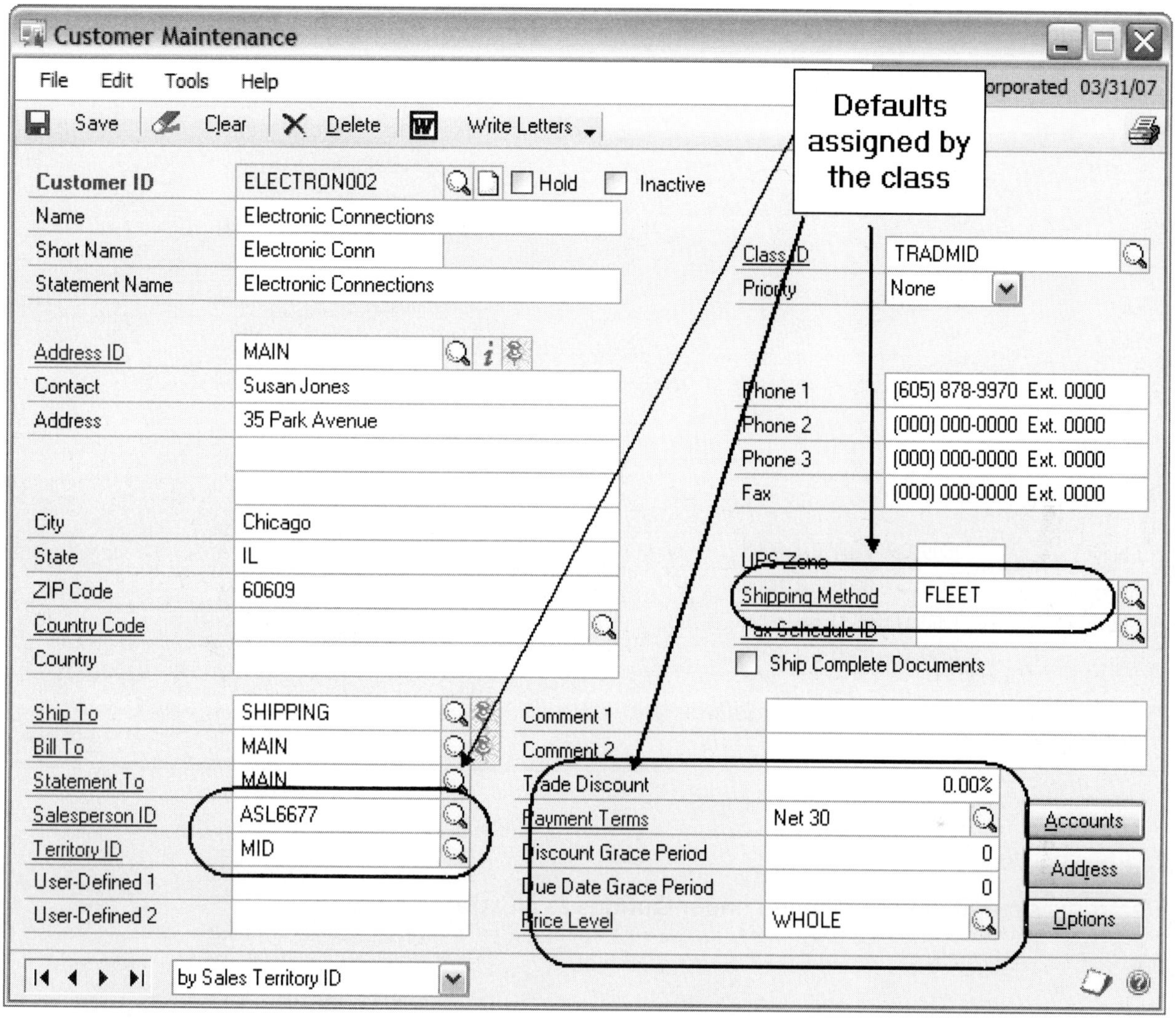

The shipping address card for Electronic is illustrated below.

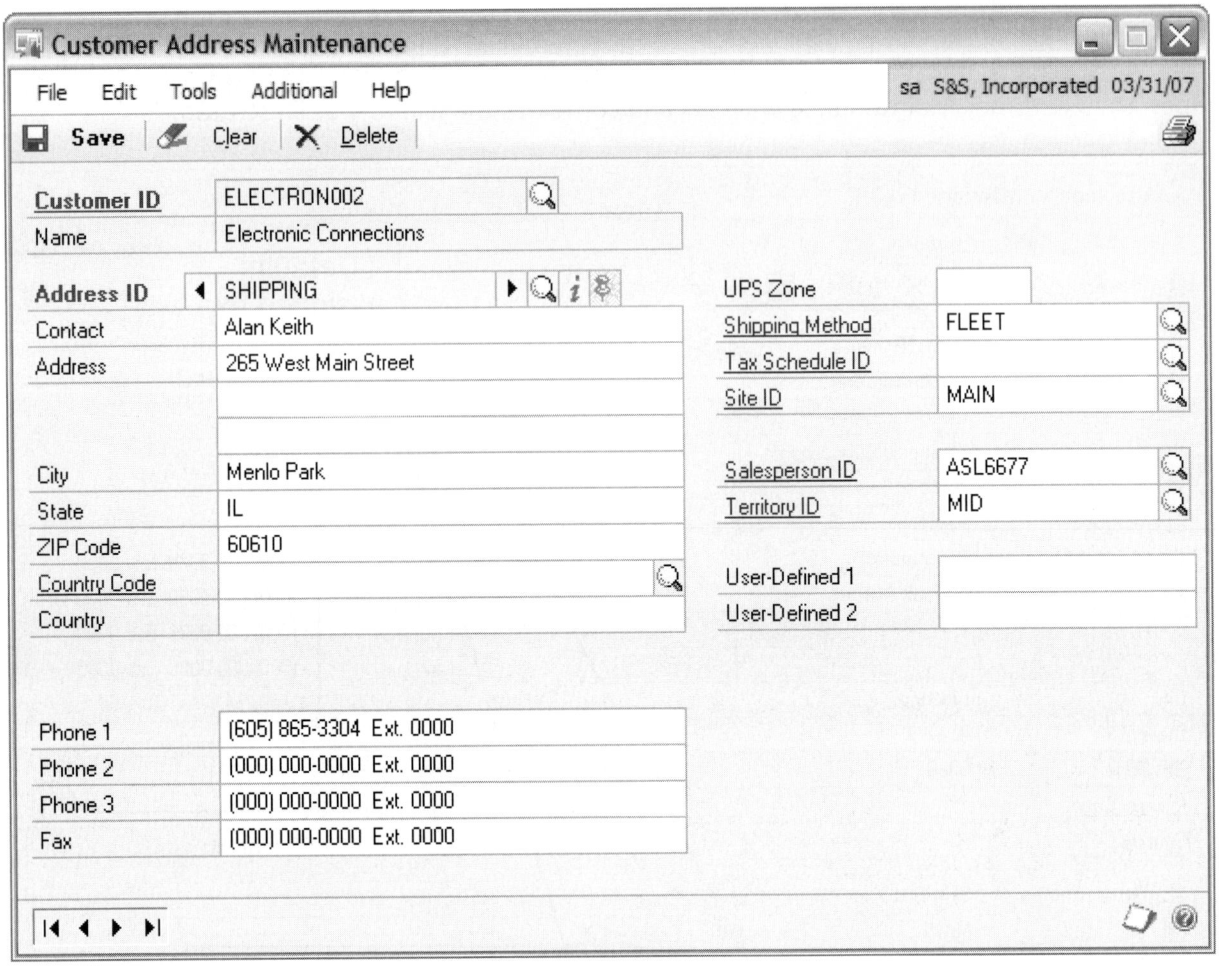

Electronic's credit limit is changed under Options as illustrated next.

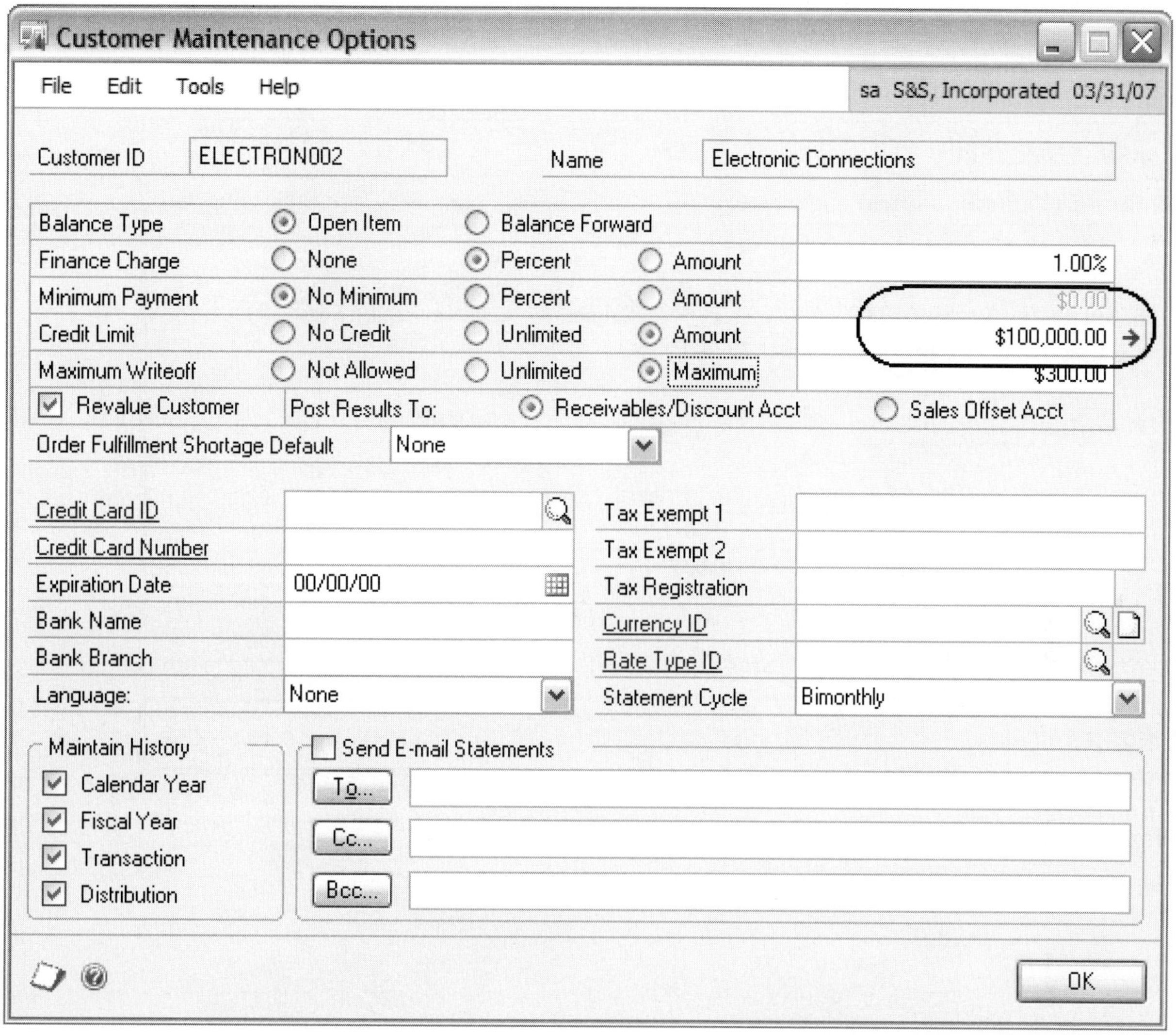

General ledger accounts are already present because they defaulted from the customer class.

E5:3 Sales Order Processing

First create the batch as shown next. Verify the date.

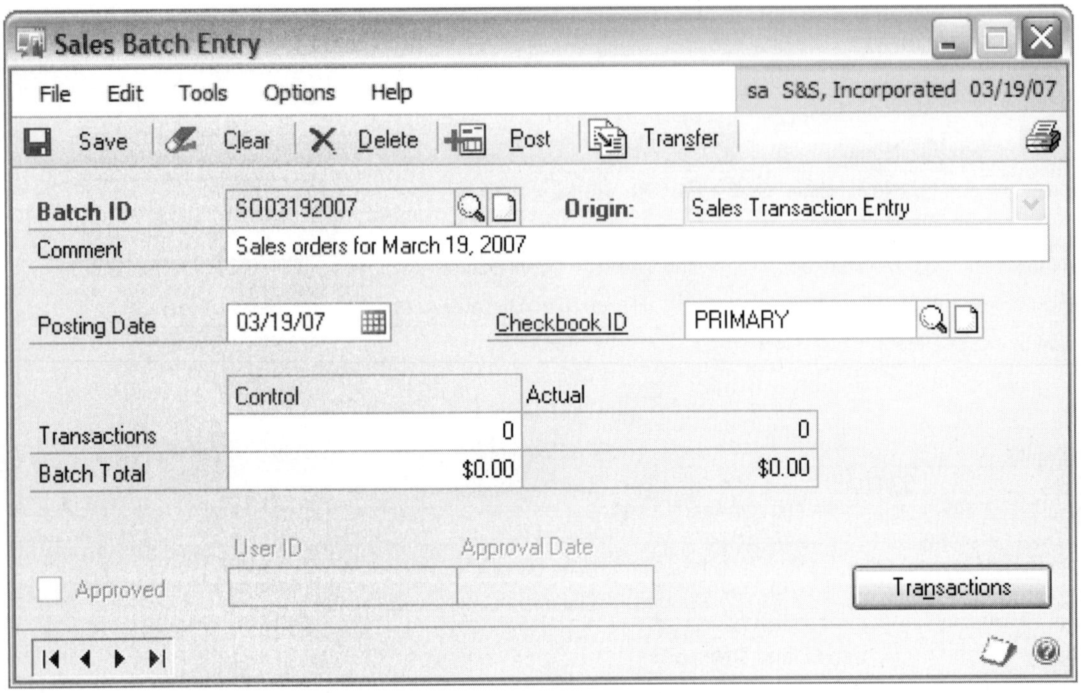

Next, create the following transaction and verify the date.

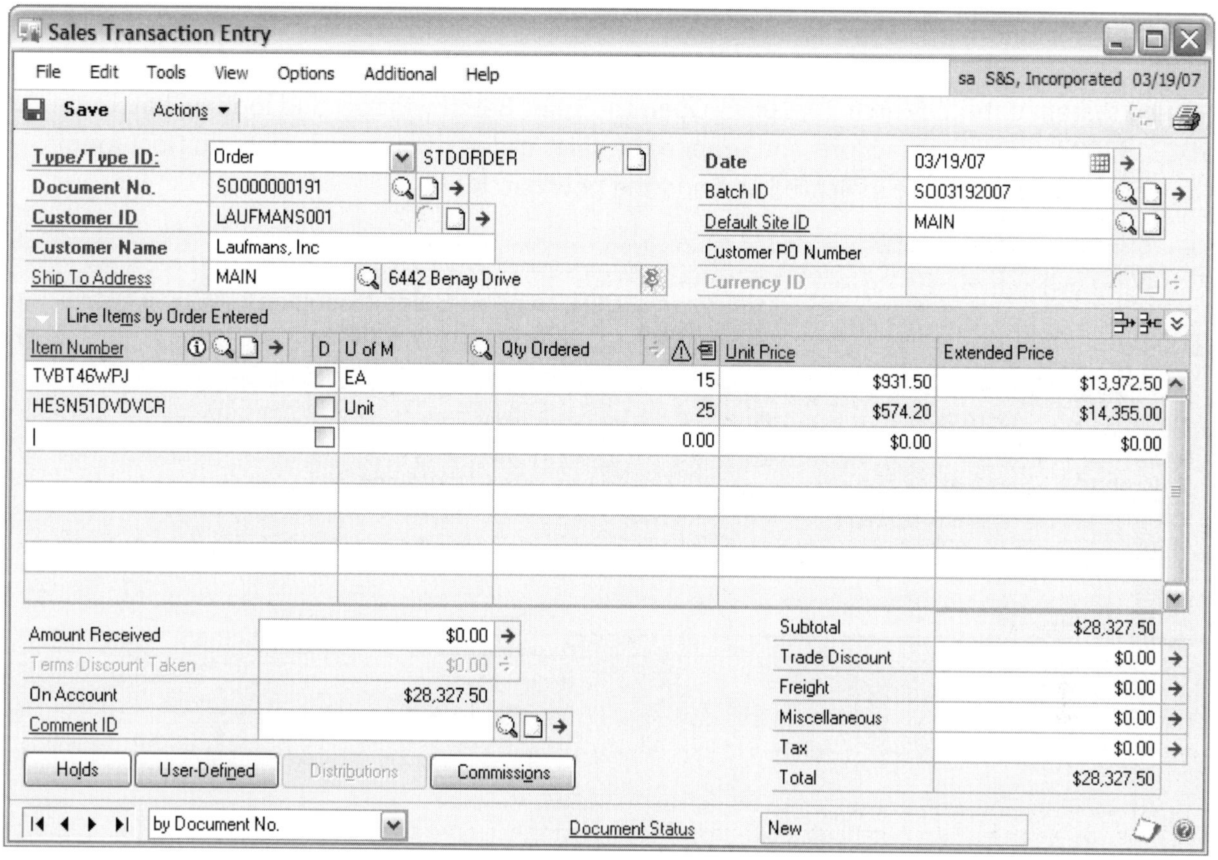

When finished, print the Batch List control report and the sales order, picking ticket, and packing slip. (Not illustrated.)

E5:4 Transfer Laufmans Order to an Invoice

Set the system date to March 20, 2007. Open the Sales Batch window and look up batch SO03192007. Click Transactions and reopen the sales order. Using the arrow on Document No, enter the batch name indicated and add the new batch.

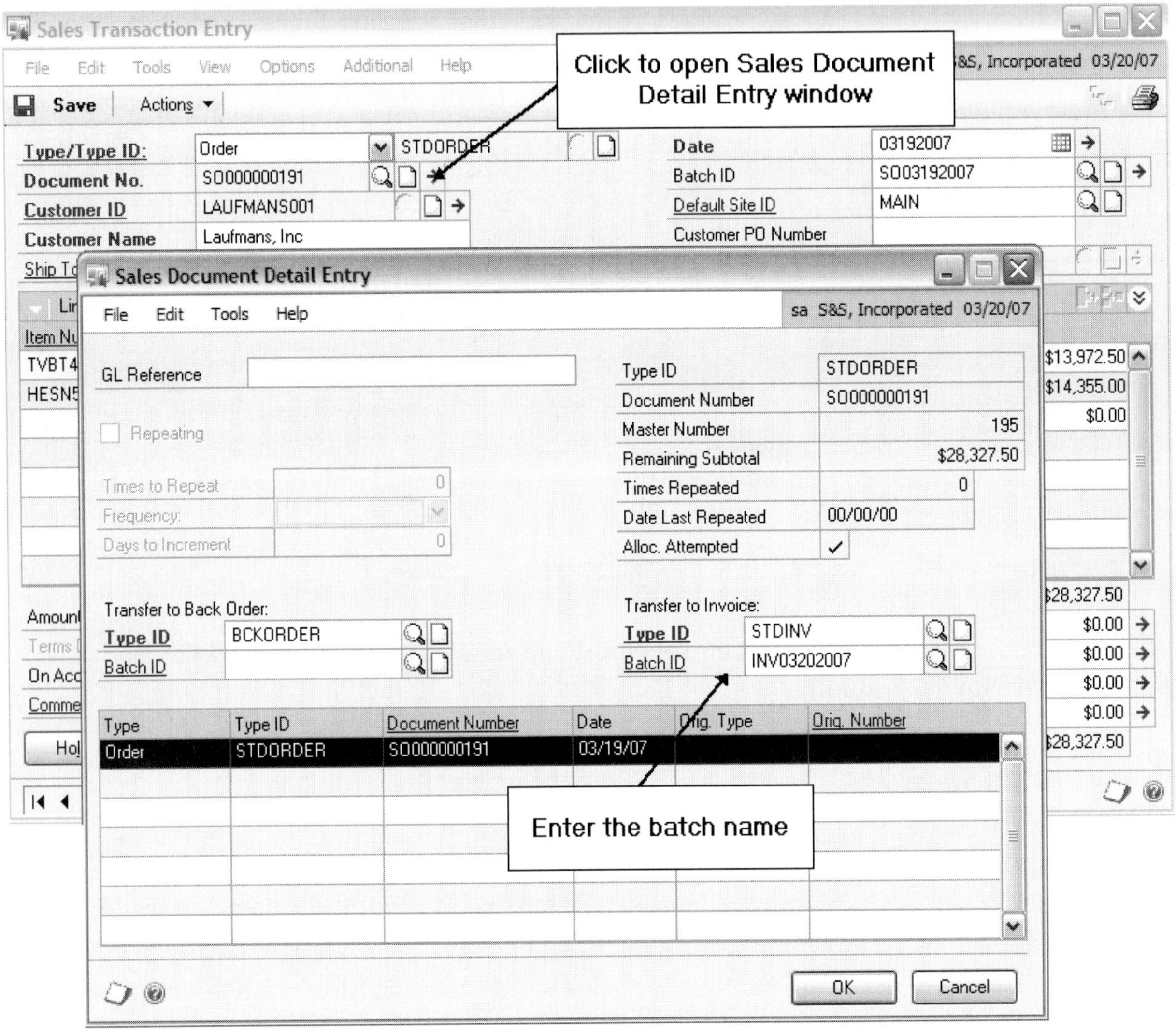

Click OK and return to the Sales Transaction Entry window. Click Actions to select Transfer. Transfer the order to an invoice and confirm that no errors occurred.

You now have a new invoice dated March 20, 2007. (See the next illustration.)

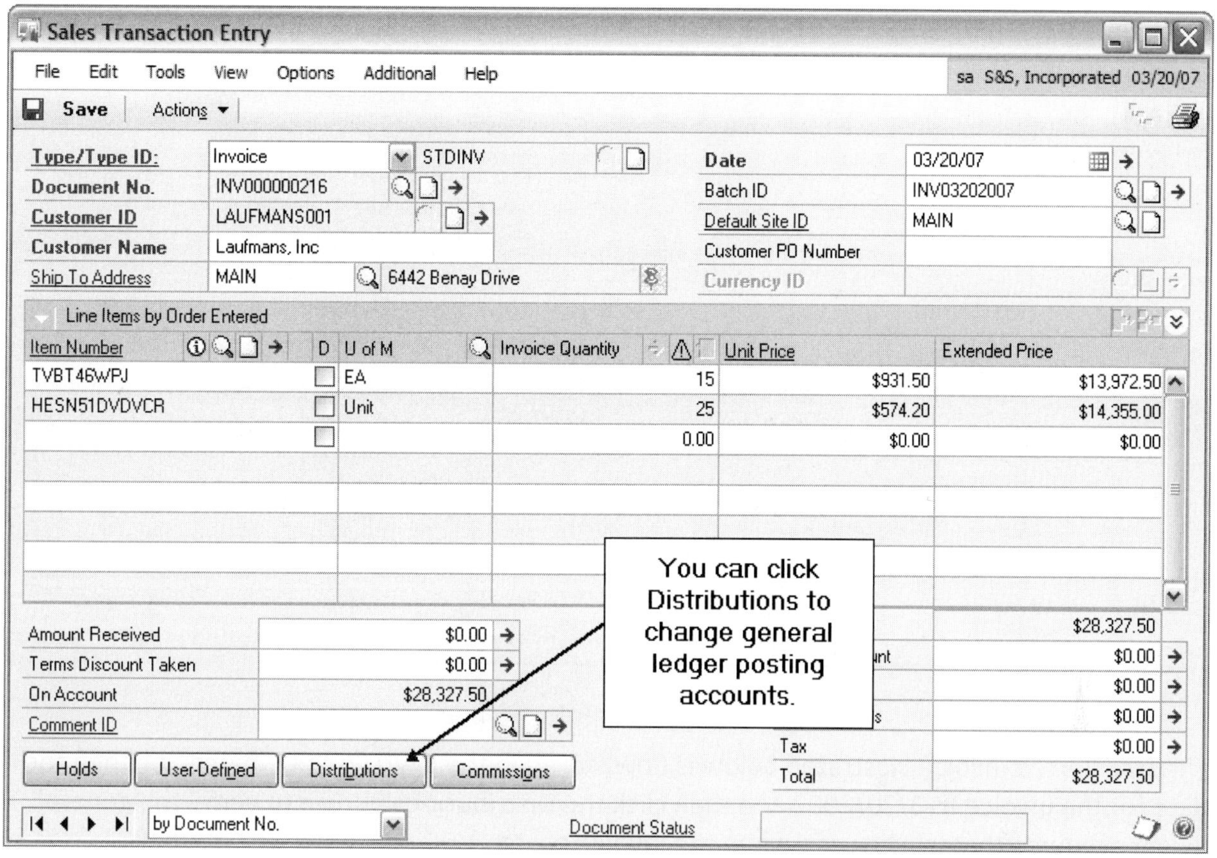

A sales clerk can change the default posting accounts by clicking Distributions and selecting a new account. Click Save.

Return to the Sales Batch Entry window and look up the new batch to complete processing. You should print the Edit List and sales invoice before posting.

After posting, the SOP Posting Journal, Inventory Sales Register, Cost Variance Journal, and General Posting Journal print. You can identify general ledger accounts on the SOP Posting Journal and General Posting Journal. All reports document the financial affect of the transaction. The last report verifies that the transaction finalized in the Financial Series.

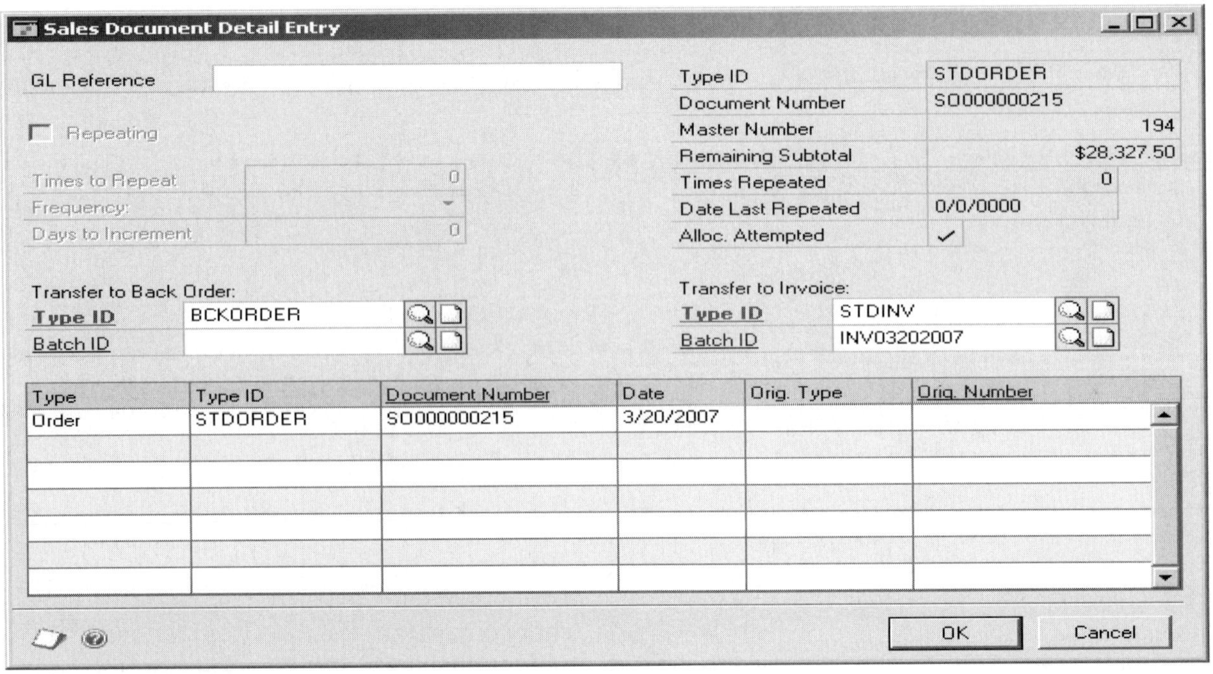

The transferred invoice illustrated below is now stored in the INV03202007 batch. Change the date for the invoice to 3/20/2007 and then click the Distributions button to verify the general ledger accounts that will be used when the invoice posts.

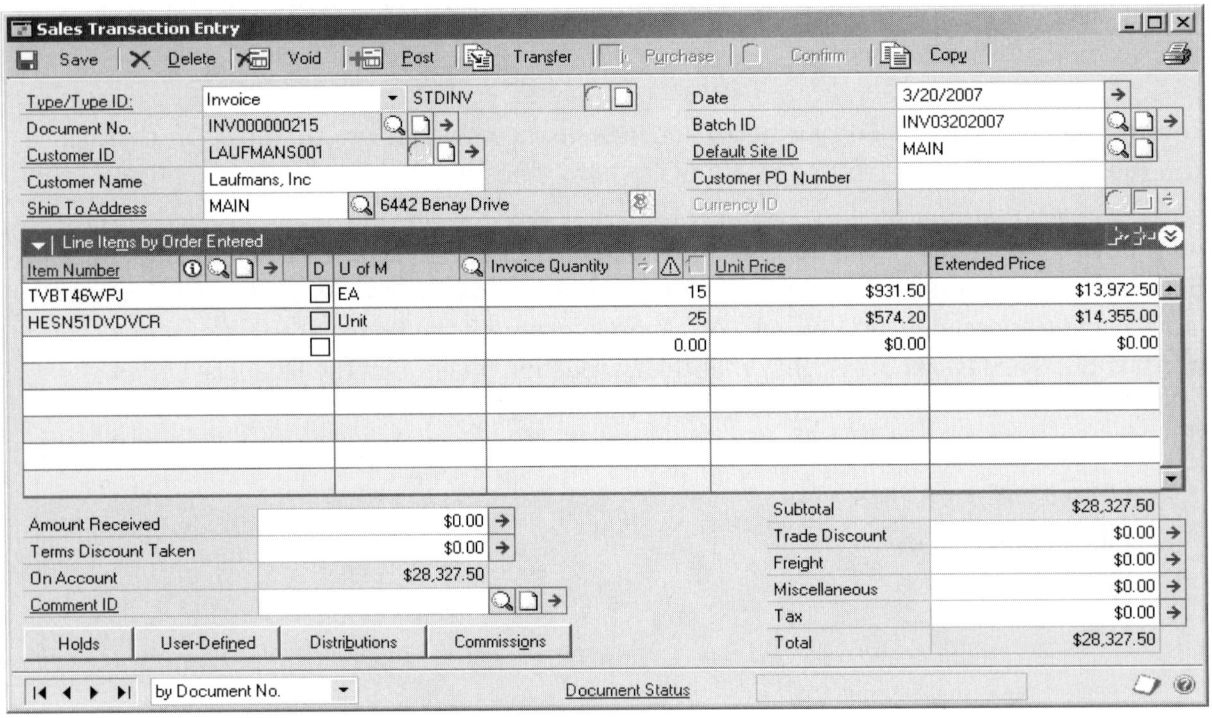

This window shows the general ledger accounts that will be used when the invoice posts. Accounts can be changed in this window when necessary. Close this window and save the invoice.

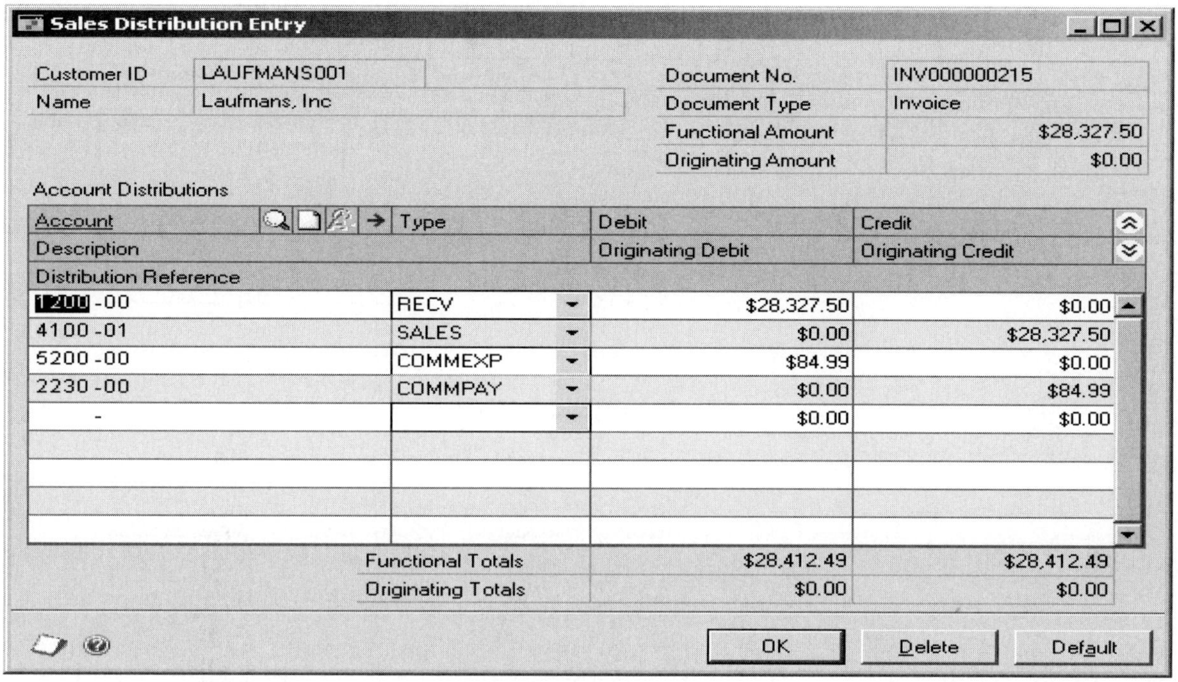

Return to the batch window and pull up the batch storing the invoice and click Post. Below are the control reports that print after posting.

Batch ID: INV03202007 Audit Trail Code: SLSTE00000083
Batch Comment: SO Trnf to Invoice

Approved: Batch Total Actual: $28,327.50 Batch Total Control: $0.00
Approved By: Trx Total Actual: 1 Trx Total Control: 0
Approval Date: 0/0/0000

Type	Document Number	Doc Date	Post Date	Customer ID	Name	Salesperson
INV	INV000000215	3/20/2007	3/20/2007	LAUFMANS001	Laufmans, Inc	CJW7872

Subtotal	Trade Discount	Freight Amount	Misc Amount	Tax Amount	Document Total	Discount Avail
$28,327.50	$0.00	$0.00	$0.00	$0.00	$28,327.50	$0.00

Item Number	Description / U of M	Site	Quantity	Markdown / Unit Price	Extended Price
TVBT46WPJ	Batoshi 46 Inch Widescreen Projection			$0.00	
	EA	MAIN	15	$931.50	$13,972.50
HESN51DVDVCR	Sunyung 5.1 Home Entertainment Combo DVD/VCR			$0.00	
	Unit	MAIN	25	$574.20	$14,355.00
					$28,327.50

Account Number	Account Description	Account Type	Debit Amount	Credit Amount
1200-00	Accounts Receivable	RECV	$28,327.50	$0.00
4100-01	Sales - East	SALES	$0.00	$28,327.50
5200-00	Commission Expense	COMMEXP	$84.99	$0.00
2230-00	Commissions Payable	COMMPAY	$0.00	$84.99
1310-00	Inventory	INV	$0.00	$21,225.00
4500-01	Cost of Goods Sold - East	COGS	$21,225.00	$0.00
			$49,637.49	$49,637.49

Salesperson Name	Sales Territory ID	Comm %	% of Sale	Sales Amount	Commission Amount
Warner, Curtis	EAST	0.30%	100.00%	28,327.50	84.99
				$28,327.50	$84.99

System: 5/16/2005 6:38:56 PM S&S, Inc Project DB Page: 1
User Date: 3/20/2007 INVENTORY SALES REGISTER User ID: sa
Sales Order Processing

Audit Trail Code: SLSTE00000083

Item Number / Document Number	Date	Customer ID	Item Description / Customer Name	Unit	Qty Invoiced	Unit Price	Markdown	Ext Price
HESN51DVDVCR			Sunyung 5.1 Home Entertainment Combo DVD/VCR					
INV000000215	3/20/2007	LAUFMANS001	Laufmans, Inc	Unit	25	$574.20	$0.00	$14,355.00
				Item Totals:	25.00000			$14,355.00
TVBT46WPJ			Batoshi 46 Inch Widescreen Projection					
INV000000215	3/20/2007	LAUFMANS001	Laufmans, Inc	EA	15	$931.50	$0.00	$13,972.50
				Item Totals:	15.00000			$13,972.50
				Report Totals:	40.00000			$28,327.50

```
System:      5/16/2005    6:39:50 PM                    S&S, Inc Project DB                                Page:     1
User Date:   3/20/2007                                 GENERAL POSTING JOURNAL                             User ID:  sa
                                                            General Ledger
* Voided Journal Entry


Batch ID:       SLSTE00000083
Batch Comment:  SO Trnf to Invoice


Approved:         No             Batch Total Actual:              $99,274.98          Batch Total Control:                  $0.00
Approved by:                     Trx Total Actual:                          1          Trx Total Control:                        0
Approval Date:


     Journal        Transaction   Transaction  Reversing   Source     Transaction                          Audit Trail   Reversing Audit
     Entry             Type          Date         Date     Document   Reference                               Code          Trail Code
---------------------------------------------------------------------------------------------------------------------------------------
          1,697     Standard     3/20/2007                   SJ       Sales Transaction Entry            GLTRX00000641

                 Account                   Description                                                    Debit                 Credit
                 ------------------------- ------------------------------------------  ---------------------- ----------------------
                 1200-00                   Accounts Receivable                                       $28,327.50
                 4100-01                   Sales - East                                                                      $28,327.50
                 5200-00                   Commission Expense                                             $84.99
                 2230-00                   Commissions Payable                                                                    $84.99
                 1310-00                   Inventory                                                                         $21,225.00
                 4500-01                   Cost of Goods Sold - East                                 $21,225.00
                                                                                           ---------------------- ----------------------
          Total Distributions:             6                              Totals:            $49,637.49             $49,637.49


      Total Journal Entries:           1
```

These reports, in order, are the Sales Order Posting Journal, Inventory Sales Register, Cost Variance Journal, and General Posting Journal. The Sales Order Posting Journal is not shown in its entirety and the Cost Variance Journal is not shown because there was no inventory cost variance. The last report to print shows this transaction posted to the general ledger. The three preceding reports show the transactions effect on the Sales and Inventory Control Series. These reports should be stored for later reference. In addition, an edit list should have been printed and reviewed prior to posting the invoice.

E5:5 Cash Receipt from Laufmans

You can post the transaction individually or through a batch. If through a batch, remember to post the suspended transaction. The Cash Receipts Entry and Apply Sales Documents windows are illustrated next.

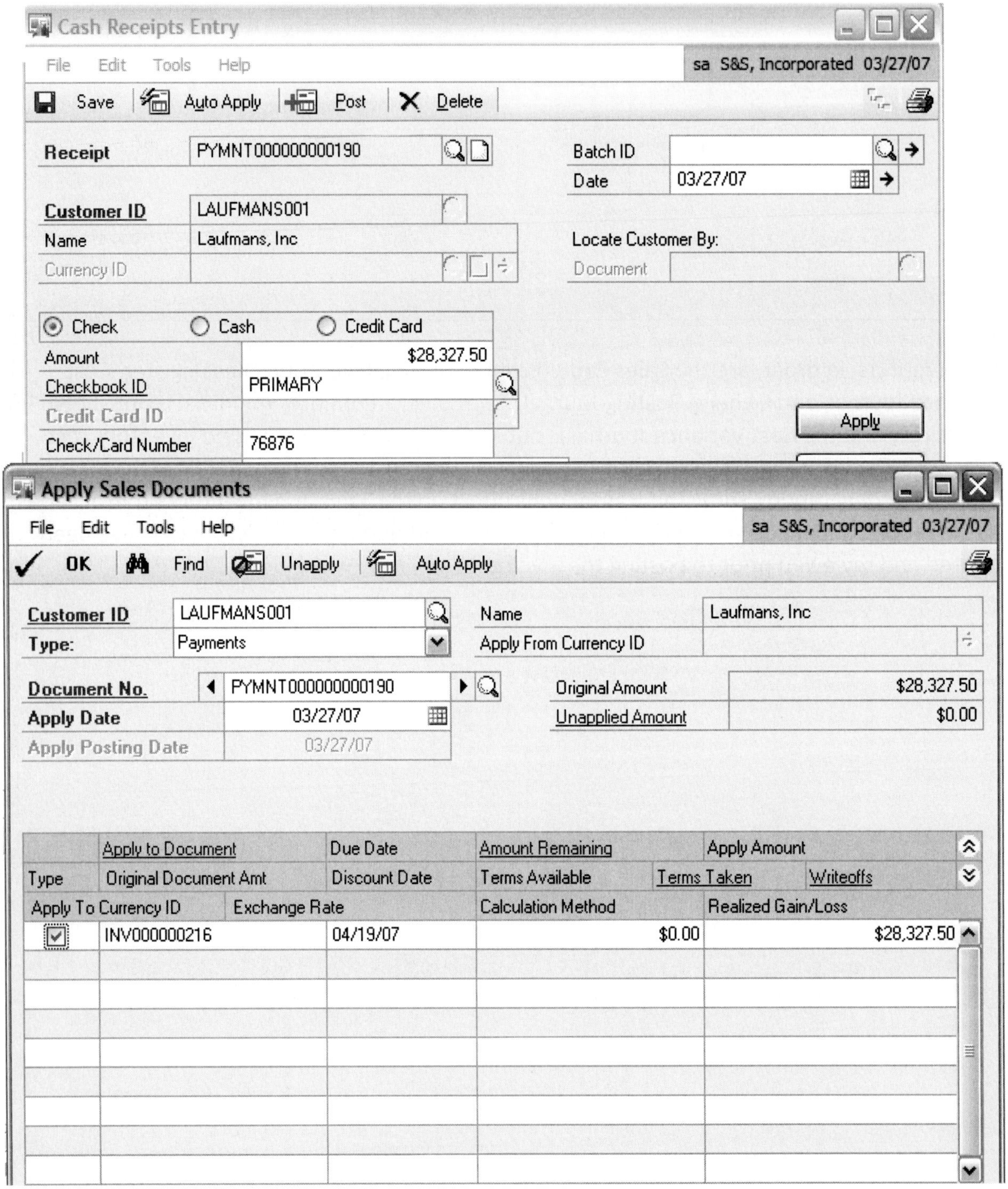

You should print an edit list before posting. This list cannot be printed if posting individually. It can only be printed by saving the transaction to a batch. The total on the edit list should be compared to the control total sent from the mailroom to verify data entry.

E5:6 Sales Series Report Practice

Click Posting Journal and select the Sales Posting Journal category. Modify the existing report as illustrated next.

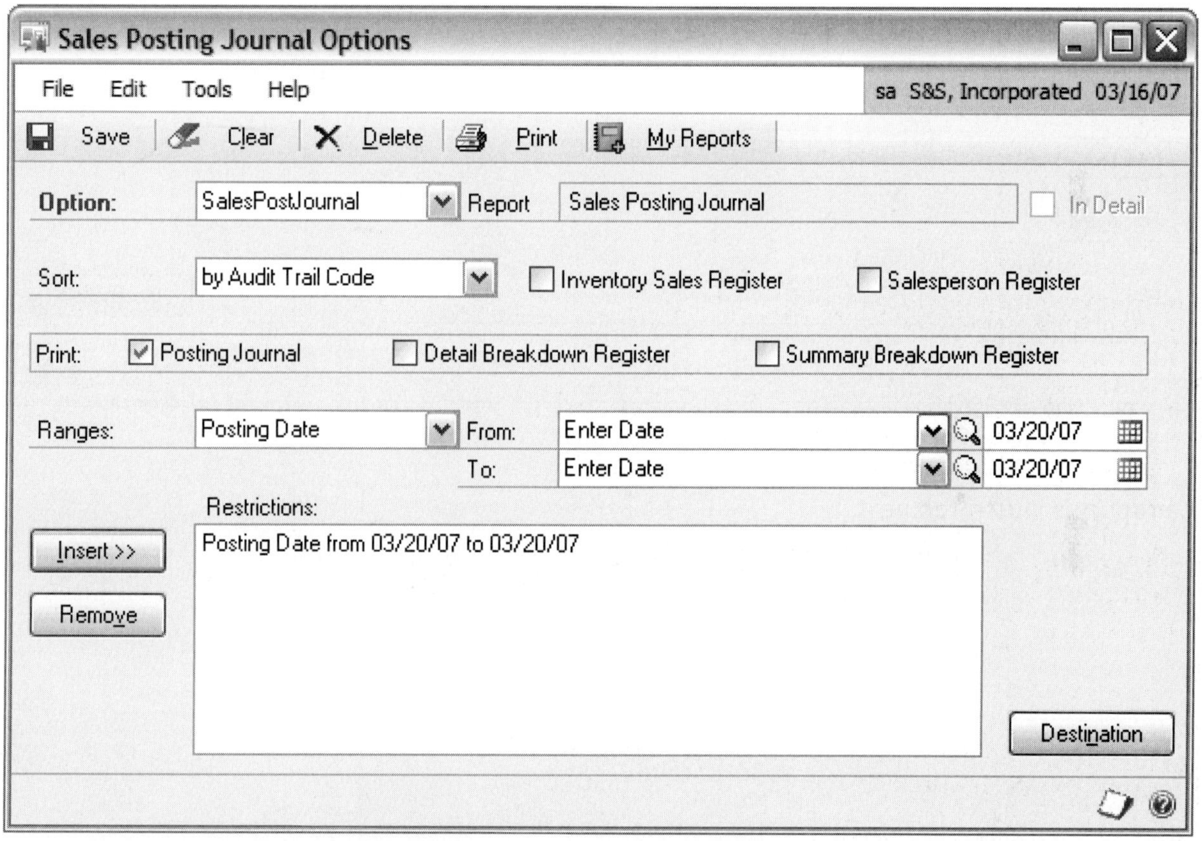

To analyze gross profit, click Analysis and modify the existing report found under SOP Document Analysis. (See next illustration.)

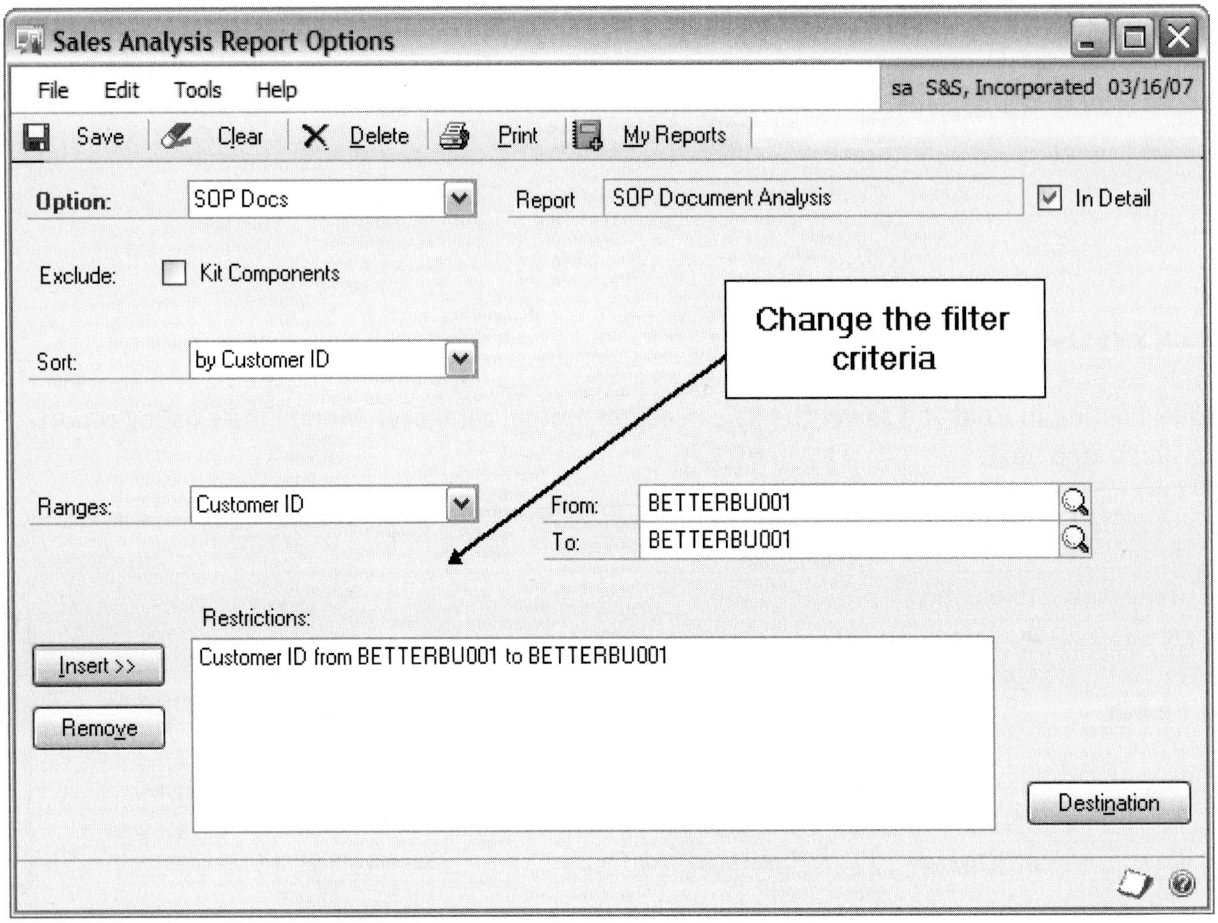

The report is illustrated next.

S&S, Incorporated
SALES DOCUMENT ANALYSIS REPORT
Sales Order Processing

User Date: 03/16/07
Page: 1
User ID: sa

Ranges:	From:	To:
Customer ID:	BETTERBU001	BETTERBU001
Document Date:	First	Last
Item Number:	First	Last

Sorted By: Customer ID   Print Option: Detailed   Exclude:

^ Drop Ship   = Kit Component   # Non-Inventory

Customer ID   Customer Name

Item Number	Description	Base U of M Quantity	Sales	Cost	Profit	% of Sales
BETTERBU001	Better Buy, Inc.					
AUDNPXM4CD	NeerPio XM Ready 4 Channel C	35	$4,462.50	$3,570.00	$892.50	20.00%
AUDNPXM4CD	NeerPio XM Ready 4 Channel C	200	$25,500.00	$20,400.00	$5,100.00	20.00%
AUDSNCDMP3	Sunyung CD/MP3/ATRAC3	50	$2,250.00	$1,800.00	$450.00	20.00%
AUDSNCDMP3	Sunyung CD/MP3/ATRAC3	200	$9,000.00	$7,200.00	$1,800.00	20.00%
AUDSNCDMP3	Sunyung CD/MP3/ATRAC3	700	$31,500.00	$25,200.00	$6,300.00	20.00%
AUDSNCDMP3	Sunyung CD/MP3/ATRAC3	40	$1,872.00	$1,440.00	$432.00	23.08%
AUDSNCDMP3AMFM	Sunyung Portable CD/MP3/AM/F	100	$6,250.00	$5,000.00	$1,250.00	20.00%
AUDSNCDMP3AMFM	Sunyung Portable CD/MP3/AM/F	350	$21,875.00	$17,500.00	$4,375.00	20.00%
AUDWW52WCD	WAWA 52 Watt X4 Channel Car	200	$15,000.00	$12,000.00	$3,000.00	20.00%
DCCN22XDZ	Canyon DigCamcord 22X Optica	130	$47,320.00	$36,400.00	$10,920.00	23.08%
AUDSNCDMP3	Sunyung CD/MP3/ATRAC3	50	$2,250.00	$1,800.00	$450.00	20.00%
AUDSNCDMP3	Sunyung CD/MP3/ATRAC3	200	$9,000.00	$7,200.00	$1,800.00	20.00%
AUDSNCDMP3	Sunyung CD/MP3/ATRAC3	700	$31,500.00	$25,200.00	$6,300.00	20.00%
AUDSNCDMP3	Sunyung CD/MP3/ATRAC3	40	$1,872.00	$1,440.00	$432.00	23.08%
AUDSNCDMP3AMFM	Sunyung Portable CD/MP3/AM/F	100	$6,250.00	$5,000.00	$1,250.00	20.00%
AUDSNCDMP3AMFM	Sunyung Portable CD/MP3/AM/F	350	$21,875.00	$17,500.00	$4,375.00	20.00%
AUDWW52WCD	WAWA 52 Watt X4 Channel Car	200	$15,000.00	$12,000.00	$3,000.00	20.00%
DCCN22XDZ	Canyon DigCamcord 22X Optica	130	$47,320.00	$36,400.00	$10,920.00	23.08%
DCJV16XDZ	Javix DigCamcord 16X Optical	50	$15,312.50	$12,250.00	$3,062.50	20.00%
DCJV16XDZ	Javix DigCamcord 16X Optical	200	$62,720.00	$49,000.00	$13,720.00	21.88%
DCJV16XDZ	Javix DigCamcord 16X Optical	20	$6,272.00	$4,900.00	$1,372.00	21.88%
AUDSNCDMP3	Sunyung CD/MP3/ATRAC3	40	$1,872.00	$1,440.00	$432.00	23.08%
AUDSNCDMP3AMFM	Sunyung Portable CD/MP3/AM/F	100	$6,250.00	$5,000.00	$1,250.00	20.00%
AUDSNCDMP3AMFM	Sunyung Portable CD/MP3/AM/F	350	$21,875.00	$17,500.00	$4,375.00	20.00%
AUDWW52WCD	WAWA 52 Watt X4 Channel Car	200	$15,000.00	$12,000.00	$3,000.00	20.00%
DCCN22XDZ	Canyon DigCamcord 22X Optica	130	$47,320.00	$36,400.00	$10,920.00	23.08%
DCJV16XDZ	Javix DigCamcord 16X Optical	50	$15,312.50	$12,250.00	$3,062.50	20.00%
DCJV16XDZ	Javix DigCamcord 16X Optical	200	$62,720.00	$49,000.00	$13,720.00	21.88%
DCJV16XDZ	Javix DigCamcord 16X Optical	20	$6,272.00	$4,900.00	$1,372.00	21.88%
DCNK4XDZ	Nikki DigiCamcord 8Mg Pixel	100	$58,880.00	$46,000.00	$12,880.00	21.88%
DCSM10XDZ	Sunyung DigCamcord 10X Optic	50	$20,475.00	$15,750.00	$4,725.00	23.08%
DCSM18XDZ	Sumsang DigCamcord 18X Optic	120	$28,860.00	$22,200.00	$6,660.00	23.08%
DP0Y4MG3XD	Olympium 4Mg Pixel 3XOptical	35	$5,689.60	$4,445.00	$1,244.60	21.88%
DP0Y4MG3XD	Olympium 4Mg Pixel 3XOptical	80	$13,004.80	$10,160.00	$2,844.80	21.88%
DP0Y4MG3XD	Olympium 4Mg Pixel 3XOptical	300	$48,768.00	$38,100.00	$10,668.00	21.88%
DP0Y4MG3XD	Olympium 4Mg Pixel 3XOptical	200	$32,512.00	$25,400.00	$7,112.00	21.88%
DPDS128MGST	DiscSun 128MB Memory Stick	50	$1,920.00	$1,500.00	$420.00	21.88%
DPFJ52MG32XDC	Fujiyama 5.2Mg Pixel 3.2X Op	40	$8,857.60	$6,920.00	$1,937.60	21.88%
DPSN51MG3XDC	Sunyung 5.1Mg Pixel 3X Optic	40	$10,320.00	$8,000.00	$2,320.00	22.48%
DVDLPRW80G	Lipsphi Progressive Scan DVD	20	$8,280.00	$6,000.00	$2,280.00	27.54%
DVDNVPCD	Navox Progressive DVD/CD	15	$517.50	$375.00	$142.50	27.54%
DVDNVPCD	Navox Progressive DVD/CD	300	$10,350.00	$7,500.00	$2,850.00	27.54%
DVDRD7PORT	Roidlop 7 Inch Portable DVD	250	$32,500.00	$25,000.00	$7,500.00	23.08%
DVDSMCD	Sumsang DVD/CD Near HD	200	$27,300.00	$21,000.00	$6,300.00	23.08%
DVDVX8PORT	VoxAudi 8 Inch Portable DVD	23	$5,830.50	$4,485.00	$1,345.50	23.08%
HEMY71C980W	MaYaha 7.1 Channel 980 watt	25	$13,530.00	$10,250.00	$3,280.00	24.24%
HESB51DVD	SEBO 38 DVD 5.1 Home Enterta	5	$9,450.00	$6,750.00	$2,700.00	28.57%
HESB51DVD	SEBO 38 DVD 5.1 Home Enterta	20	$37,800.00	$27,000.00	$10,800.00	28.57%
TVSB52W	Subishi 52 Inch Widescreen D	25	$62,775.00	$46,500.00	$16,275.00	25.93%
TVSN42W	Sunyung 42 Inch Widescreen P	2	$3,903.90	$2,730.00	$1,173.90	30.07%
TVSN42W	Sunyung 42 Inch Widescreen P	100	$195,195.00	$136,500.00	$58,695.00	30.07%
	CUSTOMER TOTALS:		$886,052.90	$669,225.00	$216,827.90	24.47%
	REPORT TOTALS:		$886,052.90	$669,225.00	$216,827.90	24.47%

E5:7 Write-Off Posting Accounts

GP was configured to post write-offs to the allowance account under the Posting Setup window explained in Chapter 3 for the following GAAP reason. S&S uses the allowance method to recognize bad debt expense. With this method, an annual estimated reserve for uncollectible accounts (i.e., bad debt expense) is prepared. This estimate is booked to allowance for doubtful accounts by either debiting or crediting the account balance to match the estimate. The offset to this entry is posted to bad debt expense. If a subsequent write-off does occur the allowance account is adjusted for the actual write-off expense because the company already recognized an expense when posting the estimate.

E5:8 Test Receivable Controls

GP located the credit limit on Barter's customer card. It then looked at Barter's outstanding account balance, added the new order amount, and compared this to the credit limit.

CHAPTER 6 EXERCISES

E6:1 Practice With Vendor Cards

1. Click Vendor under Cards and enter the following information. Notice that the Vendor ID follows Ashton's primary key scheme.

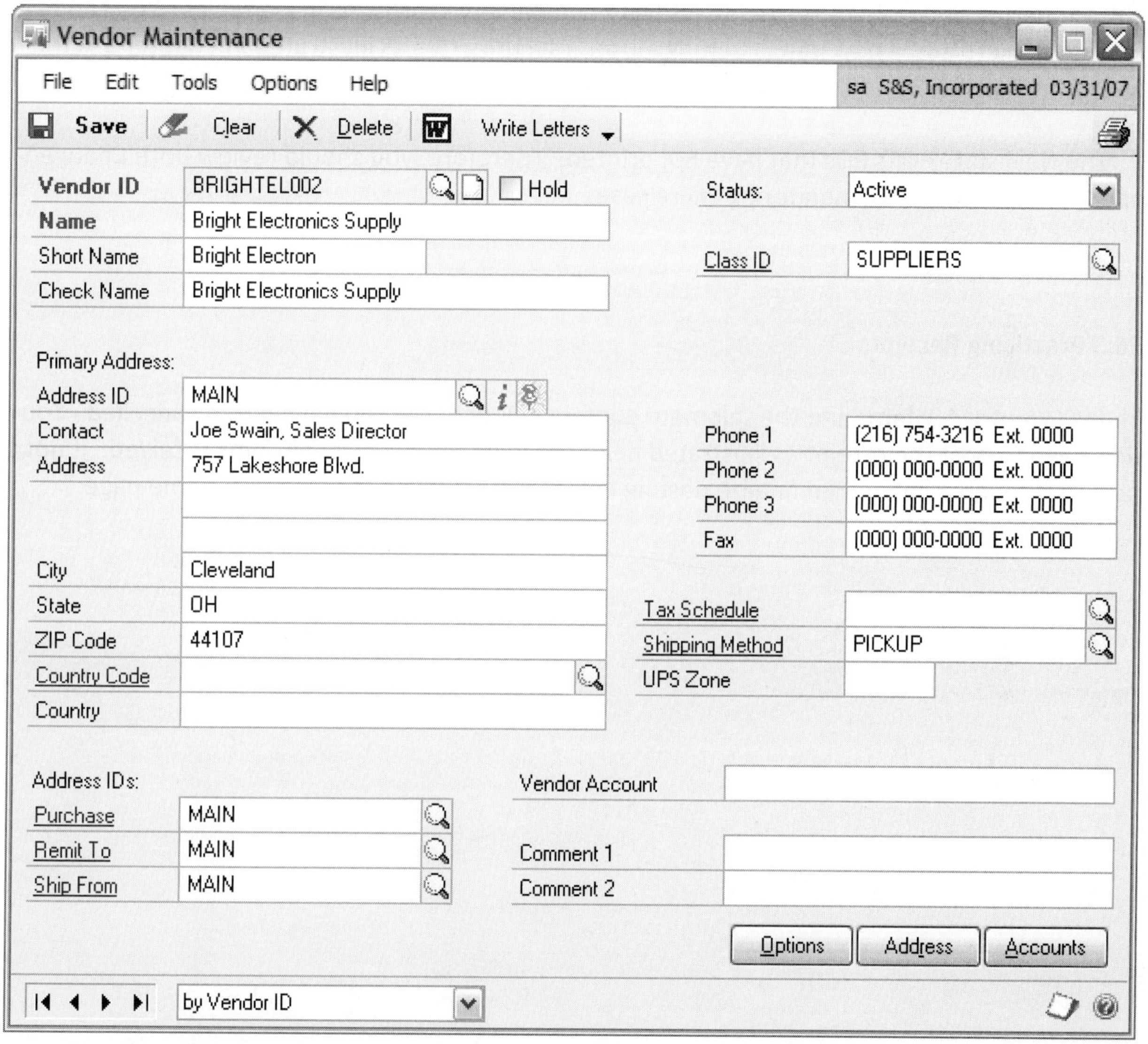

2. SumSang's Vendor ID uses the first nine instead of first eight letters of the company name. Prior to saving a new vendor, you can delete and recreate the account to assign a new ID but you cannot change the ID after saving the account. Fortunately, the error in SumSang's ID is not critical because it stills mitigates creating duplicate vendor accounts and facilitates easy use of the account lookup window. However, you will often encounter companies assigning just a numeric ID such as 1, 2, 3, etc. These companies later learn the difficulty posed on data entry because vendors are not listed alphabetically in lookup windows and users cannot type the first

few letters in the company name to advance the list. There is a utility that can be purchased to renumber IDs.

E6:2 Working with Purchase Orders

1. All hyperlinked field names in the Purchase Order Entry window access master tables. S&S's current permissions do not restrict users from adding new records to these tables. You can test this by trying to add a new item. Setting a user's security role as illustrated in Chapter 3 is the way to restrict access to these tables.

2. The New status lists POs that have not printed. Therefore, you should review both Changed and New statuses when monitoring PO release.

E6:3 Practicing Receipts

The PO was for 10 items and the shipment contained 9 with the remaining item cancelled. You first need to post the receipt as illustrated next, reducing the quantity of items received. If not posted through a batch then finalize posting using Series Post on the Financial home page.

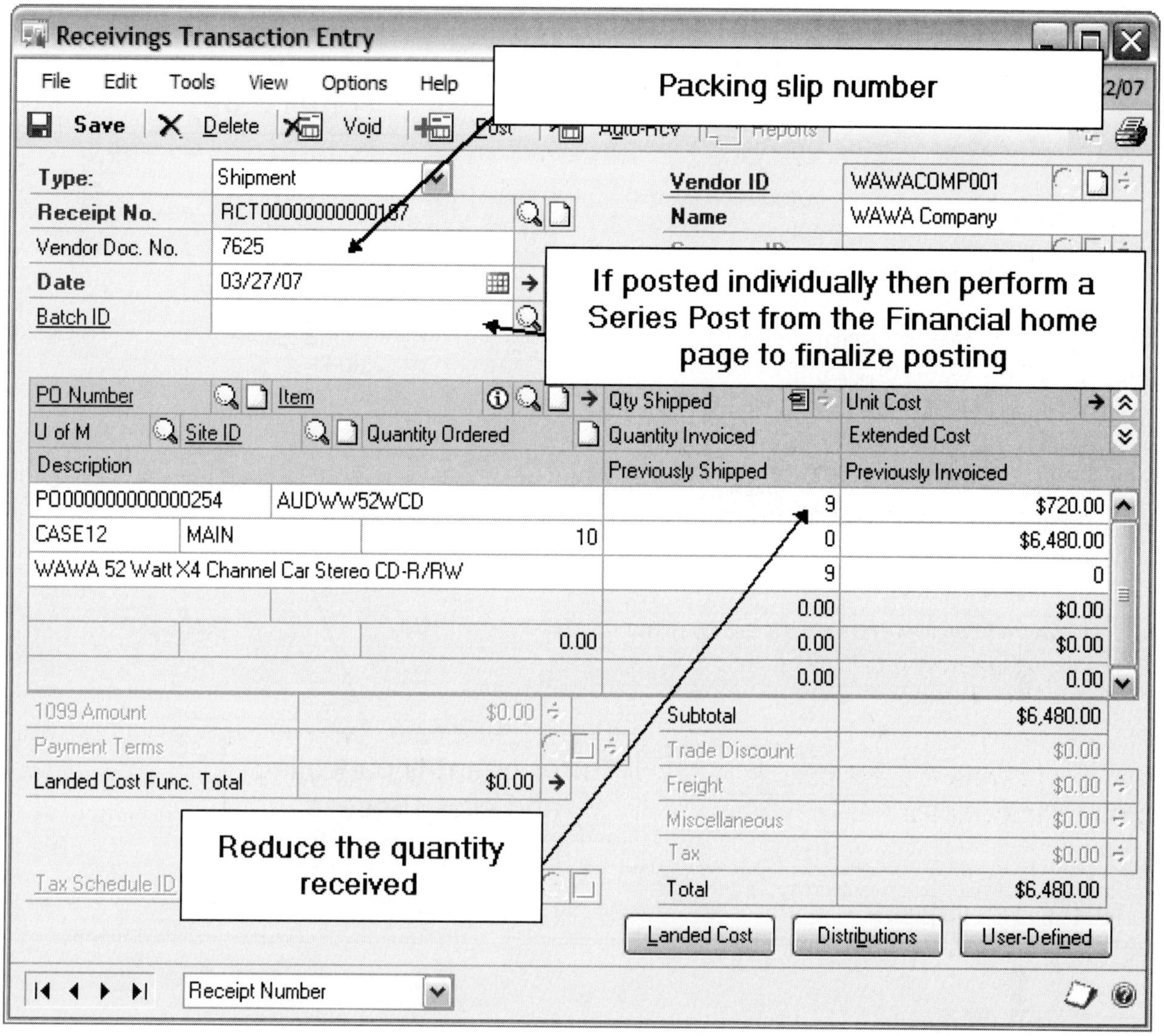

You next need to open the Edit Purchase Order Status window and cancel the remaining item as illustrated next.

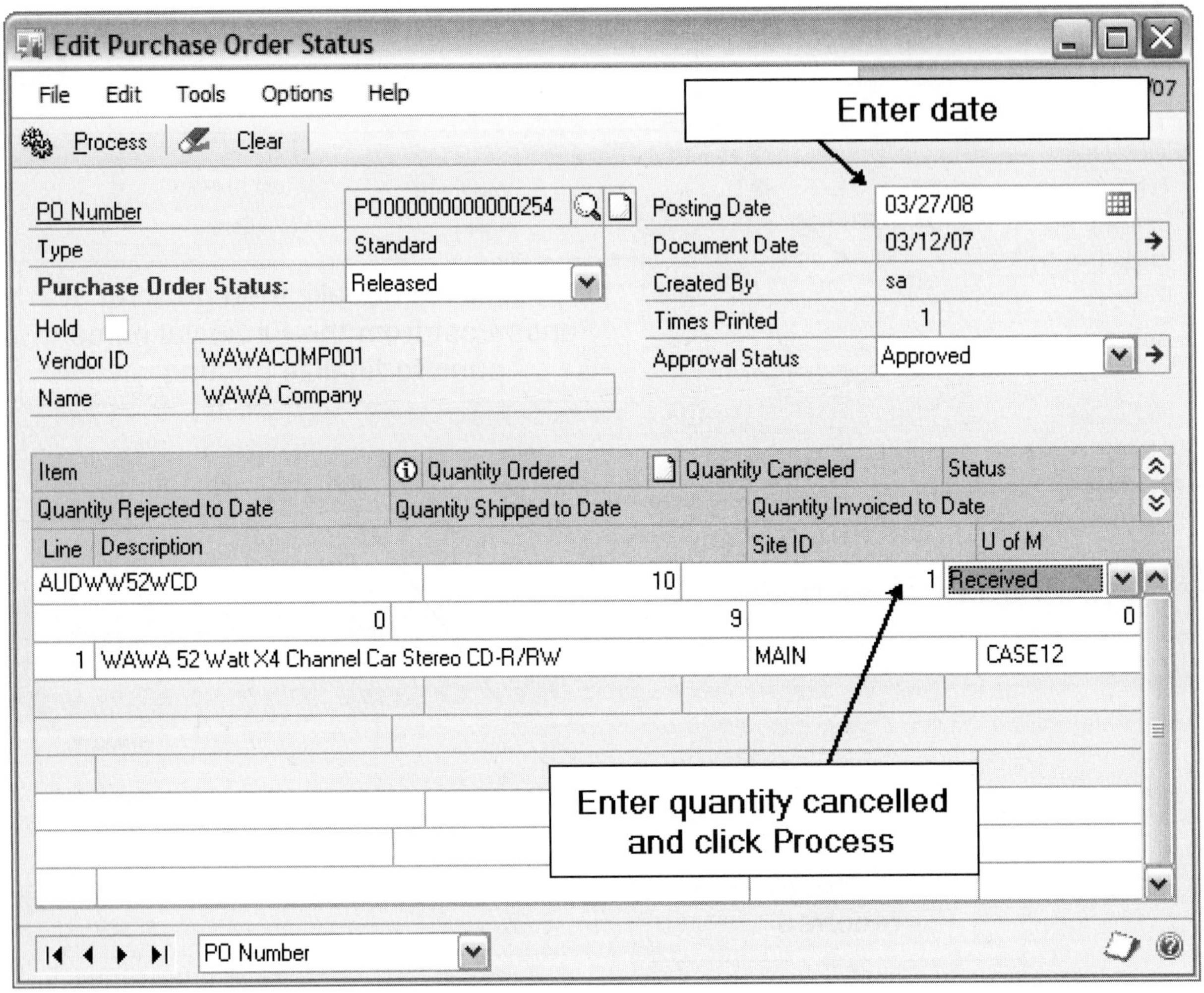

E6:4 Control Reporting for Matching Invoices to Receipts

You can print a Received/Not Invoiced report to list posted receipts awaiting vendor invoices. This report is found by clicking Analysis under Reports and selecting Received/Not Invoiced.

E6:5 Practice Posting a Vendor Invoice

You can enter the invoice through a batch or as an individual transaction by clicking Transaction Entry. If entered individually, remember to activate the Financial home page and complete posting through Series Posting.

The invoice is illustrated next and was posted individually.

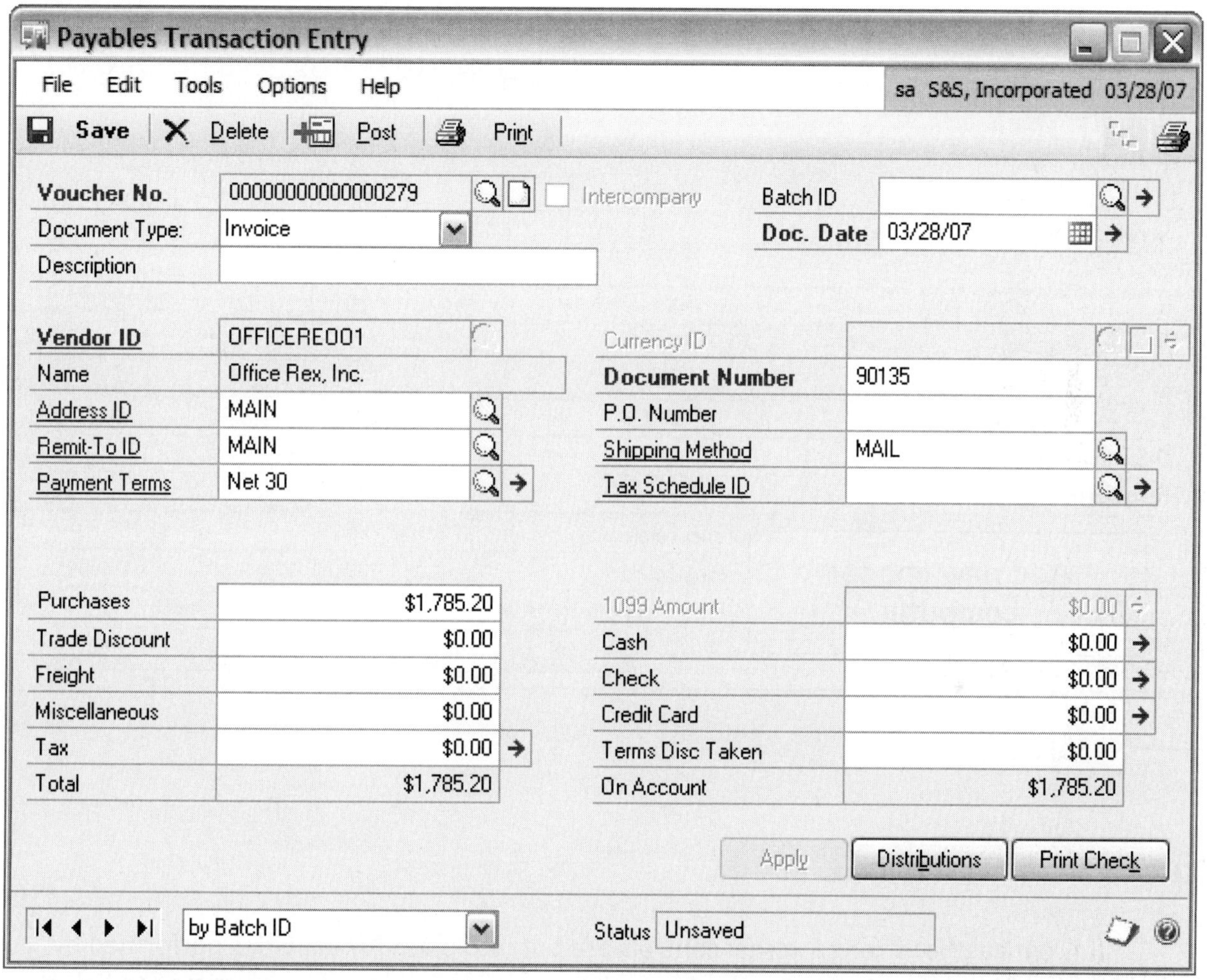

You must change distribution accounts because the invoice is for office equipment and office supplies. Distribution accounts are illustrated next.

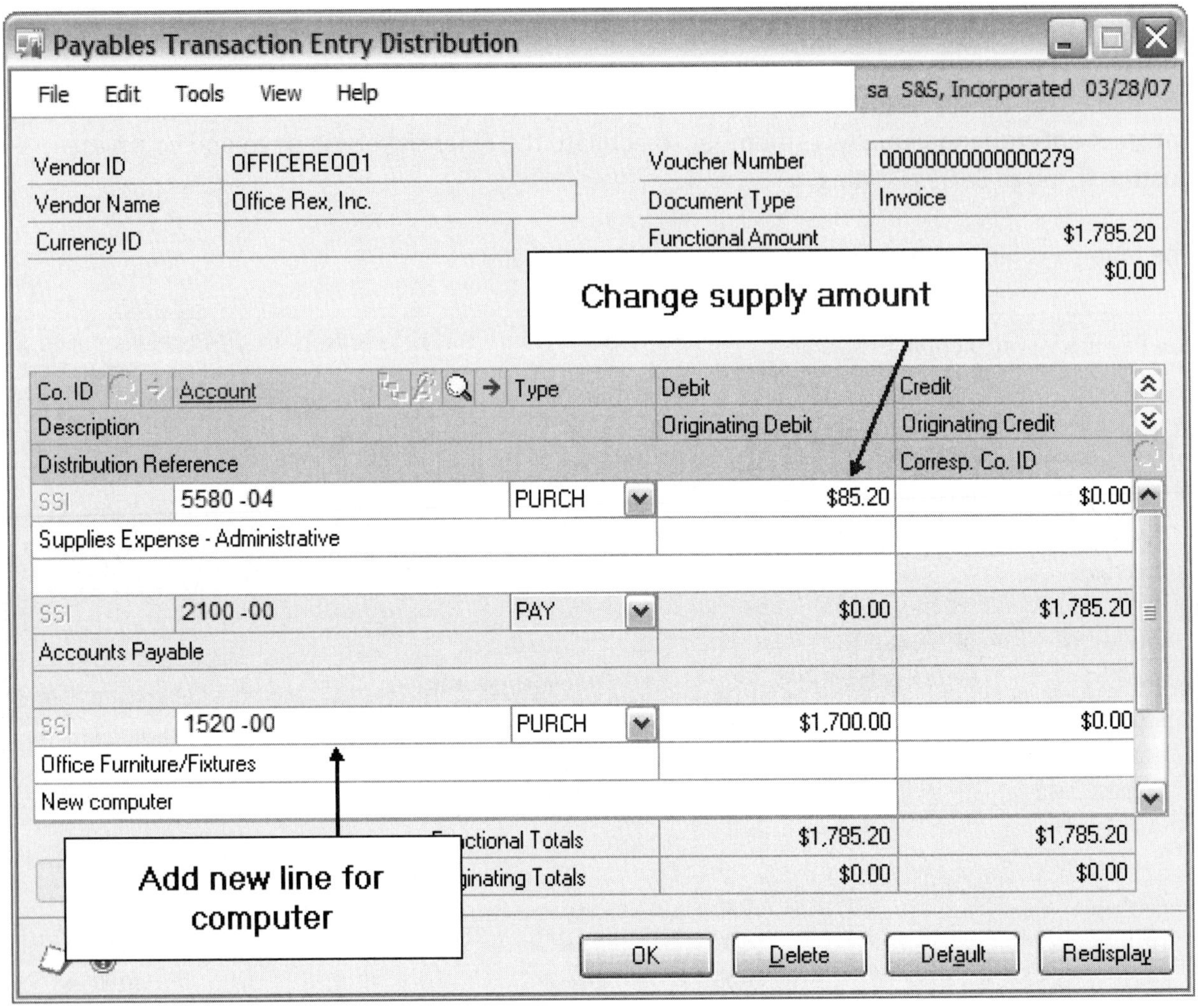

E6:6 Cashier Internal Controls

1. It is critical that strong internal controls are put into place for activities performed by the cashier department. Purchasing Series menu access should be restricted to Select Checks, Edit Checks, and Print Checks. You will also need to permit access to the Batches menu. You can permit access to Inquiry and Report menus but restrict all access to Cards, Utilities, and Setup menus.

2. Access to check stock must be protected and printing should not be unattended. You can implement these controls through a locked storage cabinet and restrict printing to controlled printers in the cashier's office. Bank reconciliations should be performed monthly by someone independent of printing checks.

E6:7 Practice Purchasing Series Reporting

1. First, prepare the historical aging report found under Trial Balance. Modify the report as illustrated next and print it to the screen. Locate the report total found on the last page under Due.

   Next, activate the Financial home page and perform a Summary inquiry as to the March 31 period balance for accounts 2100-00 Accounts Payable and 2105-00 Purchase Discounts Available. The balance sums for these two accounts must match the report total for the Series to reconcile. If balances do not reconcile, open the Financial Series Post window and confirm all transactions have finalized to the general ledger.

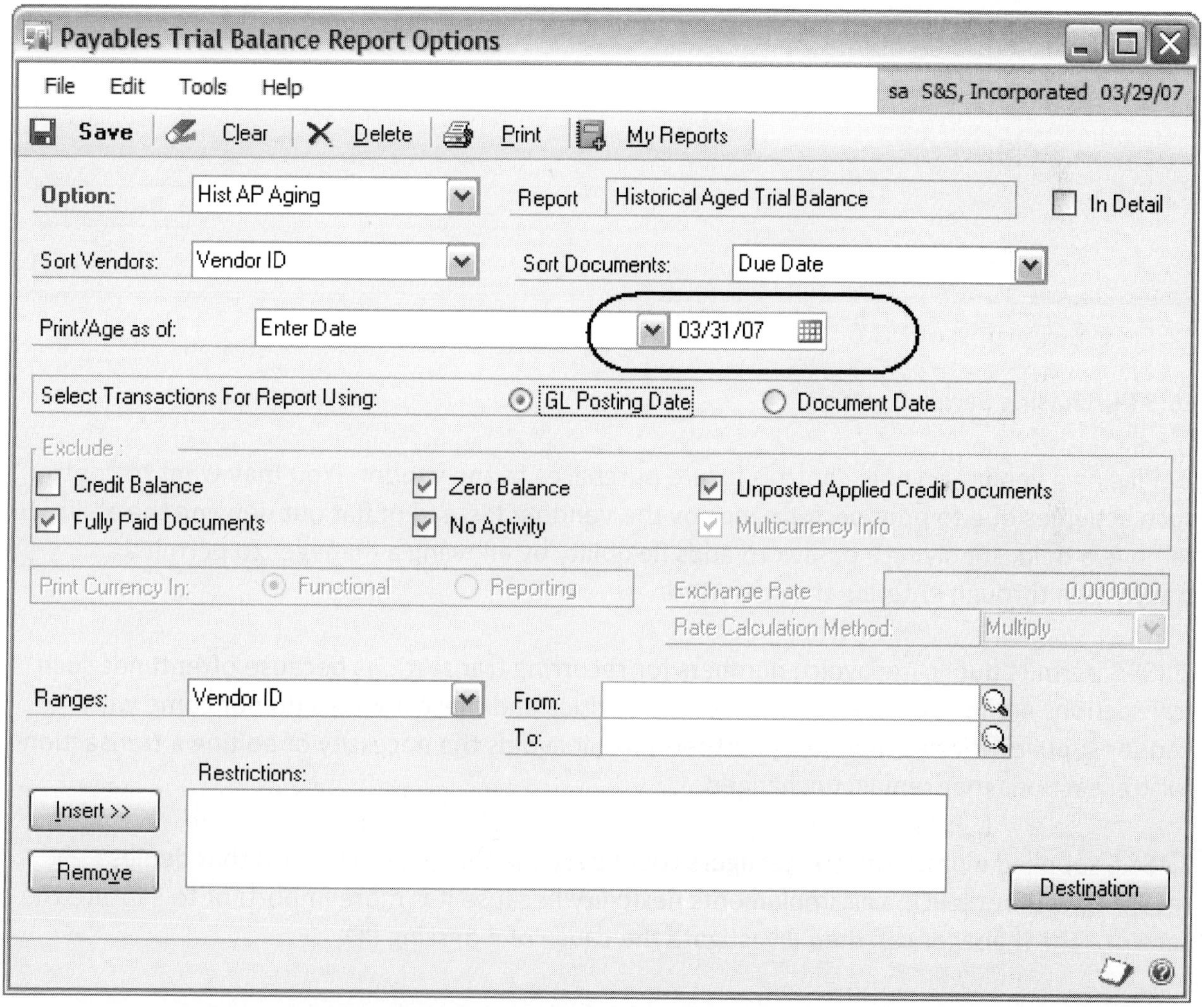

2. Prepare the report by clicking Check Information and selecting Vendor Check Register. Click New and create the following report. Make sure to set the Destination to Screen.

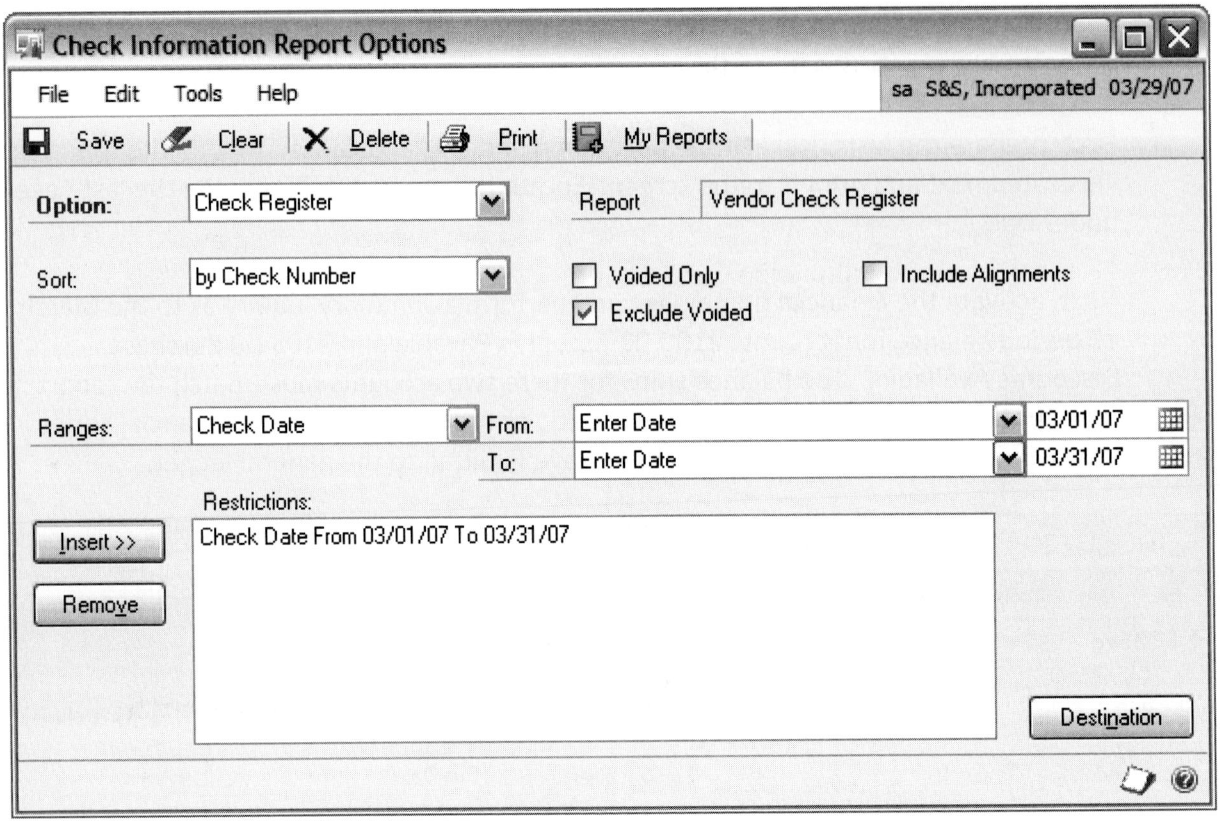

E6:8 Purchasing Series Controls

1. Placing a vendor on hold controls future purchases to the vendor. You may want to control such activities due to poor performance by the vendor. Instead of flat out denying the ability to remove a hold, supplying a password adds flexibility by allowing a manager to permit a transaction through entering the password.

2. S&S permits duplicate invoice numbers for recurring transactions because oftentimes such transactions are for expenses such as rent or utilities and these invoices do not come with vendor supplied invoice numbers. Furthermore, it avoids the necessity of editing a transaction for transactions that remain unchanged.

3. S&S supplied a password so managers could override the general control that denies receiving without a PO. This implements flexibility because it is more important to capture the receipt. The manager can then investigate the cause of a missing PO.

Chapter 7 Exercises

E7:1 Practice Identifying Pay Codes, Benefits, and Deductions

Thomas Winchester is paid hourly at $8.50 per hour and he receives overtime at $12.75 if he works more than 40 hours during the week.

His voluntary deductions are 2 percent to a 401k and family health insurance coverage costing $107.00.

The company provides a matching 401k benefit of fifty percent.

E7:2 Practice With Employee Cards

You work in the HR department so are authorized to make changes to employee master records.

The changes to Thomas Winchester's federal withholdings are shown next.

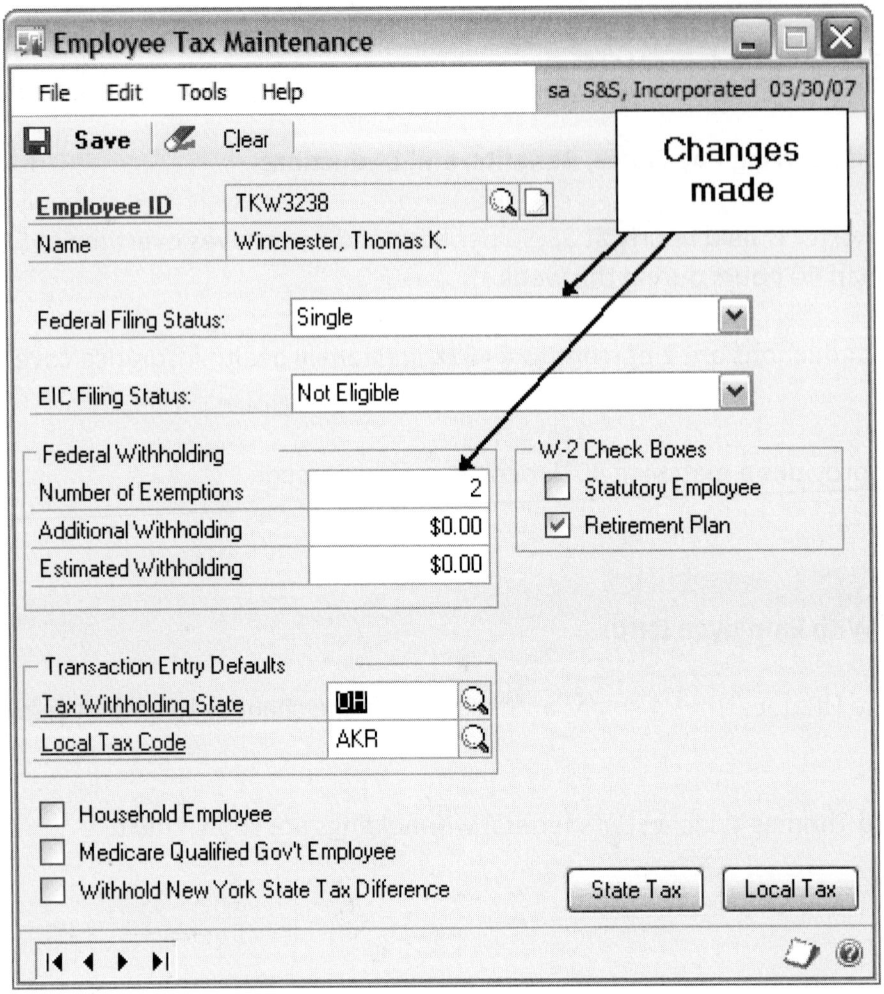

Next are changes for April Levine's 401k deductions.

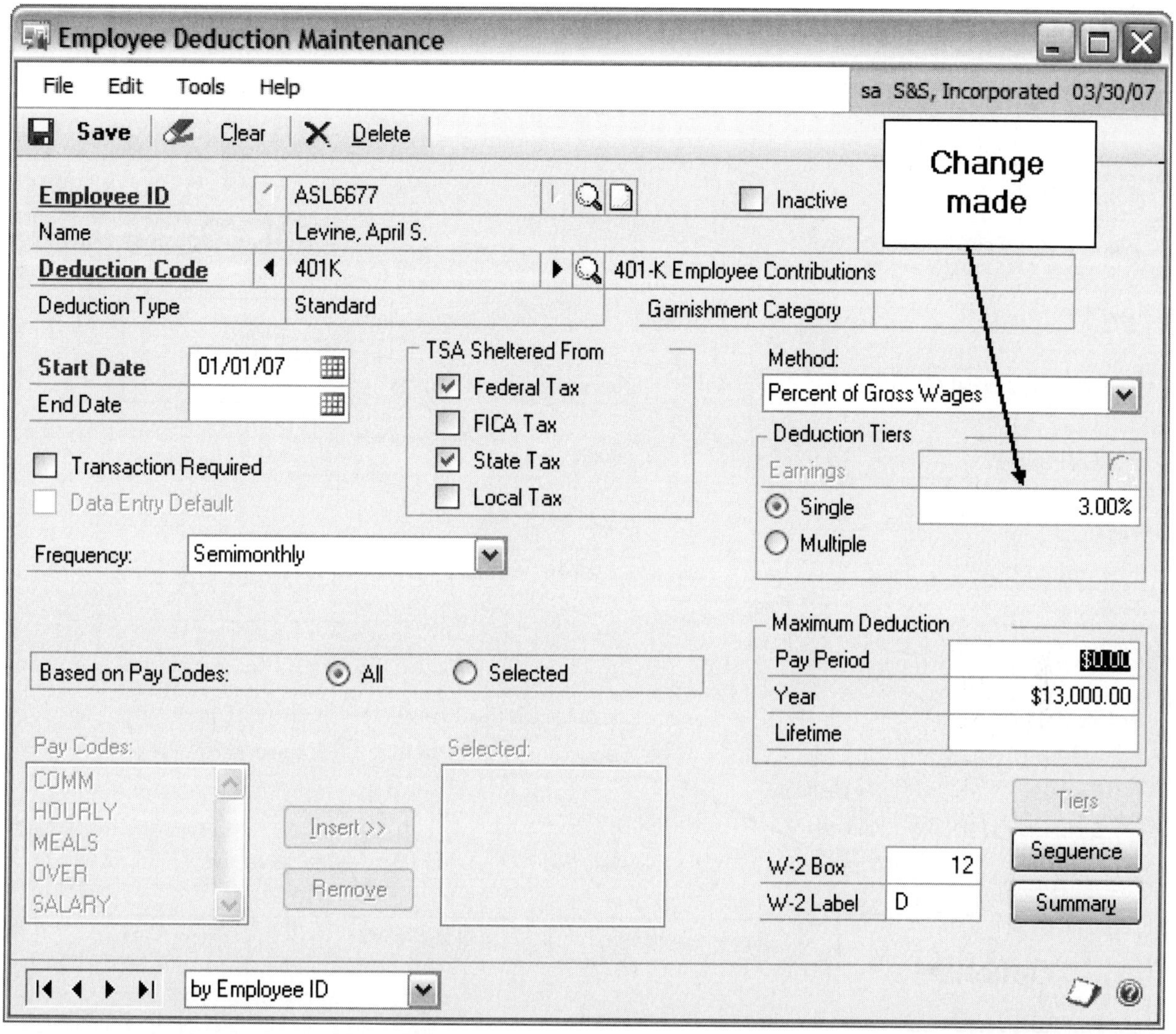

Employee Deduction Maintenance

File   Edit   Tools   Help

sa S&S, Incorporated 03/30/07

Save | **Clear** | **X** **Delete**

Employee ID	ASL6677 [🔍] [ ] ☐ Inactive
Name	Levine, April S.
Deduction Code	◄ 401K ► 🔍 401-K Employee Contributions
Deduction Type	Standard

Garnishment Category

Change made

Start Date 01/01/07
End Date

TSA Sheltered From
- ☑ Federal Tax
- ☐ FICA Tax
- ☑ State Tax
- ☐ Local Tax

Method:
Percent of Gross Wages

Deduction Tiers
Earnings
- ⦿ Single   3.00%
- ○ Multiple

☐ Transaction Required
☐ Data Entry Default

Frequency: Semimonthly

Maximum Deduction

Pay Period	$0.00
Year	$13,000.00
Lifetime	

Based on Pay Codes: ⦿ All   ○ Selected

Pay Codes:
COMM
HOURLY
MEALS
OVER
SALARY

Selected:

[Insert >>]

[Remove]

Tiers

Sequence

W-2 Box   12
W-2 Label   D

Summary

|◄ ◄ ► ►| by Employee ID

E7:3 Practice Building Paychecks

Click Build Batch and enter the following criteria.

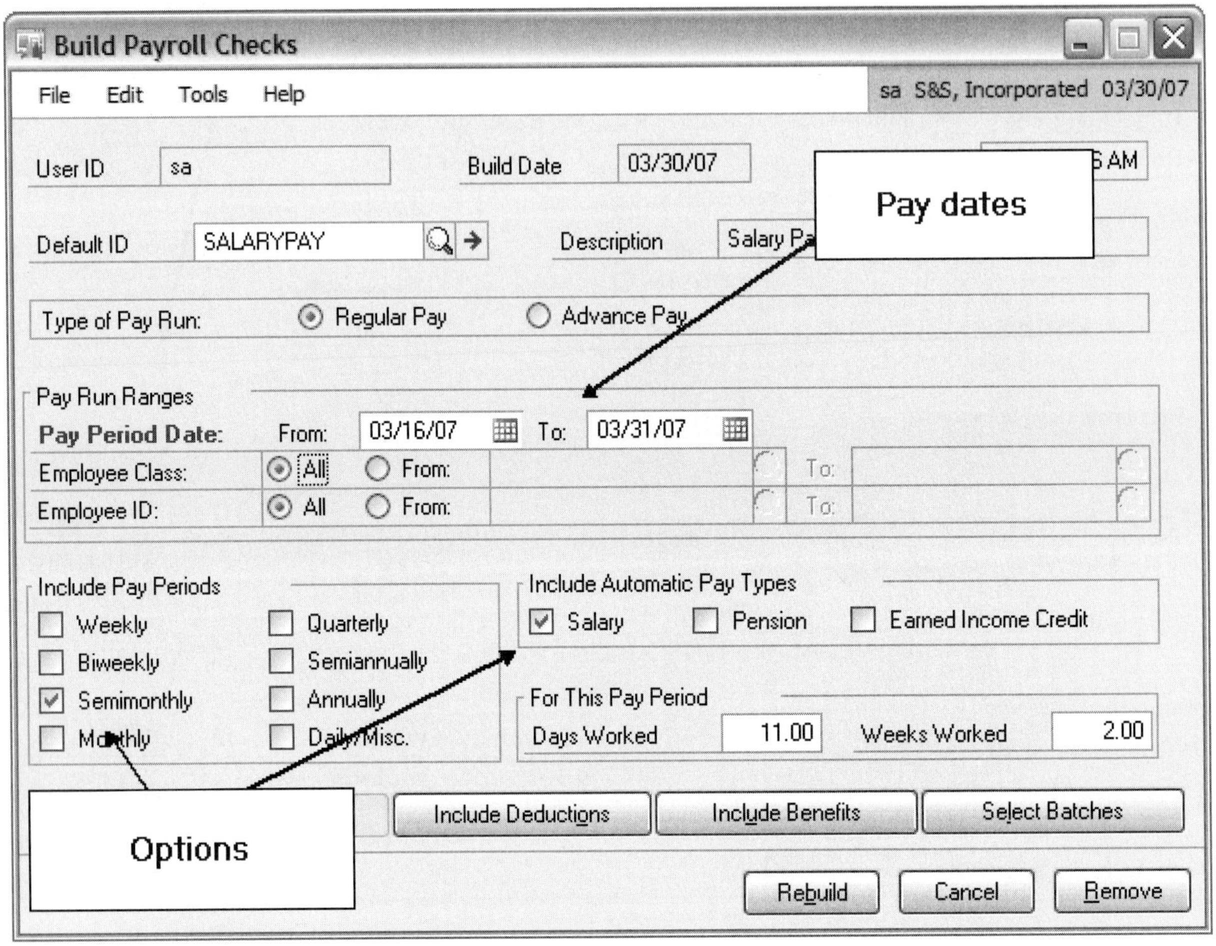

Click Include Deductions and Include Benefits to confirm that All is marked.

Click Select Batches and add the following batches.

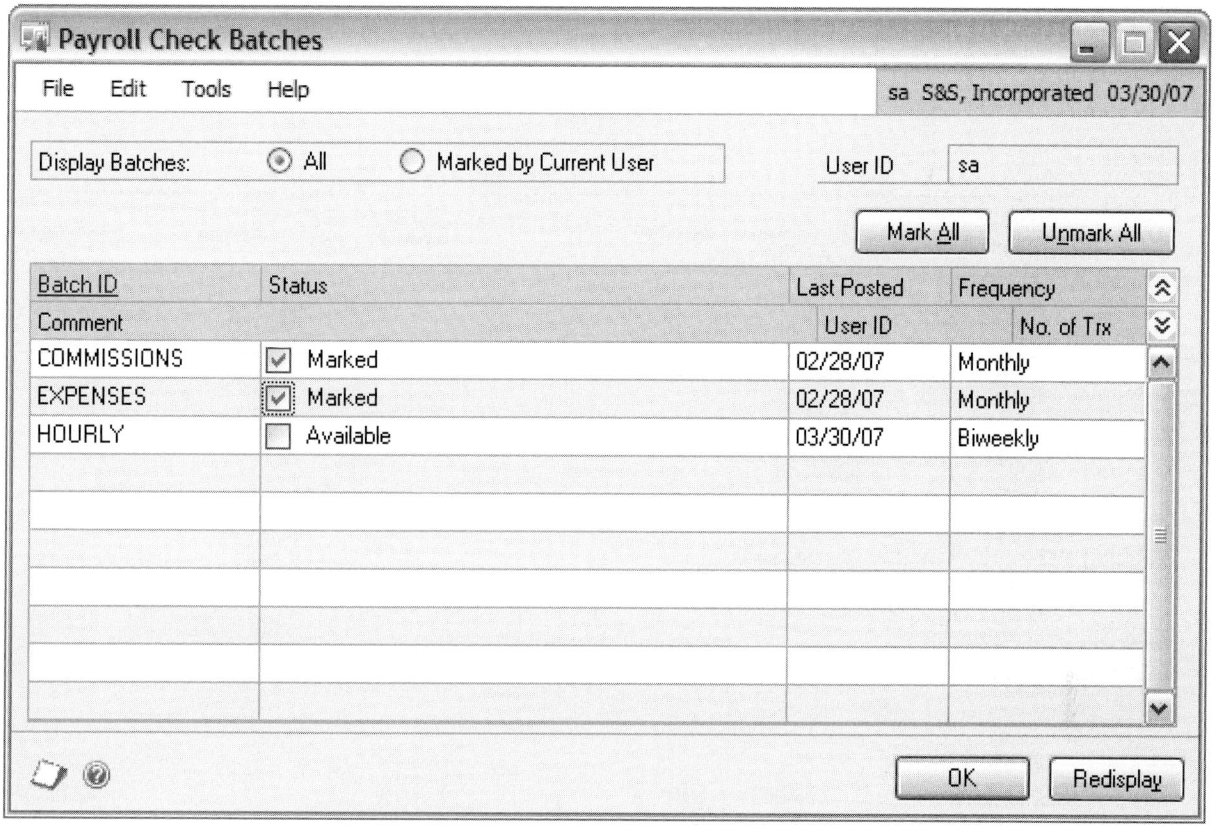

Build the batch, saving changes. The Check File report prints as follows.

```
                                              S&S, Incorporated                              Page:   1
User Date: 03/30/07                           CHECK FILE REPORT                              User ID: sa
                                                U.S. Payroll

Employee ID      Name
------------------------------------------------------------------------------------------------------------------
             Code     Description           Dept    Position  Shift           Pay Rate          Premium     Amount/Units
------------------------------------------------------------------------------------------------------------------
                State     Local                  W/Comp   SUTA      Weeks    Days                 Receipts     Batch ID
------------------------------------------------------------------------------------------------------------------
APF3232         Fleming, Ashton P
   Pay:      SALARY   Salary                ADMIN    ACCT                     $2,358.33                        $2,358.33
                OH       AKR                  2387     OH        2.00    11.00
   Benefit:  401K     401-K Employer Match                                      50.00% of Deduction
   Deduction: 401K    401-K Employee Contributions                               4.00% of Gross Wages
             HSINGL   Single Health Insurance                                 $60.00
   State Tax: OH      Ohio
   Local Tax: AKR     Akron City Income Tax

ASL6677         Levine, April S
   Pay:      SALARY   Salary                SMID     STAFF                    $1,287.50                        $1,287.50
                OH       AKR                  2387     OH        2.00    11.00
             COMM     Commission            SMID     STAFF                                                       $859.80
                OH       AKR                  2387     OH        0.00     0.00                              COMMISSIONS
             MEALS    Bus Expense           SMID     STAFF                                                        $15.25
                                              2387               0.00     0.00                              EXPENSES
             TRAVEL   Bus Expense           SMID     STAFF                                                       $120.70
                                              2387               0.00     0.00                              EXPENSES
   Benefit:  401K     401-K Employer Match                                      50.00% of Deduction
   Deduction: 401K    401-K Employee Contributions                               2.50% of Gross Wages
             HSINGL   Single Health Insurance                                 $60.00
   State Tax: OH      Ohio
   Local Tax: AKR     Akron City Income Tax
```

CJW7872		Warner, Curtis J							
Pay:	SALARY	Salary	SEAST	STAFF			$1,244.58		$1,244.58
	OH	AKR	2387	OH	2.00	11.00			
	COMM	Commission	SEAST	STAFF					$858.40
	OH	AKR	2387	OH	0.00	0.00			COMMISSIONS
	MEALS	Bus Expense	SEAST	STAFF					$30.54
			2387		0.00	0.00			EXPENSES
	TRAVEL	Bus Expense	SEAST	STAFF					$165.00
			2387		0.00	0.00			EXPENSES
Benefit:	401K	401-K Employer Match					50.00% of Deduction		
Deduction:	401K	401-K Employee Contributions					3.00% of Gross Wages		
	CONTR	Contributions					$15.00		
	HFAMI	Family Health Insurance					$107.00		
State Tax:	OH	Ohio							
Local Tax:	AKR	Akron City Income Tax							
MTM3987		Murphy, Mary T							
Pay:	SALARY	Salary	SWEST	STAFF			$1,354.17		$1,354.17
	OH	AKR	2387	OH	2.00	11.00			
	COMM	Commission	SWEST	STAFF					$2,560.23
	OH	AKR	2387	OH	0.00	0.00			COMMISSIONS
	MEALS	Bus Expense	SWEST	STAFF					$23.85
			2387		0.00	0.00			EXPENSES
	TRAVEL	Bus Expense	SWEST	STAFF					$374.16
			2387		0.00	0.00			EXPENSES
Benefit:	401K	401-K Employer Match					50.00% of Deduction		
Deduction:	401K	401-K Employee Contributions					3.00% of Gross Wages		
	HFAMI	Family Health Insurance					$107.00		
State Tax:	OH	Ohio							
Local Tax:	AKR	Akron City Income Tax							

SJP5132	Parry, Scott J							
Pay:	SALARY	Salary	ADMIN	OWNER			$2,787.50	$2,787.50
	OH	AKR	2387	OH	2.00	11.00		
Benefit:	401K	401-K Employer Match					50.00% of Deduction	
Deduction:	401K	401-K Employee Contributions					3.00% of Gross Wages	
	CONTR	Contributions					$25.00	
	HFAMI	Family Health Insurance					$107.00	
State Tax:	OH	Ohio						
Local Tax:	AKR	Akron City Income Tax						
SMG4255	Gonzalez, Susan M							
Pay:	SALARY	Salary	ADMIN	OWNER			$2,787.50	$2,787.50
	OH	AKR	2387	OH	2.00	11.00		
Benefit:	401K	401-K Employer Match					50.00% of Deduction	
Deduction:	401K	401-K Employee Contributions					3.00% of Gross Wages	
	HFAMI	Family Health Insurance					$107.00	
State Tax:	OH	Ohio						
Local Tax:	AKR	Akron City Income Tax						
Total Employees:	6							

Calculate paychecks. The Calculate Checks Report appears as follows.

```
                                        S&S, Incorporated                              Page:    1
User Date:  03/30/07                  CALCULATE CHECKS REPORT                         User ID: sa
                                           U.S. Payroll

Employee ID     Name                         Soc Sec Number
------------------------------------------------------------------------------------------------------------------------
     Code  Pay Type        Dept   Position        Pay Rate    Amount/Units     Gross Wages      Ben/Ded/Tax       Net Wages
------------------------------------------------------------------------------------------------------------------------
APF3232         Fleming, Ashton P            083-25-3232
     SALARY Salary          ADMIN  ACCT          $2,358.33                      $2,358.33
                                                                        -----------------
                                                                                $2,358.33

                                       Benefits:       401K   401-K Employer Match                       $47.17
                                                                                           -----------------
                                                                                                         $47.17

                                       Deductions:     401K   401-K Employee Contributions               $94.33
                                                       HSINGL Single Health Insurance                    $54.00
                                                                                           -----------------
                                                                                                        $148.33

                                       Taxes On Wages: FICA Soc Sec Withheld                            $146.22
                                                       FICA Medicare Withheld                            $34.19
                                                       Federal Withheld                                 $389.79
                                                       OH State Withheld                                 $89.75
                                                       AKR    Local Withheld                             $47.17
                                                                                           -----------------
                                                                                                        $707.12

                                                                                                          -----------------
                                                                                                                 $1,502.88
                                                                                                          =================
```

```
ASL6677       Levine, April S              007-65-6677
   SALARY Salary       SMID   STAFF       $1,287.50                    $1,287.50
   COMM   Commission   SMID   STAFF                        $859.80       $859.80
   MEALS  Bus Expense  SMID   STAFF                         $15.25
   TRAVEL Bus Expense  SMID   STAFF                        $120.70
                                                              -----------------
                                              Gross Wages              $2,147.30
                                              Non-Wage Business Exp      $135.95
                                                              -----------------
                                                                       $2,283.25

                                  Benefits:      401K   401-K Employer Match                 $26.84
                                                                                  -----------------
                                                                                             $26.84

                                  Deductions:    401K   401-K Employee Contributions         $53.68
                                                 HSINGL Single Health Insurance              $60.00
                                                                                  -----------------
                                                                                            $113.68

                                  Taxes On Wages: FICA Soc Sec Withheld                     $133.13
                                                  FICA Medicare Withheld                     $31.14
                                                  Federal Withheld                          $302.08
                                                  OH State Withheld                          $71.27
                                                  AKR    Local Withheld                      $42.95
                                                                                  -----------------
                                                                                            $580.57

                                                                                                     -----------------
                                                                                                             $1,589.00
                                                                                                     =================
```

CJW7872	Warner, Curtis J			088-23-7872			
SALARY	Salary	SEAST	STAFF	$1,244.58		$1,244.58	
COMM	Commission	SEAST	STAFF		$858.40	$858.40	
MEALS	Bus Expense	SEAST	STAFF		$30.54		
TRAVEL	Bus Expense	SEAST	STAFF		$165.00		

				Gross Wages		$2,102.98	
				Non-Wage Business Exp		$195.54	

						$2,298.52	

Benefits:	401K	401-K Employer Match	$31.55

			$31.55
Deductions:	401K	401-K Employee Contributions	$63.09
	CONTR	Contributions	$15.00
	HFAMI	Family Health Insurance	$107.00

			$185.09
Taxes On Wages:	FICA Soc Sec Withheld		$130.39
	FICA Medicare Withheld		$30.49
	Federal Withheld		$160.85
	OH State Withheld		$64.33
	AKR	Local Withheld	$42.06

			$428.12

$1,685.31

================

MTM3987	Murphy, Mary T			038-82-3987				
SALARY	Salary	SWEST	STAFF	$1,354.17		$1,354.17		
COMM	Commission	SWEST	STAFF		$2,560.23	$2,560.23		
MEALS	Bus Expense	SWEST	STAFF		$23.85			
TRAVEL	Bus Expense	SWEST	STAFF		$374.16			

				Gross Wages		$3,914.40		
				Non-Wage Business Exp		$398.01		

						$4,312.41		
			Benefits:	401K 401-K Employer Match			$58.72	

							$58.72	
			Deductions:	401K 401-K Employee Contributions			$117.43	
				HFAMI Family Health Insurance			$107.00	

							$224.43	
			Taxes On Wages:	FICA Soc Sec Withheld			$242.69	
				FICA Medicare Withheld			$56.75	
				Federal Withheld			$399.74	
				OH State Withheld			$152.38	
				AKR Local Withheld			$78.29	

							$929.85	

								$3,158.13
								================

SJP5132	Parry, Scott J		089-23-5132				
SALARY Salary	ADMIN	OWNER	$2,787.50		$2,787.50		

					$2,787.50		
		Benefits:	401K	401-K Employer Match		$41.82	

						$41.82	
		Deductions:	401K	401-K Employee Contributions		$83.63	
			CONTR	Contributions		$25.00	
			HFAMI	Family Health Insurance		$107.00	

						$215.63	
		Taxes On Wages:	FICA	Soc Sec Withheld		$172.82	
			FICA	Medicare Withheld		$40.42	
				Federal Withheld		$309.11	
			OH	State Withheld		$111.62	
			AKR	Local Withheld		$55.75	

						$689.72	

							$1,882.15
							================

```
SMG4255        Gonzalez, Susan M           088-23-4255
    SALARY Salary          ADMIN   OWNER          $2,787.50                      $2,787.50
                                                                          -----------------
                                                                                 $2,787.50

                                   Benefits:        401K   401-K Employer Match                    $41.82
                                                                                          -----------------
                                                                                               $41.82

                                   Deductions:      401K   401-K Employee Contributions            $83.63
                                                    HFAMI  Family Health Insurance                $107.00
                                                                                          -----------------
                                                                                              $190.63

                                   Taxes On Wages: FICA Soc Sec Withheld                          $172.82
                                                   FICA Medicare Withheld                          $40.42
                                                   Federal Withheld                               $309.11
                                                   OH State Withheld                              $111.62
                                                   AKR   Local Withheld                            $55.75
                                                                                          -----------------
                                                                                              $689.72

                                                                                                      -----------------
                                                                                                           $1,907.15
                                                                                                      =================

                                   REPORT TOTALS:
                                   WAGES                             $16,098.01
                                   NON-WAGE BUSINESS EXP                $729.50
                                   BENEFITS                             $247.92
                                   DEDUCTIONS                         $1,077.79
                                   TAXES                              $4,025.10
                                   NET WAGES                         $11,724.62
```

Print paychecks to the screen.

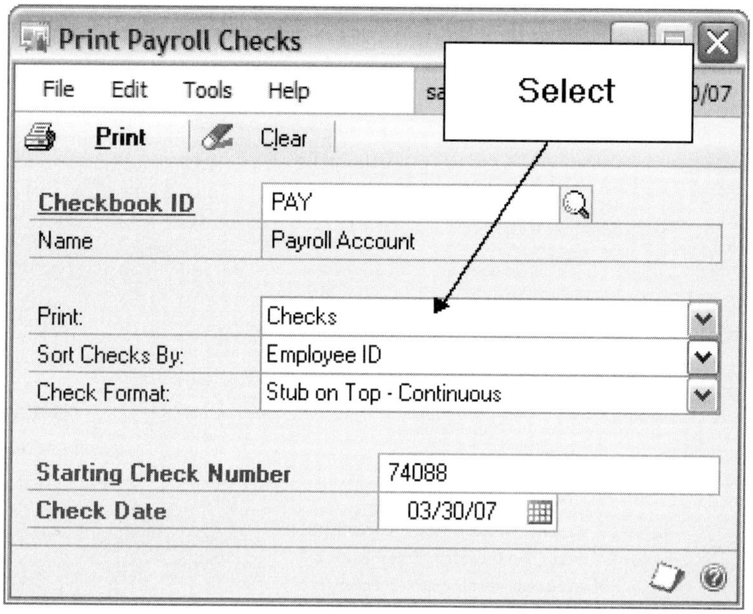

Post entries to the general ledger.

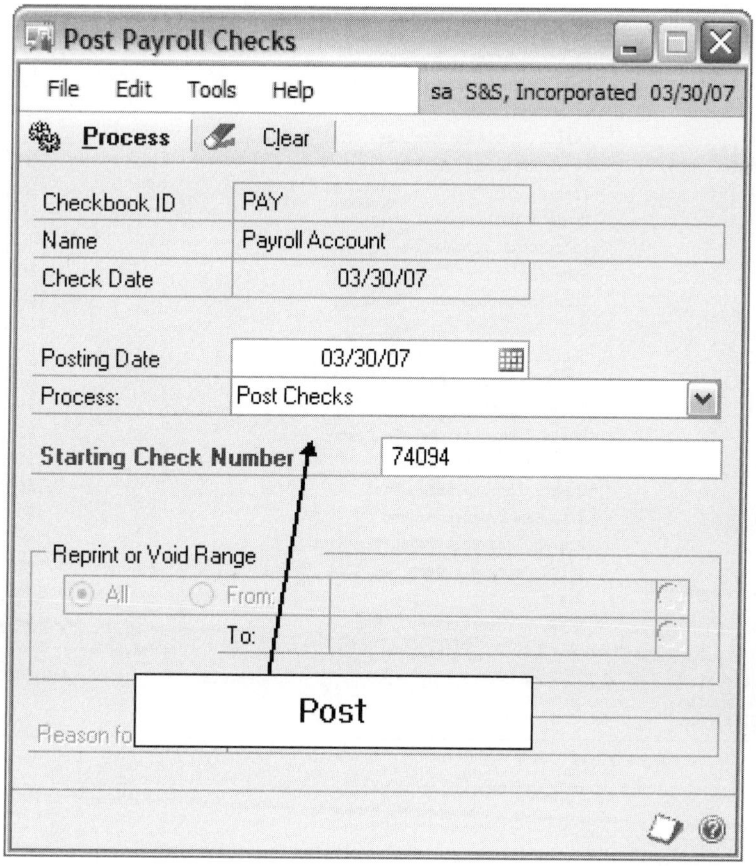

General Posting Journal appears next.

S&S, Incorporated
GENERAL POSTING JOURNAL
General Ledger

User Date: 03/30/07 Page: 1
User ID: sa

* Voided Journal Entry

Batch ID: UPRCC00000062
Batch Comment: Payroll Computer Checks

Approved: No | Batch Total Actual: $36,613.82 | Batch Total Control: $0.00
Approved by: | Trx Total Actual: 1 | Trx Total Control: 0
Approval Date:

Journal Entry	Transaction Type	Transaction Date	Reversing Date	Source Document	Transaction Reference	Audit Trail Code	Reversing Audit Trail Code
1,738	Standard	03/30/07		UPRCC	Payroll Computer Checks	GLTRX00000669	

Account	Description	Debit	Credit
2270-00	FICA Taxes Payable		$2,462.96
2275-00	Federal Withholding Taxes Payable		$1,870.68
2280-00	State Withholding Taxes Payable		$600.97
2285-00	City Withholding Taxes Payable		$321.97
5100-04	Wages/Salaries - Administration	$7,933.33	
5310-04	FICA Tax Expense - Administration	$606.89	
5410-04	Health Insurance Expense - Administration		$268.00
5420-04	401-K Expense - Admininstration	$130.81	
1130-00	Checking - Payroll		$11,724.62
2320-00	401-K Payable		$743.71
5100-02	Wages/Salaries - MidWest	$1,287.50	
5200-02	Commission Expense - MidWest	$859.80	
5310-02	FICA Tax Expense - MidWest	$164.27	
5410-02	Health Insurance Expense - MidWest		$60.00
5420-02	401-K Expense - MidWest	$26.84	
5530-02	Travel - MidWest	$120.70	
5535-02	Meals & Entertaiment - MidWest	$15.25	
2310-00	Deductions Payable		$40.00
5100-01	Wages/Salaries - East	$1,244.58	
5200-01	Commission Expense - East	$858.40	
5310-01	FICA Tax Expense - East	$160.88	
5410-01	Health Insurance Expense - East		$107.00
5420-01	401-K Expense - East	$31.55	
5530-01	Travel - East	$165.00	
5535-01	Meals & Entertainment - East	$30.54	
5100-03	Wages/Salaries - West	$1,354.17	
5200-03	Commission Expense - West	$2,560.23	
5310-03	FICA Tax Expense - West	$299.44	
5410-03	Health Insurance Expense - West		$107.00
5420-03	401-K Expense - West	$58.72	
5530-03	Travel - West	$374.16	
5535-03	Meals & Entertaiment - West	$23.85	

Total Distributions: 32 Totals: $18,306.91 $18,306.91

Total Journal Entries: 1

E7:4 Practice Payroll Reporting

1. The March Deduction Summary report appears next, listing employee voluntary deductions.

```
                                   S&S, Incorporated                          Page:     1
User Date: 03/30/07                DEDUCTION SUMMARY                          User ID: sa
                                        Payroll

 Ranges:          From:            To:
   Employee ID:   First            Last
   Class ID:      First            Last
   Department:    First            Last
   Position:      First            Last

 Date From: 03/01/07
 Date To:   03/31/07

Deduction Code                          MTD Total          QTD Total          YTD Total
-----------------------------------------------------------------------------------------
 401K                                   $1,244.25          $3,396.17          $3,396.17
 CONTR                                     $95.00            $275.00            $275.00
 HFAMI                                  $2,140.00          $5,564.00          $5,564.00
 HSINGL                                 $1,128.00          $2,784.00          $2,784.00
                                  ----------------   ----------------   ----------------
          Deduction Code Totals:        $4,607.25         $12,019.17         $12,019.17
```

2. The Payroll Summary report does not list employee state and local tax withholdings. For this information, you must print the State Tax Summary and Local Tax Summary reports.

3. The Pay Code Summary report lists employee payments by type, including commissions and expense reimbursements. The Payroll Summary report lists gross and taxable wages, which includes commissions because such payments are taxable but does not include expense reimbursements because such payments are not taxable.

E7:5 Practice Managing Codes

Click Deductions under Setup and create the following code.

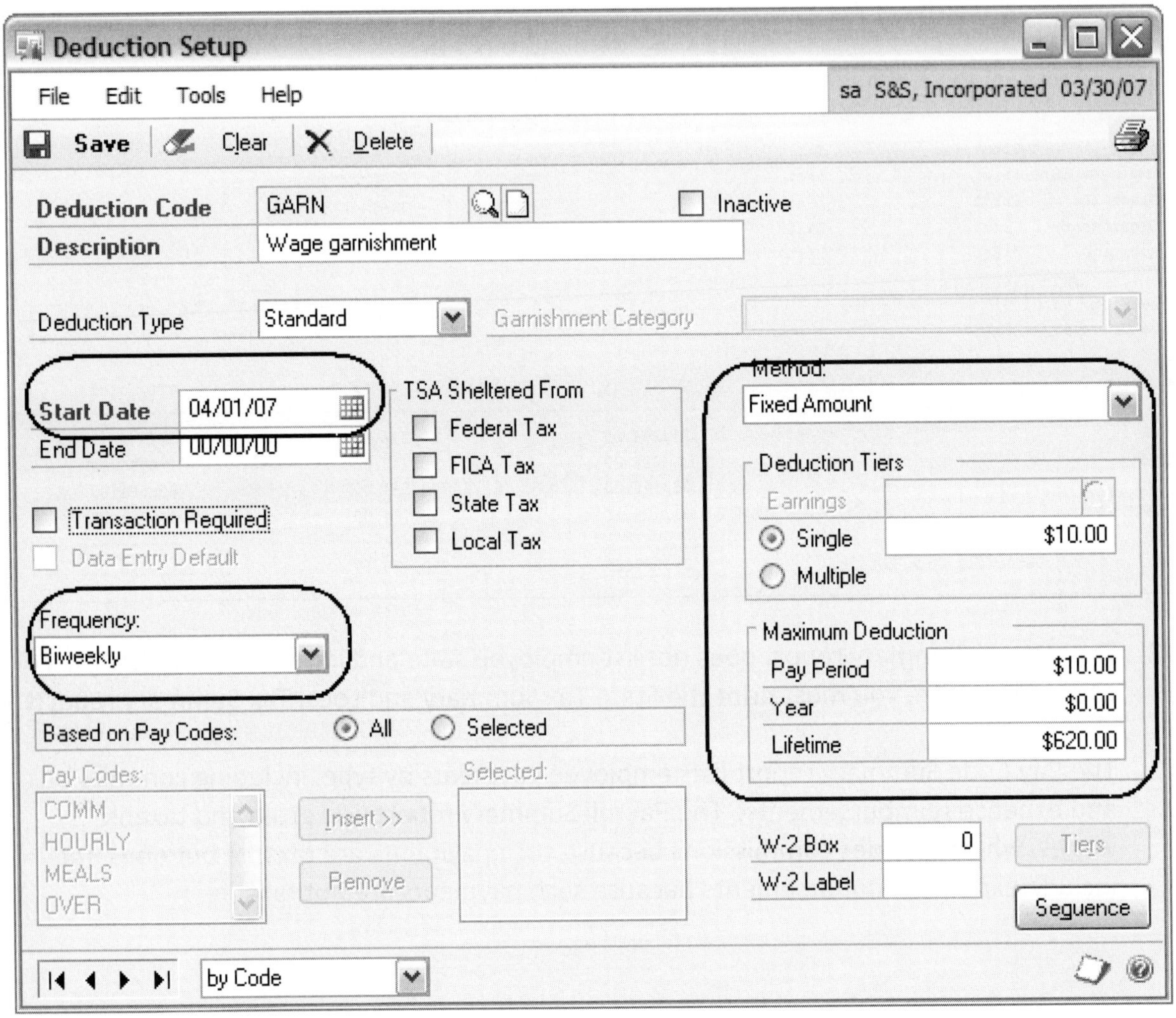

The link to George Hanratty's card appears next.

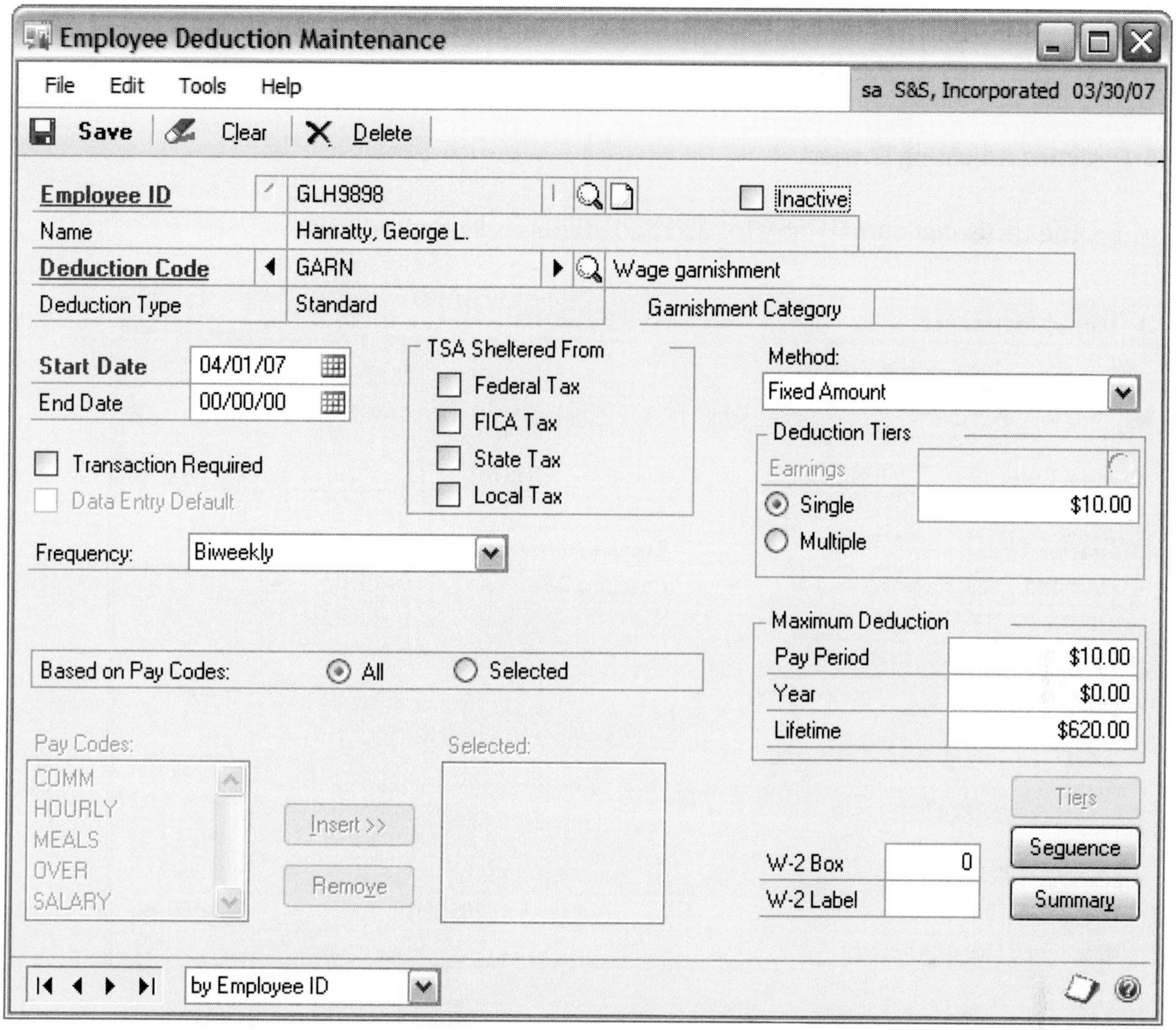

Employee Deduction Maintenance

File   Edit   Tools   Help   sa S&S, Incorporated 03/30/07

💾 Save   🖊 Clear   ✖ Delete

Employee ID		GLH9898	🔍 📄	☐ Inactive
Name		Hanratty, George L.		
Deduction Code	◀	GARN	▶ 🔍 Wage garnishment	
Deduction Type		Standard	Garnishment Category	

Start Date   04/01/07 ▦
End Date   00/00/00 ▦

☐ Transaction Required
☐ Data Entry Default

Frequency: Biweekly ▼

TSA Sheltered From
☐ Federal Tax
☐ FICA Tax
☐ State Tax
☐ Local Tax

Method:
Fixed Amount ▼

Deduction Tiers
Earnings
◉ Single $10.00
○ Multiple

Maximum Deduction
Pay Period	$10.00
Year	$0.00
Lifetime	$620.00

Based on Pay Codes: ◉ All   ○ Selected

Pay Codes:
COMM
HOURLY
MEALS
OVER
SALARY

Insert >>
Remove

Selected:

W-2 Box   0
W-2 Label

Tiers
Sequence
Summary

I◀ ◀ ▶ ▶I   by Employee ID ▼

CHAPTER 8 EXERCISES

E8:1Practice Adjusting Entries

1. The recurring journal entry for accrued utilities is illustrated next.

2. The recurring batch for depreciation appears next.

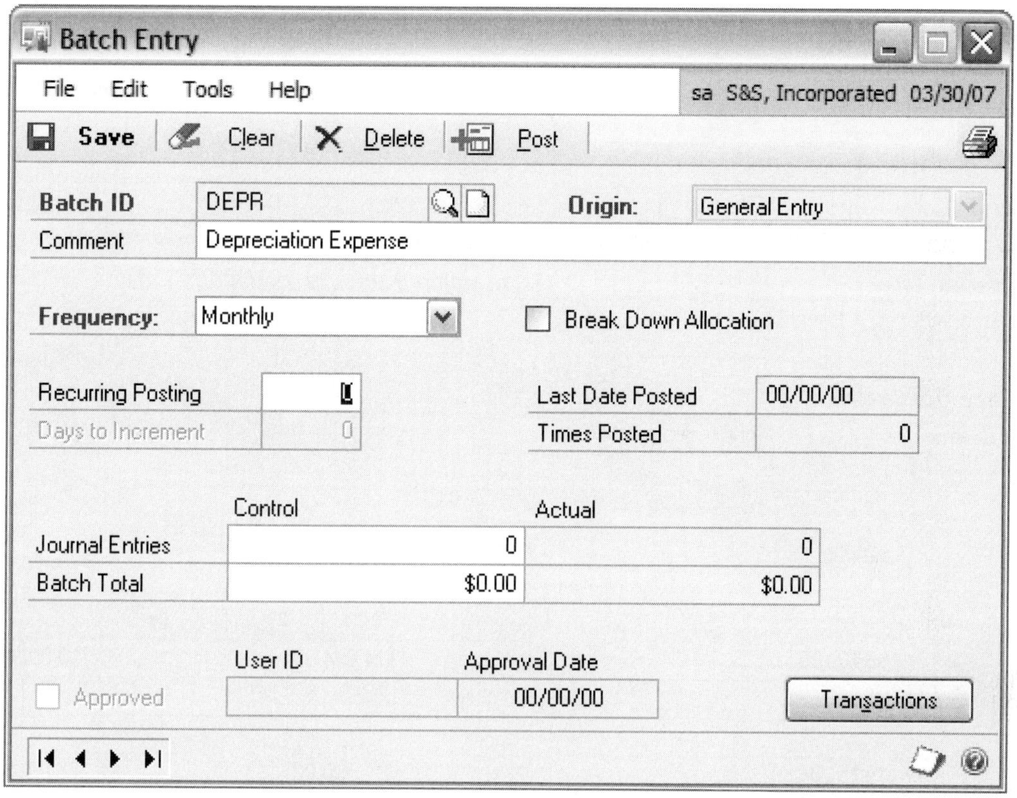

The depreciation transaction for this batch appears next.

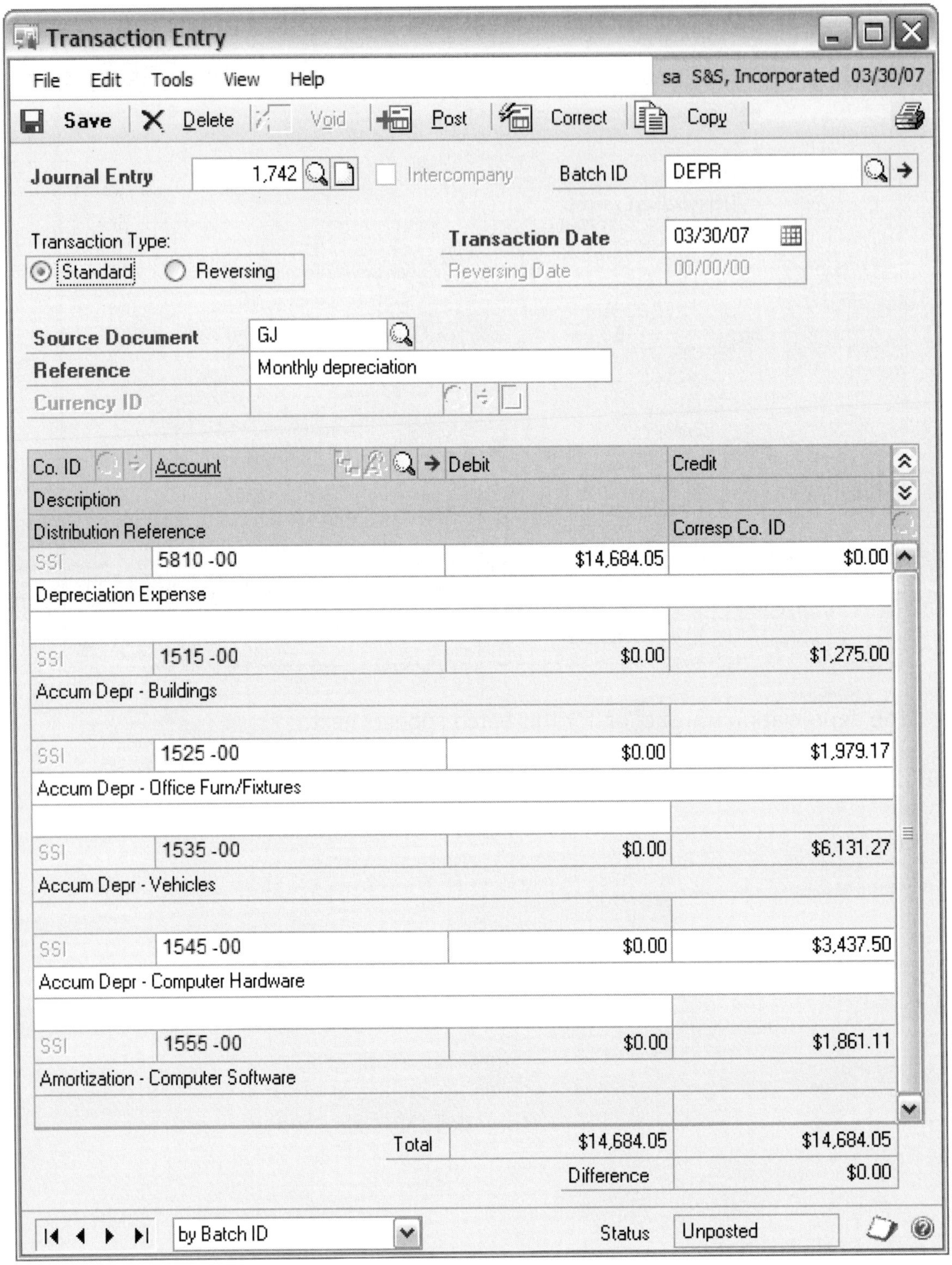

Series Posting window with batches marked to post is illustrated next.

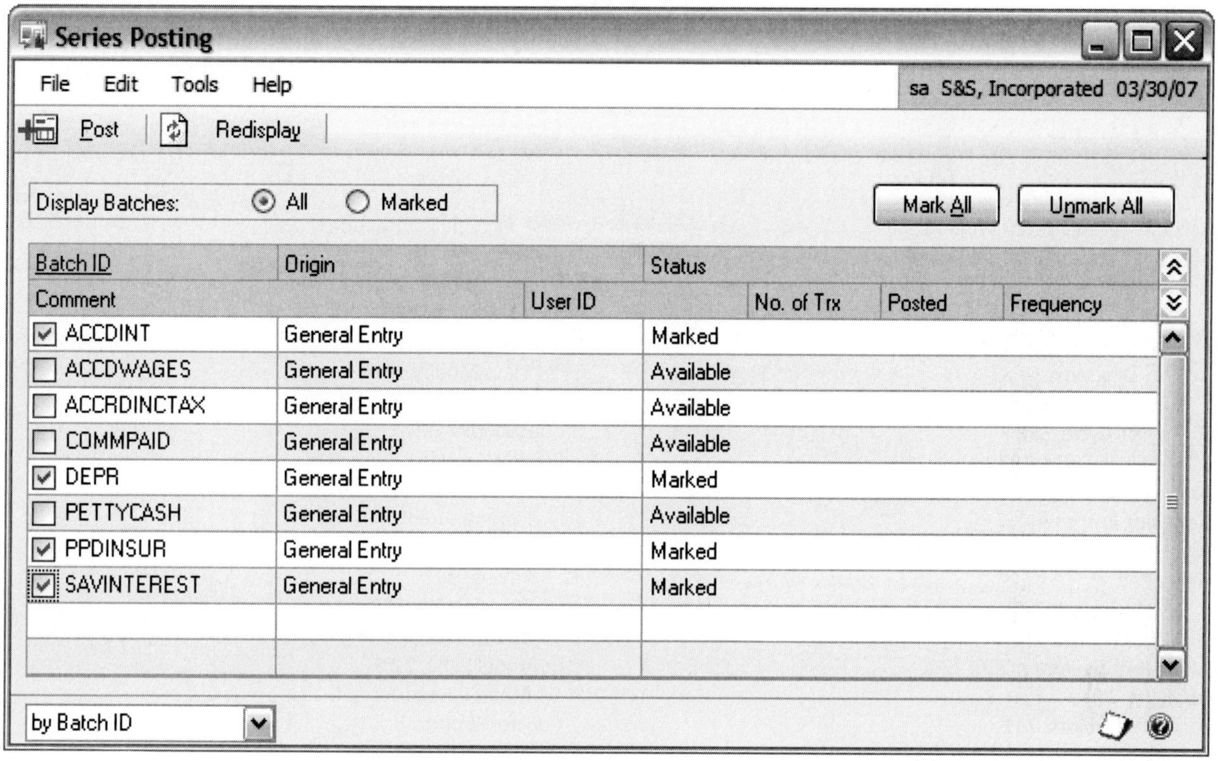

Series Posting

File Edit Tools Help

sa S&S, Incorporated 03/30/07

Post | Redisplay

Display Batches: ● All ○ Marked

Mark All Unmark All

Batch ID	Origin	Status				
Comment		User ID		No. of Trx	Posted	Frequency
☑ ACCDINT	General Entry	Marked				
☐ ACCDWAGES	General Entry	Available				
☐ ACCRDINCTAX	General Entry	Available				
☐ COMMPAID	General Entry	Available				
☑ DEPR	General Entry	Marked				
☐ PETTYCASH	General Entry	Available				
☑ PPDINSUR	General Entry	Marked				
☑ SAVINTEREST	General Entry	Marked				

by Batch ID

INDEX

E

F

R

S

T

U

V

W

Y

SINGLE PC LICENSE AGREEMENT AND LIMITED WARRANTY

READ THIS LICENSE CAREFULLY BEFORE OPENING THIS PACKAGE. BY OPENING THIS PACKAGE, YOU ARE AGREEING TO THE TERMS AND CONDITIONS OF THIS LICENSE. IF YOU DO NOT AGREE, DO NOT OPEN THE PACKAGE. PROMPTLY RETURN THE UNOPENED PACKAGE AND ALL ACCOMPANYING ITEMS TO THE PLACE YOU OBTAINED THEM. *THESE TERMS APPLY TO ALL LICENSED SOFTWARE ON THE DISK EXCEPT THAT THE TERMS FOR USE OF ANY SHAREWARE OR FREEWARE ON THE DISKETTES ARE AS SET FORTH IN THE ELECTRONIC LICENSE LOCATED ON THE DISK:*

1. GRANT OF LICENSE and OWNERSHIP: The enclosed computer programs ("Software") are licensed, not sold, to you by Prentice-Hall, Inc. ("We" or the "Company") and in consideration of your purchase or adoption of the accompanying Company textbooks and/or other materials, and your agreement to these terms. We reserve any rights not granted to you. You own only the disk(s) but we and/or our licensors own the Software itself. This license allows you to use and display your copy of the Software on a single computer (i.e., with a single CPU) at a single location for academic use only, so long as you comply with the terms of this Agreement. You may make one copy for back up, or transfer your copy to another CPU, provided that the Software is usable on only one computer.

2. RESTRICTIONS: You may not transfer or distribute the Software or documentation to anyone else. Except for backup, you may not copy the documentation or the Software. You may not network the Software or otherwise use it on more than one computer or computer terminal at the same time. You may not reverse engineer, disassemble, decompile, modify, adapt, translate, or create derivative works based on the Software or the Documentation. You may be held legally responsible for any copying or copyright infringement which is caused by your failure to abide by the terms of these restrictions.

3. TERMINATION: This license is effective until terminated. This license will terminate automatically without notice from the Company if you fail to comply with any provisions or limitations of this license. Upon termination, you shall destroy the Documentation and all copies of the Software. All provisions of this Agreement as to limitation and disclaimer of warranties, limitation of liability, remedies or damages, and our ownership rights shall survive termination.

4.DISCLAIMER OF WARRANTY: THE COMPANY AND ITS LICENSORS MAKE NO WARRANTIES ABOUT THE SOFTWARE, WHICH IS PROVIDED "AS-IS." IF THE DISK IS DEFECTIVE IN MATERIALS OR WORKMANSHIP, YOUR ONLY REMEDY IS TO RETURN IT TO THE COMPANY WITHIN 30 DAYS FOR REPLACEMENT UNLESS THE COMPANY DETERMINES IN GOOD FAITH THAT THE DISK HAS BEEN MISUSED OR IMPROPERLY INSTALLED, REPAIRED, ALTERED OR DAMAGED. THE COMPANY DISCLAIMS ALL WARRANTIES, EXPRESS OR IMPLIED, INCLUDING WITHOUT LIMITATION, THE IMPLIED WARRANTIES OF MERCHANTABILITY AND FITNESS FOR A PARTICULAR PURPOSE. THE COMPANY DOES NOT WARRANT, GUARANTEE OR MAKE ANY REPRESENTATION REGARDING THE ACCURACY, RELIABILITY, CURRENTNESS, USE, OR RESULTS OF USE, OF THE SOFTWARE.

5. LIMITATION OF REMEDIES AND DAMAGES: IN NO EVENT, SHALL THE COMPANY OR ITS EMPLOYEES, AGENTS, LICENSORS OR CONTRACTORS BE LIABLE FOR ANY INCIDENTAL, INDIRECT, SPECIAL OR CONSEQUENTIAL DAMAGES ARISING OUT OF OR IN CONNECTION WITH THIS LICENSE OR THE SOFTWARE, INCLUDING, WITHOUT LIMITATION, LOSS OF USE, LOSS OF DATA, LOSS OF INCOME OR PROFIT, OR OTHER LOSSES SUSTAINED AS A RESULT OF INJURY TO ANY PERSON, OR LOSS OF OR DAMAGE TO PROPERTY, OR CLAIMS OF THIRD PARTIES, EVEN IF THE COMPANY OR AN AUTHORIZED REPRESENTATIVE OF THE COMPANY HAS BEEN ADVISED OF THE POSSIBILITY OF SUCH DAMAGES. SOME JURISDICTIONS DO NOT ALLOW THE LIMITATION OF DAMAGES IN CERTAIN CIRCUMSTANCES, SO THE ABOVE LIMITATIONS MAY NOT ALWAYS APPLY.

6. GENERAL: THIS AGREEMENT SHALL BE CONSTRUED IN ACCORDANCE WITH THE LAWS OF THE UNITED STATES OF AMERICA AND THE STATE OF NEW YORK, APPLICABLE TO CONTRACTS MADE IN NEW YORK, AND SHALL BENEFIT THE COMPANY, ITS AFFILIATES AND ASSIGNEES. This Agreement is the complete and exclusive statement of the agreement between you and the Company and supersedes all proposals, prior agreements, oral or written, and any other communications between you and the company or any of its representatives relating to the subject matter. If you are a U.S. Government user, this Software is licensed with "restricted rights" as set forth in subparagraphs (a)-(d) of the Commercial Computer-Restricted Rights clause at FAR 52.227-19 or in subparagraphs (c)(1)(ii) of the Rights in Technical Data and Computer Software clause at DFARS 252.227-7013, and similar clauses, as applicable.

Should you have any questions concerning this agreement or if you wish to contact the Company for any reason, please contact in writing:

Multimedia Production
Higher Education Division
Prentice-Hall, Inc.
1 Lake Street
Upper Saddle River NJ 07458